The SAGE Encyclopedia of
JOURNALISM
SECOND EDITION

Editorial Board

The SAGE Encyclopedia of

JOURNALISM

SECOND EDITION

Editor

Gregory A. Borchard

University of Nevada

⑤SAGE reference

Los Angeles I London I New Delhi I Singapore I Washington DC I Melbourne

FOR INFORMATION:

SAGE Publications, Inc.
2455 Teller Road
Thousand Oaks, California 91320
E-mail: order@sagepub.com

SAGE Publications Ltd.
1 Oliver's Yard
55 City Road
London, EC1Y 1SP
United Kingdom

SAGE Publications India Pvt. Ltd.
B 1/I 1 Mohan Cooperative Industrial Area
Mathura Road, New Delhi 110 044
India

SAGE Publications Asia-Pacific Pte. Ltd.
18 Cross Street #10-10/11/12
China Square Central
Singapore 048423

Printed in the United States of America

ISBN: 978-1-5443-9115-1

Acquisitions Editor: Andrew Boney
Developmental Editor: Shirin Parsavand, Carole Maurer
Editorial Services Lead: Leticia Gutierrez
Production Editor: Megha Negi
Copy Editor: Hurix Digital
Typesetter: Hurix Digital
Proofreader: Eleni Maria Georgiou, Jeff Bryant,
          Theresa Kay
Indexer: Integra
Cover Designer: Candice Harman
Marketing Manager: Brianna Griffith

This book is printed on acid-free paper.

21 22 23 24 25 10 9 8 7 6 5 4 3 2 1

Contents

Volume 4

List of Entries

ABC News
ABP News
Access to Media
Advanced Research Projects Agency Network (ARPANET)
Advertising
Advertising, Ethics in
Advertorials
Advocacy Journalism
Aerial Photography
Africa, North
Africa, Sub-Saharan
African American News Media
Agence France-Presse
Agenda Setting
Agricultural Journalism
Al Arabiya
Al Jazeera
Al-Manar
Alternative News Media
Alumni Magazines
American Civil Liberties Union (ACLU)
Amplification
Anchors, Television
Antitrust
Artificial Intelligence and Journalism
Arts Journalism
Asia, Central
Asia, East and Southeast
Asia, South
Asian American News Media
Associated Press
Audience Research
Audiences
Audio and Video News Services
Audio Journalism
Australia and New Zealand
Automation

Bandwagon Journalism
Bangladesh
Bernays, Edward L.
Bertelsmann
Bias
Blacklisting
Blogs and Bloggers
Bloomberg
Bly, Nellie
Bots
Boycotts
Brady, Mathew B.
Brazil
Breitbart
British Broadcasting Corporation
British Broadcasting Regulation
British Commercial News Broadcasting
British Newspapers
Broadcast, or Broadcasting
Broadsheet Newspapers
Business Journalism
Business Magazines
BuzzFeed
Byline

Cable News
Cables, Undersea
Cartoonists, Political
CBS News
Celebrity and Fan Media
Censorship
Central America and the Caribbean
Checkbook Journalism
China
Chinese Television
Circulation
Citizen Journalism
Civic Journalism

Reader's Guide

The Reader's Guide is provided to assist readers in locating articles on related topics. It classifies articles into 30 general topical categories: Broadcast Organizations; Broadcast Technology; Broadcast, Past and Present; Broadcast, Practiced and Defined; Broadcast, Radio; Broadcast, Television; Cultural Issues in Journalism; Economics of Journalism; Freedom of the Press in American History; Issues and Controversies, Coverage of; Journalism Online, Practiced and Defined; Journalism, Practiced and Defined; Journalism Techniques; Journalism Types; Journalism, International; Journalism, International Organizations; Journalism, U.S.; Journalism, Visual Orientation; Law and Policy; Media Regulation and Oversight; Media Theories; Photojournalism, Issues and History; Press and Politics, The; Print Production; Print, Historical Issues and People; Print, Practiced and Defined; Public Relations, Issues and History; Social and Ethical Aspects of Journalism; Social Media Organizations; Technological Aspects of Journalism

Broadcast Organizations

ABC News
CBS News
CNN
Fox News
MSNBC
National Public Radio
NBC News
Public Broadcasting Service
Sinclair Broadcast Group
Sky News
ViacomCBS

Broadcast Technology

Audio and Video News Services
Audio Journalism

Broadcast, or Broadcasting
Digital Sound
Livestreaming
Satellite Newsgathering
Shortwave Radio
Simulcasting
Streaming Media
Video Journalism
Video News Releases

Broadcast, Past and Present

Broadcast, or Broadcasting
Commentators, Radio
Murdoch, Rupert
Mutual Broadcasting System
National Public Radio
NBC News
Newscasters, Radio
Pacifica Radio
Paley, William S.
Public Radio Journalism
Public Service Broadcasting
Radio Corporation of America
Shortwave Radio
Television News, History of

Broadcast, Practiced and Defined

Anchors, Television
Community Radio
Newscasters, Radio
Public Service Broadcasting
Sports Broadcasting
Talk and News Radio
Television Newsmagazines
Video Journalism

Broadcast, Radio

ABC News
Audio Journalism

Broadcast, or Broadcasting
CBS News
Commentators, Radio
National Public Radio
NBC News
Newscasters, Radio
Pacifica Radio
Public Radio Journalism
Radio Corporation of America
Shortwave Radio
Talk and News Radio

Broadcast, Television

ABC News
Anchors, Television
Broadcast, or Broadcasting
Cable News
CBS News
CNN
Fox News
MSNBC
NBC News
Public Television Journalism
Tabloid Television
Television Commentary
Television News, History of
Television Newsmagazines

Cultural Issues in Journalism

African American News Media
Asian American News Media
Democracy and the Media
Diversity in Journalism
Émigré News Media
Ethnic Press
Feminist News Media
Indigenous News Media
Latino News Media
LGBTQ Issues, Coverage of
LGBTQ Journalism
News Audiences, U.S.
News Avoidance
News Deserts
Race and Ethnicity, Coverage of
Religious News Media
Social Movements and
    Journalism

Economics of Journalism

Advertising
Advertising, Ethics in
Advertorials
Audience Research
Audiences
Circulation
Classified Advertising
Clickbait
Convergence
Digital Advertising
Discussion Boards
Employment
Fake News
Free Daily Newspapers
Hoaxes
Infotainment
Labor Unions in Media
Marketing
Media Conglomerates
Media Markets
Media Monopoly
Media Ownership
News Deserts
Newspaper Chains, Ownership of
Nonprofit Media
Paywalls
Self-Publishing

Freedom of the Press in American History

Commission on Freedom of the Press
Democracy and the Media
English Roots of the Free Press
Espionage Act
First Amendment
Fourth Estate
Free Expression, History of
Free Press and Fair Trial
Pentagon Papers
Publick Occurrences
Sedition Act of 1798
Stamp Act
Watergate
Zenger, John Peter

Issues and Controversies, Coverage of

Civil Unrest, Coverage of
Education, Coverage of

QQ

QQ is an instant message software developed by Chinese tech giant Tencent. It is officially known as *Tencent QQ* and has an easily recognizable penguin logo. Started as an instant messaging software (QQ IM) when first released in 1999, Tencent soon began to offer users various additional features like email service (QQ mail), a social networking site that combines personal blog and social newsfeed (Qzone), online social games (QQ game), music streaming (QQ music), voice call, and video chat for groups. Tencent aims to develop QQ as a "one-stop online service platform" that can satisfy all their users' communication, information sharing, and entertainment needs. Since its initial release, QQ has grown exceptionally. It reached 1 million users within a year and 50 million the next. As of 2020, QQ had about 850 million active monthly users worldwide. It is one of the world's most widely used social media applications. This entry examines the development of QQ, its users and business model, and its relationship with the Chinese government.

Development of QQ

QQ is the first popular instant message software in China. In the early 2000s, only about 10% of the Chinese population had cell phones, and text message wasn't cheap. To register for an account, one did not need a phone number or an email address. Teenagers without their own cellphones can easily get a QQ account going online. After filling out basic information, each user was assigned a unique series of numbers as their permanent ID. QQ mail, which was automatically assigned to every QQ user, was many young people's first adoption of an email service. Besides, the basic chat function in QQ, which later includes file transfer, voice call, and video chat, was entirely free. Young people, especially teenagers, heavily relied on QQ to communicate with friends. In a few years since its initial release, it quickly became the most popular social media in China. For over a decade since its first release, having a QQ account was nearly a necessity for young people's social life in school and at the workplace.

In the 2010s, smartphone use grew quickly in China, and Tencent also promptly developed a QQ app for smartphones to attract more users. Since then, users can log in to their accounts on multiple devices simultaneously, including desktop, laptop, iPad, and cell phone. Because all chat history would be synced across devices automatically and sharing files across platforms can be effortless, many users rely on QQ to share and store information. In the meantime, more social media websites and instant messaging apps became available in China. Nonetheless, most QQ users remained loyal even as some tried out alternatives. On the one hand, long-time users have accumulated a sizeable social network that includes virtual and real-life relationships; it would not be easy to transfer existing networks to a new platform altogether. On the other hand, many users were also used to rely on QQ mail for professional communication, QQ games and music for entertainment, and Qzone for personal blogging and social networking. Although there were many alternatives for each individual service QQ provides, most users could not abandon the whole package because of their previous time investment on the platform and the convenience of linking all these services to one account. In other words, the cost of completely leaving QQ seems to be too high for the majority of users. Although it was no longer the only social app for savvy users, it remained one of the most popular apps in China.

QQ's Users and Business Model

Most QQ users are young and tend to have less buying power as 60% of them are under 30 years old. In recent years, it has become especially popular among Generation Z in China. Most successful marketing campaigns on the platform are from brands targeting teenagers.

Unlike many social media companies in the United States, besides advertising revenue, QQ has various profitable services. It offers multiple levels of paid membership and various paid features for its instant messaging users. For example, users can customize their avatars in the QQ show, which is a sperate profile page in addition to their profile picture. Every user is assigned a default human avatar with a plain outfit according to the user's gender. One must pay for advanced customization in the QQ show, such as outfits, accessories, unique background, and stickers. Users can either pay a monthly membership fee or buy QQ coins, a virtual currency, and then purchase individual items online. Because most active QQ users are teenagers and young adults, many of whom want to customize their QQ show avatars to show off their personalities online, this service was highly popular and profitable in early years. QQ games and QQ music also offer both basic free version and paid membership with various in-app purchases for advanced features and greater flexibility. Many young people also enjoy posting updates and seeing friends' updates on Qzone, a Facebook-like social network site that is connected to their QQ account. In addition to the free default template, Tencent offers users paid options to upgrade and customize their Qzone template and layout. Paid users can also add music and stickers on their profile page as well as in their blog posts.

QQ group chat is another critical feature that is highly profitable. Every user is permitted to own up to five chat groups with up to 200 members per group for free. With different levels of paid memberships, users can form groups with up to 500, 1,000, 2,000, and 3,000 members. Users can create groups with family, friends, classmates, coworkers, and clients. Indeed, most active users who participate in social groups on QQ are mostly younger and still in school. To better reach the fan base, many celebrities have fan groups on QQ where they actively communicate with fans and also post updates in fan groups. For example, Chinese idol group The Fighting Boys (TFBoys) has 67 million followers on QQ, more than 34.8 million followers One Direction has on Facebook. There are also many fans-managed Qzone pages and fan groups that meant to support and share information about TFboys with other QQ users. Tencent also invited TFBoys to host special events with fans following them to strengthen users' loyalty to the platform. Small business users also like to use QQ groups to communicate with clients and cultivate brand loyalty.

Because the voice/video group chat function and image/file sharing feature on QQ are user friendly, reliable, and mostly free, many people in China also rely on it to communicate at the workplace. As young people are most familiar with QQ before they enter the workforce, many organizations and small businesses readily adopt it as a preferred tool for their employees to communicate and collaborate professionally. Employees sometimes can use their personal QQ account to join work groups and communicate with colleagues using QQ mail.

Because QQ was initially developed as computer software, many of its key features, like Qzone and QQ mail, were only accessible on web pages. Since the 2010s, Tencent has made a substantial effort to transition QQ to compete on the smartphone application market and made most of its services into separated apps while still allowing users to link them to their IM accounts.

QQ and Government Regulation

Owning several of the most popular social and entertainment apps in China, Tencent has followed the Chinese government's Internet surveillance and censorship policies. Over the years, numerous reports have shown that Chinese government officials can monitor conversations on various social media platforms by tracking keywords or phrases and even track users' locations when they check in on social media. Recent reports show evidence that Tencent has increased its data sharing with the Chinese government as the company's founder and chief executive, Ma Huateng, became a member of 3,000 delegates to the National People's Congress.

For instance, in 2019, security researcher and hacker Victor Gevers retrieved over 300 million chat logs from Tencent's popular app WeChat and QQ, which also contain users' personal identifying information such as citizen ID numbers, addresses, and location data. Gevers believes those data were collected in Internet cafés and sent to police stations, although it remains unclear how the government was using those data.

In recent years, the Chinese government also issued specific regulations on instant messaging group chats, including QQ groups. Unlike a public discussion board, those groups should be a private space for group discussions. Nonetheless, the Cyberspace Administration of China stated that group owners and managers have to take full responsibility for the management of the groups. In other words, if any comments are too critical of the government, group owners and managers may be held responsible and face repercussions. Also, Tencent, the same as many other online chat providers, has been asked by the government to keep the records of any group chat for at least 6 months. It remains unclear whether Tencent complies with such requests or how it decides what to share with the government.

In the meantime, the Chinese government has also pushed wireless providers to check and keep a record of new users' government-issued identification documents when they register for new cell phone numbers. People who have already registered cell phone service without providing real names were also encouraged to contact their providers and voluntarily link their government-issued ID to their existing phone numbers. Chinese officials claim such policy changes would reduce wireless fraud. QQ also has updated its policy so that new users have to provide a valid phone number for registration. Many long-time users, who registered without providing cell phone or their real names to Tencent in the beginning, cannot continue to use certain services on QQ platforms without adding a valid phone number in their profile, which is mostly likely registered with their government-issued identification documents. As a result, although Chinese users can still largely remain anonymous on QQ in front of other users, it would not be hard for the Chinese government to get identifiable information on most users from Tencent. It remains unclear whether wireless fraud has indeed been reduced since such policy was adopted. In addition, QQ users are also encouraged to report other users to Tencent for posting controversial political opinions or being too critical to the government. Users can be blocked by Tencent if such reports are confirmed valid. As a result, users have become more aware of government's surveillance and may be more careful about what they say on QQ.

It is well understood in China that if Tencent, or any other social media company, allows controversial political opinion to be widely shared on its platform, the Chinese government may simply take down the whole platform as punishment. Since the early days of the Internet, the Chinese government has shutdown many online services because they consider political posts on their platforms too radical. Because of this, while some users are not happy with such heavy-handed surveillance, many understand that this is necessary for Tencent to survive and thrive in China's unique political climate.

Meredith Wang

See also China; Social Media

Further Readings

Cook, S. (2019, March). Worried about Huawei? Take a closer look at Tencent. *Japan Times*. Retrieved from https://www.japantimes.co.jp/opinion/2019/03/28/commentary/world-commentary/worried-huawei-take-closer-look-tencent/#.XqzB-pNKhQM

Chen, C., & Deng, I. (2018, September). QQ, the grandaddy of China's social media scene, gains new life by appealing to generation Z. *South China Morning Post*. Retrieved from https://www.scmp.com/tech/article/2162288/qq-grandaddy-chinas-social-media-scene-gains-new-life-appealing-generation-z

Law, C. (2017, October). QQ: The biggest digital platform you've never heard of. *ClickZ*. Retrieved from https://www.clickz.com/qq-the-biggest-digital-platform-youve-never-heard-of/113476/

Liao, S. (2019, March). Over 300 million Chinese private messages were left exposed online. *The Verge*. Retrieved from https://www.theverge.com/2019/3/4/18250474/chinese-messages-millions-wechat-qq-yy-data-breach-police

Shen, T. (2017, September). China issues new rules for group chats for WeChat, QQ and others. *Tech Node*. Retrieved from https://technode.com/2017/09/08/china-issues-new-rules-for-group-chats-for-wechat-qq-and-others/

Wu, J. P., & Frantz, T. L. (2012). Largest IM platform in China Tecents QQ. *Journal of Business Case Studies (JBCS), 8*(1), 95–102. doi:10.19030/jbcs.v8i1.6742

You, Z. Q., Han, X. P., Lü, L., & Yeung, C. H. (2015). Empirical studies on the network of social groups: The case of Tencent QQ. *PLoS One, 10*(7), e0130538.

QUOTATION

Quotation is fundamental to human communication. Language theorists have studied the linguistic, literary, semiotic, philosophical, functional, and cognitive nature of oral and written quotation for many decades, formally labeling it reported speech and thought. Theorists of direct (quote-marked) and indirect (non-quote-marked) quotation have concentrated most heavily on direct quotation—since quote marks add an important nonlinguistic, thus uniquely rhetorical element to language captured inside quotes—and somewhat less attention to the semantics of indirect speech.

Quotation qualifies as meta-language: language about language, one person's repeating another's words, whether in fictional or factual discourses. Accurate quotation of informational sources is critical in many occupations, especially journalism. A contemporary journalistic story is, in fact, virtually nothing but a series of quotations, making the citing of news sources journalism's fundamental narrative device. Around the late 19th century, journalistic source quotation become commonplace, but there is no formal history of quotation in journalism, probably because reporters' earliest source citations were generalized glosses and very loose summations, rather than accurately quoted words.

Only since the end of the 20th century have communication scholars begun to investigate, for example, how quotation helps establish news objectivity, or accuracy and fairness to all sides of an issue; can create different "voices" within a story; or rhetorically depicts differing "subjectivities" of sources and reporters, depending on the quote mode. Some studies treat quotation transparently, as simple information transmission—for example, when different sources are counted to assess viewpoint "balance"—but sometimes without attention to quotation itself as a unique meta-linguistic act.

This entry explains factual quotation's emergence in journalism, details its linguistic and functional nature, and presents quote modes representative of contemporary print news. The focus on print is because television news features "sound bites," where sources are *seen and heard*. Similarly, radio news sources are "heard from." Only in print does the depiction of speech and thought take such a central role as a linguistic, rhetorical, and strictly standardized compositional process deserving study in its own right.

19th-Century Roots

American journalism historians say that, before the 1870s, a news writer's daring to use persons' actual remarks in stories would have been deemed inappropriate. Journalists of the day would significantly alter a person's actual comments or simply fabricate them. In antebellum America, and prior to around the 1830s, journalists were little more than political propagandists serving partisan ends, mouthing the words of their ideological patrons.

Only in the middle decades of the 19th century did reliance on commercial advertising begin to free newspapers from their previous need of political patronage, although many papers long maintained an editorial alliance to one or another political party. The reporting of stories, however, could now be done with formal "neutrality" declared, at least in principle, by the reporter. Increasingly, reporters could craft more factual, accurate, nonpartisan stories for a growing number of literate readers with diverse interests. Newspaper and magazine reporters in this way could begin to function as autonomous, professional practitioners following an occupational set of standardized newsgathering techniques.

By the 20th century, the growth of university journalism degree programs helped further certify journalism as an independent profession, including teaching formalized rules of newsgathering and storytelling—quotation being one of them. American journalism historian Michael Schudson maintains that by the 1920s, journalistic interviews resulting in source quotation was established practice. Quotation emerged, then, as an occupational means, in narrative form, of modern fact-based storytelling, marking off person-centered knowledge claims as decidedly *not* those of the reporter, whose official role was now to remain neutral. Today, a story of more than a few paragraphs will typically have at least one quoted source—and longer stories, especially investigative pieces, will have many more.

The Modes of Journalistic Quotation

Journalistic quotation can be defined as the reporter's linguistically repeating, in written form and with assumed accuracy, the words, and sometimes, the thoughts of another person. Contemporary journalistic quotation follows nearly inflexible rules pertaining to the use of quotation marks, attribution type and placement, and punctuation.

The most common verb of speech used in source attribution is "said," considered by linguists as "neutral," conveying no attitude (interpretation) on the reporter's part. However, "marked" or "infused" speech verbs—*admitted, denied, asserted, charged, claimed, warned*, and countless others—do project some specific awareness of a more narrow, often emotionally charged speaking situation inviting the reporter's interpretive assessment, via the use of these "attitude" verbs.

Formal analyses of different quote modes show the overwhelming preference for "said" as the most common speech-verb connected with direct quotation, while "marked" speech verbs occur almost exclusively with indirect quotation, alongside frequent use of "said." The use of marked speech verbs in indirect quotes is because indirect requires the reporter's careful summarization and paraphrasing of original source content, resulting in an interpretive gloss of initial source commentary. Indirect quotation also deploys synonyms and other evaluative words to stand in for whatever was said originally, giving the journalist significant interpretive leeway. Indirect is therefore

writer-centered: the "onstage" narrator hogging the spotlight is, in effect, the journalist. Indirect speech demonstrates a key feature of contemporary quotation—the reporter's authorized interpretive role in objectively, accurately, creatively reconstruing previous speaker commentary for informational clarity.

By contrast, direct quotation is *source-centered*: it presents only the source's (assumed) exact verbiage, within quotation marks, meaning the reporter shines the speaking spotlight on the source as "onstage" rhetorical presence. Direct quotation serves an important traditional storytelling role in highlighting someone's dramatic, colorful, often controversial sentiments and highly subjective, even inflammatory rhetoric: a news source, unlike the journalist, is not constrained to engage in objective discourse.

Analyses of contemporary news stories generally show indirect quotation is likely the predominant quote mode, especially in larger urban papers specializing in critical reporting, while direct quotation occurs somewhat less often, though probably more frequently in smaller newspapers covering exclusively local, personality-driven issues. The type of story can also be determinative of the number and type of quotes used. In longer, in-depth stories, more indirect quotation is likely to predominate, including more use of quotation of both human sources and documents, and a higher number of total sources, if only because reporters themselves engage in more detailed, nuanced analysis via interpretive rewording and detached, analytical presentation using multiple sources to establish central facts. Longer form news stories generally utilize sources as *conduits* of information rather than as personalized human-interest "characters." But in feature, sports, entertainment, and other human-interest stories, the use of direct quotes will likely increase, since direct speech brings source voices into the story in their own colorful words and sentiments. Here, sources are depicted as distinct "characters" and not merely as informational conduits.

Examples of the Most Common Quote Modes

To conclude this entry, it is useful to examine the most used journalistic quotation modes (as constructed by the author to highlight differences, with attributions underlined): Direct [quote-marked]; indirect [non-quote-marked] (*direct and indirect being the two most often used*); mixed [direct/indirect]; and free-indirect [a direct/indirect hybrid *without* quote marks, and often *without* clear attribution]:

- Direct: "This is an outrageous violation of my civil rights, and I won't stand for it," Smith <u>said</u>. "I'm taking this to court, and I'll win."
- Indirect (with "*said*" [neutral] speech verb): Smith <u>said</u> the law violates his civil rights and that he'll sue.
- Indirect (both *neutral* and *marked* ["attitude"] attributions): Smith <u>contends</u> the law violates his civil rights and <u>said</u> he will sue.
- Mixed quotation: The lawsuit, Smith <u>alleges</u>, is "an outrageous violation" of his civil rights, and <u>said</u> he's "taking this to court," confident he'll win.
- Free-indirect: He has no doubt it's a major violation of his civil rights—outrageous, indisputably illegal, not the kind of ridiculous legal maneuvering that could ever really stand up in the courtroom, where he <u>believes</u> he'll win.

The free-indirect example is likely less familiar to news readers. The free-indirect mingles the journalist's creative reimagining of someone's *supposed* words and thoughts. Occurring less often than formulaic direct, indirect, and mixed modes, free-indirect is a quasi-literary rendering of previous speech, often without clear attribution, thus functioning much like direct quotation, but without quote marks.

Conclusion

This entry has briefly covered only a few areas important to a basic understanding of journalistic quotation, detailing its role in securing journalism's status as a professional practice devoted to objective storytelling. Today, journalistic quotation is so thoroughly ingrained as a compositional device that a perceived source "imbalance"—the suspicion most quotes favor only one viewpoint—can launch allegations of "bias." Reporters are often, fairly or not, criticized for "misquoting" a source, which shows how the public expects quotation to stand in for neutrality, factuality, and truthfulness.

Joseph C. Harry

See also Interviewing; Objectivity; Sources

Further Readings

Harry, J. C. (2014). Journalistic quotation: Reported speech in newspapers from a semiotic-linguistic perspective. *Journalism, 15*(8), 1041–1058. doi:10.1177/1464884913504258.

Pietila, V. (1992). Beyond the news story: News as discursive composition. *European Journal of Communication, 7*(1), 37–67. doi:10.1177/0267323192007001003.

Schudson, M. (1994). Question authority: a history of the news interview in American journalism, 1860s-1930s. *Media, Culture & Society, 16*(4), 565–587. doi:10.1177/016344379401600403.

Zelizer, B. (1995). Text, talk, and journalistic quoting practices. *The Communication Review, 1*(1), 33–51. doi:10.1080/10714429509388250.

Race and Ethnicity, Coverage of

As the United States has grown increasingly diverse, journalists have recognized the importance of reporting on issues of race and ethnicity. They also realize they must earn trust from multicultural communities and include people from a wide variety of backgrounds as sources and subjects. This task is not as straightforward as it may seem. As with most other U.S. institutions, those in charge of reporting and writing the mainstream news have been predominantly white. They have covered the news based on their own attitudes, experiences, and concerns. As a result, U.S. news organizations have an uneven history of equally and fairly covering all the people who participate in civic life.

This entry discusses coverage of race and ethnicity in the U.S. media since the 19th century, efforts to boost the numbers of minority journalists in mainstream news organizations, coverage of race and ethnicity in ethnic media, and research on the coverage of race and ethnicity in the mainstream news media and on the impact of that coverage. It then looks at how coverage of race and ethnicity has been affected by changes in the news industry in the 21st century and by recent developments, such as the Black Lives Matter protests of 2020. Finally, the entry discusses techniques that can be used to provide better reporting on race and ethnicity.

Development

When the penny press first arose in the 1830s, it sought to attract a broad audience by combining a low price with plenty of crime news and human interest stories. At its center was the heterogeneous white audience, rather than marginalized racial and ethnic minorities. This financially pragmatic formula, along with the general exclusion of people of color from public and political affairs, shaped news considerations and practices for decades to come. Scholars have identified four basic approaches in coverage since those days: at different times, mainstream news outlets have (1) excluded racial and ethnic minorities altogether, (2) focused on them as a threat, (3) detailed social confrontations among racial and ethnic groups, and (4) selectively covered minority groups based on a stereotyped view.

At least until the middle of the 20th century, only community-based outlets provided any in-depth coverage of racial and ethnic minorities. The bilingual *El Misisipí* began publication for Spanish exiles in New Orleans in 1808 and stayed in print 2 years. In 1827, the first Black-owned, edited, and published newspaper for Black Americans was founded, called *Freedom's Journal.* A year later the Cherokee Nation launched its own paper, soon named the *Cherokee Phoenix and Indians' Advocate,* in English and the Cherokee language, with international circulation and the interests of other tribes in mind. The paper ran out of money in 1834, and the Georgia Guard burned its building to the ground just before the tribe's forced relocation. But the Cherokee nation was able to revive the paper and it still publishes as the *Cherokee Phoenix*. *La Prensa*, founded in 1913, merged in 1963 with *El Diario de Nueva York* and now publishes as *El Diario*. Ethnic media remain an important force in U.S. news, with devoted audiences that see themselves and their lives reflected honestly and accurately there.

Several defining moments in U.S. race relations over the past century have forced mainstream news outlets to reassess their white-centered approach. In the early 1900s, for instance, mainstream journalists comfortably disregarded the rise of Black leaders such as A. Philip Randolph, who led the drive to organize the Brotherhood of Sleeping Car Porters (when trains were still the prime means of long-distance travel); Walter White, executive director of the National Association for the Advancement of Colored People; and W. E. B. Du Bois, the influential scholar and editor of NAACP's magazine, *Crisis*. In the 5 years between 1935 and 1940, *The New York Times* ran just one page-one story mentioning Randolph and none about the others, according to a review of the newspaper's archive by journalists Gene Roberts and Hank Klibanoff. But the push for desegregation in the late 1940s, the brutal 1955 murder of Emmett Till, the Montgomery Bus Boycott of the mid-1950s, and the 1957 showdown over desegregation at Central High in Little Rock, Arkansas, challenged reporting that had ignored the lives of Black people.

Roberts and Klibanoff describe white news editors' slow realization that the civil rights movement and white supremacy resistance could no longer be overlooked. A few papers hired Black reporters, and white reporters began to venture out into the Black community. In 1948 Carl T. Rowan took a job as a copy editor at the formerly all-white *Minneapolis Tribune*; in 1950, Marvel Cooke began reporting for the *Daily Compass* in New York; and in 1952, Simeon Booker became the first Black reporter at a major newspaper, *The Washington Post*. In 1961, Dorothy Butler Gilliam became the first Black female reporter to join the *Post*.

The desegregation battles did not, however, inspire news outlets to integrate their pages in any comprehensive way. Latinos, Asians, and American Indians remained absent in coverage, except at times as criminals and threats. For the most part, it was white reporters that covered the civil rights movement for the white press. The American Society of Newspaper Editors (ASNE) had no nonwhite members at all until 1965, when it allowed the membership of John H. Sengstacke, the editor of the famed Black newspaper, the *Chicago Defender*. Some news outlets relegated coverage of Black people to one or two special pages. For the general public, it was as if African Americans, American Indians, and people of Hispanic and Asian descent never gave birth, married, achieved in their lives, or died.

In 1967, when President Lyndon Johnson appointed a commission to find out why riots had erupted in urban areas each summer for several years, its members returned with an indictment of the news media. The 1968 report of the National Advisory Commission on Civil Disorders, known as the Kerner Commission, attacked journalists for failing to apply their own tough standards to their reporting on the uprisings. They reprinted rumors, reported inflated damage statistics, and printed "scare" headlines that exaggerated the scope and damage across the country, the report concluded. News misrepresented the violence as primarily Black–white confrontations. Most importantly, based on a content analysis of television and newspapers, the commission reported that reporters, editors, and producers had neglected racial problems that had simmered across the country for years. As prominent journalist Robert C. Maynard wrote a decade later, "the vast majority of white Americans was left to suppose that for no particular reason a bunch of blacks took it into their heads to burn down the city" (Marzolf and Tolliver, 1977, p. 7).

The Kerner report pointed to deep injustices within U.S. society and warned that the nation was "moving toward two societies, one black, one white—separate and unequal." Journalists, the commission said, had failed to report the deep problems America faced and neglected to identify potential solutions. The commission, calling news outlets "shockingly backward," urged them to hire Black reporters, editors, writers, and commentators beyond token levels. Black Americans should be covered routinely in the context of overall society, they argued. Reporters should be assigned to "urban" and "ghetto" beats, and news outlets should develop relationships with their counterparts in the Black press. Black staffers should be promoted into policy and decision-making levels. The news media reflected "the biases, the paternalism, the indifference of white America," the commission found. "The media report and write from the standpoint of a white man's world."

The report's stinging words triggered a flurry of new hires, but also complaints by news editors that there just were not enough qualified ethnic minority journalists to bring on. Some universities and foundations stepped forward with programs to meet this objection—although most were short-lived. What is known today as the Robert C. Maynard Institute for Journalism Education in Oakland, California, remains one of the most successful training programs designed to integrate newsrooms and educate journalists of all backgrounds to report fully and completely on all people. It began as a training ground for entry-level minority journalists, placing graduates into jobs. The program gave a start to many outstanding journalists, such as Pulitzer Prize winners Dennis Bell of *Newsday;* Steven Holmes of *The Washington Post*; and David Reyes, Virginia Escalante, and Louis Sahagun (along with institute cofounder Frank Sotomayor) of the *Los Angeles Times*. Milton Coleman, former senior editor of *The Washington Post*; Kevin Merida, ESPN senior vice president; and Carolina Garcia, former executive editor of the *Los Angeles Daily News*, are all graduates.

Despite the flurry of hiring after the Kerner report, a conference of high-level journalists 10 years later decried the lack of progress. Minority journalists found work but often left the business within a few years, discouraged. The news still failed to report on both the realities of inner-city life and the influential culture and history of people of color. At heart, the problem really was the definition of news, concluded the group brought together by the University of Michigan. It remained fixed on white, middle-class, and male perceptions of who and what mattered in the world. What was needed, summed up one conference participant, was "greater infusions of minorities and women at a variety of levels in order to make that redefinition of journalism happen naturally through working together" (Marzolf and Tolliver 1977, p. 13). Maynard, who with his wife, Nancy Hicks Maynard, later became the first Black owners of a

major metropolitan daily, called the press one of the most segregated institutions in the United States. When only some kinds of people get to control the telling of America's story, he said, "it is impossible for all Americans to understand what they should about each other" (Marzolf and Tolliver 1977, p. 9).

The Year 2000 Goal

The Maynards and other leaders in the Institute for Journalism Education developed a plan. They lobbied the ASNE (which in 2019 merged into the News Leaders Association) to set a goal: By the end of the century, minority journalists at member newspapers should match their proportion in the nation's population. The plan passed in April 1978, and members agreed to a survey each year to assess progress. The first census found that minorities made up only 4% of newsroom employees in contrast to 17% of the population.

The ASNE goal helped stimulate additional training and recruiting programs. But as 2000 approached, more than 40% of newsrooms remained completely white despite the increasingly diverse U.S. population. About one-third failed to report their data at all.

With journalists of color still just 11.5% of professional newsrooms, ASNE members "strongly reaffirm(ed)" their commitment in 1998 and reset their parity goal to the year 2025 if not sooner. At minimum, ASNE said, all newspapers should employ journalists of color and each should reflect the diversity of its own community. The editors added women to their census, set 3-year benchmarks, and pledged to redouble their efforts.

Journalists Organize

Journalists of color encountered discrimination in hiring and, once they broke into a news operation, often faced hostility and skepticism about their abilities. They formed associations to support one another, provide training for young journalists, and promote inclusive newsrooms committed to covering all Americans fully and fairly.

In 1970, about 50 Black producers of television and film formed the National Association of Black Media Producers. They elected as president Tony Brown, who later earned fame as the host of the

Public Broadcasting Service public affairs program *Tony Brown's Journal*. He discovered a tool in the Communications Act of 1934, which declared that broadcasters, who are dependent on the publicly owned airwaves, must serve the interests of the whole community. With the help of Black community organizations, the association was able to push broadcaster doors open to Black people.

A few years later in Philadelphia, Black print and broadcast journalists created the National Association of Black Journalists in 1975 in an attempt to increase their numbers and pressure the industry from the inside. The Asian American Journalists Association formed in 1981, followed by the Native American Journalists Association and the National Association of Hispanic Journalists in 1984. These associations formed a coalition, UNITY: Journalists of Color, that lasted several decades.

The older, more broadly based journalist groups also played a role. The NewsGuild, a labor union founded as the American Newspaper Guild in 1933, had been inclusive from the start. The national level of the Society of Professional Journalists, however, only later joined the effort to press for change. In the 1990s, Society of Professional Journalists established chapters at several historically Black colleges. Reginald Stuart, at the time a reporter for *The New York Times* and later a corporate recruiter for major news companies, became the organization's first Black president in 1994.

Independently and collectively, each of these organizations have taken up the task of holding the news business accountable, monitoring both coverage and hiring practices. Scholarships and training supported students and helped professionals thrive in their jobs. Stylebooks aimed to help journalists with terminology and racially sensitive issues. Even as other industries made important strides toward integration, however, the news media fell progressively behind.

Ethnic Media

As conventional news coverage lagged in its struggle to keep up with U.S. demographic changes, community and ethnic media leapt in to fill the gap. Circulation increased rapidly for Hispanic and Spanish-language newspapers from 1990 to 2003, when it flattened a bit and then climbed again to 17.8 million by 2006, according to an analysis by the Project for Excellence in Journalism. In the years that followed, Latino-focused outlets continued to grow, if more slowly. Black-oriented media remained consistent fixtures into the 21st century but were hit by the same economic challenges as other news media and slow to move into digital offerings. The eminent Johnson Publications spun out its famed magazines *Ebony* and *Jet* in 2015, then declared bankruptcy 4 years later.

Founded in 1945, Johnson Publications had transformed white news media's perceptions of Black culture and community, leading to broader coverage of Black celebrities and business successes. Both magazines also wrote frankly about racism. In 1955, *Jet* editors made a bold editorial decision that galvanized the civil rights movement. At the request of Emmett Till's mother, they printed a photo of the brutally tortured, disfigured 14-year-old in his coffin. Two white men had kidnapped and killed the Chicago boy after he was accused of offending one of the men's wife. The killers were acquitted by an all-white jury.

Ethnic media cover their communities in far more depth than do mainstream outlets and follow news developments in areas such as immigration and civil rights more closely. Such community-oriented media also tend to include context and commentary that other journalists neglect. When covering U.S. Immigration and Customs Enforcement Agency actions, for instance, Spanish-language media often offer a level of diversity in topic and approach not achieved by other outlets. Mainstream news often concentrate on the victims of a particular enforcement raid or focus on examples of companies that hired undocumented workers. Spanish-language outlets cover similar topics in a balanced and neutral fashion and, in addition, bring in the social, historical, and political factors contributing to policy and enforcement.

Research on Mainstream News Coverage

Many scholars have studied news angles, content, and sourcing in mainstream news and found compelling evidence that overall, mainstream journalists continue to report from a white point of view. While coverage has become more inclusive, people of color often remain absent—except in crime, sports, or entertainment news. White, male voices still dominate as experts in local and national news, whether broadcast or text-based. In 2015, National Public Radio conducted an internal study of sources and found that male reporters relied on other men as sources 75% of the time. Further, Latino, Black, and Asian journalists were more likely to reach beyond white sources to gather the news.

Black people do consistently and disproportionately appear on local stations and in newspaper crime news—nearly always as suspects, researchers have found. A preponderance of Black people appearing on network news are poor, complaining, or involved with drugs and crime. University of Illinois at Urbana–Champaign communications researcher Travis Dixon analyzed 2 years of local and national news and opinion in print and broadcast and found stark misrepresentations of Black Americans. Overall, he found African American families were portrayed disproportionately and inaccurately as living in poverty, receiving welfare, with uninvolved fathers, and associated with criminality. Other studies have found journalists to be less likely to cover incidents involving nonwhite victims across subjects from missing persons to violent crime. The cumulative effects of such distortions may be profound.

In pivotal experiments testing attitudes and reactions, political scientists Frank D. Gilliam Jr. and Shanto Iyengar concluded that news watchers showed regular, unconscious tendencies to associate Black people with crime. Even when they were shown sample news stories with no perpetrator at all, 44% of viewers remembered a Black criminal. Frequent news watchers in the Los Angeles study tended toward views that the researchers called "new racism": a perception that Black people tend to violate traditional values of hard work and make illegitimate demands for government benefits.

In a 2018 survey of public perceptions on the 50th anniversary of the Kerner report funded by the Ford Foundation, more than half of 3,000 African Americans, Hispanic Americans, Asian Americans, and white Americans said that African Americans were portrayed more negatively than reality. Nearly half of Hispanic Americans and African Americans felt that Latinos were misrepresented as well. A majority of all races agreed that diversifying the staff of news media would improve news quality. While such studies have limitations and do not prove a causal link, they do give journalists cause for reflection.

Period of Awakening

In the first two decades of the 21st century, rapid changes in distribution forced news organizations to adjust or die. Headlines no longer could be simply "punchy," they had to capture eyeballs in an enormously distracting environment and perform well in search engines and social media channels. Journalism had to compete with information that looked very similar but was designed to sell—a product, an idea, a political agenda. The news industry's advertising-based business model began to collapse as Internet giants Google and Facebook vacuumed up news customers and advertisers. Takeovers and mergers convulsed the news sector, and many local news companies went out of business.

As long-time print and broadcast operations struggled, "digital natives" sprang up. While the economic shifts produced a barren news landscape in many ways, they also made room for new voices such as ESPN's "The Undefeated," which covers the intersections between sports, race, and culture; Indianz.com, operated by the Winnebago Tribe; The Root, which features Black news, politics, and culture; AsAmNews and *Hyphen* magazine, with an Asian American emphasis; and NewsTaco, with Latino news and information.

Over the first half of 2020, a series of developments upended what had already been a difficult period. The new coronavirus swept the world, bringing with it a surge of demand for trustworthy news, but also an exodus by advertisers concerned about appearing next to upsetting content. From 2008 to 2019, news organizations had shed 23% of their staff. As of April 2020, *The New York Times* estimated, another 36,000 journalists had been laid off, furloughed, or had their pay cut. Those who remained covered the wrenching story of illness and death, often risking their lives out on the street while others sheltered at home. Then, following months of stay-at-home orders, George Floyd was killed by a Minneapolis police officer who was captured on video pressing a knee into the Black man's neck for nearly 9 min. The incident, one more in an accelerating drumbeat of similar videos documenting police killings of Black men and women over recent months and years, reignited the Black Lives Matter movement. Hundreds of thousands of protesters poured into streets across the globe—and remained there.

The continuing movement, which drew participants from across the racial spectrum, became the largest ever in the United States to date. It widened from a focus on police violence to calls for justice across government, corporations, and many other institutions. Working alongside protesters, journalists were beaten, tear-gassed, and wounded with rubber bullets by the police and state troopers.

Discussions about systemic racism surged in social media and on opinion pages. The upheaval soon spread to newsrooms themselves. Reporters challenged dictums that they should stay out of the conversation unfolding online and cover racial justice dispassionately. They called attention to a double standard that often assumed bias on the part of Black, Asian, and Latino journalists and allowed white ones more freedom. Ethical questions arose: Could journalists voice moral outrage on Twitter? Could they join publicly in debate about covering race? Join protests? Journalists often freely express support of the First Amendment and free speech—is that where allowable opining ends?

In June, when *The New York Times* published an inflammatory column by Sen. Tom Cotton asserting that the government should send "an overwhelming show of force" to quell the social upheaval, *Times* journalists took to Twitter in protest. One thousand employees reportedly signed onto a letter to the publisher denouncing the decision to run it. The editorial page editor resigned, and similar reckonings at *The Washington Post*, *The Philadelphia Inquirer*, the *Pittsburgh Post-Gazette*, Refiney29, Bon Appetit, and the *Los Angeles Times* unfolded as journalists spoke up about entrenched racism in newsroom culture, traditions, and coverage. Employees at *Essence* magazine pushed the quest for

accountability into the Black press, calling out bullying and sexual harassment and asking several executives to step down. *The Wall Street Journal* newsroom wrote a letter to the editor-in-chief calling for "more muscular coverage about racial and social inequities" and more skeptical treatment of business executives and government officials in their pages.

Hiring practices across the industry still favored white journalists: In the 2019 ASNE survey, journalists of color made up 21% of salaried staff among daily newspapers that reported their data and 30.8% of staff among online-only outlets. *The Washington Post*, *The New York Times*, and *The Wall Street Journal* all promised to redouble their efforts at inclusive staffing and coverage, some making new appointments and creating job openings on the spot. That same month, the Associated Press announced it would capitalize both "Black" and "Indigenous" in its influential stylebook, after studying the question for 2 years. The change reflects "an essential and shared sense of history, identity and community among people who identify as Black," wrote John Daniszewski, AP's vice president of standards. Indigenous references "original inhabitants of a place," he added, explaining that the changes reflected a need to be inclusive and respectful in the news agency's storytelling. Inside and outside journalism, people asked for reflection: Was the U.S. press a white supremacist institution?

Techniques for Better Reporting

As cities across the nation grow more diverse, news outlets are realizing they must change their habits and recognize both their own implicit biases and the societal reactions their coverage creates. Fundamentally, news must create an information environment that is truthful. As one component of accuracy, journalists should resist habitually covering story subjects and sources in expected roles or social status positions. Reporters must learn to notice, for example, the Black women who are technology wizards, the Native Americans in the executive suite, and Latino families with three generations in community policing. Stories should include not only familiar ideas but also challenge audiences to adjust their assumptions.

Some newsroom traditions help lock in imbalance in sourcing and content. Practices such as evaluating a source's "credibility" according to title, status, and familiarity in the newsroom may lead a majority white staff to rely mainly on white sources. Perceptions of "prominence" and "proximity," or measures of the importance of a news topic, may vary according to journalists' familiarity with communities outside of their own neighborhoods and the downtown elite. Source lists handed down on a beat are less likely to reflect the racial, ethnic, and language diversity in schools, parks, shops, and workplaces across the country.

A number of mainstream news media outlets have forged partnerships with ethnic and community outlets in order to build better awareness of the people and stories they are missing. Ethnic media offer a background in the institutional and social underpinnings of their community's experience. They can share the perspectives and voices of groups that mainstream outlets find hard to access. For their part, the larger news organization can provide resources and connections to political and institutional sources that ethnic media may lack.

The Maynard Institute has long taught journalists to cover the whole community by analyzing how they perceive news and what they might be missing. Maynard identifies five forces that shape lives, experiences, and the social tensions in society: the "fault lines" of race, class, generation, geography, and gender and sexual orientation. By using this framework for self-reflection, reporters and editors can see how their own upbringing and history shape their view of the world. They can understand the shared culture within a newsroom, which often reflects society's racial and other social hierarchies and thus distorts the newsgathering process.

By assessing the ways in which these fault lines mold views about the importance and meaning of issues, journalists can do a better job deciding what to cover and how. They can learn their own blind spots and assumptions they have accumulated over time. Reporting more consciously, they can identify news they would have overlooked or avoided and locate the sources necessary for a complete and accurate story. A piece about the health of the Social Security system, for instance, will be much more complete if it explores the very different experiences across racial group, ability or disability, and gender in both earnings and benefits.

Other resources also highlight the need for diverse voices. The Poynter Institute, a nonprofit journalism education and training center in Florida, places ethics, trust, and diversity together in its training and resources. Columns on integrating the newsroom and covering developing issues ethically sit side by side on its website, signaling that inclusion is central to accuracy and fairness. The Trust Project, an international nonprofit that works with news outlets to show "trust indicators" that explain the fundamental standards and practices behind their journalism, includes diversity alongside disclosures on ethical issues such as conflict of interest, corrections, and unnamed sources. The trust indicator called "diverse voices" asks sites to describe their commitment to inclusive reporting and provide data on the proportion of staff that reflects underrepresented voices in their region.

The need to change reporting practices became especially clear in the early months of COVID-19 in 2020, as the lopsided toll of cases and deaths among Black Americans, Latinos, and Asians became impossible to ignore. Even when coverage steered clear of stereotypes, journalists typically offered limited explanations—such as underlying health problems, cramped living situations, or an inability to work from home—that came close to blaming the victims. News stories often left the public to assume that the living and working conditions exposing people of color to higher risk were somehow inevitable. Instead, journalists must learn to uncover the interlocking systems that underpin such racially stratified conditions.

In the case of underlying health conditions, for instance, racial favoritism in the channeling of resources such as healthcare, clean air and water, and clean and well-lighted spaces to exercise over time have left people of color physically more vulnerable to the ravages of the virus. Simply by using the question "Why?" to deepen their inquiry, reporters can unravel the external forces that shape people's lives in a racialized manner. They can show the layers of institutional practices, policies, and built-in bias that reflect societal power structures and act to hold inequality in place. They must study the history of race in America, including the construction of whiteness, and the way structural racism operates across neighborhoods and institutions in order to add context and awareness to their stories.

A journalist has a duty to "seek truth and report it" in service of justice and democracy, declares Society of Professional Journalists, the nation's most broad-based journalism organization, in its ethics code. Yet "truth" in the news, both journalists and communication researchers have found, can be a matter of shifting ground. Whether journalists are reporting a car accident or a riot, their own location, knowledge base, and personal history influences the "truth" they are able to see. They may not notice and report on the impact of longstanding racial power relations, and their own role within them. The mainstream news media continue to struggle, with uneven success, to report fully on the truth lived by the racial and ethnic minorities in American society.

Sally Lehrman

See also African American News Media; Asian American News Media; Civil Unrest, Coverage of; Diversity in Journalism; Ethics; Ethnic Minority Networks; Immigration, Coverage of; Latino News Media; Indigenous News Media; Newsroom Culture

Further Readings

Banaji, M. R., & Anthony, G. G. (2013). *Blindspot: Hidden biases of good people*. New York, NY: Delacorte Press.

Brown, F. (Ed.) (2011). *Journalism ethics: A Casebook of professional conduct for news media* (4th ed.). Portland, OR: Marion Street Press, LLC.

Brown, T. (2003). *What mama taught me: The seven core values of life*. New York, NY: William Morrow.

Christian, S. E. (2012). *Overcoming bias: A journalist's guide to culture and context*. Scottsdale, AZ: Holcomb Hathaway.

Dixon, T. (2017). "A dangerous distortion of our families," color of change. Retrieved from https://colorofchange.org/dangerousdistortion/

Dixon, T. L., & Azocar, C. L. (2007). Priming crime and activating Blackness: Understanding the psychological impact of the overrepresentation of blacks as lawbreakers on television news. *Journal of Communication, 57*(2), 229–253. doi:10.1111/j.1460-2466.2007.00341.x.

Dixon, T. L., & Linz, D. (2000). Overrepresentation and underrepresentation of African Americans and Latinos as lawbreakers on television news. *Journal of Communication, 50*(2), 131–154. doi:10.1111/j.1460-2466.2000.tb02845.x.

Domke, D. (1997). *Journalists, framing, and discourse about race relations*. Columbia, SC: Association for Education in Journalism and Mass Communication.

Domke, D., Garland, P., Billeaudeaux, A., & Hutcheson, J. (2003). Insights into U.S. racial hierarchy: Racial profiling, news sources, and September 11. *Journal of Communication, 53*(4), 606–623. doi:10.1111/j.1460-2466.2003.tb02913.x.

Entman, R. M., & Rojecki, A. (2000). *The black image in the white mind: Media and race in America*. Chicago, IL: University of Chicago Press.

Gilliam, F., Jr., & Iyengar, S. (2000). Prime suspects: The influence of local television news on the viewing public. *American Journal of Political Science, 44*(3), 560–573. doi:10.2307/2669264.

González, J., & Torres, J. (2011). *News for all the people: The epic story of race and the American Media*. New York, NY: Verso.

Jeffrey, G. & Barthel, M. (2020). Black, Hispanic and white adults feel the news media misunderstand them, but for very different reasons. *Pew Research center*. Retrieved from https://www.pewresearch.org/fact-tank/2020/06/25/black-hispanic-and-white-adults-feel-the-news-media-misunderstand-them-but-for-very-different-reasons/

Jha, S., & Izard, R. (2005). Who got to talk about it? *Seattle Journal for Social Justice, 4*, 101–118.

Lehrman, S. (2005). *News in a new America*. Miami, FL: John S. and James L. Knight Foundation.

Lehrman, S. & Wagner, V. (Eds.) (2019). *Reporting inequality: Tools and methods for covering race and ethnicity*. London, UK: Routledge.

Marzolf, M., & Tolliver, M. (1977). *Kerner plus 10: Conference on the minorities and the media*. Ann Arbor, MI: University of Michigan. Retrived April 22, 1977, from https://eric.ed.gov/?id=ED149382

National Advisory Commission on Civil Disorders. (1968). *Kerner report*. New York, NY: Bantam Books. Retrieved from www.eisenhowerfoundation.org/docs/kerner.pdf

Oliver, M. B., Ramasubramanian, S., & Kim, J. (2007). Media and racism. In D. R. Roskos-Ewoldsen & J. L. Monahan (Eds.), *Communication and social cognition: Theories and methods* (pp. 273–91). New York, NY: Routledge.

Pride, A. S., & Wilson II, C. C. (1997). *A history of the Black press*. Washington, DC: Howard University Press.

Schudson, M. (2011). *The sociology of news* (2nd ed.). New York, NY: W. W. Norton & Company.

Society of Professional Journalists. *Code of ethics.* Retrieved from http://www.spj.org/ethicscode.asp

Society of Professional Journalists. *Diversity toolbox.* Retrieved from https://www.spj.org/divsourcebook .asp

Wilson II, C. C., Gutiérrez, F. F., & Chao, L. (2012). *Racism, sexism and the media: The rise of class communication in multicultural America (*4th ed.). Thousand Oaks, CA: Sage.

RADIO CORPORATION OF AMERICA

The Radio Corporation of America (RCA) played a dominant role in the development of radio and television broadcasting from 1919 until the 1970s. The company's cemented its influence through the development and manufacture of communications equipment and the establishment of broadcast stations and networks. This entry examines the history of development of the RCA and examines its influence beyond radio broadcasting, including its influence on television and attempted foray into early computing.

History and Development

In the early 20th century, radio was used predominantly for ship-to-shore communications. American Marconi Corporation, a subsidiary of Britain's Marconi Company, established a monopoly on wireless maritime transmitters and receiving equipment. During World War I, the U.S. Navy took control of American Marconi's transmitters and was reluctant to return them to the foreign-owned company at the conclusion of the conflict. Meanwhile, American Marconi made plans to purchase and operate new, high-powered transmitters manufactured by General Electric (GE). Fearing that a foreign country would dominate transatlantic radio communications, the U.S. government pressured GE to buy American Marconi

and form a subsidiary to purchase and operate the new transmitters. GE established RCA as this subsidiary in 1919, with a stipulation that all board members had to be U.S. citizens and no more than 20% of its stock could be owned by foreign interests.

As the 1920s began, the radio industry turned its attention toward the development of broadcasting—using a single transmitter to disperse a signal among a wide audience. Through a series of agreements, the major players in radio communication (RCA, GE, American Telephone & Telegraph [AT&T], and Westinghouse) agreed to share patents for critical radio technologies that would allow for broadcast transmission and reception. As part of the patent agreements, GE took ownership of about 30% of RCA's stock, with Westinghouse and AT&T owning about 20% and 10%, respectively. RCA initially moved cautiously into broadcasting, hewing to its original mission of providing international and transoceanic communication. However, David Sarnoff, a holdover from American Marconi who was now a manager at RCA, pushed his superiors to dive headlong into the broadcasting industry. In the summer of 1921, RCA set up a transmitting facility at a GE factory in New Jersey to broadcast a heavyweight championship boxing match. By most accounts, the experiment was a success, as an estimated 200,000 people listened (even though the transmitter burned out minutes after the final bell sounded).

By 1923, RCA operated three broadcast radio stations: two in New York City and one in Washington, D.C. In 1926, the company purchased AT&T's popular New York station WEAF; it also signed a long-term agreement to lease AT&T's transmission lines. The lines would allow RCA to essentially interconnect individual broadcast stations and share programming among them. To this end, RCA formed a separate entity, the National Broadcasting Company (NBC), boasting that it would bring "National radio broadcasting with better programming permanently assured." The idea was that the network would originate programming in cultural centers (New York City, for the most part) where it was easier to secure popular artists and simulcast this programming over geographically dispersed stations using AT&T's transmission lines.

NBC actually established two networks: the Red Network, with WEAF as its flagship station, and the Blue Network, with RCA's other New York station, WJZ, as its flagship. The Red Network ran the most popular (and expensive) programming, while the Blue Network tended to carry less expensive programming as well as "sustaining" public service content that did not carry advertising. By the end of 1926, 19 stations were on NBC's networks; that number grew steadily over the next decade. By 1941, 221 stations were signed up with NBC, representing more than one quarter of all broadcast stations in the United States. NBC's roster also included many of the most powerful 50,000 watt stations, as well as outlets located in the largest markets in the country. The network's power and influence attracted the attention of the Federal Communications Commission (FCC), which ordered NBC to divest itself of one of its networks. In 1943, the Blue Network was sold to candy magnate Edward Noble, who rebranded it as the American Broadcasting Company.

NBC was not the only arm of RCA to receive governmental scrutiny. By the 1930s, RCA had become a leader in manufacturing radio sets for consumer use, and it had also expanded into other areas such as vacuum tube and phonograph players. The U.S. Justice Department in 1932 forced GE and Westinghouse to give up their RCA stock and to make patent pooling arrangements among the companies nonexclusive. At this point, RCA became a wholly independent company. Still, RCA's overall size and rich cache of exclusive patents for communications technologies would attract the notice of federal regulators throughout the 1940s and 1950s. "RCA occupies a premier position in fields which are profoundly determinative of our way of life," noted the FCC in its 1941 *Report on Chain Broadcasting*. "Its diverse activities give it a peculiarly advantageous position in competition with enterprises less widely based."

Influence Beyond Radio Broadcasting

RCA also inserted itself squarely in the development of television during the 1930s, investing millions of dollars in research, hiring engineers from competitors, and acquiring critical patents.

In 1938, RCA proposed that the FCC adopt standards for television transmission and reception it had developed. In the face of widespread opposition to RCA's proposal by competing companies, the FCC chose to approve "limited" commercial operation of black and white television so that various competing standards could be tested. Instead, RCA dove headfirst into marketing and manufacturing television sets, announcing at the 1939 World's Fair that television had "arrived." The FCC moved quickly to staunch RCA's overreach, and instead began a series of hearings to consider other television standards, including a color system proposed by CBS. In 1941, the FCC adopted television standards proposed by the National Television Systems Committee. These standards would rely on patents owned by RCA, and the company would continue to receive royalties on television equipment well into the 1960s.

The early 1960s were probably the high-water mark for the company's influence. Although it remained a major player in broadcasting, equipment manufacturing, and military and space communication, breakthrough innovations eluded the company. RCA's attempt in the 1970s to enter the computer business failed spectacularly, piling up losses of more than $500 million. In 1986, GE took over RCA, and quickly set about dismantling the company's various ventures or integrating them into its own operations. Today, RCA is merely a trade name owned by Sony Music Entertainment and Technicolor.

James Foust

See also Broadcast, or broadcasting; Federal Communications Commission (FCC); North America

Further Readings

Barnouw, E. (1968). *The Golden Web: A history of broadcasting in the United States.* New York, NY: Oxford University Press.

Sterling, C. H., & Kittross, J. M. (2002). *Stay tuned: A history of American broadcasting* (3rd ed.). Mahwah, NJ: Erlbaum Associates.

U.S. Federal Communications Commission. (1941) *Report on chain broadcasting.* Washington, DC: U.S. Government Printing Office.

RECORDING

"Recording" refers to written, aural, or visual evidence that has been preserved in some tangible medium. In journalism, the term is used to describe the practice of capturing and preserving selected elements of a news story. Journalists use recording devices to conduct interviews. Newspapers and magazines use transcriptions of verbatim statements of people or documents. Audio recordings preserve the voices of newsmakers. Photography and videography provide visual documentation of images of news events. All are recordings, but the word "recording" is used more specifically to refer to the preservation of words, sounds, images, and data using audio and video technologies.

Early recording systems used to store information include words on paper (symbols that inform the vocalization of human speech) and sheet music notations (instructions for singing and musical instrumentation). Some early mechanical devices also preserved instructions for sound, such as the prongs of a rotating cylinder used to pluck the strings in a music box and a perforated paper roll in a player piano. These devices did not preserve actual sounds, and for that matter, neither do more contemporary electronic devices. All rely on encoding processes to preserve some representation of sound and then decoding for reproduction in a way that is unique to a specific recording technology.

This entry discusses the history of sound recording before detailing the microphones and digital audio recording used in journalism. It then looks at the history of video recording, the development of digital video recording, and more recent developments in audio and video technology.

History of Sound Recording

The first practical device capable of recording the human voice was the "phonograph," invented by Thomas Edison in 1878. Edison thought the phonograph (a Greek word for "sound writer") would be used for dictation, for educational purposes. Major improvements followed, such as the "graphophone" (Chichester Bell and Charles Tainter, 1881), a wax cylinder machine, and the "gramophone" (Emile Berliner, 1887), a flat disc system that made storage and duplication more convenient, later sold to the Victor Talking Machine Company which became a division of the Radio Corporation of America.

Significant technological developments in radio electronics contributed to improvements in amplifier and loudspeaker technologies. Consumers adopted these early systems for home entertainment and music recording, and Radio Corporation of America Victor became a major producer of vinyl records and the company's "Victrola" player. Other methods of recording included "Phonofilm," an optical sound-on-film system (Lee de Forest, 1919) used to produce experimental short films with music, speech, and vaudeville. Before long, Fox Movietone newsreels were shown in movie theaters. In 1927, the "Vitaphone," a synchronized disc system, was used to produce the first feature-length "talkie," "The Jazz Singer."

Magnetic sound recording technologies were also developed. The first such device was called a *telegraphone* (Valdemar Poulsen, 1890s), which was used to record Austrian Emperor Franz Joseph at the 1900 Paris World's Fair, believed to be the oldest surviving example of a magnetic recording. Later devices included wire and metal tape machines that were used to record news events as early as World War I. Breaking news events demonstrated the value of sound recording, such as WLS reporter Herb Morrison's dramatic description of the Hindenburg airship crash in 1937. Radio networks and local stations recorded news or talk programs, such as Edward R. Murrow's famous broadcasts on short-wave radio from London, which were preserved on electronic transcription disc. World War II also influenced the growth of sound recording, such as the development of the "magnetophone," invented by two German companies (AEG and BASF), a machine that used iron- or ferrous oxide-coated paper or cellulose acetate tape—a recording medium that would later be known as *magnetic tape*. After the war, the American Signal Corps brought back these improved recording technologies to the United States.

Before and during the war, most radio programming was broadcasted live. The ability to record sound on magnetic tape changed radio and help launch the music industry during the postwar period. Improvements in magnetic tape recording not only enhanced sound quality, it provided engineers with the ability to mix, balance, edit, store, and produce stereo and multichannel audio. Noise reduction systems to improve quality and control "hiss," such as Dolby and dbx, were developed in the late 1960s. Various tape formats were also introduced, including reel-to-reel, endless-loop eight-track and professional cartridge, and the consumer compact audio cassette, which was standardized by the Philips Company of the Netherlands in 1962.

Analog audio technologies such as these were designed to capture and record variations in the physical characteristics of sound waves over time by imprinting their signature onto a moving physical surface or magnetized substrate. In the case of vinyl recording, the sound wave signature is encoded by carving a spiral groove onto the surface of a vinyl cylinder or disc. With magnetic tape, iron oxide particles on the surface of the tape are magnetically manipulated to create a pattern that mirrors variations in the electrical audio signal. Analog recordings capture sound continuously, in real time without interruption. Many hardware and tape formats came and went during the early decades of sound recording, but analog audio technologies remained fundamentally unchanged until the introduction of digital audiotape by Sony in 1987.

Microphones

One of the primary jobs of a journalist is to conduct and record interviews. To do so, they use microphones, which contain a transducer, an electronic component that converts acoustic energy into a low-voltage signal that can be processed and stored. By default, microphones are analog devices because the electrical signal they generate is a continuous representation of real-time changes in sound wave amplitude (perceived loudness) and frequency (perceived pitch) caused by variations in pressure and vibration from surrounding air molecules.

When a microphone is connected to an audio mixer or recording device, the low-voltage signal is amplified to make it suitable for audio processing. A "preamp" is used to increase or decrease the amount of signal attenuation. A volume-unit meter (or VU meter) displays the strength of the audio signal in decibels to ensure a proper record level. Setting the record level too low will produce unwanted background noise and setting it too high can overdrive the preamp circuit, causing *clipping*—distortion and a loss of audio fidelity. When a microphone is connected to a digital audio recorder, the signal must also pass through an analog to digital converter, where it is transcoded into binary form (0s and 1s).

The two most common microphone transducer types are *dynamic* and *condenser*. Most dynamic mics feature a relatively simple diaphragm moving coil design. Variations in sound pressure (acoustic energy) causes the diaphragm to vibrate and pulse. The vibrations are transferred to a moving coil that produces a low-voltage electric current that corresponds to the original sound wave. Reporters typically use dynamic handheld microphones when conducting field interviews or recording voiceovers. Condenser microphones include a capacitor, which require an internal battery or *phantom power*, making them more sensitive than dynamic microphones, thereby allowing them to pick up sound from further away. Most lavalier microphones fall into the condenser category and are often used for sit-down interviews and for on-air talent and guests in a television studio setting. Because they are more sensitive, "lav" mics are best used in quiet settings with minimal ambient sound.

Digital Audio Recording

In order for sound to be understood by a computer, it must be converted from its native analog form to a digital format that can be represented with discrete numerical values. Pulse code modulation (PCM), the most common codec used for recording audio as a digital stream of binary data, was conceived by British engineer Alec Reeves in 1937. His theory of pulse code modulation transmission relied on a process called *sampling* to transform a continuous signal into a sequence of regular interval discrete measurements. Each measurement (or sample) represents one instance of a sound wave's properties at a single moment in time. In digital recording, each sample is stored numerically as a binary string of zeros and ones.

The fidelity of a pulse code modulation audio stream is determined by three variables: *sampling rate*, the number of times per second in kHz units each sample is recorded; *bit depth*, the number of bits assigned to each sample; and *bit rate*, the number of bits per second transmitted during playback or streaming. All things being equal, the greater the sampling rate and bit depth, the greater the overall sound resolution and quality. During reproduction, digital representations are converted back to analog acoustical energy for human monitoring.

Digital data storage and distribution formats, such as the audio compact disc, which uses a laser to read digitally encoded information, was the dominant consumer digital audio medium for three decades. Sony and Philips introduced the optical disk format in 1982 and published the initial technical standards for digital audio recording in a document known as the *Red Book*. An audio compact disc holds up to 74 minutes of uncompressed audio, includes two channels of stereo bitstreams encoded with linear pulse code modulation, and has a sampling rate and bit depth of 44.1 kHz/16 bit.

History of Video Recording

Over time, magnetic tape recording systems evolved that enabled recording video as well as audio. In 1956, Ampex released the first analog broadcast quality video recorder. It was dubbed the quad machine, because it used 2-inch wide magnetic quadruplex tape mounted on large metallic reels. Quad recorders served the broadcast industry until 1976, when Ampex and Sony jointly released the Type C 1 reel-to-reel recorder which was smaller, significantly less expensive, and included advancements such as instant replay and slow motion.

The 1970s also ushered in the era of electronic newsgathering and an eventual end to the long-held practice of film-based recording in broadcast news. In its place, broadcast news teams began using portable electronic video cameras and videocassette recorders (VCRs), which greatly enhanced their ability to disseminate news and information in a timely manner. Initially, portable video recording required a three-person team comprised of a reporter, a videographer to operate the camera, and a recording engineer to carry the VCR and monitor levels. Eventually, bulky portable recorders such as the Sony U-matic ¾ VCR were replaced by a better device called a *camcorder*—a one-piece recording unit that combined a camera with a VCR that could be operated by one person. In 1983, Sony introduced the first professional-grade Betacam camcorder, which was widely used by electronic newsgathering professionals for more than a decade.

Digital Video Recording

Digital video converts an analog signal representing an image into numbers for magnetic, optical, or solid-state digital format devices, such as hard-disk and flash drives, memory cards, network storage, and online distribution. Digital cameras capture incoming light from objects in the field of view, turn it into a corresponding electrical signal, and then convert the energy of that signal into numbers for each picture element (pixel) representing light intensity and color in the image. Because of the large amount of information in a moving video image, newer systems use digital compression techniques (algorithms), which reduce the amount of redundant information to save storage space.

In the 1990s, various high-density optical storage technologies emerged for recording standard definition video. In 1995, Toshiba introduced the DVD (digital versatile [or video] disc) to record and distribute audio, video, and data, making this device the most widely used consumer video recording and distribution medium for motion picture film at the time. A standard DVD disc could hold 133 minutes of standard definition video content and offered desirable features consumers craved such as rapid access to program content via a visual interface with links to program chapters and bonus content. The DVD rapidly supplanted consumer reliance on antiquated analog tape formats such as VHS and Betamax. The Blu-ray disc format followed in 2006 to enable distribution of high-definition movies on a single disc the same size as an audio compact disc.

Solid-state video devices and digital video recorder systems, such as TiVo and ReplayTV, use computer technology and hard drives to enable consumers to download, manipulate (pause, fast forward, reverse, slow motion), and take advantage of instant replay functions and time-shift television programs for later viewing. Video distribution services, such as satellite, cable, and Internet protocol television systems, also provide on-demand access to stored video programming.

Many recording formats, including digital variations of magnetic tape such as digital audiotape for professional sound recording, Digital Betacam (or DigiBeta) for professional newsgathering, and MiniDV for video recording by nonprofessionals, persisted in popularity from the late 1980s until the end of the 1990s. However, with the growing popularity of *file-based recording* near the turn of the century, their effective usefulness eroded.

On a related front, broadcast and production technical standards for digital television and high-definition television were adapted. By early 2007, personal digital multimedia devices allowed Internet users to download video podcasts or "vodcasts" of television news, information, and music. As recording technology continues to evolve, on-demand systems, available online or through digital cable systems, have reduced the need for consumers to download or record television news and other programs at home.

With file-based recording, digital devices such as DSLRs (digital single lens reflex cameras), video camcorders, audio recorders, smartphones, and so forth, encode audio and video signals directly to a flash drive or memory card as digital bitstreams, a sequence of bits used to represent individual video or audio signals. High-definition video files are much larger than audio files and must be compressed before uploading to streaming video services such as YouTube and Vimeo. Distribution standards changed, and by 2020, MP4 was the established video format for streaming high-definition video on the web. Likewise, H.264 and its successor H.265 (HEVC—High Efficiency Video Coding) were the most widely used codecs for encoding video, while AAC-LC (Advanced Audio Coding-Low Complexity) was used for encoding audio.

Newer Audio and Video Tools

Hard disk, removable flash drive, and solid-state digital storage devices are more recent innovations in sound recording. Stand-alone consumer electronic devices were eventually supplanted by smartphones, which are capable of doing infinitely more, while expanding the distribution channels for news, information, and music across the Internet via Wi-Fi and cellular networks. Today, digital audio and video news stories are widely distributed online through a plethora of social media and streaming services.

Today, many journalists use smartphones to record interviews, still photos, and video images. They can also use mobile apps for editing and processing of sound, images, and video and for instantly sharing, transmitting, or publishing content wirelessly around the world. Podcasting, a convenient way to package, access, and download digital audio content, is now used by many respected journalists to provide supplemental news, information, and opinion. Mobile recording devices and apps help journalists capture everything said in an interview or press conference, especially long news events. Smartphone apps have been created specifically for such recording purposes and more. Some applications even offer a transcription function, making it possible to convert recorded sound to written words for publication.

Don A. Grady and Vic Costello

See also Audio and Video News Services; Convergence; Digital sound; Digital Television; Electronic News Gathering; Podcasting; Television; Video News Releases

Further Readings

Costello, V. (2016). *Multimedia foundations: Core concepts for digital design.* New York, NY: Routledge.

Daniels, E. D., Denis Mee, C., & Clark, M. H, eds. (1999). *Magnetic recording: The first 100 years.* New York, NY: IEEE.

Marlow, E., & Secunda, E. (1991). *Shifting time and space: The story of videotape.* New York, NY: Praeger.

Nmungwun, A. F. (1909). *Video recording technology: Its impact on media and home entertainment.* New York, NY and London, UK: Routledge: Taylor & Francis Group.

Schoenherr, S. (Revised, 2005). Recording technology history. Retrieved from http://www.aes-media.org /historical/html/recording.technology.history/notes .html

Reporters Committee for Freedom of the Press. (Summer 2012). Reporter's recording guide: A state-by-state guide to taping phone calls and in-person conversations. Retrieved from https://www.rcfp.org/wp-content/uploads/imported/RECORDING.pdf

Rumsey, F., & McCormick, T. (2014). *Sound and recording: Applications and theory* (7th ed.). Burlington, MA: Focal Press.

Whitaker, J., & Benson, K. B. (2000). *Video recording systems*. New York, NY: McGraw-Hill.

RELIGION JOURNALISM

Religion journalism is perhaps one of the most challenging subfields within journalism—it requires specialist knowledge to discern its specificities and the subject matter is so sensitive that the slightest mistake in wording can lead to angry outcries from the public. Topics such as religion are incredibly nuanced, and the ability to communicate religious issues accurately in 500 to 600 words can be challenging, to say the least. If a public is conceived of as diverse, then this creates both an opportunity and a danger for journalism on religion in a democracy.

Many countries have what Robert Putnam and David Campbell (2010) describe as a "volatile" mixture of a high religious pluralism—people of different faiths in close contact—and high religious diversity—a wide array of religions (p. 494). This would naturally raise the stakes for reporting on religion. Journalism is rooted in the history of religion itself and may be one of the most enduring subfields of journalism. Yet the religion specialty has shrunk substantially since the digital turn in the news industry, leaving much of the reporting on religion to nonspecialists. This specialty has great potential for promoting diversity and inclusion in society; yet, particularly in regard to concerns related to religiously oriented hate groups, there are substantial dangers that accompany this form of reporting.

Focuses of Religion Journalism

Religion journalism tends to be both trend oriented and focused on the individual experience. In 2019, religion journalism conducted significant reporting on the growing schism within the United Methodist Church—this schism represents the continuation of Culture Wars era trend toward church splits over social issues, and social issues appeared to be at the heart of the split within the denomination. In a similar manner, the coronavirus pandemic in 2020 provided the opportunity for religion journalists to report on churches streaming activities, digital religious groups, and online churches—none of these were new phenomena but are representative of the trend toward digital religious experiences. The reporting is also highly individualistic. In 2020, in the wake of protests following the death of George Floyd by a police officer while being arrested, U.S. President Donald Trump appeared in front of an episcopal church, holding a Bible and announcing strong measures against protesters. Religion journalism reported extensively on the pastor and members of the church where Trump appeared and local journalists focused on the responses by local religious leaders to this imagery presented by the U.S. president.

These twin focuses on the trend and the individual experience make sense given the nature of the topic. It is difficult to offer any form of generalization on religion, given that there are myriad ways that the religion is interpreted—which presents a meaningful difference from the rules of basketball in sports journalism or laws for running a country's political campaign. Even if the generalization were based on the religious scripture, this presents three issues for the religion journalist: (1) different faiths place different degrees of emphasis on the scripture, (2) scriptures are often read in widely different manners—even in faiths that place a strong emphasis on the scripture, and (3) the most interest aspects of a religion tend to occur on a more individual level. In other words, human interest is a central aspect of religion reporting. Trends are more rarely reported across religious traditions but more commonly reported within religious traditions. So, for example, the decline of brick-and-mortar church attendance in the Western world represents a trend discussed within Christianity but is less commonly discussed in Islam, Judaism, or other faiths. More commonly reported trends in Islam might be demographic changes.

Religion journalism promotes a set of best practices through the specialty's nonprofit professional group, the Religion News Association. The association conducts yearly training at its annual conference and also offers, through the website ReligionLink, a set of best practices guides and source guides for reporters in the field. The organization's essential tenet is that "good reporting is good reporting" in that while religion journalism has distinguishing features it is essentially a specialty rooted in journalism.

Evolution of the Religion Beat

The religion beat began in the mid-19th century, becoming the norm starting in the early 1900s, when most newspapers had some sort of religion section. The earliest known religion beat specialists began at the start of the 20th century. The beat quickly professionalized to the point that a new professional association for religion specialists emerged in 1949. Since then, most of the nation's largest newspapers had specialists.

In the 1980s, public attention and journalism research focused attention on the salience of religion as a topic in journalism. Scholarship of the religion beat has centered primarily on content analyses describing the amount of religion news and the topics for coverage. For example, a number of studies have found that at most 2% of all the news in U.S. newspapers is about a religion. All large-scale content studies on religion news have focused on print publications, so the percentage of online religion news at a media outlet has not been assessed. Regardless of the relatively small percentage of all news about religion, religion has remained a key topic in the news. Annual content studies from the Pew Research Center often find religion as among the key topics of the news. End-of-the-year stories similarly highlight the importance of religion.

Contemporary journalism often traces its roots to the advent of movable type, and this is a history that has a profound, if not always explicitly acknowledged, influence on religion journalism. This first mass communication technology served to develop distributable Bibles. In many ways this technology facilitated the development of both Protestant Christianity and journalism. Protestant Christianity rests in five solas—statements about the nature of how faith is determined. Sola Scriptura argues that the Christian Bible is the final authority on Christian faith and practice and the only infallible source of divine revelation. Sola Christus asserts a doctrine of the priesthood of all believers, in other words, that no priesthood is required beyond that of belief itself. Both of these beliefs rely in an essential manner on the mass distribution of Bibles—this provides a final authority for practice that would be essential for developing a priesthood of all believers. In a very similar manner, movable type facilitated the spread of information and the development of an informed public—both of which are foundational for the operation of journalism.

These shared technological roots do not imply a native marriage between journalism and religion. On the contrary, scholars have at times argued that journalism and religion share a "double blind" spot toward the activities of the other: religion often is blind to the operation and activities of journalism, and journalism is at times blind to the activities of religion. However, both journalism and Protestantism have an obvious shared foundation in their challenge to institutional power. Protestantism famously dismantled the hegemony of Western Catholicism. In a similar manner, the concept of the watchdog is an essential journalistic role, written into the rationale for the profession. This history leads scholars to argue that journalism operates with a sort of protestant normativity—that is, that journalists tend to operate with an essentially protestant set of biases.

In popular rhetoric, the news media are seen as presenting a secular and irreligious product. However, this belief does not hold up in scholarship. In a 1998 study, Mark Silk examined bias studies involving religion coverage and found them inconclusive. However, he found that when news media cover religion, the frames used are largely religious in nature. "News professionals . . . are operating with ideas of what religion is and is not, of what it ought and ought not be—with topoi—that derive, to varying degrees, from religious sources" (Silk, 1998, p. 55). These topoi account for many of the critiques of Western religion journalism in that journalistic reporting on Islam, Mormonism, and Judaism. In particular, this tends to be presented through inaccurate labeling such as a "Catholic pastor" (as opposed to "priest") or a

"Catholic sermon" (as opposed to "homily"); they are labels that take for granted a Christian Protestant point-of-reference. This represents a challenge if the journalistic goal is accuracy and fairness. Although religion specialists have been effective in this reporting, the decline in religion specialists represents a challenge to this reporting.

Since the Great Recession of 2000s, many religion reporting positions have become defunct—due to limited financial resources, difficulty in identifying advertisers for religion news sections, and too many other journalistic obligations. As papers began downsizing, those sections were closed or replaced with a token page, usually on Friday or Saturday. In the United States alone, large-scale newspapers that have shuttered their dedicated religion news coverage include The Dallas Morning News, the Cleveland Plain Dealer, the Orlando Sentinel, and The Palm Beach Post.

However, while clearly suffering some decreases in major markets, religion journalism survived the digital turn in the industry—one of the most profound shifts in the journalism marketplace since the penny press—as well as the Great Recession. Furthermore, recent surveys conducted by the Religion News Association demonstrate that the beat is more widespread in smaller circulation marketplaces than previous research suggests. Urban marketplaces may not currently see a future in religion reporting, but local and community news organizations remain committed to the religion beat. This may be a reflection of audience age and the rural nature of small and mid-sized communities, where religion often plays a significant role in social cohesion.

While these circumstances may indicate a continued commitment to religion reporting in the field, they may also indicate a continued lack of priority placed on individual religion reporters. For example, in a 2013 survey by the Religion News Association, only half of the 255 newsrooms surveyed employed an individual who regularly covered religion and there was typically only one religion journalist employed.

The segmentation of the American media marketplace as a result of the rise of Internet and mobile readership has changed the shape of religion news. More than 20 years ago, scholars argued that religion reporting was becoming less

localized, but Religion News Association surveys from 2013 indicate that the pendulum may have swung the opposite direction. Although the survey data suggest strength in the local reporting of religion, few surveys have substantially measured religion news at many small circulation newspapers. As opposed to having less coverage of local religion, the circulation size of newsrooms conducting religion reporting may indicate that more local religion reporting is happening than in previous years. That said, religion reporting at larger circulation newspapers is in decline, yet larger urban area newsrooms have been the ones that historically had the resources to cover national-level religion stories. This raises the question—who will be covering such stories if not large urban newspapers? A number of vibrant online-only sites are providing a growing trove of religion content free to members, including Patheos, OnFaith, and Religionnews.com.

Dangers and Opportunities

This form of journalism presents both dangers and opportunities for journalists. Religion news requires sensitivity in reporting, and as a result, careful reporting can provide an opportunity to showcase the nature of how journalists think about their work. While not a reporting activity in particular, the decision regarding the 2006 publication of the Mohammed cartoons, in which the Prophet Mohammed is shown with a bomb strapped to his chest, was nevertheless a journalistic decision. The New York Times declined to publish the cartoons, but French newspaper Le Monde chose to publish them. The difference in decision making between the two news organizations indicated that they operate under two different journalistic paradigms. In reports in which they detailed why they decided what they decided, Dan Berkowitz and Lyombe Eko (2007) note that the journalism took the opportunity provided by the Mohammed cartoon controversy to remind readers of the purpose of journalism and, by doing so, reaffirmed their journalistic paradigm.

The cartoons presented the opportunity to engage in paradigm maintenance, but the running of the cartoons also presented a danger: it represented a worst-case scenario in relations between religion and the press—any decision made would result in a right being infringed on. In both cases, a belief was infringed upon—by journalists in the United States who argue that press had been censored and by Muslims in France who argued that their prophet should not be depicted.

Journalism provides a normative lens in making judgments about what constitutes good religion as opposed to bad religion. The way journalists make these judgments is in part through their work as an interpretive community. As a community, journalists make sense of stories regarding religion for the public. Journalists tend to be more politically savvy than religiously savvy, which may explain why religion is often collapsed onto politics. This appears through the use of labels used in attribution—journalists attempting to distill a more recognizable political term from a person's description of their faith (e.g., "conservative Catholic"; "fundamentalist Muslim").

In a similar manner, journalists faced with reporting on the Mormon Baptism for the Dead had to discern the appropriate means with which to undertake reporting. In this case, the reporting centered on two minority religious groups in the United States—Jews and Mormons—whose religious and legal battles were mediated in the press. In the Mormon doctrine of the Baptism for the Dead, Mormon's have a responsibility to baptize their ancestors—by proxy—even after they have died. It does not force them to be Mormon, but it does grant them the opportunity, according to doctrine, to choose Mormonism if they had never encountered it. This caused a conflict when it was reported that Mormons had been baptizing Jews who had died during the Holocaust. Journalists, rather than emphasizing the conflict, worked to decrease the sensationalism of the conflict through peacemaking processes such as diminishing differences between parties and minimizing sensational claims related to the case. Gregory P. Perreault, Margaret Duffy, and Ariel Morrison (2017) argue that this occurs as a result of the danger implicit in the cultural unease caused by the conflict. Hence, journalists here took the opportunity presented by the event to engage in peacemaking in order to ease the conflict between the groups.

While religion as a topic crosses over with numerous specialties—perhaps most noticeably in politics and science—there are certain specialties in which the topic has been shown to be less likely to appear. As religion specialists have decreased, these crossovers have become more essential in the dissemination of religion news. In sports journalism and gaming journalism, however, such crossovers have been less common.

In sports journalism, the appearance of religion journalism is often tied to human interest stories on individual athletes, but even in those cases sports journalism is rooted in an essential way to sports play. Hence, unless the religion is particularly tied to sports play in a meaningful way—such as professional golfer Tiger Woods's discussion of his Buddhist faith as a part of a public apology for marital infidelity—such faith is less likely to appear. When it does appear, sports journalists tend to report on religion in a more surface-level manner than would be expected outside of the religion specialty. In other words, an athlete's faith would be considered a part of describing their personality but might be less likely to be considered as a motivating force in their lives.

In a similar manner, video games commonly feature significant symbology of religion—games host religious guilds, and game players themselves can interact with gaming in a religious manner—yet little of this appears in gaming journalism, in part because gaming journalism tends to be rooted in issues related to game play. Again, if the religion is not somehow material to playing of the game, it is less likely to appear in the reporting of a piece of gaming journalism. Gaming journalists have described the religion in gaming as a sort of "wallpaper"—it is set dressing designed to set the tone but does little material to the entirety of the game. For example, gaming journalism reported extensively on player and industry response to a scene in the video game Bioshock Infinite in which the player—in a first-person perspective—is required to be baptized in order to begin the game. One Christian player took offense to this requirement and made public statements attacking the game and also requested a refund. In this case, as in the case of Tiger Woods, the religion journalism appeared in part because of its synergistic tie to the core of the other journalistic specialty.

Gregory Perreault

See also Peace Journalism; Religious News Media

Further Readings

Berkowitz, D., & Eko, L. (2007). Blasphemy as sacred rite/right: the Mohammed cartoons affair and maintenance of journalistic ideology. *Journalism Studies, 8*(5), 779–797. doi:10.1080/14616700701504757.

Perreault, G. P., Duffy, M., & Morrison, A. (2017). Making a Mormon?: Peacemaking in US Press Coverage of the Mormon Baptism for the Dead. *Journal of Media and Religion, 16*(4), 141–152. doi:10.1080/15348423.2017.1401410.

Putnam, R., & Campbell, D. (2010). *American grace: How religion divides and unites us.* New York City, NY: Simon & Schuster.

Silk, M. (1998). *Unsecular media: Making news of religion in America* (Vol. 12). University of Illinois Press.

RELIGIOUS NEWS MEDIA

The first newspaper in British colonial America, *Publick Occurrences, Both Forreign and Domestick* (1690), assumed a religious point of view. Its purpose, editor Benjamin Harris wrote, was to report news of the day so "That Memorable Occurrences of Divine Providence may not be neglected or forgotten, as they too often are." Harris, an Anabaptist, set out to produce a newspaper of record, not a religious medium, but he was so steeped in the Protestant culture of New England that he simply assumed the events he reported reflected the providence of God. A report in *Publick Occurrences* about a mourning widower who hanged himself said, "The Devil took advantage." Another story reported that "Merciful Providence" fed the English colonists who were fighting the French in Canada. American colonies were largely established by men and women who saw the world through the lens of religious faith, so religion was a part of the institutions they created, including the press.

Today's distinction between unbiased news about religion and news from a religious perspective stems from the 1830s with the development of the first electronic medium of communication, the telegraph. Use of the telegraph during the era of the penny press contributed to the development of disinterested religion journalism distinct from parochial religious journalism. Indeed, subsequent changes to religious news media also followed the introduction of new electronic media. The rise of the radio and then television broadcasting propelled religious news media towards conservative hermeneutics and politics, and the emergence of the online digital age splintered consumers of religious news media into niches. This entry discusses the history of religious news media in the United States and the state of religious news media in the 21st century.

Print Media

The breach between disinterested reporting about religion and religious journalism began in the 1830s with the development of the penny press. Enterprising newspaper editors, seeking to expand circulation, replaced subsidies with expanded advertising, lowered the price of an individual newspaper to one cent and began selling issues one at a time, and increased timeliness by publishing reports they received by telegraph from faraway places. Telegraphed news was made affordable by sharing costs with newspapers in distant locations regardless of their editorial philosophy, which required telegraphed news to become neutral reports comprised of verifiable facts.

With the development of the penny press, commercial media began to report disinterested news about religion, leaving more interpretive and sectarian reporting to religious publications. Such reporting of religion in James Gordon Bennett's *New York Herald* outraged competing newspapers and clergy, who campaigned to drive his newspaper out of business. But the so-called Moral War of 1840 failed, and the *New York Herald* and other commercial newspapers continued to publish independent, candid reports about religion to receptive readers.

Ceding control of news to profit-driven enterprises did not come easily to American religious groups. Not only did religious groups become perennial critics of commercial media, but from time to time they operated news operations of their own designed to serve both as models of public interest journalism and as viable alternatives to commercial operations. Their success varied. Today's daily *Deseret News* was begun in 1850 by Mormon pioneers in Salt Lake City who set out to record their activities for posterity. Similarly, today's *Christian Science Monitor* was begun in 1908 by Mary Baker Eddy, the founder of the Church of Christ, Scientist, who wanted to publish a general interest newspaper that she said would injure nobody but rather bless all humankind, unlike the sensational yellow journalism of Joseph Pulitzer and William Randolph Hearst. Roman Catholic laypersons began *The Sun Herald* of Kansas City to report the day's news through the perspective of Christian values in 1950, only to fold 2 years later. Another short-lived newspaper, the biweekly *National Courier*, began in 1975 to report the news of the day from an evangelical Christian perspective, but poor management led the publication into bankruptcy after just 2 years.

The controversial founder of the Unification movement, Sun Myung Moon, founded the conservative *Washington Times* in 1982 in order, he said, to tell the world the truth about God. Through his news media company News World Communications, Moon bought the international news agency, UPI, in 2000, and in 2013, *The Washington Times* joined with Herring Broadcasting to start One America News, a politically conservative 24-hour cable television news channel.

Commercial newspapers may have captured an increasingly large part of the market for religion news since the middle of the 19th century, but religious magazines that supplied information and interpretation for the faithful multiplied during this time. Religious magazines have been published in North America since 1743, when *Christian History* began circulating weekly reports of the advancement and resurgence of faith in Great Britain and colonial America. Denominational publishing began in 1789, when Methodist missionaries Francis Asbury and Thomas Coke started the monthly *Arminian Magazine*. In the 19th century, the number of religious magazines grew as immigration increased, the country expanded, denominations proliferated, and audiences segmented. By 1885, more than 650 religious magazines were published in the United States, nearly double the number published at the end of the Civil War.

Religious magazines are still vital today, as attested to by the hundreds of institutional members of religious press associations including the Associated Church Press, the Evangelical Press Association, the Catholic Press Association, and the American Jewish Press Association. Many of these publications are local. In 2019, for instance, Roman Catholics published 34 diocesan magazines and 42 national magazines in the United States. The most influential national religious magazines are *The Christian Century* and *Christianity Today* (Protestant), *America* (Catholic), and *Commentary* (Jewish). Their circulations, however, are small, ranging from a low of 26,000 for the conservative *Commentary*, 36,000 for the progressive *Christian Century*, and 45,000 for liberal *America* to a high of 130,000 for the evangelical *Christianity Today*, a far cry from the millions of readers of commercial magazines such as *Time*, *People*, and *Good Housekeeping*.

Broadcast Media

Religious radio began at the dawn of broadcasting in the 1920s with local ministers preaching on commercial radio stations on Sunday mornings and religious radio stations such as Where Jesus Blesses Thousands in Chicago and KFSG (Foursquare Gospel) in Los Angeles featuring evangelists such as Paul Rader and Aimee Semple McPherson. A half century would pass before radio featured Christian News/Talk programming, a format that corresponded with the rise of the religious right after the 1970s.

One of the first religious broadcast news programs was *Christian Perspectives on the News*, which was hosted by Don Cole, the so-called radio pastor for the network of radio stations run by Chicago's Moody Bible Institute from 1971 until 2008. Around this time, evangelical Christian television host Pat Robertson changed his popular daily variety program, *The 700 Club*, into a magazine show that included news and opinion. Robertson's Christian Broadcasting Network followed in 1986 with *CBN News Tonight*, a nightly half-hour television program that offered news, features, and Christian commentary. CBN would expand its news programming with the daily newscasts *Faith Nation* and *NewsWatch*, weekly programs such as *Christian World News* and

Jerusalem Dateline, and news analysis programs such as *Faithwire* and *The Global Lane*. CBN News reports both secular and religious news from the perspective of the Christian right.

As Robertson was beginning to expand CBN's news programming, a conservative radio talk-show host from Dallas was starting a Christian news and talk radio network. Founded in 1985 by outspoken evangelical Christian Marlin Maddoux, USA Radio Network eventually supplied round-the-clock programming to 500 radio stations worldwide. Maddoux said that his *Point of View* talk show advanced a biblical worldview and complemented the fairness and balance of USA Radio Network's news stories, which included reports of Christian ministries, the persecution of Christians, and other stories that he believed church people would find interesting. Maddoux died in 2004, but USA Radio Network maintains its conservative Christian character. A recent lineup of USA Radio Network's programs included *Bible's Greatest Heroes*, *Chosen Generation with Pastor Greg Young*, and *USA Christian Internet News*.

The evangelical Christian firebrand Donald Wildmon, who created what would become the American Family Association in Tupelo, Mississippi in 1977, established American Family Radio (AFR) in 1991. With a mission to champion Christian activism, AFR set out to eradicate immorality in American culture by converting unbelievers to true Christian faith and by instituting family values as found in a literal reading of the Bible. AFR paid a staff of 10 journalists and seven technology specialists to supply 24/7 news to 1,200 broadcast, print, and online affiliates in 45 states and 11 foreign countries. The Southern Poverty Law Center listed the American Family Association as a hate group because of the organization's campaigns against LBGTQ rights and Islam.

Christian broadcasting networks have benefited from the repeal of the Federal Communications Commission's fairness doctrine in 1987 and the enactment of the Telecommunications Act of 1996, which ended the cap on the number of radio stations any one company could own. The fairness doctrine had required radio stations to broadcast controversial public issues from diverse political perspectives. By far, the religious broadcasting news operation that capitalized on these two changes the most was the Salem Radio Network (SRN). Begun in 1993, SRN now runs 115 radio stations, mostly in large metropolitan areas, and SRN News is also heard on more than 2,700 affiliates across the nation. SRN News operates out of Washington, DC, boasting on its website of being the only Christian news service using state-of-the-art broadcast facilities with full-time correspondents at the Capitol and the White House.

Online Media

Like their commercial counterparts, religious news media changed with the introduction of the World Wide Web in the 1990s. Online sources for religious information and opinion, including the evangelical online newspaper The Christian Post and the online Jewish magazine Tablet, proliferated as religious groups and individuals seized the opportunity to communicate news about their faith in new, dynamic ways. Older religious news organizations such as Catholic News Service launched websites, while other websites such as World Religion News sprung up to carry news about multiple religions. An online library and center for blogs, Patheos launched in 2009 as the go-to source for news, information, and dialogue on spirituality and religion, attracting more than 30 million page views by 2015. SRN not only made podcasts of previous newscasts available online but also produced ChristianHeadlines.com, a website of news reports, blogs, columns, and slideshows indexed alphabetically from *A Christmas Carol* to YouTube.

Ironically, with all of the channels available in the digital age, providing the public with religious news became increasingly difficult. Part of this difficulty was the nature of the public. Corresponding with the expansion of the World Wide Web was the rise of a population who became known as the nones, Americans who identified with no religious tradition. By 2019, an estimated 26% of Americans were religiously unaffiliated. Although 65% of American adults described themselves as Christian, this was down by 12 percentage points from a decade earlier, according to Pew Research Center. Since the end of the 20th century, secularism has been on the rise.

Social media have also made providing the public with religious news more difficult. Many online media attract more homogeneous populations, which often share stories of interest on social media with like-minded people. In the digital age, media users tend to use media that support the way they see the world, even in the case of online news sites that make their content free to nonsubscribers. Print and broadcast sources increasingly reach older consumers and younger consumers focus on digital media. With the proliferation of blogs, the distinction between information and opinion blurred online and trust in media declined generally. A 2019 survey by the Pew Research Center found that five in 10 Americans reported having little or no confidence in the news media to act in the best interests of the public. Four in 10 said the same about religious leaders. The result, in the early 21st century, is a society divided, among other things, by religion and media use. Using print and various electronic media, religious news providers attempt to impress their point of view onto those they reach, but a growing minority is having none of it.

John P. Ferré

See also Blogs and Bloggers; Broadcast, or Broadcasting; Fairness Doctrine; Internet: Impact on the Media; Religion Journalism; Telecommunications Act of 1996

Further Readings

Fackler, M., & Lippy, C. (1995). *Popular religious magazines of the United States*. Westport, CT: Greenwood Press.

Grant, A., Sturgill, A., Chiung, H., & Stout D. (Eds.) (2019). *Religion online: How digital technology is changing the way we worship and pray*. 2 vols. Santa Barbara, CA: Praeger.

Lochte, B. (2006). Christian radio: The growth of a mainstream broadcasting force. Jefferson, NC: McFarland & Co.

Pew Research Center. (2019, October 17). In U.S., decline of Christianity continues at rapid pace: An update on America's changing religious landscape. https://www.pewforum.org/2019/10/17/in-u-s-decline -of-christianity-continues-at-rapid-pace/

Publick Occurrences both Forreign and Domestick (1690, September 25). Retrieved from http:// nationalhumanitiescenter.org/pds/amerbegin/power /text5/PublickOccurrences.pdf

Rodgers, R. (2018). The struggle for the soul of journalism: The pulpit versus the press, 1833–1923. Columbia: University of Missouri Press.

REUTERS

Reuters, an international news agency founded in London in 1851 by German Paul Julius Reuter (1816–1899), first served clients in the city of London and on stock exchanges (bourses) in Europe with financial and commercial services. London newspapers became subscribers beginning in 1858. Throughout its existence, while developing a range of products for the media, Reuters financial and commercial services (and from the 1960s, the computer terminals feeding them) were its main moneymaker. In the later 19th and early 20th centuries, Reuters' growth was linked to the expansion of the British empire.

Reuters differed from other international news agencies (e.g., New York Associated Press; France's Havas agency) in not collecting news from the provinces and limiting its British news collection to the capital, the clearing-house for political, diplomatic, and financial news. Rather, it developed a close, almost symbiotic connection with the leading British domestic agency, the Press Association (founded in 1868), which later became one of its owners.

Acquired by the Thomson Group in 2008 through a "reverse merger" largely engineered by Reuters then-CEO Tom Glocer, a mergers and acquisitions lawyer, the Reuters news agency has undergone a series of corporate changes since its inception. Initially a privately owned family concern, in 1865 it went through the first such change: incorporation. Many changes followed. The most significant occurred in 1984 when the company was floated on the London stock exchange. Its then-owners, in the form of a trust set up in 1941, including London newspaper publishers, profited handsomely. Many employees acquired company shares and monitored the ups and downs of its share price.

This entry details many of these changes as it discusses the services Reuters provides and the various issues with which it contends as an international news agency.

Financial Services

Paul Julius Reuter himself was a businessman who, having failed in previous ventures, saw the immense potential of electric telegraphy for rapid reporting of financial markets worldwide. Before 1858, no newspaper subscribed to the Reuters agency service. Reuters's first subscribers, such as the Rothschild bank, signed on to the service for its coverage of financial and commercial news from Britain and abroad. The agency was founded just as a telegraph link between London and Paris, facilitated by submarine cable between Dover and Calais becoming operational. The London Stock Exchange and the Paris Bourse each learnt before the end of the day's transactions the opening prices of shares, bonds, and commodities, in the other capital. This was the premise of what later would be called trading "in real time"; speedy transmission evolved over decades into instantaneous transmission.

The "follow the cable" policy of Paul Julius Reuter was later transmuted under his successor, Gerald Long (general manager from 1963 to 1981), as real-time reporting of financial markets worldwide. Indeed, the rapid growth of what had become in the 1950s a money-strapped company was accelerated by the company providing the networks and equipment, including computer terminals, used by banks and credit organizations to conduct and conclude "trades."

General News Services

The financial underpinning of the agency sometimes takes second place, in people's perceptions of Reuters, to its coverage of world news. Its service of general news—covering a host of news categories (political, diplomatic, sports, entertainment, crime, human-interest, religion, science)—has been, since the later 19th century, the main reason why it gradually became well-known and prosperous. "Gradually," because as a wholesaler of news, the company generally accepted that it remained in the background: for decades, many newspaper subscribers did not credit the agency as a news source—or did so only when the reliability of a news report was questioned.

As a German (who acquired British nationality in 1857), Reuter gained acceptance in the British elite; he was made a baron in 1871, presented to Queen Victoria in 1860. Many of his early employees, when the company was still a modest affair, were German; his first news editor, more journalist than Reuter himself, Sigmund Engländer came from Moravia in the Habsburg Empire.

Partly because the expansion of the Reuters network accompanied that of the British Empire in the later 19th century, Reuters' fame was furthered by colonial news. During the Boer War (1899–1902), the news of "the relief of Mafeking," of a besieged British force in a South African township, caused massive celebrations in London and elsewhere. After a 217-day siege (October 1899-May 1900), the news of its relief delivered by Reuters brought the agency valuable publicity.

Reuters had developed a special service covering colonial news, partly financed by the British news agency serving provincial newspapers, the Press Association (PA) and the Newspaper Proprietors' Association (NPA). Reuters covered primarily international news and London diplomatic and political news; it had developed close ties with the PA founded in 1868. In this respect, it was unusual among major international news agencies, like Havas in France, Wolff in Germany, and the Associated Press in the United States, all of which had journalists covering domestic and provincial news, as well as, to a certain extent, international news. The PA paid Reuters for its international news service and Reuters paid the PA for British provincial news. The relation between the two grew ever closer; and in 1941, the PA and London national newspapers, the NPA, acquired a stake in Reuters. Reuters and the PA dominated the market for general news in Britain. A British royal press commission noted in 1947, "Reuters is a monopoly as far as foreign news coverage is concerned."

Recurrent Issues

Over the decades, several recurrent issues have haunted the agency: relations with the British government and (less so) other governments; "new" technologies; the nature of the news services and of requirements of its journalists and other staff.

Relations With Governments

A news agency "must live in good intelligence" with the government of the country where it is headquartered. This remark, made by an employee of the French Havas agency, applied to all international news agencies. A government, the machine or bureaucracy of the state, is an invaluable source of news. At the same time, Reuters did not in any way wish to seem beholden to the British government. Impartiality in news coverage guaranteed professional success: newspaper subscribers of various political persuasions relied on it for factually correct reports (at least correct at the time when transmitted). Reuters tried, and generally succeeded, to reconcile the two. The result was a relatively staid style of news reports.

Engländer, news editor from 1852 to 1875, claimed he was responsible for Reuters's adherence to a factually correct, sober style. Yet even he, on occasion, sought to introduce more "color." In the early 1890s, he urged an international society gossip column. In the 1930s, Rickatson Hatt, an editor who had worked in the United States, encouraged a more vivid style of newsreporting. Yet on sensitive news, such as stories about Wallis Simpson, the American divorcée and intended wife of the then-king, Edward VIII, he told staff not to mention her without his clearance. The tension between factual reporting and "color" was long present. In the 1940s, just after World War II, Reuters both admired and feared the Associated Press's "rocket-star" style.

A factor conducive to an officious reporting style stemmed from what was known as *the news agency alliance*. Initially, Paul Julius Reuter wanted to expand his agency in Germany as well as across the British Empire, implementing his "follow the cable policy." He even funded a cable link between Britain and north Germany (the Norderney Company) to further expansion eastward. But as Prussia led the creation of a united Germany, and Prussian chancellor Otto von Bismarck became Germany's chancellor, Reuters came into conflict with the German government-backed agency, Wolff (later the Continental) where Bismarck's closest financier, Gerson von Bleichröder, held sway.

In the 1850s–1860s, ambitions of the three major European agencies—Reuters, Havas, and Wolff—to each expand beyond the country where they were headquartered ended when each, reluctantly, decided it was better to confirm their respective dominance of their "home" market by sharing "the rest of the world" between them. They agreed not to sell their service in the markets or "territory" (the contractual term) of their allied agencies; they relied primarily on the relevant allied agency for the news coverage of its territory, while remaining free to send their own reporters there.

This news agency alliance, fashioned in 1859, strengthened subsequently, as many national agencies were founded and joined the alliance, which held by and large for 70 years. But many such agencies were government-controlled: their coverage of their territory relayed primarily official news. Reuters often protested that allied agencies favored such news, sometimes supplemented by extracts from the press of the relevant territory, itself often mostly state-controlled. In a Europe of nascent power blocs, led by the Triple Alliance dominated by Bismarck's Germany, along with the Habsburg Empire and Italy, in the late 1880s, Reuters feared it might have to choose between their agencies and Havas.

Such nationalist pressures culminated with the outbreak of World War I. This threatened to end the news-agency alliance: the German agency promoted German news and interests, as did Havas the French; Reuters, not wanting to appear a tool of the British government nonetheless "rallied around the flag," in an ambiguous manner. An ambiguity epitomized by Roderick Jones, Reuters chief executive from 1915 to 1941 and very much a pillar of the British establishment and empire, taking a post with the British propaganda machine. In a period of censorship, agency star reporters were not allowed access to the front line. Reuters archivist, John Entwisle, noted that British advances were reported, but German advances, which were sometimes greater, were not.

News-editorial independence from the government was frequently trumpeted. Reuters' credibility depended on this. The state often helped otherwise, by offsetting transmission costs, for instance.

Technology

The advent of a new communications technology periodically challenged Reuters. It was slow to adapt to the advent of the telephone in the 1870s and 1880s. Wireless radio transmission was used early by the agency, but in the 1930s, it feared BBC international transmission might compromise its telegraph and radio transmissions across the Empire.

It was better positioned when the computer age dawned. Indeed, much of its late 20th-century prosperity stemmed from its research and development investments in computer-fed screen services for the financial and business community of traders and banks; these in effect generated the revenue for the agency to also develop a range of news services for governments and the media. There was even a time, in the 1970s, when Reuters computer networks and terminals were used by traders, bankers, and others to both get the latest stock price news and conclude trades (for a fee) via its network. The halcyon years ended with the rise of Bloomberg, with its more user-friendly terminal, in the 1980s. Bloomberg had better access to a range of U.S. financial instruments, an ever-growing importance as globalization progressed. Furthermore, under Peter Job, chief executive from 1991 to 200I, and its then board of directors, Reuters was seen as having delayed in adapting to the Internet.

Nature of the News Service

In the I950s, Reuters was considered a low-profile company starved of cash by the British press. The vast revenue it subsequently generated was due largely to the renewal of its commercial services, piloted initially by its Comtelburo service, whose staff was often disparaged by agency newsmen. Feeds of commercial and financial news to clients worldwide underpinned the agency's recovery.

How truly international was the agency's coverage over the years? The British empire long loomed large; the importance of the United States grew and grew: for the allied news agencies, Reuters was the contact agency with the U.S. ally, the Associated Press. World Wars both stressed the importance of international coverage and increased the difficulty in separating news from propaganda. Subsequent conflicts involving Britain—the Suez invasion in 1956 and the Falkland crisis in 1982—saw Reuters successfully demonstrating its independence of the British government.

Staff

Reuters archives show that in 1936 it had over 1,000 full-time employees, 676 correspondents abroad, and news-exchange agreements with many national agencies. Agency bureaus abroad both covered local news and sold agency services to local clients. In December 2006, Reuters employed 2,400 journalists operating in 196 news bureaus in about 130 countries (in a world of some 200 countries). Correspondents might cover several countries from a regional base; some traveled widely as "firefighters" in a news "hotspot." In other hotspots, local reporters were employed. For instance, in Afghanistan, Reuters' local Afghan reporter Sayed Saluhaddin reported the fall of the Taliban regime and U.S. bombs on Kabul in the pursuit of Osama bin Laden after the attacks of September 11, 2001.

Reuters, like other international news organizations, has a long roll call of correspondents killed while doing their job. Kurt Schork (1947–2000), its American reporter who covered the wars in former Yugoslavia, was hunted by Serb forces and killed in Sierra Leone in 2000. An indication of the importance of human interest color, his story about the killing of two young lovers, a Serb boy and a Moslem Bosnian girl, with its shades of Romeo and Juliet locked in a mortal embrace, was the piece often consulted in the weeks following his death.

In November 2001, two Reuters' men were killed in Afghanistan and the Taliban once arrested Saluhaddin as a spy. Like many other journalists, Saluhaddin produced for a multimedia environment. He preferred TV film shots and still photos to filing text "copy." Decades earlier, most Reuters' journalists filed only text. The diversification of the news product, stretching back to photo and radio, intensified in recent decades. "Show not tell" was a frequent Reuters instruction in the early 1990; the agency then increased its worldwide TV reporting presence. In the early 2000s, a Reuters news editor, sitting in on confidential international finance meeting, tweeted news developments to his staff outside.

Since the Reuters Company acquisition by Thomson in 2008, via the Thomson family's private holding company Woodbridge, the agency is one of the best-known assets of the Thomson-Reuters group.

Michael Palmer

See also Agence France-Presse; Associated Press; Havas

Further Readings

Read, D. (1992). *The power of news. The history of Reuters.* Oxford, UK: Oxford University Press.

Michael, B. P. (2019). *International news agencies: A history.* Cham, Switzerland: Palgrave Macmillan, Springer.

Risk and News

The number of impactful news stories to which people are exposed influences their perceptions of risk. The rise of social media and the instantaneous transmission in multiple formats (especially by audiovisual means) of news stories on terrorism, health crises, climate emergencies, and the rise of the extreme right fit into the paradigm of the risk society theorized by German sociologist Ulrich Beck. Most especially, the emergence of newer risks means that the decisions faced by humanity involve novel problems and hazards that contradict the institutional language of control.

Globalization contributes to a growing complexity and interdependence of both local and global interactions, which, in turn, increases the probability of unforeseeable crises such as that caused by COVID-19. A 2002 book by David Altheide that contextualizes the nature and use of the word *fear* in U.S. media concludes that most industrialized societies have developed toward the risk society paradigm, organized around communications oriented to police surveillance, control, and prevention. In addition, the vocabulary of fear is central to certain forms of media that rely on this to make an impact.In this context, journalism and the mass media play a crucial role. The mass media multiply our collective information on dangers, insecurities, uncertainties, or fears through stories that are instantly disseminated worldwide, yet their intervention is considered essential to risk coverage. As pointed out by Bakir (2010), the media (a) provide knowledge that informs citizens, (b) modulate the public acceptability of different risks, (c) motivate the public to act responsibly, and (d) provide meaning frames for risks. This entry discusses the reporting of risks in the mass media, ways of reporting responsibility, and how new forms of media offer new ways of communicating about crisis situations.

Risks of Interest

Journalistic mediation is crucial to risk coverage. Public opinion in the face of significant risks needs to be addressed, as readers and viewers need help when deciding whether to buy a certain food, use a certain means of transportation, or remain at home as ways of limiting risk. This rationalization process forces the media to extract multiple interpretations and draw on a wide range of information sources. Individuals take into account the amount of information available when assessing risks.

The social responsibility of the informant and the media is crucial in the choice of linguistic resources used in situations of risk. Misuse of an expression may be involuntary but may also mask the express intention of the media or the informant to magnify, exaggerate, or minimize an event. The journalist's responsibility in a risk society is not just to report rigorously and responsibly but also to combat inaccurate and fake news.

The transformation brought about by social media, which allow the exchange of unverified information, renders journalists even more responsible for the dissemination of accurate information on risks and catastrophes. At the same time, however, the interest aroused by tragedies leads to contradictory feelings in information professionals who face complex challenges in the exercise of their profession. The essential problem when reporting risk is that the concept is abstract and invisible until it is manifested in a specific accident or disaster.

In disaster coverage, information rights, professional ethics, and victims' rights to their honor, integrity, and image converge. The journalistic interest stems from the interest of the public that consumes the information. Based on sociological, psychoanalytic, and cognitive arguments, Van Dijk (1988) argues that the public appreciates learning about catastrophic events out of a sense of satisfaction at not being affected by the event themselves. Negative news, however, can also cover information on prevention or services for the public. In other words, tragic news is a form of simulating possible incidents that we ourselves may experience in the future.

Reporting Responsibly

Journalism in the face of risk can apply four basic precepts to help improve media coverage: (1) avoid fearmongering, (2) avoid politicizing information, (3) facilitate forums for cooperation and debate, and (4) historically contextualize the emergency.

One of the most important issues in reporting news about risk is to avoid fearmongering, that is, fostering a sensation of alarm. It is important to carefully choose words and to avoid the kind of language that only generates fear. In the first moments of an emergency, it is recommended to avoid the temptation to politicize the situation and point the finger of blame, whether at an actor (government body, company, and emergency manager), a behavior, or a fact.

Part of the journalist's responsibility is to report on all aspects of the risk or crisis and also to facilitate cooperation, that is, to help the public by publishing contact details for help of all kinds, including administrative/governmental, psychological, and economic assistance. News organizations also need to indicate ways that the public can contact them with information that journalists can verify for dissemination.

It can be a good practice to present emergency news in comparative terms with other similar events. Recalling other historical moments and events contextualizes a situation in terms of other moments of crisis, allowing the public to grasp the real magnitude of an event and therefore reducing the potential for alarmism.

Reporting on emergency situations requires that the facts be explained in detail and that some essential questions be answered: When did the event happen, where did it happen, what happened, what is the risk? To the extent possible, early coverage of an emergency needs to discuss who or what may be responsible for the situation, provide a chronological account that can help members of the public better understand and process information, and include contact information for bodies in charge of managing aspects of the emergency as well as nongovernmental organizations, associations, companies, and banks where economic and material contributions can be made to alleviate the consequences of the disaster. It is also important to disseminate crucial information for those coping with the emergency, such as on where to take refuge and how to obtain supplies such as food, blankets, and water. Information provided in an emergency should include links to online resources that can provide additional detailed, quality information on the event, its causes, and its consequences.

Graphic information should include good maps of risk areas, which should be relative to the territorial scope of the media. Comparative statistics that relate the event to previously experienced similar situations can put scope of the event in perspective. Other aspects of the presentation that should be considered are providing images of the situation and what wording to use to indicate when new or crucial information is being reported. Some news organizations tend to dramatize emergency situations with shocking images or banner headlines, but a more measured approach may help avoid provoking alarmism.

New Media, New Opportunities

Social media can be useful in crisis situations thanks to their immediacy and the ability for users to collaborate in communicating information. With the emergence of social media, the emission of messages in situations of risk is no longer exclusive to public bodies and the media, as citizens can now actively participate in the propagation of content in an emergency. With social media, citizens are direct participants, providing information and freely giving their opinion. Multiple studies support the use of Twitter in emergency situations for efficient information transmission. Watson, Finn, and Wadhwa (2017), for instance, assert that big data produced in social media platforms can have a positive impact on both the management and the prevention of emergencies. However, a 2016 study by Eriksson and Olsson found a mismatch between how citizens and crisis communications professionals used Facebook and Twitter, indicating that if public agencies rely on social media at times of crisis, it could interfere with the public receiving crucial information. Since the emergence of Web 2.0, when a crisis occurs, media newsrooms call on citizens to participate and contribute comments, images, and even videos. This participation, if the information is verified, has been shown to make a substantial contribution to news stories that complement reporting by professional journalists.

Carles Pont-Sorribes

See also Citizen Journalism; Civil Unrest, Coverage of; Natural Disasters, Coverage of; News Values; Social Media; Terrorism, Coverage of

Further Readings

Altheide, D. L. (2002). *Creating fear. News and the construction of crisis.* New York, NY: Aldine de Gruyter.

Bakir, V. (2010). Media and risk: Old and new research directions. *Journal of Risk Research, 13*(1), 5–18. doi:10.1080/13669870903135953

Beck, U. (2009). *World at risk.* Cambridge, UK: Polity Press.

Coats, R. (2001). Online: Plan now for the next time. In W. Watson (Ed.), *Crisis journalism: A handbook for media response.* Reston, VA: American Press Institute.

Eriksson, M., & Olsson, E. K. (2016). Facebook and Twitter in crisis communication: A comparative study of crisis communication professionals and citizens. *Journal of Contingencies and Crisis Management, 24*(4), 198–208. doi:10.1111/1468–5973.12116

Finkel, K. (2001). Tips on how copy desks can handle big stories well. In W. Watson (Ed.), *Crisis journalism: Handbook for media response.* Reston, VA: American Press Institute.

Fog, A. (2002). *Mass media and democracy crisis.* Retrieved from http://www.agner.org/cultsel/mediacrisis.pdf

Grin, G. (2001). How to report, layer and present crisis news. In W. Watson (Ed.), *Crisis journalism: Handbook for media response.* Reston, VA: American Press Institute.

Hazlett, C. (2001). Ten things newspapers should do. In W. Watson (Ed.), *Crisis journalism. Handbook for media response.* Reston, VA: American Press Institute.

Liu, B. F., Austin, L., & Jin, Y. (2011). How publics respond to crisis communication strategies: The interplay of information form and source. *Public Relations Review, 37*(4), 345–353.

Murdock, G., & Horlick-Jones, T., & Petts, J. (2001). *Social amplification of risk: The media and the public.* Contract Research Report: Health & Safety Executive (HSE).

Pont-Sorribes, C. (2013). *Comunicar las emergencias* [Communicate the emergencies]. Barcelona, Spain: Editorial UOC.

Pont-Sorribes, C., & Cortiñas Rovira, S. (2011). Journalistic practice in risk and crisis situations: Significant examples from Spain. *Journalism, 12*(8), 1052–1066. doi:10.1177/1464884910388233

Van Dijk, T. A. (1988). *News as discourse.* Hillsdale, NJ: Erlbaum.

Watson, H., Finn, R. L., & Wadhwa, K. (2017). Organizational and societal impacts of big data in crisis management. *Journal of Contingencies and Crisis Management, 25*(1), 15–22. doi:10.1111/1468–5973.12141

Watson, W., Kellogg, J., & Ureneck, L. (2001). Packaging and presentation: Underscore the gravity of the event. In W. Watson (Ed.), *Crisis journalism. Handbook for media response.* Reston, VA: American Press Institute.

RT AND SPUTNIK

Sputnik and RT are state-funded Russian media outlets usually described as propaganda outlets controlled by their government to improve its image, especially that of President Vladimir Putin. Both Sputnik and RT maintain websites, but RT is a television-based operation with a web presence. This entry describes the history and growth of both operations, and how they figured into investigations of Russian interference in the 2016 U.S. presidential campaign.

Sputnik

The Sputnik name may appear familiar to many people who grew up during the Cold War. It was the name for the first satellite launched to orbit Earth, and Sputnik effectively began the space race in 1957. As a symbol of success and past Soviet glory, the name was given new life as a Russian news agency, website, and radio service.

Prior to the start of Sputnik in 2014, RIA Novosti functioned as a comparatively well-regarded news agency. As RIA Novosti dissolved in 2013, Sputnik emerged and rose in importance. Operating under Rossiya Segodnya as a subsidiary, Sputnik has resembled the old Soviet Union propaganda efforts rather than the more professional

TASS and RIA Novosti. Sputnik presents itself as an alternative source of news, while attempting to undermine public trust in established sources of news reporting. This lends support to Russian intelligence operations of disinformation that tend to be cost efficient and benefit from those who spread lies framed as alternative facts.

One of Sputnik's more notable disinformation campaigns was pushing false claim that Seth Rich, a staff member of the Democratic National Committee (DNC) who was murdered in 2016, was involved in leaking DNC emails during the 2016 presidential campaign, fueling conspiracy theories about his murder. Russian intelligence used Sputnik to encourage others to believe that Rich was responsible for providing emails to WikiLeaks, despite U.S. intelligence agencies' conclusion that Russian intelligence officers hacked and leaked the emails.

Sputnik's Internet orientation gives it an advantage over traditional news production outlets. It has operated in 30 cities around the world producing content in as many languages. This orientation enables it to provide significant coverage to politicians in various countries who support Russia, or to politicians who challenge their own countries' ways of doing things on issues such as health care, education, or immigration. These political outliers have their views presented, often without a counter or mainstream perspective. Sputnik has not been successful in every location, however, as some Scandinavian sites did not survive more than a year or so. In some cases, governments have taken action against Sputnik. Lithuania, in 2019, decided that Sputnik should be banned for violating its copyright law. That same year, the United Kingdom Foreign Office would not issue press credentials for Sputnik and RT to attend a media freedom conference because of their efforts to spread disinformation. In contrast, Sputnik has been more successful with its local sites in the Balkans, such as in Serbia. Sputnik may be more influential than RT because of these local sites being freely available and appearing familiar because of their native Internet style.

RT

The name RT is based on the television outlet's original name, Russia Today. It was established in 2005 to serve as an information weapon for the Russian government and as an expression of Putin's propaganda strategy. RT's content has shifted as the Russian economy and international politics have necessitated revised alliances with individuals and governments.

Putin attempted, and largely succeeded in, centralizing money, power, and an authoritative image. As part of this process, Putin eliminated as much competition as possible. He pushed out the oligarchs who had their hands on the independent television stations so his government could oversee the stations. The stations' managers began meeting with Putin's handpicked political planner to learn what would be covered and how the news would be presented. Putin saw television as a way to craft the views he wanted the public to hold.

Russia Today's birth was announced by Margarita Simonyan, a young journalist from Southern Russia near Georgia. Simonyan quickly moved up the ranks in Russian media from working as a television correspondent to head of the new Russia Today, by demonstrating loyalty to Putin as a member of the Kremlin press pool. The key to success was not challenging Putin during interviews. Russia Today was established as a nonprofit entity working out of the RIA Novosti headquarters. Its motto is "Question More." Simonyan has taken the position that the United States is not a democracy nor a lecturing role model for other nations. To question more is to question Western narratives.

The presentation style looked conventional from the start, at least on the surface. A 1-hour broadcast began with news reporting then the final 30 minutes sharing lighter topics such as features and sports. Satellite broadcasts could reach the United States and Europe. Staffers tended to be inexperienced journalists, and Russia Today appeared to prefer those who spoke English as natives—often with native British accents.

Initially, the Russia Today programming reflected the rationale for its government's operations. Putin's growing strength coincided with an economic success based on oil prices. Russia Today began when these oil prices were boosting Putin's popularity. But as the oil business worsened, Russia Today changed as part of Putin's strategy to maintain control in times of chaos. Over time, the message has been that Putin was making Russia wealthy, that only Putin could stabilize Russia when times were bad, and other countries were in worse shape than Russia.

Russia Today would rebrand as RT for an international audience to make its association with Russia less visible. It is difficult to estimate the size of RT's television or Internet audience. Throughout its periods of different names and mediums, RT has embraced radicals and critics of Western governments, from noted American linguist Noam Chomsky to WikiLeaks founder Julian Assange and Brexit promoter Nigel Farage. It has even hosted those who espouse Holocaust denial or neo-Nazism or who claim the terrorist attacks of September 11, 2001, were an American operation.

RT prided itself on its London office's view of the British Security Service (MI-5) and proximity to Secret Intelligence Service (MI-6), respectively the internal security agency and international intelligence agency of the United Kingdom. It has also been one of the most vocal mouthpieces for the Russian government regarding its invasion of Georgia and Ukraine. Despite evidence to the contrary, RT pushed the false narratives that the conflicts were simply the product of ethnic Russians (so-called separatists) protecting their heritage and claiming their territories for Russia. In one case, RT edited an interview with a Ukrainian rabbi in Crimea to make it sound like he was leaving because of anti-Semitism, rather than the real cause of Russian-originated conflict.

RT has received attention for signing American television personalities past their height of popularity. RT contracted to run two independently produced Larry King programs after his CNN show ended in 2010, while Ed Schultz joined RT as an anchor in 2016. Aspiring journalists have taken jobs at RT, resulting in some vocal departures. One American, Liz Wahl, resigned while on the air in 2014, and has since run for Congress on a platform challenging Russian propaganda and Putin's politics.

Russian Interference Investigations

Because of the prominent attention paid to Russian disinformation efforts during the 2016 election campaigns and the U.S. Department of Justice's Report On The Investigation Into Russian Interference In the 2016 Presidential Election (nicknamed the Mueller report), RT and involved entities had to register with the Justice Department under the Foreign Agent Registration Act. Upset at the move, Russia placed new limitations on American media operations.

The entity behind RT's American production, T&R Productions, registered as an agency, and T&R identified ANO TV-Novosti as the foreign principal. T&R reported it had editorial control of RT's programming. Russia stated such registration was unnecessary because its outlets were similar to the unregistered British Broadcasting Corporation and France 24.

Another result from the Mueller report and journalistic investigations was Twitter's banning of Sputnik and RT from advertising on its platform, although both would be allowed to keep their nonadvertising accounts. In response, RT accused Twitter of applying heavy sales pressure on RT to advertise.

Michael Flynn, who briefly served as President Donald Trump's national security advisor in 2017, became embroiled in controversy for his associations with Russia, including his prior acceptance of tens of thousands of dollars to speak at RT's 10th anniversary event and sit with Putin. Both Sputnik and RT were accused by the U.S. Department of National Intelligence of promoting Trump's candidacy in 2016 and framing American news coverage as biased against Trump, all part of Russia's intelligence campaign. RT ran propaganda associating Trump's opponent Hillary Clinton with ISIS funding and illegal use of charity funds.

Timothy Roy Gleason

See also Europe; Fake News; Press and Government Relations; Propaganda; Russian Federation; TASS and Russian News Agencies; WikiLeaks

Further Readings

Eastern Partnership Civil Society Forum. (2015). Messages of Russian TV: Monitoring report 2015. Brussels, Belgium: Author. Retrieved from http://www.media-diversity.org/additional-files/documents/Monitoring_report_Russian_TV.pdf

Feinberg, A. (2017, August 1). My life at a Russian propaganda network. *Politico*. Retrieved from https://www.politico.com/magazine/story/2017/08/21/russian-propaganda-sputnik-reporter-215511

Ioffe, J. (2010, September/October). What is Russia today? *Columbia Journalism Review*. Retrieved from

https://archives.cjr.org/feature/what_is_russia_today
.php

Pisnia, N. (2017, November 15). Why has RT registered as a foreign agent with the US? *BBC*. Retrieved from https://www.bbc.com/news/world-us-canada -41991683

Pomerantsev, P. (2015, October). Authoritarianism goes global (II): The Kremlin's information war. *Journal of Democracy, 26*(4), 40–50.

RUSSIAN FEDERATION

The Russian Federation, commonly referred to as *Russia*, is a country in Eastern Europe that was the core member of the former Union of Soviet Socialist Republics, also known as the *USSR* and *Soviet Union*. It was an ally of the United States and Great Britain during World War II, but its aim of spreading forced socialism put it in opposition to its former allies. It employs propaganda as a governmental tool. It is one of the most dangerous places for journalists to operate. The government has established numerous laws prohibiting freedom of expression.

The Russian Federation is the product of its history as a monarchy and socialist state, resulting in an environment where the press has been controlled by the government in power. The governance and oppression of monarchal and socialist eras continue to shape how the Russian Federation applies formal control over, or pressure on, the news media. The Soviet era and the current Russian Federation share a tendency to view the source of its problems as coming from the West, especially the United States. The Russian media have reproduced this view in concert with the government. This entry discusses the history of the Russian Federation, its news organizations and propaganda outlets, formal controls on the country's press, and dangers facing the country's journalists and news organizations.

Monarchy

Monarchies are not democratic institutions. They are established through maximizing power over time, and monarchs attempt to pass control down through generations of the same family. In those places where the monarchy controls the government, the press does not have freedom of expression.

The first Russian tsar, also spelled czar in English, was Ivan IV, who ruled between 1533 and 1584. *Tsar* came from the word *caesar* and was used to mean emperor in Russia. The Romanov family came to power in 1613, and they would rule Russia until the revolution of 1917. Tsar Nicholas II, the last tsar, made a contribution to Russian and future Soviet news when he ordered the merger of two news agencies into the St. Petersburg Telegraph Agency, which dealt with economic and political news. Tsar Nicholas II could not have expected his effort would assist his enemy. An oppressive monarchal government was replaced by a new form of oppression that would take over the tsarist media and significantly increase the use of the media to help govern citizens.

Union of Soviet Socialist Republics

The Russian Revolution of 1917 led to a competition for power among different socialist groups and wealthy elites that was ultimately won by one of the socialist groups, the Bolsheviks. The leader of the Bolsheviks, meaning the majority, was Vladimir Lenin. The Bolsheviks were the most radical revolutionaries, and Lenin was the most radical of the radicals. Lenin rose to power and believed Russia was at the front of a global revolution of the proletariat—the working class. He saw the value of newspapers and used printing for propaganda. The St. Petersburg agency was taken over and renamed Petrograd as a rejection of the past. Russians in news and politics felt that Western Europe had a cartel over news distribution, and both the new Soviets and World War I were breaking that cartel.

After Lenin died, Joseph Stalin formally took power in 1924. Stalin, born as Iosep Jughashvili, worked to expand the new Soviet empire. Stalin saw the potential of the media as a tool of propaganda. The Soviet people were constantly exposed to propaganda in news and entertainment. The Soviets rejected the American and Western European models of watchdog journalism. The newspaper *Pravda*, established in 1918 and meaning "truth," was the most famous Soviet newspaper to Westerners and was actually the organ of the Communist Party. Soviet journalism was about promoting the Soviet ideology and maintaining power, such as *Za Stalina!* (For Stalin!). Newspaper stories, photographs, and films were often aimed to motivate people to work harder to meet the government's goals and then to celebrate those who accomplished it.

Several leaders followed Stalin, and what also followed was a process of de-Stalinization. This process included reorienting journalists for the purpose of rejecting some of Stalin's practices and policies, and which led to a more dynamic style of reporting. The press was to be less of a tool for persuasion and more of a historian of the Soviet Union for the public and proponent of the state. Journalists had to increasingly face the reality that Soviets were illicitly exposed to foreign news that would question the so-called reality of Soviet news. Furthermore, in the 1970s, the Soviet press recognized that Western news was becoming more energetic with images and sounds, and they were behind the West in many ways. This was the era Russian President Vladimir Putin grew up in, and which would influence his work as a Soviet spy and politician.

The final Soviet head of government was Mikhail Gorbachev, who took charge in 1985 and had a media-friendly persona in the West. Gorbachev's policy of glasnost brought some openness of ideas, and the policy of perestroika was a movement toward a marketplace economy. Glasnost was Gorbachev's effort to allow Russians to examine their own history, albeit within a scope allowed by the government. Unfortunately, the social history was one of mass poverty, food and other shortages, a lack of democracy, and a sense of fatalism. This was one of the rare moments in Soviet history when journalists could publicly question authorities, albeit minimally, without significant retaliation. Gorbachev's circle tried to shift the direction of Soviet journalism by engaging with two publications, the *Ogonek* and *Moskovskie Novosti*, to lead the way, and trying to change the leadership of *Izvestiya*.

The New Russian Federation

The Russian Federation is the name for the Russian state after the Soviet Union dissolved. While the Russian state existed throughout the 1900s within the Soviet Union, the power and soul of the union was in Russia. In December 1991, Gorbachev announced the Soviet Union had ended after all but one of the other Soviet republics officially left the Union. Gorbachev introduced reforms to save the Soviet Union, but they could not undo decades of oppression and the observation that the Western nations were prospering in comparison.

Gorbachev survived a 1991 coup attempt by important members of the Communist Party who did not like the country's reformist direction. Boris Yeltsin, a Gorbachev ally who thought the reforms were moving too slowly, stood on a tank outside of Parliament rallying support for Gorbachev and reforms in front of the public and media cameras for the world to see—something that would not have been visible in the Soviet era. The attempted coup lasted 3 days, but Gorbachev's presidential career was slated to end anyway. Gorbachev turned the country over to Yeltsin after he won the presidential election. For the new leader, press control was a function of necessity. A 1993 failed coup attempt led President Yeltsin to censor more than a dozen newspapers and a television show, a reminder of the Soviet oppression of freedom of expression. Yeltsin tried to increase his popularity through light media coverage, such as dancing onstage at a rock concert, but aging, former Soviet politicians were not experienced in promoting themselves through Western-style media events. Yeltsin named former spy Putin, who was versed in disinformation and media imaging, his prime minister.

The opening of the Russian economy ignited a race to profit from the move from communism to capitalism, including media ownership. The fall of communism meant government-owned enterprises would have to be privatized, but there were not adequate controls to prevent corruption. The chances of buying a state entity for privatization—including media operations—could depend on a potential buyer's support of the leadership.

The newly independent, or quasi-independent, outlets had to adjust to new business practices. For example, *Izvestiya*, a newspaper sometimes translated as *Izvestia* and *Izvestiia*, had been a reliable Soviet mouthpiece, but in 1991 it declared it was free of Soviet oversight. The paper, like others, previously survived because the Communist Party provided important funding. After a ban against *Izvestiya* failed to be effective, the Communist Party hurt the newspaper by pulling funding.

Russia applies a variety of tools to try to prevent former Soviet republics and allied countries from developing formal relationships with Western Europe. Russia has used military force, traditional media, and social media to create conflict in other countries and encourage foreign loyalty to Russia, with disinformation being the most cost-effective weapon.

Russia's counter-Western European efforts include anti-European Union efforts, as well as opposing the North Atlantic Treaty Organization. The former includes providing media exposure to politicians and parties calling for the break-up of the European Union, such as the Brexit effort in the United Kingdom and the radical right wing in France. Nigel Farage, a right-wing populist who was among the loudest proponents of Brexit, appeared on the state-funded RT television network multiple times.

Putinization of Television

Putin, who has served as prime minister or president since 1999, has a reputation for appreciating the power of television. Putin realized that television news was the way to reach the public, largely because of the war with Chechnya, the Chechen Republic.

Yeltsin did not want Chechnya to break away and force was used to keep it part of the Russian Federation. As the war worsened, so did Yeltsin's prospects for reelection. Television is especially important because that is how Russians tend to get their national and political news. Television could not improve military tactics, but it could improve the public's perception of the war.

Putin envisioned remodeling the new, quasi-capitalist television to something closer to the Soviet experience. Russian entertainment television would not be that entertaining, but the news would fit the propaganda model of Lenin's journalism. An authoritarian approach, such as Putin's, is one of maintenance much more than change because an authoritarian government tries to keep its power in place.

To counter a return to centralized television, California-based Internews, a nonprofit, opened a

Moscow office in 1992. It established a network of private television outlets of more than 100 outlets with a combined audience of more than 100 million people by 1996, called the *Independent Broadcasting System*. Internews provided equipment and training throughout the former Soviet Union, such as in Belarus and Ukraine, as well as in the new Russia. The Russian government pressured journalists to follow its preferred framing of the war with Chechnya, but Internews-trained journalists were some of the notable resisters to the government.

Internews also created programming, such as *Vremya Mestnoe* and *Esli*. *Vremya Mestnoe* stood out for compiling reports from outlets into a broadcast. *Esli* was created as a transitional series that explained the legal issues and process after the fall of the socialist system. The Educated Media Foundation took over the operations of Internews Russia through a merger near the end of 2006. The next year, the Russian government tried to shut down its operations.

By 1999, the beginning of the Putin era, there were four important television networks based in Moscow: NTV, ORT, RTR, and TV-6. NTV had the largest viewership and was owned by Vladimir Gusinsky, who established MOST, a bank that loaned money to new businesses.

ORT (Russian Public Television) had a mix of private investors and state ownership. It has been common in Russia for investors to have ties to high-level government officials. At ORT, Boris Berczovsky was an investor and one of Yeltsin's closest friends, who quickly became wealthy as the owner of a car dealership. ORT became known as *Channel One*.

RTR (Russian State Television) is known as *Channel 2*. Despite its reach, it was not the most popular. Lastly, TV-6 became the first commercial television station established.

Without an established journalistic routine in television news, some stations experimented to get viewers. One Moscow station, M1, had naked women read the news on the program *Golaya Pravda*, or "The Naked Truth."

In recent years, three channels have dominated Russia as the landscape of television has changed under Putin. Channel One and Russia One are outright owned by the government and serve as propaganda outlets. Another is NTV, which is a property of Gazprom, the government-controlled energy firm, and hardly an independent voice in contemporary Russia. Tricolor is the leading satellite business.

Gazprom's takeover of NTV exemplifies the problems of conducting business and doing journalism in Russia. Unlike others who bought former Soviet operations, Gusinsky started comparatively from scratch. His support for a struggling Yeltsin—after his NTV critically reported on Yeltsin's poor performance on Chechnya—enabled Gusinsky to acquire Channel 4. Gusinsky invested in expansion, which hurt him when the economy crashed in 1998. An investment group led by American Ted Turner, the founder of CNN and TBS in the United States, wanted to invest in Gusinsky's NTV, as long as the Russian government would guarantee it would not interfere in its operation.

Gusinsky made enemies during his climb as a would-be media mogul. Gusinsky wanted to purchase a telecommunications company at the time government officials decided bids would have to be made in order to complete a sale. After losing his bid, Gusinsky used his media to attack those officials. NTV became the powerful, dissenting voice on TV when the war with Chechnya was restarted in 1999. This upset the Russian prime minister at the time, Putin, who would go onto the higher position of president.

To raise funds, Gusinsky made a deal with Gazprom. This would lead to his downfall. In 2000, now-President Putin had police raid his media office, and then arrested Gusinsky to force him to sign away his controlling interest in his media empire, Media Most, for his freedom. Media Most controlled NTV, Seven Days publishing firm, *Itogi* magazine, and Ekho Moskvy radio. A business that was valued at more than $1 billion before the economic crash and renowned for quality and independence in Russia, became part of the Putin-oligarchy control. In 2004, the European Court of Human Rights determined Russia had violated Gusinsky's rights.

Newspapers and Propaganda

While television is the dominant source of news and entertainment in Russia, newspapers are still active but vary in their role as propaganda tools.

As of 2017, there were more than 400 daily newspapers serving Russia, typically aligned with government policy. Newspapers and their websites have the opportunity to play a more journalistic role than radio in Russia, where FM music is popular.

Putin and the government have supported various news outlets that can serve as propaganda outlets for foreign audiences. One is *Russia Beyond*, an advertising supplement for Western publications. *Russia Beyond* began in 2007 as *Russia Beyond the Headlines*, a publication printed in different languages and run by the Russian-government newspaper the *Rossiyskaya Gazeta*. At one point, readers of *The Washington Post* website could read *Russia Beyond the Headlines* on the *Post* website via a dedicated section. It also developed its own mobile app for online readers, and has accounts on various social media channels. Social media has been used to soften Putin's image, such as by promoting a video of Putin's four best jokes. By 2016, it came under the control of TV-Novosti. The next year, 2017, *Russia Beyond the Headlines* was shortened to just *Russia Beyond*. It has run as a supplement in a variety of newspapers, such as *The New York Times* and London's *Daily Telegraph*.

Izvestiya, meaning the news, is the most prominent Russian newspaper, and also a supporter of the Putin government. Gazprom took control of the newspaper during the Putin-Gusinsky affair, but sold its majority ownership to the SOGAZ insurance company in 2008. The sale occurred during Putin's second stint as prime minister. SOGAZ was controlled by the Bank Rossiya (Bank of Russia) and its head, Yuri Kovalchuk, frequently described as Putin's banker. Bank Rossiya figures prominently in the Panama Papers and investigations into how Putin and his inner circle became profoundly wealthy.

Prominent newspapers include *Kommersant*, *RBK*, and *Vedomosti*. They received attention in the West for publishing the same editorial and similar front pages in support of a journalist, working for an independent website, who was held prisoner by the Russian government. The site, Meduza, is based in Latvia in order to operate, but it covers Russia by Russians. *Kommersant* is a business newspaper owned by a Putin ally, and its reputation took a hit when two respected journalists were forced to resign and several of their colleagues resigned in protest.

Formal Controls

A variety of formal controls have been placed on the press and nongovernmental organizations in order to limit reporting on Putin, the government, and oligarchs.

The Russian Federation followed the Soviet tradition of strictly limiting demonstrations. While the Russian Federation does not prohibit all demonstrations, it tightly controls the required permits to demonstrate. This power enables the Russian government to refuse permission to any kind of demonstration it does not want, and it can arrest demonstrators without a permit for holding a demonstration that is illegal under Russian law.

One of the ways Putin restricted reporting was creating laws against nongovernmental groups. In 2006, Putin made such a move that included press organizations. The action was met with international discomfort because it empowered Putin to shut down organizations for flimsy reasons. There have been numerous more laws restricting freedom of expression.

Protests in 2012 led to a foreign agent law targeting nongovernmental groups. Putin believed, or at least stated, that outsiders were responsible for stirring up trouble in Russia, including protests. This is one of the reasons why Putin and Russian intelligence opposed Hillary Clinton in the 2016 U.S. presidential election, because Putin thought Clinton had created dissent when she was U.S. secretary of state by criticizing the Russian election process and results. As of 2012, the Russian government can block websites without a court order.

In 2013, a law was established to ban gay "propaganda," limiting communications on gay relationships and LGBT rights. The United Nations feared the law would worsen homophobia and other biases in Russia. The same year, Russia made it illegal to hurt someone's feelings regarding religion, but the law is so vague that it enables the government to punish critics of the state-aligned Russian Orthodox Church, which has a history of favoring autocrats. Also, in 2013, the Lugovi Law was put in place to block online access to sites that are the sources of information on unsanctioned mass actions, such as protests. A criminal code also made it illegal to call for territorial separation from the Russian Federation.

A 2014 law forced bloggers with at least 3,000 daily unique visitors to register with the government. Bloggers became legally responsible not just for their own content, but for comments posted on their sites. Another law prohibits supporting Nazism and giving false information about Soviet activities during World War II. The law has been criticized for being vague, and could be used against people reporting atrocities committed by the Soviets.

Laws in 2014 and 2015 limited the foreign ownership of a media company to 20%. Those non-Russian owners who had more than 20% control had to either sell off part or all of their shares to buyers who knew the foreign owners had to sell or close.

A 2016 law targeted news aggregators by requiring them and search engines to remove information the government deemed not truthful. Also as part of counter-terrorism laws, the government prohibited communication online that would justify terrorist acts.

In December 2019, Putin signed a law that identifies journalists and bloggers working with foreigners as "foreign agents" themselves. A journalist or blogger is considered a foreign agent for reporting for the foreign media or distributing foreign news. The law followed massive street protests in the summer of 2019.

Threats and Attacks

Russia is a dangerous place for journalists to operate. In 2006, *Novaya Gazeta* reporter Anna Politkovskaya, who was known for her critical coverage of the Chechen war, was assassinated in Moscow and her killing has become symbolic of the dangers facing journalists. As of 2014, six men had been found guilty of participating in a conspiracy to kill her, but the person(s) who ordered the assassination remained safe. Politkovskaya's story resonates with journalists because she was twice poisoned and even tortured, yet she remained a committed investigator until her death.

The Committee to Protect Journalists (CPJ) reports 38 journalists were killed in Russia between 1992 and 2019 because of their work.

The CPJ could not confirm that another 24 were killed because of their journalism. Twenty more are believed to have been killed while covering news. For 2019, CPI ranked Russia as the 11th-worst country for the prosecution of cases involving murdered journalists.

Because of these dangers, the number of news outlets willing to take on Putin and his government is small. *Novaya Gazeta* remains a critical and independent voice, and is joined by radio's Ekho Moskvy and Dozhd TV. Some Russian journalists decided that the threats they received could have led to violence and decided to leave. Ekho Moskvy's Karina Orlova, for example, left Russia for the United States because of threats from Chechens after a cohosted show about a murderous attack on the staff at *Charlie Hebdo*, a French magazine. Another Ekho journalist, Ksenia Larina, went to Europe after a colleague, Tatyana Felgengauer, survived being stabbed multiple times in her throat while working at the Ekho office. Russian television outlets run by the state have loudly criticized journalists like Felgengauer.

The dangers facing journalists extend to nongovernmental, human rights activists like Natalia Estemirova, who is believed to have been killed in 2009 by Chechens aligned with the Russian government. Putin's Russia has tried to limit or prevent the activities of nongovernmental groups acting in different roles, such as watchdogs of the government and promoters of democracy. One way to do this is to threaten and attack the activists, like Estemirova, and another is to place legal restraints on those that accept foreign money.

Timothy Roy Gleason

See also Europe; Press and Government Relations; Propaganda; RT and Sputnik; TASS and Russian News Agencies

Further Readings

Becker, J. (2004). Lessons from Russia: A neo-authoritarian media system. *European Journal of Communication, 19*(2), 139–163. doi:10.1177/0267323104042908

British Broadcasting Corporation. (2020, January 7). Russia profile—media. Retrieved from https://www.bbc.com/news/world-europe-17840134

Browder, B. (2015). *Red notice: A true story of high finance, murder, and one man's fight for justice.* New York, NY: Simon and Schuster.

Committee to Protect Journalists. (2019). Russia. Retrieved from https://cpj.org/europe/russia/

History.com editors. (2020, September 11). Collapse of the Soviet Union. Retrieved from https://www.history.com/topics/cold-war/fall-of-soviet-union

Luhn, A. (2015). 15 years of vladimir putin: 15 ways he has changed Russia and the world. *The Guardian.* Retrieved from https://www.theguardian.com/world/2015/may/06/ vladimir-putin-15-ways-he-changed-russia-world

McNair, B. (1991). *Glasnost, perestroika and the Soviet media.* London, UK: Routledge.

Nance, M. W. (2018). *The plot to destroy democracy: How Putin and his spies are undermining America and dismantling the west.* New York, NY: Hachette Books.

PEN International. (2019). Russia's strident stifling of free speech 2012–2018. Retrieved from https://pen-international.org/app/uploads/PEN-Russia-ENG-FullLayout-FINAL-1.pdf

Rogerson, K. (1997, September). The role of the media in transitions from authoritarian political systems: Russia and Poland since the fall of communism. *East European Quarterly, 31*(3), 329–353.

Gov.UK. (n.d.). Foreign travel advice: Russia. Retrieved from https://www.gov.uk/foreign-travel-advice/russia

U.S. Department of State. (n.d.). Russia. Retrieved from https://www.state.gov/countries-areas/russia/

S

SATELLITE NEWSGATHERING

Satellite newsgathering (SNG) is the transmission of video or sound news reports using communication satellites. SNG allows real-time electronic media reporting from far distant locations. Its use has helped reduce the one-time divide between local and national reporting.

Contemporary uses of SNG can include deployment of a Digital Satellite News Gathering van, which can be mobilized practically anywhere. The van beams signals to a geostationary satellite and the van, and between the satellite and a control room run by a broadcast station or network with advanced systems using internet protocol. Broadcast engineers are currently working on designs for remotely controlled, robotic DSNG vehicles that can be teleoperated in hostile environments such as battle zones, deep space missions, and undersea explorations without endangering the lives of human operators.

Communication Satellites

The demands of military missiles and communications drove and largely funded the initial development of communication satellites. First theorized by science fiction author and inventor Arthur C. Clarke in a 1945 article, the concept of orbiting satellites some 22,300 miles above Earth would allow three of them to communicate with the entire globe. At that altitude, they would appear to remain stationery (hence "geostationary" orbit) above the same spot. Clarke thought it might take 50 years to develop what he predicted—in fact, it took less than 20.

The world's first low-orbit artificial satellite, *Sputnik,* was launched by the Soviet Union in October 1957. Its appearance sent shock waves through government and military circles in the United States and greatly increased federal funding to develop U.S. intercontinental missiles and orbiting satellites. Coverage of rocket launches from Cape Canaveral, Florida, became a regular beat in everyday print and television journalism—starting with the disastrous failed launch of the *Vanguard* satellite in December 1957, which was carried live on television. A year later, the *SCORE* satellite carried a prerecorded message from President Eisenhower that was transmitted back to Earth. AT&T's *Telstar* satellite of mid-1962 allowed the first live television transmissions between Europe and the United States for the limited windows of time when the satellite was orbiting over the Atlantic. The *Relay* satellite later that year helped link the United States and Japan with voice communications. But all of these were low-altitude (a few hundred miles above Earth) satellites that could be used only intermittently for a few moments during each Earth orbit.

The breakthrough to Clark's geosynchronous orbit came with *Syncom* early in 1963, the first communications satellite to reach the 22,300-mile altitude. It and the two to follow quickly proved Clark's thesis by being useful 24 hours a day, unlike brief orbital "windows" for the earlier satellites. The United States created the Communications Satellite Corporation (Comsat) to develop civilian satellite applications, which, in turn, led a year later to the formation of Intelsat to do the same globally. A steadily improved series of Intelsat satellites, starting with Early Bird in 1965, slowly expanded the global satellite communications system.

In the United States, a growing number of domestic satellites (domsats) laid the groundwork for a wholly new way to interconnect broadcast stations and cable systems, doing away with expensive terrestrial links. Equipped with uplink and downlink antennas, networks, and stations could now exchange or distribute programs in real time (minus a tiny time lag for the signal to travel a total of 44,600 miles) at a fraction of the cost of traditional terrestrial coaxial cable or microwave links. Furthermore, signals could go either way and multiple channels could be accommodated. By the late 1980s, American broadcast and cable networks were all using satellite distribution, and television receive-only (TVRO) "dishes" had become ubiquitous at stations and cable systems.

SNG Development

The first direct application of SNG appears to have taken place in 1975 when Chicago television station WBBM sought to cover the conspiracy trial of heiress Patty Hearst in San Francisco. The process involved using a portable video camera (itself a relatively new innovation) with a device to transmit (uplink) the signal to one of the first communications satellites. Back in Chicago, station engineers could then downlink that signal for processing into news reports. Though expensive, this early example of breaking down the "local–national" dividing line between network and local station journalism was a portent of the future.

Just 7 years later, when Britain decided to contest Argentina's military occupation of the Falkland Islands in the spring of 1982, satellite news communications got a world debut. All news reports from the fighting front had to be transmitted over the 8,000 miles separating the remote South Atlantic islands from London. British army signals units established analog links using satellites, and transmitted both official military information and civilian news reports, usually time-shifted anywhere up to 24 hours.

This one news story demonstrated the drawbacks of SNG as well as its benefits. First, the process was still costly and the equipment was cumbersome. It was difficult to transport the needed ground equipment, which was heavy and bulky, and it took time to set up and calibrate with the needed satellite. Few commercial users could afford the expense or risk. Further, transmissions were often affected by radio interference on the satellite up- and downlinks.

Within the next decade, however, SNG links had improved markedly. In 1984, Consus Communications began the first American SNG cooperative, which used a fleet of SNG-equipped vans. By 1992, more than 150 television stations were affiliated. They had a lot of competition, for the broadcast and cable networks were also increasingly active in SNG; NBC had 67 SNG trucks, CBS 54, and ABC 48 of them. Sites of major news stories (such as political conventions or important court trials) soon began to resemble crowded parking lots as the satellite vehicles gathered.

SNG was next put to the test in 1990–1991 in coverage of the first Gulf War. CNN's Peter Arnett was able to report from Baghdad over a period of weeks by using portable satellite news equipment. He was employing one of the first "fly-away" SNG antennas that could be packed into wheeled cases and carried on a commercial airliner. The smaller antennas could be precisely aimed at satellites—and thus attracted less (possibly hostile) attention. The White House was soon SNG equipped to allow quicker communication with news media and the public.

Within a year, the International Telecommunication Union and various national groups were working on consistent technical standards to enable SNG transmissions. The first were approved in 1992 and the process continued with digital SNG standards into the mid-2000s. But not all SNG issues were technical—use of the devices was sometimes contingent on getting local government or telecommunications authority permission.

Changing Impact

Where one network needed equipment that filled 75 to 100 shipping cases in order for it to cover the attack on Afghanistan in 2002, within a year that same capability could be fit into just five or six cases. By the time of the Iraq War, beginning in 2003, the effect of a steady trend of miniaturization and streamlining was evident. Combining small cameras with desktop video meant that digitally edited reports could be transmitted day and night to networks and stations back home. Breaking news could also be sent by satellite telephone, which used far less bandwidth, though it provided jerky and low-resolution pictures (these sufficed for talking head reports that did not need to show much movement).

Thanks to the improving equipment, SNG is increasingly able to fulfill its role as a temporary link arranged on short notice. The continued reduction in equipment size, weight, and complexity—and cost—was aided further by conversion to digital technology over the past decade or so. Many companies provide equipment or full SNG links on a lease basis. Any SNG transmission still requires several pieces of equipment. Other than the satellite itself (by far the most expensive portion of the process), a means of transmitting up to the satellite (the uplink antenna) and back again (downlink) is essential, as well as processing equipment at both ends to receive and edit the video material received. Once the satellite signal is on Earth, it can be forwarded to a studio or elsewhere using microwave links (studio-transmitter links, STL) using different spectrum frequencies than are applied for SNG.

Steadily improving digital SNG equipment has contributed to the end of the traditional distinction between local and national (and international news). With readily portable SNG units down to 70 pounds and a cost of about $130,000 by the mid-2000s, even small market stations can make use of the devices and receive or report stories far from the station.

Christopher H. Sterling

See also Audio and Video News Services; Convergence; Digital Journalism Tools

Further Readings

Bird, P., & Butt, K. (2002). Digital satellite news gathering: More features in less space. *Broadcast Engineering,* July 2002.

Butrica, A. J. ed. (1997). *Beyond the ionosphere: Fifty years of satellite communication (NASA History Series).* Washington, DC: Government Printing Office.

Higgins, J. (2004). *Introduction to SNG and ENG Microwave (Media Manuals).* Burlington, MA: Focal Press.

Higgins, J. (2007). *Satellite newsgathering* (2nd ed.). Burlington, MA: Focal Press.

International Telecommunication Union. (2009). Series SNG: Satellite News Gathering.

Newsgathering—The next generation. Satellite Evolution (July–August 2007): 20–24.

Satellite news gathering: Special report. Electronic Media (April 7, 1992): 29–34.

Wendland, M. (2003). From ENG to SNG: TV technology for covering the conflict with Iraq. *Poynter Online,* March 6, 2003.

SATIRE OF NEWS

Satire is a literary genre that employs humor when making commentary on individuals or activities and their perceived vices, shortcomings, or mistakes. In satire, humor is used to underscore an opinion or point about an issue or event. Most often, satirists use wit to criticize or attack something of which they disapprove. Parody (or spoofs), sarcasm, exaggeration, and analogy are defining literary tools of satire that help create its humorous tone.

In journalism, satire most commonly pokes fun at the news, or uses parody portrayed as conventional news. While satirical news is defined by its comedic nature, using deadpan humor to create spoofs of the news, its underlying objective is to make statements about real people, events, and trends, often with the intent of influencing change. In this way, it is usually fundamentally biased. This objective also highlights a key difference between satire of news and parody of news: While parody uses humor for humor's sake, news satire employs humor to attain the greater result of social criticism and/or promote change. Politics and current events are common themes in news satire, although the genre is not limited to them. This entry discusses the origins of news satire before looking at its prevalence and popularity and its effects.

Origins

An early example of satire in news is *The Spectator,* a British newspaper published in the early 1700s. Created by popular writers Joseph Addison and Richard Steele, the newspaper consisted of one long essay narrated by a fictional character that would report and critique a single aspect of the news each day. Unlike a typical newspaper that would report hard news, *The Spectator* was satirical in a number of ways. First, the use of a fictional character to present real information allowed for variation in tone and a less systematic reporting style, providing a sense of intimacy through storytelling and creating an element of entertainment. Furthermore, *The Spectator* provided commentary beyond objective news reporting with the distinct intent to influence change in societal behavior and mindset. This fundamentally satirical goal was clearly evidenced by the newspaper's mission to "enliven Morality with Wit, and to temper Wit with Morality."

Newspapers

Newspapers are the oldest form of news satire, at least as old as conventional journalism in the United States. In American journalism, one of the most famous news satirists was Samuel Clemens, more popularly known as *Mark Twain*. In the 1870s, Clemens worked as a young reporter for the Virginia City *Territorial Enterprise,* a newspaper in Nevada. He was relieved of his position at the *Enterprise* for publishing occasional spoof articles that were misconstrued by editors and readers as real. Clemens went on to publish what were deemed "hoaxes" in other newspapers across the country, for which he was also reprimanded.

While the genre of news satire has been around for centuries, its prevalence within American journalism dramatically increased with changes in technology. From the rise of the telegraph before the Civil War, to the birth of broadcasting in the early 20th century, and on to the opening of the Internet to commercial use in 1995, technology has intensified the speed and breadth of mass communication and brought a new, grander scope to the genre of new satire. Today, news satire is disseminated rapidly on a wide scale due to the interconnectedness of modern technology, permeating popular culture, and serving as a source of news information for tech-savvy American youth.

One of the most popular satirical news publications is *The Onion,* a newspaper created in 1988 that has since expanded into a multifaceted satirical news organization. *The Onion* was first published by Tim Keck and Christopher Johnson, two juniors at the University of Wisconsin–Madison. In

1996, the paper's website began, quickly garnering national attention. It was bought by Comedy Central in 2000, at which point the print version began national distribution. *The Onion* went on to develop a daily web video broadcast in 2007, The Onion News Network, and in 2008 a film based on the newspaper appeared as *The Onion Movie.* The print edition ceased distribution in December 2013, mirroring the decline of the traditional newspaper industry and its transition to predominantly digital-based forms of news reporting.

The Onion is satirical in that it parodies traditional news in its articles, reporting fake stories about local, national, and international events and politics, usually to create underlying social or political commentary. In the early 2000s, it parodied the style of *USA Today* with its use of bright graphics and statistical pie charts, as well as featured sections such as "News in Brief," "Opinion," "American Voices" ("What do *you* think?"), and "Infographic." *The Onion* even has a fictional history with a list of fictional contributing writers and editors.

Television

Broadcast news satire arose with the advent of radio news in the early 20th century, but became more prevalent during the satire boom of the late 1950s in the United Kingdom. A generation of satirical writers popularized satire on television. A cornerstone of this satire renaissance was the television show *That Was the Week That Was,* a popular satirical news program that aired on BBC Television in 1962 and 1963. In the United States, the NBC television network adapted this British program into *Rowan and Martin's Laugh-In,* a predominantly political comedy show that aired from 1968 through 1973. A satirical news sketch that aired as part of the show is an early example of popular televised news satire in the United States. The segment "Laugh-In Looks at the News" parodied network news with a fake anchor giving a comical report on recent news stories, both fake and real. The sketch also satirized historical events and predicted bizarre events far into the future.

Along with *Rowan and Martin's Laugh-In, Saturday Night Live*'s "Weekend Update" segment helped usher in the satire boom in the United States, reaching an audience of about 30 million people every week during its formative years of

1975 through 1980. "Weekend Update" is a satirical news sketch that parodies political and current events. The segment was created and originally hosted by *Saturday Night Live* comedian Chevy Chase and was introduced on the show's original broadcast on October 11, 1975. Developed during a pivotal time that included President Richard Nixon's resignation after the Watergate scandal and the end of the Vietnam War, it makes light of current events while emphasizing the perceived shortcomings of American politics and parodying mainstream broadcast journalism.

Perhaps the best-known broadcast news satire program in the early 21st century is Comedy Central's *The Daily Show*. It premiered in 1996 but rose to popular notoriety when Jon Stewart replaced Craig Kilborn as host in 1999. Stewart hosted the show until he was succeeded by Trevor Noah in September 2015. *The Daily Show* parodies political figures and mainstream media while satirizing real news, drawing most of its stories from American politics and then mockingly criticizing them.

The popularity of *The Daily Show* led to the creation of a spin-off, *The Colbert Report,* hosted by Stephen Colbert, who had portrayed a conservative "correspondent" on *The Daily Show*. This news satire program aired from 2005 to 2014 and parodied political pundit shows such as Fox News's *The O'Reilly Factor* (1996–2017). HBO's satirical news show *Last Week Tonight*, which premiered in 2014, is hosted by John Oliver, a previous correspondent and fill-in host for *The Daily Show*. In 2016, *Full Frontal With Samantha Bee* premiered on TBS as a late-night news satire show with long-time *The Daily Show* correspondent Samantha Bee as host. As often is the case with news satire as opposed to straight parody, both Comedy Central programs, *Last Week Tonight* and *Full Frontal,* are seen as politically biased, most often using sarcasm to mock and criticize conservative people and politics.

On the Web

The web has also heightened access to and popularity of news satire. It has also exacerbated some of the problems with spoof news.

Although news satire has been on the web since its beginning, *The Onion*'s website, created in 1996, has been the most influential source of satirical news online. Since its inception, myriad news satire articles have been posted across the Internet, often as website articles or on blogs, and hundreds of satirical news websites have been created. Some have been designed to collect popular news parody articles. HumorFeed.com, for example, runs a news satire headline feed with over 40 contributing news parody sites.

A fundamental problem with news satire is its ability to be misinterpreted as real by audiences and even mainstream media. Its use of deadpan humor, which is more covert than typical comedy, makes the "fakeness" of news satire comparatively less apparent and more easily misperceived as actual news. The web intensifies this because of its abilities to repost pieces of news satire out-of-context and disseminate such pieces so speedily. The result is heightened room for misapprehension and confusion concerning what is real and what is parody.

Furthermore, satire is often criticized for defying the conventions of traditional journalism. Neither conventional news nor blatant comedy, satire often escapes the editorial processes of conventional journalism and is less subject to censure. Web publications, including blogs and articles posted on personal websites, are even less subject to review because they may be posted by anyone and escape any process of editing, thereby heightening the confusion. In recent years, the rapid propagation of unchecked information and "fake news" on web-based social media platforms such as Facebook has come under criticism in the United States, even likened to the spread of a virus by academic institutions, suggesting that misinterpretations of news satire taken out of context can be similarly distributed. The result is widespread dissemination of satirical pieces whose take on the news has not been checked for accuracy and is less likely to be censured.

Prevalence and Popularity

News satire's integration in American popular culture is demonstrated by the popularity of these programs and publications. *The Daily Show* is a notable example. In March 2007, the Pew Research Center's Project for Excellence in Journalism asked Americans to name the journalist they most admire.

Jon Stewart, then host of *The Daily Show*, ranked fourth on the final list, following network news anchors Brian Williams, Tom Brokaw, and Dan Rather. The presence of a satirist on such a list underlines the integration of news satire within American culture. Senator John Edwards used *The Daily Show* as a forum to announce his candidacy for the Democratic presidential nomination in September 2003, serving as another example of the conflation of satirical and real news.

Furthermore, a 2014 Pew Research Center analysis found that a portion of American adults actually got news from *The Daily Show* and *The Colbert Report*. Pew found that 10% of online adults got news from The *Colbert Report* the previous week, which was comparable to true news outlets such as *The Wall Street Journal* and *USA Today*. Furthermore, 76% of those The *Colbert Report* viewers also got news from *The Daily Show*, with many also receiving news from CNN, NPR, local television news, and other sources. These statistics suggest that such programs serve as a primary source of information for many—particularly young men. A 2014 Pew survey found that 22% of 18- to 29-year-old men in the United States got news about politics and government in the previous week from *The Colbert Report*.

Statistics on readership and viewership of satirical news publications and programs further demonstrate the popularity of news satire. *Full Frontal* first aired in February 2016, and by the end of that year the show had 1.32 million viewers. By the beginning of 2020, *The Daily Show* had won 24 primetime Emmy Awards, *Last Week Tonight* had won 16, and the *Colbert Report* had won 7. In 2006, the *Merriam-Webster* dictionary publisher named *The Colbert Report's* neologism "truthiness" Word of the Year.

Effects

News satire has had measurable effects on the public in recent years. In a 2017 Ohio State University study, researchers found that people with low or little interest in American politics tended to watch satirical news shows over true news, and that satirical programs affected citizens' belief that they can influence political systems. These findings suggest that satire is able to draw people into politics that may otherwise avoid matters of state. The study also found that people choose satirical

programs that align with their political beliefs, and that those programs reinforce their partisan leanings as much as true news.

The Daily Show is a commonly cited barometer for the effect of satirical news on political opinion. For example, a 2006 study by Jody Baumgartner and Jonathan Morris demonstrated that *Daily Show* viewers exposed to political comedy tended to rate politicians parodied by the show more negatively than nonviewers. Likewise, *Daily Show* viewers demonstrated higher levels of cynicism toward both media and the electoral system at large. Yet these same study participants reported comparatively high levels of confidence in understanding current American politics.

More recently, a 2017 study examined American attitudes toward Syrian refugees after watching a satirical segment on *Full Frontal With Samantha Bee* that was sympathetic to refugees. Findings showed that support for refugees increased significantly after viewing the segment, and that support was still found after 2 weeks.

The use of satirical news as primary news source has had discernible effects on the political awareness and participation of American audiences. In 2004, the National Annenberg Election Survey found that viewers of news satire were better informed on political happenings and current affairs than those who relied solely on traditional news media. A quiz given to nearly 20,000 American adults in mid-2004 demonstrated that news satire watchers had more knowledge about the backgrounds of political candidates and candidates' stances on issues than those who did not watch political satire. Moreover, *Daily Show* viewers knew the most about election issues, as compared to viewers of conventional news and straight comedy shows such as *The Tonight Show With Jay Leno* and *Late Show With David Letterman*. However, a 2008 study published in the *Journal of Communication* came to a different conclusion, suggesting that news entertainment programs like *The Daily Show* were less effective at producing political knowledge retention in 18- to 64-year-olds than traditional news media, which resulted in more memory-based processing of political information.

While concern has been raised regarding the high levels of political cynicism associated with news satire viewers, a 2008 study by Xiaoxia Cao and Paul Brewer linked political comedy viewing with increased levels of political participation. This study concludes that exposure to political comedy shows, including satirical news programs, is positively associated with increased participation in political campaigns and membership in a political organization. This political participation might be skewed toward the liberal end of the political spectrum; Pew Research Center reported in 2014 that survey respondents who got news from *The Daily Show* and *The Colbert Report* were more consistently liberal than conservative. For example, about 72% of *The Daily Show* audience held left-of-center political views.

Satire has affected journalism and journalists as well. A 2007 study by communications researcher Lauren Feldman underscores the point that, during a year when young Americans' traditional news media consumption was decreasing, their attention to late-night comedy programs as sources of political information was on the rise. Through examination of discourse surrounding satire programs such as *The Daily Show,* the study found that many journalists have recognized this trend and begun using such programs as forums to reflect upon the nature of their work and the current state of journalism in general. The study concludes that the once rigid distinction between news and entertainment is blurring and that journalists themselves are reconsidering the dividing conventions between straight and satirical news.

Conclusion

In journalism, satire has been employed as a form of commentary on political issues and current events, using parody, sarcasm, and similar forms of deadpan humor to emphasize a point or critique such subjects. Its popularity has proliferated as communication technology has made news satire more easily and quickly accessible to the masses. Today, *The Onion, The Daily Show With Trevor Noah, Saturday Night Live*'s "Weekend Update," *Last Week Tonight With John Oliver*, and *Full Frontal With Samantha Bee* are all examples of influential satirical news in American popular culture. Myriad studies have demonstrated palpable effects that news satire has on audiences as a result of their great popularity, subsequently blurring the lines between conventional and satirical news.

Marisa A. Lubeck

See also Entertainment Journalism; Fake News; Hoaxes; Internet: Impact on the Media; Parody of News; Satirists, Political

Further Readings

Andrews, E. L. (2019, October 9). How fake news spreads like a real virus. *Stanford Engineering Magazine.* Retrieved from https://engineering.stanford.edu/magazine/article/how-fake-news-spreads-real-virus

Baumgartner, J., & Morris, J. S. (2006). The daily show effect: Candidate evaluations, efficacy, and American youth. *American Politics Research, 34*(3), 341–367. doi:10.1177/1532673X05280074

Baym, G. (2007). Representation and the politics of play: Stephen Colbert's Better Know a District. *Political Communication, 24,* 359–376. doi:10.1080/10584600701641441

Cao, X., & Brewer, P. R. (2008). Political comedy shows and public participation in politics. *International Journal of Public Opinion Research, 20*(1), 90–99. doi:10.1093/ijpor/edm030

Feldman, L. (2007). The news about comedy: Young audiences, the daily show, and evolving notions of journalism. *Journalism, 8*(4), 406–427. doi:10.1177/1464884907078655

Feldman, L., & Chattoo, C. B. (2018). Comedy as a route to social change: The effects of satire and news on persuasion about Syrian refugees. *Mass Communication and Society, 24*(3). doi:10.1080/15205436.2018.1545035

Gottfried, J., & Anderson, M. (2014, December 12). For some, the satiric "Colbert Report" is a trusted source of political news. Pew Research Center. Retrieved from https://www.pewresearch.org/fact-tank/2014/12/12/for-some-the-satiric-colbert-report-is-a-trusted-source-of-political-news/

Kim, Y. M., & Vishak, J. (2008). Just laugh! You don't need to remember: The effects of entertainment media on political information acquisition and information processing in political judgment. *Journal of Communication, 58*(2), 338–360. doi:10.1111/j.1460-2466.2008.00388.x

Knobloch-Westerwick, S., & Lavis, S. M., (2017). Selecting serious or satirical, supporting or stirring news? Selective exposure to Partisan versus mockery news online videos. *Journal of Communication, 67*(1), 54–81 doi:10.1111/jcom.12271

Marek, L. (2013, November 8). Onion quits print. *Crain's Chicago Business.* Retrieved from https://www.chicagobusiness.com/article/20131108/NEWS06

/131109836/onion-ceases-print-editions-pivots-to
-sponsored-digital-content#

Mitchell, A., Gottfried, J., Kiley, J., & Matsa, K. E. (2014, October 21). Political polarization & media habits. Pew Research Center, Retrieved from https://www.journalism.org/2014/10/21/political-polarization -media-habits/

Palmeri, F. (2003). *Satire, history, novel: Narrative forms, 1665–1815*. Newark, DE: University of Delaware Press.

Pratt, J. (2001, October/November). 'To enliven morality with wit': The spectator. *History Magazine*. Retrieved from http://www.history-magazine.com/spectator.html

Reincheld, A. (2006). "Saturday Night Live" and Weekend Update. *Journalism History, 31*, 190–197. doi:10.1080/00947679.2006.12062688

Rosen, R. M. (2007). *Making mockery: The poetics of ancient satire*. New York, NY: Oxford University Press.

Rowan, D., Martin, D., Keyes, P. W., & Gibson, H. (1968). *Rowan and Martin's laugh-in*. New York, NY: Samuel French.

Simpson, P. (2003). *On the discourse of satire: Towards a stylistic model of satirical humor*. Amsterdam, Netherlands: John Benjamins.

Travers, B. (2019, October 30). Samantha bee is already preparing 'full frontal' for the 2020 election. IndieWire. Retrieved from https://www.indiewire.com /2019/10/samantha-bee-interview-full-frontal-2020 -election-1202185903/

SATIRISTS, POLITICAL

Political satire is a subgenre of political journalism, and a complex ironic practice of political criticism mixed with rhetorical hyperbole, entertaining humor, deliberate misstatement, and personal insight. Political satire frequently defines (and on occasion, exceeds) the accepted limits of professional journalism because the practice draws attention to biases and subjectivity inherent in newsgathering and editing, as well as society in general. Satire in general plays this role for literature, folklore, pop culture, and film.

Political satire has roots deep in Western history and has flourished in different historical periods and cultures of representative democracy. Like all satire, political satire holds current events and social relationships up against a set of idealized ethical norms such as basic fairness, humanitarianism, and democracy. Political satire can function as topical humor when actual events fall short of proclaimed ideals, or when responsible individuals, organizations, or governments are seen as openly hypocritical. Political satire can simultaneously offer humor and social criticism. Political cartoons are a well-known subset of political satire using graphic design, illustration, and physical exaggeration to engage in political commentary. Political satire in essay form utilizes exaggeration, irony, hyperbole, double entendre, and other rhetorical devices to simultaneously create humor and social and political commentary.

While parody and political satire share many attributes, not every political satire is parody and not all parody is satire, political or otherwise. Parody is usually a necessary-but-not-sufficient element to satire. However, both parody and political satire often test the limits of freedom of press and the specifics of libel, slander, cultural sensitivity, privacy rights, and copyright and trademark protections. In 1994, the U.S. Supreme Court in *Campbell v. Acuff-Rose Music* found that, "parody has an obvious claim to transformative value." Within the Copyright Act of 1976, section 107 defines fair use. The Supreme Court decision clearly stated that "parody like other comment or criticism may claim fair-use under §107."

This entry discusses the origins of political satire and political satire in the early United States before turning to political satire since the start of the 20th century. The entry also looks at the relationship between the cultural specificity of satire and a globalized media environment and provides examples of some contemporary political satirists and outlets for political satire.

Origins and Development

The most well-known example of early political satire was the Dionysian theater rituals in classical Greek democracy. During these festivals, performers lampooned political leaders and elaborate skits were performed in the public arenas as a form of acceptable open criticism. As Greek society transitioned to a written culture, these performances were recorded and became lasting records of political satire. Most famous among Greek theatrical satirists was Aristophanes, whose plays are still performed and retain much of their original satire of power. Several pre-Socratic philosophers also engaged in spoken and written political satire. So powerful were political satire and early theater that Plato harshly criticizes them in *The Republic.* Plato is cautious of "poets" and other writers because they have an ability to destabilize a democratic regime by appealing to the base entertainment desire of the audience. These same practices were continued by the Romans in the form of Saturnalia rituals and the stoic and satirical writings of Seneca, Horace, Juvenal, and others.

In Western cultures, satire and political satire were preserved during the Middle Ages by traveling minstrels and bards who obliquely offered social criticisms through lyrics to popular songs performed in informal settings. These coded satires were often of reigning monarchs and the feudal system itself. Many of these folklore songs were eventually collected and written as nursery rhymes and fairy tales, such as "Three Blind Mice" and "Jack and Jill." Simple satires of religious institutions were coded into performances of mystery plays and church dramas. Erasmus's *In Praise of Folly* satirized both the institution of the church and self-delusion on the part of the readers. Political satire regained popularity with the beginning of the Enlightenment era and greater literacy rates in European countries. Political upheavals around the redistribution of wealth and the rise of a mercantile middle class were the subjects of this satire.

British literary satirists including Jonathan Swift and Alexander Pope influenced and encouraged an American colonial tradition of political satire. While attempting to break into establishment newspapers and magazines, Benjamin Franklin and other colonial printers used political satire both to speak out against the excesses and unfairness of British colonial rule and as an effective means of self-promotion. Franklin's *Poor Richard's Almanack* traces a fine line between satire, legitimate agricultural information, and outright hoax. This mixture of serious and satirical information is also found in his *Autobiography of Benjamin Franklin.* Such political satire occurs throughout colonial works of journalism, which both reported on current affairs and offered scathing satires of King George III of England. Satire was suppressed along with other political journalism leading toward the American and French revolutions.

Early American Political Satire

Political satire continued to be a noticeable feature in 18th- and 19th-century journalism from Fleet Street publishers in London to French and American newspapers. While political satire is not unique to English-language journalism, it has made a more powerful impact in these societies. Political historians have argued that satire continued to flourish because these societies valued and enshrined a freer and more open press. Other theories for the continued popularity of satire in the Anglophone world in general and the United States in particular are that economic power is more widely spread, literacy rates are comparatively high, political engagement is socially encouraged, and political power is frequently balanced in a two-party system.

As printing technologies improved, illustrated political cartoons began to appear in newspapers as engravings and lithographs. Early political cartoons were a powerful form of political satire at a time when newspapers had large circulations but a large percentage of the population was not functionally literate. From Franklin's simple "Join or Die" woodcut to the increasingly elaborate cartoons of Thomas Nast in *Harper's Weekly* to the nuanced illustrations of *Punch* and *The New Yorker,* editorial and satirical cartoons have had an enormous impact on the style and substance of journalism. Enduring images such as Uncle Sam, the Republican elephant, and the Democratic donkey were all created within cartoons as a form of political satire. Many neologisms of the time, such as *gerrymandering* and *muckraking,* passed into the written satire of the 19th century and into the political lexicon of contemporary journalism. Viral online image macros or "memes" serve a similar function to earlier political cartoons, but allow for non-professionals to customize political satire images to fit quickly evolving news stories.

In the United States, satire acted at its most serious when used within the abolition movement and during the U.S. Civil War (1861–1865). The continued rise of literacy and the proliferation of periodical magazines created a unique and new literary market in the mid-19th century. Many of these publications turned to satire, particularly political satire, to reach out to new audiences. Satirical books influenced political essays in *Harper's Weekly* and used satire to indirectly criticize the institution of slavery, political corruption, war profiteering, and U.S. imperialism when direct criticism would have been difficult or impossible.

Like Franklin, Mark Twain (the nom de plume of Samuel Clemens) began his long career as a writer and essayist working as an assistant to a printer. Twain frequently made use of satire for political means. While working for a series of newspapers during Reconstruction (1865–1877), Twain used the "travelogue" genre as a vehicle for his satire, for example *The Innocents Abroad* and *Roughing It*. Among the political targets of Twain's satire were growing American imperialism, social elitism, phony frontiersmen, and religious dogmatism. His satirical journalism and his novel writing frequently cross-pollinated each other. Twain's famous essay "The Celebrated Jumping Frog of Calaveras County" was originally published in *The New York Saturday Press*, which launched his career as both a satirist and a journalist. In a similar career to that of Twain, Ambrose Bierce also championed political satire within newsgathering and journalism. Bierce gained popularity as one of the first permanent columnists for the Hearst newspapers, then as the editor of *The Wasp*, a satirical magazine.

Twentieth-Century Political Satire

In the early 20th century, the term *debunkers* was broadly applied to political satirists working as journalists. H. L. Mencken, Don Marquis, and Upton Sinclair each used satire to similar effect, and Mencken and Sinclair occasionally lampooned the very institutions they promoted. Due to his open criticism and satire of U.S. involvement in both world wars, Mencken was frequently considered to be anti-Semitic and pro-German, despite his outspoken writing to the contrary. In the early 20th century, these same political satirists also began calls for a civil rights movement, took aim at prohibition, and championed immigrant rights.

Both Mencken and Marquis pioneered the sharp-tongued, mordantly ironic writing style that would later become the hallmark of political satire in magazine writing, as it began to distinguish itself from newspaper writing. *The Smart Set, Punch,* and other early monthly publications founded and popularized by Mencken, Marquis, and Sinclair eventually led to the style of *The New Yorker, Vanity Fair,* and other literary and lifestyle magazines. These magazines prided themselves on

Figure 1. A satirical, political cartoon that appeared in *Harper's Weekly* in November of 1877 by Thomas Nast. Titled "The Lightning Speed of Honesty," the cartoon depicts Uncle Sam seated on a snail named 45th Congress, as he carries army and navy payroll and money, with the Resumption Act in his pocket. The Resumption Act sought to reduce the amount of greenbacks (used to finance the Union side of the Civil War) in circulation.

Source: Library of Congress.

a highbrow literary style, sharp wit and irony, and an eclecticism that reflected the growing literary movement of urbanity and sophistication in the period between the two world wars. The Algonquin Round Table was an unofficial group of journalists, playwrights, and satirists in the 1920s that moved quick wit, sardonicism, and satire from populist lampooning into high culture and political commentary. Among this group, Dorothy Parker and Robert Benchley were literary essayists and satirists; Alexander Woollcott and Heywood Broun were professional journalists; and other members of the group, such as Harpo Marx, were

Broadway and Hollywood actors. While diverse, the group was held together by their use of literary satire for cultural and political aims.

Colleges have also been hotbeds for satire, where student groups published newspapers and magazines such as the *Harvard Lampoon,* continuing the tradition of highbrow satire. The growth of specialized humor magazines has led to more accepted publications for satire such as *National Lampoon, Mad,* and *Rolling Stone* that frequently mix political satire with farce, pop culture reporting, and music reviews. These magazines retain some of the political satire of college publications, but add a unique blend of consumer culture graphic design and lowbrow shock value. Later examples include *The Onion* and other alternative press publications that have moved toward mainstream journalism.

The "gonzo journalism" of the countercultural movement of the 1960s was another form of political satire influenced by the libertine ideals of drug and hippie culture. Freely mixing facts with outlandish fictions and personal opinions, this form of satire involved reevaluating serious topics in a sarcastic manner while eschewing objectivity. Championed by writers Hunter S. Thompson, Tom Wolfe, and George Plimpton, gonzo journalism as satire outlasted its hippie origins and continued into the 1980s and continues to influence contemporary journalists. Gonzo journalism celebrated anarchic popular culture and the civil rights movement, while satirizing U.S. involvement in the Vietnam War, the Watergate scandal, the consumerism of the 1970s and 1980s, and the Cold War policies of U.S. President Ronald Reagan in the 1980s.

Political Satire in Broadcast and Online Media

Political satire continued its dynamic relationship with political journalism in the late 20th century and into the 21st century. While print journalism continues to include satire, television and online media have become more central vehicles for the genre. Since the late 20th century, satirical TV shows have taken off in the United States, Great Britain, and Canada, with some of them finding popularity across Anglophone countries. *That Was the Week That Was* was a satirical sketch comedy show in the United Kingdom in the 1960s that directly influenced later broadcast news satire programs such as

Not the Nine O'Clock News (1979–1982) and *Brass Eye* (1997–2001) in the United Kingdom, *Not Necessarily the News* (1982–1990) in the United States, and *This Hour Has 22 Minutes* (1993–) in Canada. *Monty Python's Flying Circus* (1969–1974) was an absurdist British sketch comedy show known for its randomness and a deconstructivist approach to television that continues to influence the style of parody and political satire.

North American sketch comedy programs such as *Laugh-In* (1967–1973), *SCTV* (1976–1981), and *Saturday Night Live* (1975–) engaged in frequent political satire. However, these programs maintained their parody and contrivances openly. By contrast, satirical news shows such as *The Daily Show* (1996–), *The Colbert Report* (2005–2014), and *Last Week Tonight* (2014–) have walked a fine line between offering satire and presenting legitimate news, and false or prank news.

During political campaigns and beyond, political satire is frequently, and sometimes deliberately, mixed with disinformation, rumors, and hoaxes. Many social media sites now affix tags designating satirical content as such. Misinformation in the guise of satire continues to circulate via media channels despite editorial oversight by broadcasters and notifications by social media platforms.

Satire and Global Cultures

Satire often does not work in terms of media globalism because the irony it employs can be linguistically or regionally very specific. For example, the political satire within Bollywood films in India is generally lost on Anglophone audiences. Within bilingual and multilingual countries, such as Canada and Switzerland, satirical newspapers and television shows, such as the Canadian *La fin du monde est à 7 heures* (The End of the World Is at 7 O'Clock, 1997–2000) are usually not translated because the essential humor component is lost.

The publication of cartoons of the prophet Mohammed by Danish newspaper *Jyllands-Posten* in 2005 and French satirical weekly newspaper *Charlie Hebdo* in 2011 were conceived as social and political satire of theocratic Islam, iconoclasm, and the process of cultural assimilation. The strong public reaction and controversy the publication created highlighted the differences in responses to political satire by different cultures in a globalized media world. Mistranslations and misunderstanding in globalized media have occasionally led to unintentionally funny occurrences: In 2002, *The Beijing Evening News* translated and ran a satirical story from *The Onion* that humorously claimed that the U.S. Congress had demanded a retractable dome be built to replace the Capitol building. Even after the story was revealed as a U.S.-based satire, the editors of the paper refused to publish a clarification or retraction.

Contemporary Political Satire and Satirists

"The Capitol Steps"

Formed in the early 1980s in Washington, D.C., this rotating group of comedians performs both parody pop songs and improvised comedy satirizing current political events. In 1994, a U.S. Supreme Court ruling allowed them to perform parody and satire without paying royalties for being within legal "fair use." Several different casts remain active in live performances and public radio appearances.

Samantha Bee (1969–)

Samantha Bee is a Canadian comedian and TV host of *Full Frontal With Samantha Bee* since 2016. She began her career in sketch comedy and writing in Toronto, and joined *The Daily Show* as the first female correspondent in 2003. After 12 years, she left *The Daily Show* and became the head writer and producer for her own show satirizing politics and news. Bee is also known for additional acting and voice acting roles.

Charlie Brooker (1971–)

As an English writer and satirist, Brooker is best known for the science fiction anthology series *Black Mirror* (2011–). He began his career writing for the BBC with *The 11 O'Clock Show* (1998–2000) and later wrote and hosted *Screenwipe* beginning in 2006. In 2009 and 2010, Brooker produced and hosted *Newswipe* with a format of news satire and criticism of journalism. As of 2020, he continued to be involved in news criticism, hosting *Wipe* specials and appearing on other United Kingdom and American television specials.

Stephen Colbert (1964–)

Colbert began his career as a writer and performer and gained popularity on *The Daily Show*. His television show *The Colbert Report* was a spin-off of *The Daily Show* that pushed satire to extreme levels, with Colbert playing a pompous conservative also known as *Stephen Colbert*. In 2006, Colbert was a featured entertainer at the White House Correspondents' Association Dinner, and in 2010, joined Jon Stewart in the "Rally to Restore Sanity and/or Fear" while remaining in the character of his alter ego. In 2015 he dropped his satirical character and became the host of the CBS late-night program *The Late Show With Stephen Colbert*.

Al Franken (1951–)

Franken is a liberal political satirist who began his career as a writer for *Saturday Night Live* in the 1970s and continued to write and perform occasionally through the 1990s. Franken wrote a series of books satirizing conservative media, particularly radio talk shows. He was elected as U.S. senator representing Minnesota in 2008, and resigned the office in 2018 after allegations of sexual harassment.

Greg Gutfeld (1964–)

Beginning his career as a magazine editor, Greg Gutfeld became the editor of *Stuff* and the UK edition of *Maxim* where he brought an element of gonzo journalism and political satire to each magazine to increase readership. Gutfeld was an early writer for *The Huffington Post* before hosting the late-night program *Red Eye* on the Fox News Channel from 2007 to 2015. He was known for controversial humorous polemics. In 2011 he became a panelist on *The Five*, and in 2015 began hosting *The Greg Gutfeld Show*, both on the Fox News Channel.

Garrison Keillor (1942–)

Keillor is a public radio personality and commentator who began his radio career on Minnesota Public Radio in the late 1960s. He created the radio show *A Prairie Home Companion* in 1974 and hosted it until 2016 before stepping down. The show, a blend of variety show, monologue, sketch comedy, and political satire, continued under the same name with host Chris Thile until 2017, and for 3 years after that as *Live From Here*. The show's name was changed after Minnesota Public Radio terminated its contracts with Keillor in 2017 amid allegations of inappropriate behavior toward an employee. Keillor has written several books excerpting stories from his radio show.

Bill Maher (1956–)

Maher began his career as a stand-up comedian and achieved popularity on late-night television in the 1990s with *Politically Incorrect*, a program that blended the roundtable interview format with comedy routines. Maher has been an active proponent of blogging and new media and involved in disparate political movements. In 2008 he starred in the comedic documentary *Religulous*. He began hosting late-night talk show on HBO, *Real Time With Bill Maher*, in 2003.

Trevor Noah (1984–)

Noah is a comedian and TV host born in South Africa where he began as a presenter and host for the South African Broadcasting Corp. (SABS). He produced and hosted *Tonight With Trevor Noah* (2010–2011) before moving the United States and joining *The Daily Show* in 2014. In 2015 he replaced Jon Stewart as the host of *The Daily Show* and has produced other television specials.

The Onion

Founded in the late 1980s as a local college humor newspaper in Madison, Wisconsin, *The Onion* gained popularity after the launch of its website in 1996. The publication was distributed in several major cities in the United States and blended parody and satire with entertainment news and interviews. The print version was discontinued in 2013 but the website remained. Several satire news stories from *The Onion* have been republished accidentally as legitimate news stories both within the United States and internationally.

John Oliver (1969–)

John Oliver began his career as a stand-up comedian and a member of the Cambridge Footlights comedy troupe during college. Oliver hosted several stand-up comedy shows and *Mock the Week* (2005–) for the BBC before joining *The Daily Show* in 2006. In 2014 he became the host of *Last Week Tonight* on HBO. Like other late-night news programs, the satire and criticism of the show have had demonstrable political effects. Oliver is the namesake of the "John Oliver Effect," referring to changes in policy and culture in the United States resulting from the show.

P. J. O'Rourke (1947–)

O'Rourke is a conservative political satirist who began his career writing for *The National Lampoon* and *Rolling Stone*. While originally considered a gonzo journalist, he later satirized the genre in a series of books and media appearances. He continues as a freelance writer and political commentator for public radio.

Jon Stewart (1962–)

Stewart is a television host and political satirist best known for hosting *The Daily Show*, from 1999 to 2015. Stewart began his career as comedian and master of ceremonies for sketch comedy and worked as a substitute host and writer for late night television shows. After stepping down from his position as host and producer for *The Daily Show*, he continued to write satirical books and making public appearances and issue advocacy.

William A. Hanff Jr.

See also Cartoonists, Political; Column-Writing; Editorials; Parody of News

Further Readings

Baym, G., & Jones, J. P. (Eds.). (2013). *News parody and political satire across the globe*. Abingdon, UK: Routledge.

Caron, J. E. (2016). The quantum paradox of truthiness: Satire, activism, and the postmodern condition. *Studies in American Humor, 2*(2), 153–181. doi:10.5325/studamerhumor.2.2.0153

Carretta, V. (1983). *The snarling muse: Verbal and visual satire from pope to Churchill.* Philadelphia, PA: University of Pennsylvania Press.

Colletta, L. (2009). Political satire and postmodern irony in the age of Stephen Colbert and Jon Stewart. *The Journal of Popular Culture, 42*(5), 856–874. doi:10.1111/j.1540-5931.2009.00711.x

Fletcher, M. D. (1987). *Contemporary political satire: Narrative strategies in the post-modern context.* New York, NY: University Press of America.

Granger, B. I. (1960). *Political satire in the American revolution 1763–1783.* Ithaca, NY: Cornell University Press.

Hirst, M. (1998). From gonzo to pomo: Hunting new journalism. In M. Breen (Ed.), *Journalism theory and practice* (pp.196–219). Paddington, NSW, Australia: Macleay Press.

Hmielowski, J. D., Holbert, R. L., & Lee, J. (2011). Predicting the consumption of political TV satire: Affinity for political humor, the Daily Show, and the Colbert Report. *Communication Monographs, 78*(1), 96–114. doi:10.1080/03637751.2010 .542579

Jackson, L. (2018). Null and nuller? Laughing about injustice, from Jon Stewart to John Oliver. *Philosophy of Education Archive,* 154–163.

LaMarre, H. L., Landreville, K. D., & Beam, M. A. (2009). The irony of satire: Political ideology and the motivation to see what you want to see in the Colbert Report. *The International Journal of Press/Politics, 14*(2), 212–231. doi:10.1177/1940161208330904

Plato. (1914). *The republic.* New York, NY: Hearst's International Library.

Stewart, J., Karlin, B., & Javerbaum, D. (2004). *America (the book): A citizen's guide to democracy inaction.* New York, NY: Warner Books.

Tower, S. (1982). *Cartoons and lampoons: The art of political satire.* New York, NY: Julian Messner.

Legal Citations

Campbell v. Acuff-Rose Music, 510 U.S. 569 (1994).

SCIENCE AND TECHNOLOGY JOURNALISM

Science and technology journalism provides public meaning to scientific issues that would otherwise never be widely discussed in public. It is a subset of journalism practice that can take on a wide variety of forms but is focused on communicating science to specialist and nonspecialist audiences. While it has historically been linked to the promotion of science and gee-whiz stories that seek to fascinate people, through time its roles have diversified to showcase that one strength of science journalism as a profession is a critical stance on scientific and technology issues. This stance helps science journalism draw both on the power of science to learn about our world and the power of journalism to take a serious and thoughtful view on connections between science and society. Even as legacy mass media in some countries falter, imperiling jobs, many make the argument that a growth in misinformation makes good, independent, and evidence-based science journalism more important than ever. This entry discusses how scientific journalism has been defined, different approaches to science journalism, some common themes in discussions of the field, and challenges facing science journalism.

Definition(s) of Science Journalism

There is no standard definition of science journalism that is unequivocally accepted by all. Journalists, scientists, scholars, and critics have long debated the essential elements that could make up a robust field of science and technology journalism. Should it focus on the *translation* of complex scientific findings into jargon-free journalism to inform nonspecialists? Or make its mission the *critique* of scientific endeavors and new technologies for the public good? Perhaps, the goal is simply to *engage* audiences in the slow process of scientific discovery? Many additional questions and combinations of answers have been proposed, often with the underlying thread that journalism is one important connection between science and society. For science reporters such as Cornelia Dean, whose 2009 book *Am I Making Myself Clear?* is an invitation to scientists to talk to the public, science journalism involves four steps:

1. "Paying attention" to developments in science and technology;
2. Talking to the researchers that generate these developments;

3. Seeking to understand the ideas behind them; and

4. Communicating (through media production) this understanding to the public.

The importance of Dean's four steps is clearly situated in arguments that this is how we stay knowledgeable about how science is, and will continue to, change our world. This is seen through issues such as climate change, gene editing, ethical robots, pandemics, black holes, the loss of biodiversity, space exploration, quantum computing, and so many other topics that require incisive social learning and public deliberation. Such scientific topics, however, can represent some of most difficult forms of discourse to untangle without background knowledge.

The work of science journalists to publicly untangle science is often a highly personal endeavor. Each science journalist has their own preferences in terms of scientific topics, multimedia formats, tactics for explaining complex topics, trusted scientists to interview, and distinguishing styles. This, of course, is combined with sharing various common professional practices, a culture, set of norms, and a political and economic context situated in a desire to link scientific developments to public knowledge. In his 1997 book chapter, "Covering Science for Newspapers," Boyce Rensberger outlines five criteria newspaper science writers use when deciding whether a story is newsworthy:

1. Fascination value—science journalists speak to human curiosity;
2. Size of the audience—science journalists want topics that impact many people;
3. Importance—science journalists want their story to resonate, to mean something;
4. Reliability—science journalists want science that is good, convincing, peer-reviewed, and notes its limitations (other scientists will back it up); and
5. Timeliness—science journalists want a "new" discovery.

Not every science journalist will agree with or prioritize all these criteria, but they suffice to show that science journalism can look a lot like other journalism, which Sharon Dunwoody notes is due to media coverage patterns making use of similar production infrastructure as opposed to content specifics.

Science journalists have long had a strong community with professional associations such as the World Federation of Science Journalists (WFSJ) and its 63 member associations from across the world, as well as books providing guidance to science journalists. A restrictive view of this work sees the clearest, defining examples of science journalism in the specialist news reporting found in, for example, the science section of the *New York Times* or in magazines such as the *New Scientist*. A larger view recognizes that almost any general journalist can find themselves covering a science and technology issue, and importantly, that there is an increasingly diverse set of online and social media outlets aimed at conveying information about science to their audiences (e.g., Ars Technica, Live Science, Gizmodo).

The recognition of a growing array of online information sources about science has led to renewed calls for science journalism to better define itself. A group of 50 science journalists and experts at the 1st Kavli Symposium on the Future of Science Journalism in 2014 noted the need to clarify their connection to direct communications from scientists, scientific institutions, industry, and other sources. These journalists wondered if these direct communications would employ the standards of the field or would serve conflicting interests. On a thorny issue, this group focused on a definition of science journalism, suggesting it involves:

1. Finding and interviewing scientific experts;
2. The use of scientific explanation and argumentation in its published work;
3. The use of what Dunwoody terms weight-of-evidence reporting, in which scientific evidence is assessed and weighted; and
4. The desire to connect science to everyday experience and important cultural, economic, political, and social contexts.

These four components clearly seek to situate science journalism as more than just transferring understandable scientific information to nonspecialist audiences. Instead, there is an articulation of a form of journalistic practice with the core values of verification and critique, which ultimately seeks to hold science to public account. The list also implies that one main job of science journalists is finding appropriate sources. This does not exclude that some science journalism will rightly be of the gee whiz variety or will prioritize entertainment value or will see its primary usefulness as linked to science literacy.

History of Science Journalism

Since mass media channels have existed, stories about new technology and scientific discoveries have been produced. Dorothy Nelkin in *The Culture of Science Journalism* (1987) recounts how, as early as the 1830s, the London newspaper *Athenaeum* was publishing on the Geological Society of London, and the *New York Tribune* sold tens of thousands of copies of John Tyndall's physics lectures in 1872. It was a time of science hoaxes too, with the press in the 1800s writing about bat-like humans on the moon, and people living without eating (an early indicator of the role of sensationalism in science news).

As of 1845, *Scientific American* was founded—with *Popular Science Monthly* (1872) and *National Geographic* (1888) following soon after—and began to set down how journalism about science could be used to inform people about their world, fascinate them about the future, and be mindful of the values driving progress and the power of technology. *Scientific American* still takes pride in trying to be the first to pinpoint emerging scientific trends before the news reaches the general population.

Writers who have sought to describe the history of science journalism note that initial efforts were from scientists who wanted to broadly share their knowledge and discoveries. This showcases how science journalism practice, while situated in many traditional journalistic norms, also has a unique history of its own, impacted by the particularities of science and the evolution of the field of science communication.

There is much to learn from historical books written on these subjects (in particular, historian John Burnham's formative 1987 book *How Superstition Won and Science Lost: Popularizing Science and Health in the United States*). Dunwoody (2014) describes an example from late 18th-century Britain: Scientists at the time assumed people would substantially gain from the inclusion of scientific information in their lives. Many scientists obliged by actively discussing their work in public forums. In turn, scientific institutions, it was thought, would gain from this publicity through increased appreciation and acceptance of their research activities.

The improvement of science literacy was central to this early mission. In the United States, leading American scientists from 1900 to 1930s pursued an agenda that science needed to be communicated widely for this very reason. Scholar Robert Logan (2001) describes some of the philosophies from this time, which included passionate arguments to communicate science so as to:

Cultivate the idea of lifelong learning for citizens;

Help people live healthier and longer lives by promoting scientific awareness;

Encourage support for the scientific method as a strategy for public officials to assess complex public affairs choices;

Help citizens and public officials better understand the connection between investment in science research and the United States' economic future;

Improve public investment in science;

Foster more interest in science as a career among youth;

Enhance public goodwill and support for science among taxpayers; and

Nurture a public will to support science as a nonpartisan staple of national investment in the future of the economy and culture.

Many of the top-down approaches to these philosophies were eventually disputed as deficit models of public understanding of science were heavily critiqued, and the importance of bottom-up approaches to inclusion and public engagement were recognized. Science journalism would also have its own reckoning about being a cheerleader for science, as the importance of critical and independent stances on science became more widely recognized in the 1960s.

By the early 20th century, science had rapidly advanced to encompass a complex set of expert knowledge, which became less and less accessible without schooling. With the development of specific training programs in science, a particular vocabulary, and reward systems based in research productivity, the communication of science to nonspecialists became less of a priority. Scientists retreated to their peer groups, instead allowing popular science stories to be created by journalists. American scientists such as Edwin Slosson and Paul Heyl recognized the importance of journalists, and how they could broadly disseminate scientific findings. They even made appeals in the 1920s to news magnates like E. W. Scripps to create a science news beat.

Alongside the early efforts from scientists, there was a burgeoning subset of journalists interested in specializing in the coverage of science and technology. By some accounts, science journalism emerged as a viable profession in North America at the beginning of the 20th century, spurred on by postwar concerns, nuclear incidents, space programs, and biotechnology. The numbers of science journalists in many countries would continue to increase during the 20th century, with the amount of journalism on science and technology also growing.

Dunwoody, however, reminds us that, while any journalist can cover science, specialized science journalists have always been a small subset of the journalism profession. In addition, she points to research on Greek newspapers to highlight that the amount of general news coverage of science in Greece did not exceed 2.5% of total news (politics sat at 25% and sports 15%, in comparison). There are, of course, numerous other media outlets for science, and with the advent of online news contemporary science journalism began to diversify its approach.

Approaches

Today, it is well accepted that science and technology journalism produce a framework of expectations that gives public meaning to otherwise isolated scientific issues. Without this journalism, many of these science topics would never be widely discussed in public.

In her 1995 book, *Selling Science: How the Press Covers Science and Technology*, Nelkin argues that science journalism should help people to: (1) stay up-to-date on scientific advancements

and new technologies, (2) assess the appropriateness of scientific research, and (3) make choices when faced with competing scientific arguments related to their environment, health, and well-being. These three goals for contemporary science journalism, and criticism over whether they are being met, center on how science journalists can best turn scientific research into accessible stories for nonspecialist audiences.

Four Models of Science Journalism

Recently, scholarship has begun to address these expectations with the use of models to conceptualize and clarify the wider frameworks used to communicate science. For those just learning about science journalism, or for the analysis of thorny questions of its normative purpose and practical effectiveness, this approach is instructive for how it opens up the varying theoretical purposes of science journalism practice.

Various contemporary models of science journalism can broadly be grouped into two main categories: traditional models that view science as the legitimizing form of knowledge and aim at transmitting scientific knowledge to audiences; and more emerging nontraditional models that value knowledge outside of science and aim at presenting science information tied to its ability to engage people and build trust among groups. Such models represent one approach to conceptualizing how journalists might produce, and how audiences might respond to, contemporary science journalism. Importantly, they are only a point of reference; one intended to help us think about science journalism, and simply offer a representation of the complex processes of science journalism. The following is a summary of four models presented in a 2013 article by David Secko, Elyse Amend, and Terrine Friday.

Model A: Science Literacy (Traditional)

Much of science in the news media is event and publication driven, seeking to inform audiences about science. A new scientific paper gets published, and journalists cover it. This approach falls under a science literacy model, which seeks to "translate" scientific information for people and to provide the information needed to make decisions in their daily lives. Such journalism is often driven by conflict and the "wow factor" (novelty).

For a journalist, this model involves the use of traditional journalistic norms, such as objectivity, and views audiences as lacking scientific knowledge (deficit model). It uses scientific experts as main sources. Model A is oriented to education, seeking to raise science literacy, or the level of understanding publics have about science, and thereby seek to gain popular support for science. Science in this context is fixed and certain—it can be used to make decisions and the scientific method justifies any knowledge presented.

Theoretically, this model represents a linear, top-down transmission structure where knowledge from scientists is provided to journalists, who translate it into accessible journalism. Versions of the science literacy model had been extensively critiqued for making people passive participants, avoiding their personal and contextual information needs, supporting uneven power relations between those viewed as having knowledge (scientists) and those that do not (audiences), and dismissal of other forms of (nonscientific) knowledge.

Model B: Contextual (Traditional)

Not all science journalism is driven by new research papers in scientific journals like *Science* and *Nature*. Some is focused on events, issues, concerns, and cultural realities tied to specific populations.

For a journalist, this contextual approach seeks to inform communities about science as it relates to their context(s). Model B still makes use of experts as its main sources, treating audience members as concerned spectators, and is there still a traditional approach to "top-down" information delivery (holding onto notions of knowledge deficits in audiences, and science as fixed and certain). But journalists working in this style acknowledge that science means different things in different geographic locations and social settings. This is an important acknowledgment, as context can shape how individuals receive, process, and respond to scientific information. This journalism pays close attention to the construction of messages as linked to the needs and situations of their audiences.

Theoretically, Model B wants a more cooperative relationship between science and the public, identifying audiences as able to gain knowledge quickly about relevant topics. However, while the contextual model seeks to increase knowledge and change attitudes, it has been criticized as just another version of the deficit model that places scientific knowledge above other forms of knowing (i.e., science and society remain separated as different worlds), where only a mastery of science journalism can bring peace to disputes. Audiences do not have any direct participation within this form of science journalism.

Model C: The Lay-Expertise Model (Nontraditional)

The main difference in the lay-expertise model is that it situates local knowledge as equal to scientific knowledge. The goal is to disrupt the idea that science–society relationships are the result of differing worlds, and that it is possible to incorporate the knowledge and interests of specific populations—their lay-expertise—in science journalism.

For a journalist, this model values knowledge in its own right, with science seen as limited and uncertain, requiring "expertise" from sources outside of science to examine issues and their social connections. This means working to empower local communities in the scientific process, diversifying sources to those outside science, asking nonspecialists to supply questions they want answered, and viewing stories as not solely scientific. Accuracy does not slip away, but this community dilemmas drives this journalism, as the community provides solutions to uncertain science, and journalists adopt a style that reflects active engagement. Scientists and experts only act as secondary sources, with their roles limited to providing background and context.

Theoretically, this model seeks to foster confidence that individuals have valuable knowledge to share on a scientific topic. However, there are challenges in this model. Critics suggest balancing expert, lay-expert, and nonexpert knowledge is impossible. They note that the inequality of information from different groups is a constant obstacle.

Model D: The Public Participation Model (Nontraditional)

In the age of social media and interactive journalism, it should not be a surprise that science journalists are seeking new ways to engage with people. Science is a slow process. The processes that drive scientific discovery, the consequences of choices, and the personalities involved, all point to the importance of science as a social activity. The public participation model attempts to make the scientific process more interactive and encourages public debate on scientific issues.

For a journalist, this model is less focused on science literacy, or any knowledge gaps that may exist, and instead wants stakeholder groups to be more involved in a scientific issue (especially policy issues) to build trust among these groups. Scientists here are not presented as someone special and science stories focus on the processes behind the science. The desire is to promote media channels for more active, nonlinear discussion, where it is made clear science can lead to both certainty and uncertainty but is definitely embedded in wider social issues.

Theoretically, this model is nontraditional as it wants to break from a linear transmission structure present in legacy journalism. The public participation model focuses on a holistic mapping of a multitude of stakeholder viewpoints, and aims to engage audiences in pluralistic debate. The public participation model has been subject to criticisms as well, such as addressing politics and policy issues over public understanding of science, and emphasizing the process of science while discounting the actual content. This approach is also only able to address smaller, particular audiences at a time.

Common Discussions in Science Journalism

A quick search will find hundreds of books, journal articles, pieces of journalism, commentaries, videos, podcasts, and social media posts on science journalism written during the 2010s alone. A quick snapshot of some of these themes is warranted to help understand today's science journalist and their challenges.

Science or Journalism First?

Science journalists are often asked where their allegiances lie. Many make it clear that they are journalists first, who happen to cover science, though in recent years an increasing number of science journalists have come to the profession with a scientific degree and/or laboratory bench training, in addition to journalism training or learning on the job. Viewed as specialist reporters they hold different values than their generalist peers, but often note their integrity and the need for the mental freedom that independence provides. Science journalists see themselves as solely responsible for the content and frame of their work, regardless of what they place first.

Scientist–Journalist Interactions

Reported research demonstrates that there is an interconnectedness between journalists and scientists—journalists need scientists for information for their stories, and scientists' need journalists to popularize their research. With journalists working under strict time pressure, accessibility is one of the main factors that draw these individuals together. Simply put, those scientists who are easily reachable or call journalists back are more likely to be used in stories. However, there appears to be a growing trend of scientists increasingly being strategically oriented to the media, where use of online media may reinforce this reciprocal relationship.

Are Science Journalists OK?

Similar to all journalism, science journalism continues to be in flux. For example, science sections at newspapers throughout North America and Europe have seen significant cuts, with fewer and fewer science journalists now holding full-time legacy media jobs. Research on the effect is scant, but the little that exists points to many science journalists now being on their own, working as freelancers and entrepreneurs. A 2013 study suggested that job satisfaction remained high. Of the 592 respondents giving information on employment, 51% were in full time staff positions (more than half for 10 years or less).

The Digital Age

As the Internet continues to gain importance as the main source of scientific information, and search patterns change, questions have naturally arisen about how scientists and audiences now compete with science journalists for the production of scientific narratives. In a special 2011 issue of the journal *Journalism*, scholar Stuart Allan discusses this new digital era, where direct and open engagement is possible, but is accompanied by the emergence of a 24/7 news cycle and an endless variety of rapidly produced science media content. Speed and brevity hold sway. Science journalists are expected to be multiskilled across numerous media platforms, while being able to separate facts from hype and misinformation.

Criticism of Science Journalism

During a time of increasing demand for online science content, science journalists continue to be criticized. Much of the research literature points to inaccuracy, sensationalism, a lack of methodological details, uncritical reporting, a focus on scientific progress that makes use of a narrow range of expertise, and inclusion in a cycle of hype. Some work suggests science journalists are ultimately unsure how their audiences make use of journalism to understand science. Worries about homogenous coverage also continue, being attributed to recurring sourcing practices (e.g., journalists consistently using the same sources), unlimited press releases, and time constraints that undermine in-depth coverage. Yet some scholars continue to show optimism over the potential to meet these challenges through improved understanding and innovation.

Challenges on the Horizon

Science journalists continue to produce excellent, inspiring work. They are well recognized for their enthusiasm and commitment to the societal value of science journalism. However, it is a time of peril and excitement, with questions over who should be considered a science journalist. Media organization affiliations are giving sway to hybrid careers where people work as scientists and freelance journalists, somewhat evoking the historical times described earlier.

Some see science journalism entering a new golden age. For instance, science journalism educators Thomas Hayden and Erika Check Hayden (2018, p.1) write, "there has never been more, better quality science and environmental journalism produced than there is today," while acknowledging that "the careers of individual science and environmental journalists have never been more precarious." Regardless, Hayden and Hayden see science journalists banding together to "assert the value of rigorous, factual, independent coverage and scrutiny." Others raise more alarm about the cutbacks to news organizations in recent years and their effect on science journalism. Dunwoody (2014, p. 27) writes: "science journalism is an increasingly imperiled occupation that, perversely, is needed now more than ever."

David M. Secko

See also Environmental Journalism; Health and Medical Journalism; New Media; Risk and News; Theories of Journalism

Further Readings

Amend, E., & Secko, D. M. (2012). In the face of critique: A metasynthesis of the experiences of journalists covering health and science. *Science communication, 34*(2), 241–282. doi:10.1177/1075547011409952

Bos, M., & Nuijens, F. (2020). Science journalism. In F. van Dam, L. de Bakker, A. M. Dijkstra, & E. Jensen (Eds.), *Science communication: An introduction* (pp. 119–144). Hoboken, NJ: World Scientific Publishing.

Carr, T. (2019). Revisiting the role of the science journalist. Undark Magazine. Retrieved from https://undark.org/2019/07/15/science-journalism-communications/

Dunwoody, S. (2014). Science journalism. In M. Bucchi & B. Trench (Eds.), *Routledge handbook of public communication of science and technology* (pp. 27–39). New York, NY: Routledge.

Hayden, T., & Nijhuis, M. (Eds.). (2013). *The science writers' handbook: Everything you need to know to pitch, publish, and prosper in the digital age*. Boston, MA: Da Capo Lifelong Books.

Hayden, T., & Check Hayden, E. (2018). Science journalism's unlikely golden age. *Frontiers in communication, 2*, 24. doi:10.3389/fcomm.2017.00024

Logan, R. A. (2001). Science mass communication: its conceptual history. *Science Communication, 23*(2), 135–163. doi:10.1177/1075547001023002004

Nelkin, D. (1987). The culture of science journalism. *Society, 24*(6), 17–25. doi:10.1007/BF02695570

Nelkin, D. (1995). *Selling science: How the press covers science and technology.* New York, NY: W. H. Freeman.

Rensberger, B. (1997). Covering science for newspapers. In D. Blum and M. Knudson (Eds.), *A field guide for science writers* (pp. 7–16). New York, NY: Oxford University Press.

Secko, D. M., Amend, E., & Friday, T. (2013). Four models of science journalism: A synthesis and practical assessment. *Journalism Practice, 7*(1), 62–80. doi:10.1080/17512786.2012.691351

SEARCH ENGINE OPTIMIZATION (SEO)

Search engine optimization (SEO) refers to the practices and strategies aimed to increase the visibility and traffic a website or a web page receives from search engine results. Search engines are one of the most widely used services to navigate the Internet and retrieve information from it. For instance, web pages and other content such as videos, photos, or images are shown and ranked based on what the search engine considers most relevant to users. SEO involves designing a website to make it appear in search engine results more frequently and more prominently. For news organizations, SEO is like displaying a print newspaper or a magazine on the front row of the newsstand. This entry discusses search algorithms, the use of SEO in journalism, concerns raised by SEO tactics and efforts to deal with them, and recent developments in search engine technology.

Search engines are an important source of the traffic to many news websites. According to the Reuters Institute for the Study of Journalism, search remained a significant gateway to the news in many countries as of 2019, including Brazil, Germany, France, Italy, Poland, Turkey, and the United States. The American Press Institute reported in 2014 that about half of Americans said they received news in the previous week from search engines and online news aggregators.

In general, the higher and more frequently a news website appears in the search engine results page (SERP), the more visitors it will have from the search engine's users. Researchers have found that the first Google search results page generates as much as 92% of all traffic from an average search.

As more people depend upon the web for news, search engines are becoming increasingly influential news gatekeepers. As a result, it is important for news organizations and journalists to understand the importance of optimizing content for the web and utilizing SEO. News organizations are even restructuring news production processes to deal with the new challenges they face because of news users' increasing reliance on search engines.

Search Algorithms

Search engines employ algorithms to find and collect information about web pages. Search engines use complex algorithms that can give access to resources users may not otherwise be aware of or familiar with. In general, a search algorithm is a problem-solving procedure that takes the user's word or phrase, sifts through a vast database of cataloged keywords with their URLs, and then returns a listing of best-matching web pages according to the search criteria.

Though specifics of search algorithms are not always made public, they generally take as input a sequence of words (search terms) and return as output links to web pages that contain the most relevant information the user seeks. Because search terms may be equivocal or applicable to multiple subjects, or because multiple people looking for the same information might enter substantially different search terms, search engines develop very particular sets of rules whereby they guide inputted search terms into proper directions to locate the requested information.

Any search engine has a crawler that collects information about all the content it can find on the Internet. Crawlers referred to as *spiders* visit web pages and index the information in a database. Search engine algorithms, then, identify, from a search's textual input, what to select from the search engine's index of the web to return an output. These algorithms decide, from the multitude of web pages that contain some or all of the search terms, which to rank higher and which to rank relatively lower in the output. The decisions a search engine makes in this process inevitably prefer some information and rule out other information.

Search algorithms can be divided into three broad categories: on-page algorithms that assess on-page factors looking at the elements of a page (e.g., keywords in content or meta tags); whole-site algorithms that consider the relationship of site elements (e.g., architecture of pages, linking between pages); and, finally, off-site algorithms that examine the incoming links. All three types are generally part of a larger algorithm.

In general, the search results depend on the perceived quality of the page in accordance with the algorithm and a number of factors such as location, frequency of keywords, links or click through rates, apparent authority and trustworthiness of a website, number and quality of inbound and outbound links (for example, links going to and leading out from a website), and both connectivity with and popularity among social networks. For example, the PageRank of Google is a metric that assesses the importance of website pages by counting the number and quality of links to a page. Even slight changes in these choices can lead to significant differences in search results. Therefore, it is not unusual for one search engine to return different results from another search engine for the same search request.

SEO in Journalism

According to the Pew Research Center, visitors who arrived via a search engine accounted for at least 20% of the traffic to 11 of 26 top news sites studied in 2014. If a story's headline, URL, and metadata include the same keywords people are searching for, the story has a better chance of being found and read. While SEO appeared almost in parallel with the appearance of the first search engines in the late 1990s, SEO strategies only began to have a direct impact on journalistic workflow in many newsrooms in the 2010s, creating new challenges for media professionals and news organizations.

Many media outlets across the world (for example, *The New York Times*, *The Washington Post*, CNN, the *Daily Mail*, the *Guardian*, the *Los Angeles Times*, and *The Daily Telegraph*, to name a few) have recently employed SEO specialists to increase the visibility of their content and position their stories at the top of the search rankings. BBC trains all its journalists about basic SEO. Investing in the appropriate systems and training, news organizations can alter or modify their content to attract the interest of the bots and thus improve the exposure of their news stories in search engines.

Application of SEO practices to digital media outlets can be divided into three broad categories: On-page, off-page, and technical SEO. On-page optimization includes the management of all factors associated directly with a news website, such as keywords, appropriate content, internal link structure, and html elements. Many news publishers today around the world strive to create news rich in keywords: They create SEO-friendly titles, use metadata, include relevant keywords in the initial paragraphs (synonyms, plural variations, or other forms), and use multimedia content in the form of videos, photographs, podcasts, and so forth. On-page SEO also contains the page title (or HTML title tag), on-page headlines, description of web pages (or meta description tag), and URLs.

Off-page optimization includes all the actions performed outside the news website, such as link building or social signal strategy. For example, a news organization can obtain as many quality incoming links as possible or disseminate the news content via social media platforms. Finally, technical SEO may include actions such as the use of special formats for the mobile web, good information architecture, or an increase in website speed.

Given the increase of online news consumption and the dependence of the media outlets on digital platforms, news publishers constantly try to find techniques to improve the prominence and visibility of their stories in search engines and direct the traffic to their news sites. SEO practices reflect the essential needs of web users to find information, while also securing long-term promotion for journalism.

Criticism of SEO

Scholars have noted the power that search engines and the optimization for search ranking have by bringing greater exposure to certain websites over others, and the political ramifications of this. Laura Granka has lamented a lack of transparency in many search engines and their algorithms, while Victor Asal and Paul Harwood (2008) have argued that understanding the mechanics of search engines dispels the notion "that the Internet is an egalitarian space" (p. 4).

Some news organizations and journalists attempt to deceive search engines using illicit techniques to intentionally improve search engine ranking. Those techniques are usually called *black-hat SEO* and do not follow the search engines' guidelines. The techniques include, among others, keyword stuffing (filling a web page with particular words and phrases likely to be included in a search) and link farms (websites created to raise the search ranking of another site by linking to it).

Search engines deal with the attempts to game the rankings by constantly changing their algorithms. In 2011, Google launched the Panda update to lower the search ranking results of "low quality" sites in search results and to improve rankings for "high quality" sites. A 2012 update, Penguin, was in response to black-hat SEO tactics of so-called link schemes to send traffic from one website to another. In 2013, the Hummingbird update added contextual search, as Google had begun to look at the relationship between terms to interpret context.

Another dark side of SEO is that the dependence on SEO techniques may diminish publishers' autonomy as well as the autonomy of journalism in general. Search engines may influence not only the news agenda journalists choose but also the way journalists write their stories. Although SEO is value-neutral, some worry that efforts to implement it in news organizations take away focus from delivering news in service of the audience and ensuring coverage of a range of topics.

Journalistic work can benefit when SEO is implemented consciously and professionally, however. The core of journalism is what content is covered and how it is created. Creating compelling, meaningful, and useful content will likely influence a news website more than any other factors. The content has to be characterized by reliability, interest, and quality. New techniques designed to ensure high ranking in search results need to be cautiously implemented, keeping essential news values in mind. The need to pay attention to what the audience cares about cannot be downplayed. In a 2012 article describing SEO efforts at the BBC, Martin Asser claims that SEO is not just about increasing traffic to a story but also staying connected with the essential needs of web users, helping them find the information they need and want.

Developments in Search Engine Technology

The algorithms of search engines are constantly evolving, with artificial intelligence becoming a leading area in the evolution of SEO. In 2015, Google began using RankBrain, a search algorithm based on machine learning, to help push more relevant results to users.

In 2018, Google introduced a neural network-based technique for natural language processing called *Bidirectional Encoder Representations from Transformers*, or *BERT*. BERT is designed to allow for searches using more complex or conversational language by incorporating a better understanding of how language is used and the context of individual words within searches.

Speakable (BETA) by Google Assistant is another signal showing the evolution of SEO. Speakable can return up to three relevant articles as a response to people's questions about specific topics and provide audio playback using text-to-speech markup. Implementing such a markup can be lucrative for news organizations because when the assistant provides an answer, it also attributes the source and sends the full article URL to the user's mobile device.

Chang Sup Park

See also Artificial Intelligence and Journalism; Bots; Google; Internet: Impact on the Media

Further Readings

American Press Institute. (2014, March 17). *How Americans get their news*. Retrieved from https://www.americanpressinstitute.org/publications/reports/survey-research/how-americans-get-news/

Asal, V., & Harwood, P. G. (2008). Airing grievances online: Search engine algorithms and the fate of minorities at risk. *Journal of Information Technology*

& *Politics*, 4(3), 3–17. doi:10.1080/193316808
01915009

Asser, M. (2012, September 6). Search engine
optimisation in BBC News. *BBC*. Retrieved from
http://www.bbc.co.uk/blogs/internet/posts/search_
engine_optimisation_in

Giomelakis, D., & Veglis, A. (2015). Employing search
engine optimization techniques in online news
articles. *Studies in Media and Communication*, 3(1),
22–33. doi:10.11114/smc.v3i1.683

Granka, L. A. (2010). The politics of search: A decade
retrospective. *The Information Society*, 26(5),
364–374. doi:10.1080/01972243.2010.511560

Ledford, J. L. (2015). *Search engine optimization bible*
(Vol. 584). Indianapolis, IN: Wiley & Sons.

Malaga, R. A. (2007). The value of search engine
optimization: An action research project at a new
e-commerce site. *Journal of Electronic Commerce in
Organizations (JECO)*, 5(3), 68–82. doi:10.4018/
jeco.2007070105

Mitchell, A., Jurkowitz, M., Olmstead, K., Eva-Matsa,
K., Keegan, M., Boyles, J. (2014). Social, search &
direct: Pathways to digital news. *Pew Research
Center*. Retrieved from https://www.journalism.org
/2014/03/13/social-search-direct/

Newman, N., Fletcher, R., Kalogeropoulos, A., &
Nielsen, R. K. (2019). *Reuters institute digital news
report 2019*. Oxford, UK: Reuters Institute for the
Study of Journalism.

Secrecy and Leaks

Government secrecy and the leaking of state
secrets are not new, but have come to the forefront
of attention in the United States in recent years
during the presidential administrations of Barack
Obama and Donald Trump. Previously, between
1917 with the passage of the Espionage Act
through 2009, only one person had been convicted under the statute for leaking government
documents to a news organization. Since 2010,
the Obama and Trump administrations have prosecuted at least 15 individuals under the statute for
such actions. Although no journalists have been
prosecuted for government leaks through the first
half of 2020, questions still arise about the competing interests of government secrecy and security versus freedom of the press.

This entry first discusses the U.S. government
system for classifying documents and the use of
national security as a justification for withholding
information. Second, the entry looks at prosecutions under the Espionage Act. Finally, the entry
turns to the legal and ethical considerations for
journalists in regard to government secrecy, as
well as concerns about the potential for government secrecy impinging on freedom of the press.

Government Classifications of Documents

In 1951, President Harry Truman passed an executive order creating a classification system of government information, resulting in the expansion of
the amount of information deemed secret or classified, including at the state and local levels. David
Davies (2006) called the executive order a "low
point of press-government relations in the 1950s"
(p. 860–861) as the relationship between the two
parties began to be more adversarial. Whereas the
press often practiced self-censorship during World
War II, the new classification system led several
reporters and editors to push against the withholding of information in peacetime, calling it unnecessary and against the values of a free press.

The U.S. government classification system
includes three levels:

- "Confidential" is the lowest level of
classification, which covers information that, if
leaked, could damage national security.
- "Secret" classification covers information that
could cause serious damage to national security.
- "Top secret" is the highest level of classification
and covers disclosures of information that could
cause exceptionally grave damage to national
security.

Government officials and employees needing to
view or otherwise use documents classified at any
of these levels require clearance at the same level
to do so.

National Security as Justification for Withholding Information

A common justification for government secrecy is
the protection of information that could, if

released, cause damage to national defense and foreign relations. For example, in 1971, the U.S. Supreme Court was tasked with determining whether *The New York Times* and *The Washington Post* could publish a Defense Department study detailing the history of U.S. activities in Vietnam that was leaked by military analyst Daniel Ellsberg. President Richard Nixon and his administration argued that a prior restraint, meaning preventing the newspapers from publishing excerpts of or the entirety document, was necessary to protect national security.

The Court in *New York Times v. United States*—what has become known as the "Pentagon Papers" case—ruled in a *per curiam* opinion that the Nixon administration had not overcome the "heavy presumption" against prior restraints. Justice Hugo Black wrote in a concurring opinion that:

> [T]he word 'security' is a broad, vague generality whose contours should not be invoked to abrogate the fundamental law embodied in the First Amendment. The guarding of military and diplomatic secrets at the expense of informed representative government provides no real security for our Republic. (*New York Times v. United States*, 1971)

The Pentagon Papers case was far from the only instance of the government seeking to prevent a publication from publishing information with national security as the main justification. In 1979, a judge in the U.S. District Court for the Western District of Wisconsin issued a preliminary injunction on national security grounds prohibiting the publication of a story by *Progressive* magazine detailing how to build a hydrogen bomb. Several publications would go on to publish the information anyway as the injunction only applied to *Progressive*.

The federal government can also invoke national security as a reason to prevent disclosure of information in court. Under the state secrets privilege, the government can assert that it should not be forced to provide information during litigation when doing so would reasonably harm national security. The privilege can be a potent tool for the government to stop lawsuits because if invocation of the claim succeeds, the case may lack sufficient grounds to proceed.

Espionage Act Prosecutions

Where government secrecy and freedom of the press come to a head is instances of the press publishing or broadcasting leaked government documents, raising questions about whether news organizations and reporters can be targeted. Although it has not been used to prosecute a traditional journalist who published leaked documents, the Espionage Act has been used more frequently in recent years to prosecute government leakers.

On June 15, 1917, two months after the United States entered World War I, Congress passed the Espionage Act, which prohibited the obtaining, recording, or copying of information that could result in the injury of the national defense and/or foreign relations. The act was also passed to target individuals seen as obstructing enlistment or causing disloyalty to the U.S. military.

In 1919, the Supreme Court upheld the convictions of three individuals viewed by the federal government to be dissenting voices and threats to the war effort. The Court in *Schenck v. United States* first upheld the conviction of socialist Charles T. Schenck, who circulated a flyer arguing that the draft violated the Thirteenth Amendment prohibition of involuntary servitude. In *Debs v. United States (1919)*. The Court also ruled against Eugene Debs, who had delivered a public speech, which the Court found would have "the probable effect" of preventing military recruiting (Debs v. United States, 1919). Finally, the Court in *Abrams v. United States* (1919) upheld the conviction of Jacob Abrams and four other individuals under the Espionage Act after the group had thrown from a window two separate leaflets, one in English and one in Yiddish, denouncing World War I and the sending of American troops to Russia. The majority found that the Espionage Act criminalized the actions of these "anarchists," "rebels," and "revolutionists." However, Justice Oliver Wendell Holmes Jr. wrote a dissenting opinion in which he came to a different conclusion than he had in *Schenck* and *Debs*, ruling in favor of Abrams and holding that the First Amendment protects the right to dissent and disagree with the government's viewpoints and actions. Justice Holmes also articulated the "marketplace of ideas" theory, writing that "the ultimate good desired is better reached by free trade in ideas— that the best test of truth is the power of the thought to get itself accepted in the competition of the market, and that truth is the only ground upon which their wishes safely can be carried out. That, at any rate, is the theory of our Constitution" (*Abrams v. United States*, 1919).

During the Obama administration, the Espionage Act began to be used more frequently to target the sources of government leaks. One such individual was Chelsea Manning, a former Army intelligence analyst, who in 2010 leaked over 700,000 pages of classified U.S. documents to WikiLeaks, a nonprofit organization known for publishing leaked government information. The documents included incident logs from the Afghanistan and Iraq wars, dossiers on Guantánamo Bay detainees held without trial, diplomatic cables from American embassies, and a video of a helicopter attack in Baghdad that killed two journalists. A military court found Manning guilty on six counts of violating the Espionage Act, as well as on 14 lesser charges in July 2013. On August 21, 2013, Manning was sentenced to 35 years in prison, with President Obama commuting most of the remaining prison sentence in January 2017. Manning was later jailed once again on contempt charges in 2019 after refusing to testify before a grand jury investigating WikiLeaks and founder Julian Assange, though she was released when the grand jury was dismissed in 2020.

Another leak case involved Edward Snowden, a former National Security Agency (NSA) contractor who leaked a trove of classified information to *The Guardian* and *The Washington Post* in 2013. The information that Snowden provided to journalists documented the widespread scope of U.S. intelligence agencies' surveillance efforts worldwide. The programs Snowden revealed fall generally into two categories: (1) domestic collection of telephone and email metadata authorized under sections 214 and 215 of the USA PATRIOT Act; and (2) generalized collections of communications authorized under section 702 of the Foreign Intelligence Surveillance Act (FISA). On September 2, 2020, the U.S. Court of Appeals for the Ninth Circuit held that the NSA's warrantless mass surveillance of Americans' telephone metadata violated FISA and may have violated the Fourth Amendment, but the ruling was likely to be appealed. In the wake of the disclosures, Snowden fled to Russia in June 2013, where he remained as of mid-2020 to avoid possible prosecution in the United States.

In one case, James Risen, a Pulitzer Prize winning journalist and author, was swept up in an Espionage Act prosecution by the Obama administration. In 2010, federal prosecutors indicted former Central Intelligence Agency (CIA) officer Jeffrey Sterling, alleging that he had provided classified information for Risen's book, *State of War*. In 2011, then-U.S. Attorney General Eric Holder authorized a subpoena ordering Risen to testify at Sterling's trial. Risen refused, contending that he had a First Amendment right to protect his source. In 2013, the U.S. Court of Appeals for the Fourth Circuit overturned a district court order, which had prevented prosecutors from asking Risen to disclose the name of his source. After the Supreme Court declined to hear Risen's case, he faced potential jail time for contempt. However, the DOJ did not seek Risen's testimony during Sterling's actual trial. Sterling was ultimately convicted under the Espionage Act and sentenced to 42 months in prison. In January 2018, he was released after serving over 2 years of the sentence.

The Trump administration also targeted several leakers, continuing the trend started by the Obama administration. The first such prosecution concluded on August 23, 2018, when former NSA contractor Reality Winner was sentenced to 63 months in prison and 3 years of probation for leaking classified documents detailing Russian involvement in the 2016 U.S. presidential election, among other information. On October 18, 2018, Terry James Albury, a former Minneapolis Federal Bureau of Investigation (FBI) agent who leaked agency documents detailing surveillance of journalists, among other topics, was charged with two counts of violating the Espionage Act and sentenced to 4 years in prison.

Additionally, in March 2017, the CIA experienced its largest loss of confidential information in the history of the agency, with thousands of documents detailing the CIA's surveillance and hacking of electronic devices being leaked. Over 1 year later, in May 2018, the U.S. federal government identified Joshua A. Schulte, who formerly worked for the CIA and NSA, as a prime suspect, charging Schulte with three counts under the Espionage Act. The Trump administration also charged U.S. Air Force intelligence analyst Daniel Everette Hale, who was accused of obtaining classified information illegally and disclosing it to a reporter. In October 2019, the DOJ charged Defense Intelligence Agency (DIA) employee Henry Kyle Frese with two counts under the Espionage Act for leaking classified national defense information to two journalists, one at CNBC and the other at NBC News.

New York Times reporter Ali Watkins was swept up in the DOJ's 2018 prosecution of James A. Wolfe, the former U.S. Senate Select Committee on Intelligence (SSCI) director of security. Wolfe agreed to plead guilty to one count of making a false statement to the FBI in connection to an investigation into alleged leaks to the press. As part of the investigation, federal officials secretly seized several years' worth of Watkins' phone and email records, potentially in violation of DOJ policies regarding the obtaining of journalists' records by law enforcement.

Perhaps the closest the federal government has come to prosecuting a news organization for its involvement in publishing leaked government documents was the May 2019 charges against Julian Assange, the founder of WikiLeaks. On May 23, 2019, the DOJ released an indictment alleging 17 counts under the Espionage Act against Assange. The indictment also included an additional count of violating the Computer Fraud and Abuse Act (CFAA). According to the indictment, the DOJ claimed that Assange and WikiLeaks encouraged individuals with security clearances to leak classified information so it could be published.

The charges against Assange prompted significant concern from journalists and press advocates that the indictment was the next step toward prosecuting traditional journalists under the statute. For example, in a May 24, 2019, HuffPost article, Jane Kirtley, the Silha Professor of Media Ethics and Law at the University of Minnesota, said, "Whatever happens to Julian Assange could potentially happen to any journalist, anywhere—including someone who the government would

acknowledge has a more traditional journalistic role" (Robins-Early, 2019).

Legal Considerations for Journalists and Government Secrecy

There are three additional areas of law at the intersection of government secrecy and freedom of the press, each of which illustrate the complicated legal landscape around protections for and the right to publish information related to the federal government. The first is the reporter's privilege to protect journalists from having to reveal confidential sources or unpublished information. The 1972 Supreme Court case *Branzburg v. Hayes* brought the issue of a reporter's privilege to the forefront of national attention. Although the Court sided against the press, it was a limited decision that focused only on journalists appearing before a grand jury in relation to revealing confidential sources. The majority ruled that because citizens are not constitutionally immune from testifying before a grand jury under a subpoena, this same standard should be applied to the press.

However, the majority in *Branzburg* "le[ft] state legislatures free, within First Amendment limits, to fashion their own standards in light of the conditions and problems with respect to the relations between law enforcement officials and press in their own areas" (*Branzburg v. Hayes*, 1972). Known as "shield laws," several states have passed legislation providing an absolute or qualified privilege for reporters to protect their confidential sources and, in some cases, information. Other states recognize such a privilege in their state constitutions, common law, or court rulings. However, there is no federal shield law, though different federal circuits recognize the privilege in different ways. Additionally, in *Cowles v. Cohen* (1991), the Supreme Court held that journalists can face liability for violating an agreement with a source.

There have been some limited instances where journalists have been jailed for contempt of court after refusing to disclose their sources of leaked government information. In 2005, the D.C. Circuit upheld a ruling by a federal judge, who found *New York Times* reporter Judith Miller in contempt after she refused to appear before a federal grand jury tasked with determining who had leaked the identity of CIA agent Valerie Plame. Miller spent 85 days in prison before Lewis Libby, Vice President Dick Cheney's chief of staff, formally released her from a pledge of confidentiality. Miller then testified that she had two conversations with Libby about Plame, although she never wrote about her. Similarly, in 2006, federal prosecutors issued a subpoena to freelance blogger Joshua Wolf to appear before a grand jury. Wolf had made a video recording of a protest in San Francisco during which someone had struck and seriously injured a police officer with a pipe. Although the video had not been aired, Wolf refused to turn it over. The Ninth Circuit ultimately held that Wolf could not claim the reporter's privilege for nonconfidential material, leading the blogger to serve 226 days in jail for contempt. Wolf was released after he agreed to post the video on his website, though it did not depict who had struck the police officer.

A second area of law dealing with protections for journalists who publish leaked documents was involved in a string of cases decided by the Supreme Court in the 1970s and 1980s, including *Cox Broadcasting Corp. v. Cohn* (1975), *Oklahoma Publishing Co. v. Oklahoma County District Court* (1977), *Landmark Communications, Inc. v. Virginia* (1978), *Smith v. Daily Mail Publishing Co.* (1979), and *Florida Star v. B. J. F.* (1989). These cases established what became known as the *Daily Mail* principle, which holds that a media organization should not be punished for disseminating truthful information of public significance where the media organization had no role in any illegality

In the *Daily Mail* series of cases, the Supreme Court held to be in violation of the First Amendment statutes prohibiting the media from publishing certain lawfully obtained and truthful information, including (1) the name of a rape victim, (2) the name of a juvenile defendant, and (3) the confidential proceedings before a state judicial review commission. Although the press does not have an absolute right to publish truthful information under the First Amendment, the Supreme Court ruled that in certain cases, "absent a govern-mental need of the highest order," the press has a First Amendment right to publish (Bartnicki v. Vopper, 2001).

The Court also addressed the question "concerning what degree of protection, if any, the First Amendment provides to speech that discloses the contents of an illegally intercepted communication," but is also truthful information, in *Bartnicki v. Vopper*. The Court cited the *Daily Mail* line of cases and the Pentagon Papers, holding that "a stranger's illegal conduct does not suffice to remove the First Amendment shield from speech about a matter of public concern" (*Bartnicki v. Vopper*, 2001). The Court thus held that, at least in the particular circumstances of the case, the First Amendment right of publication exceeded the government's interests, therefore protecting the press from government punishment of publication where it did not participate in, but only received, the illegal interception of communications.

Finally, the right to publish has little value if there is nothing to publish. Public records laws play an important role in that regard by facilitating public access to government records. Public records laws generally impose a duty on agencies and officials to release a wide range of records related to governmental activity. In the United States, the federal Freedom of Information Act (FOIA) governs access to records of federal agencies, while state public records laws govern access to records of state and local governments.

FOIA imposes disclosure obligations on federal agencies, but it does not apply to the president, vice president, Congress, or the federal courts. Access is not absolute, however. Agencies may withhold (1) properly classified material implicating national security or foreign policy; (2) internal agency personnel rules and practices; (3) information specifically exempted from disclosure by statute; (4) trade secrets and privileged or confidential commercial information; (5) inter-agency or intra-agency correspondence; (6) personnel and medical files when disclosure would invade someone's personal privacy; (7) certain material compiled for law enforcement purpose; (8) information related to government supervision of financial institutions; and (9) geological and geophysical information about wells. Agencies must respond to requests within 20 days, although agencies often have significant processing backlogs that well exceed this response time requirement. Meanwhile, every U.S. state has a public records law of some sort on the books, as does the District of Columbia. Though the laws are similar in purpose, they can vary widely in the scope and level of access to records, applicable exemptions, fees, response time requirements, and enforcement provisions.

The press has played an important role in the development, use, and enforcement of public records laws in the United States. Virtually every day, news organizations produce stories based on public records, including daily police blotters, investigative reports, and long-form features. But journalists are not necessarily the most frequent requesters of public records. At least at the federal level, multiple studies indicate that commercial requesters tend to be the most prolific users of FOIA overall, often filing requests in an effort to resell the records for profit, gather intelligence on competitors, and better understand the regulatory landscape.

Ethical Considerations for Journalists and Government Secrecy

Government secrecy and the leaking of secrets is not just a legal issue but also has important ethical considerations for journalists. Journalism groups and news organizations have adopted ethics codes that implicate both government secrecy and interactions with anonymous sources.

The Society of Professional Journalists (SPJ) Code of Ethics says journalists should recognize their watchdog role in holding government accountable. This includes championing government transparency and working to ensure that all people have access to public records. The Online News Association says its members should be able to access information to the same extent as other news outlets so as to promote the principles of FOIA. Some news organizations have similar ethical provisions. For instance, the *Wisconsin State Journal*'s Code of Ethics says it is the newspaper's responsibility to defend the First Amendment and the state's public records and open meetings laws on the public's behalf and to challenge efforts that would diminish such rights.

Interactions with sources is another ethical dimension. SPJ says journalists should evaluate the motives of sources before promising them anonymity, and that when sources are used anonymously, news organizations should explain the reason for granting anonymity. SPJ also calls for journalists to provide anonymity to sources only when they face danger or retribution, and when the information cannot be obtained from another source.

Likewise, the Associated Press (AP) Statement of News Values and Principles says its journalists may grant sources anonymity only when three conditions are met: (1) The source is providing information instead of speculation or opinion; (2) granting anonymity to the source is the only way in which the information can be obtained; and (3) the source has proven to be reliable and would have access to information that is accurate. AP reporters must get approval from a supervisor before filing a story with an anonymous source, and the supervisor has an obligation to evaluate the material supplied from the anonymous source.

Government Secrecy Versus Freedom of the Press

Rhetoric by the Trump administration further raised the possibility that the federal government could, and perhaps would, target journalists for prosecution over the publication of government leaks. On May 16, 2017, President Trump suggested to then-FBI director James Comey that he should consider putting reporters in prison for disseminating classified information. During an August 4, 2017, news conference, then–Attorney General Jeff Sessions indicated that the DOJ was evaluating departmental policies regarding subpoenas for members of the press and suggested that the DOJ would consider targeting journalists as part of leak investigations. Finally, during a January 15, 2020, confirmation hearing, Sen. Amy Klobuchar (D-Minn.) asked then–U.S. Attorney General nominee William Barr, "If you're confirmed, will the Justice Department jail reporters for doing their jobs?" Barr responded that he could "conceive of situations" where such actions could be taken as a "last resort," such as when a news organization publishes or broadcasts information "that will hurt the country" (Wemple, 2019).

Scott Memmel and Jonathan Anderson

See also Censorship; First Amendment; Freedom of Information Act (FOIA); Gag Orders; Investigative Journalism; Pentagon Papers; Prior Restraint; Shield Law; Supreme Court and Journalism; WikiLeaks

Further Readings

C-SPAN (Producer) (2019, January 15). Attorney general confirmation hearing, Day 1. Retrieved from https://www.c-span.org/video/?456626-1/attorney-general-nominee-william-barr-confirmation-hearing

Davies, D. R. (2006). *The postwar decline of American Newspapers, 1945–1965.* Westport, CT: Praeger.

Dilanian, K., & Madani, D. (2019). Wikileaks co-founder Julian Assange indicted on 17 new charges under Espionage Act. *NBC News.* Retrieved from https://www.nbcnews.com/news/us-news/wikileaks-founder-julian-assange-indicted-new-charges-under-espionage-act-n1009441

Easley, J. (2017). DOJ warns the media could be targeted in crackdown on leaks. *The Hill.* Retrieved from https://thehill.com/homenews/administration/345316-justice-to-review-media-subpoenas-policy-in-crackdown-on-leaks

Robins-Early, N. (2019, May 24). Assange's espionage act charge sets up a fight over the first amendment. *HuffPost.* Retrieved from https://www.huffpost.com/entry/assange-espionage-first-amendment_n_5ce8457ae4b00e03656dfc5e

SPJ Code of Ethics. (2014). Retrieved from, https://www.spj.org/ethicscode.asp

Sterne, P. (2017). Obama used the Espionage Act to put a record number of reporters' sources in jail, and Trump could be even worse. *Freedom of the Press Foundation.* Retrieved from https://freedom.press/news/obama-used-espionage-act-put-record-number-reporters-sources-jail-and-trump-could-be-even-worse/

Wemple, E. (2019, January 15). William Barr on jailing journalists: "I know there are guidelines in place". *Washington Post.* Retrieved from https://www.washingtonpost.com/opinions/2019/01/15/william-barr-jailing-journalists-i-know-there-are-guidelines-place/

Legal Citations

Abrams v. United States, 250 U.S. 616 (1919).

Bartnicki v. Vopper, 532 U.S. 514, 522 (2001).

Branzburg v. Hayes, 408 US 665 (1972).

Cohen v. Cowles Media Co., 501 U.S. 663 (1991).

Cox Broadcasting Corp. v. Cohn, 420 U.S. 469 (1975).

Debs v. United States, 249 U.S. 211 (1919).

Florida Star v. B. J. F., 491 U.S. 524 (1989).

In Re: Grand Jury Subpoena: Joshua Wolf (9th Cit. 2006).

In Re: Grand Jury Subpoena, Judith Miller (D.C. Cir. 2005).

Landmark Communications, Inc. v. Virginia, 435 U.S. 829 (1978).

New York Times v. United States, 403 U.S. 713, 719 (1971).

Schenck v. United States, 249 U.S. 47 (1919).

Smith v. Daily Mail Publishing Co., 443 U.S. 97, 103 (1979).

United States v. Moalin, No. 13-50572, 2020 WL 5225704 (9th Cir. Sept. 2, 2020).

United States v. Progressive, Inc., 467 F. Supp. 990 (W.D. Wis. 1979).

United States v. Reynolds, 345 U.S. 1 (1953).

Section 230, Communications Decency Act

Section 230 of the U.S. Communications Decency Act is the centerpiece American Internet law. It greatly limits the legal liabilities of those who facilitate and transmit others' content electronically. For this reason, it has encouraged everyone to participate in the Internet, enabled that medium to grow, and thereby allowed its electronic content to dominate communications. But for the same reason, it has engendered criticism and concern, particularly because of the almost unlimited freedom it has given large technology companies to grow and dominate the Internet, largely based on customer content for which, under Section 230, they have no liability. This entry examines pre-Internet laws and several early legal cases that led to the development of Section 230 of the Communications Decency Act. This entry further examines the enactment of Section 230 of the Communication Decency Act and ongoing opposition to the Act.

Pre-Internet Law

To understand Section 230, one must understand preexisting law. Traditional publication law made practically everyone in the path of publication liable for unlawful or tortious published content, such as statements or articles that were libelous or invaded someone's privacy. In the classic case of a newspaper that published a libelous article, this meant potential liability for everyone in the chain of publication—reporter, editor, publisher, even a newsstand operator.

The law distinguished between knowing participants in publication (the reporter, editor, and publisher) and mere distributors unfamiliar with the content. So distributors were liable only if they knew of the wrongful content. A newsstand operator was safe when the bundle of newspapers was plopped on the store's doorstep. But once someone told the newsstand operator (or other distributor) that a particular newspaper contained libelous content, it would face liability if it continued to sell the challenged material.

Under this broad publication liability system, publishers took care as to every item they published. News editors carefully edited reporter's copy, advertising managers checked out advertising content, and editorial page editors vetted reader letters before publishing them. Because wronged persons had full remedies against those in the direct chain of publication, distributors were rarely challenged. This publication liability system covered newspapers, magazines, books, and broadcasting, as well as less traditional media such as videotapes, electronic games, and recordings. A "common carrier" exemption excluded telephone companies from this system; common carriers were not liable for the content they carried.

Online Service Cases

Prior to the widespread commercial use of the Internet, several commercial online services introduced the public to electronic news and information. Two cases stemming from those services revealed the consequences of applying the traditional publication liability system online.

In *Cubby v. CompuServe*, the online service CompuServe was sued for libel based on an article, published on Rumorville USA, an online newsletter, which was included in CompuServe's Journalism Forum, one of the 150 forums that CompuServe made available to its subscribers. The court viewed CompuServe as akin to a distributor of publications, and thus liable only once

it had notice of tortious conduct, such as the allegedly disparaging messages carried on Rumorville USA. CompuServe evaded liability in that case, but the decision gave potential plaintiffs a roadmap—to make an online service liable, one only need give it notice of the illegal content it was carrying.

The next case, *Stratton Oakmont v. Prodigy*, went farther. The online service Prodigy, unlike CompuServe, engaged in some content screening. (Seeking to be family-friendly, it screened for, and excluded, content containing the so-called seven dirty words.) In assessing Prodigy's potential liability to a libel plaintiff, a court followed a similar analysis as in *Cubby v. CompuServe*, but found that Prodigy fell into the "publisher" category, because it had engaged in content editing. Prodigy thus was as much liable for the alleged libelous article as the article's author.

The *Stratton Oakmont* case came down in 1995, just as it was becoming apparent that the Internet, then still predominantly used by government and universities, would soon be opening up to broad commercial and public use. If *Stratton Oakmont* (and *Cubby*) were the law, Internet service providers could become directly liable for all of the content they carried. Under *Stratton Oakmont*, any service that edited content took on direct liability. And even if a service did not screen or edit content, as Prodigy did, a wronged party's notice could make a distributor liable under *Cubby*. To avoid liability, service providers would have to hire teams of reviewers to vet user content, and to be safe, they would have to take down all questionable and challenged content. This would give anyone bold enough to object an automatic veto on Internet content.

Enactment of Section 230

The nascent Internet service provider industry went to Congress and lobbied for the law that became Section 230. The industry asked for special rules making the traditional publication liability system inapplicable on the Internet. While the industry was concerned with the outcomes of both *Cubby* and *Stratton Oakmont*, the lobbying and debate focused on *Stratton Oakmont*, because its holding was so contrary to public policy—it penalized those who sought to improve content more than those who did nothing. Congress listened to the industry and enacted a law with two key provisions—a liability exclusion for online service providers as to third-party content they carried, and a "Good Samaritan" provision that specifically approved of, and immunized, good faith content screening and editing.

Though Section 230 represented a major change in the law, it was approved with relatively little controversy, probably largely because the Internet service providers who lobbied for it were strong and united, and there was no countervailing lobbying effort. The discussions during congressional deliberations generally echoed the purposes set forth in the bill's preamble: that it was necessary to enable the Internet and its promise for free and open communications by all.

Title

Section 230's placement within the major legislation known as the *Telecommunications Act of 1996* led to a curious title. Another part of the Telecommunications Act sought to prohibit dissemination of indecent material on the Internet. That part, the Exon Amendment, was placed together with Section 230 into a chapter titled the "Communications Decency Act." The Exon Amendment was challenged and found unconstitutional in 1997 in *Reno v. American Civil Liberties Union*, leaving only Section 230 within the chapter named for its unconstitutional statutory neighbor. Section 230 is often referred to by the ill-fitting chapter title or its CDA abbreviation.

Terms

Section 230 is codified in the federal Communications Act; its full citation is 47 U.S.C. § 230. The section begins with a statement of congressional findings and policy, expressing the purpose of the act to promote the continued development of the Internet and interactive media, and to preserve its vibrant and competitive free market, largely unfettered by regulation. These precatory preamble has significantly influenced the interpretation of the act.

The operative subsection, part (c), contains two provisions: (c)(1), the basic immunity provision, worded such that online intermediaries may not be "treated as the publisher or speaker of any information provided by another," and (c)(2), the Good Samaritan provision, immunizing actions taken in good faith to restrict or take down material. Further sections of the act define terms and set its limitations, including its nonapplication to intellectual property and federal criminal laws.

Because of the intellectual property exemption, Section 230 does not apply to claims of copyright or trademark infringement. Some courts have also classified common law right of publicity claims as exempt because of their intellectual property-like nature. Service providers have a different statutory immunity, in section 512 of the Copyright Act, enacted 2 years after Section 230, as part of the Digital Millennium Copyright Act. Rather than a blanket immunity like Section 230, section 512 sets up a notice-and-takedown scheme, protecting service providers while also providing a means for copyright owners to pursue online infringers. No special statute covers trademark infringement, so service providers continue to have potential contributory liability for their users' trademark infringement once they have notice of the infringement.

Application of Section 230

In practice, Section 230 has immunized most activities of Internet intermediaries like service providers, search engines, social media sites, website, and message board operators, and similar providers, to the extent that they carry third-party content.

Two cases decided shortly after enactment of Section 230 interpreted its grant of immunity very broadly, and proved influential in shaping subsequent cases. The first, *Zeran v. America Online*, involved a post by an unidentified user on American Online (AOL) that made false and defamatory accusations against the plaintiff, Kenneth Zeran. He sued AOL (at least in part because he did not know the identity of the post's creator). The U.S. Court of Appeals for the Fourth Circuit held that Section 230 barred claims, like Zeran's, seeking to hold a service provider liable for its exercise of a publisher's traditional functions, such as deciding whether to publish, withdraw, postpone, or alter content.

Referring to the prefatory policy sections of the act, the court identified Section 230's key purposes as to not deter online speech by imposing tort liability on online intermediaries (since such liabilities would inevitably lead them to censor their customers' content), and to encourage service providers to self-regulate, taking advantage of the section's Good Samaritan provision. To Zeran's argument that AOL was a distributor (and hence potentially liable after notice, like CompuServe in *Cubby*), the court held that distributor liability was a kind of publisher liability, and all such liabilities were immunized by Section 230.

The second case, *Blumenthal v. Drudge*, tested whether Section 230 would immunize a service provider even when it approved and profited from the content at issue. AOL had paid for Matthew Drudge to create content for its service, and had retained contractual authority to approve or remove "Drudge Report" content. But when plaintiff Sidney Blumenthal sued AOL for defamatory content on the "Drudge Report" hosted on AOL, the court found AOL immunized by Section 230 even in these circumstances. All that mattered for Section 230 purposes, the court held, was that the content in issue was third-party content— "material disseminated by them [AOL] but created by others [Drudge]." The court characterized Section 230 as a "tacit quid pro quo" in which Congress exchanged immunity as an incentive for service providers to self-police the content they carry.

Scores of Section 230 cases followed *Zeran* and *Blumenthal*, but the vast majority of them followed their reasoning and results. Even the few notable cases that have not ruled in favor of service providers, often at early procedural stages of litigation, identified only narrow gaps in its immunity. The Ninth Circuit decision in *Fair Housing Council of San Fernando Valley v. Roommates.com, LLC*, for example, held that a provider may be liable for content if it prescribes or mandates a portion of the content that is challenged as tortious or otherwise illegal. By contrast, many decisions hold, and *Roommates.com* acknowledges, that providers are not liable if they provide only customary editing to a third party's content.

Opposition to Section 230

After its breath and effectiveness in shielding service providers became apparent, various parties began attacking Section 230, on different grounds. In *Wild West 2.0: How to protect and restore your online reputation on the untamed social frontier*, for example, Michael Fertik and David Thompson claimed that Section 230 left people defenseless from online communications, including anonymous disparagement and hateful harassment.

In 2018, Congress significantly restricted Section 230 for the first time, after the online classified advertising forums Craigslist and Backpage repeatedly used Section 230 to successfully defend themselves from allegations that human traffickers were using their services. Congress enacted FOSTA-SESTA, the Fight Online Sex Trafficking Act, and Stop Enabling Sex Traffickers Act, which created an exception to Section 230 that seeks to make website service providers responsible if third parties are found to be posting ads for prostitution on their platforms. As of April 2020, a constitutional challenge to FOSTA-SESTA was pending.

More general concerns about Section 230 grew as the Internet economy changed. When Section 230 was enacted, in the mid-1990s, the Internet was generally seen as an open and diverse medium, full of potential for everyone. By the second and third decades of the 21st century, many people had soured on its promises and focused instead on online content and practices that they found objectionable. Few critics directly criticized the core function of Section 230—allowing third party content free of the need for service providers to preview all content and prohibit that which could be legally actionable. Rather, criticism focused on what critics felt Section 230 allowed or facilitated: (1) a content free-for-all, often with misleading (sometimes deliberately so), mean-spirited, or partisan messaging, and/or (2) the Internet business landscape, dominated by tech companies like Google, Facebook, and Amazon, so profitable and powerful that they were effectively insulated from government controls or user preferences.

Various changes to Section 230 have been suggested, including creation of a notice-and-takedown system similar to section 512 of the

Copyright Act; removing the Good Samaritan provision or modifying it to make intermediaries liable for their changes to user content; applying a common carrier standard (slightly more limited protection than Section 230); or making intermediaries liable for user content, but limiting remedies against them (for example, only injunctive relief). Some kind of "fairness doctrine" or ideological balance requirement has also been suggested, although such a change seems unlikely to pass constitutional muster.

Section 230 has significantly influenced the development of online communications and culture in the United States. Its successor, if there is one, will do the same.

Mark Sableman

See also Censorship; Editing, Online and Digital; First Amendment; Free Expression, History of; Internet: Impact on the Journalism; Libel; Telecommunications Act of 1996

Further Readings

Blumental v. Drudge, 992 F.Supp. 44 (U.S. District Court for the District of Columbia, 1998).

Communications Decency Act, 47 U.S.C. § 230. (1996).

Cubby Inc. v. CompuServe, Inc., 776 F.Supp. 135 (U.S. District Court, Southern District of New York, 1991).

Fair Housing Council of San Fernando Valley v. Roommates.com, LLC, 521 F.3d 1157 (U.S. Court of Appeals for the Ninth Circuit, 2008).

Fertik, M. & Thompson, D. (2010). *Wild West 2.0: How to protect and restore your online reputation on the untamed social frontier*. New York, NY: AMACOM. doi:10.1080/10875301.2010.525448

Goldman, E. (2019). Why section 230 is better than the first amendment. 95 Notre Dame L.R. 33.

Kosseff, J. (2019). *The twenty-six words that created the internet*. Ithaca, NY: Cornell.

Kosseff, J. (Dec 19, 2019). What's in a name? Quite a bit, if you're talking about section 230. *Lawfare blog*. Retrieved from https://www.lawfareblog.com/whats-name-quite-bit-if-youre-talking-about-section-230.

Stratton Oakmont, Inc. v. Prodigy Services Co., 23 Media law reporter 1794 (Supreme Court, Nassau County, New York, 1995).

Tushnet, R. (2008). Power without responsibility: Intermediaries and the first amendment. 76 Geo. Washington L.R. 986.

Zeran v. America Online, 129 F.3d 327 (U.S. court of appeals for the fourth circuit, 1997).

SEDITION ACT OF 1798

In 1798, the U.S. Congress passed four laws known collectively as the *Alien and Sedition Acts* regulating immigration, citizenship, and the rights of aliens, or noncitizens, in the United States, and setting legal limits on political speech. The Sedition Act forbade citizens from writing or speaking critically about the president and the Congress in a defamatory way. It was seen as an effort by the Federalist Party, headed by John Adams and Alexander Hamilton, to muzzle its opponents, the Democratic-Republican Party headed by Thomas Jefferson and James Madison, and a violation of the freedom of speech enshrined in the First Amendment of the U.S. Constitution.

This entry first describes the political concerns and unrest in the years leading up to the Alien and Sedition Acts, as well as the political role of newspapers in the early United States. It then looks at the rationale for passing the Alien and Sedition Acts, opposition to the Sedition Act, and prosecutions under the Sedition Act. Finally, it discusses the impact of the Sedition Act on newspapers and free speech in the United States.

The Alien and Sedition Acts were the result of several cross currents at work in the early American republic. When drafting the U.S. Constitution, many delegates feared the federal government would hold too much power, threatening the authority of the individual states as well as the people's civil liberties. In response, the first Congress passed the Bill of Rights guaranteeing the freedom of speech and the press in the First Amendment to the Constitution and asserting that any power not specifically granted to the federal government by the Constitution was reserved to the individual states in the Tenth Amendment.

In addition to apportioning power between the federal government and the states, the Constitution balanced power between the three branches of government. The goal of government, in part, was to maintain stability and insofar as it damaged people's confidence in their rulers, criticism of the government as well as factions and political parties were seen as destabilizing forces that should be limited.

In 1789, the year George Washington became president, the French revolution erupted. While most Americans initially welcomed the revolution's commitment to human rights, equality, and liberty, as the events in France became more chaotic, many Americans became disillusioned and fearful that its disorder would spread. In 1793, Edmond Genet, the French representative to the United States began to outfit privateers to attack British ships, with whom the French were then at war. In response, Washington proclaimed that the United States was a neutral in the conflict between Britain and France. Jefferson and Madison, however, argued that the president did not have the power to issue such a proclamation. Hamilton, in contrast, argued that Washington did have that authority.

Partially at the urging of Genet, Democratic-Republican Societies were formed to oppose Washington's neutrality proclamation. These societies viewed the French Revolution as the continuation of the American Revolution, opposed Hamilton's fiscal policies and saw Washington as a betrayer of the country. When farmers in western Pennsylvania rebelled against a tax imposed on them by the federal government, Washington blamed the Democratic-Republican societies for the unrest. Politically, the United States was beginning to cleave politically into two camps—the Federalists and the Democratic-Republicans.

The Political Role of Newspapers

Like the very structure of government, in the 1790s, the role of public opinion and the people in governing was unsettled. The Federalists generally believed the people should vote in elections and then support the government and their leaders. Criticism reduced confidence in the governors threatening government stability. The Democratic-Republicans saw the public opinion and the press as safeguards against tyranny.

Public opinion was expressed and ideas debated through a wide range of vehicles including public gatherings, the submission of petitions to the government officials, meetings, parades, pamphlets, and newspapers. In April 1789, John Fenno

established the *Gazette of the United States* to serve as the voice of the Federalist government, then located in New York City. Until then almost all American newspapers were integrated into larger, more comprehensive printing operations. Their pages were often open to a large array of contributors. Many newspapers relied on the local government for printing contracts, so they were careful not to antagonize people in power. The *Gazette of the United States* was different. The newspaper was tied so closely to the Federalist government, that when the capital moved from New York to Philadelphia, the newspaper moved as well.

With the *Gazette* regularly publishing essays by Adams, Hamilton, and their supporters, politicians surrounding Jefferson and Madison felt the need to respond. In 1790, Jefferson cajoled Philip Freneau, a classmate of Madison's at Princeton University, to launch *The National Gazette*, which served as a platform for the Democratic-Republicans.

Neither the *Gazette of the United States* nor the *National Gazette* were successful financially. But the impulse for newspapers to ally themselves politically took hold. In 1794, Benjamin Franklin Bache, Benjamin Franklin's grandson, founded *America Aurora* in Philadelphia. The newspaper was notorious for its vituperative attacks on Federalist politicians including George Washington and John Adams. As more newspapers became politicized, leading politicians worried that governments could withstand the newspapers' assaults. Jefferson opined that public opinion was so powerful that even the worst government could remain in power with its support and without it even the best government would fail.

Passing the Alien and Sedition Acts

In 1794, John Jay, then the chief justice of the United States, led a delegation to Great Britain to resolve issues remaining since the end of the American revolution. Washington and Hamilton supported the treaty he negotiated. Jefferson opposed it, contending that its terms favored Great Britain at the expense of France. France also objected to the treaty. To avert war, in 1798, President John Adams sent a delegation to France. In what is called the XYZ Affair, the peace mission failed. It appeared that war with France was inevitable, polarizing the nation.

Fearful that immigrants from France and Ireland would destabilize the U.S. government, the Federalist-led Congress passed the Alien and Sedition Acts. The Sedition Act defined sedition as speaking, writing, or publishing false, scandalous, and malicious words against the government of the United States, either house of the Congress of the United States, or the President of the United States with the intention of defaming them. The rationale was that freedom of the press should not be extended to those who wanted to destabilize the government. While freedom of the press conferred the liberty of writing, publishing, and speaking a person's thoughts, that person was answerable to the party injured by those words, including the government.

Opposition to the Sedition Act

The Democratic-Republicans fought the passage of the Alien and Sedition Acts with mass meetings and demonstrations as well arguing their case through newspapers and pamphlets. For example, George Hay, who defended one of the journalists indicted under the Sedition Act, asserted that any legislative control of the press would be an abridgement of its liberty. The Democratic-Republicans also argued that restrictions on the press would eventually lead to restrictions on the right to assemble, to petition the government and other civil liberties.

The most concerted opposition came in the form of the Kentucky and Virginia Resolutions, passed by the legislatures of those states. Thomas Jefferson initially drafted the Kentucky Resolution. He argued that the acts violated the First and Tenth Amendments of the Constitution. Moreover, justifying the acts through the clause in the Constitution empowering the federal government to promote the general welfare gave the executive branch power not authorized by the Constitution. Jefferson contended that since the Constitution was a compact created by the states, when the federal government assumed undelegated powers, those laws were unauthorized and consequently void and of no force. The states had the right to decide the constitutionality of federal laws. Jefferson warned that if the federal government usurped

undelegated power, revolution and bloodshed could follow. The Kentucky legislature passed a milder version of Jefferson's draft, and called on the other states to declare the acts unconstitutional.

James Madison authored the Virginia Resolution urging repeal. He demanded that the states take the necessary and proper measures to maintain their authority and the liberty of the people. Although generally the judiciary checked the general government, Madison conceded, this case required the intercession of the states because the acts threatened the right to freely examine public characters and measures, which safeguarded every other right.

The theory that the states had the authority to judge the constitutionality of federal law and nullify those laws found to be unconstitutional was not embraced by the other states. Ten states condemned at least one of the resolutions. Only Tennessee joined Virginia and Kentucky in demanding the repeal of the acts. The Massachusetts legislature declared that the concept that each state could decide the unconstitutionality of laws undermined the idea of union and sapped the federal government of any authority.

Public opinion also initially supported the Federalist position on the Alien and Sedition Acts. In the elections of 1798, the Federalists maintained control of both houses of Congress.

Sedition Act Prosecutions

Between 1797 and 1801, at least 17 and perhaps as many as 28 indictments for sedition were initiated. Of the 17 best known cases, three were brought under the common law for sedition and 14 were charged under the Sedition Act. The first indictment for sedition was brought under common law against Benjamin Franklin Bache, the editor of *American Aurora*, in June 1798, prior to the final codification of the Sedition Act. Bache had printed a letter from the French foreign minister about the XYZ affair before it had been translated and released by the administration. Before the trial, Bache died of yellow fever.

The first person to be charged under the Sedition Act itself was Matthew Lyon, a printer who established a newspaper in Vermont in an ultimately successful effort to get elected to Congress.

Lyon was indicted on October 5, 1798, for publishing letters that purportedly defamed the president. Convicted on October 8, Lyon was fined $1,000 and commanded to remain in jail until the fine was paid. Lyon continued to write from jail and later that year won reelection to Congress while still imprisoned. Eventually, Lyon's fine was paid through funds raised from leading Democratic-Republicans, including Jefferson and Madison.

Over time, in addition to editors, the Sedition Act was brought against a variety of people who criticized the Adams administration including James Bell, a tavern owner in Carlisle, Pennsylvania. Benjamin Fairbanks of Massachusetts was prosecuted for erecting a liberty pole with a placard atop it denouncing Adams and supporting Jefferson.

The Impact of the Sedition Act

The Sedition Act expired on the last day of the Adams administration in March 1801. As an instrument of political suppression, it largely failed. Only a few newspapers closed, and editors charged with sedition continued publishing while their trials were underway. Some were able to make their voices heard even from jail. Far from stifling Democratic-Republican sentiment, the Acts stimulated it. Of the approximately 71 newspapers established in 1800, around 30 identified with the Democratic-Republicans. The Democratic-Republicans won the election of 1800 and when Jefferson took office, every major city and many smaller towns had a newspaper supporting his views.

While the Sedition Act expired, sedition, defined as criticism of the government and its officials, continued to be a crime at the state level. The defense against a charge of sedition laid out in the Sedition Act was eventually incorporated into state sedition laws. Those changes represented a broadening of the scope of free speech compared to the common law of sedition, which had traditionally been applied. As opposed to the common law, the Sedition Act only punished false speech that was maliciously uttered. Both the truth of the speech and the intention had to be considered. Moreover, juries decided both the facts and the

law in sedition cases. Under common law, juries only decided if the person was responsible for the offending words. Judges decided if the words were libelous. The last case of criminal sedition involving the federal government came when President Theodore Roosevelt unsuccessfully brought suit against the *New York World* and the *Indianapolis News* in 1909.

Elliot King

See also Democracy and the Media; Espionage Act; First Amendment; History of Free Expression, History of; Partisan Press

Further Readings

Bird, W. (2016) *Press and speech under assault: The early Supreme Court, the Sedition Act of 1798, and the campaign against dissent.* New York, NY: Oxford University Press.

Bradburn, D. (2008). A clamor in the public mind: Opposition to the Alien and Sedition Acts. *The William and Mary Quarterly, 65*(3), 565–600.

Garrison, A. H. (2009). The Internal Security Acts of 1798: The founding generation and the judiciary during America's first national security crisis. *Journal of Supreme Court History, 34*(1) 1–27. Retrieved from https://papers.ssrn.com/sol3/papers.cfm?abstract_id=1530614

Halperin, T. D. (2016). *The Alien and Sedition Acts of 1798.* Baltimore, MD: Johns Hopkins University Press.

Smelser, M. (1954). George Washington and the Alien and Sedition Acts. *The American Historical Review, 59*(2), 322–334. doi:10.1086/ahr/59.2.322

Smith, J. M. (1956). *Freedom's fetters: The alien and sedition laws and American civil liberties.* Ithaca, NY: Cornell University Press.

SELF-PUBLISHING

The term *self-publishing* is used to describe processes used when an author publishes works of fiction or nonfiction without the use of a commercial publishing house, which typically buys the copyright of a creative work in return for royalties paid to the author. This entry describes key moments in the development of self-publishing, from the invention of the printing press through to the current day when the affordances of 21st-century digital technology have allowed for more than 1 million self-published titles to be created in 2018. According to the 2018 Bowker Report, self-publishing is in the strongest growth period in its history.

For centuries, publishing depended on access to the means of mass production. This changed irrevocably after the development of digital means of production to the point that today the author, not the platform, can be the publisher. This entry examines early forms of publishing and the various forms of self-publishing through the centuries.

Early Publishing

For hundreds of years following the invention of the Gutenberg printing press in 1439, the costs associated with owning the means of production were prohibitive, so mass publication was provided by a limited number of publishing houses. The model for these businesses is to purchase the rights to a work from the author in return for royalties on sales. Royalty percentages are determined by the publishing house and the author (and the author's agent, if they have one). The commissioning editor coordinates peer review of the manuscript proposal and/or sample chapters before taking the proposal to an Editorial Board that determines whether the proposal is worth publishing. This decision is a professional judgment as to the projected sales of the published work. Authors are paid an advance on their royalties, based on minimum projected sales.

A second peer review, of the full manuscript, is organized when the manuscript is submitted. Authors are typically set up with a staff editor, who may make adjustments and structural changes to the manuscript and will organize production processes such as indexing. The house takes on the responsibilities and costs of designing, editing, printing, distributing, and marketing the book.

Vanity and Subscription Publishing

One of the earliest self-publishers was American inventor Benjamin Franklin, who had the financial means from his other businesses and investments to use his own printing press for 26 years to publish his annual *Poor Richard's Almanack* from 1732. The book, an early form of personal journalism containing essays and an annual weather forecast, became one of the most popular publications in colonial America, selling an average of 10,000 copies a year. This form of self-publishing was known for many years as *vanity* publishing because the author published to a market without the work being evaluated by a commercial publishing house for its potential commercial success. Instead, the author paid a publisher to print and distribute a publication. For example, English author Jane Austen paid London publisher Thomas Egerton to publish her first novel *Sense and Sensibility* in 1811 after it was rejected by commercial publishers. In the 20th century, French author Marcel Proust paid for the publication of his early works after publishers declined to do so.

In the later 1800s, an early form of direct marketing emerged whereby subscriptions to the books were sold door-to-door by salespeople. *Subscription publishing* was considered a "low-class" method of publishing. It was the owner of a subscription publisher, American Publishing Company, who approached Samuel Clemens (Mark Twain) in 1867 to compile a book from his *Sacramento Union* articles describing his travels in Europe, Egypt, and the Holy Land. The resulting book, *Innocents Abroad*, was sold door to door in installments.

Vanity publishing still exists today. It differs from self-publishing in that the author assumes all the risk and pays the publisher. While vanity presses do offer services like cover design and editing, the publisher typically owns the copyright to the work.

Zines

In the 1970s, self-publishing was popularized in various subcultures, especially in the United Kingdom. These publications called *zines* were first produced using inexpensive offset printing technology, which was also used to create alternative newspapers and underground comics. By the punk rock era of the 1970s, xerography had become commonplace, enabling fans to easily produce their own do-it-yourself publications for distribution at concerts and in record shops. Zines differed from other publications through their heavy use of collage, paper cutouts, and a rough "undersigned" look. Today, printed zines continue to be produced alongside digital zines, which sometimes replicate the cut-and-paste aesthetic of paper zines.

Print on Demand

Self-publishing has been further enabled by advancements in technology, such as the development of desktop publishing software. Printed material was distributed by mail-order or via consignment in bookshops and was the forerunner of print-on-demand (POD). With POD, books can be published one at a time or in very small print runs. This means that publishers no longer have to commit resources and funds to large print runs or, maintain large inventories, and that the texts stored digitally could be made on demand indefinitely. POD has opened the market up to more small presses and independent publishers.

However, there is a disadvantage with this form of self-publishing: restricted distribution. Without the support of a traditional publisher, access to potential readers can be limited, as bookstores may be hesitant to stock self-published titles. Such titles carry a greater risk to the book seller because unsold stock cannot be returned to the publisher, and the biggest self-publishing service company, Amazon, directly competes with book stores for sales.

Online Publishing

Following access to the World Wide Web in 1989, a slew of new companies emerged to service those who wanted to self-publish. At first, this self-publishing was broadcast focused—for example, personal websites—but soon user-generated taxonomies emerged, such as weblogs, wikis, and syndications. Fan fiction, whereby enthusiasts publish their own fiction for other enthusiasts, also emerged as a genre.

Contemporaneously, weblog (blog) hosting services such as Blogger and Wordpress made it easy for people to instantly publish themselves on the Web without being able to write code. In more recent years, weblogs have been redeveloped into e-books, such as *Julie and Julia: 365 Days, 524 Recipes* (2002). Mashable, a blog started by a self-publisher in 2005, generated revenue of $2 million per month in 2017. In 2005, Reddit, a social news aggregation, web content rating, and discussion website, was launched. Registered Reddit members submit to the site content such as links, text posts, and images, which are then voted up or down by other members. Reddit is also on the video-sharing website YouTube, where users narrate curated versions of Reddit posts and comments.

Individual journalists have developed huge followings by sharing their views online, and alternative media such as Neiman Lab has flourished in the online environment. As of 2021, there are hundreds of blogs around the world devoted to journalism. Nonjournalists have also influenced public opinion through personal blogging. In fact, the top five influential blogs in 2020 were by technology billionaire Bill Gates, musician Alicia Keyes, Indian Prime Minister Narendra Modi, author Paul Coelho, and athlete Usain Bolt. These famous individuals, who have millions of people following their thoughts and opinions, self-publish directly to their audiences.

Big technology has responded to the emergence of user-generated content by engaging more with consumers. In fact, in 1995, Amazon began to publish user-generated content in the form of product reviews. These changes demonstrate the significant erosion of the traditional role third-party publishers in mediating between author and audience.

Crowdfunding for creative production became more common from 2009 when creators used social media platforms such as KickStarter to seek financial support from by interested future readers or listeners. In 2020, Kickstarter reported on 12 journalism projects supported by backers.

Platforms like Lulu and Createspace (now part of Amazon), among others, provide authors with tools to format books, design covers, and convert PDFs to e-books. They also provide enhanced services such as editing and marketing for a fee. These platforms and their services allow authors to not only publish without the involvement of agents and traditional publishers but also to make their self-published print and e-books available globally.

The rising influence of social media provides further affordable promotional opportunities for self-publishing authors. Companies such as Smashwords and BookBaby assist writers in using social media to promote and distribute their work. Social networking sites such as Facebook, Twitter, and Instagram can be used to market self-published works—and the peer review is subsequently done by consumers. This lack of professional peer review is perhaps the most significant difference between traditional and self-publishing because it means that the quality varies in terms of the writing and presentation. Self-published works may also not be subject to fact-checking and copyright checks that traditional publishers require.

The Commerce of Self-Publishing

Digital publishing lacked a payment mechanism until 1998, when pioneering publishers and authors began to sell books online. Sony released the first e-book reader in 2004, followed by Kindle e-Reader from Amazon in 2007, which came with a vast retail store attached. This meant that only an online distributor-retailer now stood between writer and reader. Kindle Direct Publishing (KDP) enables indie authors to sell the digital version of their books on Amazon.com (or other Amazon country websites). There is no charge to upload the file. Authors receive royalties of 35% to 70% of the sale price, depending on whether the book is sold on KDP or through another Amazon service called *KDP Select*.

Although this process brings authors three steps closer to their readers, content is still mediated by large corporations such as Amazon, Apple, and Google. The vast majority of "indie" authors earn their income from a single distributor-retailer, Amazon. In 2020, Amazon was by far the biggest player in self-publishing in the United States and the United Kingdom and growing swiftly in other countries where it has a presence. But other distributors of e-books are helping authors reach additional territories. For example, Kobo Writing Life supports self-publishing in a format whereby authors own copyright, set prices, and promote their products. PublishDrive is software for authors and publishers to distribute and manage e-books, print, and audiobooks, and

StreetLib is a distribution platform for e-books, audiobooks, POD books, online literature, comics, and magazines in any language.

None of the aforementioned platforms invest in the publishing process—neither do they license publishing rights. *The author*, not the platform, is the publisher.

The public's increasing preference for mobile devices presents a challenge for self-publishing, as smaller screens are less suited for reading, and large documents can be unwieldly to download. Publishers continue to develop technological solutions, such as audio books. Services such as the Creative Penn and Authors Republic are devoted to the creation and distribution of self-published audio books. Another service, Findaway Voices, focuses on the digital production of audiobooks and reaches markets not served by Amazon. Future trends in self-publishing will likely focus on delivering visual content.

Lynette Sheridan Burns

See also Audio Journalism; Citizen Journalism; Social Media

Further Readings

Cope, B (Editor). (2006). *The future of the book in the digital age*. Oxford, UK: Chandos Publishing.

Poynter, D. (2007). *Dan Poynter's self-publishing manual: How to write, print and sell your own book*. Santa Barbara, CA: Para Publishing. doi:10.33137/pbsc.v19i1.17417

O'Reilly, T. (2009). *What is Web 2.0?* Sebastopol, CA: O'Reilly Media Inc.

Boler, M. (2008). *Digital media and democracy*. Cambridge: Massachusetts Institute of Technology.

Singletary, D. A. (2017). Self-publishing: How did mark Twain's first book make it to print? Retrieved from https://medium.com/@Don_37722/self-publishing-how-did-mark-twains-first-book-the-innocents-abroad/.

SELF-REGULATION

News media self-regulation is defined as a system of voluntary accountability of journalists to the public. It is based on agreed principles of professional ethics and includes mechanisms of complaints review, monitoring, and conflict resolution in the field of their professional activity. Common elements of media self-regulation throughout the world are professional codes, press councils, and public editors, as described in this entry.

The interdependent reasons for a media organization to develop self-regulation include the following:

- to preserve editorial freedom from interference by media proprietors, advertisers, and the government;
- to advance market position by achieving higher media quality and standards than others while proving its own effective public accountability; and
- to help audiences access the media and engage with journalists, thus gaining public trust.

In the public eye, responsibility for keeping news credible rests with the media. At the same time, trust in the free media is not based on the belief of its "infallibility" in a democracy, but rather on skepticism, experience, and knowledge of how the media operate. Public trust depends on journalistic integrity and availability of effective self-regulatory complaint mechanisms. That is why those in the press react strongly when that trust is challenged by journalists who misbehave or betray the public, for example, by lying about facts or plagiarizing.

While the first elements of the self-regulation of the press came into existence at the turn of the 20th century, self-regulation has largely developed following World War II. Its popularity among journalists and the public was, in particular, a result of the conclusions of the work of the Commission of Freedom of the Press in the United States and the first Royal Commission on the Press in the United Kingdom in late 1940s.

Professional Codes

An important condition for media self-regulation is the presence of a full-fledged professional media community that recognizes itself as such and commits to specific behavior considered to be professionally correct for journalists and the media in their daily activities. These ideas and values are codified in sets of ethical standards for good journalism, usually titled as codes of professional ethics or codes of conduct. They are typically adopted by the national associations of journalists after thorough consultations in search of consensus, or by media companies, with the consent of the reporters, editors, and managers. There also exist specific codes for particular types of media actors, such as broadcast journalists, press photographers, opinion journalists, magazine editors, comics magazine publishers, business media, and chess journalists.

Most of the codes provide general guidelines for good practice, and others also include specific recommendations. Some foresee sanctions for violations of their norms. These codes are constantly supervised and regularly revised.

The provisions found in the majority of codes from around the world relate to six core areas:

1. truthfulness in newsgathering and reporting;
2. fairness and impartiality in reporting (e.g., respect of copyright and/or right of reply, avoidance of conflicts of interest);
3. protection of free expression;
4. tolerance and nondiscrimination on the basis on one's personal characteristics, such as race, religion, or ethnicity;
5. respect for the sources and their integrity, accuracy, and privacy, including "limitation of harm," which means minimizing harm to other's rights when reporting;
6. independence of journalists from outside influence, such as advertisers, while staying accountable to the public.

Search for truth remains the main value of journalism as a profession. The major global association of media workers, the International Federation of Journalists (IFJ), has proclaimed the Global Charter of Ethics for Journalists, setting out respect for the facts and for the right of the public to truth as the very first duty of the journalist. In the pursuit of the truth, according to the IFJ, the journalist shall, at all times, deem it their duty to faithfully "defend the principles of freedom in the honest collection and publication of news and the right of fair comment and criticism." The journalist is called to "report only in accordance with facts of which he/she knows the origin." The IFJ further pledges that journalists shall not suppress essential information or falsify documents. If any published information is still found to be inaccurate, the journalist shall do the utmost to rectify it. These principles are shared by national associations that are members of the IFJ, as well as followed by the grounding documents of the national self-regulation bodies.

In the United States, the first nationwide code of ethics for the news industry was adopted by the American Society of Newspaper Editors in 1923. In 1926, the Society of Professional Journalists (SPJ), the nation's most broad-based journalism organization, particularly dedicated to stimulating high standards of ethical behavior, adopted its own canons of journalism, under the title "SPJ Code of Ethics."

Press Councils

Crafting a strong professional code is a start, but to work, there needs to be some mechanism in place, such as the press council (or media or news council). Press councils can be national or regional in scope, competent in the matters of all the media, or specifically designed for print, broadcast, and/or online. Each established press council is unique, the result of its country's particular history and media environment.

Nevertheless, at least in Europe, press councils possess the following common features. They are self-regulatory nonprofit entities that are voluntarily set up by the media themselves—although usually given a high degree of operational independence. Despite possible state intervention at their start-up stage, they achieve independence as to their management and functioning. In actuality, a reason for their establishment is the threat of governmental regulation of the media. The best way to finance a press council that secures its independence is through clear procedures and transparent mechanisms. Ideally, there should be a diversity of sources of funding, with the largest contribution being made by the media industry, or shared equally by owners and journalists. In the countries in the early stages of developing self-regulation, a major role is played by international donors.

Press councils are collective bodies, often consisting of both professionals, appointed by the founding media and journalists' associations, and laypersons. Sometimes, when they function at a professional association, press councils are closed for participation of the latter.

The primary function of press councils is the administration of an agreed-upon professional code, which may include a set of complaint procedures. Through these, anyone can complain for free and without legal representation, thus helping generate trust in the quality and transparency of news. Another function of press councils is to maintain freedom of expression and pluralism of opinions in society, both in their decisions and other public activities.

The Alliance of Independent European Press Councils and the World Association of Press Councils are the main international umbrella organizations. They coordinate activities of their members and the exchange of information online and at regular conferences.

The practice of press councils in the United States is patchy and provides just two examples. In both cases, the councils did not have direct support from news organizations, relying instead on foundation support and individual donors. They are the Washington News Council, closed in 2014 after a 15-year run, and Minnesota News Council, which folded in 2011 after 41 years of providing public/professional adjudication of journalism disputes.

The Swedish Press Council, founded in 1916, is considered the oldest in the world; it receives about 300 complaints each year.

Public Editors

A significant number of media outlets worldwide hire—as an instrument of self-regulation—an independent public editor often called *readers' editor* or *news ombudsman*. The role of public editors, regardless of the formal title they are given, is to investigate and reply to comments and complaints from the audience concerning published or broadcast news and feature stories. To do so, they enjoy administrative autonomy in the editorial offices, as they present the complaints to the appropriate persons on the editorial team in order to get answers or resolutions to those complaints. They also obtain explanations from relevant journalists and editors for readers, viewers, or listeners and oversee the tracking of editorial mistakes and announce corrections. Public editors are usually guaranteed column space or time in their media to provide clarity about editorial decisions and processes, answer credible complaints, and point out when the news organization fails to meet its own professional standards and best practices. Public editors also responsible for explaining these standards both to the public and to editorial employees. Public editors may shuttle tips and story ideas from readers and viewers to the staff, so as to ensure that underreported issues and groups are given sufficient coverage. Often, the public editor is the person available to present the news outlet's accountability record to citizen, church, business, and educational groups.

Editorial standards editors, while not dissimilar to public editors, are typically less autonomous and lead efforts to maintain ethical practice throughout the newsroom, occasionally seeking to explain the workings of journalism to their audiences.

Although hiring a public editor can make financial sense (*The Guardian* in United Kingdom found that legal costs declined by as much as 30% once an ombudsman was placed there to find solutions to conflicts that otherwise could end up in a lawsuit), it is considered a luxury at a time when the traditional media industry is going through a decline. Many of the major U.S. networks and newspapers dropped the position in the late 2010s as a cost-saving measure, citing the rise of real-time feedback in social media.

The first newspaper public editor was appointed in 1967 to serve the readers of *The Courier-Journal* and *The Louisville Times* in Louisville, Kentucky. This experiment became known in other parts of the United States, in Canada, the United Kingdom, Sweden and other European countries, the Mediterranean, and in Latin America, where similar public editors came to existence. This trend led to the establishment, in 1980, of the international Organization of News Ombudsmen and Standards Editors that comprises an active cohort of executives from around the world who handle editorial standards and editorial complaints.

Public editors within the individual editorial offices should be distinguished from national media ombudsmen, such as in Ireland, Lithuania, South Africa, and Sweden. National media ombudsmen are usually affiliated with the national press councils and handle complaints regarding the editorial content of all participating news outlets from those who feel unfairly treated by the media. Public editors must be also distinguished from media critics (columnists and bloggers), who are influential scrutinizing voices on professional practice across all media, thus becoming an instrument of media literacy, or critical thinking on the matters of the media transparency and accountability. Media critics contribute to a better understanding by media users of how the news industry works, by explaining different types of media content and evaluating stories for truthfulness, reliability, and value for money. This allows the audiences—confronted with challenges brought about by the abundance of information and the proliferation of new forms of communication—make informed choices about content selection and use.

In publicly controversial situations, there may be also independent reports commissioned by media outlets but prepared by outside experts to review the practices in the newsroom. For example, during the 2004 U.S. presidential election, CBS News consistently reported on the poor record of the incumbent, President George W. Bush, in the Texas Air National Guard during the Vietnam War, relying on damaging documents that later proved to be false. An independent report, commissioned by the TV network, found serious flaws in the newsgathering procedures, which led to the resignation or firing of four news executives.

Self-Regulation of Public Service Media

Traditionally, public service media set the example for private media by providing a model for professional standards in reporting and for accountability in general. Likely, all public service media in the world today employ an editorial code and mechanisms of public accountability.

In the United States, the remaining full-time public editors of major news outlets are embedded in the offices of the Public Broadcasting Service and the National Public Radio. Following professional standards is a fundamental commitment for the British Broadcasting Corporation (BBC) in the

United Kingdom, required under the agreement accompanying the BBC Royal Charter from 2017 (as well as earlier ones). In particular, the standards require using firsthand sources, checking and cross-checking facts, validating the authenticity of documents and other (increasingly digital) materials, and corroborating claims and allegations made by contributors.

Online Media

Originally designed for the printed press, self-regulation mechanisms spread in the 1990s to the broadcasting environment and since the 2010s to online media. With the widespread proliferation of propaganda-driven disinformation comes numerous new challenges for journalists, standards of journalism, and media self-regulation. Self-regulation of online content can be particularly difficult. Social media have no geographical frontiers in the virtual world: Bloggers and other authors can be hosted in countries far away from their target audience and outside of the reach of the self-regulatory body that would take the complaint and try to administer professional standards. Therefore, self-regulation of user-generated content and blogs often comes down to corporate self-regulation of the online platforms and major content providers. It can be in the form of an oversight board of laypersons and media professionals, awareness-raising on the standards applied, and/or special marks of the posts.

In Europe, self-regulation is strongly recommended by intergovernmental organizations as a key instrument of governance for online information and platforms. In particular, users of online media are to be informed about the possibility of addressing complaints to journalists, editors, or professional associations, similar to those existing offline. Internet service providers are encouraged to empower their users to report "fake news" or "hate speech," make it known publicly, as well as voluntarily correct factually wrong content, publish a reply, and/or remove false or hateful content.

A number of media councils regulate online publications. For example, the United Kingdom's Independent Press Standards Organisation oversees, in addition to traditional media, more than 1,100 online titles that are subject to the Editors' Code of Practice.

Andrei G. Richter and Olga Mamontova

See also Advertising, Ethics in; Commission on Freedom of the Press; Conflicts of Interest; Corrections Policies; Ethics; Fact-Checking Movement; Fake News; Letters to the Editor; Media Criticism; Media Literacy; Ombudsman; Photojournalism, Ethics of; Plagiarism; Press Freedom; Privacy; Propaganda; Public Relations, Ethics in; Transparency; Trust in Journalism

Further Readings

Dennis, E. E., & Merrill, J. C. (2006). *Media debates: Great issues for the digital age.* Belmont, CA: Wadsworth Publishing Co.

Dvorkin, J. (2020). The modern news Ombudsman: A user's guide. Retrieved from https://www .newsombudsmen.org/the-ono-handbook/

Hullin, A., & Smith, J. (2008). *The media self-regulation guidebook: All questions and answers.* Vienna, Austria: OSCE Representative on Freedom of the Media.

Hullin, A., & Stone, M. (2013). *The online media self-regulation guidebook.* Vienna, Austria: OSCE Representative on Freedom of the Media.

International Federation of Journalists (IFJ). (2019, June 12). Global charter of ethics for journalists. Retrieved from https://www.ifj.org/who/rules-and-policy/global -charter-of-ethics-for-journalists.html

Mayes, I. (2007). *Journalism right and wrong: Ethical and other issues raised by readers in the "Guardian's" Open Door column.* London, UK: Guardian Books.

Nordenstreng, K. (2010) Pottker, H. and C. Schwarzennegger. Self-regulation: A contradiction in terms? Discussing constituents of journalistic responsibility. In *Europäische Öffentlichkeit und journalistische Verantvortung* (pp. 417–438). Köln, Germany: Herbert von Halem Verlag.

Richter, A. (2019). Accountability and media literacy mechanisms as counteraction to disinformation in Europe. *Journal of Digital Media & Policy, 10*(3), 311–327. doi:10.1386/jdmp_00005_1

SENSATIONALISM

Sensationalism, a type of news reporting that emphasizes shock value over facts, is a key ingredient of what in the United States became known in the late 19th century as "yellow" journalism (after a cartoon character). Yellow or sensational journalism is noted for stories that exploit, distort, or exaggerate the news. Sensationalism triumphs over factual reporting as stories are twisted into forms designed to attract readers and (more recently) viewers. The same style of sensationalized news reappeared in the muckraking journalism of the early 20th century, in the tabloid newspapers of the 1920s, and in print and electronic media in the years since.

Sensational news, however, dates back at least to the news sheets of the 17th century. Critics complained about an overemphasis on crime and disaster stories even then. The rise of the penny press popular newspapers in the 1830s often depended on sensational human interest stories offering graphic details even if the technology of the time could not provide matching pictures.

"Yellow" Origins

Yellow journalism achieved its peak fame in 1896 with the journalistic practices of competing New York City daily newspaper publishers Joseph Pulitzer and William Randolph Hearst. Newspaper sensationalism dated back much earlier.

In a sense, Benjamin Day and James Gordon Bennett introduced the idea of sensational treatment of news during America's penny press era in the 1830s, thanks to their reliance on human interest stories. Everything and everyone, especially the underdogs of society, the butcher, the baker, the shoemaker, and especially the mistress or prostitute, was considered (and thus made) newsworthy. What Day and others did was to place emphasis on the common or unusual person (including those rarely covered in the news to that point) as he or she reflected the political, educational, and social life of the day. Their formula was to blend stories of murder, catastrophe, and love with elements of pathos to produce the human side of news. Pulitzer and Hearst built their publishing empires using this model decades later.

In the late 19th century, the development of yellow journalism reflected a society in transition. America was shifting from a predominantly rural to largely urban society. Fueled by a wave of immigrants from Europe, the nation's cities grew by nearly one-third. At the same time, the United

States flexed its military might as the army evolved from a small frontier force to the army and navy that in 1898 challenged the remains of Spanish power in the Western hemisphere. As a result of war with Spain—one heavily promoted by Pulitzer and Hearst—the United States collected Puerto Rico, Cuba, the Hawaiian Islands, and the Philippine Islands. The victory had one unintended effect—it helped promote the belligerent nationalist tone of much of the American press.

Sensationalist yellow journalism became synonymous with the journalism practiced by Pulitzer and Hearst, and soon others as well. Pulitzer's successful *St. Louis Dispatch* allowed him to enter New York journalism in 1883 with purchase of *The World*. Pulitzer's *World* utilized modest typography with headlines in small light-face type that appeared above stories of murder, mayhem, and mystery, every bit as sensational as those of one of the then-popular police gazettes.

By September 1884, *The World* reached a circulation of 100,000; within 2 years, circulation soared to 250,000. When Pulitzer introduced the *Evening World* in 1887, the combined circulation of both editions was 374,000. Meanwhile, his Sunday edition alone reached 250,000 though half was advertising.

Pulitzer's journalism soon affected the character of much of the nation's daily press. He upset the status quo and furnished a new formula for the metropolitan daily by crafting a new concept of news, utilizing many illustrations, employing a crusading tone, and, though less obvious, revitalizing his editorial page and aggressively selling advertising space. His chief contribution was his invention of a formula that Hearst and others later adopted—sex on the front page and a kind of spurious morality on the editorial page.

Pulitzer helped introduce a new definition of sensationalism that, at its most basic, included self-promotion, an updating of the paper's layout, and adoption of an aggressive reporting style. *The World,* for instance, regularly boasted on its front page about its high circulation figures and that it printed more advertising than any other paper in the country.

He made stunts a daily fixture in newspapers by 1890. They were often entertaining, sometimes educational, and nearly always attracted readers. His most ambitious was sending Elizabeth

Cochran, better known to readers as "Nellie Bly," on a world voyage in an effort to beat the record of the hero of Jules Verne's *Around the World in Eighty Days*.

Thanks to improving printing technology, Pulitzer also introduced colored supplements, including an eight-page comic section, in 1893. The highlight of this section was Richard F. Outcault's "Hogan's Alley," a social satire that depicted life in a New York tenement. The leader of the gang was a one-tooth ragamuffin, "The Yellow Kid," whom *World* printers clothed in a bright yellow dress. He would come to symbolize the Pulitzer-Hearst brand of sensational journalism in the 1890s.

During the 1890s, yellow journalism was founded upon what journalism historian Frank Luther Mott called "familiar aspects of sensationalism—crime news, scandal and gossip, divorces and sex, and stress upon the reprint of disasters and sports." Its distinguishing characteristics included:

- often-huge headlines, in black or red, that "screamed excitement, often about comparatively unimportant news";
- pictures, many without real news significance;
- impostors and such frauds as faked interviews;
- a Sunday supplement, with color comics (something adopted by many decidedly unsensational papers in the years to come);
- and a "more or less ostentatious sympathy with the 'underdog,' with campaigns against abuses suffered by the common people."

This approach to journalism spread rapidly, influencing most metropolitan newspapers. And it clearly attracted an audience. Two types of readers, immigrants and women, were especially drawn to the yellow press. Department store advertising, directed chiefly to women in the home, also encouraged female readership.

Many who might otherwise criticize the "bottom feeding" approach of sensational news agreed that it served as something of an integrating force, helping to meld the flood of immigrants into the American mainstream. Attracted by the color and pictures, they soon learned to read the words. Further, many readers admired yellow journalism's

crusades against privileged and powerful business and political interests, especially when they exposed corruption in municipal government. This motive soon morphed into the muckraking journalism of the early 20th century, which applied some of the content and methods of sensationalism to a concerted crusade against the malfeasance of big business.

The assassination of President McKinley in 1901 contributed to a decline in yellow journalism. In his first message to Congress, President Theodore Roosevelt said that McKinley's assassin had probably been inflamed by reckless journalism that appealed "to dark and evil spirits." A decline in both *The World*'s and the *Journal*'s circulation was further evidence of the public's declining interest in old-style yellow journalism.

Muckraking and Tabloids

The years leading to World War I saw an important variation of yellow journalism. Called *muckraking* (after the muck rake in *Pilgrim's Progress*), it was a kind of aggressive investigative reporting aimed at demonstrating the shortcomings of big business and its leaders appeared in books and magazines even more than newspapers. Muckraking authors and reporters hammered constantly at the shortcomings of the Gilded Age, often graphically demonstrating how wealth was produced from the hard efforts of working men and women.

Ida Tarbell's multipart magazine series in *McClure's* magazine exposing the methods John D. Rockefeller used to develop his Standard Oil monopoly (1904) and Upton Sinclair's novel *The Jungle* (1906) are two often-cited examples of dogged reporting that looked under rocks and described things that needed change or the weak and defenseless that needed help. Child labor was one favorite target in an attempt to get children out of factories and into schools. The thriving Progressive political movement contributed to muckraking and gained useful ideas from it.

But following on years of yellow journalism, the muckrakers soon exhausted their readers as well. It is hard to maintain a state of ready awareness and crusading fervor all the time. Soon one social shortcoming seemed much like the next. Some readers found the constant barrage of stories so overwhelming that it seemed nothing could be done to address the problems identified. By about 1912, the muckraker's time had passed.

The appearance of tabloid newspapers in several of the largest markets in the 1920s provided the next step in sensational news. Chief among them were the *New York Graphic* and the *New York Mirror*. The tabloid offered ease of handling and illustrations—but was built on story selection that emphasized crime and scandal. The tone of such stories was less that of the crusader than of the informer or tattletale. Tabloid stories were intended to titillate more than promote change. The sensational stories were designed to build circulation (which for many years they did) while attracting advertisers who, in turn, sought exposure to the huge readership of the new tabloid papers. The *New York Daily News* managed to sneak a camera into the execution of a murderer and ran the fuzzy resulting photo on its front page. Short, punchy headlines emphasized the most titillating aspects of *Daily News* stories.

Modern News Sensationalism

In recent decades, news sensationalism has continued in several different forms. Tabloid papers declined after 1980 as television, cable, and online resources drew readers from newspapers.

By the 1950s, television began to add its own version of sensational news. Requiring pictures to hold viewer attention, television stations early on discovered the visual excitement of fires, accidents, and both natural and man-made disasters. The old line "if it bleeds, it leads" all too often applies to both print and broadcast news which focus on the sensational rather than what may be more important in many cities. Local television news typically centers on stories of murder, robbery, and other mayhem, sometimes to the near exclusion of other stories.

A growing focus on celebrities and disasters across print and electronic news media in the late 20th and early 21st century suggests a different kind of sensationalism. Here the emphasis is on the personal as well as professional lives of show business and sports figures (and sometimes people in other occupations) to the detriment of reporting other, usually more important stories. "Gang" or "crowd" reporting where masses of reporters and photographers all congregate around one story is an example. The televised trial of O. J. Simpson in the mid-1990s illustrated the lasting appeal of crime news and helped lead to the creation of Court TV, a cable network focused on such things. By the early 21st century, murders of children often dominated headlines in print and on the air for months thereafter.

In the end, sensational news reporting can be seen as pandering to the news audience's lowest concerns—fear (of crime or disease, for example) or morbid fascination (as with those struck by disaster, celebrities in a scandal, or murder victims). On the other hand, publishers and broadcasters often defend their sensationalized news as "giving the public what it wants"—there is an element of truth in the claim as circulation and viewership often increase when such sensationalized stories are covered—rather than what some critics argue the public may really need, such as important economic or political news.

Christopher H. Sterling and Anthony Fellow

See also Celebrity and Fan Magazines; Criminal Justice and Journalism; Ethics; Hard Versus Soft News; Hoaxes; Human Interest Journalism; Infotainment; Investigative Journalism; Muckrakers; Tabloid Newspapers; Tabloid Television

Further Readings

Brian, D. (2001). *Pulitzer: A life.* New York, NY: Wiley.

Campbell, W. J. (2003). *Yellow journalism: Puncturing the myths, defining the legacies.* Westport, CT: Praeger.

Chiasson, L. Jr. (Ed.) (1997). *The press on trial: Crimes and trials as media events.* Westport, CT: Praeger.

Fox, R. L., & Van Sickel, R. W. (2007). *Tabloid justice: Criminal justice in an age of media Frenzy* (2nd ed.). Boulder, CO: Lynne Rienner.

Jensen, C. (Ed.) (2002). *Stories that changed America: Muckrakers of the 20th century.* New York, NY: Seven Stories Press.

Krajicek, D. J. (1998). *Scooped! Media miss real story on crime while chasing sex, sleaze, and celebrities.* New York, NY: Columbia University Press.

Mott, F. L. (1962). *American journalism: A history: 1690–1960* (3rd ed.). New York, NY: Macmillan.

Nasaw, D. (2000). *The chief: The life of William Randolph Hearst.* Boston, MA: Houghton Mifflin.

Serrin, J., & Serrin, W. (Eds.) (2002). *Muckraking! The journalism that changed America.* New York, NY: The New Press.

Spencer, D. R. (2007). *The yellow journalism.* Evanston, IL: Northwestern University Press.

Stevens, J. D. (1991). *Sensationalism and the New York Press.* New York, NY: Columbia University Press.

SEXUAL HARASSMENT IN JOURNALISM

For centuries, women journalists have been harassed physically, verbally, and, more recently, online, simply for doing their jobs. Historically, women who dared to step out of the home's private sphere and into the male-dominated public realm of work faced sex discrimination as well as verbal and physical assaults. Women journalists have fought against misogyny, sexual harassment, and discrimination through lawsuits, public discourse, and online movements and protests. Still, sexual harassment today remains the most reported harassment complaint to the U.S. Equal Employment Opportunity Commission.

Women journalists who report abuse and discrimination on the job sometimes face retaliation, and some remain silent. Sexual harassment persists while feminist movements, including #MeToo, continue to resist. This entry discusses sexual harassment of and discrimination toward women journalists in the United States since the 1800s. It also looks at news coverage of sexual harassment from the time of its initial recognition in U.S. law to the exposure during the 2010s of numerous cases of sexual harassment involving journalists and powerful media figures.

Groundbreaking Women in Journalism

Sexual harassment is not a new problem for women journalists. From the early days of the press, women were present in newsrooms and print shops, and some faced abuse. Public records from the 19th century show women in the workplace endured discrimination, harassment, sexual assault, and rape. In the late 1800s, pioneering women journalists such as Nellie Bly and Ida B. Wells-Barnett reported the news while bearing harassment, threats, and attacks. Elizabeth Jane Cochran, known professionally as *Nellie Bly*, worked for the *New York World* and became famous for her undercover expose that chronicled women's horrific treatment in a mental institution. Bly, who also wrote about her trip around the world, was criticized widely, including by men who believed women who worked outside the home were immoral and that journalism was too dangerous for women. Some told her to stop reporting and "go back to the kitchen."

Wells-Barnett, whose newspaper published accounts of violent lynchings to expose atrocities in the American South, was attacked on several fronts. A white mob burned down her Memphis newspaper, the *Free Speech and Headlight.* She was physically removed from a train for refusing to ride in a segregated car. After many death threats in the South, she relocated to New York City. Her 1892 book *Southern Horrors: Lynch Law in All Its Phases* revealed white men's repeated assault and rape of Black women in the South after the Civil War. She never stopped revealing the truth about racial crimes despite the attempts to intimidate and silence her.

In the decades following this groundbreaking work, women in newsrooms primarily were assigned to the "women's sections," which focused on the four "F's": food, fashion, family, and furnishings. But change was coming.

Lawsuits Break Barriers

While sexual harassment was part of women journalists' jobs for most of American history, women in the 1970s began legal actions to gain the right to work the same jobs as men. In 1970, 46 women who worked at *Newsweek* magazine sued their employer, claiming sex discrimination in hiring and promotion. At the time, a 52-member reporting staff included only one woman, while the rest of the women worked as researchers for male reporters. The women won the right to be promoted. In 1972, women at *The New York Times* also sued for sex discrimination, citing unequal pay and lack of hiring and promotion of women. These and other lawsuits against media organizations, including the Associated Press, NBC, Time Inc., *The Washington Post, Reader's Digest,* and *Newsday,* forced news media companies to hire and promote more women, who flooded into heavily male-dominated newsrooms. Women found new opportunities to work as journalists, editors, and publishers. They also faced new venues for sexual harassment.

In 1974, journalist Lin Farley led a team that coined the term *sexual harassment* after students in a class she was teaching at Cornell University sought a name for what was happening to them in the workplace: unwanted sexual come-ons, unwanted physical contact, uninvited sexual jokes and sexual references, display of sexual images, and other discriminatory treatment. It took 12 more years, until 1986, for the U.S. Supreme Court to rule that sexual harassment was illegal under Title VII of the Civil Rights Act of 1964.

The Anita Hill–Clarence Thomas Hearings

The first major public test of sexual harassment came in 1991, when lawyer Anita Hill testified before an all-white-male Senate Judiciary Committee considering the confirmation of Clarence Thomas to the U.S. Supreme Court. Anita Hill, a lawyer who had worked for Thomas at two U.S. government agencies, the Office for Civil Rights in the U.S. Department of Education and the Equal Employment Opportunity Commission, testified that Thomas had sexually harassed her at work. The hearings were nationally televised. Hill testified that Thomas repeatedly asked her to go on dates with him, talked about his sexual prowess, described pornography, and made crude sexual jokes in the workplace. The visual images of the hearings, with a lone Black woman facing intrusive and repetitive questions about the specifics of the harassment from an all-white male panel led by Senator Joe Biden, focused national discourse on sexual harassment. Finally, sexual harassment became clearly defined as unwelcome, persistent remarks, advances, physical contact, and/or demands based on sex. Thomas, who was eventually confirmed to the Supreme Court, disputed Hill's account and called the hearings a *high-tech lynching*. In 2019, when he launched his campaign for U.S. president, Biden said he regretted what Hill went through during the hearings.

After the hearings, public attention focused on sexual harassment and its consequences. Women and men began to scrutinize such behavior as a hindrance in the workplace and felt more empowered to report it. Reforms, including state laws and the U.S. Civil Rights Act of 1991, gave victims of sexual harassment more legal recourse. In 1992, dubbed "The Year of the Woman," more women were elected to Congress than ever before. The hearings and responses to them laid the foundation for the #MeToo movement.

#MeToo

Academic studies from the 1990s through the present day show a majority of women journalists report they have been sexually harassed while working in newsrooms and while reporting in the field. A 2018 study by the International Women's Media Foundation found two-thirds of women journalists had been harassed on the job, both in person and online. Many of them kept silent for years in fear of being doubted, told to tolerate it, labeled as troublemakers, receiving retaliation, or losing their jobs. However, a social media hashtag and other efforts helped provide a way for them to bond with others who had suffered the same kind of abuse and to call out their harassers.

In 2006, civil rights activist Tarana Burke created the #MeToo movement to raise awareness of sexual assault and abuse and to support and advocate for survivors. A decade later, women in Hollywood began using the #MeToo hashtag on social media to draw attention to sexual abuse by film producer Harvey Weinstein and other men. Women in the journalism industry also had begun to speak out about harassment and abuse in their profession. In 2011, CBS journalist Lara Logan recounted being sexually assaulted by a mob of men while reporting the fall of Hosni Mubarak in Cairo's Tahrir Square. That same year, Lynsey Addario, a *The New York Times* photojournalist, recounted being kidnapped and sexually assaulted while reporting in Libya. According to the Committee to Protect Journalists (CPJ), 15% of women journalists worldwide have experienced sexual violence connected with their jobs. CPJ's website offers advice on ways to mitigate such attacks.

In 2016, Fox News anchor Gretchen Carlson filed a sexual harassment complaint against Roger Ailes, CEO of the cable news network. Several other women journalists at Fox News later spoke out about Ailes's decades of sexual harassment. Ailes eventually was removed as head of the network, which settled Carlson's lawsuit for $20 million.

In 2017, a "Shitty Media Men" list, an anonymous crowdsourced spreadsheet, circulated among women journalists, accusing specific men of sexual misconduct and leading to the investigation and firing of several of the men named. More women began to post on social media under the #MeToo hashtag and speak publicly about harassment in journalism. In this climate of #MeToo activism and women's public pushback, several other prominent media men were fired or forced out of their jobs for sexual misconduct. They included Charlie Rose of CBS and PBS; Matt Lauer of NBC's Today show; Bill O'Reilly of Fox News; Les Moonves, chairman and CEO of CBS; Michael Oreskes, a former *The New York Times* editor who headed NPR's news division; Robert Moore, managing editor of the *New York Daily News*; Mark Halperin, a veteran political journalist; and dozens of others. By firing these men, journalism organizations demonstrated they would no longer tolerate sexual harassment and abuse. Still, some women journalists continued to fear judgment or retaliation from colleagues and supervisors for speaking up. Some, according to studies, said they simply left the profession rather than tolerate sexual harassment.

Cyberharassment

Gendertrolling is a term coined by author and editor Karla Mantilla to describe online threats and harassment of women. Men are harassed online as well, but primarily because of their opinions or ideas, while women often are attacked simply for having an online presence. Researchers have found that women journalists, often required by employers to operate social media accounts, are three times more likely than male journalists to be harassed, showing that misogyny is entrenched in cyberspace. Women journalists risk their safety and emotional well-being every day.

A 2016 video featuring two sports journalists, Julie DiCaro and Sarah Spain, shows unsuspecting "regular guys" reading violent, harassing tweets that the journalists received. The words are shocking. "One of the players should beat you to death

with their hockey stick like the whore you are," reads one tweet. Another targets DiCaro for writing about her personal experiences: "I hope you get raped again." The climate of online abuse can subject women journalists to emotional distress and humiliation. Sometimes, it forces them to exit social media platforms, effectively silencing them. Jessica Valenti, a columnist for *The Guardian* newspaper, temporarily abandoned Twitter in 2016 after a rape and death threat against her 5-year-old daughter. Social media companies have done little to curb online abuse, so journalists are forced to accept gendered attacks as part of their jobs.

Threats of violence may cause journalists to avoid reporting certain stories, therefore damaging press freedom. Online attacks are no exception. Women journalists of color face online racism as well as sexism. The Committee to Protect Journalists has documented cyberharassment of women journalists across the world and found a majority fear for their safety because of online abuse. Some women have left journalism jobs because of the constant threats and pressure. One organization fighting against online abuse is Troll-Busters, a nonprofit that provides support and protection for women writers and journalists targeted with cyberharassment. However, social media companies continue to protect the free speech of harassers when confronted with user abuse. Recently, some individuals have challenged the rights of harassers and have won. In December 2019, a man was charged with assault for sending journalist Kurt Eichenwald a tweet with a strobe GIF that triggered his epilepsy. Twitter suspended Martin Shkreli, a hedge fund manager later convicted of securities fraud, after he posted lewd tweets about journalist Lauren Duca. Twitter also suspended far-right-wing writer Milo Yiannopoulos after he incited his followers to post sexist and racist tweets about comedian and actress Leslie Jones.

Despite some progress in wage equality, women in journalism continue to be underpaid compared with men. A 2019 study by the Washington Post Newspaper Guild showed women in the *Post*'s newsroom earned less than men with the same duties, with women of color earning $30,000 less per year than white men. Journalists under 40 had the widest gender disparity in pay. In the magazine industry, women also received lower compensation than men doing the same jobs.

With exposure to in-person and online harassment and lower compensation than their male counterparts, it is no wonder women often leave the journalism profession. *The American Journalist in the Digital Age*, a 2013 study, showed that men and women enter the journalism profession in equal numbers, but that after 5 years, women leave at higher rates than men do. Women say they leave journalism because of lower pay than men, lack of opportunity for promotion, lack of mentoring, and inflexible job schedules, according to a 2007 study published in *Newspaper Research Journal*.

Women Journalists and Allies Expose Harassment

Brave women journalists have exposed wrongdoing since the days of Wells-Barnett and Bly. It is only fitting that in many cases women journalists exposed some of the worst sexual harassment offenders of recent years. Megan Twohey and Jodi Kantor of *The New York Times* won the 2017 public service Pulitzer Prize for breaking the story of Harvey Weinstein's long-standing abuse of women in Hollywood. They shared the prize with Ronan Farrow of *The New Yorker*, who also reported on Weinstein's misdeeds. Kim Masters of the *Hollywood Reporter* subsequently reported on Weinstein and other Hollywood men accused of sexual misconduct, including harassment against her. In 2017, Irin Carmon and Amy Brittain of *The Washington Post* revealed the sexual abuse allegations that brought down Charlie Rose of CBS and PBS. Emily Steel, a *The New York Times* business reporter, reported with Michael S. Schmidt in 2017 on allegations against Bill O'Reilly that led to multimillion dollar sexual harassment lawsuit settlements and O'Reilly's firing from Fox News. In 2015, Maryclaire Dale, an Associated Press reporter, exposed accounts that comedian Bill Cosby had drugged and raped women.

Tracy Everbach

See also Bly, Nellie; Feminist News Media; Wells-Barnett, Ida B.

Further Readings

Bly, N. (1887). *Ten days in a madhouse*. New York, NY: Ian L. Munro.

Committee to Protect Journalists. (2019). Physical safety: Mitigating sexual violence. Retrieved from https://cpj.org/2019/09/physical-safety-mitigating-sexual-violence.php

Everbach, T., & Flournoy, C. (2007). Women leave journalism for better pay, work conditions. *Newspaper Research Journal, 28*(3), 52–64. doi:10.1177/073953290702800305

Gibbons, S. (Fall 2019). More studies document wage disparities; salary data shared. *Media Report to Women, 47*(4), 1–3.

Gilger, K. G., & Wallace, J. (2019). *There's no crying in newsrooms: What women have learned about what it takes to lead*. Lanham, MD: Rowman & Littlefield.

Hill, A. (1997). *Speaking truth to power*. New York, NY: Penguin Random House.

International Women's Media Foundation. (2018). Attacks against female journalists are career-altering, survey says. International Women's Media Foundation. Retrieved from https://www.iwmf.org/2018/09/attacks-against-female-journalists-are-career-altering-survey-says/

Just Not Sports. (2016, April). #MoreThanMean—Women in sports face harassment. [Video]. Retrieved from https://www.youtube.com/watch?v=9tU-D-m2JY8

Kroeger, B. (1994). *Nellie Bly: Daredevil, reporter, feminist*. New York, NY: Times Books/Random House.

Mantilla, K. (2015). *Gendertrolling: How misogyny went viral*. Santa Barbara, CA: Praeger.

Mayer, J., & Abramson, J. (1994). *Strange justice: The selling of Clarence Thomas*. Boston, MA: Houghton Mifflin.

Povich, L. (2012). *The good girls revolt: How the women of Newsweek sued their bosses and changed the workplace*. New York, NY: Public Affairs.

Robertson, N. (1992). *The girls in the balcony: Women, men, and The New York Times*. New York, NY: Random House.

Stelter, B. (2011, April 28). CBS reporter recounts a "merciless" assault. *The New York Times*. Retrieved from https://www.nytimes.com/2011/04/29/business/media/29logan.html

Vickery, J. R., & Everbach, T. (2018). *Mediating misogyny: Gender, technology & harassment*. Cham, Switzerland: Palgrave MacMillan.

Vox. (2019). 263 celebrities, politicians, CEOs, and others who have been accused of sexual misconduct since April 2017. Retrieved from https://www.vox.com/a/sexual-harassment-assault-allegations-list.

Wells, I. B. (1892). *Southern horrors: Lynch law in all its phases.* New York, NY: New York Age Print.

Willnat, L., & Weaver, D. (2013). *The American journalist in the digital age: Key findings.* Bloomington: School of Journalism, Indiana University.

Websites

Dart Center for Journalism and Trauma: https://dartcenter.org/

TrollBusters: www.troll-busters.com

SHIELD LAW

Journalists sometimes get information from sources who do not want to be identified in news stories because they fear retribution or embarrassment. Often, this information helps journalists uncover illegal or unethical behavior by people in powerful institutions. Many journalists adhere to a long-standing professional tradition of protecting confidential sources' identities, so that these and future sources will trust reporters with sensitive information. However, if the source's information indicates the source may have information relevant to a crime or helpful to a civil litigant, the journalist may receive a legal order to reveal the source's identity. Such situations create conflicts between journalists' professional standards and their duties as citizens to obey valid legal orders or risk consequences such as large monetary fines or imprisonment.

Because journalists often are seen as performing a service in a democratic political system by informing the public about what powerful institutions are doing, legislative bodies sometimes provide protection for journalists' relationships with sources through statutes known as *shield laws.* These laws are designed to help resolve conflicts between journalists' professional duty to protect sources and the justice system's need for truthful information. In general, shield laws give journalists a right to conceal source names and other unpublished information unless there is no alternative source and the information is important and relevant to a legal controversy. This entry discusses the protection offered by shield laws and the limits of these laws when digital communications are involved.

In the United States, the Constitution's First Amendment states that "Congress shall make no law . . . abridging the freedom of speech, or of the press," but whether that means that journalists cannot be required to identify sources is disputed. There is no national statute protecting journalists and their sources, although the U.S. Congress has considered such legislation at various times. Support for a federal shield law withered after WikiLeaks revealed thousands of U.S. military and diplomatic documents on its website, leading to fears that a shield law would protect that organization and similar ones.

The U.S. Supreme Court ruled in *Branzburg v. Hayes* in 1972 that journalists had no constitutional right to conceal information from criminal investigatory bodies known as grand juries. However, the nine members of the Court were almost evenly divided on the issue and left open the question of whether journalists could conceal sources from courts in criminal trials and civil cases. The Court also invited Congress and state legislatures to provide such protection through statutes. The court decision was followed by a sharp rise in the number of subpoenas issued to journalists nationwide.

In the lower federal appellate and trial courts, the divided opinion in *Branzburg* led many judges to rule that the First Amendment provides limited protection to journalists seeking to conceal the names of confidential sources and other unpublished information. However, not all federal appellate jurisdictions recognize the privilege, and there is disagreement among those that do about who and what are protected. The federal courts' privilege rulings also have little effect on state courts and vice versa.

Each of the 50 states has its own legal system that is separate from the federal system yet coexists with it. Maryland in 1896 became the first state whose legislature passed a shield law for journalists; there are now 38 state statutory shields plus one in the District of Columbia, a city-state that comprises Washington, the national capital. New Mexico and Utah courts have adopted statewide evidence rules that include prohibitions on forcing journalists to identify sources unless certain conditions exist. In the states without legislatively created shield statutes, courts in most have recognized some form of limited protection for journalists through case law interpreting the First Amendment or state constitutions. A federal evidence rule instructs federal courts to consult common law, including state court decisions, to determine whether a privilege not to testify exists.

Specific statutes to protect journalists from being forced to reveal their sources to investigators or courts are rare outside of the United States. Other nations that give journalists at least some protection from official coercion usually do so through court interpretations of constitutional guarantees of press freedom or through general codes of evidence or court procedure. Russia's Federal Law on the Mass Media is one of the few national laws providing for source protection, and many nations from the former Soviet Union have adopted similar legislation. However, the law allows the government to require news organizations to reveal sources if needed for a criminal investigation, and Russian journalists have found the protection to be stronger on paper than in reality. A change in Russia's Criminal Procedure Code in the mid-2000s made it harder to punish the media for refusing to reveal sources.

International law also recognizes a limited right of journalists to protect sources. The European Court of Human Rights in 1996 interpreted the European Convention on Human Rights' Article 10, which guarantees freedom of expression, as providing journalists with the right to conceal source identities. Also, the International Criminal Tribunal for the Former Yugoslavia recognized a limited right of war correspondents to keep their sources confidential in 2002 and affirmed the decision in 2005.

Who Is Protected

One of the most vexing problems with creating a legal privilege is defining the word "journalist." In *Branzburg v. Hayes*, the U.S. Supreme Court stated that the First Amendment press clause protects the rights of all individuals equally, whether or not they work for the institutional press. The Court said it would be highly difficult to define a group called "journalists" that would receive extraordinary First Amendment protection because journalists were not licensed or otherwise remarkable from other citizens who might inform the public about current events. Legislation, however, allows a government to define special classes of people who receive benefits, as long as the legislation does not strip from other people rights guaranteed by the federal or state constitutions.

In the case of journalist shield laws, U.S. states have taken several approaches to defining the class of persons who can conceal sources of information. Some, like Colorado, extend protection to persons employed by the traditional print media, wire services and news and feature syndicates, and electronic media, including broadcasting stations and cable television systems. Other states, such as Nebraska and Oregon, use the same list as Colorado and add persons who publish books and pamphlets. Maryland includes specific media like Colorado but also includes persons associated with "any printed, photographic, mechanical, or electronic means of disseminating news and information to the public" (Reporter's Privilege Compendium). Other state shield laws are vague about who is protected, saying it may be anyone connected with an organization involved in producing news or just "the news media." Delaware, Florida, Indiana, Texas, and West Virginia require that persons seeking protection from subpoenas be earning income for journalistic work before they can claim to be protected by those states' laws.

State courts tend to narrowly interpret shield laws or other privileges because they may impede the judiciary's search for truth. Therefore, it may be preferable, from journalists' viewpoint, to have broad definitions in the legislation. For example, in 2005, a federal appellate court determined that the Alabama shield law did not protect a magazine writer because the law did not specifically mention magazines. However, in that case, *Price v. Time, Inc.*, the court determined that a limited First Amendment privilege protected the writer from revealing his sources.

Newer state laws and amendments to older laws include specific protections for persons who produce news on the Internet or "online" or have broad catch-all provisions for persons working for electronic media. Questions remain about whether bloggers or other Internet-based communicators without ties to traditional media organizations are protected by existing shield laws or case precedents. In 2006, a California state appellate court determined that an Internet magazine, or "e-zine," was protected under the state shield law even though the law did not mention Internet-based publishers. However, a federal court in Oregon and the New Jersey Supreme Court both rejected bloggers' claims that they were protected by laws in those states, saying their activities and profiles did not comport to common characteristics of professional journalists.

What Is Protected

All of the American state shield laws protect journalists from being forced to reveal the names of confidential sources. About two thirds of them also protect unpublished information that might not have been obtained in confidence, such as reporters' notes, unpublished photographs, and outtakes from television stories. It may seem counterintuitive to protect journalists' work product, particularly when it is nonconfidential, but many journalists would argue that the added protection makes sense. Supreme Court Justice Potter Stewart, in his dissenting opinion in the Branzburg case, suggested that reporters needed protection from subpoenas not only to keep news flowing from sources to reporters to the public but also to protect the press's independence from government interference. Going a step further, protecting the press from subpoenas for all types of information would enhance its independence and keep it from being forced into becoming an unofficial investigative branch of the government. Journalists have also argued, and courts have sometimes agreed, that news organizations are uniquely vulnerable to subpoenas because they gather information and broadcast that fact, creating an undue burden for the media.

Some states, including Louisiana, New York, and North Carolina, specifically protect "nonconfidential" information. Other states, however, imply such protection by listing the types of things protected, including notes, documents, photographs, films, recordings, tapes, and reports, to use one example from Colorado. Other state laws simply say that journalists do not have to disclose "any information" or something similar. Personal observations of criminal activity generally are not protected.

Scope of Protection

In the Branzburg decision, Justice Stewart's dissent argued that the government should not be able to order journalists to appear before grand juries without first showing that the information being sought was highly relevant to the investigation, critically important, and unavailable from other sources. Federal courts interpreting the federal constitutional privilege often use the Stewart three-part test for balancing the needs of journalists and those seeking information from them. The test is included in most state shield laws. The test creates a qualified or limited privilege, meaning that unless someone can satisfy the test's three requirements, they cannot require a journalist to testify or provide documents.

Some shield laws, however, including those in California and Nevada, do not have qualifying language and thus can be read as absolute. These laws do not provide exceptions to the rule that journalists cannot be forced to cooperate with officials or civil litigants. While this is true in theory, it is not always true in practice. In California, for example, the state's highest court ruled in *Delaney v. Superior Court* (1990) that journalists could be required to testify whether failing to do so might harm a defendant's constitutional right to a fair trial. In Nevada, the state Supreme Court ruled twice that the shield law had been superseded by another state law requiring disclosure before reversing itself in 2000 and finding that the law created a qualified privilege, despite its absolute language. New York's shield law is a bit of a hybrid, providing absolute protection for confidential information and qualified protection for non-confidential material.

Digital Age Complications

A 2017 report by UNESCO raised serious concerns about the efficacy of protections for journalists around the globe. The report noted that many countries used anti-terrorism laws and other national security measures to override protections for journalists. Meanwhile, enhanced surveillance powers and methods meant that officials in many countries could monitor phone and email traffic of journalists and their sources, often with no notice to those being monitored. The report warned that laws designed to protect journalist–source relationships were rapidly becoming outdated in most nations because they did not deal with new technologies and surveillance methods.

In the United States, state shield laws generally are silent on whether journalists have a right to be informed if their phone and email records are searched without their knowledge in pursuit of someone who leaked classified information to the press. Federal case law is also limited and generally denies journalists the right to intervene against searches of their electronic communication records.

In response to concerns about monitoring by government officials, some journalists have turned to encrypted email apps such as WhatsApp and Signal. However, an indictment against a U.S. Senate staff member accused of leaking classified material to journalists revealed that government officials had figured out how to obtain his WhatsApp and Signal messages through gaps in the encryption. A computer system known as SecureDrop was believed to be more effective at protecting communications between journalists and sources, but it was complicated to use and relatively expensive, limiting its adoption to mostly well-established media organizations.

Conclusion

Shield laws protecting journalists from being forced to reveal sources or to provide documents to courts or investigators are largely an American phenomenon. These state laws generally define who is protected and whether those persons may also conceal information such as notes, photographs, and outtakes that are not confidential. The laws generally are qualified, allowing people seeking information from journalists to persuade courts to order the journalists to cooperate. Even those that are absolute in tone have not been interpreted that way by courts.

As the Internet has become more of a news outlet, tensions have arisen over whether persons associated with new media fit the definition of "journalist" in state shield laws. Some states specifically include persons reporting online under definitions of who is protected, but in other states, courts have struggled to determine when a blog or other online publication fits the definition of journalism.

The same new technologies that are allowing more people to assume the role of journalists in informing the public also may make it easier for government officials to track communications between journalists and sources through cellular telephones and emails. There are concerns that laws meant to protect the confidentiality of reporter–source relationships are not equipped to deal with new challenges posed by technology and anti-terror laws. Technology may also be the solution to the problem, but most efforts to create encrypted messaging solutions have not proved up to the task.

Anthony L. Fargo

See also Blogs and Bloggers; First Amendment; Free Expression, History of; International and Comparative Journalism Law; Presidential Scandals, Coverage of; Press and Government Relations; Russian Federation; Secrecy and Leaks; Theories of Journalism; War Correspondents

Further Readings

Fargo, A. L. (1999). The journalist's privilege for nonconfidential information in states with shield laws. *Communication Law and Policy, 4*, 325–354. doi:10.1080/10811689909368681

Jones, R. A. (2008). Avalanche or undue alarm: An empirical study of subpoenas received by the news media. *Minnesota Law Review, 93*, 585–669.

Posetti, J. (2017). *Protecting journalism sources in the digital age*. New York: UNESCO Publishing.

Reporter's privilege compendium. (2002, 2021). Reporters Committee for Freedom of the Press. Retrieved November 12, 2019, from https://www.rcfp.org/reporters-privilege/

Smith, D. C. (2014). The real story behind the nation's first shield law: Maryland 1894–1897. *Communication Law and Policy, 19*, 3–53. doi:10.1080/10811680.2014.860828

Youm, K. H. (2006). International and comparative law on the journalist's privilege: The Randal case as a lesson for the American press. *Journal of International Media & Entertainment Law, 1*, 1–56.

Legal Citations

Branzburg v. Hayes, 408 U.S. 665 (1972).
Delaney v. Superior Court, 789 P.2d 934 (Cal. 1990).
O'Grady v. Superior Court, 139 Cal. App. 4th 1423 (Cal. Ct. App. 2006).

SHORTWAVE RADIO

Shortwave radio is a means of broadcasting over great distances, one that has been used for decades for international propaganda. Since the late 1990s, depending on the service, shortwave has been increasingly superseded by satellite-distributed broadcasts and audio streaming on the Internet.

Origins

Experiments with shortwave radio transmission date to the early 1920s, with much of the important work being done by amateur or "ham" operators. Guglielmo Marconi and other radio innovators also played a part in the technology's development. Pioneer American AM station KDKA in Pittsburgh established an experimental shortwave transmitter in Nebraska in the early 1920s to try retransmitting its signal to the west coast—and farther. A few other stations did likewise, but the limited number of shortwave receivers held back development. Amateur operators sent the first shortwave signal across the Atlantic in 1923. Shortwave was also used for long-distance telephone service across oceans—transatlantic service opened in 1927.

Shortwave came to be called *short* as it was developed because its wavelengths (associated in numerous specific bands within the 3- to 30-MHz portion of the spectrum) are shorter than the long wavelengths then widely used. Shortwave today is also called high-frequency radio.

Shortwave broadcasts proved themselves in tropical climates in the late 1920s where standard (AM) radio signals were often blotted out by atmospheric interference. Furthermore, the shortwave transmitters needed less power to disseminate a good signal than did the standard stations. By the 1930s, shortwave broadcasting was becoming an established presence in many tropical areas.

Journalism on the Air

Shortwave became a vital part of global journalism in the late 1930s as a growing number of foreign correspondents used the technique to send their reports to and from various continents, especially between Europe and the United States. This was innovative technology at the time, and it amazed American listeners to be able to hear Hitler or other European leaders, as well as American correspondents, broadcasting live rather than by means of delayed recording.

CBS led the way in applying shortwave technology among American networks. Cesar Saerchinger arranged all sorts of CBS broadcasts from Britain and Europe, most of them focusing on cultural or entertainment events and venues. NBC's Max Jordan covered Europe in somewhat the same way, slowly moving from arranging light fare to covering hard news. A young Edward R. Murrow, replacing Saerchinger in 1938, began by simply continuing what his predecessor had done—until events forced a change.

During the September 1938 Munich crisis, Murrow worked with a number of stringers to pull together reports for the network (always referred to simply as "New York"), providing the first multicity roundups of reports from journalists in Berlin, Vienna, Rome, Paris, and London, where he was based. This involved working closely with European broadcast organizations, split-second timing, and "getting air" from New York. Back in New York, H. V. Kaltenborn virtually lived in a studio for a month, catching breaks and sleep as he could. Only in that way could the multilingual journalist provide running commentary as well as translations of important overseas broadcasts given the time zone differences between the continents.

But shortwave transmissions could be notoriously unpredictable, as weather conditions, time of day, and other factors could make a voice fade and then get louder and then fade again—if static didn't obliterate the material entirely. So while broadcasts could be carefully scheduled, and laboriously prepared, they did not always get through. This was a problem of the physical properties of the spectrum used by shortwave signals and could not be overcome. It troubled international radio links for decades.

By the early 2000s, many broadcasters had abandoned shortwave service to some parts of the world. The BBC World Service, for example, now relies on web-based service for North America, Australia, and New Zealand, where high penetration of computers and web access makes such an approach viable as well as far less expensive (not a minor factor as budgets and personnel came under pressure to cut costs). German shortwave broadcasters, among others, soon followed suit.

International Services

Starting in the late 1920s and accelerating over the next decade, international shortwave served a variety of purposes. One was to link distant colonies to the home country, something the Dutch first accomplished in 1927, and the French began in 1931. The British Broadcasting System inaugurated its "Empire Service" in 1932, tying worldwide colonies to the mother country. In 1935, King George V was able to send a Christmas message to the whole Empire using shortwave. A closely related purpose was to broaden interest in and the appeal of a nation's culture—indeed, this turned out to be the most lasting role of shortwave transmission. Carrying the music, art, language, and history of a country to listeners elsewhere was a continuing appeal of the service. In 1933, Radio Luxembourg began a commercially based music and entertainment service that proved hugely popular when European domestic systems were devoted to culture and highbrow entertainment. The appeal of this station troubled other countries who could do little about it.

Probably the best known rationale for shortwave broadcasts was for political or religious persuasion. Radio Moscow was one of the first international broadcasters to utilize shortwave when it began service in 1929, soon joined by most European Nations. What little U.S. international radio there was in the 1930s was in the hands of private operators, including networks (NBC was particularly active) interested in expanding markets and religious broadcasters seeking converts while retaining those already in the fold. There was little interest in shortwave listening within the United States.

With Europe spiraling toward war, shortwave propaganda broadcasts from Germany and Italy began a veritable "radio war" with British and French radio services. In early 1942, the official U.S. shortwave Voice of America began operations. And during the fighting yet another role for shortwave appeared—so-called Black propaganda stations that while originating outside a country were made to sound as though domestic dissidents were broadcasting to their fellow countrymen. Propaganda services reached a peak during World War II with all fighting powers adding to the on-air cacophony. Some countries sought to "jam" reception of the enemy broadcasts by transmitting noise on their channels. "Tokyo Rose" broadcast to American troops from Japan and "Lord Haw-Haw" to allied forces from Berlin in an attempt to weaken their fighting morale. They encouraged tuning in by playing the latest popular music among the propaganda rants. In many cases, the fighting men enjoyed the music and ignored the rest.

The cold war between the late 1940s and 1990 made international shortwave radio even more intense. The Voice of America sought to counter the growing broadcasts from the Soviet Union and its satellite nations, all of them transmitting in many different languages. The United States also began (but hid their official funding of) Radio Free Europe and Radio Liberty, which targeted their news and cultural programming to Eastern Europe and Russia, respectively. New voices were heard—China became an important international broadcaster in its own and many western languages. Albania provided its own shrill version of communist propaganda. Some neutral nations—India among them—broadcast their own views.

The end of the cold war drastically changed international shortwave as traditional enemies began to work together. Radio Free Europe and Radio Liberty essentially merged and began to operate out of cities they had once targeted and extend their programming into the Middle East. The United States began transmitting other shortwave (as well as FM) radio services into the same region, plus less successful shortwave transmissions into Cuba (Radio Martí) and China (Radio Free Asia), both of which were heavily jammed by their target country's governments.

At the same time, evangelical Christian stations greatly increased their shortwave transmissions, often using many more languages (more than 100) than official government services. And a growing number of advertiser-supported commercial services targeted Africa and other regions lacking entertainment (chiefly music, which travels well across borders and cultures) in their own domestic service.

By the 1990s, the benefits of direct satellite broadcasting became increasingly apparent and shortwave transmissions began to decline in favor of the newer technology. The arrival of the Internet in the mid-1990s and its accelerating availability over the next decade created yet another option for effecting international communications at far less cost than big and expensive shortwave transmitters.

Christopher H. Sterling

See also Audio and Video News Services; Foreign Correspondents, Electronic; Satellite News Ggathering; Streaming Media; U.S. International Communications

Further Readings

Anderson, A. T. (2003). Changes at the BBC World Service: Documenting the World Service's Move from Shortwave to Web Radio in North America, Australia, and New Zealand. *Journal of Radio Studies, 12,* 286–304.

Berg, J. S. (1999). *On the Short Waves, 1923–1945.* Jefferson, NC: McFarland.

Ettlinger, H. (1943). *The axis on the air.* Indianapolis, IN: Bobbs-Merrill.

Kaltenborn, H. V. (1938). *I broadcast the crisis.* New York, NY: Random House.

Leutz, C. R., & Gable, R. B. (1930). Historical review. In *Short Waves* (pp. 11–32). Altoona, PA: C. R. Leutz.

Rolo, C. J. (1942). *Radio goes to war.* New York, NY: Putnam.

Saerchinger, C. (1938). *Hello America!* Boston, MA: Houghton Mifflin.

Wood, J. (1992, 2000). *History of international broadcasting.* Vols. 2. London, UK: Institute of Electrical Engineers.

World radio-TV handbook (2022). New York, NY: Billboard, annual.

SIMULCASTING

To simulcast is to provide the same program at the same time over two or more electronic media (broadcast, cable, or satellite) channels—a simultaneous broadcast. Most typical is simulcasting of broadcasts over an AM and FM station in the same market, or over both a radio and a television station. But there are many variations, and the most common today is a radio station simulcasting its signal over the Internet. The relevance of simulcasting to journalism is found most strongly in sportscasting.

Origins

The first widespread use of simulcasting in the United States utilized AM and FM stations in the late 1940s. As the new FM service developed, network and AM broadcasters argued that the most efficient way to build its audiences was with popular AM program fare, both news and entertainment. Given that the new service had little or no money to invest in program personnel or content, the idea made some sense. Of course simulcasting also obviated any reason for consumers to buy FM receivers given their existing radios could provide all the available programming. Indeed, some critics argued simulcasting was really just a plot by the AM business to prevent FM from developing into a competitor. Further, the American Federation of Musicians struck many stations, arguing that musicians should be paid twice if their performances were going to be carried on both AM and FM stations.

The musician's demand was finally resolved among the parties, but the larger AM-FM simulcasting issue took longer, put to rest in the 1960s with a series of "nonduplication" decisions by the Federal Communications Commission. These required colocated AM and FM stations to program at least half their time on the air separately. The policy argument held that simulcasting was a waste of spectrum space. Broadcasters argued their programs were none of the government's business. But the Federal Communications Commission decisions were upheld despite numerous court appeals. By the early 1980s, the now independently programmed FM business surged ahead of AM listening nationwide—and by the early 21st century accounted for nearly 80% of all radio listening.

Another application of simulcasting came in the late 1950s with experimental stereo radio broadcasts, usually of music. Before Federal Communications Commission approval of FM stereo technical standards in 1961, colocated AM and FM stations could share a broadcast with one providing the left sound channel and the other the right, though their quality was unequal. Likewise, a television and radio station (ideally FM, so both audio channels were of the same quality) could provide, say, right and left stereo channels of a music performance. An early British example came in 1974, when the BBC broadcast a recording of Van Morrison's London Rainbow Concert simultaneously on both its BBC2 television channel and on Radio 2. American public television and radio stations were the most likely to offer such broadcasts, especially when airing a live concert.

Broadcast and Internet Simulcasting

WXYC, a student-operated station at the University of North Carolina in Chapel Hill, began simulcasting its off-air (broadcast) signal on the Internet on November 7, 1994, using technology developed at Cornell University. It claims to have been the first radio station in the world to offer a concurrent Internet simulcast of an off-air signal. Many stations soon followed suit, and by the early 21st century, such simulcasting (also termed audio streaming) had become common, aided by the spread of broadband connections. Listeners could tune in to stations well beyond off-air listening range. Satellite radio services also simulcast their hundreds of channels of music and talk programming for subscribers over the air (to special receivers) and on the Internet.

In September 2006, CBS became the first network to offer a live simulcast of its evening news broadcast over the Internet. CBS also made the CBS Evening News available as an on-demand program accessible after the simulcast and allowed viewers to build their own broadcast online by choosing individual reports from each program.

Sports

Professional sports events often feature simulcast play-by-play broadcasts on radio and television. Typically, one or two announcers provide coverage on both media. The practice was common in the early years of television when many people lived far from a station, but since the 1980s, most teams have employed separate on-air personnel for television and radio coverage. Chick Hearn and Rod Hundley were the last broadcasters in professional basketball to simulcast. In baseball, Vin Scully continues to simulcast the first few innings of games. By the early 2000s, the National Hockey League had two remaining teams of broadcasters that simulcast: Daryl Reaugh and Ralph Strangis (in Dallas) and Rick Jeanneret and Jim Lorentz (in Buffalo).

In December 2007, a professional football game between the New England Patriots and the New York Giants was carried on the NFL Network (which is available on cable in fewer than 40% of the nation's homes) and was simulcast on both CBS and NBC, thus reaching virtually every television home.

Changing Technology

As a part of American radio industry consolidation and cost-cutting efforts since the mid-1990s, simulcasting has often involved transmitting the same programming over multiple stations owned by the same entity. Talk and music programming heard in one market may be presented in others at the same time, sometimes using a centrally located announcer or newscaster using voice tracking technology.

Cable television systems simulcast network programs. On some cable systems, analog–digital simulcasting (ADS) means that analog channels are duplicated as digital subchannels. Digital tuners are programmed to use the digital subchannel instead of the analog. This allows for smaller, cheaper cable boxes by eliminating the analog tuner and some analog circuitry. The primary advantage of analog–digital simulcasting is elimination of interference and, as analog channels are dropped, the ability to transmit 10 or more standard definition television (or two high definition) channels in their place. The primary drawback is the common problem of overcompression, which can result in fuzzy pictures or pixelation (breaking up of the image).

Simulcasts using satellite links raise a different challenge, as there is a significant delay because of the uplink and downlink distances required (nearly 50,000 miles round trip). Likewise, any simulcasting involving video compression also has a significant additional delay, which is noticeable when watching a local signal from a direct broadcast satellite.

One other application is common in Canada because of heavy viewing of American television programs along the common border. Signal substitution (also known as simulcasting, sim-subbing, or commercial substitution) occurs when a cable or satellite company inserts the signal of a Canadian television station onto the channel of an American station that is showing the same program at the same time. Canadian cable and satellite operators only perform commercial substitution when requested to do so by a Canadian network or station—in which case by Canadian law, they must comply.

Christopher H. Sterling

See also Federal Communications Commission (FCC); Streaming Media

Further Readings

Keith, M. C. (2007). *The radio station* (7th ed.). Boston, MA: Focal Press.

Marriott, S. (2007). *Live Television: Time, space and the broadcast event*. Los Angeles, CA: SAGE.

Sterling, C. H., & Keith, M. C. (2008). *Sounds of change: A history of FM broadcasting*. Chapel Hill: University of North Carolina Press.

SINCLAIR BROADCAST GROUP

Sinclair Broadcast Group founder Julian Sinclair Smith began with one FM radio station in Baltimore, Maryland, in 1971, and since then, his family has built one of the largest media corporations in the United States. Julian was an engineer who decided to go into business for himself and created the Chesapeake Television Corporation. The Sinclair Broadcast Group was founded in 1986 and went public in 1995. The group is traded on the NASDAQ Global Select Market under the ticker symbol SBGI (Sinclair Broadcast

Group, Inc.). The company owns, operates, and/or provides services to 191 television stations in 89 designated market areas. Sinclair's rise coincides with the decisions of the Federal Communications Commission (FCC) on ownership rules. This entry examines Sinclair Broadcast Group's origins, its battle with the FCC, its expansion, and the ethical concerns that continue to be raised by the Sinclair Broadcast Group.

Early Years—Origins of a Behemoth

Julian Sinclair Smith purchased one of the first UHF stations, WBFF-TV in Baltimore, MD, in 1971. By 1986, he and his four sons, David, Fred, Duncan, and Rob, had acquired two more UHF stations, one in Pittsburgh, Pennsylvania, and one in Columbus, Ohio. The family appointed Robert Simmons as the President and CEO of the company.

The 1990s was a period of growth for the Sinclair Broadcast Group. Newly hired CEO, David Smith, found a way around FCC ownership rulings. He created the country's first major market local marketing agreements (LMA) with WPTT-TV in Pittsburgh. This enabled Sinclair to program a second station in the market where it already owned a station. In 1994, Sinclair acquired four stations plus two LMAs in Milwaukee and Baltimore. By the end of the next year, Sinclair Broadcast Group consisted of 18 TV stations in 12 markets. The company realized US$111.5 million in fund future acquisitions. David Smith attempted to buy as many broadcast stations as possible, concentrating on secondary markets, including Memphis, St. Louis, and San Antonio where operation costs were not as expensive as the costs to run stations in New York or Chicago.

Sinclair Broadcast Group has battled with the FCC since the deregulation of the industry began in 1996. The Telecommunications Act of 1996 overhauled the existing regulations of telephone and broadcasting. The deregulation enabled more competition in local areas, by removing restrictions on media ownership and resulted in consolidation within the industry. The new regulations forced local carriers to share their communication facilities with competitors at established fair and equitable rates. Before the Telecommunications Act, a single corporation could not own more than 12 stations and was limited in their reach. The companies were limited to reaching 25% of the households in the United States. Sinclair Broadcast Group continued to acquiring stations and purchased River City Broadcasting. The acquisition of River City Broadcasting expanded the company into radio. At the end of 1996, Sinclair owned 28 TV stations in 21 markets and 23 stations in seven markets. The company's growth helped expand its profit margins.

In 1998, Sinclair doubled its size with acquisitions of Heritage, Sullivan Broadcasting, and Max Media. It had now become one of the largest television broadcasting companies in the United States, with 59 TV stations in 39 markets. It also became one of the top 10 radio broadcasters with 51 radio stations in 10 markets.

Digital Battle With the FCC

Sinclair had become a force to be reckoned with by 1999 by divesting its radio group to focus on television, anticipating the launch of digital television. The company moved their headquarters from WBFF studios in Baltimore to a new location in Hunt Valley, Maryland. Sinclair Broadcast Group campaigned to change digital television transmission standards when the FCC was considering the transition from analog to digital. The FCC intended to make 8-VSB the standard but Sinclair argued that the quality of the reception was unacceptable for indoor antennas and pushed for the Coded Orthogonal Frequency Division Multiplexing (COFDM) standard, which was also Europe's predominant method of DTV delivery. Sinclair wanted the FCC to test the two transmission signals and chose the superior version or at least let broadcasters choose between the 8-VSB standard and the COFDM. Sinclair conducted demonstrations at six sites in Baltimore to demonstrate 8-VSB's indoor reception problems and documented reception problems at 34 other sites. After a successful demonstration of the COFDM transmission to Congress, the FCC continued with their demand for the 8-VSB. FCC engineers concluded that 8-VSB transmission and tower construction would be less expensive for broadcasters. In the final ruling, the FCC conclusion stated, "We believe that the course we are taking will provide the certainty that many broadcasters, equipment

manufacturers and consumers need to invest with confidence in new technology while at the same time preserving the flexibility to accommodate innovation and experimentation. In doing so, we believe our decision will provide many benefits to American consumers."

In 2006, television stations were required to transition from analog to digital transmission. Congress authorized the distribution of an additional broadcast channel to every full-power TV station that the station would be able to launch a digital broadcast channel while simultaneously continuing analog broadcasting. It wasn't until 2009 that the stations stopped broadcasting analog transmissions.

Duopolies and Expanded Reach

In 1999, the FCC permitted duopolies in large markets but forbade them in areas with small number of stations, LMAs. Previously, the LMAs were exempt from any operator's ownership tally. The FCC rules forbid one company to control two TV outlets in markets containing fewer than eight separately owned stations. The 1999 decision made several of Sinclair's LMAs out of bounds. Sinclair would have been forced to divest their LMAs in Columbus and Dayton, Ohio; Charleston, South Carolina; and Charleston, West Virginia; if the federal judges upheld the decision. Sinclair's defense insisted that the "voice test" was a drastic solution that failed the U.S. Supreme Court's "strict scrutiny" test, which requires infringements on free-speech rights to be defined in narrow terms. The FCC ruled that the "public interest" standard must be applied to justify media ownership rules.

The battle with the FCC was unsuccessful. CEO David Smith commented, "We knew that asking a court to reconsider its original decision is generally an uphill battle. We remain gratified that the court initially ruled in our favor in finding that the FCC's duopoly rules were arbitrary and capricious" (McConnell, 2002, p. 20). Sinclair would spend the next two decades challenging the FCC's ownership rules.

The 2000s opened with the 9/11 attack, the national economy went into recession and with it the greatest decline in advertising spending since Sinclair's founding. The economy slowly improved and Sinclair's Board of Directors approved the company's first ever common stock dividend. By 2005, Sinclair completed the build out of its digital television platform and provided multichannel video programming distributors, such as cable and satellite and telecommunications companies, with programming and became the first broadcaster in the United States to request retransmission consent agreement fees. The fees provided a new revenue stream and the company built a war chest for reinvestment and acquisition. After reshuffling their network affiliations, Sinclair becoming the largest FOX affiliate group in the United States.

After the 2008 recession, Sinclair began a wave of industry consolidation. In 2011, the company purchased Four Points and Freedom Communication stations. Three years later, Sinclair had acquired 109 stations, adding over US$3 billion in assets. The company also launched new programing distribution and network content material. Sinclair claims it was producing 2,200 hours of local news per week, making the company the largest producer of local news content in the country.

From 2004 to 2014, Sinclair went from 62 stations to 167 stations, eclipsing the next rival, Nexstar by 59 more stations. Sinclair was in 77 markets, reaching nearly 40% of the U.S. population. In 2015, Sinclair created *Full Measure with Sharyl Attkisson*, a Sunday morning national news program and the COMET network, the first ever science-fiction over-the-air multicast network that is partnered with MGM. By the next year, Sinclair expanded its live sports programming and created the network STADIUM.

In 2017, the company appointed their third CEO and President, Christopher Riley. His appointment launched the company's first mission statement, "Connecting People with Content Everywhere". That same year, after the National Broadband Plan Spectrum Auction, mandated by Congress and the FCC, three station licenses were sold in Baltimore, Harrisburg, and Milwaukee for US$311 million. And in 2019, the company acquired 21 regional sports networks at a value of US$10.6 billion.

As of March 2020, Sinclair operates 191 TV stations, 607 channels, operating in 89 markets. The company continues their technological assertiveness with three technology groups with in their company. One Media, Acrodyne, and Dielectric are subdivisions implementing technical solutions and innovating new platform technologies.

Controversial Ethical Practices

The reach of Sinclair has resulted in critical evaluation of its practices. Sinclair attempts to concentrate its editorial control from its headquarters and expand its message to its affiliates. Sinclair produces and distributes mostly conservative-opinion segments, called News Central, about national and international affairs, for its local affiliate newscast. Sinclair describes the segments as a cheaper way to offer news. The partisan stance of the company is often camouflaged within newscasts as news stories. Many Sinclair viewers may not know the source of the information or recognize the name of the owner of their local affiliate but instead connect the information to the network (ABC, CBS, NBC, or FOX). Scholarly critics believe this disconnect between viewers and the affiliate ownership has implications for civic discourse, particularly if issues of media bias or local news coverage cause the news consumer to be unsure of the credibility of local news stories.

The conservative practices and ethos of the company are visible in the programming of the local affiliates. In 2004, Sinclair pulled an episode of *Nightline*, on which Ted Koppel read the names and showed the faces of dead U.S. soldiers, from all eight of its ABC affiliates. Just before the 2004 presidential election, Sinclair attempted to force its station to air a documentary that featured Democratic candidate John Kerry in an unfavorable light, accusing Kerry of worsening the plight of Vietnam prisoners of wars because of his "Winter Soldier" crusade during the war.

In 2016, President Donald Trump's son-in-law, Jared Kushner, admitted that the presidential campaign struck a deal with Sinclair to guarantee favorable coverage in return for access.

The FCC fined Sinclair US$13.3 million for running paid programming during news programs without disclosure of its sponsors. It was the largest fine ever proposed for violation of the FCC's sponsorship identification rules. Preproduced 60- to 90-second stories from the Huntsman Cancer Institute aired during news programs to look like independently generated news coverage.

In 2017, the FCC denied a merger of Sinclair with Tribune Media Company. The merger, a

US$3.9 billion deal, would have given access to 73% of the U.S. households. The merger attempt launched an internal investigation of the FCC over decisions made by FCC chair, Ajit Pai, because of the appearance the deal was significantly more beneficial for Sinclair. Sinclair's close ties with President Donald Trump added to the controversy. President Trump called the FCC's decision not to approve the deal "sad and unfair" but critics cited that the conservative company would provide favorable news coverage to the president. Sinclair stations required their stations, which include local affiliates of all four major broadcast networks, to air "must-run" segments produced by a former Trump official Boris Epshteyn, a conservative pundit.

In 2018, Sinclair was heavily criticized for its editorial control of its local television stations. Sinclair news anchors were required to read identical promo ad script criticizing, "False news and fake stories." A viral video posted by Deadspin revealed Sinclair's practice.

In the aftermath of the viral video, it was revealed that Sinclair would question job applicants about their positions on abortion and other political issues. Some applicants were turned down if they were "too liberal". News directors were solicited for donations to Sinclair's political action committee. The company has a political action committee supporting conservative agendas, notably deregulation of the media. This form of politicking is similar to the partisan newspapers of the 1800s, when newspapers openly propagandized for a particular political party. The papers were rewarded with patronage jobs or government printing contracts; for Sinclair, the partisan activity was meant to lobby the Trump administration to greenlight the Tribune merger.

A study by Kylah J. Hedding, Kaitlin C. Miller, Jesse Abdenour, and Justin C. Blankenship (2019) identified a "Sinclair Effect" on local news. Sinclair stations are more likely than non-Sinclair stations to employ sensational "palace intrigue" frames, partisan sources, and commentary. The study concluded by saying, "Media conglomerates, while invisible to the average news viewer, have the potential to exert ideological, operational or professional influence on local news organizations, in which Americans place a great deal of trust."

Dean C. Cummings

See also "Broadcast, or Broadcasting"; "Federal Trade Commission (FCC)"; "Media Conglomerates"; "Media Markets"; "Media Ownership"; "Telecommunications Act of 1996"

Further Readings

Berg, M. (2018). Meet the billionaire clan behind the media outlet liberals love to hate. Forbes.Com.

DiCola, P. (2007). Choosing between the necessity and public interest standards in FCC review of media ownership rules. *Michigan Law Review, 106*(1), 101–134.

Downs, R. (2017). FCC fines Sinclair Broadcasting Group $13M for airing paid content as news. *UPI Top News.*

Federal Communications Commission. (1996, December 27). Fourth Report and Order. Retrieved from https://transition.fcc.gov/Bureaus/Mass_Media/Orders/1996/fcc96493.txt

Feldstein, M. How Sinclair became the most insidious force in local TV news. *Washington Post*, April 10, 2018. Gale In Context: Opposing Viewpoints. Retrieved March 26, 2020, from https://link.gale.com/apps/doc/A534051229/OVIC?u=gasouthernuniv&sid=OVIC&xid=aa0d7ebb (ch)

Hedding, K. J., Miller, K. C., Abdenour, J., & Blankenship, J. C. (2019). The Sinclair effect: Comparing ownership influences on bias in local TV news content. *Journal of Broadcasting & Electronic Media, 63*(3), 474–493. doi:10.1080/08838151.2019.1653103

Jensen, E. (2005). Sinclair's shadow: Canned news and conservative commentary . . . Coming soon to a station near you? *Columbia Journalism Review, 44*(1), 49–50.

Kasakove, S. (2018). The spread of Trump TV. *Nation, 306*(7), 6.

Lester H., & Jackson, H. (n.d.). TV anchors decrying fake news puts spotlight on Sinclair Broadcast Group. *NBC Nightly News.*

Lieberman, D., & Cox, J. (2004, October 19). Sinclair broadcasting takes a beating; controversial Kerry documentary isn't its only problem: [FINAL edition]. *USA Today*. Retrieved from https://search.proquest.com/docview/408912649?accountid=11225

Matsa, K. E. (2014, May 12). The acquisition binge in local TV. Pew Research Center. Retrieved from http://pewrsr.ch/1jakbXG.

McConnell, B. (1999, October 11). Sinclair hurls DTV gauntlet. *Broadcasting & Cable, 129*(42), 19.

McConnell, B. (1999, November 22). DTV plot thickens. *Broadcasting & Cable*, 129(48), 19.

McConnell, B. (1999, December 13). FCC hasn't warmed to Sinclair pitch. *Broadcasting & Cable*, 129(51), 128.

McConnell, B. (2001, May 14). Sinclair asks for more time. *Broadcasting & Cable*, 131(21), 11.

McConnell, B. (2002, August 19). Sinclair loses on LMA ruling: station group may be out of luck in four cities, after federal court rejects its appeal (Washington). *Broadcasting & Cable*, 132(34), 20.

Sinclair Knocks FCC Duopoly Rules. (2001, September 3). *Broadcasting & Cable*, 131(37), 20.

Sky News

Sky News—Europe's first 24-hour news channel—began life on February 5, 1989, one of four channels launched by Australian-born media magnate Rupert Murdoch. Based in London, the channel represented a challenge to the two main public service broadcasting news services run by the BBC and ITN. Thirty years on, Sky News is recognized as a quality news service providing extensive national and international news equal to that provided by the BBC and ITN. This entry discusses the channel's history and ownership, its attempts to balance breaking news with more in-depth stories, its reputation, and its potential future direction.

Launch

Whatever the commercial risks of the overall project, Rupert Murdoch was taking a particular risk in launching a news channel that would have to compete against, and inevitably be compared with, the two highly regarded existing British television news services run by the BBC and ITN (the news provider for the main commercial network ITV). Both services, steeped in the culture of public service broadcasting, were regarded as among the leaders in global broadcast news. Murdoch's only previous experience of TV news was in the rough and tumble of the highly competitive television environment of Australia in which the three commercial channels sought to compete

more in terms of sensation than serious news content.

The man Murdoch recruited to launch the channel was John O'Loan, a highly experienced journalist who had spent the previous 15 years working for two of Australia's commercial news channels. O'Loan arrived in London in August 1989, facing the monumental task of starting a 24-hour news channel from scratch in just 6 months, knowing he had to create a way of doing television news that was distinctive from that of both the BBC and ITN. With that in mind he hired journalists not just from the two broadcasters but also from radio and from newspapers. These journalists, he believed, would bring new styles and approaches to the business of television news.

Controversy and Fears

Because of Murdoch's buccaneering reputation, and in particular because of his controversial ownership of the tabloid *Sun*—which only 2 years previously had been involved in a lengthy and toxic dispute with British trade union—there were fears that Sky News would be a tabloid news service with a notably right-wing stance. One of its first presenters, Frank Bough, suggested that the channel would be best compared to the mid-market *Daily Mail*, leading media commentator Steve Barnett, to observe that should this formula not work then the channel could be forced to adopt the more sensationalist news values of Britain's best-selling down-market tabloid, the *Sun*.

In their 2009 article "Towards a 'Foxification' of 24-Hour News Channels in Britain? An Analysis of Market-Driven and Publicly Funded News Coverage," Stephen Cushion and Justin Lewis sought to investigate whether Sky News had indeed become, in their words, "Foxified" (following the model of Murdoch's Fox News channel in the United States). They defined this as sensationalist news values (as opposed to public service news traditions), speculation as opposed to factual reporting, and partisanship as opposed to impartiality. They categorized stories as either "tabloid" or "broadsheet"—a rough and ready, but sufficiently robust distinction (used by other scholars) to analyze the extent to which between 2004 and 2007 Sky News's overall coverage differed from that of the BBCs 24-hour news channel. Their finding was that there was little difference between the news agendas of the two broadcasters.

Breaking News

Another aspect of the tabloidization charge related to what critics saw as Sky's overuse of the "Breaking News" on-screen moniker. In a separate 2009 article, Lewis and Cushion found that BBC News's channel used the moniker on 7% of their news items compared with Sky, who used it on 14%. The researchers suggested that the growth of the "Breaking News" concept symbolized a preference for style over substance—what they called giving news a constant feel of "newness," irrespective of whether or not it was.

But the "Breaking News" caption was about more than just about giving a sense of the newness to the channel's output. Rupert Murdoch, more than most, was aware that a 24-hour news channel would never make money (or at least that was the case until the invention of Fox News). Sky News had a different purpose. Murdoch knew that his new television network would need to win over, and then maintain the support of, the regulators, the politicians, and other sections of elite opinion. Capturing this audience was as important—if not more so—than capturing a significant audience share. An important way this was achieved was by the "Breaking News" ticker-tape at the bottom of the screen.

O'Loan has said he knew that in the offices of the people Sky News wanted to reach, televisions would be on without sound and the "Breaking News" caption was a way of capturing and holding the attention of this audience. The success of this strategy was evidenced in a British Government investigation into the BBC's news channel, which observed that most newspaper newsrooms and government offices had their televisions tuned to Sky News with the sound turned down, rather than tuning them to the BBC.

Impartiality

Critics were also concerned about the extent to which Murdoch's ownership of Sky News would result in a Fox-style right-wing slant to the news. O'Loan has reported that in his 5 years at the helm, Murdoch made only one editorial intervention—to complain about the way the channel was presenting the weather. And despite the suspicions of the critics, most observers, both academic and professional, have agreed that Sky News' political coverage has been even-handed. Backing for this came during the 2010 general election, when some Labour Party supporters claimed that Sky News was anti-Labour; the claim was rebutted by left-wing journalist Mehdi Hasan who, writing in the Labour-supporting *New Statesman*, said there was no evidence whatsoever to suggest that Sky News was biased against Labour.

Audiences

Sky News's budget has always been significantly lower than that of the BBC. Nonetheless, over the years, Sky News has garnered many industry awards and plaudits (it has won the Royal Television Society's News Channel of the Year Award 13 times). Writing in 2009, media commentator Steve Hewlett, who had held senior editorial positions with BBC and ITV, noted that Sky News was widely recognized as a service of genuine quality.

Despite winning awards and reaching elite audiences, for the first few years of its existence, Sky News barely registered in terms of the general audience, sometimes achieving viewing figures that registered as zero in the ratings survey. Its breakthrough came with the U.S.-led invasion of Iraq in 2003, which established in the British audience the "habit" of turning to 24-hour news when there was a major news story breaking. The boss of rival channel ITV, Chris Shaw, observed "extraordinary things happened to TV news" as people became addicted to rolling war coverage, with Sky News "the clear victor," increasing its audiences by a factor of seven.

In 1996, the channel's weekly reach in Britain had been around 3 million, but 2 years after, the Iraq War that figure had increased to 11 million. Since that time, its viewing figures have remained fairly constant with approximately 7% of U.K. adults citing Sky News as their most important source of news (this figure includes the audience for the channel's comprehensive website).

Just News?

One issue that successive editors of Sky News have battled with is how to strike the balance between providing rolling news and offering a service which gives more breadth and depth to the news. Initially, the channel attempted to do this by running news for the first 30 minutes of the hour and then switching to feature programs in the second half hour. But in the early days, the Sky network was faced with a titanic battle for survival with a rival satellite broadcaster, BSB, and although it offered no real news service (just 2 minutes of "rip and read" headlines), the network's overall losses meant that Sky News had to cut its budget by 10% and ditch its feature programs to become just a rolling news service.

O'Loan has said his only regret was that he was never able to sustain the sort of in-depth coverage that he thought would add significantly to the channel's coverage. In 2005, Nick Pollard, who was by then at the helm of Sky News, tried to resurrect the idea of including non-news programming. He created a series of new programs, including a daily *World News Tonight* program with James Rubin, a former spokesman for the U.S. State Department, billed as an "hour of analysis and context." But just 3 months after the relaunch, low ratings forced the channel to return to its previous diet of rolling news and Pollard moved on to pastures new.

Ownership

Big changes were to come in 2018, not in terms of Sky News's content but in terms of ownership when Murdoch ceded control of Sky as part of a restructuring of his wider media empire. He was hoping that 20th Century Fox, which he then owned, would able to take over the 61% of the Sky TV empire that was not under his control. However, after a tortuous 2-year battle, he was eventually outbid by the American telecoms giant Comcast, which also controlled NBC. During the battle, the future and independence of Sky News played a crucial role in the takeover battle, with the U.K. government intervening to secure the news channel's long-term viability. When Comcast finally won, they were required to pledge that they would maintain Sky News current funding for at least 10 years and were obliged to establish an independent board to oversee its editorial policy.

Viewers' Verdict

Over the 30 years of Sky News's existence, it has gained a solid reputation for providing fast and reliable news on a par with the best of British public service broadcasting news. Perhaps most striking, in terms of marking its acheivements, were the results of 2019 research undertaken by the UK's media regulator OfCom for its annual news consumption report. It asked those who had nominated the two 24-hour news channels as their main source of news and had a positive view of them, their opinions on a number of qualities. Of Sky News regular viewers, 80% said it was "high quality" compared with 79% for the BBC, 76% said it was accurate compared with 71% for the BBC, 73% said it was "trustworthy" compared with 71% for the BBC, and perhaps most markedly of all (given the controversies at its launch) 68% said Sky was impartial compared with just 59% of BBC regular viewers. This may have partly reflected controversies that have surrounded the BBC's political coverage since 2016.

Going Forward

The question that Sky News has wrestled with down the years—whether it should attempt to be more than a rolling news service—never really went away. Sky News head John Ryley has outlined what he saw as Sky News's mission in announcing a move away from being only a rolling news channel to one covering debate, discussion, and opinion. The channel's audience may support this move, given that a majority told Ofcom in its 2019 survey that Sky News provided "a depth of content and analysis not available elsewhere." So after a number of attempts to shift Sky News away from simply being a rolling news service to providing more depth and analysis, with its funding assured for the foreseeable future, this time round it might just succeed in achieving something that its first head wanted to do more than 30 years ago.

Ivor Gaber

See also British Broadcasting Corporation (BBC); British Broadcasting Regulation; British Commercial News Broadcasting; Comcast; Murdoch, Rupert

Further Readings

Barnett, S. (1989). Broadcast news. *British Journalism Review, 1*(1), 49–56. doi:10.1177/095647488900100111

Barnett, S., Seymour, E., & Gaber, I. (2012). From Callaghan to credit crunch: Changing trends in British television news 1975–2009 University of Westminster. Retrieved from https://westminsterresearch .westminster.ac.uk/download/8f1960fa621b98d00ffe4 ad84105db01b305936dff29c0f87b40a4d4d7637de5 /1088495/From-Callaghan-To-Credit-Crunch-Final -Report.pdf.

Chippindale, P., & Franks, S. (1991). *Dished: the rise and fall of British Satellite Broadcasting*. London, UK: Simon & Schuster.

Cushion, S., & Lewis, J. (2009). Towards a "Foxification" of 24-hour news channels in Britain?: An analysis of market-driven and publicly funded news coverage. *Journalism, 10*(2), 131–153. doi:10.1177/146488490 8100598

Gaber, I. (2018). New challenges in the coverage of politics for UK broadcasters and regulators in the "post-truth" environment. *Journalism Practice, 12*(8), 1019–1028. doi:10.1080/17512786.2018.1498297

Hewlett, S. (2009). For TV news, the news isn't all bad. *British Journalism Review, 20*(2), 41–46. doi:10.1177/0956474809106670

Lewis, J., & Cushion, S. (2009). The thirst to be first an analysis of breaking news stories and their impact on the quality of 24-hour news coverage in the UK. *Journalism Practice, 3*(3), 304–318. doi:10.1080/17512780902798737

Ofcom. (2019). News consumption in the UK: 2019. UK Office of Telecommunications. Retrieved from https:// www.ofcom.org.uk/__data/assets/pdf_file/0027 /157914/uk-news-consumption-2019-report.pdf

Shaw, C. (2003). TV news: Why more is less. *British Journalism Review, 14*(2), 58–64. doi:10.1177/09564748030142010

SNAPCHAT

Snapchat is a multimedia messaging application that features the ability for users to take photos and record short videos to send to contacts. When a user sends a message, or *snap*, using the default settings, it automatically disappears from the recipient's device once it is seen. A feature called *Snapchat Stories* lets users share longer posts that are automatically deleted after 24 hours.

By 2020, Snapchat was reported to have more than 200 million daily active users. The app is especially popular with members of Generation Z (those born after 1996), and journalists have begun to incorporate it in their reporting practices. This entry discusses the history of the app, its use by news organizations, and research on the app and its relationship to journalism.

While students at Stanford University, Evan Spiegel, Bobby Murphy, and Reggie Brown launched a photo app in 2011 that was originally called *Picaboo*, before Spiegel and Murphy relaunched it 2 months later as Snapchat. Brown filed a lawsuit alleging they pushed him out of the company without compensation. In 2014, Spiegel and Murphy settled the lawsuit with Brown for $157.5 million, with Snapchat releasing a statement giving Brown credit for the original concept for the app. In March 2017, Snapchat's parent company Snap Inc. became a publicly traded company valued at more than $30 billion, although in more recent years that valuation fell by a considerable amount.

Like other social media platforms, Snapchat has faced criticism concerning data sharing, privacy, and transparency. In May 2014, the U.S. Federal Trade Commission (FTC) brought charges against Snapchat alleging the company misled users when it promised that messages sent through the service would disappear. In actuality, third-party apps allowed users to save photo and video messages they received through Snapchat. The FTC also said Snapchat deceived consumers over the amount of personal data it collected and the security measures taken to protect that data from misuse and unauthorized disclosure. The settlement prohibited Snapchat from misrepresenting its enforcement of privacy, security, or confidentiality of users' information. In addition, the settlement required Snapchat to implement a privacy program monitored by an independent professional for the subsequent 20 years.

The app itself has evolved to feature more than messages that disappear when they are read. In

October 2013, Snapchat launched Snapchat Stories, allowing users to see photos and videos of their friends and organizations they follow for a 24-hour period. Two years later, Snapchat created Official Stories for verified brands and influencers. Around that time, organizations such as CNN, ESPN, Vice Media, Comedy Central, Buzzfeed, and others began using Snapchat Stories to share information catered to their followers. In August 2016, Instagram launched its own, similar-looking Instagram Stories.

In January 2015, Snapchat launched Snapchat Discover, which resembles an interactive magazine and includes video and text articles from selected publishers. In Discover, news organizations such as *The Washington Post* and *The New York Times* would share short segments or feature information with longer stories. In November 2016, Snapchat added the magazines *Entertainment Weekly* and *Essence* to its Discover service to provide more coverage of entertainment, lifestyle, and politics. In June 2020, Snapchat added a news aggregator in the Discover tab called *Happening Now*, with stories categorized under topics such as politics, entertainment, and sports.

As of 2015, 41% of smartphone users aged 18 to 29 used apps that automatically delete sent messages, such as Snapchat, according to Pew Research Center. By the end of 2015, Snapchat's format included videos with accompanying text-based articles, graphics, and links to additional digital content. While minor updates have been made to the interface and display, Snapchat today looks and operates similarly to the way it did in 2015.

There are challenges to using Snapchat for journalism, because Snapchat content is only available for a limited amount of time before it disappears. As Snapchat posts stories on a temporary basis, followers are encouraged to view the content close in time to when it was created, and content cannot always be located when a viewer wants to revisit it.

Snapchat was quickly integrated into newsrooms because of its reach. Snapchat, like Facebook, Instagram, and Twitter, has a live function that news organizations use to stream events or give feedback in real time to their audiences. In addition, Snapchat QR codes allow users to quickly follow news organizations that bear the Snapchat Ghost logo. These organizations included early adopters CNN, NBC's *Today* show, NBC Sports, Vice, *The Washington Post*, and *The New York Times*. In 2018, many news organizations became part of Snapchat Partners, an organization that allowed them to mix their own content with content that users share publicly using the Our Stories feature. The Our Stories feature allows partners to reuse this content on their own websites and social channels.

Paul Bradshaw published a guide in 2016 on how journalists can integrate Snapchat Stories into their news work with professional consistency. The guide highlighted how Snapchat allows journalists to download snaps to use or share on other platforms later. Using Snapchat requires understanding the app layout and adjusting to updates, including changes to the length of time material can appear on Snapchat and how the algorithm prioritizes content. The platform thrives on being informal, which has been a challenge for reporting and sourcing.

The Reuters Institute released data concerning data and messaging applications, including Snapchat, in 2019. It found platforms such as WhatsApp and Facebook Messenger were growing rapidly among those older than 25, but Snapchat and Instagram resonated most with those 18 to 25 years old.

Journalism scholars have examined changes in journalism practice resulting from the introduction of digital technologies and social media. However, research specifically dealing with Snapchat and journalism, including how journalists and news consumers interact with and use the platform, has surfaced only recently. Studies have identified the promotional and relational aspects of Snapchat, the frequency of hashtag use, and how people use the platform to share content.

Mildred F. Perreault

See also Facebook; Instagram; Social Media; Twitter; WhatsApp

Further Readings

Adornato, A. (2017). *Mobile and social media journalism: A practical guide.* CQ Press.

Beckett, C., & Mansell, R. (2008). Crossing boundaries: New media and networked journalism. *Communication, Culture & Critique, 1*(1), 92–104. doi:10.1111/j.1753-9137.2007.00010.x

Bell, E., & Owen, T. (2017, March 29). The platform press: How Silicon Valley reengineered journalism. *Columbia Journalism Review.* Retrieved from https://www.cjr.org/tow_center_reports/platform-press-how-silicon-valley-reengineered-journalism.php

Bossetta, M. (2018). The digital architectures of social media: Comparing political campaigning on Facebook, Twitter, Instagram, and Snapchat in the 2016 U.S. election. *Journalism & Mass Communication Quarterly, 95*(2), 471–496. doi:10.1177/1077699018763307

Bradshaw, P. (2016). *Snapchat for Journalists.* Victoria, BC: Leanpub.

Clark, L. S. (2016). Participants on the margins: #BlackLivesMatter and the role that shared artifacts of engagement played among minoritized political newcomers on Snapchat, Facebook, and Twitter. *International Journal of Communication, 10*(1), 235–253. Retrieved from https://ijoc.org/index.php/ijoc/article/viewFile/3843/1536

Colhoun, D. (2015, August 3). Snapchat's news experiment is working—For now. *Columbia Journalism Review.* Retrieved from http://www.cjr.org/analysis/snapchat_discover_yahoo_warner_buzzfeed.php.

Dave, P. (2017, Jan. 24). Snapchat: From an idea at Stanford to Southern California's biggest-ever IPO. *Los Angeles Times.* Retrieved from https://timelines.latimes.com/snapchat-stanford-ipo/

Dowd, C. (2016). The new order of news and social media enterprises: Visualisations, linked data, and new methods and practices in journalism. *Communication Research and Practice, 2*(1), 97–110. doi:10.1080/22041451.2016.1155339

FTC (2014, May 8). Snapchat Settles FTC charges that promises of disappearing messages were false. Retrieved from https://www.ftc.gov/news-events/press-releases/2014/05/snapchat-settles-ftc-charges-promises-disappearing-messages-were.

Gallagher, B. (2018). *How to turn down a billion dollars: The Snapchat story.* New York, NY: St. Martin's Press.

Gambarato, R. R., & Tárcia, L. P. T. (2017). Transmedia strategies in journalism: An analytical model for the news coverage of planned events. *Journalism Studies, 18*(11), 1381–1399. doi:10.1080/1461670X.2015.1127769

Lee, E. J., & Kaufhold, K. (2019). Journalistic professionalism and user motivations for Snapchat video. In Khosrow-Pour, M. (Ed.), *Journalism and ethics: Breakthroughs in research and practice* (pp. 597–612). Pennsylvania, PA: IGI Global.

Masunaga, S. (2017, March 1). The guy who came up with the idea for Snapchat got $158 million and vanished from public life. *Los Angeles Times.* Retrieved from https://www.latimes.com/business/la-fi-tn-reggie-brown-20170301-story.html

Newman, N. (2018). Journalism, media and technology trends and predictions 2018. Reuters Institute. Retrieved from https://reutersinstitute.politics.ox.ac.uk/our-research/journalism-media-and-technology-trends-and-predictions-2018

Picard, R. G. (2015). Journalists' perceptions of the future of journalistic work. Reuters Institute. Retrieved from https://reutersinstitute.politics.ox.ac.uk/our-research/journalists-perceptions-future-journalistic-work

Shaw, L. & Barron, R. (2015, January 29). The creative and offbeat ways journalists are using Snapchat. *American Journalism Review.* Retrieved from http://ajr.org/2015/01/29/creative-offbeat-ways-journalists-using-snapchat/.

Soffer, O. (2016). The oral paradigm and Snapchat. *Social Media+ Society, 2*(3), doi:10.1177/2056305116666306

Švecová, M. (2017). Journalism on social media: How to tell stories and news to young people. *Ad Alta: Journal of Interdisciplinary Research, 7*(2), 216–218.

Wenger, D. H., Owens, L. C., & Cain, J. (2018). Help wanted: Realigning journalism education to meet the needs of top U.S. news companies. *Journalism & Mass Communication Educator, 73*(1), 18–36. doi:10.1177/1077695817745464

SOCIAL JUSTICE JOURNALISM

Social justice journalism is a genre of journalism that emphasizes injustices and inequalities in society. Depending on the model of news organizations, social justice journalism might also advocate for social change and justice.

Since the new millennia and around the world, there has been a rise in social movement and protest activity. These movements call attention to social injustices and disparities that exacerbate inequalities around the world. However, beyond the viral discussions on social media that accompany most of these recent movements, various forms of journalism can play an essential role in pushing forward social justice, by bringing light to social injustice, educating publics, and pushing forward solutions-centered narratives that challenge rather than maintain the status quo.

Traditional journalism's foundations were rooted within what many scholars now view as a faulty premise of objectivity, fairness, and accuracy. This includes the idea that journalists can neutralize their position in their reporting, that "both" sides of the story should and can always be reported, and the idea that there are only two sides to begin with. The concept of objectivity helped build the reporting techniques and traditions that characterize the science of reporting in traditional journalism.

While achieving objectivity is a noble goal, journalists, editors, and newsrooms often fall short. He said/she said journalism can only create an illusion of fairness, especially when not everything everyone says is true. In addition, journalists are not actually capable of getting the perspectives of everyone and everything in a single news story. These strategies have consequences. A canon of literature indicates that news coverage does not fairly represent some groups, communities, issues, and institutions. In many cases, marginalized groups are represented negatively and stereotypically, and these representations have a lasting negative impact on the people they portray, public perceptions, opinions, and policies.

The shortcomings of journalism have encouraged both expansion within the traditional model and beyond the traditional newsroom. To expand on the coverage of social issues, social grievances, and, in some cases, social movements, a branch of journalism—social justice journalism—centers the discovery and narratives of social issues. Social justice journalism has various manifestations, but most work as an effort to expose issues that do not rise to the forefront of news cycles, to explore the parameters of social issues that are not expanded upon in traditional journalism, and to actively participate in creating justice by uncovering injustice.

Importantly, the term has only recently appeared in discourse about journalistic practice, and there are various perspectives on the boundaries of social justice journalism, as well as distinct differences in how social justice journalism looks within and outside the traditional press. In other words, social justice journalism serves as a genre of reporting within the traditional journalism framework and a type of journalism that caters more specifically to affected communities and social justice movements. Conceptualizations of social justice journalism also include elements of other genres of journalism that seek to remedy the shortcomings of traditional journalistic models and routines, including community, advocacy, solutions, and constructive journalism. What follows is a discussion and comparison of social justice orientation within mainstream media, alternative media, activist and ethnic media, and social media.

Social Justice in Traditional Journalism

The foundation of journalism includes an ethical commitment, which creates expectations for what journalism is supposed to be. Journalism is supposed to be comprehensive and loyal to the public and to serve as a check on those in power. Journalists play a variety of roles in society, such as disseminators and interpreters of information, and adversaries or watchdogs of governmental actions and institutions. From a normative perspective, the ideology of good journalism and the role designation of journalists weave at least some components of social justice-oriented reporting into the fabric of traditional journalism.

However, for decades, critics and scholars of news media have concluded that mainstream forms of journalism have routinely suppressed the voices of marginalized communities and dissent from citizens. For example, news coverage of Black and Indigenous rights protests has a lengthy history of being represented in denigrating, demonizing, and marginalizing ways. These negative patterns of representation of movements that bring light to social issues continue in the present day. Industry norms, newsroom culture, general routines, practices that accompany the production of news, and the illusion of and alliance to the concept of objectivity each contribute to the patterns that ultimately show how marginalized people, groups, and issues go unheard or poorly represented in the press. Problems related to professionalism, objectivity, and perceptions of neutrality that circulate in journalistic communities contribute and sustain these patterns.

As it appears within the framework of traditional journalism, social justice journalism is a dedicated effort of storytelling that supplements the aforementioned shortcomings. Social justice journalism is a genre or beat of journalism focused on highlighting a social issue, collective action, demands for change, and solutions and remedies for social ills and injustice. The exposure of discrimination and exploitation is central to social justice journalism and generally includes topics related to inequities in the topics such as criminal justice, health, racism and racial inequalities, civil rights, health, immigration, and environmental issues.

Because many of these topics and issues are routinely underexplored in the mainstream press, attention and exposure are at the core of social justice journalism. Journalists often feel they contribute to the mission of social movements and advocacy entities just by giving visibility to the issue. Exposure is critical; news coverage is often on the frontlines of exposing audiences to social issues. Such efforts can spark outcries, revitalize social movements, and rejuvenate political activity among citizenry. Such was the case in 2019 in U.S. territory Puerto Rico. The *Centro de Periodisimo Investigativo* helped expose behind-the-scenes conversations among high-ranking political officials (including the governor) that included sexist, racist, and homophobic commentary. The coverage was key to igniting an extended and massive citizen uprising. Another example is the work of *Milkwaukee Journal Sentinel* reporter Raquel Rutledge work. Rutledge spent extensive time

uncovering harmful working conditions faced in the coffee industry, exposing workers' routine exposure to diacetyl, a carcinogenic chemical. After renewed attention to police brutality in the United States, many noted that there was not a comprehensive record of police use of force or victims of police-involved shootings. Both *The Guardian* and *The Washington Post* produced social justice journalism projects and public databases that sought to remedy this problem and bring light to the pervasiveness of the issue. *The Washington Post* journalist Susan Ferriss's work also raised attention to the protocol of invasive searches by U.S. Customs and Border protection officers and other federal agents.

The 1619 Project, spearheaded by Nikole Hannah-Jones, is another example of social justice journalism appearing in the mainstream. The project was launched as an insert in *The New York Times* on the 400-year anniversary of the arrival in the colonies of the first African slaves. This project illuminated the horrors of slavery in the United States and connected this history with the institutional and systematic challenges and disparities that Black people face.

As shown by these examples, social justice journalism, as it is produced within the mainstream, is often deeply connected with investigative journalism efforts. Investigative journalism also of investigative journalists that produced social justice journalism include, for example, those that helped expose the Panama Papers, an expansive record of an illegal offshore finance industry that benefited powerful and wealthy individuals for decades. After the papers were published, investigations were held in more than 75 countries, protests against corruption were held around the world, and several elites, politicians, and celebrities were investigated and prosecuted. Stories from *The New York Times* journalists Jodi Kanton and Megan Twohey, and Ronan Farrow, writing for *The New Yorker*, exposed the abuse of Hollywood producer Harvey Weinstein. The stories highlight the sexual assault and harassment accusations from numerous women, which ultimately led to Weinstein's arrest and conviction. These stories were also catalysts for the modern #MeToo movement. Pulitzer Prize-winning series named as investigative series have brought light to police misconduct, drug trafficking, labor issues, and abuses of power by elites. These projects are also connected with social justice journalism.

Alternative Media and Social Justice Movements

Given the shortcomings of traditional media, marginalized people, entities, and movements often benefit from alternatives to the mainstream, which can include digitally native, alternative, and ethnic media news outlets. Alternative media amplify awareness about social justice issues and center marginalized voices. These news organizations often overtly depart from the ideological position and paradigm of "objectivity," and instead (re)position narratives and arguments to serve a particular social justice issue or marginalized group. Such organizations thereby utilize journalistic practice to represent the people and momentum of a movement. In the stratified digital sphere, alternative media are often a collective of media organizations, united by interest in a particular ideological position that typically also aligns with a social justice issue and solidarity. Adbusters, for example, is a group of global media makers, journalistic and artistic, that critiques consumerism and capitalism. Democracy Now! follows a more traditional journalistic approach to the production of content but focuses primarily on social injustice and activism.

From this perspective, social justice journalism also assumes a corrective position to traditional journalism, emphasizing specific issues, problems, and solutions; pushing against hegemonic power structures; and centering the voices from marginalized communities.

Oftentimes, journalists within this framework of social justice journalism are connected with or embedded in issues, affected communities, and movements. This means reporters are usually connected community members and are sometimes involved in other advocacy efforts. Journalists have extensive knowledge of the innerworkings of the community's networks, dimensions of the problem and how it affects the community, and access to movement leaders and advocates. Journalists are thus able to acquire expertise and access to community perspectives. This is unlike the episodic traditional journalism that often utilizes parachute models with issues considered

fringe or communities considered marginalized. Journalists producing activist media are active members of the communities they report for.

Social justice journalism in the context of alternative media utilizes a notably different business model than traditional newsrooms. While traditional newsrooms are designed as businesses that make profits, social justice journalism's business model is community oriented and serves as a mechanism that connects people with the information and resources needed to unravel in justice. As such, alternative media publications and periodicals show up in variety of forms, including newspapers, magazines, journals, radio and television broadcasts, and zines.

Activist and Ethnic Media as Social Justice Journalism

Activist and ethnic media publications are also forms of social justice journalism, and what follows is a brief and thus incomprehensive illustration of how these presses and publications have worked to promote social justice by providing the narratives of change that were absent in mainstream press publications. Activist and ethnic presses have a rich history in documenting the trials that accompany major social changes around the world.

Such was the case with the abolitionist movement in the United States. Unable to have Black voices heard in the mainstream press, *The Freedom's Journal* was created to "plead our own cause"—a declaration central to Black presses still today. Early Black newspapers and publications focused on public discussion of colonialization, slavery, and elevating Black people in the United States and beyond. These publications were useful in educating and mobilizing communities. The *Chicago Defender*, founded in 1941, included central information for Black communities during turbulent times that went unconsidered and unreported in white-run mainstream presses. Papers like the *Chicago Defender* notably housed many of the debates about ways in which Black people would achieve civil rights.

The social justice journalism in support of women's rights found its roots in Black publications, with Black women like Maria Stewart at the helm. In general, women also struggled to gain access to the power of the mainstream press and were privy to a series of struggles that sought to silence their voices. But, as the Civil War approached, tensions between abolitionists and suffragists mounted, and white feminists began a legacy of publications that emphasized women's rights and reimagining the role of women in society, with varying and sometimes contradictory levels of progressiveness. Today, organizations such as The 19th (www.19thnews.com) continue the work of amplifying the voices and concerns of women and gender diverse people. This media outlet takes a new approach to digital news production, reporting news with gender, identity, and politics in mind, but also avoiding editorial and opinion articles in an effort to remain nonpartisan.

The first U.S. Native American newspaper, *Cherokee Phoenix* (1828), was a bilingual publication that advocated against the Indian Removal Act of 1930. Today, the publication remains a multiplatform publication that serves the Cherokee community. Lesbian, gay, bisexual, transgender communities have also utilized advocacy models of social justice journalism to advocate for recognition and equality, and create and form communities.

Advocacy-centered models of social justice journalism often reimagine traditional ideas of sustainable business models. Many publications have short life spans, fueled by volunteerism and personal dedication but lasting only few months or years. Others have a decades-long history of serving communities and addressing social justice issues. The advent and adoption of digital technologies revolutionized opportunities for social justice journalism to flourish. The role of information technology in media for social justice in society is unmistakable. New technologies and communication channels expanded the breadth of all forms of media and allowed new ways for people and journalists to harness the media power needed to liberate communities. In the context of activist and ethnic media, journalism for social justice continues to thrive online, and advocacy remains essential for many online publications. Social justice journalism has played an important role in unraveling, documenting, and validating some of the world's most egregious human injustices.

Social Justice Journalism in a Digital Age

The creating, adoption, and accessibility of new technologies like cell phones, high-speed Internet, and social media have also drastically change how we understand journalism and journalists, and how social movements and advocacy function. New iterations of social justice journalism are intimately tied to this shift in media production and access. Social media have helped connect communities and movements in unprecedented ways. The viral spread of videos that document the human tragedies that accompany injustices of racism, sexism, homophobia, and ableism have been pivotal for pushing public awareness about social inequalities. Hashtags have helped link conversations across social media platforms and networks, giving organization and structure to mediated public discourse and citizen reporting. Social media posts connected to this hashtag activism offer updates, mobilization information, editorials or opinions, and other features that are characteristic of social justice journalism. Data from social media users around the world were a critical part of empowering publics across time and space, and social media have been at the helm of connecting some of the massive protests in recent years such as the Arab Spring, which included protests against oppressive governments and social inequality starting in Tunisia in 2011 and spreading across many countries; the 2017 #MeToo movement, which pushed against sexual abuse and violence; and March for Our Lives movement (#enoughisenough) that followed the Parkland, Florida, mass shooting at a high school in 2018. Social media were also essential facilitators for the Black Lives Matter movement, which principally pushed against racism and police brutality. The 2014 killing of Michael Brown in Ferguson, MO, thrust the social movement popularly referred to as the *Black Lives Matter movement* to the forefront of public attention. Social media helped drive mainstream media attention to the social justice issue, and as such, social media have become an invaluable resource for the further production of social justice journalism.

It is important to note though that in the mainstream press, attention is cyclical and is often driven by human tragedy. In other words, more press attention is granted when violence and injustice must be elevated and amplified by networked media and on social media. But this does not necessarily constitute social justice journalism. Scholars have shown that while social movements benefit from the exposure, the coverage in traditional media often pushes forward a narrative that marginalizes or demonizes social movements, collective action efforts, and movement demands. But for some issues, coverage is more negative than others, and so the degree to which the mainstream media contributes to really representing the breadth of a social justice issue and its movement is contingent. As such, while social media help facilitate attention to social justice issues and advocacy, the resulting mainstream coverage is not the equivalent of social justice journalism.

Technology accessibility, adoption, and advancements have diversified the media landscape and upended the stronghold traditional media organizations used to have on disseminating information. Media creators across a broad spectrum have been able to contribute to the public narrative and discussion through digital means. This shift requires us to rethink what journalism is and diversify our understanding of how journalism can center and prioritize the human condition and contribute to its democratic role. Social justice journalism offers an opportunity to emphasize the importance of journalists as watchdogs for democracies and is aimed at eradicating injustice. Journalism within the mainstream, in alternative spaces, for specific communities and about specific issues are essential forms of social justice journalism that can be seen in the media landscape today.

Danielle K. Kilgo

See also Advocacy Journalism; Alternative News Media; Constructive Journalism; Ethnic Press; Investigative Journalism; Solutions Journalism

Further Readings

Downing, J. D. (2000). *Radical media: Rebellious communication and social movements*. Los Angeles, CA: Sage.

Gitlin, T. (2003 [1980]). *The world is watching: Mass media in the making and unmaking of the new left*. Berkeley: University of California Press.

Harlow, S. (2017). *Liberation technology in El Salvador: Re-appropriating social media among alternative media projects*. London, UK: Palgrave Macmillan.

Kilgo, D. K., & Harlow, S. (2019). Protests, media coverage, and a hierarchy of social struggle. *The International Journal of Press/Politics, 24*(4), 508–530. doi:10.1177/1940161219853517

Lumsden, L. J. (2019). *Social justice journalism: A cultural history of social movement media from abolition to #womensmarch*. New York, NY: Peter Lang.

Mourão, R. R. (2019). From mass to elite protests: News coverage and the evolution of antigovernment demonstrations in Brazil. *Mass Communication and Society, 22*(1), 49–71. doi:10.1080/15205436.2018 .1498899

Nelson, J. L., & Lewis, D. A. (2015). Training social justice journalists: A case study. *Journalism & Mass Communication Educator, 70*(4), 394–406. doi:10.1177/1077695815598613

Nikunen, K. (2018). *Media solidarities: Emotions, power and justice in the digital age*. London, UK: Sage.

Ostertag, B. (2006). *People's movements. People's Press: The Journalism of Social Justice Movements*. Boston, MA: Beacon Press.

Steinke, A. J., & Belair-Gagnon, V. (2020). "I know it when I see it:" Constructing emotion and emotional labor in social justice news. *Mass Communication and Society, 23*(5), 608–627. doi:10.1080/15205436 .2020.1772309.

Weaver, D. H., & Wilhoit, G. C. (1996). *The American journalist in the 1990s: US news people at the end of an era*. Mahwah, NJ: Lawrence Erlbaum.

Williams Fayne, M. (2020). The great digital migration: Exploring what constitutes the Black Press Online. *Journalism & Mass Communication Quarterly, 97*(3), 704–720. doi:10.1177.10776990 20906492

SOCIAL MEDIA

The primary functions of social media are for individuals to create a profile, build connections (e.g., friends or followers), and to communicate with those connections through the site. Today, social media are prolific in part due to their presence as mobile applications (apps) on cell phones, as well as their ability to be accessed through the Internet.

Arguably the first social media site was SixDe-grees, launched in 1997. SixDegrees had users identify family and friends and operated from the idea that there are only six degrees of separation between people around the world. Users could log in to the website and see how their connections spread out through their network. The site never gained traction and was shut down in 2001. It would open the door for other attempts at social media, however, such as Friendster in 2002, MySpace in 2003, and Facebook in 2004. With Facebook came a large shift in how individuals engaged with and conceived of social media; Friendster had a decidedly interpersonal slant, and MySpace had been born out of the music industry. Facebook would, from its earliest years, be used not just for networking with friends, but for the organization of groups to discuss a wide range of topics. When Facebook went public in 2006, greater shifts were seen wherein the creation of Pages for anyone from celebrities to politicians to news sources created the opportunity to connect with users and share content. Facebook—along with Twitter, founded in 2006, and Instagram, launched in 2010—represent the core commonly used social media sites today.

In a review of the past decade of technology trends, a December 2019 report from the Pew Research Center noted that roughly 72% of adults in the United States are users of social media and turn to social media not only to connect with friends and family but also to read the news and engage with politics. In an increasingly digital world, it is important to reflect on the role of social media within journalism, taking account of key sites, practices, and challenges that can be faced.

Facebook

Since its inception in 2004, Facebook has grown to over 2 billion monthly active users. Facebook is a social media site where individual users can connect and communicate with friends and family by sending "friend requests." Facebook users are also able to "follow" public organizations, famous personalities, and other notable public figures through their Page. Facebook's ecosystem offers a plethora of communication tools for journalists to employ, such as Pages (a profile for journalists or news

organizations), Facebook Live Video (livestreaming of content), Instant Articles (distribution of news directly through the site), and Stories (a feature that allows short videos or images that can link to additional news content from the top of the newsfeed).

The Pew Research Center also stated that as of 2019, 55% of American adults get news from Facebook compared to that of 2018, which ranked at 43%. Even though Facebook can satiate the news diet for its users, it also gratifies journalists in different aspects.

Facebook offers news organizations the opportunity to engage with the public through sharing their content, which subsequently drives more traffic to their website, creating a mutually beneficial partnership between news organizations and Facebook. Pages are not just for news organizations; individual journalists can also have a Page on Facebook. By creating a Page, freelance and individual journalists can interact with their potential audience within their community by talking to followers about recent work they have published in different outlets, while also gaining insight on Facebook user's opinions about topics they are researching for future publication. Facebook offers an ambient environment for journalists so they can monitor new trends of collective intelligence—loosely organized groups of people who work together electronically to communicate, share specific knowledge, and discuss events—while tapping into immediate access of information (see Hermida, 2010). Collective intelligence is analogous to the notions of crowdsourcing, peer production, wisdom of crowds, and wikinomics. Essentially, today's journalists are able to monitor Facebook as a part of their daily newsgathering routine.

Facebook not only allows journalists to obtain immediate access to information, but it is also utilized as an official news source. Depending on the subject matter, it is not uncommon for individual citizens to be directly quoted in news stories based on comments or videos shared on the site. Facebook is a platform that provides a large variety of sources that journalists might not have been able to access before, whether it be users livestreaming events that provide video and/or audio for a breaking news story (e.g., protests, terrorist attacks) or commenting in response to news shared. Journalists can engage more directly with the public and can draw on their resources to offer a more in-depth look at the news.

Twitter

Launched in 2006, Twitter is a primarily text-based social media site that relies on short-form limits (originally 140 characters, now 280). On Twitter, users can "follow" other accounts, which allows their posts to be shared in a common feed, similar to Facebook. Twitter accounts can be made private, limiting access to tweets to just one's followers, or public, allowing anyone who knows a user's Twitter handle to view their tweets. Public accounts are ideal for news organizations and individual journalists to gain new followers and to connect with their broader audience. While one of the lesser used social media sites overall with roughly 300 million active monthly users, those who do use Twitter often cite the app as a primary location for their daily news consumption. Twitter's popularity as a news source is highest with 30- to 49-year-olds and 18- to 29-year-olds (Pew Research Center, 2018).

The posts made by users on Twitter are called *tweets* and can include the attachment of a link to a website, a picture, GIF, or short video in addition to the 280 character-limit text. Users can "like" a tweet (previously called *favorite*), "retweet" or share a tweet, and comment (respond) to a tweet. Users are encouraged to use hashtags in their posts (e.g., #breakingnews) to identify the core content as a way to connect with other users on the site.

Hashtags and other commonly used words or phrases in tweets are identified as "trending topics" on Twitter, which can be viewed based on the country one is in. Hashtags can help to give attention to key topics in the news as well as generate topics that subsequently may be covered in the news (e.g., #MeToo). Of concern is the potential for trending topics to spread misinformation, particularly during or immediately after breaking news stories (see "Challenges" section later in this entry).

In addition to everyday people engaging with breaking news on Twitter, the site has created the opportunity for journalists and publishers to build relationships with their consumers. While the most followed accounts on Twitter are primarily celebrities, the CNN Breaking News Twitter account (@cnnbrk) was identified as the 15th most followed account on Twitter as of June 2021 with over 61 million followers; CNN's main account (@CNN) was ranked #21 with 53.7 million followers, followed by *The New York Times* (@nytimes) account ranked at #25 with 49.8 million followers. Internationally, BBC Breaking News (@BBCBreaking) ranked #27 with 47.8 million followers. Twitter can also be useful for freelancing journalists, who seek a platform to share their content created with followers beyond the primary publisher.

Instagram

Instagram launched as a mobile app in October 2010, filling a gap in the existing social media market by relying on images and videos instead of text. While Facebook incorporated all three components, and Twitter led with text as most important, Instagram put the visual front and center, encouraging users to apply filters to square images. Users of Instagram create a short profile and post their own images and/or videos. They can follow other accounts that subsequently populate their newsfeed and can use the "Explore" tab to view popular posts across the site. Unlike Facebook and Twitter, Instagram is primarily a mobile app, although users can access and view content from the Internet as well. In 2012, Facebook acquired Instagram, allowing users to link content shared on Instagram to their Facebook profile. As a result, several newer features of Facebook are also on Instagram (e.g., livestreaming, stories).

Compared to Facebook and Twitter, Instagram has been used to a lesser degree for the news. However, Instagram is one of the most popular social media sites for young people today, with over 1 billion active accounts on the site (more than double that of Twitter). Facebook, as the owner of Instagram, saw the potential to connect to a broader audience, and in 2019 instituted Instagram Local News Fellowships as part of the broader Facebook Journalism Project. This allowed journalism students to intern in newsrooms to help publishers grow their Instagram following.

One of the most popular features on Instagram is the use of interactive Stories, which has over 500 million daily active users. In an interactive story, a journalist can pose questions, polling users on anything from what news they would like to see more of to their opinion on a preselected topic. Another popular feature on the site is Instagram TV (IGTV). On IGTV, users can upload longer, vertical videos to the site. IGTV creates the opportunity to embed longer segments from televised broadcasts to share with a digital audience. Journalists and publishers also can rely on the use of geotagging to increase the reach of their content on Instagram. Geotagging allows a user to identify the location of their post, which can increase the visibility of the content when other users on the site search that location. Unlike Twitter and Facebook, users cannot embed hyperlinks directly into a post on Instagram. However, they can include a hyperlink in their Instagram biography (bio) that allows followers to learn more about content off-site. For news organizations, using external services to allow them to link to multiple stories from their bio can be useful.

Challenges

According to a Pew Research Center October 2019 report, one in five adults in the United States receive their news through social media, overtaking print newspapers. With this rise in consumption comes a need for journalists to be aware of the concerns that exist with social media use. These include but are not limited to fake news, fake accounts, unknown algorithms, fragmented audiences, and an increased opportunity for citizen journalists to provide access to content outside of the industry standard, creating uncertainty about breaking news stories.

Fake news can be understood as content shared online that lacks a foundation in reality, viewed as deliberate misinformation to the public. Fake news stories range from over-the-top human-interest stories to important political issues (e.g., the 2016 U.S. presidential election and Brexit). One of the greatest benefits of social media (reach) becomes then a challenge as users struggle to know which news they see is real. In response, sites like factcheck.org and snopes.com have gained in popularity so Internet users can verify if what they are reading is real.

The concern of "fake news" was attached to Facebook after the 2016 U.S presidential election, wherein it was revealed that several of the most popular news stories shared on the site in the lead up to the election contained misleading and sometimes false information. Facebook has faced increasing pressure since to protect the data of its users, delete fake accounts, and to fact-check impugned news articles. Twitter also faced backlash over the spread of fake accounts (e.g., bots) and fake news on the site, facing scrutiny for how the site has been used during elections around the world. The ability for hashtags to go viral as a result of these fake accounts has been the topic of debate. During the 2019 gubernatorial election in Kentucky, the effects of fake news were on full display, when an account tweeted that they had "shredded a box of Republican mail in ballots." Retweeted out almost immediately, the message spurred the hashtag "#StoptheSteal," and even though the account was suspended shortly after, flagged as a bot, the message would subsequently lead to a recount of votes, delaying the final results of the election by days. Instagram is also not immune to fake news concerns, having recently dealt with "deepfake" videos (i.e., videos that have been altered to distort reality) and edited images that are shared on the site. One example of this was a video of Representative Nancy Pelosi wherein she appeared to be drunk; it was revealed that the clip came from a video that had been slowed down and altered to create the appearance of inebriation. In January 2020, Facebook announced a new policy aimed at the identification and removal of deepfake videos, highlighting the continued need to modify and extend the parameters of acceptable content on social media as misinformation can spread easily online.

In 2009, Twitter worked to combat fake accounts trying to represent organizations and people through the site by introducing "verified accounts"—if an account was verified as real and belonged to the person or organization that claimed to run the profile, Twitter would place a blue and white checkmark next to the username (e.g., @nytimes is the verified account for *The New York Times*). Other sites (e.g., YouTube, Instagram, and Facebook) have since added similar verification markers, meant to help users know the content shared is real. While this helps to combat misinformation from well-known accounts, the ability for fake news to spread from lesser known accounts remains an issue. In recent years, Facebook and Twitter have both taken greater steps to verify accounts and news shared, with the opportunity for users to flag suspicious activity.

The ability for social media sites to manipulate what users see is also an increasing challenge faced by journalists and news organizations today. While a newspaper may create content to share through sites like Facebook and Twitter, there is no guarantee that users will see it due to algorithms and other unknown, often proprietary reasons. The Pew Research Center, in an October 2019 report, highlights this issue in noting that 88% of Americans are aware that social media can control what news they see and that 62% believe social media sites have too much control, resulting in a worse mix up of news.

The sorting algorithm is another issue Facebook users face when using the platform. The sorting algorithm is one of the most popular forms of algorithms on social media networks. The sorting algorithms collect as well as examine input data to create a streamlined output for users (see Johnson, 2017). In other words, users' data creates users' personal streamlined "News Feed," which reflects the personal interests of each user of a given site. Individualized news feeds create a barrier for journalists because there is not a free-flowing marketplace of ideas. Instead, users have their filtered realities online and can easily miss a news article that appears in the News Feed of one user but not another. Until a story more broadly trends on social media, the chances that a user knows about that content are decreased as a result.

A final challenge of social media is users taking on the role of citizen journalists. The ability for any user of social media to share news online can, at times, privilege speed over accuracy. One such example was the Boston Marathon Bombing that occurred in 2013. News of the bombing and images from users who were in attendance were shared and reshared as it became a trending topic on Twitter. Users began to speculate, using images shared by other users, about potential suspects in the bombing. False claims were made and retweeted through the site, leading to a misidentification of who was responsible for the bombing. This kind of citizen journalism has grown increasingly common on social media sites like Twitter, wherein users can engage with messages and create viral opportunities for connecting with more people around the world on a given topic.

Future Directions

Increasingly, younger users of social media have shifted away from the core sites (e.g., Facebook) in favor of new technologies that offer features they find to be more appealing. Indeed, as social media users become increasingly concerned with issues related to privacy and fake news, new social media can fill in to create opportunities for publishers to connect with a new generation of consumers.

Snapchat is an image and video-based social media application. The niche of the site, when released in 2011, was that posts ("snaps") were ephemeral instead of staying constant on someone's profile; users would have one chance to watch the short video or view an image (anywhere from 1 to 10 seconds) before it disappeared, unable to be retrieved. Snapchat would later allow users to save posts, which would alert the creator of the original snap. The addition of the "Discover" feature in 2015 created the opportunity for news organizations to capitalize on the use of Snapchat; sites like CNN are able to have "channels" that Snapchat users can watch for video content to take in the daily news. A report from the Pew Research Center in 2018 suggests Snapchat is used more than twice as much for news consumption for 18- to 29-year-olds compared to older generations, suggesting that the site is an opportunity to connect with a younger audience who may be less likely to watch the news in more traditional formats.

TikTok, launched in 2017, is a video-sharing platform, and one of the newest social media apps, with over 500 million active users. Users can share original video content ranging from 3 to 60 seconds, depending on the type of content. A heavy amount of the content on TikTok overlays a user's own video with music or audio from viral clips. Users can click through a video to see other content that relies on the same audio or music across the site. TikTok has emerged as a branding opportunity for individual reporters and news organizations, although some organizations (e.g., NBC News) are sharing news through the app as well. Meanwhile, *The Washington Post* has engaged the meme-culture of the site by sharing videos that use common hashtags and audio clips as opposed to curated news stories. TikTok, like Snapchat, is geared toward younger audiences, with the majority of users between 16 and 24 years of age.

YouTube, founded in 2005, is a video-sharing platform that straddles the line of social media but is often included in reports on social media use. In their 2018 report on social media consumption, the Pew Research Center noted that YouTube had seen one of the largest increases in users that got their news from the site, up by 6%. On YouTube, accounts in good standing can post videos up to 12 hours in length, while all users have the ability to upload videos up to 15 minutes long. YouTube has provided the opportunity for segments from shows (e.g., *The Today Show*) to be shared digitally sooner after they air, increasing the reach of news produced. Several news organizations have also created content solely for digital purposes that they share through their account with subscribers. In 2011, YouTube added YouTube Live as part of the site, which allowed users to livestream content to their subscribers. News organizations like C-SPAN, Fox News, and USA Today have used the livestream feature to connect with viewers on the site. Unlike other social media, YouTube has also emerged as a cross-generational site, used as much by young adults as older generations, increasing its value for journalists to connect with a diverse audience.

Final Thoughts

Social media have become an everyday tool for communication by hundreds of millions (and in the case of some sites, billions) of people worldwide. The immediacy, spreadability, and reach of many of these sites make them ideal for journalists and publishers to connect with potential consumers, benefiting both the publisher and social media site. With each new site launched, additional benefits and challenges for journalists and publishers arise. By attending to the features of those sites that can enable opportunities to connect and share the news, journalists can stay current and reach a broader audience than if they used traditional sources of media consumption.

Natalie Pennington and Serena Hicks

See also Citizen Journalism; Facebook Snapchat; Fake News; Snapchat; Twitter; YouTube

Further Readings

Auxier, B., Anderson, M., & Kumar, M. (2019, December 20). 10 tech-related trends that shaped the decade. Pew Research Center. Retrieved from https://www.pewresearch.org/fact-tank/2019/12/20/10-tech-related-trends-that-shaped-the-decade.

Bruno, N. (2011). *Tweet first, verify later? How real-time information is changing the coverage of worldwide crisis events*. Oxford, UK: Reuters Institute for the Study of Journalism.

Ellison, N. B., & boyd, d. (2013). Sociality through social network sites. In W. H. Dutton (Ed.), *The Oxford handbook of internet studies* (pp. 151–172). Oxford, UK: Oxford University Press.

Hermida, A. (2010). Twittering the news: The emergence of ambient journalism. *Journalism Practice, 4*(3), 297–308. doi:10.1080/17512781003640703

Johnson, J. D. (2017). Ethics, agency, and power toward an algorithmic rhetoric. In A. Hess & A. L. Davisson (Eds.), *Theorizing digital rhetoric* (pp. 196–208). New York, NY: Routledge, Taylor & Francis Group.

Ju, A., Jeong, S. H., & Chyi, H. I. (2014). Will social media save newspapers? Examining the effectiveness of Facebook and Twitter as news platforms. *Journalism Practice, 8*(1), 1–17. doi:10.1080/17512786.2013.794022

Katz, J. E., & Mays, K. K. (2019). *Journalism and truth in an age of social media*. New York, NY: Oxford University Press.

Lewis, S. C., & Molyneux, L. (2018). A decade of research on social media and journalism: Assumptions, blind spots, and a way forward. *Media and Communication, 6*(4), 11–23. doi:10.17645/mac.v6i4.1562

Shearer, E., & Matsa, K. E. (2018, September 10). News use across social media platforms 2018. Pew Research Center. Retrieved from https://www.journalism.org/2018/09/10/news-use-across-social-media-platforms-2018/.

Shearer, E., & Grieco, E. (2019, October 2). Americans are wary of the role social media sites play in delivering the news. Pew Research Center. Retrieved from https://www.journalism.org/2019/10/02 /americans-are-wary-of-the-role-social-media-sites -play-in-delivering-the-news.

Schmidt, C. (2019, June 18). Meet TikTok: How the Washington Post, NBC News, and The Dallas Morning News are using the of-the-moment platform. Neiman Lab. Retrieved from https://www.niemanlab .org/2019/06/meet-tiktok-how-the-washington-post -nbc-news-and-the-dallas-morning-news-are-using-the -of-the-moment-platform/.

Tandoc E. C., Jr., Lim, Z. W., & Ling, R. (2018). Defining "fake news." *Digital Journalism, 6*(2), 137–153. doi:10.1080/21670811.2017.1360143

Twitter: Most followers (2020, February). Friend or follow. Retrieved from https://friendorfollow.com /twitter/most-followers/.

Wilson, Y. (2019). *The social media journalist handbook*. New York, NY: Routledge.

SOCIAL MOVEMENTS AND JOURNALISM

The term *social movements* is generally used to refer to organized campaigns developed by citizens focusing on a particular topic, often political or social in nature. These movements can take place in small, local communities or across nations. Modern social movements utilize technology to mobilize large groups of people and to spread the word about their efforts. This entry traces the development of several social movements and discusses social movements' relationship with the media, journalists, and technology.

Social Movements

Social and political change has occurred worldwide due to the efforts of those involved in social movements. In the United States, women's suffrage, the growth of labor unions during the Industrial Revolution, and laws to protect the civil rights of Black people all resulted from social movements. Worldwide, movements have changed governments, driven out leaders, and brought sweeping social change. Movements differ from protests in that they are sustained, organized, and long lasting.

In Europe in 1848, unrest regarding years of economic depression and difficult living conditions led to a series of revolutions dubbed the "People's Spring." Across Europe, citizens banded together in cities and capitals to force governments to embrace democracy. These movements had some short-term successes, and one outcome of this movement was Karl Marx's creation of the Communist Manifesto, which would eventually fuel the movement for communism. Ultimately, the monarchies and governments of Europe remained largely intact, but this movement inspired, at least in name, the Arab Spring. However, the Arab Spring movement had modern tools to hasten its spread.

The Arab Spring, a series of uprisings against authoritarian governments in the Middle East and North Africa that began in 2010, was similar to the People's Spring in that it stemmed from citizens' unrest over living conditions and treatment by governments, and also that it spread beyond the borders of one nation. Modern technology afforded the ability to spread movements both within and outside of the affected areas through the use of Internet and mobile applications. The movement began with a protest in Tunisia that led to that country's authoritarian dictator fleeing the country. Word of this act spread quickly via news reports online, and organizers were able to activate large groups more quickly thanks to email, SMS, and Twitter. Via Twitter, journalists and citizens around the world were able to watch the protests unfold in real time. Similar protests spread quickly and led to regime change and even civil war in some nations.

In the United States, as well as in other Western nations, many different movements since 2000 have focused on social and political policy change. Beginning in 2011, the Occupy Wall Street movement was born in the United States. Occupy Wall Street was focused on economic inequality and resulted largely from the 2008 financial crisis. Protestors of various backgrounds and political leanings camped out on Wall Street in the heart of New York's financial district to draw attention to economic policies that led to drastic inequalities among citizens. Although this movement was focused on the United States, it was likely inspired by similar acts of protest and occupation occurring across Europe.

One of the most well-known social movements in the United States is the Black Lives Matter movement, which grew out of the 2012 shooting death of unarmed, 17-year-old African American teenager Trayvon Martin in Sanford, Florida. Martin was killed by a member of the neighborhood watch, George Zimmerman, who in 2013 was acquitted of the crime. The movement was started by three women, Opal Tometi, Patrisse Cullors, and Alicia Garza, to raise awareness of violence against African Americans and address the systems that have led to and support this violence.

Tools of the Black Lives Matter movement have informed organizers of subsequent movements, including the #MeToo movement and Moms Demand Action. Both of these movements were also created by women to address social issues that impacted their ability to live full and safe lives. Tarana Burke began using the phrase "me too" in online blog posts in 2006 to call attention to sexual violence perpetrated against women, but the use of the #MeToo hashtag on social media took off in 2017 in response to reporting on sexual assault allegations against Hollywood producer Harvey Weinstein. As revelations of sexual harassment and assault by other powerful men in Hollywood and other industries followed, the hashtag became the name of a movement against sexual violence.

The Moms Demand Action movement was started by Shannon Watts the day after the Sandy Hook Elementary School shooting in 2012. This movement also began online, on Facebook, and has since developed a strong following on Facebook, Instagram, and Twitter, as well as leading to local chapters of members who meet in person in all 50 states. These movements, Black Lives Matter, #MeToo, and Moms Demand Action, represent an important shift in social movements—their ability to grow from online environments to real-world communities of people working for a common cause. Their ability make this shift is related to their relationship with the media.

Journalism

Social movements depend on the work of journalists in order to be successful. Indeed, before the Internet, information spread to the masses largely via mass media. In those times, getting the attention and interest of journalists was critical to spreading the word regarding a movement's platform. However, getting the attention or interest of a journalist was not the only hurdle. Activists and organizers also had to get the support of the journalists' editors and news organization in order for their message to get out.

Journalists at traditional media outlets must work though editors in order to publish their reports. Editors work for media companies, and even in democratic countries, special interests can put pressure on news organizations to squash coverage or influence what is covered. In addition, news organizations depend on having audiences and, in most cases, advertisers, whose willingness to subscribe or advertise could be influenced by their satisfaction with the news being covered. For example, during the civil rights movement in the 1960s, mainstream news organizations were largely staffed by white males, while their leadership was largely white and male as well. Institutionalized racism and a lack of understanding between journalists and the people they were covering would influence how reporters covered protests in local communities during this era.

In the United States, the news media and communities have become more diverse, and with the evolution of the Internet, reporting is not solely in the hands of the mass media. However, it cannot be overlooked that many social movements occur in countries where there is no democracy or free press. In some nations, reporters may work for government-controlled media that could choose not to report on movements that they prefer not spread, or report mistruths about activists and protestors.

Hong Kong, a semiautonomous Chinese city, once had a reputation as one of the most open Asian cities for flow of news and information. However, in the 2000s, more journalists reported self-censoring due to pressure from China, which in recent years has moved to restrict Hong Kong's freedoms. During protests in Hong Kong in 2019 over plans to allow extradition to Mainland China, Chinese reporting often sharply differed from that of the world press and some journalists in Hong Kong. In cases such as these, individuals looking for truth regarding protests and social movements must turn to trusted sources to determine what is happening. In today's media landscape, trusted sources often include information consumed or discovered via social media platforms.

Social Media

Modern social movements use social media to amplify their message and connect with audiences. As evidenced particularly by the Black Lives Matter, Moms Demand Action, and #MeToo movements, online discussions can lead to real-world, organized action. These movements have high-profile sponsors and volunteers and have influenced policy in communities across the United States.

The Internet is fallible and, for some groups, inaccessible. Even for those with a smartphone, Internet access is not free and, for some marginalized communities, often those most impacted by the work of social movements, it is out of reach. Some of the world poorest citizens, those most victimized by unethical regimes, do not have access to the Internet. In addition, governments and big companies can limit or shut down Internet access. However, in an increasingly globalized world, journalists and citizens who wish to chronicle events are more easily able to travel and capture video and reports of what is happening in communities. Further, this information is not dependent on mass media to be spread. Those who do have access to the Internet can read and share contently rapidly.

This sharing of information happens millions of times per day, across dozens of social media platforms. Students attending a rally in the United States can livestream video of the event to be viewed by friends and family worldwide. It is not uncommon for individuals with such video footage to be contacted by mainstream media outlets and asked to share their content via traditional media channels, or online. In this case, what is shared socially is amplified by the coverage from mass media. In addition, police dashcam or body-cam footage is often shared by activists in the Black Lives Matter movement to draw attention to acts of police brutality toward African

Americans. In this situation, activities that were previously unaccounted for are not only captured, but there is a mechanism through which to bring attention to them.

Many news organizations in the United States have seen declines in viewership, subscriptions, and attention. However, many journalists have an active presence on social media that can provide an opening for their work to be seen by those who are united by their views on an issue. A journalist covering an event can simply post to social media using a hashtag associated with a topic and link to the online version of their story to broaden its reach among those interested in the issue. Journalists with large social media followings can bring significant attention to their stories. The ability for people to discover content via hashtag is significant for the spread of social movements but can also lead to the spread of misinformation.

Users on social media can read information in posts delivered to them in a newsfeed. The information in the newsfeed differs by platform. It generally comes from people the user has chosen to connect with but can also include posts from advertisers. Researchers have shown that users rely on peripheral cues when determining the credibility of such content and often miss or disregard the source of the content. This reliance on cues has led to the spread of false information online, including false information about social movements. Some sources of false information are nefarious, or politically motivated. However, much false information is simply opinion read as fact or the work of writers who have not properly researched their topic.

Kate Keib

See also Civil Unrest, Coverage of; Social Justice Journalism; Social Media

Further Readings

Callison, C., & Hermida, A. (2015). Dissent and resonance: #Idlenomore as an emergent middle ground. *Canadian Journal of Communication*, 40(4), 695–716. doi:10.22230/cjc.2015v40n4a2958

Hermida, A., Lewis, S. C., & Zamith, R. (2014). Sourcing the Arab Spring: A case study of Andy Carvin's sources on Twitter during the Tunisian and

Egyptian revolutions. *Journal of Computer-Mediated Communication, 19*(3), 479–499. doi:10.1111/jcc4.12074

Keib, K., Himelboim, I., & Han, J. Y. (2018). Important tweets matter: Predicting retweets in the# BlackLivesMatter talk on Twitter. *Computers in Human Behavior, 85,* 106–115. doi:10.1016/j.chb.2018.03.025

Papacharissi, Z., & de Fatima Oliveira, M. (2012). Affective news and networked publics: The rhythms of news storytelling on# Egypt. *Journal of Communication, 62*(2), 266–282. doi:10.1111/j.1460-2466.2012.01630.x

Tilly, C. (2019). *Social movements, 1768–2004.* Milton Park, UK: Routledge.

Tufekci, Z. (2017). *Twitter and tear gas: The power and fragility of networked protest.* New Haven, CT: Yale University Press.

SOLUTIONS JOURNALISM

The term *solutions journalism* was used before the turn of the 21st century but gained popularity and legitimacy among journalists and journalism scholars in the years after the 2013 launch of the independent, nonprofit Solutions Journalism Network, which defines the practice as rigorous reporting on responses to social problems. In other words, solutions journalism is evidence-based news reporting that focuses on how people are working to solve problems rather than focusing solely on the problems themselves.

This entry begins by defining solutions journalism more thoroughly. Then, it provides a justification for such an approach and acknowledges criticisms of the approach. Examples are provided of news organizations and individual news stories that exemplify the practice. Finally, the impact of this journalistic approach is discussed.

Definition of Solutions Journalism

Solutions journalism news stories focus on what people are doing to effectively address social problems. For example, in 2020, mainstream news outlets focused their coverage on the death toll of the global COVID-19 pandemic and its accompanying social hardships and economic fallout.

Proponents of solutions journalism acknowledge that exposing society's ills is a core function of the news media, but they argue that informing the public of society's successes, or at least of legitimate attempts to solve problems, are equally as important. Solution-based stories on the pandemic focused their attention on what individuals, organizations, or institutions were doing to reduce the number of people infected by the virus and ease its widespread impact. By flipping the frame and reporting on responses to problems rather than solely on the problems themselves, journalists aim to empower audiences and push society forward.

The Solutions Journalism Network—which supports the practice by training journalists and collaborating with newsrooms and universities across the globe—says that in order to qualify as solutions journalism, a news story must include certain qualities. A story must describe a response to a problem, include evidence that the response is working, provide insights that can help others, and discuss the limitations of the response. Academic research has bolstered those criteria, detailing that the response must make up the bulk of the story rather than be tacked onto the end, for example. The Solutions Journalism Network also has identified what they call imposter stories; for example, a story that simply praises a single individual's good deed would not qualify as a solutions journalism news story. A good idea for a potential solution would also not meet the criteria, as solutions stories must document responses that have already shown signs of progress.

Justification and Criticism

Solutions journalism is one of many types of journalism identified by scholars and practitioners worldwide in recent years. The development of so many new journalistic approaches indicates a dissatisfaction with conventional journalistic norms and practices. Indeed, scholars and practitioners have coined several terms describing forms of journalism that highlight a commitment to social responsibility, such as civic journalism, public journalism, peace journalism, advocacy journalism, constructive journalism, and more. Like these similar forms of news, solutions journalism was born in part to serve as an antidote to the negativity bias present in mainstream news. A large body of literature has documented that the mainstream news media focus on problems and conflict and such coverage has a detrimental impact on individuals' mental and physical health, attitudes, and behaviors. Specifically, consuming mainstream news—especially television news—can cause individuals to feel anxious, depressed, and stressed.

In addition to the overabundance of negative news, the journalism industry has faced substantial challenges in recent decades. The business model based on print advertising collapsed with the growth of the Internet, resulting in a significant number of layoffs and newsroom closures. Levels of public trust in the media have steadily declined in recent decades, at least in most Anglo-Saxon countries. Further, political partisanship has grown more extreme and media criticism more rampant. While U.S. president, Donald Trump frequently referred to journalists and news organizations as *the enemy of the people*. Solutions journalism offers a response to a lengthy period of journalistic disruption and disillusionment.

Some have expressed skepticism of solutions journalism on the grounds that it is a slippery slope to publishing purely positive news at best and propaganda at worst. Critics are concerned that solutions journalism might delegitimize the longstanding watchdog function of the press, which involves holding the powerful accountable by exposing corruption and other misdeeds. Proponents say these critics do not fully understand the practice and insist that solution-focused stories, when done effectively, are not feel-good stories but rather are critical examinations of societal problems that have widespread social significance.

Solutions journalism strives for the journalistic ideal of objectivity, at least insomuch as objectivity is possible. Solutions journalism, and similar genres, ascribe to the media sociology perspective that journalists are not detached observers who simply report facts, but rather play a role in shaping stories. Solutions journalists take a more active rather than passive role by framing their stories in terms of possible solutions rather than sustained conflicts. Some critics call this bias or advocacy, but proponents of solutions journalism argue that all journalists shape the stories they report and choosing to focus on a solution is no more or less

objective than choosing to focus on a problem. Further, solutions journalists say that adhering to the Solution Journalism Network's standards for writing a solutions story—that being a rigorous, evidence-based approach—limits bias or advocacy.

Perhaps more valid criticisms than that solutions journalism veers too close to advocacy are that such stories might cast issues too simplistically, as many problems are complex and do not have clear solutions, and that leaders of nondemocratic societies might encourage the publication of pro-government stories under the veil of solutions journalism. This style of reporting is not a cure-all for journalism's problems, and it might not be appropriate for all news stories, such as breaking news, or in all journalistic landscapes, such as in countries without a free press.

Examples and Impact

Examples of solutions journalism can be found in news outlets on every continent. The Solutions Journalism Network's Story Tracker, a database that houses solutions-oriented news stories, included nearly 9,000 stories from 173 countries in mid-2020. Journalists are practicing this approach in countries such as South Africa, Uganda, Kenya, China, Colombia, and more.

The approach is perhaps the most popular in Europe, where the term *solutions journalism* is often used interchangeably with constructive journalism. The U.K. magazine *Positive News* is credited as being the first news outlet dedicated to publishing constructive news. French nongovernmental organization Reporters d'Espoirs (Reporters of Hope) launched a group of journalists and media professionals dedicated to promoting solutions journalism in 2003. In Denmark, DR, or the Danish Broadcasting Corporation, hosts a radio show centered around solving problems in the community. Dutch news website De Correspondent launched in the Netherlands in 2013 after raising more than 1 million euros in 8 days to finance its work in constructive journalism. The news platform replicated its crowdfunding success in 2018, when it raised more than $2.6 million in 30 days to fund a counterpart English-language website, The Correspondent. The English-language site launched in September 2019 but discontinued publishing new articles as of January 2021. Early supporters of The Correspondent had expressed disappointment with the decision to keep the new site's headquarters in Amsterdam after the fundraising campaign gave the impression it would be based in the United States.

Other European news outlets that publish solutions journalism include SVT in Sweden, *Tages-Anzeiger* in Switzerland, and *Perspective Daily* in Germany, among others. More well-known news organizations in Europe have also shown a commitment to solutions journalism. The BBC began publishing solutions-oriented news under the title BBC World Hacks after the United Nations called on the media giant to do so. And British daily newspaper *The Guardian* launched a series called *The Upside*, which publishes solutions-focused news stories. *The Guardian* reporter Sarah Boseley received the Future of Journalism Award, given by the Solutions Journalism Network and another independent center called the *Constructive Institute*, in 2019 for her story "The Big Sleep," which investigated how the Democratic Republic of Congo, one of the most troubled countries in the world, had all but eradicated the tropical disease called *sleeping sickness*.

In the United States, news outlets big and small are experimenting with solutions journalism, many of them in conjunction with the Solutions Journalism Network. *The New York Times* launched a series in 2010 called *Fixes* that publishes solutions journalism stories covering topics such as the opioid epidemic and other health care issues, incarceration, and racial injustice. *The Seattle Times* has published solution-oriented stories about problems plaguing the education system in Washington state since 2013. Its journalists have reported on approaches to improve school discipline, parent education, and math instruction. In 2018 and 2019, *POLITICO Magazine* launched two series, *What Works* and *What Works Next*, that included articles about a Houston-based health app preventing flood damage, a successful Baltimore after-school program, and millennials' unique responses to societal problems.

Solutions journalism appears to have a promising impact, both economically and socially. Utah's *Deseret News* adopted a solutions focus as a way to increase readership after a number of layoffs. In 2013, it became the fastest growing newspaper in the United States based on circulation. After training its reporters in solutions journalism in an effort to refocus its coverage, the *Montgomery Advertiser* in Alabama reported an increase in pageviews and engagement time on its solutions stories in 2018. Several newsroom projects centered around solutions journalism have received grant support, such as the *Arizona Daily Star*'s 2018 piece, "Fixing Our Foster Care Crisis."

Academic research regarding solutions journalism has mostly suggested that these types of stories engage news audiences. Although research has traditionally indicated that audiences are attracted to shocking stories, exemplifying the "if it bleeds, it leads" adage, and attention-grabbing headlines have become increasingly popular in the age of clickbait, other research suggests that although news stories with high levels of conflict attract audiences, at least initially, the excessive amount of negatively skewed news has also caused audiences to become apathetic to human suffering and to disengage with the news entirely. Compared to news stories focused on conflict, experiments have revealed that solutions stories can cause readers to feel more positive and have greater intentions to engage with the content. Several studies have also shown that those who read solution stories report higher levels of self-efficacy, or the belief that they can contribute to the solution themselves. Some studies have shown further benefits of solutions stories such as increased intent to share the stories or to act in a way that supports the solution, but these results have not been conclusive.

Although most early research has focused on the effects of text-based solutions journalism stories among adults, some scholars have examined solutions journalism as it relates to the photos published alongside text stories, its effects on children, teaching solutions journalism to university students, and journalists' own perceptions of the practice. Journalists in the United States reported favorable attitudes toward solutions journalism in a 2016 survey. Although existing research paints an optimistic picture for the future of the practice, more work needs to be done before conclusions can be drawn about the impact of this approach.

Karen McIntyre Hopkinson

See also Constructive Journalism; Europe; Framing; News Audiences, Decline ofU.S.; News Avoidance; News Values; Objectivity; Peace Journalism; Social Justice Journalism

Further Readings

Benesch, S. (1998). The rise of solutions journalism. *Columbia Journalism Review, 36*(6), 36–39.

Curry, A. L., & Hammonds, K. H. (2014). The power of solutions journalism. Retrieved from http:// engagingnewsproject.org/enp_prod/wp-content /uploads/2014/06/ENP_SJN-report.pdf

Curry, A. L., Stroud, N. J., & McGregor, S. (2016). Solutions journalism and news engagement. Retrieved from https://engagingnewsproject.org/wp-content /uploads/2016/03/ENP-Solutions-Journalism-News -Engagement.pdf

Dyer, J. (2015, June 11). Is solutions journalism the solution? Nieman Reports. Retrieved from http:// niemanreports.org/articles/is-solutions-journalism-the -solution/

Green-Barber, L. (2018, October 8). What we know (and don't) about the impact of solutions journalism. *Solutions Journalism Network*. Retrieved from https:// thewholestory.solutionsjournalism.org/what-we-know -and-dont-about-the-impact-of-solutions-journalism -61ae0c4a0890

Lough, K., & McIntyre, K. (2018). Journalists' perceptions of solutions journalism and its place in the field. *#ISOJ Journal, 8*(1), 33–52.

McIntyre, K. (2019). Solutions journalism: The effects of including solution information in news stories about social problems. *Journalism Practice, 13*(1), 16–34. doi:10.1080/17512786.2017.1409647

Wenzel, A., Gerson, D., Moreno, E., Son, M., & Morrison Hawkins, B. (2017). Engaging stigmatized communities through solutions journalism: Residents of South Los Angeles respond. *Journalism, 19*(5), 649–667. doi:10.1177/1464884917703125

SOURCES

Journalistic sources are defined as actors who journalists get information from using newsgathering techniques such as interviews and observations. This information can include quotes, background information, story suggestions, or eyewitness accounts. Sources are therefore actors outside the news organization itself who provide information subsidies and can be actors who are interviewed by e-mail, in person, or by telephone, as well as documents containing relevant information. This entry discusses the types of sources and their use in the news process, ethical and legal aspects of sourcing, power in journalist-source relations, the use of online sources, journalists' verification of sources, and audiences' views on journalistic sources.

Sources can be differentiated into types, which some authors classify in a source hierarchy based on perceived trustworthiness from the perspective of the journalist. The most trustworthy sources are official sources such as ministries and other government institutions, followed by professional sources, which include, for example, nongovernmental organizations or companies from the economic sector. The third type is nonprofessional sources such as citizens who are not in the public eye for professional reasons. A fourth type, actors from the media system itself such as correspondents and news agencies, can be added. This classification is based on the proximity to journalistic standards that sources usually exhibit when presenting information. Official and especially journalistic sources are used to adapting their communication style to the needs of journalists. Nonprofessional sources such as private citizens, on the other hand, usually do not take journalistic demands into account when posting reports of their experiences on social media platforms.

In journalism research, as early as 1979, Herbert Gans postulated that it was sources that led journalists to the topics of reporting. Zvi Reich called sources the *cornerstones* of journalistic activities such as detecting, researching, and verifying news. They provide journalists with information and thus the raw material on which further reporting is based. As a rule, it is sources, not journalists, who witness events that are potentially worth reporting. In academic definitions of journalism, sources also play a prominent role: Denis McQuail defines journalism as construction and publication of contemporary events based on reliable sources. Journalists need sources, especially when facts are not verifiable or are controversial. Sources can be used to manifest the facts and lend authority to information.

Sources in the News Process

Despite their ascribed importance, in journalism research, sources were somewhat underrepresented for a long time. The theory of news values and research on gatekeepers and social psychological approaches conceptualize news decisions from the perspective of journalists without placing sources at the center of consideration. Activities of journalists in relation to sources are often summarized under the terms of newsgathering or sourcing. Also, theories of news production localize sources mainly at the beginning of the process as suppliers of information, which are consulted by journalists.

As a result of the sociological turn in journalism research, journalists were then increasingly viewed in an organizational context and the idea of an autonomously acting gatekeeper who selects sources was rejected. With this change of perspective, the sources of information inevitably move more into the focus of interest, although the actual relationship to sources is only present in an approach that places sources in the context of social interactions. In reciprocal models, the relationship between sources and journalists is described as a process of exchange and ongoing social relationship, in which the gathering of information is not a single event but the result of complex interactions between the two actors. This process of "finding the truth" is described as epistemology of news reporting, which is defined by rules and routines that operate within a social setting, and determines how journalists obtain their knowledge. Knowledge is not understood as the product of an objective and rational analysis of reality, but as the result of an intersubjective negotiation process. Barbie Zelizer refers to the place where meanings are constructed, shared, and redefined as the interpretive community of journalism. According to this approach, the relationship between journalists and their sources can be described as a negotiation of meaning between multiple groups, each of which is located in different interpretative communities with their own patterns of interpretation.

Ethical and Legal Aspects of Sourcing

In this negotiation, journalists have the obligation to protect their sources. Source protection is a central component of numerous codes of ethics, according to which it is always wrong not to protect the source. This ethical responsibility toward journalistic sources is, however, also legally anchored in some countries in the form of the so-called *shield laws*. In Sweden, for example, journalists can be prosecuted for disclosing their sources.

Source protection as a legally protected good is the exception rather than the rule; nonetheless, journalists face potential sanctions if they do not protect their sources. Without certain protective mechanisms, potential sources could be deterred from passing on important information to journalists, who would then no longer be able to adequately perform their task as the fourth estate. The protection of sources gains special importance in the case of whistleblowers where investigative reporters and sources collaborate to reveal abuses of power. For journalists, this kind or reporting can pose challenges, such as the establishment of secure communication channels and considerations about surveillance of their own activities.

Power in Journalist–Source Relations

In the description of the relationship between sources and journalists, a substantial part of the literature has focused on which voices get heard in the news. In many cases, this research is framed under the label of power and examines dependency in the relationship between sources and journalists. The power relations between reporters and their sources depend on various contextual factors: the story itself, the source, and social, cultural, political, and economic contexts. Thus, the reporter–source relationship can range from a goal-oriented exchange of information to a struggle for the sovereignty of interpretation in the presentation of information.

The level of dependency on sources can be differentiated according to the stages of news production. In the news discovery phase, the agenda-building theory assumes that issues arise in an interplay between media, politics, and society. Particularly in routine reporting, journalists are guided by planned events such as press conferences or press releases and news agencies and tend to remain passive. In the news selection phase, not only the perceived relevance of an issue contributes to the decision to select it for coverage, but also the availability of sources and the accessibility of information. Sources who adjust their information to journalistic needs are, therefore, privileged in news reporting.

In the newsgathering phase, sources gain in importance because journalists try to identify additional perspectives and cross-check previous information. In the presentation phase, Gaye Tuchman described strategic rituals journalists use to preserve objectivity. Sources play a major role in these rituals. For example, they enable journalists to distance themselves from the information displayed in the journalistic piece.

Empirical research on the relation between sources and journalists has often referred to the tango-metaphor to ask who exerts greater influence in shaping the news. Gans stated that sources usually lead the tango. More recent studies found power relations to be dependent on context factors such as cultural differences, the kind of story journalists cover, and working conditions of journalists. However, most studies agree that authoritative sources such as government officials or academic experts dominate the news. Citizens are mainly present as eyewitnesses in crisis events, breaking news situations, or to represent the public opinion in vox pops. In routine coverage, citizens only play a minor role.

Digitalization and Journalistic Sources

The rise of digital media has significantly changed the relationship between sources and journalists. First, sources no longer depend on journalism to spread their messages to the audience. For example, populist politicians heavily use these new possibilities to communicate directly. This also has consequences for power in the relationship between sources and journalists, because sources can bypass the filter and journalistic coverage is not the only channel to reach a broader audience.

Second, the ability of journalists to access content generated by users dramatically increased. The availability of user-generated content as potential raw material and the presence of diverse voices online led scholars to assume that journalistic coverage would begin to include more nonelite sources. However, this optimism was not fulfilled as user-generated content often does not fulfill journalistic standards, which increases the hurdle to be integrated in news coverage. Some studies have noted an increase in social media in the news, but also stated that this material is mainly used to illustrate opinions of a range of sources. Other studies have found that journalists seldom base stories on online sources and rather use them as a supplement. Overall, the impression prevails that journalists, at least in routine reporting, use digital tools only as a new access route to established sources.

Third, social media not only offer unlimited access to raw material but also pose the challenge of how to determine the trustworthiness of sources and the credibility of their material. Techniques such as geo-location of pictures or forensic processes to identify fake videos are incorporated in newsrooms or offered as a service by external organizations. Additionally, not only the direct use of social media material is problematic with regard to verification, but also using social media as a tool for story detection in the sense of ambient journalism involves risks for journalists. Large-scale disinformation campaigns could bias the public opinion journalists perceive when monitoring social media.

Verification of Journalistic Sources

Bill Kovach and Tom Rosenstiel describe journalism as a "discipline of verification," which has developed norms such as objectivity, rules, and routines in the collection, selection, and presentation of valid information. Journalists need to determine if a source tries to be accurate and honest, or if they only offer self-serving information. Verification is essential for the ability of journalism to provide fair and accurate reporting. The drive for accuracy is a core value of journalism and defines acceptable professional behavior in the sourcing and presentation of information.

In the context of digital media, journalism must develop strategies to deal with the speed and abundance of material on social media platforms. The conflict between accuracy of information and speed of reporting is particularly present in the online context. Breaking-news situations are the point of culmination when the flow of information is usually chaotic and contradictory, and journalists' verification efforts are also visible to recipients. According to the findings of some studies, verification is neglected in these crisis situations and verification is only carried out after publication.

The standards for assessing the trustworthiness of sources from the perspective of journalists have apparently changed as a result of social media. Since verification is a very time-consuming and resource-intensive process, several authors have identified alternative ways in which journalists can arm themselves against attacks on their objectivity without having to investigate every last detail of information. Studies dealing with the process of verification have found that in many cases, journalists rely on trust relationships with sources to shorten the process of verification. Other studies have tried to investigate the steps journalists follow when verifying sources.

Audience Perspective on Journalistic Sources

Sources do fulfill different functions for journalists in the phase of news discovery and gathering but also in the phase of news presentation. Journalists use sources to fulfill the norm of objectivity, which requires the presentation of supporting evidence and conflicting possibilities. How transparent journalists are with regard to their sourcing practices differs, and this in turn affects the audience.

How the audience views journalistic sources is not at the center of journalism research and has received less attention compared to journalistic sourcing. Nonetheless, journalists' handling of sources is crucial for the audience's evaluation of the quality of journalism. In general, the news audience seems to value quotes, the mentioning of sources, their proximity to the news event, and a high status of the source. On the other hand, some types of sources such as public relations are rated as untrustworthy in general. If sources provide uncertain information that is nonetheless newsworthy, journalists have to solve the dilemma by providing the audience with enough information to judge the source and at the same time avoiding the impression that the whole journalistic piece is untrustworthy. In this case, transparency about

sources can evoke uncertainty on the side of the audience.

With regard to online sources of information used in news stories, empirical evidence is mixed suggesting that the audience do not perceive the use of off-line sources as more credible than online sources. Only very eye-catching displays of social media posts within a story, such as screenshots of tweets, might negatively influence the credibility. Additionally, the need for transparency seems to differ between online and off-line recipients of news. People who regularly use online news expect journalists to disclose more details about sources than off-line users do.

Florian Wintterlin

See also Fake News; Fourth Estate; Gatekeeping; New Media; Sources, Anonymous; Trust in Journalism

Further Readings

Berkowitz, D. A. (1991). Assessing forces in the selection of local television news. *Journal of Broadcasting & Electronic Media, 35*(2), 245–251. doi:10.1080/08838159109364121

Blumler, J. G., & Gurevitch, M. (1981). Politicians and the press. In D. D. Nimmo & K. R. Sanders (Eds.), *Handbook of political communication* (pp. 467–493). Beverly Hills, CA:

Sage.Brandtzaeg, P. B., Lüders, M., Spangenberg, J., Rath-Wiggins, L., & Følstad, A. (2015). Emerging journalistic verification practices concerning social media. *Journalism Practice, 10*(3), 323–342. doi:10.10 80/17512786.2015.1020331

Ekström, M. (2002). Epistemologies of TV journalism. *Journalism: Theory, Practice & Criticism, 3*(3), 259–282. doi:10.1177/1464884902003300301

Franklin, B., & Carlson, M. (2010). *Journalists, sources, and credibility: New perspectives*. New York, NY: Routledge.

Gans, H. (1979). *Deciding what's news: A study of CBS Evening News, NBC Nightly News, Newsweek, and Time*. Evanston, IL: Northwestern University Press.

Kovach, B., & Rosenstiel, T. (2001). *The elements of journalism. What newspeople should know and the public should expect*. New York, NY: Crown Publishers.

Lecheler, S., & Kruikemeier, S. (2016). Re-evaluating journalistic routines in a digital age: A review of research on the use of online sources. *New Media & Society, 18*(1), 156–171. doi:10.1177/14614448 15600412

Mancini, P. (1993). Between trust and suspicion: How political journalists solve the dilemma. *European Journal of Communication, 8*(1), 33–51. doi:10.1177/0267323193008001002

McCombs, M. E. (2004). *Setting the agenda: the mass media and public opinion.* Cambridge, UK: Polity.

McManus, J. H. (1994). *Market-driven journalism: Let the citizen beware?* Thousand Oaks, CA: Sage.

McQuail, D. (2013). *Journalism and society.* Thousand Oaks, CA: Sage.

Reich, Z. (2009). *Sourcing the news: Key issues in journalism—An innovative study of the Israeli press.* Cresskill, NJ: Hampton Press.

Schlesinger, P. (1987). *Putting "reality" together: BBC news.* London, UK: Constable & Robinson Ltd.

Sigal, L. V. (1986). Sources make the news. In R. Manoff & M. Schudson (Eds.), *Reading the news* (pp. 9–37). New York, NY: Pantheon Books.

Tuchman, G. (1972). Objectivity as strategic ritual: An examination of newsmen's notions of objectivity. *American Journal of Sociology, 77*(4), 660–679.

Tuchman, G. (1978). *Making news: A study in the construction of reality.* Michigan: Free Press.

Zelizer, B. (1993). Has communication explained journalism? *Journal of Communication, 43*(4), 80–88. doi:10.1111/j.1460-2466.1993.tb01307.x

SOURCES, ANONYMOUS

From the perspective of journalists, the anonymity of sources can have at least two meanings: First, a source can be anonymous in the sense that its identity is not known to the journalist. Second, the source can insist on anonymity in reporting, but disclose itself to the journalist. In literature, the phenomenon of anonymous sources is treated under various headings. One of the most prominent is unnamed sources, which describes sources who do not want their names to appear in journalistic coverage. Other terms, such as distant sources, refer to sources that are at least partly anonymous for journalists. This type of source is mainly characterized by the fact that journalists usually do not have the opportunity (or the interest) to meet the actors personally. Instead, their content is researched via digital media and integrated into the news.

Both forms of anonymity have consequences for journalistic norms and practices as well as for the public's perception of journalistic reporting. In journalism research, especially how journalists deal with unnamed sources and ethical debates underlying their use have been examined. With regard to sources anonymous to the journalist, research has extensively examined social media sources in the news, how they are verified, and the consequences of using anonymous (citizen) sources for the relationship between journalists and their audience. This entry discusses the opportunities and challenges of sources anonymous to the journalist and sources unnamed in the coverage and describes how anonymity affects journalistic processes.

Anonymous Sources and Journalistic Norms

Anonymous sources are important to journalists' role as independent watchdog because they can allow for a fuller exploration of a story and offer alternative viewpoints on positions articulated by those speaking on behalf of organizations or political parties. This kind of sensitive information is often communicated only under the shield of anonymity and thus offers the journalist a possibility to access otherwise unobtainable information. Criticism of the use of anonymous sources is particularly ignited in cases where the use of anonymous sources has led to false and distorted reporting.

Journalists are called upon to protect their sources and yet be as transparent as possible to the public. This dilemma already plays a major role in everyday source work, but it becomes even more pronounced with anonymous sources. The individual journalist makes himself or herself vulnerable because he or she cannot shift responsibility onto the source by naming it. Instead, the journalist is taking an active role by granting anonymity to the source and acting as the only authority accountable for the information presented. This has several consequences both for the relationship between journalist and source and for journalistic reporting as such.

First, at the level of journalistic reporting, strategic rituals to ensure the journalist's objectivity, such as the presentation of different points of view or transparency about the sourcing process, are no longer applicable, because it is not possible to name the source. Instead, the journalist must personally ensure the correctness of the facts. In the event of an error, responsibility for the incorrect coverage falls directly back on the journalist. The risk for the journalist is increased, because of the high interdependence with the source and concerns that the source could take advantage of the anonymity granted by the journalist to manipulate the journalist or news organization.

Second, in their relationship with anonymous sources, journalists have to develop mechanisms to cope with this risk. In the case of distant sources, journalists often use cross-checks or digital methods of verification. In the case of anonymous sources, it is crucial that a relationship of trust already exists between the journalist and the source, which is based on previous experiences and reduces the journalist's uncertainty about relying on the source for reporting. This is particularly prevalent in the case of whistleblowers, where verification by cross-checks is restricted. However, also in routine reporting, journalists regularly rely on (background) information from sources they are not allowed to name in their coverage.

How often journalists are confronted with the challenge of anonymity is dependent on the area they are working at. Compared to most news reporters, investigative journalists more regularly deal with anonymous sources. Political journalists often use background information from politicians in their reporting without naming them. In a historical analysis of norms surrounding the use of anonymous sources displayed in guidelines and textbooks, Matt Duffy found that anonymous sourcing was not always an accepted practice but gained acceptance in the 1970s, while few textbooks offered guidelines how to cope with anonymity of sources.

Third, if one takes a closer look at distant sources, where journalists often do not know the name of the source themselves, additional conflicts of norms arise. The central question here is the relevance of the material supplied by the source and how this relevance is weighed against the anonymity of the source. In other words, the journalist must decide whether the source's information is so relevant that the limited possibility of verification can be accepted. Studies have shown that not only relevance but also temporal factors such as the dynamics of news situations play a

role for the publication of such information. The use of distant sources is common in crisis reporting, where reports have to be made in the shortest possible time from inaccessible areas. However, the problem of how to cope with distant sources is also present in routine reporting, albeit in a different form. Especially in the case of entertaining content with low social relevance, verification is sometimes dispensed with and the material is integrated with a general reference to online networks without questioning the anonymity of the source.

Online Sourcing and Anonymity

Even though journalists had already used sources that they could not meet in person before digitization, the amount of material available has grown exponentially through the Internet. In research, this form of material is often referred to as *user-generated content* (UGC) and describes content created by nonprofessional communicators that is (partially) publicly accessible. By definition, UGC is characterized by the fact that the material does not come from sources that belong to the circle of established sources of journalists. As a rule, the source is, therefore, not already known to journalists, but the source does not necessarily have to be anonymous either.

One can differentiate between various degrees of anonymity of UGC, which also have an impact on journalistic processes. First, users can hide behind a pseudonym and not reveal any personal information even when asked. For journalists, this form of source is at best sufficient as a starting point for further research. Second, users can refuse to reveal personal information, but provide evidence that prove their presence at a location by photographing street signs or current newspapers. Third, users can disclose all information, and their anonymity can only be based on the fact that journalists are not able to meet them in person. This form of source is best used by journalists because it already meets many journalistic standards.

However, there might be situations where the anonymity of sources is not decisive for journalistic sourcing. For example, if journalists report on areas that are not accessible to them, it may not be individual tweets or posts that are of interest, but an impression that is created by a mass of tweets with similar content. Whether the individual sources are anonymous or not is irrelevant at this point. Additionally, the importance of anonymity varies with the expectations journalists have of the source material. When it comes to finding topic ideas and drawing attention to certain events, the anonymity of the source is less problematic. However, when it comes to verifying information or when the source provides exclusive information, the anonymity of a source poses a problem for journalistic norms such as the reliability and verifiability of information.

Whistleblowers as Anonymous Sources

Whistleblowers represent a special form of source that guarantees journalists exclusive information. These sources enable journalists to fulfill their control function to a special degree, because they provide insights into structures and contexts that are otherwise not visible to journalists. Whistleblowers witness wrongdoing and feel the need to turn to an outsider to correct the perceived violations under a significant personal risk. Legally, whistleblowers are often not protected, and they may be prosecuted after their revelations if their identity becomes public.

Media studies that have focused on whistleblowing as an act of publishing internal information through news media have looked at relationships between journalists and whistleblowers, how journalists decide which information to publish, and effects of third-party interests on journalistic work as a result of revelations by whistleblowers. For journalists, whistleblowers represent a special challenge due to the uniqueness of the process and ethical questions. Whistleblowers want to make authorities responsible for their actions; however, their motives are often unclear and can range from promoting the common good to revenge campaigns, which makes judging their trustworthiness crucial. Whether a whistleblower is trusted depends on factors such as fairness to the target and motivations for disclosure and is heavily determined by a process of trust building through frequent contacts.

From the perspective of the sources, the disclosure of information also involves a considerable risk, which is further increased by digital communication. Paul Lashmar questions whether the Snowden revelations and the subsequent discussion about mass surveillance have led to sources being deterred from talking to journalists because they are more aware of surveillance capabilities by authorities. This addresses the problem that journalists are not always able to guarantee the anonymity of the source and the general dilemma of source protection and publication of information relevant for society.

Anonymous Sources From the Perspective of the Audience

Not naming sources in journalistic coverage has consequences not only for journalistic practices but also for how the audience perceives journalism. On the one hand, journalists who use unnamed sources such as "government officials" display their connectedness to influential people and might gain authority themselves. On the other hand, journalists who regularly rely on anonymous sources are quickly suspected of being in cahoots with sources and of concealing the true motives of the source. In the case of unnamed sources, the audience is left with no option, but to trust the information reported by the journalist. As this trust becomes more difficult to gain and practices such as citizen or collaborative journalism establish a cultural shift toward transparency, the use of anonymous sources must be justified to the public as well as within the journalistic organization.

Despite their importance for journalistic practices, research on the use of anonymous sources is scarce. Much of the research refers to legal aspects of source protection and the frequency with which journalists use unnamed sources. How the audience perceives unnamed sources is seldom examined, except in studies noting that the credibility of journalistic pieces is harmed by the use of unnamed sources. In general, there is a need for research on how the audience perceives source attribution in general, the estimated trustworthiness of different ways to incorporate anonymous sources, and the effects on general attitudes toward journalism. This is especially true for changes in audience behavior due to the use of anonymous sources. For example, does the lack of naming the source encourage recipients to search for information themselves, thus promoting a more self-contained approach to news? Or, on the contrary, is it the case that not naming the source leads to reactance to the news content and increases distrust in journalism?

In the case of distant sources, journalists often do not name the source and use rather broad categories such as "Internet" to describe the origin of the source. Social media material is used by journalists to fill the news vacuum after breaking news, to report on crisis areas, or as a substitute for vox pops from the street. In recent years, journalism research has dealt extensively with this type of source and examined on a content level and from the perspective of journalists how social media material is integrated into news reporting. The general assumption is that social media are an enrichment for journalism, complement the repertoire of sources, and increase interactions between the audience and journalists.

Little attention has been paid in research to the difficulties associated with using social media sources. This becomes particularly evident in the case of anonymous sources that could not be clearly verified by the journalist. In these cases, journalists sometimes use a disclaimer in their coverage indicating that the information could not be completely verified. In doing so, they follow the norm to be transparent about sources but at the same time distance themselves from their responsibility to report accurate facts. The task to evaluate the origin of the source is transferred to the recipient of news. There is some empirical evidence that this practice increases the recipient's uncertainty about the reported facts, but more research is needed on how the audience perceives unverified anonymous sources in the news.

Florian Wintterlin

See also Ethics; Fourth Estate; Investigative Journalism; Secrecy and Leaks; Social Media; Sources; Transparency

Further Readings

Andén-Papadopoulos, K., & Pantti, M. (2011). *Amateur images and global news.* Bristol, UK: Intellect Books.

Carlson, M. (2011). Whither anonymity ? Journalism and unnamed sources in a changing media environment. In B. Franklin & M. Carlson (Eds.), *Journalists, sources, and credibility: New perspectives* (pp. 37–48). New York, NY: Routledge.

Carlson, M. (2011). *On the condition of anonymity: Unnamed sources and the battle for journalism.* Urbana: University of Illinois Press.

Duffy, M. J. (2014). Anonymous sources: A historical review of the norms surrounding their use. *American Journalism, 31*(2), 236–261. doi:10.1080/08821127.2014.905363

Edgerly, S., Mourão, R. R., Thorson, E., & Tham, S. M. (2020). When do audiences verify? How perceptions about message and source influence audience verification of news headlines. *Journalism & Mass Communication Quarterly, 97*(1), 52–71. doi:10.1177/1077699019864680

Hellmueller, L., Vos, T. P., & Poepsel, M. A. (2013). Shifting journalistic capital? Transparency and objectivity in the twenty-first century. *Journalism Studies, 14*(3), 287–304. doi:10.1080/1461670X.2012.697686

Lashmar, P. (2017). No more sources? The impact of Snowden's revelations on journalists and their confidential sources. *Journalism Practice, 11*(6), 665–688. doi:10.1080/17512786.2016.1179587

Lewis, S. C., & Molyneux, L. (2018). A decade of research on social media and journalism: Assumptions, blind spots, and a way forward. *Media and Communication, 6*(4), 1–36. doi:10.1093/oxfordhb/9780198733522.013.17

Martin-Kratzer, R., & Thorson, E. (2007). Use of anonymous sources declines in U.S. newspapers. *Newspaper Research Journal, 28*(2), 56–70. doi:10.1177/073953290702800204

Sternadori, M. M., & Thorson, E. (2009). Anonymous sources harm credibility of all stories. *Newspaper Research Journal, 30*(4), 54–66. doi:10.1177/073953290903000405

Waters, S. (2020). The ethical algorithm: Journalist/whistleblower relationships explored through the lens of social exchange. *Journalism and Communication Monographs, 22*(3), 172–245. doi:10.1177/1522637920947719

SOUTH AMERICA

Journalism in South America encompasses myriad forms and functions, making simple generalizations impossible. However, some trends have been observed across various nations in recent years that have impacted the regional panorama of the continent's news media, including the following: a digital transformation that has radically changed South American approach to news; political battles for new legislation to shift ownership patterns; grassroots movements to demand more pluralism and a wider representation of perspectives; a decrease in public trust in media; and worsening conditions for the exercise of independent journalism, as media–state relations deteriorate in numerous countries.

The Evolving Press Models of News

Journalism has a long history in South America. While forms of mass communication existed before colonial powers arrived by the late 19th century most South American nations had established Spanish- and Portuguese-language presses. Hybrid press models melding partisan and commercial funding mechanisms would emerge and blend in South America during much of the 20th century. One model was in the tradition of European partisan press, whereby journalists acted as advocates for particular political or ideological perspectives, infusing articles with opinion, rather than remaining neutral observers. Here, journalists had "missions": to espouse certain political views, earn public support for a government or political party, and promote or interpret certain political realities. Political conflicts played out on front pages, or could even birth new outlets, as researcher Silvio Waisbord noted was the case in Colombia, including *El Espectador* in 1887 and *El Tiempo* in 1911. Political leaders became publishers and editors, such as Argentinian Bartolome Mitre of *La Nación*. The idea of journalists as active advocates or political militants continues to some extent, in various parts of Latin America. Outlets directly tied to partisan interests and transparent in their ideological loyalties exist among South American newspapers and broadcasters, particularly in countries where political parties are strong, as in Colombia and Uruguay. However, by the early 20th century, another model had arrived to the continent.

The second model of journalism adhered more to one seen in the United States, emphasizing a separation away from official influence over content and toward an "objective," information-centered style of reporting, whereby markets generate revenue for news outlets. In comparison to the partisan model, newspapers were commercial enterprises geared for mass audiences, rather than select sectors. Waisbord discussed how this model arrived on the heels of global transformation, as a wave of globalization swept Latin American countries. New communication technologies and media services—such as photography, film, and wire services—and reorganization of newsrooms pushed transformation, as did a shift toward commercial logics to maximize audiences. At the same time, a growing middle class, emerging private sector, and spread of market research influenced the adoption of a business model. Various newspapers shifted to a version of this model, including Argentina's La Nación, Chile's El Mercurio, O Estado de São Paulo of Brazil, and El Comercio of Peru.

However, in South American newsrooms, the U.S. model of the journalist as an "impartial" purveyor of so-called "objective" information did not fully consolidate. The state remained an important variable in how journalists and media professionals could ply their professions. Media organizations' abilities to survive without important government subsidies and favorable regulatory decision making in the face of limited market potential and economic and political upheaval was precarious. After various Latin American nations began nationalizing important advertising sectors, such as telephones, airlines, electric companies, and mining industries, the state had more financial control over media. Democratic instability could mean contentious relations with various governments, and those who found their editorial line at odds with regime leaders could find their organization censured or closed, as was the case with La Prensa and Argentinian President Juan Perón's administration in the early 1950s. Other times, media executives formed tight relations with political actors, in the name of partisanship, national security, and economic policy. During the Salvador Allende presidency in Chile in the early 1970s, the daily El Mercurio called for the overthrow of the president. In Brazil, top newspapers supported a 1964 coup d'état.

Alternative and Community Media Versus State Media

In contrast to mainstream media, South America's alternative presses have functioned under various types of regimes in previous decades, as alternative voices to the political, economic, or social "dominant orders," as Waisbord (2011) described them. Community radio networks in Bolivia owned or affiliated with mining unions or miners have served important functions in regions where geography, poverty, and illiteracy affect media access. Still its effects have diminished as it was limited to specific geographic areas.

Starting in 2007, civic society groups, emerging without government support, have successfully lobbied for legislative and political changes in media systems. Indigenous and underrepresented groups, students, and academic and diverse professionals tried to secure wider representation in news content. Maria Soledad Segura and Slivio Waisbord explained that these civic society proposals provided an unprecedented but cautious opening for citizen participation in media policy development, especially in Argentina, Paraguay, Peru, and Uruguay, shaping the public discussion, public opinion, and government agenda. These efforts resulted on the creation or reemergence of state or public media in at least seven South American countries. In 2015, Daniela Inés Monje reported that Argentina, Brazil, Paraguay, Bolivia, Ecuador, and Venezuela showed an increase in public TV and radio stations and developed new audiences.

Despite these advancements, most of these new public media business models had strong government dependencies in terms of control, content, and financing. With the exception of Uruguay, which Reporters Without Borders considers a "regional model" for its 2007 and 2014 broadcast legislation that allowed for more access and a Communication Council independent from the government, these laws and regulations failed to deliver on the promise of pluralism in the news, but not in other cultural areas. In most South American countries, the public media remains closely aligned with the government and has problems including opposition voices or dissidents in their news segments, analysis, and opinions. In extreme cases, the public media have created weekly programs such as "Aló Presidente" in Venezuela, or "Enlace Ciudadano" in Ecuador, with the only purpose to applaud government performance.

In a more positive direction for press freedom, some of these civic society proposals, helped by international organization recommendations, have had an impact on decriminalizing journalism practice in several Latin American countries, such as no longer punishing journalists with prison sentences for defamation or slander. Uruguay is the most successful example since its 2009 reform which decriminalized many press offenses such as the defamation of public officials.

Watchdog Journalism

One important shift that occurred in South American journalism in the late 20th century was the shift of watchdog reporting to mainstream media. Watchdog media are those that critically scrutinize events, issues, and power actors to publish information others would not want in the public eye. In regions struggling with deep inequality, a weak rule of law, and ongoing political or economic instability, such reporting has important roles in ongoing processes of democratization. Watchdog media have brought attention to human rights abuses and broaches of civil liberties, high-level corruption, mismanagement, and other wrongdoing. Such reporting can lead to government investigation, judiciary proceedings, resignations, or jail time for those found guilty.

Waisbord chronicled various examples of watchdog reporting in South America. Reporting by Peruvian newsweeklies such as Caretas on high-level corruption and state-sanctioned killings in the 1980s and 1990s (others implicated the administration of then-President Alan García in fraud) was one of them. Brazil's Folha de São Paulo covered high-level corruption, plans to buy votes toward presidential reelection, and payoffs in construction of a railway. Argentine media unveiled official involvement in human rights abuses, illegal weapons sales, and homicide within military ranks. And Colombian outlets like El Espectador and Cambio 16 showcased terrorism wreaked by paramilitary forces and drug cartels, and secret dealings between those forces and public officials.

Observers of Latin American journalism attribute the emergence of muckraking and more assertive forms of reporting in the region to influences operating simultaneously within, between, and external to newsrooms. Increases in private sector advertising, decreases in partisan direct controls, and continuing democratization allowed space to report on official misconduct. As audiences responded to publications of scandals, market competition increased, spurring further publication of official misdeeds. Politicians noted the growing importance of such stories in election outcomes, and strategic release of information could work to derail opponents or lend a hand to allies. In other cases, journalists' focus on public sphere values changed newsrooms. These "newsroom entrepreneurs," in writer Sallie Hughes's words, steered newsroom coverage in new directions; organizational ideologies influenced reporting toward, or conversely, away from particular political and economic power actors.

A shift to digital platforms in recent years has also aided a proliferation of investigative and in-depth journalism outside of mainstream and in some cases to the funding and training of regional and international organizations. Some examples are Ojo Público in Perú, Ciper in Chile, Chequeando in Argentina, Agencia Pública in Brazil, La Silla Vacía in Colombia, Armando Info in Venezuela, and Blueforesta in Bolivia.

Audiences and Digital Access

The use of digital technology has changed the way many South Americans consume news. According to United Nations estimates, the population of South America by the end of 2019 was over 428.8 million, with Brazil (211.7 million), Colombia (50.5 million), and Argentina (49.9 million) forming the most populated countries. More than three fourths of the continent's populations live in urban areas. In Argentina, Brazil, Chile, Uruguay, and Venezuela, the percentage of the population living in urban areas is even higher. Colombia, Peru, Bolivia, Paraguay, and Ecuador have somewhat larger rural populations, comparatively. By 2019, almost 70% of the South American population were online, up from 50% in 2014. A 2019 analysis of Argentina, Chile, and Brazil done by the Reuters Institute of Journalism revealed that online was the main news sources for around eight out of 10 digital consumers, although seven out of 10 also used TV, and three out of 10 used print. But despite these advances, broadband access and use still remains elusive for many. Together, Brazil, Colombia, Peru, Argentina, Venezuela, Ecuador, Bolivia, Chile, Paraguay, and Uruguay still need to connect 145.4 million people, according to the United Nations. The South American region has the highest level of inequality, and one of the least affordable mobile Internet service for the poorest 20% of the population reported the State of Mobile Internet Connectivity in 2019.

For most of Latin America, cellphone technologies provide a gateway to the Internet. Ninety-five percent of the Latin American population is covered by a 3G or higher mobile broadband network. Almost eight out of every 10 persons in Argentina, Chile, and Brazil access the news from their smartphones. And, online news is now the main source of news for Latin America, reports the Reuters Institute of Journalism. More than four in 10 (42% of the population) in Chile and other Latin American countries prefer to access news through social media. Facebook is the main social media platform for news, but Instagram and WhatsApp use is increasing in Argentina, Brazil, and Chile. In Brazil, more than half of the Internet news users prefer WhatsApp for news, while a quarter use Instagram.

Following the example of other global news media, Argentina, Chile, and Brazil news media companies have started to shift their content distribution from social media and aggregators to reader payment under the promise of more quality reports. Despite recent media campaigns, the percentage of South Americans who pay for digital journalism remains low, reaching only 9% in Chile, 11% in Argentina, 17% in Mexico, and 27% in Brazil (Statista 2021). A positive note for press, radio, and television is that South America has better financial expectations regarding the process of digital transition than the traditional media in North America and Europe, concluded Francisco Campos-Freire and colleagues in a 2017 analysis of the media trends of 19 Latin American countries.

Ownership and Call for Pluralism

Many Latin American media scholars agreed that since the beginning of the 21st century the legislative and policy reforms to communication policies in most of Argentina and Ecuador did not tackle the systemic problem of media concentration, as they mainly targeted "unfriendly media." Advertising and audiences are now concentrated in very few companies in most parts of the region. Researchers agree that media concentration reduces the "market of ideas," and the diversity of perspectives necessary for citizens to be able to have a meaningful participation in a democratic process. Corporate sector and family-owned businesses control most of the news media in Argentina, Brazil, Colombia, Ecuador, and Peru, concluded the Media Ownership Monitor and several annual reports from Reporters Without Borders, and the owners are using this outlet to influence public opinion as if it were "capital." This type of consolidation, explained Marquéz Ramírez, is not only the result of the market free flow; it is linked to politics and alliances with strong governments, which historically have provided protection, benefits, contracts, and subsidies to their media allies.

In Argentina, from 2015 to 2019, President Mauricio Macri's deregulation decrees eliminated restrictions on concentration in big media groups. As a result, the Media Ownership Monitor (MOM) from Reporters Without Borders reports that with the exception of the Clarin TV network, most popular TV stations are now owned by foreign investors. Only four media conglomerates control more than 45% of the Argentinian audience, while Group Clarin controls 25%. In Colombia, the MOM warned in March 2018 that the TV and the Radio had the highest level of media concentration, with 80% of the audience divided between four private TV channels (Caracol, RCN, city TV, and RCN Telenovelas). Three media groups control 57% of the content that society can access on radio, TV, online, and print media. Reporters Without Borders identified the media intertwined with business empires and politics.

In Peru, 6 of the 10 media groups are in the hands of family-owned corporations, which are not directly involved in politics, but have different economic interests, according to the 2016 MOM.

El Comercio Group concentrates 80% of the print circulation and almost 80% of the readership. In addition, 68% of the estimated online news audience in the country is in the hands of a single group.

Chile, one of the countries where population still prefers reading the news, faces a print press duopoly with El Mercurio y Copesa managing more than 95% of the circulation. Brazil's top four media groups concentrate more than 70% of the national audience on TV, radio, print, and online, reported the 2017 MOM. Journalists from both countries complain that the owners of these companies are connected to most of the targets of investigative journalism, making their job almost impossible.

Media–State Relations and Public Trust

Several case studies illustrate changing media–state relations. Neopopulist presidential administrations such as former Argentinian president Cristina Fernández de Kirchner, former Ecuadorian President Rafael Correa, and former Venezuelan President Hugo Chavez each spearheaded successful smear campaigns against what they perceived as opposition press, using their own social media accounts. These strategies, which also included bypassing the traditional press to communicate directly with their constituencies, resulted in significant portions of the population not trusting the traditional news outlets agreed Vigón, Juliet, and Martínez-Bustos. In Chile, the Social Barometer Surveys showed a decrease in print and TV news confidence in favor of radio and social media, coinciding with a corporate news coverage of the 2019 weeks-long street protests that sided mostly with the government of president Sebastián Piñeda, and failed to acknowledge state violence until international organizations reported it. Importantly, despite these setbacks, audiences in many South American countries such as Argentina, Chile, Brazil, and Uruguay still have a higher trust "on most of the news, most of the time" than the audiences in the United States had during the 5 years prior to 2020.

South American news media are also seeing less public trust from their audiences, following trends seen in other regions of the world. Since 2010,

Reuters and Reporters Without Borders annual studies have reported a significant decline on the level of the confidence in the traditional news outlets in most of the South American countries. A variety of factors have contributed to this trend across this vast region. The success of neopopulist rejections of an independent press in favor of "speaking directly with the people" via social media reflected what theorist Manuel Castells calls "mass self-communication," a new form of historical communication of global society digitally connected by networks.

During 2018 and 2019, the rise of "fake news" during election times also impacted journalism and trust in news media. In a 2019 Reporters Without Borders survey, Brazil registered the highest index, among 38 countries, showing concern about misinformation. Eighty-five percent of the Brazilian participants said they worried about what is real and what is false on the Internet. In Chile, it was 67% and in Argentina 62%. Another worrying factor has been the increase in the number of South American people who actively avoid the news. Argentina leads with 45% avoiders, followed by Chile (42%) and Brazil (34%).

Practicing Journalism

Across the continent, numerous problems exist for the practice of journalism according to Western standards of a free press, from corruption to impunity and even government violence. These barriers and threats manifest themselves in different ways depending on the country. In South America, in countries such as Colombia, Venezuela, and Brazil, journalists risk their life when investigating corruption or drug issues. The Bolivian government of Evo Morales (2006–2019), and the Venezuelan governments of Hugo Chavez (1999–2013) and of Nicolás Maduro (2013–), have journalists "under constant pressure" as they use "all possible means to censor independent media outlets," as concluded in the 2019 *World Press Freedom Index Summary* from Reporters Without Borders. In contrast, defamation laws in Ecuador and Perú are still used to threaten, intimidate, and prosecute journalists covering corruption and other investigative stories, especially in remote parts of the country. An exception is Uruguay, considered a regional model. Policy reforms such as the

decriminalization of media offenses or the community broadcast regulations have contributed to create a more plural and favorable "environment for journalism," Reporters Without Borders reports. As a result, the 2019 *Freedom and the Media* report identified only the Chilean and Uruguayan Press as "free;" while the Ecuadorian and Venezuelan Press were "not free," and all the rest, including the press in Argentina, Brazil, and Colombia, were considered "partially free."

Challenges for Free Press: Violence, Media Concentration, and Clientelism

The Western ideal of a press free from state bonds and located within a context of democratic institutions working in the public interest has for decades mixed with European values regarding socially responsible presses in South America. By the late 20th century, many countries overcame periods of authoritarian rule, and direct threats to journalists (such as kidnappings and killings) faded somewhat as democratic administrations came to power. Liberal market policies prompted growth of private sector advertising, and various news organizations gained a measure of economic distance from the state for a while. The emergence of investigative media outlets has increased independence and regional collaboration. At the same time, Argentina and Uruguay have decriminalized their defamation laws.

Various scholars and watchdog groups have argued, however, that during the first two decades of the 21st century and despite the already mentioned advances and, with the exception of Uruguay, the overall climate of South America press freedom has deteriorated due to several factors affecting the region. In Colombia and Brazil, there was a resurgence of the government and organized crime violence against journalists. In Argentina, Perú, Ecuador, Colombia, and Brazil, policy and legislative reforms have facilitated or failed to stop the consolidation of an already concentrated media market. Finally, a government shift from a softer indirect attempt to control journalists to a renew on authoritarianism and confrontational tactics occurred in Venezuela, Ecuador, Bolivia, and Argentina. All of this is exacerbated by extreme poverty, economic crisis, and social inequality for a large part of the population.

Media organizations across much of the region have struggled with constant change in their political and economic environments. This unevenness has had implications for performance, as outlets have had to walk a fine line between, as Waisbord put it in his 2000 article tittle, "the rock of the state and the hard place of the market." Television was launched to further state or military interests in various countries; many also saw it as a tool for social development. In Uruguay and Chile, universities and churches owned stations mandated to promote educational and cultural goals. But broadcaster relations with the state varied, especially with changes in regime type. Military regimes in Peru and Argentina weakened commercial broadcasting and instituted direct control over content; in Brazil, close relations developed between military leaders and national broadcasters, resulting in less critical coverage of those in power. In Chile, administrators appointed by the military regime held key positions in governing television programming.

By the 1980s and 1990s, deregulation and privatization liberalized media markets and broadcasting became more market oriented. Even with extensive privatization and deregulation, states still retained various means of media control. Regulation may give the state political control over media, including broadcast licensing, permit requirements, content restrictions, tariffs on technology, and taxation, and in some cases, with little public input. During these decades, one of the Latin American governments' methods of media control was allocating or removing their public advertising according to their affinity with media companies. By the time democratic rule returned to Chile in the 1990s, writer Rosalind Brenham described the presence of an "impressive array of independent media" existing in the country. However, scholars charge that the newly democratic Chilean state failed to support these diverse voices, awarding state advertising primarily to outlets aligned with official views, and with few constraints on ownership concentration, cross-ownership, and foreign investment.

Licensing requirements impeded development of independent broadcast voices, as the required technical report for a license was expensive and something smaller independent entities could rarely afford. In several cases in Chile, during the rule of Augusto Pinochet, Pinochet's advisorsutilized their elite positions in a central state-owned bank to take over ownership of important newspapers and magazines. A more recent example can be found in the use of public advertising and other subsides to covert a newly created public media, aimed to expand the plurality of voices, in an extension of the communication strategy of Argentinian President Cristina Fernández de Kirchner. In 2020, 5 years after her departure, many of them have disappeared, as President Mauricio Macri terminated the subsidies.

Despite the encouraging reforms in Uruguay and Argentina, new criminal laws were enacted in Venezuela and Ecuador to control media content. Criminal libel laws remain in effect in various parts of Latin America and can be used to silence those who criticize powerful actors, according to the Committee to Protect Journalists. In some nations, perceived insults or affronts to dignity toward public officials can be punished in the form of desacato (insult) laws. Conversely, legal infrastructure to protect or aid journalists is often superficial, or lacking altogether. Shield laws, or legislation that protects journalists from revealing confidential sources, may not be in force, or if they are, could necessitate expensive court proceedings. Legislation and initiatives to provide access to public information recently expanded in Argentina (2017), Uruguay (2014) Brazil (2011); Chile (2008); Ecuador (2004); and México and Peru (2002), yet actual compliance is, in various cases, not fully realized or enforced. State officials may still deny requests for information or ignore them altogether, and the strategic use of state information for particular benefit remains systemic in Latin America. Journalists often must depend on personal relationships for information, rather than access to databases or records. In Venezuela, both President Hugo Chavez and his successor Nicolás Maduro have maintained a contentious relationship with the country's private media, resulting in a strict legal environment for journalists and an expanded state role in media. Venezuelan presidents have increased punitive measures for breaking desacato laws, substantially increased spending in state media, and expanded a law of "social responsibility" that limits media content decisions, including mandated transmission of official messages by broadcasters.

Furthermore, disparate journalistic standards and training affects how well information is conveyed. Lack of access to formal training in new technologies or education, including an emphasis on normative principles, can be problematic. Low salaries and long hours compound the problem. Alleged reports of journalistic corruption in the region, in the forms of bowing to pressure to temper critical content, self-censoring, or engaging in other ethical compromises, have surfaced periodically.

Final Thoughts

Journalism in South America remains a mix of influences, subject to the seemingly constant flux of political and economic environments, publishing for disparate audiences mired in deep inequality, and sometimes in the face of limited access to educational and training opportunities or to newer communication technologies. More recent turns to democratic governance and market policies throughout South America have reduced somewhat the direct influence of the state in media function, but most governments retain strong forms of control over media enterprises. Ongoing processes of ownership concentration continue to place media holdings in the hands of a few corporations, a trend seen in other regions of the world. Although newer communication technologies have revitalized independent journalism and provided new spaces for investigative journalism throughout the continent, during the second decade of the 21st century, several South American presidents successfully pioneered the use of social media for smear campaigns, managing to discredit and harass unfriendly journalists and their news outlets. These factors pose significant challenges for a substantial portion of the region's population. A weak rule of law that plagues the region has implications for media function, particularly when it comes to investigations into illicit dealings.

South American journalists have managed to overcome formidable challenges in presenting information in the public interest. Exposure of high-level instances of corruption, abuses of human rights, reports on ties between *narcotraficantes*, or drug cartels, and public officials, and fraud continue, even when such publication have resulted in physical retaliation against journalists.

Perhaps the most positive sign is the reemergence of "public journalism" with the creation of more than 800 digital native, non-for-profit journalistic projects all over Latin America. A study from SembraMedia reported that these organizations represent a shift in the "news ecology" of the region and foster a well-informed conversation on issues concerning the citizens such as corruption, abuses of power, poverty, crime, impunity, and environment.

Mercedes Vigón and Juliet Pinto

See also Central America and the Caribbean; Comparative Models of Journalism; Development Journalism

Further Readings

Becerra, M. (2015). Medios públicos: el agujero negro de la política de medios. De la concentración a la convergencia. Políticas de medios en Argentina y América Latina. *Buenos Aires: Paidós, 3*, 83–106.

Bogdan-Martin, D. (November 9, 2019). Measuring digital development facts and figures 2019. ITU, United Nations agency for information and communication technologies. Retrieved from https://itu.foleon.com/itu/measuring-digital-development/offline-population/ (accessed January 2020).

Campos-Freire, F., Yaguache, J., & Ulloa, N. (2017). Trends in the media industry of South America in the digital transition. *Revista de Comunicación, 16*(2), 33–59.

Castillo, A. (June 2018). The new wave of public service journalism in Latin America." WACC Communication. Retrieved from http://waccglobal.org/who-we-are/our-organization/about-wacc (accessed January 2020).

Freedom House. 2019 Freedom and the Media: A Downward Spiral Press Freedom Dark Horizon. Retrieved from https://freedomhouse.org/report/freedom-and-media/2019/media-freedom-downward-spiral (accessed June 2021).

Herrscher, R. (2019). Chile despertó es momento que despierte el periodismo. *New York Times*. December, 16. Retrieved from https://www.nytimes.com/es/2019/12/12/espanol/opinion/medios-protestas-chile.html

Hughes, S., & Lawson, C. (2005). The barriers to media opening in Latin America. *Political Communication, 22*(1), 9–25.

ITU, United Nations Agency for Information and communication Technologies. (December 2019).

World Telecommunication/ICT Indicators Database online, 23rd Edition. Retrieved from https://www.itu .int/pub/D-IND-WTID.OL-2019. (January, 2020).

Marquez Ramírez, M., and Guerrero, M. A. (2017). Clientelism and media capture in Latin America. In A. Schiffrind (Ed.), *In the Service of Power: Media Capture, and the Threat to Democracy* (pp. 43–58). Washington, DC: Center for International Media Assistance.

Mastrini, G., & Becerra, M. (2009). *Los dueños de la palabra* [the owners of the word]. Buenos Aires: Prometeo.

"Media Ownership Monitor." Reporters Without Borders, RSF. Retrieved from https://www.mom-rsf .org/en/countries/ (accessed June 2021).

Mioli,T. (2018). Smartphones reign supreme for news consumers in Latin America. Journalism in the Americas Blog. *Knight Center*, June. Retrieved from https://knightcenter.utexas.edu/en/blog/00-19846 -smartphones-reign-supreme-news-consumers-latin -america-according-reuters-institute (accessed December 2020).

Monje, D. I. (2015). The country that does not fit. Policies of citizen access to public audiovisual systems in South America. *Chasqui.Revista Latinoamericana de Comunicación, 129*, 41–59.

Prado, P. (2011). The impact of the internet in six Latin American Countries. *Western Hemisphere Security Analysis Center, 6*. Retrieved from https:// digitalcommons.fiu.edu/cgi/viewcontent.cgi?article= 1005&context=whemsac (accessed December 2019).

Repucci, S. (2019). Freedom and The Media 2019: A Downward Spiral. *Freedom House* June (2019). Retrieved from https://freedomhouse.org/report /freedom-media/freedom-media-2019 (accessed June 2021).

Reuters. "Annual Digital Reports" (June 2020). Retrieved from https://reutersinstitute.politics.ox.ac.uk/sites /default/files/2020-06/DNR_2020_FINAL.pdf (accessed June 2021).

Saldaña, M., & Mourão, R. R. (2018). Reporting in Latin America: Issues and perspectives on investigative journalism in the region. *The International Journal of Press/Politics, 23*(3), 299–323.

Segura, M. S., & Waisbord, S. (2016). *Civic society and media policy reform in Latin America*. Chicago: The University of Chicago Press.

Vigón, M., Pinto, J., & Martínez-Bustos, L. (2018). Environmental news coverage in Ecuador: New resources, old media-state tensions and practices. In B. Takahashi, J. Pinto, M. Vigón & M. Chávez (Ed.),

News media coverage of environmental challenges in Latin America and the Caribbean. Mediating demand, degradation and development. London: Palgrave MacMillan

Waisbord, S. (2011). Between support and confrontation: Civic society, media reform, and populism in Latin America. *Communication, Culture & Critique, 4*, 97–117.

Waisbord, S. (2000). Media in South America: Between the rock of the state and the hard place of the market. In J. Curran and M. Park (Ed.), *De-Westernizing Media Studies* (pp. 50–62). New York: Routledge.

World Freedom Index 2019: Authoritarism and disinformation worsen the situation in Latin America. (April, 2019). Reporters Without Borders, RSF. Retrieved from https://rsf.org/en/2019-rsf-index -authoritarianism-and-disinformation -worsen-situation-latin-america (accessed December 2019).

Spectacle

Dozens of police cars slowly following a white Ford Bronco broadcast live on television. A hearse carrying a flower-laden coffin drives by with hundreds of mourners watching and crying. Spectators in a crowded arena cheer as a presidential candidate shouts about restoring a country's past greatness. These images, beamed to millions of television viewers live and repeatedly replayed in subsequent news reports and printed in newspapers and online, comprise examples of spectacles—characterized by simplified narratives, emotional appeal, and attention-grabbing visuals.

The concept of spectacle as related to mass media theory derives from the writings of French philosopher Guy Debord, whose highly influential *The Society of the Spectacle*, first published in 1967 and reprinted with an updated preface by the author in 1994, offered a series of theses describing a postcapitalist society wherein lived reality had become separated from a media-created reality. The spectacle metaphor originates in the idea of theater, upon whose stage occurs the processes and results of the interactions of political actors removed from the spectators—that is, the people of a society—who passively watch rather than becoming involved in the workings of the world and taking part in their own destiny.

Spectacle by nature means a show or display created with purpose by its producers that is then packaged and presented to a viewing audience. The concept of spectacle as conceived by Debord becomes relevant when evaluating the role of mass media in a society based in a capitalistic economic system; the presentation of "facts" and "reality" according to mediated packaging serves as a reified example of the spectacle at work. In this entry, Debord's concept of the society of the spectacle is explained, followed by a discussion of its application to journalistic practice. Variations on the concept of spectacle are discussed; these involve media and news coverage of out-of-the-ordinary events that both require and often subsequently become content for continuing and sensational treatment by the press. Reflective of a certain political economy bound by the dictates of the media industry, media and news spectacles offer sites at which journalism ethics and moral considerations come into play. Examples of news coverage that invoke the spectacle are described, as well as how spectacle intertwines news with entertainment and celebrity with significance, and how it has become more and more a part of how political campaigns and issues are produced and then covered by news organizations.

The Spectacle in Society

Anticipating the proliferation of media technology beyond television, Debord's *The Society of the Spectacle* provides a foundation for approaching media spectacles through the lens of critical theory. Borrowing from Karl Marx's analysis of the capitalistic society in which workers are separated from their labor, with the production and consumption of commodities serving as society's all-important goal, Debord takes this further. Whereas Marx discussed an emphasis on having rather than being, for Debord the emphasis in society was on appearing rather than having. The accumulation of commodities had conquered the whole of social life to the point that now one literally buys the representation of social life transmitted through media images created by an industry whose purpose is to produce images of life as lived by others. Asserted Debord in Thesis 1, which

opens his book: "The whole life those societies in which modern conditions of production prevail presents itself as an immense accumulation of *spectacles*" (p. 12). Further, this accumulation of spectacles observed and consumed replaces the directly lived life, separating individuals from each other as they individually consume that accumulation of images presented on the stage of mass media.

As explained by James Compton in *The Integrated News Spectacle: A Political Economy of Cultural Performance* (2004), the spectacle society fosters the noninvolved spectator, with only second-hand stories of "real life" delivered through mass media representing in part the entire workings of that society as a whole. Rather than directly experiencing life for themselves, people "contemplate it in a passive way via images constructed and administered by others" (p. 36).

Debord weaves the profit-making aspect of media industries into his description of the society of the spectacle, including the phenomenon of media monopolization together with the spectacle producers' self-interest to uphold the status quo. As "administrators" of the existing system, the media thus become inseparable from the state while simultaneously separating the people under the rule of the state from each other, the power of state, the spectacle (the images presented in mediated form where the "action" of society occurs) itself, and their own power. This separation function occurs because the "communication" in mass communication goes in only one direction. Thus, power in the society of the spectacle emanates from those who serve as the actors on the spectacle's stage and those who package that action in mediated forms. As consumers of the spectacle, we, the viewing audience, perpetually play the part of spectator rather than participant in our own society.

Under this model of one-way communication, the mass media serve not only as conduits of the amalgamated spectacle of representations of social life, but media messages become commodities in and of themselves, to be consumed by a passive audience. Debord mentioned media forms and content that reify the theory of the spectacle; these include news, propaganda, advertising, and entertainment. In some way or another, everything presented by the media upholds the existing system, becomes a way to sell commodities (such as the advertising of products and services), or is a commodity itself (entertainment). In sum, Debord's notion of spectacle, according to Douglas Kellner (2010), "constituted the overarching concept to describe the media and consumer society, including the packaging, promotion, and display of commodities and the production and effects of all media" (p. 117).

News and the Spectacle

Debord's description of the spectacle may appear overly abstract, but a concrete example of the spectacle at work in the media coverage of the 1989 fall of the Berlin Wall appears in his preface to the 1994 edition of *The Society of the Spectacle*. The way in which this complex historical event was covered and framed by a simplified narrative—the triumph of democracy and a free market economy—together with images of an actual and symbolic wall being dismantled illustrated the "striving of the spectacle toward modernization and unification" (p. 9). Rather than delving into a deep analysis of the events leading up to it, news coverage told the story of the victory of the West, and its accompanying ideology of capitalism. This simplification of storytelling characterizes the way in which the mass media frame events to be easily consumed by the passive spectator, while upholding the power structure maintained by the spectacle—the version of the world that those in power want us to see.

As the spectacle presents a version of life created by media, so, too, do celebrities serve as "spectacular representations of living human beings," wrote Debord (p. 38), providing substitutes that take the place of spectators' real lives, which pale in comparison. In a media culture, noted Kellner (2003), celebrities are "the gods and goddesses of everyday life" (p. 4). Celebrity news adds to the spectacle by providing models for spectator identification, while fulfilling the spectacle's purpose of distracting by entertaining.

The combination of news and entertainment also marks the society of the spectacle, with "infotainment" reflective of the commercial logic of the spectacle which requires getting and maintaining the attention of the audience. The 24-hour news organizations, notably cable channels, have the ability to disseminate information nonstop and integrate that content via the television and computer screen. While sensationalism and news stories with high emotional appeal, easily understood narratives, and drama have always marked what we know as "news," the intensity and scale with which news media cover events has increased, thanks to the capabilities of technology such as satellites and the internet.

Kellner (2003) used the term *news spectacle* to describe "media extravaganzas, sporting events, political happenings, and those attention-grabbing occurrences" we commonly place under the category of news (p. 2), with the term *megaspectacle* describing hyped-up news spectacles that not only distract spectators from daily life, but can define time periods of history and culture. Megaspectacles thus mark a society's very timeline, demarcating the spectacular in terms of crime, scandal, and disaster that define eras. For example, during the 1990s, megaspectacles included the murder trial of former sports star O. J. Simpson, the impeachment scandal of President Bill Clinton, and the death and funeral of Princess Diana.

News spectacles and megaspectacles feature simple narratives that the audience understands, and their unusualness plays into the sensationalism upon which media rely. Coverage of conflicts and war thus become much like an ongoing serialized television show, framed in simplistic us-versus-them terms and packaged with dramatic music, graphics, and titles such as "Crisis in the Gulf," for the Gulf War of 1990–1991, and coupled with live reports from the battlefield during the Gulf War and again during the U.S. invasion at the start of the Iraq War in 2003. Compton (2004) noted the way in which war in recent decades has become aestheticized by news outlets such as CNN.

The megaspectacle of the September 11, 2001, terrorist attacks on the United States marks the historical time periods of a pre- and post-9/11 world. Kellner (2003) pointed out how the event and its aftermath brought drama to the globalized coverage, with the constant replaying of video of the two planes hitting the twin towers of the World Trade Center, the towers falling, and of the smoldering wreckage of the Pentagon. Drama and aesthetics heightened the spectacular nature of the story, with slogans and slickly produced introductions to coverage with titles such as "War on America," and the assumption made by news outlets that the United States was already at war, noted Kellner (2005). The megaspectacle of these images and phrases converged with the response by President George W. Bush, whose rhetoric invoked the simplified language of the Old West with the phrase to describe the person ultimately held responsible for the attacks as being "wanted: dead or alive." As explained by Compton (2004), "The Manichean logic of good versus evil quickly became the frame within which most mainstream news organizations structured their stories" (p. 87). The spectacular nature of 9/11 thus became one of the biggest news stories in recent history, with the media-centric society of the spectacle poised for its coverage in terms of technology. The reaffirmation of U.S.-Western values that undergirded the power structure of that very society became interwoven into the news coverage of the event itself, as theorized by Debord.

Deaths and public funerals of prominent news makers and celebrities serve the spectacle intrinsically, becoming global news spectacles, such as the death of Pope John Paul II in 2005. In that coverage of celebrity funerals have been known to double the daytime television audience, noted Compton (2004), major networks vied for the best locations for broadcasting live from the Vatican and other locations in Rome during the pope's final days. In the weeks and days leading to Pope John Paul II's passing, the entire world seemed to be watching and waiting in sympathy as the 84-year-old pontiff appeared, frail and weak, to the faithful who had gathered in St. Peter's Square. In that the Vatican itself was considered one of the most secretive organizations in the world, the transparency of the pope's illness and medical condition was ironic. Sophie Arie (2005), in the article "Illness as Media Spectacle," addressed the ethics of making a literal spectacle and show of the Pope's death, with some in the media saying that the coverage had gone too far. This combined with how the pope himself had encouraged the Vatican to use the media, his welcoming of media coverage of the spectacles of his appearances around the world, and the example he set about facing death with serenity, suggest a nebulous morality surrounding the spectacle.

The Spectacle of Political News Coverage

Because "politics is understood as a form of theatre that implies the existence of a spectator rather than being understood as an intercommunity of action," as noted by Kati Röttger (2017, p. 33), news coverage of political campaigns amplifies the show that surrounds them. Presidential elections make for ideal fodder for the spectacle, both via the representation and images of candidates as well as the physical staging of events so as to make for good visuals. Political spectacle allows for a simplified narrative of the contest and conflict, with "showdowns" between political parties and within parties an easy way to frame stories, with explanations of policy and pragmatics aspects of government pushed to the side.

In recent years, U.S. presidential campaigns—and their aftermaths—have taken on the proportions of the megaspectacle, with media coverage dramatizing unprecedented occurrences and serializing developments like a reality show. The contested outcome of the 2000 election between George W. Bush and Al Gore in 2000; the media spectacles that surrounded the 2008 candidacies of two women, Republican vice presidential nominee Sarah Palin and Hillary Clinton, who was vying to be the Democratic presidential nominee; and the worldwide celebrations that marked the 2008 victory of Barack Obama as the first African American president, all illustrated the fusion of news, drama, and entertainment of the political spectacle.

Kellner, in his 2003 book *Media Spectacle*, observed that in the age of spectacle, media "are complicit in the generation of spectacle politics, reducing politics to image, display and story in the forms of entertainment and drama" (p. 160).

The 2016 presidential campaign of its eventual victor, Donald Trump, over the first female major-party presidential candidate, Hillary Clinton, embodied key elements of the spectacle as explained here based on Debord's theory: a simplified campaign slogan, celebrity status, and a showmanship based on a keen understanding of how to gain media attention through optics and visual pageantry. A primary mechanism that marked the political theatre and spectacle created by the Trump campaign was the fusion of entertainment and personal image of the candidate, whose star power had already been cemented by the media culture. The 2016 Trump presidential campaign served as the epitome of the spectacle, as media coverage fixated on the spectacle it created and treated it as entertainment. According to Heather Yates (2019), the optics and visual appeal of rallies in large venues, a "carnival-like atmosphere" in which concession stands sold merchandise featuring the campaign's slogan, extreme personalization over policy, and offering voters excessive expectations all were ways that the spectacle itself was manipulated by the candidate. The artful use of social media, through outrageous tweets on the public medium of Twitter, noted Kellner (2016), dominated the news cycle, adding fuel to the already "surreal" campaign (p. 6). These tactics continued as the Trump presidency unfolded.

Robert Zaretsky, opining in *The New York Times* in 2017, addressed the implications of the spectacle as described by Debord in the late 1960s and how it still resonates in the Trump era, perhaps ever more so with the rise of social media and reliance of journalism as a source of news and commentary. Even with the pessimism that characterized Debord's notion of a spectacle society in which images have replaced lived reality, and spectators are removed from their own power, collective actions that appear to resist the power of the spectacle yet also take on the qualities of the news spectacle have occurred, notably the massive Women's March in January of 2017. Such events and the media coverage that accompanies them become even more urgent, and invite us, as journalists and citizens, to consider Zaretsky's question: "Do the critical counter-images that protesters create constitute true resistance, or are they instead collaborating with our fascination with spectacle?"

Erika Engstrom

See also Cable News; Celebrity and Fan Media; CNN; Democracy and the Media; Election Coverage, U.S.; Entertainment Journalism; Ethics; Infotainment; Sensationalism

Further Readings

Arie, S. (2005, April 9). Illness as media spectacle. *The BMJ, 330*, 850. doi: 10.1136/bmj.330.7495.850

Compton, J. (2004). *The integrated news spectacle: A political economy of cultural performance*. New York, NY: Peter Lang.

Debord, G. (1994). *The society of the spectacle* (D. Nicholson-Smith, Trans.). Brooklyn, NY: Zone Books.

Kellner, D. (2003). *Media spectacle*. New York, NY: Routledge.

Kellner, D. (2010). Media spectacle, presidential politics, and the transformation of journalism. In S. Stuard (Ed.), *The Routledge companion to news and journalism* (pp. 116–126). New York, NY: Routledge.

Kellner, D. (2016). *American nightmare: Donald Trump, media spectacle, and authoritarian populism*. Boston, MA: Sense Publishing.

Röttger, K. (2017). Spectacle and politics: Is there a political a political reality in the spectacle of society? In G. Gandesha & J. Hartle (Eds.), *The spell of capital: Reification and spectacle* (pp. 133–148). Amsterdam: Amsterdam University Press.

Yates, H. (2019). *The politics of spectacle and emotion in the 2016 presidential campaign*. Cham, Switzerland: Palgrave Macmillan.

Zaretsky, R. (2017, February 20). Trump and the "society of the spectacle." *The New York Times*. https://www.nytimes.com/2017/02/20/opinion/trump-and-the-society-of-the-spectacle.html

SPIN

Spin is a pejorative term that is associated with manipulative communication practices typically used during media relations. Frequently, the practice is associated with so-called spin doctors who are media relations professionals who use their insight and media techniques to influence public opinion through the press. In the age of social media, spin is something that can be used in multiple channels including traditional media, but also personal websites, social media, and advertising. However, spin is frequently associated with an organization's or person's ability to shape their organizational or personal image in a way that heavily influences public perception. Skills include being able to persuasively communicate with the public, the press, and even individuals in a way that influences their opinions and perceptions.

Spin is sometimes associated with public relations (PR), although that association is highly criticized by PR practitioners and educators. Part of the reason for this association with PR is that spin is associated heavily with persuasion, which is related to PR practice. The difference between spin and PR, however, is that PR practice is rooted in ethical norms and practices of the field, such as those established by professional organizations. Conversely, spin is a communication practice that is exclusively self-serving, focusing on the image and influence of the speaker. Although frequently associated with politics, spin is also associated with business, nonprofit organizations, or any situation where news events are framed in a positive way by an interested party. Typically, this results in media framing of an issue that benefits one specific perspective or portrayal of an event.

This entry focuses on spin as a term and as a concept, especially with regard to PR, media relations, and politics. It concludes with a discussion of contemporary connotations and associations of the term and concept.

Spin as a Term

As a practice, *spin* as a term is closely related to the term *spin doctor*, which made its appearance in the English vernacular in the 1980s and 1990s in the United States. A spin doctor is a person who practices spin as a professional communicator. The genesis of the term *spin doctor* is closely associated with the term *spin* because both gained traction as communication terms during the 1980s in the United States. During the 1980s, spin doctor was frequently used to refer to a person working in the political communication context who had skills at media relations. One of the first descriptions of spin doctors in 1980s was in national newspapers, such as *The New York Times* and *The Washington Post*, which frequently associated them with political campaigns. In a 1986 *The New York Times* article titled "Calling Dr. Spin," William Safire noted that *spin doctors* was a term that emerged during the 1984 Ronald Reagan-Walter Mondale presidential debates. He credited *The New York Times* as having used the term in an editorial after the debate, and *The Washington Post* reporter Elisabeth Bumiller as using the term later and describing the profession as related to media relations. Safire said that the spin doctors emerged in postdebate analysis in the press room

where surrogates (i.e., spin doctors) interacted with journalists advocating for their candidate.

This association with political debates leads to another term associated with spin—the "spin room." Spin rooms are places reporters, candidates, and campaign staffers reiterate talking points created by the campaigns. The point of these spin rooms is for candidates and campaign staffers to influence postdebate analysis that frequently focuses on who won or lost a particular debate. By 1988, *CBS This Morning* even had a segment that looked at spin doctors as part of a political campaign. In his analysis of spin, Safire associated spin as a political media concept to the older phrases involving "spinning" balls and stories. The phrase "spinning a yarn" has been used as a phrase to identify a preposterous or highly inaccurate story that is frequently flattering to the storyteller. Putting a "spin" on a ball indicates creating a pitch that has a purposeful direction. Therefore, spinning is the use of communication in the form of narrative that leads to a purposeful result for the communicator.

PR practitioners typically eschew the term *spin* altogether because it conflicts with their core values of ethics in communication, transparency, and public trust. The use of the term *spin* as a part of a communication professional's skills or title is uncommon. Typically, the term *spin* takes on a negative connotation because it is portrayed in the media as a form of pure advocacy for an individual or organization, as evidenced by early uses of "spin" in postdebate analysis. In fact, spin is a form of pure advocacy that has the goal of persuading an audience of the speaker's position. Spin does not necessarily have to include untruthful information but is part of opinion creating and shaping in the light most favorable to the speaker's view.

The association with spin and politics is close. Some writers have even equated to political news making, especially at the presidential level, as a type of spin. For instance, historian David Greenberg wrote a book titled the *Republic of Spin*, which details how presidencies and polling have influenced American politics starting with the administration of Theodore Roosevelt through the modern era. He argues that the use of spin by presidents took hold in the 1960s with the advent of the permanent presidential campaign, a phenomenon in which the president acted in a campaign mode during his tenure in office. The use of the term *spin*, especially as it relates to politics, took hold in the American lexicon in the 1990s as seen with television programming *Spin City*, an ABC sitcom about a New York City mayor's office, and the title *No Spin Zone: Confrontations With the Powerful and Famous in America* written by Bill O'Reilly in 2001.

Spin as a Concept

As a concept spin, or influencing public perception over an event, has a long history in the United States that is rooted in the growth of awareness of public opinion and public sentiment, especially in a political context. American press has frequently been an instrument for shaping popular opinion. As the press grew, so did its use for promotional purposes. P. T. Barnum, the famous showman and circus owner, frequently used staged events to obtain free publicity for his business. However, by the turn of the 20th century there was a growing awareness that media and the press had significant impact on popular opinion concerning government, politics, and causes. Beginning in World War I with the Committee on Public Information (CPI), PR history has acknowledged the role of spin and the use of deceptive communication practices to achieve political results. However, spin is not a concept that is limited to the 20th century. In fact, spin is something that is not necessarily insidious. It sometimes is practiced explicitly, especially in terms of U.S. presidential politics.

Every president of the United States beginning with George Washington is credited with having some level of self-awareness of public image and public attitudes. This frequently required what today would be called *media* or *press relations*. Part of this media relations and image formation required presidents to create deliberate images of themselves and current issues. This type of presidential spin has been on display since the beginning of the presidency. However, professional advisors adept in working the press and crafting public opinion has led the way in how presidential spin works. Beginning with Amos Kendall, who served in the famed "Kitchen Cabinet" of Andrew Jackson, to media-savvy Donald Trump,

there is a belief that image creation and maintenance is a key part of presidential politics. Press secretaries, press events, speeches, and formal events, such as the State of the Union address or pardoning of the Thanksgiving turkey, have been argued to be part of presidential spin. In fact, the political use of spin is closely related to the media cycle and influence of media on public perception.

Scripted and planned communication became a norm for U.S. presidents with President William McKinley and refined under Theodore Roosevelt. In fact, Theodore Roosevelt is credited with having a keen awareness of how the press framed the presidency, and his use of media relations helped him craft his public image. Other presidents including Franklin Roosevelt, John F. Kennedy, and Ronald Reagan have been credited with effectively using media to frame their image and presidencies. Roosevelt's fireside chats, Kennedy's ease with television, and Reagan's speeches coupled with background optics are viewed as important strategies that helped define their presidential agendas. Similarly, the institutionalization of press secretaries for presidents and other politicians have become a norm within U.S. politics, further illustrating the importance of crafting a media narrative.

As media and politics developed, a more complex relationship in the television age, the concept of spin grew. This was particularly true as political debates, increased press briefings, and political events became media events. Campaign surrogates using spin rooms after debates frequently try to create spin that favors a particular issue of the candidate because that spin has the impact of influencing the media framing of an issue. If a particular spin is put on an issue, then that particular perspective becomes a powerful lens in which public opinion is shaped.

Spin is closely related to the concept of shaping public opinion. The concept of the power of public opinion in relations to politics is rooted in discussions of democratic government. However, understanding the public sentiment about political issues became of greater interest during the late 19th century. In fact, the social science or study behind spinning is rooted in the growth of social science in the late 19th century in Europe. This awareness of public opinion became more sophisticated over time, especially as the electorate expanded during the 19th and 20th centuries.

The creation of spin as a concept is an outgrowth of understanding the importance of public opinion. Social scientists in the 19th century, notably Gabriel Tarde and Gustav Le Bon, first identified some of the issues surrounding public opinion and crowd behavior. Their work showed that people could be influenced heavily by the words and messages of others. By the early 20th century, the awareness and importance of public opinion became more solidified. Political campaigns and political officeholders recognized that the press played an important role in shaping public opinion. By the 1930s, academic interest in public opinion grew with the creation of *Public Opinion Quarterly*, first published in 1937. Public opinion polling has become more sophisticated during the 20th and 21st centuries with the advancement of polling and increased use of computerized statistics. Today the use of large sets of data can indicate public opinion on a variety of issues.

This created a greater awareness of the power of public opinion and the communications that shaped it. The concept of spin is closely related to the concept of propaganda, which is a deceptive communication practice that is used to manipulate public opinion. In the United States, propaganda first became an issue during World War I when the Woodrow Wilson administration established the CPI, also known as the *Creel Committee* (because it was chaired by George Creel). The result of the CPI was a sophisticated U.S. communication strategy that sought to boost morale for World War I and also discredit criticism of the war and counterpropaganda issued from the Central Powers.

In 1922, journalist Walter Lippmann wrote a highly influential book entitled *Public Opinion*, which detailed how public opinion was formed and how people made decisions and how certain parameters in cognition make people think in a particular way. Early PR practitioner Edward Bernays, who has been referred to by biographer Larry Tye as the "Father of Spin," sought to reintroduce the term *propaganda* as a form of practice during the 1920s with his book *Propaganda*, published in 1928. Bernays's view was that propaganda could actually be a good thing because opinion leaders could influence the public to support certain views that were in the public's best interest. However, Bernays's attempt to repurpose the term *propaganda* largely failed by the advent of World War II. In fact, Adolph Hitler thought that propaganda during World War I was so effective that it led to the Allies' victory. His book *Mein Kampf* included two chapters on propaganda and the importance propaganda, or manipulative communications, had on shaping public attitudes.

With the awareness of propaganda in post-World War I United States, there was an increased interest in the power of persuasion. There was a fear by some that deceptive communication practices were harmful to society, and that public education could serve to educate the public against manipulative practices of deception. One organization, the Institute for Propaganda Analysis, was formed in 1937 to combat the effects and impact of propaganda on the public. This organization sought to educate the public about the power of propaganda, and how to be more aware consumers of information, particular biased information that may impact political beliefs. Still, others in the communication field disagreed with the fear of persuasive communication. During World War II, the Nazi propaganda became so reviled that the term became associated with deceptive information practices and with negative connotations.

After World War II, communication practice became more sophisticated in the corporate context, and the rise of psychographic information, consumer psychology, and polling became a way to gauge public opinion. This led to an increased professionalization of communication, but also led to criticisms about media power and control. Scholars and social critics wrote about how disinformation and propaganda were regularly used to influence public opinion to support wars and to promote biased packaging of content by corporate media. Several theories began to emerge about media's effect on society, and how individuals processed information. Theories such as the hypodermic needle theory, two-step flow, agenda setting, and later uses and gratifications began to demonstrate how media were selected and processed by individuals. However, even though media theories had different perspectives on how people used and processed media information, the idea that media content was important to shaping public attitudes and beliefs is something that was addressed by many media theories. Perhaps the closest theoretical framework that addresses spin is framing theory, which argues that communication frames issues in a certain way that is later understood within those frames by people. However, framing is not considered the same as spin, as it has an ethical undertone to its definition and application to media.

Contemporary Connotations and Perceptions

Today's use of the term *spin* carries the baggage of older debates about propaganda and unethical communication. Its use in the political sphere remains, but its connotation spans from advocacy (least pejorative use) to outright manipulation of facts and use of lies (most pejorative use). This use of spin to mean manipulative communication has led to a cottage industry of books and articles that attempt to show how the public is persuaded by manipulative communication. In 1957, the book *The Hidden Persuaders*, written by journalist Vance Packard, detailed how Americans were persuaded by advertisers who used psychological information about consumers to make them buy products. By 1961, historian Daniel Boorstin wrote *The Image: A Guide to Pseudo-Events in America* that detailed how news in America was packaged in a way such that real news actually was not reported. Instead, Boorstin argued that "pseudo-events" or news-like events replaced news in a way that most Americans could not tell the difference between real and pseudo news. Part of the rationale for this consumption of pseudo-event news is that Americans expect news to entertain, so pseudo-events that are created by individuals or organizations (frequently with PR help) came to dominate news coverage.

Frequently, spin as a concept is associated with PR practice. Books about the term *spin* have PR connections such as Stuart Ewen's *PR!: A Social History of Spin*, which argues that PR practice uses spin to promote certain organizational objectives. He associates the rise of the spin in PR with Edward Bernays and details how corporate America used particular communication tools to achieve their desired results by shaping public opinion. Another book that associates PR profession with

spin is Bob Burton's *Inside Spin: The Dark Underbelly of the PR Industry*, which details how corporations have used communication to achieve organizational goals, often at the expense of societal well-being. While these books are merely examples of associating PR with spin, they represent a larger common perception that the PR industry is primarily motivated by spinning facts in a favorable way to corporations. This is rooted in a larger skepticism about the honesty of corporate communications, and some high-profile corporate crises that have garnered negative media attention.

The PR industry eschews the label of "spin" because of the negative connotations of the term. In fact, the term *public relations* has even become used in a derogatory way because of its association with the concept of "spinning." The four models of PR articulated by James Grunig and Todd Hunt state that there are four types of PR communication: press agentry, information model, two-way asymmetrical, and two-way symmetrical. The concept of spin is something that is associated with press agentry, a 19th century type of PR practice that used stunts and promotions to facilitate publicity to an organization. Modern PR practice has embraced the two-way symmetrical model of PR, which does not use pure advocacy or spin to communicate with publics. In fact, this model of PR argues that spinning content actually creates public distrust, which harms the image of an organization.

PR practice today views itself as a relationship management communication practice that may use advocacy as one tool to communicate with key publics. Spinning an event for a client would likely be viewed as unethical, especially because honesty is a cornerstone of the field as indicated in the Public Relations Society of America Code of Ethics. Using deceptive means to minimize or advocate for an organization harms the credibility of the profession of PR and actually ends up harming the clients because it negatively impacts their reputation.

Media are not so disinterested as to accept spinning as a regular practice without fact checking the communicators involved. Because of that, regular PR practice has routinely accepted ethical practices of honesty and fair-dealing with the press and publics.

Cayce Myers

See also Propaganda; Public Relations; Public Relations, Ethics in; Public Relations, History of

Further Readings

Bernays, E. (1928). *Propaganda*. New York, NY: Liveright.

Boorstin, D. (1962). *The image: A guide to pseudo-events in America*. Manhattan, NY: Harper & Row.

Burton, B. (2008). *Inside spin: The dark underbelly of the PR industry*. Crows Nest: Allen & Unwin.

Ewen, S. (1996). *PR!: A social history of spin*. New York, NY: Basic Books.

Grunig, J., & Hunt, T. (1984) *Managing public relations*. New York, NY: Holt, Rinehart and Winston.

Lippmann, W. (1922). *Public opinion*. San Diego, CA: Harcourt, Brace and Company.

O'Reilly, B. (2001). *The no spin zone: Confrontations with the powerful and famous in America*. Manhattan, NY: Broadway.

Packard, V. (1957). *The hidden persuaders*. Lombard, IL: McKay Co.

Safire, W. (1988, August). Calling Dr. Spin. *New York Times*, SM8.

Tye, L. (2002). *The father of spin: Edward L Bernays the birth of public relations*. London, UK: Picador.

SPORTS BROADCASTING

Sports broadcasting has become ubiquitous in the 21st century. Content is available on various devices and in nearly any form (e.g., ESPN's coverage of college football's national championship game on eight distinct channels with unique approaches to each outlet). It was not always this way, but is the new norm. From nationally broadcast but sometimes tape-delayed "game of the week" to 24-hour access, sports broadcasting remains as a last frontier of live consumption in traditional mass media form. The foundation of television production remains the core of sports broadcasting, despite access points (e.g., Twitter, MLB.tv) that no longer restrict an audience to watch from home or a place of mass gathering.

Sports offers an unmatched spectacle of excitement and unknown outcomes. The Olympic Games and soccer's FIFA World Cup provide a global audience with billions of viewers cheering for their respective nations while witnessing sporting events that are only available every 4 years. The Olympic Games are available in summer and winter formats that alternate every 2 years. The FIFA World Cup hosts a men's event and a women's event in consecutive years but each iteration is limited to a 4-year cycle. Thus, the events garner billion-dollar television and multimedia contracts that fuel the spectacle.

Outside these events that are global in scope and not annually available, professional sports leagues and U.S. college sports provide the content that fuels the business model and regular programming for sports broadcasting. Highlights of the marquee events include the National Football League (NFL) Super Bowl, the College Football Playoff, the National Collegiate Athletic Association (NCAA) men's basketball tournament (i.e., March Madness), the National Basketball Association (NBA) finals, Premiere League soccer, and golf and tennis major championships. The "regular season" games and matches in each of these respective sports leagues and associations provide the consistent programming that broadcast networks seek—and subsequently pay billions of dollars—in order to reach a highly engaged fan base willing to spend their time and money consuming sports.

The history of sports broadcasting traces to five key times that provide context for its pervasive reach: (1) the 1936 Olympic Games in Berlin, Germany; (2) sports as spectacle; (3) satellite technology and the rise of superstations; (4) ESPN and the legal fight for college football; and (4) online and streaming technology. These five elements are significant because they outline the role of sports broadcasting in a social transition from access to the construction of sports fandom through consumption. The increase in opportunities for consumption has been expanded by new technologies that have impacted audience reach.

Broadcast Potential and the 1936 Olympic Games

The rise of sports' popularity in media started in newspapers in the late 1800s around the same time that sports gained social significance beyond physical exercise. The creation of modern sports league was underway with baseball and the construction of the college sports system in the United States. Newspapers provided daily space to recap what happened in sports, not just locally, but across the country and the world. However, that was yesterday's news. Live programming of sports provided a way to participate in and engage with sports even if not attending an event as a spectator. The first broadcast of a sporting event was a radio transmission of the 1921 World Series. It was another 18 years before U.S. viewers would "see" a baseball game via television. This would forecast two interesting effects of sports broadcasting: visibility and profitability. Sports presented a vested audience for advertisers to reach and a financial windfall for sports leagues that positioned them as economic drivers for media.

In between those benchmark dates and long-term implications, the 1936 Olympic Games in Berlin gave rise to the broadcast potential for sports. Germany wanted to highlight the nation through Olympic prowess on its home soil as a support to the early rise of Nazi control under Adolf Hitler. Therefore, Germany offered radio transmission free to anyone willing to carry the signal. This was well-received in the United States where CBS and NBC both tapped into the broadcast in their battle for early radio supremacy. The first glimpse of what "transoceanic" transmission could offer through sports programing provided a way for an audience to experience a place only seen by few elite travelers who could afford to visit.

The 1936 Olympic Games in Berlin also offered the first visual broadcast of a sporting event through film technology. Theaters in Germany "showed" what the Olympic Games looked like, not just what could be heard or read. The film had to be processed and shipped before it could be seen beyond Germany's closed-circuit signal. However, the visuals that film provided helped produce how the events are historically and socially remembered. Jesse Owens, a Black athlete, won four gold medals, a symbolic afront to both Hitler and segregation in the United States. In addition, the story of the removal of Jewish athletes from competition was visible through their omission. The opportunity to visually access the Games had a lasting impact, despite poor broadcast quality. As Michael J. Socolow (2016) noted, "The Berlin Games represented the first alignment of multilateral global broadcast technology with sophisticated propaganda technique. The combination of compelling sports narrative and new modes of modern telecommunication created the blueprint for all future sports broadcasting" (p. 7). The opportunity to offer sports for its perceived transcendental impact on social issues as well as a space to glorify athletes to a growing sports audience with disposable income was why broadcast networks started to spend heavily on sports programming.

Sports Spectacle and the Sports/Media Complex

Following World War II, broadcast networks turned to sports as a supplement to primetime and news programming. Sports were reaching front pages of newspapers, and the creation of *Sports Illustrated* in 1954 was another harbinger of access that blended the power of the visual element in sports coverage. *Sports Illustrated* also impacted the depth of journalistic coverage devoted to sports and recognized an audience willing to pay for content beyond the record-keeping of winners and losers. The British Broadcasting Corporation (BBC) and U.S.-based networks CBS and NBC were willing to pay for programming that they considered extremely valuable in a growing financial model centered on advertising.

The early transmission of broadcast signals was limited to closed-circuit viewing, which meant a transmission was sent to a central location to see the content, usually movie theaters. Boxing was the primary sport in this early process, which Florian Hoof noted made sense because of the limited physical space occupied by two participants. These ideas expanded with microwave technology to send a video signal. The 1948 Olympic Games in London were broadcast to viewers within a limited geographic distance from Wembley Stadium. The 1956 Olympic Games were significant for two reasons. The Summer Games in Melbourne, Australia, became the first sporting event to sell broadcast rights, and the Winter Games were introduced as another competition. Broadcast content was limited to news stories that were edited and shipped to networks to rebroadcast as highlight packages. Technology was not yet advanced to transmit live sports beyond a geographic region limited by linear transmission of air waves (i.e., local markets).

This represented recognition of sports as a spectacle that viewers were willing to watch, even in a significantly delayed manner. The overlap between sports and media forged a symbiotic relationship that eventually positioned broadcast networks in a battle for limited, yet highly competitive, professional sports content. Sut Jhally defined this as the sports/media complex, whereby sports as broadcast programming became a material commodity that networks negotiated to own, and in the process, converted audiences into commodities to be sold to advertisers. This evolution of the role of sports broadcasting accomplished two goals. First, it turned marquee sporting events into a spectacle of consumption. Second, and as a byproduct of this first achievement, sports programming gained significant economic value that elevated sports' social significance.

The Super Bowl became the single-day sporting event to command significant money from broadcast networks, and it helped position the NFL as the leader in the sports/media complex with significant leverage. In less than a decade of existence, the Super Bowl surpassed the Kentucky Derby and the World Series as the most-watched sporting event in the United States. However, the Super Bowl was positioned as more than a football game. Media hype leading to the game, the commercials embedded in the live transmission, and the coverage of the event afterward constructed the Super Bowl as the annual spectacle of sports, given that the Olympic Games were every 4 years. Each of these marquee events were retransmitted through a broadcast network that controlled the output, and thus viewers were limited to access through antennas at homes within geographic proximity to the transmitted signal.

Satellite Communication and Liveness

Once access and consumption were evident within the potential impact for sports broadcasting, satellite communication was the transcendent space to elevate sports broadcasting into a global empire for television. BBC was a trendsetter with satellite transmission of the Olympic Games and European Cup Finals that reportedly reached at least 30 countries as early as 1960. This started to enhance soccer as the "global game" because it was played in nearly every nation and, thus, moved the world's best players from stadiums into living rooms. In the United States, NBC dominated World Series coverage from 1950 to 1976 and CBS and NBC alternated the first 18 Super Bowl telecasts. However, ABC forged its way into the network battle with the creation of *Wide World of Sports* in 1961 and *Monday Night Football* in 1970. The reach of these shows to a sports audience that wanted content beyond the weekend and outside traditional approaches to sports broadcasting pushed technical boundaries. These two shows also introduced on-air personalities within sports broadcasting, including Jim McKay and Howard Cosell. Despite this new reach for networks, sports were not offered live in many areas because of their conflict with primetime programming in different time zones. Thus, tape-delayed events were a normal occurrence dictated by the networks.

The regulation of cable companies and satellite communication helped sports reach more viewers than was limited to the traditional three broadcast networks in the United States. In 1972, the Federal Communications Commission (FCC) was granted regulatory agency over satellite signal transmission that eventually opened space for the concept of subscription-based access to sports broadcasting content. Where satellite technology helped sports flourish was the ability to reach a live audience through the developing cable subscription-based system. In 1975, Home Box Office (HBO) transmitted the signal of the "Thrilla in Manila" boxing match between Muhammad Ali and Joe Frazier to cable subscribers who paid to receive HBO. According to Hoof, this initial moment of experiencing the "liveness" of sports provided through satellite transmission started a landslide of sports programming opportunities through the 1970s and 1980s.

In addition to simply reaching fans beyond their geographically accessible teams, satellite technology assisted in making fans. For example, before the construction of all-sports broadcast channels, TBS and WGN launched as superstations through satellite technology in 1976 and 1978, respectively. Ted Turner bought the Atlanta Braves in the same year he started TBS, and he used the Braves broadcasts as flagship programming for his network along with the NBA's Atlanta Hawks. WGN-TV started as an independent station in Chicago in 1948, and the station launched with a sports broadcast of the Golden Gloves boxing finals from Chicago Stadium. Therefore, WGN as a superstation simply began simulcasting the local broadcast offerings from Chicago to anyone who could access the superstation. Chicago Cubs baseball games had been televised locally on WGN since 1948. Through satellite expansion, this extended the reach of Cubs, the NBA's Chicago Bulls, and to a lesser extent, the Cubs' crosstown rival Chicago White Sox because of fewer televised games, noted Robert V. Bellamy and James R. Walker. WWOR in New York followed the WGN model of retransmitting its signal in 1979 and provided viewers with access to New York Mets games. These broadcast opportunities through superstations provided the local station, and subsequently the teams, a financial head start over other Major League Baseball (MLB) teams before the emergence of regional sports networks. The superstations maintained for a few decades, and despite their disappearance, the impact they had on merging sports with the potential for global reach was historically significant.

One element that lagged behind was overall production value and multiple camera angles to create an immersive experience for the audience, in an effort to replicate the drama of in-person spectatorship. With use of up to three cameras in early sports production, television offered a mostly wide-angle perspective that placed the viewer in a stadium through visuals and sound. According to Garry Whannel, one overriding benefit that sports broadcasting offered versus in-stadium experience was the use of replay. This technological enhancement provided viewers with recall and better understanding of what occurred and how it could be interpreted. However, the experience was not immersive until the late 1980s and especially in the 1990s, when the concept of all-sports networks took shape.

ESPN and the Rise of College Sports

After superstations emerged, ESPN launched in September 1979. Dubbed the Entertainment and Sports Programming Network, ESPN started as an idea to help expand the reach of University of Connecticut athletics and the New England (later Hartford) Whalers professional hockey team to a rabidly developing fanbase. The "Worldwide Leader in Sports" was born after ESPN's founders recognized a more cost-efficient use of satellite technology used by HBO and others. If *Sports Illustrated* highlighted a significant value on visuals and long-form journalism, ESPN amplified sports journalism as a newsgathering source but also an available space to enhance the quantity of live sports broadcasting opportunities on a daily basis. Thus, ESPN influenced the blurred overlap between sports-as-news and sports-as-entertainment, first through its creation of *SportsCenter* and the central value of highlights and second for its live and entertainment programming.

Before becoming a global media empire, ESPN offered sports coverage of events that were not considered mainstream, ranging from world's strongest man competitions and Australian rules football to sports trivia and replays of home run derbies from the 1960s. However, maintaining a business model central to sports provided a foundation for a viewership that clearly was building around daily sports content being available. ESPN eventually landed contracts with professional sports leagues, fostered through the network's ability to create spectacle out of events that were not actual sports competition, such as the NFL Draft and College Gameday.

At the core of ESPN's business plan was the use of college sports as a brand to build upon because of its core fan base and an abundance of programming options. ESPN televised opening rounds of the NCAA basketball tournament that was a financial boom for CBS for the Final Four events, so ESPN televised opening round games as early as 1980 and helped develop the "March Madness" moniker that is affiliated with the 3-week long tournament. However, the greatest impact for ESPN was a U.S. Supreme Court ruling in *NCAA v. Board of Regents of the University of Oklahoma* in 1984. The University of Oklahoma and the University of Georgia sued the NCAA for the right to have more football games televised beyond the NCAA broadcast contract that limited national appearances. The Supreme Court ruled in favor of the universities and shifted negotiating power for college football from the NCAA to the individual conferences that included groups of eight to ten schools. ESPN capitalized as a 24-hour space available to assist in the rapid expansion of college football as a live sports programming powerhouse, but one that had ramifications that moved college sporting events to any day of the week and amplified the commercialization of college sport despite its desire to be marketed as amateurism, noted Travis R. Bell.

During its history, ESPN has contracted to televise every U.S. professional sports league as well as golf and tennis professional tours. Regardless, college sports have remained a staple that has expanded to include every college championship event, and ESPN was crucial for college sports, especially in the 12-year agreement to host the College Football Playoff beginning in 2017. Other broadcast networks such as CBS and FOX showcase college sports, but ESPN is cobranded through the creation of conference platforms including the Longhorn Network, SEC Network, and ACC Network that devote around-the-clock and exclusive coverage to these power conferences and schools. ESPN combined access, spectacle, and distribution potential to gain control over how and where fans consume college sports.

Internet, Mobile, and Streaming Technology

The final frontier (for now) in the ubiquity of sports broadcasting is the intersection of Internet, mobile, and streaming technologies. These opportunities exist because of the rapid advances in high-definition equipment that has made sports broadcasting an immersive, and sometimes interactive, experience through the combination of multiscreen options. Camera and audio equipment advanced so far that viewers can see a visual perspective from a game official or hear conversations between coaches and players during timeouts. These technological advancements enhanced the viewing experience, but it was the rapid evolution of access points beyond a television screen that pushed the reach of sports broadcasting.

Major League Baseball was at the forefront of tapping into these advances through a subscription service known as *MLB.tv*. Each MLB team

has its own independent broadcast contract with a regional sports network to engage their local viewers. Then MLB offered a cohesive broadcast package to subscribers whereby they can watch or hear the radio broadcast for nearly every baseball game with the exception of the viewer's home market, which is blacked out to maintain the exclusive contract for the regional sports network. For example, a viewer in Florida who previously relied on WGN to watch Cubs games could access everything, including the play-by-play radio broadcast that was once relegated to Chicago-area residents limited by signal strength. This model generated additional revenue and audience for MLB without any extra production costs.

That transference of over-the-air content to online and streaming platforms targeted unique subscribers and "cord-cutters" who wanted to minimize growing cable fees. Other professional sports leagues followed a similar MLB model to offer their broadcast partner content in some capacity through the league's online and mobile platforms. A desire by fans to watch away from home forced broadcast networks to target mobile users through tangential sports broadcasting opportunities including incorporating fantasy sports statistics into broadcasts. Major networks such as ESPN created streaming-specific platforms to simulcast over-the-air offerings as well as content branded solely to the streaming platform to supplement the loss of cable subscriptions. Third-party services such as YouTube TV and Sling TV offered less-expensive options to cable with an emphasis on sports channels as a draw for subscribers. In addition, platforms such as Amazon and Hulu partnered with leagues to simulcast and create unique content as multiple ways for audiences to engage with sports broadcasting from anywhere.

These streaming platforms targeted sports fans of long-standing legacy sports, but new audiences emerged with the construction of eSports and its translation to visual media for fan consumption. It is a testament to how advanced video game technology has become and an avid fan base that desire user-engaged programming. Similar to how the sports/media complex rapidly developed through increased availability of programming for consumption, eSports has followed that same trajectory with potentially greater synergy between media consumption and desire to participate, according to Kenon A. Brown and colleagues. eSports have increased in viewership and sold out arenas for audiences to watch global eSports championship events in the same manner as baseball and basketball. Thus, sports broadcasting has evolved to engage a new audience of consumers.

Ironically, the COVID-19 pandemic in 2020 pushed the technological boundaries of sports broadcasting because it forced live sports to a global halt. The pandemic had negative implications for start-up sports leagues such as the XFL, which canceled midseason and shuttered the league after filing for bankruptcy. This highlighted how reliant sports are on live broadcasting content to remain a salient business. The broadcast networks that partner with sports leagues in the symbiotic relationship turned to a combination of real athletes competing in eSports to engage viewers through what looked like sports broadcasting. NASCAR and the Indy Racing League were leaders in this area with iRacing televised on FOX. NBA players competed against each other on ESPN in an NBA 2K video game tournament. Lastly, ESPN produced a HORSE competition among eight current and former NBA and WNBA players in social isolation from their home basketball court. The transmission signal strength harkened to original sports programming of the 1940s that was blurry and minimal, yet still showed sport. The long-term sustainability of the sports/media complex came into question because of the pandemic and could force a restructuring of how sports broadcasting looks in the future. However, what the pandemic showed was a reliance on technology to find innovative ways to produce desirable sports content.

Travis R. Bell

See also Sports Journalism; Sportswriters

Further Readings

Bell, T. R. (2020). Remembering NCAA v. Board of regents: The supreme court foundation of a mediated college football cartel. In J. Carvalho (Ed.), *Sports media history: Culture, technology, identity*. New York, NY: Routledge.

Bellamy, R. V., & Walker, J. R. (2001). Baseball and television origins: The case of the Cubs. *NINE: A Journal of Baseball History and Culture, 10*(1), 31–45.

Brown, K. A., Billings, A. C., Murphy, B., & Puesan, L. (2018). Intersections of fandom in the age of interactive media: Esports fandom as a predictor of traditional sport fandom. *Communication & Sport, 6*(4), 418–435. doi:10.1177/2167479517727286

Crepeau, R., & Nathan, D. A. (2000). Review: Two views of ESPN. *Journal of Sport History, 27*(3), 525–531.

Hoof, F. (2020). Liveness formats: A historical perspective on live sports broadcasting. In M. Jancovic, A. Volmar, & A. Schneider (Eds.), *Format matters: Standards, practices, and politics in media cultures* (pp. 81–103). Lüneburg, Germany: Meson Press.

Jhally, S. (1984). The spectacle of accumulation: Material and cultural factors in the evolution of the sports/media complex. *Critical Sociologist, 12*(3), 41–57. doi:10.1177/089692058401200304

Real, M. R. (1975). Super bowl: Mythic spectacle. *Journal of Communication, 25*(1), 31–43.

Rothenbuhler, E. W. (1988). The living room celebration of the Olympic Games. *Journal of Communication, 38*(4), 61–81. doi:10.1111/j.1460-2466.1975.tb00552.x

Sanderson, A. R., & Siegfried, J. J. (2018). The role of broadcasting in national collegiate athletic association sports. *Review of Industrial Organization, 52*(2), 305–321.

Socolow, M. J. (2016). *Six minutes in Berlin: Broadcast spectacle and rowing gold at the Nazi Olympics*. Champaign: University of Illinois Press.

Stead, D. (2010). Sport and the media. In B. Houlihan (Ed.), *Sport and society: A student introduction* (pp. 184–200). London, UK: Sage.

Whannel, G. (2005). Pregnant with anticipation: The pre-history of television sport and the politics of recycling and preservation. *International Journal of Cultural Studies, 8*(4), 405–426. doi:10.1177/1367877905058342

SPORTS JOURNALISM

Sports journalism is an umbrella term that includes print, broadcast and cable television, and online news and feature reporting, writing, and photography about amateur and professional sports. Sports journalism reports about an amateur and professional sports industry that *Forbes* estimated was worth $73.5 billion in 2019 in the United States. Sports journalism has become, over the past century, an important segment of American journalism and has rapidly grown in parallel with sports and athletic competition.

The popularity of sports worldwide has led to significant news resources assigned to covering both professional and amateur sports. Sports journalists routinely cover major annual championships and daily sports events, from FIFA World Cups to the Olympics Games to NFL Super Bowls to the NCAA Final Fours, and to local high school basketball, football, and other team sports each year. Soccer, or *fútbol* in Spanish, for example, attracts millions of fans to matches around the world each year. U.S. professional and college football draws large numbers as well. Furthermore, millions attend motor racing events around the world and millions of fans watch basketball games, baseball games, golf tournaments, horse racing, cricket, rugby, and bicycle racing annually around the world. Sports journalists and their news organizations have taken on the responsibility to cover it all.

This entry first provides an overview of contemporary sports journalism in the United States, then discusses the history and development of sports journalism in the United States and the different segments, coverage areas, and topics of sports journalism. It then looks at the education and preparation of sports journalists and expectations of professional journalists. Finally, it discusses books by sports journalists and organizations of and for sports journalists.

Contemporary Sports Journalism

Sports journalism continues to evolve as a result of both societal changes and rapid advancements in technology. Technology, in particular the advent of computer networks, hand-held tablets, and smartphones, has changed how sports news is distributed and consumed as well as resulting in new approaches to how sport itself is covered.

A recent development in sports and in journalism involves collection of data and analysis of databases. Popularized with the sports public with the 2011 film *Moneyball* about the use of data analytics in professional baseball, the approach takes advantage of digital tools for observing behavior and recording it in databases. At the same time that sports teams were using analytics to improve strategies and performance in competition and in selection of players, sports journalists were using similar techniques in their own analyses of competition, fans, athletes, and even the communities where teams competed. Sports journalists do their own analyses using player and team metrics to understand performances better. While some data analysis in sports and sports journalism is basic and employs publicly available data and widely available tools such as Excel, analytics can also be highly sophisticated and involve multiple databases with millions of records, requiring specialized expertise and the use of advanced software.

Amateur and professional sports audiences are growing both in person and through daily broadcast, online, and print news media sports journalism. In the United States, college sports are drawing large attendance numbers in arenas and stadiums, but also audiences on television and other screens. This has led to a corresponding growth in demand for information about players, teams, leagues, and even participation in various levels of amateur sport.

Sports business and economics have experienced remarkable change in the past century. From what were basically small family-style businesses at best, professional sports and college amateur teams have become multimillion dollar and even billion-dollar corporate businesses using facilities valued in the hundreds of millions to more than one billion dollars. Businesses manufacturing sports equipment, such as Nike or Adidas, have become billion-dollar global corporations. All this has led to writers and reporters who focus on sports business-related issues.

With growing audiences, participation, and business, sports reporters have also needed to become knowledgeable in sports law and business management. An entire legal industry in sports law now exists to deal with salaries, contracts, injuries, individual access and participant rights, and other legal matters involving participants, agents, sports facilities, and teams. Similarly, the need to cover and understand sports organizations and their management teams is also required today in sports journalism.

History and Development of Modern American Sports Journalism

Sports journalism has paralleled the growth of the role of sports in the United States. For the nation's first century and a half, Americans did not devote much attention to sports. Most early leisure activity was recreational rather than highly competitive. But as the 18th century ended, sports and athletic competition were on their way to becoming a force in society.

The first half of the 19th century was not a time for sports or sports journalism as we know it today. Americans engaged in many recreational and leisure time activities, such as boating, horse racing, cockfighting, shooting contests, and swimming, but these were seldom covered in daily or weekly newspapers. News was dominated by political and business reporting. Of course, many activities commonly considered sport in the 21st century, such as hunting, fishing, or sailing, were necessities in the early United States.

By 1815, North American industrialization resulted in a slow shift from outdoor to indoor work. Interest in spectator sports grew and the first sports journal in the United States, the *American Turf Register and Sporting Magazine*, devoted to horse racing, began in 1829. A second sports publication, *Spirit of the Times*, began in 1831 and continued for seven decades. It was edited by William Trotter Porter, who had founded the *American Turf Register*. Gradually, some newspapers began to report about horse racing and boxing. As religious groups loosened policies that previously forbade recreational activity on Sundays, participation and interest in sports grew.

New York newspapers began to cover prize fights, horse racing, and early track competition by the mid-1830s. Henry Chadwick began writing on sports for *The New York Times* and *New York Tribune* by offering to cover and write about cricket and baseball for free. The first news story of a game was likely published in *Spirit of the Times* on July 9, 1853, with the headline, "Base Ball at Hoboken," a brief item with a box score.

Sports news was first separated from the rest of the newspaper in the 1870s in New York. During this era, sportswriters themselves became known to readers by name. Joe Vila from the *New York Sun* is credited with developing play-by-play summaries for football games. Damon Runyon experienced fame from writing for the *Denver Post* and *New York American*.

Forest and Stream was founded in 1873 with articles about hunting and fishing. Interest in athletics in general was growing with baseball, football, and other team sports particularly popular. Journalists began to write about these topics. Henry Chadwick produced the *Ball Players' Chronicle*. Francis C. Richter developed the *Sporting Life* in Philadelphia, publishing correspondents nationwide on a wide variety of subjects and noting it was the largest sports and baseball magazine in circulation in the 1880s.

Sports were becoming organized at the end of the 19th century. New sports were introduced at all levels of society. It was also an era when women began to write about sports. Nellie Bly, a pen name of Elizabeth Cochrane, was a highly regarded reporter for the *New York World* who wrote about prize fighting. *New York Times* reporter Middy Morgan wrote about horse racing.

In 1869, the Cincinnati Red Stockings became the first professional baseball team. Spectator sports became the most popular weekend activity for many Americans in the Northeast and Midwest and, as they grew, so did daily coverage in newspapers. At the beginning of the 20th century, the modern summary lead became a fixture. Up to that point most sportswriting was chronological.

Another factor contributing to the growth of spectator sports in the early 20th century was communication technology. The wireless telegraph, which Associated Press used to cover sports as early as 1899, was important in sending scoring summaries and racing statistics from city to city. In 1916, for the first time, a play-by-play story was transmitted by Associated Press from the World Series host stadium to all newspapers and other customers on the system.

General magazines were beginning to take an interest in sports. By 1920, articles on sports and recreation were popular reading in publications such as *The Atlantic Monthly*, *The Century Magazine*, *Harper's Magazine*, and *Scribner's Magazine*, and in mass circulation magazines such as *Collier's*, *Munsey's*, *McClure's*, *Everybody's*, and *Saturday Evening Post*, and a number of women's magazines.

The end of World War I was another turning point for sports journalism. The pageantry of sport had taken over the public's imagination. Events such as the Kentucky Derby, Indianapolis 500, World Series, Soap Box Derby, and the original four college football bowl games on New Year's Day meant that sports journalism had a ready market for its product.

Another major development was the decision by Associated Press to create a separate sports wire that debuted on opening day of baseball season, April 16, 1945. To expand the scope of newspaper coverage, from the largest dailies to small ones in nonmetropolitan markets, regional sports wires were developed in the late 1940s.

Modern sports magazines were developed at the end of World War II. *Sport* began in 1946 and *Sporting News* continued to grow despite competition from new, specialized sports publications. With an increase in public and private facilities for participant and spectator sports, new specialized publications entered the marketplace, giving sports journalists still more outlets. *World Tennis* was introduced, as was *Golf Digest* and the *Daily Racing Form*. Baseball magazines were still popular. Boating magazines, such as *Yachting*, began publication. Football, growing in popularity as a professional sport as well as a college sport, was represented by *Football Annual*. *Sports Digest* (1944), *Sport* (1946), *Sports Graphic* (1946), *Sports Album* (1948), *Sports Leaders* (1948), *Sport Life* (1948), and *Sports World* (1949) began publication. In 1954, Henry Luce, publisher of magazine giants of the era, *Time, Fortune,* and *Life,* published the first issue of a new weekly known as *Sports Illustrated.*

Daily newspapers and general consumption magazines paid increasing attention to recreational activities. It was a gradual trend, but one that reflected the change in attitude toward sports. By the end of World War II, Americans wanted not only to participate in sports on weekends and vacations but to read about these sports.

In the 1950s and 1960s, newspaper and magazine sports journalism adjusted to live and edited sports on television. As with the adjustment to sports on radio in the 1920s and 1930s, print sportswriters were forced into a transition period by television and other developments in broadcasting and film. Live sports on television changed newspaper coverage remarkably. Boxing was one of the first sports to be televised live with any regularly. Television enhanced baseball's popularity in the 1950s and 1960s. Professional football benefited from national television exposure as well. Prize fighting continued to be popular at that time with its new exposure on television backed by print coverage. Film and television attention brought the Olympics increased audiences. The rapid growth of sports broadcasting forced print sportswriters to react. New tools assisted them in doing their jobs better. Enhanced communication allowed writers to transmit stories to the newsroom much more quickly. Teletype systems had been adapted to permit stadium-to-newsroom communication.

By the 1960s, sports publication circulation, as well as attendance, increased. And because of new broadcasting outlets and development of color television, radio and television audience numbers grew with each new season. It was another era of transition for print sports journalism. The range of sports stories broadened considerably by the late 1960s.

Nationwide, women's amateur sports received more attention, more women's sports developed, and more women began to take an interest in sports journalism careers. Boosted by passage of federal civil rights laws that included Title IX in 1972, women's sports opportunities grew in high schools, colleges, and universities. Women's professional sports such as golf and tennis, and soon basketball slowly grew along with audience interest and sports media coverage.

Interest in sports-related news that occurred off the field and court also increased. Sports reporters began to look beyond locker rooms into boardrooms, courtrooms, and training rooms. Yet there was still an appeal in reading about the game. Instead of replacing newspaper and magazine sports reporting, television seemed to simply enhance it. People who attended a game or watched it on television also wanted to read about it in-depth the next day. Thorough reports and investigations combined with analysis and interpretation became a salvation of print sportswriting in this era.

Television expanded sports coverage and in the 1950s and 1960s sports sections grew in both allotted space and scope. Participant sports continued to grow and expansion in the coverage of these activities skyrocketed, resulting in the development of special sections devoted to participant sports features and columns for the late 1960s and the 1970s. There was movement toward more objective sportswriting, with less local team "cheerleading" in coverage beginning in the late 1960s. This drift away from boosting the home team flourishes in many areas today. And in suburban and rural areas, an emphasis on local sports continues to be a priority despite developments in wire service coverage.

Sports Journalism Specializations by Media

Daily and weekly newspapers as well as regularly published magazines continue to publish considerable sports news despite a significant decline in circulation, advertising revenue, and readership in the past 25 years. While some print publications have closed outright, others have moved to the World Wide Web and various other networked platforms. Print publications struggle to retain audiences and advertisers and seek new approaches to sustain themselves. For example, one daily newspaper in Arkansas, the *Arkansas Democrat-Gazette*, took the bold step in 2019 to give paid subscribers their own iPad tablet computers at no cost to enable access and encourage use of its online products as the company cuts back its printed editions.

Immediacy has become a critical factor in sports journalism in the online news era. This has pressured traditional print media to react much as it did when faced with the impact of sports on television beginning in the early 1960s. Print sports journalism is redefining itself again in terms of content in response, not just moving existing content to online access. This means more features and less spot results coverage in print editions. It means more in-depth analysis, using both investigative reporting approaches and sophisticated statistical analyses of players, teams, and leagues. It also means using different kinds of storytelling such as mixed media and multimedia.

Broadcast and cable sports journalism has experienced growing audiences since the 1960s and offers numerous cable sports networks today. Broadcast and cable sports coverage consists of much more than just live broadcasts of games at local, regional, and national levels. Broadcast sports journalism now offers a wide range of programming beyond games on these channels (which can often also be streamed to apps on portable devices). These programs include current events talk shows featuring experts, highlights programs, and preview coverage. The channel-wide programming is highly specialized as well, devoted to specific professional leagues such as the National Football League, and professional teams, or individual conferences, such as the Southeastern Conference or the Atlantic Coast Conference, among colleges and universities. Some universities, such as the University of Texas, have their own national cable network.

Online sports journalism takes multiple forms. It is found on websites, but also on smartphone and tablet apps. Online sports journalism, in its original form, was little more than print content copied to a legacy print news organization's website. Content has changed quite a bit since those mid-1990s beginnings. While legacy print newspapers and magazines continue to post content on their websites, online-only organizations are also now covering sports through specialized websites, and sports journalism can also be found on blogs, video websites, and social media. This has created new ways for sports journalism to reach audiences and to promote itself and its brands, but it has also created new responsibilities for many sports journalists. In the past 25 years, online sports journalism has experienced exponential growth at the same time print news media coverage of sports has declined.

Sports Journalism Specializations by Role

At the core of sports journalism are the sportswriters themselves, some of whom write on many sports and aspects of sports and others who take on specialty beats. Traditionally, sportswriters worked for newspapers and magazines, but they have found places in the online news world as well.

Generalists cover all sports at all levels and take on whatever is needed at any given time and during any season. Beat specialists are dedicated, first and foremost, to covering an assigned area. These can be teams or leagues, such as a college football team or basketball team, or the league within which those teams might compete. Some specialists are broader in approach, such as covering a sport at all levels in a market for an audience. For example, some writers cover just soccer and cover a local professional team, college teams, and high schools as well. This is particularly true in metropolitan areas. Smaller markets usually require fewer specialists and more generalists.

Sports journalism, like other forms and specialties within journalism, requires editors and managers. These individuals lead departments, hire and maintain full-time staff, coordinate assignments, schedule resources, determine budgets, often handle payroll, find and manage part-time staff, and set policies for coverage. These individuals are among the most experienced on a sports department staff. Some editors or managers continue to write and report and others write opinion and commentary in daily or less frequent columns.

But sports journalism is not writers, reporters, and editors alone. In today's heavily visual world in print and online, photographers, videographers, information graphics specialists, and other visual communicators have taken critical roles in storytelling about individuals in sports as well as about the competition itself. These professionals are responsible for supporting written content at all times, whether it be breaking news or features. In modern newsrooms, many times sportswriters and reporters are also photographers, but visual specialists contribute reporting and stories, too.

At some news organizations, especially smaller and mid-size ones, sports journalists are also content producers for websites and social media accounts. These individuals may create their own content or use that of others, such as colleagues or wire services, to prepare pages on websites or to post on blogs and social media.

Covering Social Issues in Sports

Sports are often the common ground uniting diverse groups. Sports journalists have increasingly placed their time and resources toward reporting about the role of sports in society. Contemporary sports journalism focuses on numerous social issues, including race and ethnicity. During the 20th century, sports contributed to racial and ethnic social integration and sports journalists have written about these critical moments in the social evolution of the nation.

Similarly, sports journalism today is giving increasing attention to gender issues. A recent example is the widespread abuse of young female athletes in gymnastics by physicians and coaches. Another is the recent efforts of the U.S. women's soccer team players and coaches to earn salaries and benefits equal to those of the U.S. men's team following three decades of top 10 world rankings and four World Cup championships.

Social justice has also become an important focus of sports journalism. One prominent recent example involves NFL quarterback Colin Kaepernick, who was playing for the San Francisco 49ers when he began refusing to stand for the playing of the American national anthem before games in 2017 as a way of calling attention to racial injustice in the United States. He was eventually released from the team, causing even greater controversy.

Sports injuries and sports medicine have become increasingly important topics for sports journalism. Perhaps the best example of this is the considerable attention given to traumatic head injuries suffered by high school, college, and professional football players during the first two decades of the 21st century. Coverage has not only focused on individuals who have been injured and unable to play, but on the long-term effects of chronic traumatic encephalopathy that can result from participation in an often-violent sport and on the safety of equipment used in the sport.

Some sports journalists specialize in investigative reporting about sports competition, athletes, teams, leagues, and their interaction with communities they serve. These sports reporters have sophisticated reporting skills using public records, online resources, databases, interviewing techniques, observational skills, and other tools to search deeply into subjects such as race relations, treatment of women, pay inequality, and health, safety, and care for injured athletes. This type of sports journalism requires special abilities, experience, and considerable time and is not found commonly among sports media. But it is an approach that may be used when events and issues require it, even bringing in non-sports journalists to team with sports journalists.

Sportswriters and the Olympics

Since the Olympic Games were reinstituted in 1896, they have become major global events for news and sports media to follow at all levels. While there have historically been highly politicized Olympic games (such as Berlin in 1936), games with social change and protest (Mexico City in 1968), those with terrorist attacks (Munich in 1972), and those with national teams boycotting (Moscow in 1980 and Los Angeles in 1984), most coverage focus has been on the competition and the thousands of athletes involved.

The Professional: Education and Preparation

Education

Sports journalists today are not like those of earlier generations. Today, news organizations seek educated individuals, often with bachelor's degrees in journalism or mass communication, to work as sports journalists. Increasingly, sports journalists and those planning to enter the field are also earning master's degrees with specializations such as journalism and mass communication, sports and recreation, business, international relations, or media management.

Knowledge Areas

Sportswriters are now expected to know not only the sports they cover but to have a grounding in the liberal arts, including languages, history, sociology, psychology, and the sciences. At some news organizations, a thorough knowledge of computer tools and certain software is expected. Sportswriters are both generalists and specialized journalists. Because sport transcends just athletics and competition in this era, sportswriters must know a wide range of subjects at least at an introductory level.

The Role of Experience in Athletics

Sportswriters often have some experience in athletics. Some have been an athlete while others worked in other team or league roles. The degree of that experience varies from simple schoolyard competition and childhood teams to the highest levels of collegiate and professional sport. But such experience is not a requirement nor always an advantage. It has become a desired resume item for television and radio sports journalists more than for newspaper, magazine, and online sports journalists, but experience in athletics is widely viewed as beneficial to preparation of anyone covering sports.

Professional Expectations

Sports journalism can be a demanding career. Today, it is 24/7/365, always on. There is a continuous news cycle in the modern era. For individuals working in sports journalism, this means long days and weeks during any single sport's season. Writers and editors are expected to produce stories and other content for multiple platforms of today's news media that cover sports. This means sports journalists must not only have deep knowledge of the sports that they cover and have reporting and writing skills, but they must also be able to create blog content, post on their news organization's social media sites, take publishable photographs, shoot professional-caliber video clips, and produce content for the organization's website. Furthermore, sports journalists based in print and online news media must often develop skills for occasional work in other news media, such as radio and television.

Professional Ethics in Sports Journalism

Sports journalists subscribe to general ethical guidelines of professional journalism. Numerous news organizations look to the Code of Ethics of the Society of Professional Journalists for guidance. Some, such as *The New York Times*, have prepared their own ethical standards. Ethical standards emphasize not only following and respecting legal rules of society, but also the unique values of sports journalism. These general guidelines, according to the Society of Professional Journalists, focus on seeking truth, minimizing harm to those people and entities journalists cover, acting in an independent manner, and being accountable and transparent in how journalists do their work.

Beyond reporting and writing truthfully, a key value for sports journalism is maintaining independence. Sports journalists must avoid conflicts of interest, such as working for the teams they cover and loyalty to a team they cover, and avoid taking gifts, such as valuable items, from sources and organizations. These gifts and offerings come with expectations that can compromise the practice of journalism.

Fiction and Nonfiction: Sports Books

Books about sports and athletes are often written by sports journalists and former sports journalists. Many are about favorite players and teams or well-known coaches. Sometimes, news organizations have published books consisting of their coverage of championship seasons of local teams. At times, sports journalists ghostwrite books for sports personalities or they write as their coauthors. For example, sportswriter Gene Wojciechowski worked with former University of Oklahoma football coach Bob Stoops for his memoir *No Excuses: The Making of a Head Coach*, published in 2019.

The late nonfiction author George Plimpton took his view of professional sports a step further with a series of books about his limited participation in a professional sport, such as football, hockey, boxing, and golf, to give readers an insider's view of the highest levels of the sport. His first such book, *Paper Lion*, published in 1966 is perhaps the best-known example, telling readers what summer training camp for players in the NFL was like.

Sports Journalism Professional Organizations

There are numerous professional organizations focused on sports journalism in the United States and around the world. In the United States, women in sports journalism are represented by the Association for Women in Sports Media. It was founded in 1987. The International Sports Press Association places emphasis on the Olympics, soccer, track and field, and other international competitions.

Based in North Carolina, the National Sports Media Association began in 1959. It was founded as the National Sportswriters and Sportscasters Association and renamed itself in 2016. The organization created a sportswriters and sportscasters Hall of Fame shortly after it was founded. It has a partnership with the International Sports Press Association and membership is open to sports media professionals and students interested in careers in sports journalism.

The National Sports Journalism Center was founded in 2009 at Indiana University to bring students into sports media and sports journalism. It hosts the Associated Press Sports Editors, a large national professional organization of editors and news managers who work in sports journalism.

There are also numerous professional sports journalists groups that are organized around specific media or an individual sport, such as radio and television (American Sportscasters Association), baseball (Baseball Writers Association of America), tennis (International Tennis Writers Association), and golf (Golf Writers Association of America).

Bruce Garrison

See also Bly, Nellie; Column-Writing; Sports Broadcasting; Sportswriters

Further Readings

Andrews, P. (2014). *Sports journalism: A practical introduction* (2nd ed.). London, UK: Sage.

Coutinho, R. (2017). *Press box revolution: How sports reporting has changed over the past thirty years.* New York, NY: Sports Publishing.

Fleder, R. (2003). *Sports illustrated: 50 Years of great writing, 1954–2004.* New York, NY: Sports Illustrated Books.

Froke, P., Bratton, A. J., Garcia, O., McMillan, J., & Schwartz, J. (Eds.) (2019). Sports guidelines and style. In P. Froke, A. J. Bratton, O. Garcia, J. McMillan, & J. Schwartz (Eds.), *The Associated Press stylebook.* New York, NY: The Associated Press.

Garrison, B. (with Sabljak, M.). (1991). *Sports reporting* (2nd ed.). Ames: Iowa State University Press.

Gisondi, J. (2018). *Field guide to covering sports* (2nd ed.). Thousand Oaks, CA: CQ Press/Sage.

Reinardy, S., & Wanta, W. (2015). *The essentials of sports reporting and writing* (2nd ed.). New York, NY: Routledge.

Schultz, B. (2016). *Sports media* (3rd ed.). New York, NY: Focal Press.

Schultz, R. (2017). *Secrets of sports broadcasting: Practical advice for sportscasting success*. San Francisco, CA: Udemy.

Stofer, K. T., Schaffer, J. R., & Rosenthal, B. A. (2019). *Sports journalism: An introduction to reporting and writing* (2nd ed.) Lanham, MD: Rowman & Littlefield.

Stout, G. (annual) (Series Ed.). *The best American sports writing*. Boston, MA: Houghton-Mifflin Harcourt.

Swan, J. (Ed.) (1996). *Sports style guide & reference manual: The complete reference for sports editors, writers, and broadcasters*. Chicago, IL: Triumph Books.

Wilstein, S. (2002). *Associated Press sports writing handbook*. New York, NY: McGraw-Hill.

SPORTSWRITERS

Sportswriters are journalists who cover amateur and professional sports. The term originally referred to journalists who work full-time and part-time for daily and weekly newspapers and regularly published sports magazines writing and reporting about sports, but it has been liberalized to refer to all journalists who cover sports, particularly print, online, and broadcast-cable.

Sportswriters are part of a rich history of writing about sports in all forms. Many of the best-known sportswriters start their careers writing about competitions, covering a particular team or sport for a daily newspaper, and then move to column and opinion writing about sport. While some remain based at daily or weekly newspapers, others move to national or international sports magazines. The best writers often also write nonfiction and fiction books about sports and top athletes. This entry introduces some leading 20th and 21st century sportswriters and highlights the work of a selection of award-winning sportswriters.

Contemporary Sportswriters

Sportswriters help readers understand and keep current about happenings in the worlds of amateur and professional sports. Sportswriters not only cover the competition as breaking news, they also provide analyses about competition outcomes and, where appropriate, commentary, analysis, and opinion about the outcome. Some sportswriters specialize in writing about the interaction of sports and society, local teams and their communities, and use of community resources to support teams and leagues. Some specialize in sports law or sports business and sports management. Some do investigations. Some specialize in analysis of performance of players, teams, and leagues.

Best-Known Sportswriters From 1900 to Present
Early 20th Century Sportswriters

At the end of the 19th century, women began to write about sports. Nellie Bly, whose name was Elizabeth Cochrane, was a highly regarded reporter for the *New York World*. Bly wrote about boxing. *New York Times* reporter Middy Morgan wrote about racing and livestock activities. Sportswriters who became regionally and nationally known at the turn of the 20th century were Arthur Brisbane (*New York Sun*), H. R. H. Smith (*The New York Times*), Jack London (*New York Herald*), Charles Dryden (*Philadelphia North American*), Ring Lardner (*Chicago Tribune*), Irvin S. Cobb (*New York World*), and John H. Reitinger (Associated Press). A number of these writers moved on to other writing careers, creating short stories, novels, and plays for the theater. It is often hard to tell who wrote what in newspapers in this period since much sportswriting was published without bylines.

Often sportswriters for large dailies were as popular as the athletes of whom they wrote. Sports columnists could earn a good living. It was, after all, the time of Babe Ruth, Ty Cobb, and Bobby Jones. Among these top sportswriters were Grantland Rice, Damon Runyon, Heywood Broun, Paul Gallico, and Ring Lardner. The popular Rice, for example, is most often remembered for his highly quoted *New York Herald Tribune* "four horsemen" game story about the Notre Dame football victory over Army, 13–7, in 1924. Flowery in language and liberal with use of images, his work still captures the imagination of readers a century later.

Some 1920s sportswriters, typified by Rice and Gallico, made athletes and sports bigger than life.

Other sports reporters were cynical and critical in their approach. Gallico wrote for the *New York Daily News* for more than a decade, 1923–1936, before leaving sports journalism. With a series of more than two dozen sports titles and other books, Gallico exemplified the high-caliber writer attracted by the challenges of 1920s' sports journalism who eventually evolved to other forms of nonfiction and fiction.

William McGeehan wrote for the *New York Herald Tribune*, the same newspaper as Rice. The style and approach modeled by McGeehan and Westbrook Pegler became popular during the 1930s. John Kieran wrote for *The New York Times* from 1916 to 1922, then for the *Herald Tribune* and the *American* before rejoining *The Times* in 1927. At this time, he began the newspaper's first signed daily sports column called *Sports of the Times*.

Popular Sportswriters of the Mid-20th Century

Major sportswriters at the beginning of the 1950s included Westbrook Pegler (*New York WorldTelegram*), Arthur Daley (*New York Times*), Shirley Povich (*Washington Post*), Bob Considine (International News Service), Red Smith (*Philadelphia Record* and *New York Times*), Stanley Woodward (*New York Herald Tribune*), Edward Burns (*Chicago Tribune*), Dave Egan (*Boston Daily Record*), and Kieran (*New York Times*). Rice, who died in 1954 at age 73, was still producing six columns a week for the North American Newspaper Alliance at the time he died.

Smith, a long-time columnist for the *New York Herald Tribune* and the *New York Times*, started his career in the 1920s at the morning *Milwaukee Sentinel* and wrote later for the *St. Louis Star* and the *Philadelphia Record*. He moved to New York in the mid 1940s, beginning at the *Herald Tribune* and then to the *New York Times* in 1966. Smith rose to national fame while at the *Herald Tribune*, but he won a Pulitzer Prize while at the *New York Times*. He worked for a half century in sports journalism.

Many well-respected and widely read writers moved from sports to other positions in news. Pegler, for example, switched to write columns for the editorial page in the 1930s. Others became sports section managers, as many major newspapers in metropolitan areas began to create positions through expansion at the end of the 1930s. These individuals handled administrative duties almost exclusively and left day-to-day editing and column writing to others.

Leading Sportswriters of 1950s and the Modern Era

A new style of sportswriter emerged during the 1950s and 1960s. Americans began to read Jim Murray (*Los Angeles Times*), Dave Kindred (*Louisville Courier-Journal*, *The National* and *Sporting News*), Frank Deford (*Sports Illustrated* and *The National*), Dave Anderson (*The New York Times*), and Tom Boswell (*Washington Post*).

Another new generation of sportswriters developed in the 1970s and 1980s, setting the stage for the modern era. Writers such as Damon Runyon generated writers of the caliber and style of Jimmy Cannon. Writers of the quality of Arthur Daley came from the mold of writers like Grantland Rice. Styles of the 1980s and 1990s were represented by Murray (*Los Angeles Times*), Blackie Sherrod (*Dallas Morning News*), Skip Bayless (*Dallas Times-Herald*), Dave Kindred (*Louisville Courier-Journal*, *The National* and *Sporting News*), John Shulian (*Philadelphia Daily News*), Edwin Pope (*Miami Herald*), and Mark Whicker (*Orange County [Calif.] Register*).

Modern-era sportswriters not only write for their base newspapers and branded online sites but are often also seen on sports television such as local market stations and national networks like ESPN. They are also present on numerous social media platforms such as Twitter, Facebook, and Instagram, stretching their personal name brands and giving their sports coverage and commentary a much broader exposure than the generations of sportswriters who came before them. One such example is South Florida's Dan Le Batard, who began during college as a part-time sportswriter for the *Miami Herald* and matured into one of that newspaper's most popular sports columnists. His career expanded and led to broadcasting appearances and opportunities, and eventually to his own podcasts and sports talk shows on ESPN radio and ESPN television.

A Select List of Award-Winning Sportswriters

Compiling any list of outstanding professionals in a field is challenging. The following listings are alphabetical by last name and are not ranked. Both men and women as well as older generation and modern-era sportswriters have been included. Some better-known writers on this list began their careers writing about sports, then expanded to write on other subjects and publish in different genres.

Mitch Albom

Mitch Albom (1958–) is best known today as a writer of best-selling inspirational books such as *Tuesdays With Morrie* and *The Five People You Meet in Heaven*. From New Jersey, Albom began his professional journalism career as a writer for a weekly in Flushing, NY, while in college. After school, he freelanced before joining daily newspapers in Fort Lauderdale, FL, and in Detroit, MI. After winning top sportswriting awards for his work at the *Fort Lauderdale News* and *Sun Sentinel*, he was hired as a sports columnist for the *Detroit Free Press*. One of the most awarded sportswriters of his generation for his appealing columns, he also wrote nonsports commentaries on Sundays for the newspaper's opinion page. In addition to his nonfiction inspirational books, he has authored books about Michigan college football and basketball and collections of his columns. He has been a radio host, written plays, worked on films, and has appeared regularly on sports and other television shows.

Jimmy Cannon

Jimmy Cannon (1909–1973), an award-winning writer, made his reputation writing about boxing and was honored with a place in the International Boxing Hall of Fame. Working mostly for New York area newspapers (*Daily News*, *Post*, *Journal-American*, and *Newsday*) and news distributors such as King Features in the early and mid 20th century, Cannon recognized the significance of Black athletes beyond those in boxing. Cannon wrote a daily column in an era when sportswriters and columnists' voices were at their loudest.

Henry Chadwick

Henry Chadwick (1824–1908) was one of the first sportswriters to focus on baseball, working in its earliest days in the late 19th century. Originally from England, he was honored with induction into the Baseball Hall of Fame for his work. He is credited with creating box scores and player and team statistics and is given credit for the "K" symbol in baseball scoring that represents strikeouts. He edited the first baseball guide and wrote about the sport from the 1860s until the early 1900s. He wrote for newspapers in addition to editing baseball guides for Spalding.

Bob Considine

Bob Considine (1906–1975) was a sportswriter and much more during his professional news career. He began his sportswriting life covering tennis at *The Washington Herald* and later worked as a war correspondent for the International News Service during World War II. Considine set the model for many modern-era writers by demonstrating high skill in covering sports as well as other major news of the day. During his long career, he also authored best-selling books about sports (*The Babe Ruth Story*) and war (*Thirty Seconds Over Tokyo*). He became one of the early sportswriters to work in radio and television.

Arthur Daley

Arthur Daley (1904–1974) served as a columnist and sportswriter for *The New York Times* for almost a half century beginning in the 1920s, not long after he was graduated from college. A Pulitzer Prize winner in 1956 for commentary about sports, Daley was a college athlete at Fordham University in the 1920s and served as sports editor for the campus newspaper. The native-born New Yorker was *The Times*'s sports columnist for more than three decades, covering major global sports events and the routine sports of New York.

Mary Garber

Mary Garber (1916–2008) is an original among women sportswriters. Award-winning, Garber was the first female sportswriter honored with induction into the U.S. Basketball Writers Hall of

Fame. She began her career during World War II, covering a wide range of news, but not sports. Immediately after the war ended, she began her career covering sports for the *Twin-City Sentinel* (and later the *Winston-Salem Journal*) in Winston-Salem, NC. For three decades, she was the only woman in her city who covered sports such as basketball and football in the college-level Atlantic Coast Conference.

Dan Jenkins

Dan Jenkins (1928–2019) is best known for his books about sports and his numerous articles in *Sports Illustrated*, but he also covered sports for the *Fort Worth Press* and *Dallas Times Herald*. He grew up in the Fort Worth area and played golf at Texas Christian University. His sportswriting career spanned six decades and left a legacy of hundreds of articles in *Sports Illustrated* as well as monthly columns for *Golf Digest* and best-selling books such as *Semi-Tough*.

Sally Jenkins

Sally Jenkins (1960–), daughter of sportswriter Dan Jenkins (see previous subsection), has been honored as the top sports columnist in the United States by the Associated Press Sports Editors professional organization four times while working as a columnist for *The Washington Post*. Before working in Washington, she was a senior writer for *Sports Illustrated*. She is the author of 12 books about sports and sports people, including a popular volume written with University of Tennessee women's basketball coach Pat Summitt and a book written with bicycle racer Lance Armstrong. Her work has appeared in numerous magazines and she has regularly appeared on sports network television and radio.

Dave Kindred

Dave Kindred (1941–) became best known as a *sportswriter* and *columnist* for the *Louisville Courier-Journal*. He also covered sports and wrote columns for the *Washington Post*, the *Atlanta Journal-Constitution*, *The National*, *Sporting News*, and *Golf Digest*. Winner of numerous awards for his work, including Associated Press Sports Editors' national Red Smith Award, given for lifetime achievement in sportswriting. He is author of at least nine sports books on topics such as golf, baseball, basketball, football, and boxing.

Roger Kahn

Roger Kahn (1927–2020), a native New Yorker, may be best known for his classic baseball book *The Boys of Summer*. The book, rated by *Sports Illustrated* as one of the best sports books of all time, is the story of the Brooklyn Dodgers baseball teams of the early 1950s. He authored 20 or more books, both nonfiction and fiction. However, many of them focused on baseball. He started his career working at the *New York Herald-Tribune* at the end of World War II and rose to cover the Brooklyn Dodgers. He later became sports editor of *Newsweek* on Long Island.

Ring Lardner

Ring Lardner (1885–1933), a highly creative Midwesterner, wrote about sports as a columnist and developed a national reputation for his fiction in the form of short stories. His professional career began covering sports in South Bend, Indiana, but he soon moved to Chicago and wrote about sports for several newspapers, including the *Chicago Tribune*. For a brief time, he wrote in St. Louis for *Sporting News* before returning to the *Tribune*. He wrote at least one novel, about baseball, and he had success as both a playwright and song composer.

Jim Murray

Jim Murray (1919–1998) perfected his craft as a national sports columnist for the *Los Angeles Times*. He wrote a nationally distributed column for almost four decades. Much honored, he earned the Pulitzer Prize for commentary in 1990 for a series of 1989 columns. He also worked at *Sports Illustrated*, *Time*, and *Los Angeles Examiner*. His career began in his native Connecticut with stints at the *New Haven Times* and *Hartford Times*. He was author of six books, including an autobiography and collections of his columns written for *The Times*.

Westbrook Pegler

Westbrook Pegler (1894–1969) began his professional career at the beginning of World War I as a war correspondent for United Press and was reportedly the youngest reporter from the United States. Following the war, he turned to write columns about sports and general interest stories. He moved to the *Chicago Tribune* and then Scripps Howard news group. By this time, he was writing about politics, crime (winning a Pulitzer Prize in 1941), and other subjects for syndicated audience of about 6 million readers.

George Plimpton

George Plimpton (1927–2003) is widely known for a series of insider books about professional sports. His first, *Paper Lion: Confessions of a Last-String Quarterback*, was a close-up look at professional football from summer training camp and preseason games. He founded the literary *Paris Review*, but his first-hand participant reporting won international recognition and sold millions of books. Titles included his experiences in playing and practicing with a professional hockey team, playing on the professional golf tour, going several rounds with a professional boxer, among others. An article for *Sports Illustrated* in the late 1980s titled "The Curious Case of Sidd Finch" about an athlete with a remarkable 168 mph fastball that no one could hit, created quite a stir as well. An April Fool's Day joke, the article noted how this young phenomenon was going to revolutionize Major League Baseball. The article was so popular that he turned it into a novel with the same title. Plimpton's career included literary criticism, writing sports fiction, and acting. He also appeared regularly on television.

Edwin Pope

Edwin Pope (1928–2017) developed his reputation as a sports reporter and columnist at *The Miami Herald*. While he was widely known for decades of coverage of professional tennis at Wimbledon and covering professional football's Super Bowl year after year, his diverse columns brought national attention and numerous awards. His professional career began at the small newspaper in Athens, Georgia, and as a student at the University of Georgia. From there, he worked for United Press International, the *Atlanta Journal*, and the *Atlanta Constitution* before moving to Miami in 1956. Pope covered sports there for more than a half century. He was a columnist and the section's sports editor, but writing columns and commentary about sports, both national and very local, both professional and amateur, was his love.

Shirley Povich

Shirley Povich (1905–1998) was synonymous with sportswriting, reporting, and commentary at *The Washington Post* for about five decades. He began as a sports columnist and section editor for *The Post*, but briefly was a Pacific Theater war correspondent during World War II. Povich returned to sportswriting when the war ended and continued until he retired in 1973. But for the next 25 years until his death, he authored hundreds of additional columns and commentaries, and he continued to cover the World Series each year. He was winner of numerous national writing and commentary awards and honors.

Grantland Rice

Grantland Rice (1880–1954), often called a writer's writer, is widely known for his descriptive skills with words in describing the drama and personalities of sports in the early 20th century. He was a former college athlete, playing football and baseball for Vanderbilt University. He even coached the 1908 baseball team for Vanderbilt. Originally from Middle Tennessee, Rice began sportswriting by covering golf. He worked for the *Atlanta Journal*, *Cleveland News*, and *Nashville Tennessean*. He became a columnist for the *New York Tribune*, authoring "Sportlight." His sportswriting career spanned more than a half century.

Damon Runyon

Damon Runyon (1880–1946) was master of many forms of journalism and general writing specializations in the first half of the 20th century but is perhaps best known for his short stories and sportswriting. While he was most famous for his fiction, he wrote about sports for a wide range of

Hearst newspapers and news and feature distribution services over several decades. He was a baseball columnist for Hearst Newspapers and is recognized for helping define how baseball is covered. He also wrote often about professional boxing.

Red Smith

Red Smith (1905–1982) built his sportswriting and sports commentary reputation in Philadelphia (*Record*) but sealed it with sports columns based in New York City (*New York Herald Tribune* and *The New York Times*). He spent more than 50 years covering sports and was honored with a Pulitzer Prize for distinguished commentary in 1976 for his columns about sports. Usually ranked among the top sportswriters in American journalism history, Smith's column was syndicated and published across the United States and around the world. His most common subjects were horse racing, baseball, football, fishing, and boxing.

Stanley Woodward

Stanley Woodward (1895–1965) served two terms as sports editor of the *New York Herald Tribune* in the 1930s–1940s and 1950s–1960s in addition to writing a regular column. Originally from Massachusetts, he played football for Amherst College. After World War I, he began his professional news career for his hometown *Worcester Gazette* as a reporter, moving to the *Boston Herald* where he soon became sports editor. He left for the *New York Herald Tribune* to become sports editor. While managing the section, he wrote columns about college football.

Bruce Garrison

See also Column-Writing; Sports Broadcasting; Sports Journalism; Sportswriters.

Further Readings

Fleder, R. (2003). *Sports illustrated: 50 years of great writing, 1954-2004*. New York, NY: Sports Illustrated Books.

Garrison, B. (with Sabljak, M.). (1991). *Sports reporting* (2nd ed.) Ames: Iowa State University Press.

Stout, G., (annual) (Series Ed.). *The best American sports writing*. Boston, MA: Houghton-Mifflin Harcourt.

Kahn, R. (1972). *The boys of summer*. New York, NY: Harper & Row.

Plimpton, G. (1966). *Paper lion: Confessions of a last-string quarterback*. Guilford, CT: Lyons Press.

Washburn, P. S., & Lamb, C. (2020). *Sports journalism: A history of glory, fame, and technology*. Lincoln: University of Nebraska Press. doi:10.1080/08821127.2021.1865105

Stamp Act

The Stamp Act sparked much controversy between Great Britain and the colonies in America and laid the groundwork for the conflict that produced the American Revolution. It was a tax aimed at raising money for the British government, but it seemed to also restrict the ability of the colonies to criticize the government when they disagreed with it and the issue of free press produced much of the argument. This entry examines why the Stamp Act was introduced, its potential impact, reactions to the Stamp Act with a focus on printers' opposition to the Act, and the result of Stamp Act protests.

Background for the Adoption of the Stamp Act

Following the victory over France in the French and Indian War in 1763, Great Britain found itself 130 million pounds in debt and quickly sought new sources of revenue in the growing American colonies to help pay off the war debt and cover the costs of protecting the borders of the colonies. The first effort was the Sugar Act passed in 1764 which placed duties on refined sugar. Then came the Stamp Act, passed on March 22, 1765, and scheduled to become effective on November 1. The act required that all newspapers, licenses, bonds, and legal documents be printed on stamped paper that carried a special tax. The decision to pass this legislation was one of the worst political mistakes in history because British leaders seemingly did not think about who this act would impact. The groups most impacted by this legislation were some of the best educated and most publicly involved citizens in the colonies—merchants, lawyers, and printers. All three of these groups viewed the tax as excessive and were very upset when it was passed.

Potential Impact of the Stamp Act

Printers in particular faced immediate financial disaster because taxes were to be paid at the rate of a half penny for each copy of a two-page paper, a penny for each copy of a four-page paper, and two shillings for each advertisement. This cost would be equal to most of their income because printers received only a small portion greater than the required taxes from subscribers and advertisers. Taxes on job printing were just as high, and printing in foreign languages was taxed at double the standard rate. Fines for violating the Stamp Act ranged from 40 shillings to 10 pounds. If a printer chose to publish anonymously without stamps, they would be tried in an admiralty court (previously established to try maritime cases) without a jury. This seemed to be a violation of the colonial people's traditional rights to try cases of local offenses in local courts before juries of local citizens. Striking as hard as it did at printers, the tax gave them a special reason to use their newspapers to oppose the Stamp Act. Initially, they seemed to be unsure what to do, but they soon began to stiffen their resolve in the face of what they saw as tyranny and increasingly spoke out in their newspapers about the actions of the British government that they considered wrong.

General American Reactions to the Stamp Act

Perhaps no law in American history evoked such violent opposition as the Stamp Act did. Preachers denounced it in sermons. Town meetings and colonial legislatures passed strong resolutions against it. The Stamp Act Congress met in New York City in October and denounced the Stamp Act as an unconstitutional invasion of colonial rights and liberties. Merchants organized boycotts against British imports. Sons of Liberty groups formed throughout the colonies and took actions to prevent the enforcement of the Stamp Act. On May 30, Patrick Henry introduced to the Virginia House of Burgesses a resolution proclaiming the colonials' right as Englishmen to possess the sole power of taxation. He described anyone who dissented against such a right as an "Enemy to this his Majesty's Colony." British authorities were particularly disturbed by this pronouncement because Virginia was the first and most populous colony.

Many government officials expressed concern that Henry's statement would spark protests and other problems throughout the colonies. Meetings called to discuss the Stamp Act sometimes turned into brawls, particularly in Boston where the stamp master Andrew Oliver was hung in effigy and the Middle Colonies where much property was destroyed, and opponents devised rallies and other strategies to keep the law from being enforced. Newspapers reported on these meetings throughout the colonies. They also printed numerous letters and essays by people in their communities that condemned the tax. Trade with Great Britain drastically dropped, and colonials refused to pay their British creditors. On June 3, the *New York Post-Boy* reported that only one fifth as many ships were working the West Indian routes than before the Stamp Act was enacted. Hard cash was increasingly difficult to find. Business experienced "a most prodigious shock." John Hancock and other merchants lamented that the economic situation was becoming tough to deal with.

Printers Oppose the Stamp Act

Led by the bolder among them, printers gradually came into full opposition to the law. The press war against the Stamp Act started in Boston, which is not surprising given the importance of the city of Boston in the colonial economy. Awakened to the dangers building against them, printers there took to their printing presses to argue against the act as a frontal assault on the liberty of the people in general and the freedom of the press in particular. Eventually, newspapers spoke as if with one voice in opposition to the Stamp Act, as though they had become one "mass medium." They carried detailed accounts of public opposition to the act, noting pointedly the names of tax collectors and stories of their being hanged in effigy. As a result of all the protests and criticism, all of the stamp distributers in the mainland colonies resigned, thus leaving printers on November 1 in a dilemma.

The law required that they use nothing but stamped paper, but the paper was not available. The absence of paper did not void the penalties for violation of the law. Printers had to determine what path to take. None intended to pay the tax, but deciding how to proceed was not easy. A few newspapers, mainly in the South, temporarily suspended publication, but others challenged the law in one way or another. Some came out defiantly, appearing without the detestable stamp and declaring that the Stamp Act was a direct attack on liberty itself, whereas others took a "safer route" and stated that no stamped paper was available. To protect themselves from authorities, some printers claimed that they continued publishing because of threats from Patriots. On November 7, 1765, John Holt ran an "anonymous" letter in his *New York Gazette and Weekly Post-Boy* threatening his business and his body if he did not publish. But in the same issue, he also stated that he would ignore the act because the motto of his paper was "The United Voice of all His Majesty's free and loyal subjects in America: LIBERTY, PROSPERITY AND no STAMPS." Others, unfamiliar with the Stamp Act's fine print, attempted to evade the law by changing their newspapers' names and publishing anonymously. Similarly, some tried to sidestep the letter of the law by removing their serial numbering, thus changing their official status from newspapers to broadsides or handbills, which were not subject to the act. Even many of those newspapers that suspended temporarily objected vehemently. In late October, the German-language *Philadelphia Staatsbote* outlined its front page in black borders with a skull at the top. On October 31, the day before the act was to take effect, six other papers published with similar make-ups. The *Pennsylvania Journal and Weekly Advertiser* assumed perhaps the most eye-catching design. It published with the text surrounded by black columns that looked like a tombstone, topped with a skull and crossbones, mourning over the death of press liberty. The motto for this issue was "EXPIRING: In Hopes of a Resurrection to Life Again." Whatever the course pursued, it is notable that not a single newspaper in the mainland colonies published on stamped paper (but there were papers in the West Indies who published on stamped paper).

Impact of the Protests Against the Stamp Act

Because of the impact on trade, British merchants asked Parliament to repeal the Stamp Act in the hopes that the trade decline would end. In March 1766, Parliament, recognizing that the Stamp Act was unenforceable and that the economic impact on trade was too large, repealed it. By then,

colonial newspapers already had been inspired to oppose British authority. Every newspaper in the colonies protested the Stamp Act in some way and published stories about protests throughout the colonies, thus showing the widespread disagreement with the tax. The continuing opposition of the newspaper printers helped bring Americans together to protest British actions and thus helped lead Americans to the Revolution.

Carol Sue Humphrey

See also Civil Unrest, Coverage of; Democracy and the Media; English Roots of the Free Press; Free Expression, History of

Further Readings

Hoffer, P. C. (2015). *Benjamin Franklin explains the stamp act protests to parliament, 1766.* Oxford, UK: Oxford University Press.

Hutchins, Z. M. (Ed.) (2016). *Community without consent: New perspectives on the stamp act.* Dartmouth: Dartmouth College Press.

Morgan, E. S., & Morgan, H. M. (1953). *The stamp act crisis: Prologue to revolution.* Chapel Hill: University of North Carolina Press. doi: 10.1086/ahr/59.1.132

Schlesinger, A. M. (1958). *Prelude to independence: The newspaper war on great britain, 1764-1776.* New York, NY: Alfred A. Knopf. doi: 10.1086/ahr/64.1.119

Sloan, Wm. D., & Williams, J. H. (1994). *The early American press, 1690-1783.* Westport, CT: Greenwood Press. doi: 10.1080/08821127.1995.10731734

STARS AND STRIPES

Stars and Stripes is the daily newspaper published for American military servicemen and U.S. Department of Defense civilians, contractors, and their families. Unique among the many military publications in the world, *Stars and Stripes* operates free of any government control or censorship. It has been published continuously in Europe since 1942, and since 1945 in the Pacific. *Stars and Stripes* has one of the widest distribution ranges of any newspaper in the world; between the Pacific and European editions, it is read in over 50 countries where there are American bases, posts, ships, or embassies. The newspaper publishes approximately 80,000 copies in the Pacific and Europe combined, 363 days each year.

Origins

This military newspaper was first published during the American Civil War, the initial issue produced when Union soldiers of three Illinois regiments set up camp in Bloomfield, Missouri, in November 1861. Upon finding the local newspaper offices abandoned, four ex-newspaper writers decided to print a one-page newspaper for their regiments, relating the troops' daily activities. They named it *Stars and Stripes* but ceased publication when the Union forces continued their advance a few days later. The Department of Defense has officially recognized Bloomfield as the birthplace of the paper, and the *Stars and Stripes* Museum and Library is located there.

The World War I version first appeared in February 1918 in Paris. An all-military staff produced it weekly to provide information to the doughboys of the American Expeditionary Force. At its peak, it had eight pages and claimed more than a half-million readers. It relied upon the improvisation of its staff, many of whom became famous and influential members of postwar American media (editor Harold Ross, for example, returned home to found *The New Yorker* magazine). The *Stars and Stripes* ceased publication after the war ended in November 1918.

In April 1942 in a London print shop, a small group of servicemen founded a four-page weekly version of *Stars and Stripes* for American soldiers in Britain; the new version quickly grew into an eight-page daily newspaper. It was graced by the work of talented young journalists such as Andy Rooney, Steve Kroft, Louis Rukeyser; author Shel Silverstein; and cartoonists Vernon Grant and Bill Mauldin. The latter's famous "Willie and Joe" cartoons laid the foundation for his later work, which garnered two Pulitzer Prizes. Eventually, several editions were published simultaneously in the European theater, some printed very close to the fighting fronts in order to get the latest information to the most troops. At one time, there were

as many as 25 publishing locations in operation in Europe, North Africa, the Middle East, and Hawaii. Throughout the war, *Stars and Stripes* had a friend and protector in General Dwight Eisenhower, Supreme Allied Commander in Europe, who issued a "hands-off" policy and defended the paper against protests by others. By V-J Day, August 15, 1945, circulation had risen to a million readers.

When World War II ended, the paper was instructed by the Department of Defense to continue to publish as long as U.S. troops remained abroad. As wartime enlisted staff were demobilized, the newspaper built an experienced staff of full-time civilian journalists, augmented by a small contingent of military journalists and photographers. The paper's reporters joined the troops in the field throughout the Korean and Vietnam conflicts. During the 1991 fighting in Iraq, the paper established a Middle East bureau for reporting the war, as circulation of *Stars and Stripes* nearly doubled within weeks. During the early 2000s Iraq War, reporters from the paper were embedded with military units in Kuwait and Iraq, as well as on Navy ships in the region. Staffers are still reporting from those countries, and thousands of copies of the paper are being printed daily in Iraq and Afghanistan for distribution.

Stars and Stripes Today

In the face of rising costs, in the 1990s the production of *Stars and Stripes* was reorganized. A central editorial office was established in Washington, D.C., that receives news stories, photos, and advertisements from bureaus around the world through a high-tech electronic publishing system with editors then creating electronic pages for different editions that are sent to printing plants around the world by satellite. Since the reorganization, the website has been expanded, a *Stars and Stripes* version for ships at sea was developed, and, in 2004, online electronic subscription service was pioneered. The paper is distributed at no charge to troops in combat theaters, offered for sale in coin boxes and military exchanges at bases, and has home delivery to subscribers in several countries. After the restructuring, advertising grew from $3 million to nearly $10 million a year by 2007.

Stars and Stripes maintains news bureaus in Europe, the Pacific, and the Middle East. In addition to national and international news and sports stories, the newspaper seeks to provide all the elements of the hometown papers servicemen left behind, from columns to coupons, comics, and crossword puzzles. The "Letters to the Editor" pages have long been a popular feature and forum for lively discussions on issues of interest to members of the military services. In 2008, five daily editions were published: Mideast, Europe, Japan, Korea, and Okinawa. The regional editions, besides the above, offer topical information on political, cultural, and sporting events at the theater military bases and in surrounding communities.

Unlike many of its military media counterparts, *Stars and Stripes* takes no editorial position of its own but strives to maintain a balanced presentation of issues and opinions. The staff, a combination of military and civilian personnel, has been trained in the traditions of American journalism. An ombudsman, usually a civilian ex-editor, protects the paper's First Amendment rights and investigates any allegations of censorship or news management by government departments or officials. As revised Department of Defense Directive 5122.11 states:

> *Stars and Stripes* is a Department of Defense-authorized daily newspaper distributed overseas for the U.S. military community. Editorially independent of interference from outside its own editorial chain-of-command, it provides commercially available U.S. and world news and objective staff-produced stories relevant to the military community in a balanced, fair, and accurate manner. By keeping its audience informed, *Stars and Stripes* enhances military readiness and better enables U.S. military personnel and their families stationed overseas to exercise their responsibilities of citizenship.

Stars and Stripes is recognized by both journalists and readers as the "G.I.'s newspaper" and has a proud history of being a credible news source. The paper has but one specific mission: to bring American military personnel and their dependents the same international, national, and regional news and opinion from sources available to newspapers throughout the United States.

Historically, *Stars and Stripes'* role becomes most visible in times of overseas conflict, when it expands dramatically to serve a growing number of military personnel. But throughout its tenure as the servicemen's newspaper, it has served to connect American servicemen abroad with each other and with the American home front.

In 2013, the paper faced job cuts, printing-schedule changes, a pay-raise freeze, and travel limitations for staff under the federal budget sequestration. In 2016, the Pentagon considered additional budget cuts. In 2020, an order for the newspaper to shutter was issued, but the order to close was rescinded.

Rex Martin

See also First Amendment; Military and the Media; War and Military Journalism; War Correspondents

Further Readings

Cornebise, A. E. (1984). *The stars & stripes, doughboy journalism in world war I.* Westport, CT: Greenwood Press.

Harris, B. (1999). *Blue & gray in black & white: Newspapers in the civil war.* Washington, DC: Brassey's.

Mitgang, H. (Ed.) (1996). *Civilians under arms: The stars and stripes, civil war to Korea.* Carbondale: Southern Illinois University Press.

Sweeney, M. S. (2006). *The military and the press: An uneasy truce.* Evanston, IL: Northwestern University Press.

Winterich, J. T. (Ed.) (1931). *Squads write! A selection of the best things in prose, verse and cartoon from the stars & stripes, official newspaper of the A.E.F.* New York, NY: Harper & Bros.

STOCK PHOTOGRAPHY

Stock photography is the creation, storage, and sale of photographs to clients who want to purchase already-made images. Photographers face various challenges in making a living as a stock photographer. Many stock photographers, if not most, do it as a part-time job. Stock photography's origins began in the 1800s, but it has changed to reflect business practices and social values. This entry begins with an overview of the roots of stock photography and then examines modern stock photography agencies and the hiring of photographers to produce high-quality images on demand. Finally, the entry discusses criticisms of stock photography.

Background

The roots of stock photography are visible in the manufacture of stereographs and the carte de visite of the late 1800s. These were photographic products for mass audiences. Stereographs were two photographs taken side-by-side and printed on a card. Viewers would use a special device to look at the pair of images, resulting in a 3D effect. The carte de visite was a photograph printed on a thick stock. Well-to-do individuals would have them created to share with friends, and consumers could buy cards displaying the portrait of a celebrity. The manufacturing of both kinds of cards involved mass production for many consumers. People created businesses for the manufacture and distribution of cards. They hired many photographers to create images for these businesses, often giving them incomes in addition to their work as studio and portrait photographers.

Another influence on stock photography was the photo agency, run by a management company or a group of photographers. Photo agencies handle the business end of photography, often around particular kinds of photography such as news and documentary photographers. Agencies recruit clients, assign photographers when a client contacts the agency, pay the bills, and handle contracts. Traditionally, stock photography companies would sell existing images, and photo agencies would deal more in specific assignments. However, some photo stock agencies are taking on some of the roles of a photo agency, such as contracting photographers to produce photographs. In all these cases, a photography industry was being established that involved the essential characteristics of modern stock photography.

Modern Stock Photography Agencies

As of 2021, stock photography businesses either sell only existing images or merge the stock photography model with the photo agency. The industry has experienced consolidation as a few have bought out some of their competitors. Photographers face shaky ground as digital photography has encouraged more people to participate, which has led to lower pay rates.

There are two basic models for the stock-only agency. The more traditional model is one that is built around agreements with particular photographers. The expenses of the past involved story photographic slides or other material and communicating by mail. Stock agencies built a relationship with clients, so agencies preferred reliable photographers. This model still exists but looks like boutique agencies because of their specialization, rather than library size. Clients use these agencies because they have a reputation for having particular kinds of high-quality photography. Commonly known as *macrostock*, these agencies have moved into the digital environment but continue to rely on quality and relationships as the basis of their operations.

Although these more traditional stock agencies still exist, they receive less press coverage than the start-up, microstock businesses that seek investors and photographs from anyone. Microstock prices are low, which means the businesses and photographers need to sell massive numbers of photographs to make a worthwhile profit. These businesses are popular with amateur photographers who started with smartphones and who can simply edit an image and upload it to the site. Microstock agencies sort of follow a model established by Amazon for attracting customers who want to save a lot of money and seller-photographers who would otherwise not be able to make money in a traditional business model. Compared to traditional stock agencies, the images are crowdsourced with less concern for quality. Commonly referred to as *microstock*, this stock photography business model depends on digital technology. Digital cameras have become so advanced that it takes little knowledge to make a usable image, and the images circulate completely in a digital environment.

Stock Meets Photographers' Agency

To expand their businesses, some stock businesses have adopted elements of a photo agency—one that represents its own photographers—by hiring photographers to produce high-quality images on demand. This appeals to photographers who want a full-time job and a consistent income. They have less freedom over what to photograph but this is offset by the predictability of a salary.

Corbis Falls, Getty Rises

Corbis and Getty are the most prominent high-end stock agencies because of their massive library, including historical images. Corbis' origins are in Microsoft founder Bill Gates' Interactive Home Systems, which became Corbis Corporation and established its reputation with the 1995 purchase of the Bettmann Archive. Corbis suddenly owned 16 million images and significantly expanded this image library, especially with the 1999 purchase of the renowned Sygma, a France-based European news agency. Its growth was rivaled by Getty Images, which strove to remain in competition with Corbis. Getty has approximately 200 million images, including those of PhotoDisc, a company once reviled for its clip art but which helped create the low-cost, online sales model, and the respected Tony Stone Images collection.

Corbis developed a reputation in the industry for poor management and sold its assets to the Unity Group, part of the Visual China Group, and the new owners would take over the contracts of Corbis's photographers. It was announced in 2016 that Getty would be the distributor for Corbis's images. The competition between the two agencies was viewed as good for professional photographers, who included commercial, editorial, and news photographers. The Corbis Images website now automatically directs visitors to Getty Images.

Top Microstock Agencies

Several microstock companies gained traction in the new digital environment. One of these was iStockphoto, a Canadian company. Established in 2000, its success led to its acquisition by Getty in 2006 for $50 million. Now named iStock, it claims to have created the business of crowd-sourced stock imagery with six employees. Offering photography, illustrations, and video, it now has hundreds of employees. At this time, its cheapest plan is 10 images for $29 per month. The agency provides online tips and market trends for its contributors.

Its main competitor has been Shutterstock, which may be better known to the general public than iStock. Boasting a library of more than 300 million images with 200,000 being added every day, Shutterstock also sells music. For the same $29, Shutterstock offers two images per month as the cheapest plan. Shutterstock offers its Custom platform for clients who want to be paired with a creator for on-demand images that is just for them.

Other microstock agencies exist, such as Adobe Stock, Big Stock Photo, and Dreamstime. Adobe Stock, formerly Fotolia, is aimed at Adobe software users who need stock photography.

Criticisms of Stock Photography

Although the quality of microstock photography has risen over the years, it has received criticism for multiple reasons. One reason is the low pay accepted by microstock photographers has supposedly pushed down the rates professional photographers can charge. Another complaint, similar to complaints made about Instagram, is that images tend to look generic or repetitive. Contributors are encouraged to make images that will sell, not necessarily move photography forward or challenge photographers' creativity. In 2004, Dell and Gateway computer companies were criticized for using stock images showing the same model from apparently one photoshoot for its back-to-school promotional ads.

More recently, a complaint has been directed at the reliance on stereotypes. Part of the blame may be shared with the legacy stock agencies' older collections. However, critics have accused microstock agencies of not being cognizant enough of diverse representations. In 2014, Pam Grossman, who was director of visual trends at Getty, created the Lean In Collection from the archives. Grossman saw this as just a start because she saw stock images of female professionals in heavy makeup being posed unnaturally.

In response to being frustrated at trying to find images of Black people for his clients, the web designer and tech guru Kenneth Wiggins created a beta stock agency in 2015 to promote better and more diverse representations in his BlackStockImages, also known as BlackStock. The effort had limited success because of Wiggins's death in 2017.

There has been a general trend in commercial and editorial illustration photography toward a more natural style, reflected in the lifestyle look. Some of the credit for the change in style goes to the economy. People struggling financially may not want to see an out-of-touch world. Another cause is Instagram, where the natural style is popular. Stock photography has followed these trends, with models appearing more like good-looking neighbors and using less obviously constructed scenes. This may also contribute to more diversity in stock imagery as some Instagram users expand into stock production, because Instagram appears to be used by more women and non-whites than those who were part of legacy stock agencies and early microstock efforts.

Timothy Roy Gleason

See also Advertising; Photo Agencies; Photo Editors; Photography; Photojournalists

Further Readings

500px blog. (2020). What commercial stock photography looks like in 2020. *500px*. Retrieved from https://iso.500px.com/stock-photography-trends/

Giorgis, H. (2015). Stock photos of Black people are finally moving beyond racist stereotypes. *New Republic*. Retrieved from https://newrepublic.com/article/122557/stock-photos-black-people-are-finally-moving-beyond-racist-steroty/

Hall, C. J. (2020). Is this the end of microstock photography? *PetaPixel*. Retrieved from https://petapixel.com/2020/06/08/is-this-the-end-of-microstock-photography/

Tate, R. (2014). The woman fighting female stereotypes, one photo at a time. *Wired*. Retrieved from https://wired.com/2014/02/secret-weapon-pics-of-women/

STREAMING MEDIA

As a concept in media, streaming describes the networked delivery of audio or video data that are rendered immediately upon arrival on a digital device, rather than being stored there first. In other words, an audio or video file does not have to be downloaded from a remote location before it can be played but starts playing as soon the data arrive onto the device.

The emergence of streaming as a dominant mode of media consumption signified two major shifts in the media and content markets. First, it transformed how content is delivered, and second, it brought significant change to the business models associated with media and content marketplaces as well as the types of companies who operate in those spaces.

Storage Versus Bandwidth

Because a video or audio file is not necessarily stored after it has been streamed and played on a device, there is a much smaller need for local storage. However, this reduction in storage requirements is offset by a need for bandwidth; if the network connection between sender and receiver is poor, the content is also delivered poorly, with a poor user experience as a result. To address this, most streaming media delivery employs some form of *compression* technology, which reduces the amount of data needed to provide an acceptable audiovisual experience.

In 1972, Indian American computer scientist Nasir Ahmed developed the main principles behind the digital video compression. In 1988, two standards organizations, the International Organization for Standardization and the International Electrotechnical Commission, established the Motion Picture Experts Group (MPEG), tasked with developing standards that would decrease the amount of data required to render acceptable quality digital video. The aim was not to stream video over the Internet, but to enable feature films and television content to be distributed on physical, digital media such as LaserDiscs and, later, DVDs and Blu-ray discs.

Because streaming required transmission of a high data volume, early streaming initiatives often happened at the local level. Local area networks were faster than Internet connections, and hence, early streaming experiments happened in places with multiple networked computers powerful enough to facilitate streaming. One such institution was the Computer Laboratory at Cambridge University in the United Kingdom, where researchers set up what is considered the world's webcam next to a coffee machine. Providing a networked video feed to everyone on the network through a small software client, the camera gave everyone the option to check whether fresh coffee had been made. The feed was started on the local network in 1991, but began streaming to the wider Internet in 1993, after web browsers gained support for video.

In 1992, students at Cornell University in the United States developed CU-SeeMe, a client program similar to the one from Cambridge, to provide the opportunity for video conferencing, which was otherwise very expensive. The quality obtainable through Internet-based video streaming was still lower than what consumers were generally willing to accept. An example of this is the film *Wax or the Discovery of Television Among the Bees* by independent filmmaker David Blair. Originally released in 1991, the film was made available on its own website in 1993, but it could only be viewed at a speed of two images, or frames, per second, making the viewing experience somewhat jerky. In June 1993, researchers at Xerox PARC in Palo Alto, California, demonstrated their streaming technology, MBone, by letting the band Severe Tire Damage play a concert live over the Internet. MBone hosted a few other bands, before the Rolling Stones took to the platform in November 1994 and transmitted 20 minutes of video and audio from a concert in Dallas, Texas. However, watching the latter concert live required both computing power and an Internet connection that cost far more than what regular consumers could afford, and only 200 computers around the world were logged on to watch the livestream.

Lifecasting

While such high-profile experiments gained attention in the media and technology worlds, commercial video streaming of prerecorded material was already on offer from vendors whose clientele was less concerned with perfect image quality. In the pornographic industry, European producers and distributors such as the Dutch company Red Light District custom-built their own streaming solutions and began publishing clips in 1994. This was also the year webcams became available at a consumer-friendly price level, with the monochrome Connectix QuickCam being the first to enter the market at

a price under U.S.$100. When color webcams entered the market 2 years later, the porn industry made the seemingly natural transition from phone sex services to video chats via the Internet, once again relying on custom-built solutions rather than commercially available services. Technologically, these video chats were early versions of what two decades later would constitute the livestreaming phenomenon.

Also in 1996 conceptual artist Jennifer Ringley pioneered *lifecasting* by setting up a webcam in her dorm room at Dickinson College in Pennsylvania, and soon after, began charging money for access to the feed. Over the next 7 years, Ringley's website, JenniCam, broadcast all aspects of her home life, including very intimate moments of a more sexual nature. This voyeurism was the attraction for some visitors to her site, which attracted four million views per day at its peak, while others followed Ringley out of sociological curiosity.

Internet Radio

Because audio takes up significantly less bandwidth than video, streaming audio reached a wide audience first, mostly providing content normally found on the radio, such as music, news, and sports. In fact, streaming audio first broke through to a wider audience by retransmitting AM/FM broadcasts over the Internet. During 1994, students on the campuses of University of North Carolina, Chapel Hill; Georgia Tech University; and University of Kansas used their technical skills to bring their college radio stations online. But compression still played a crucial role, and Internet radio did not really take off until the year after, when the Seattle-based tech company Progressive Networks debuted a compressed audio format for streaming named RealAudio. Partnering with ESPN, the company demonstrated its capability by livestreaming a baseball game between the Seattle Mariners and the New York Yankees.

In 1994, Internet entrepreneurs Todd Wagner and Mark Cuban took an interest in Cameron Audio Networks, a small company aiming to broadcast sports games live on the Internet. By September 1995, Cuban and Wagner had renamed the company AudioNet and began streaming college football games using RealAudio. A year later, AudioNet.com was home to hundreds of local radio stations from all over the United States and was livestreaming sports events and concerts by major music artists. AudioNet also featured a "CD Jukebox" with more than 700 full-length CDs available on-demand, an early herald of the music streaming services to come. With streaming video becoming an increasingly substantial part of AudioNet's offerings, the company changed its name to Broadcast.com in 1998 and became a public company.

MP3 Compression Format

Despite these efforts, music consumers abandoning CDs were not moving into streaming, but remained in the download paradigm, aided by the MP3 compression format for music, made public for the first time in 1993 by MPEG. With technology developed by the Fraunhofer Society in Germany, digital music files extracted from CDs could be compressed to around one tenth of their original size, enabling large collections of music to be stored on small units or even remotely. The small size of the MP3 format also made it possible to exchange music files over the Internet illegally, and the ease of illegal downloads—versus visiting a record store—made on-demand music appealing to many consumers.

A search engine for illegal music downloads, Mp3.com became a giant success in 1998, and eventually went public, but only after the music industry forced it to distance itself from pirated music. That role was instead taken over by Napster, created by 19-year-old college student Shawn Fanning. Napster's peer-to-peer service gave access to other users' MP3 repositories, where someone seeking a specific song might find it. Napster's growth was so explosive in its first 10 months that some network administrators reported that up to 61% of their traffic was Napster activity. Having peaked at 80 million users, a court order spurred on by music rights organizations shut down Napster in 2002, but similar services such as Kazaa, Gnutella, LimeWire, and Audiogalaxy quickly replaced it. Although MP3s belong in the download paradigm rather than the streaming paradigm, they helped users develop an expectation of a large catalog that was easy accessible without

per-unit purchases—which was the formula adopted by later streaming services.

The iPod

In 1999, Microsoft launched Windows Media Audio and Windows Media Video as streaming and downloadable alternatives to RealNetworks's formats and MP3. Apple was promoting their own QuickTime format as well as MPEG's Advanced Audio Coding. With the availability of several formats, many consumers were confused about how to organize and store their collection of MP3s. It did not help that the available portable MP3 player devices ranged from small, RAM-based players such as the Rio Diamond, to hard drive–based players that could contain most of a normal CD collection, like the Creative NOMAD Jukebox. Each had its own way of transferring and organizing music files, adding to the confusion until Apple launched its portable, hard disk–based iPod player in October 2001. Its close integration with iTunes, the MP3/music file player Apple had launched 9 months prior, made the whole process of ripping CDs, organizing the music files, and allowing individuals to take their collection with them much more effortless.

On-Demand Music Streaming

However, most iPods contained at least some music files that had been obtained illegally. To respond to this, the music industry tried to open two legal online music stores in 2001, the RealNetworks-run MusicNet and PressPlay. Although they both offered low-quality streaming in addition to downloads, and in the case of PressPlay, a subscription plan, they never achieved the success of later streaming services. The problem was that the stores only contained music from the major music labels that were invested in them, and fans had to find out which record label put out their favorite artist's music in order to purchase it legally. It was more convenient for consumers to download it illegally instead. Such piracy continued until Apple launched the iTunes Music Store in 2003. Other one-stop-shops and alternative outlets such as eMusic and OD2 had emerged in the United States and Europe, but because millions of iPod owners were already in the iTunes ecosystem, Apple's music store quickly became a near-monopoly for mainstream music purchases online. Its focus on downloads delayed the streaming era for a few years.

One of the events that helped push things along was the emergence of social media and recommendation technology. The first major social networking site, Friendster, was rapidly gaining members in 2003 when MySpace was launched as a rival. MySpace went on to become the first social network site with more than 100 million users, partly driven by music artists who could make streams of their music available to fans. Similarly, the launch of SoundCloud in 2007 enabled music and other audio streams from creators who wished to circumvent the main industry distribution methods. SoundCloud streams were easy to embed in websites, which a lot of blogs in the then-rapidly growing blogosphere made use of.

In 2005, Pandora Radio was launched. Since streaming music on-demand had yet to be brought to the mainstream, but Internet radio was wildly popular, Pandora placed itself in between the two. Pandora differentiated itself by playing a constant stream of music based on the listener's preferences, enabled by a proprietary recommendation engine. By 2013, Pandora claimed to have 70 million monthly users, commanding 70% of all Internet radio traffic in the United States.

Spotify, Netflix, and the Á La Carte Model

Globally, digital music distribution was still entrenched in the download paradigm when Spotify launched in Sweden. Scandinavia's music rights structure is characterized less by corporate interests and more by creator-controlled rights organizations, making it easier for music streaming services to obtain music streaming licenses. The same is the case in France, which is among the reasons why three of the independent services that initially dominated the streaming music market—Spotify, TIDAL, and Deezer—were initially founded in Sweden, Norway, and France, respectively. What these, and most other music streaming services had in common, was the "á la carte" subscription model, whereby customers could stream as much music as they wanted for a low monthly fee. As a business model, the per-unit sales mattered less than the

number of paying subscribers, with the upside for the vendor being that revenue is generated automatically as long as customers feel that unsubscribing is not worth it. The benefits and stability of continuous revenue generation is seen as superior to any profit advantages presented by the more labor-intensive per-unit sales model.

The success demonstrated by particularly Spotify and Netflix as they adopted this model eventually led to the model being adopted outside the streaming media realm, fueling a great deal of the personal cloud computing trend of the 2010s and 2020s, and leading consumers to think less about *ownership* of anything from cars to gardening equipment and instead paying for *access* to it. This convenience-focused approach elevated Netflix to its position as an early leader in the streaming video market, and even its first iteration as a DVD rental-by-mail service was founded on the same principle. Netflix initially started in 1998 by offering single-DVD rentals with a per-unit rental price. The DVD would be mailed to the customer, who only had to drop it in the mail within 30 days, as opposed to going to a video store where the movie would have to be returned within 24 hours. Within a year, Netflix had shifted to a model whereby users could rent multiple DVDs at a time for a single, monthly subscription fee. By 2000, Netflix was subscription-only. As adoption of high-speed Internet connections grew, the Netflix leadership considered how the company could offer movies for on-demand streaming via the Internet. By 2005, Netflix had acquired the rights to do so for enough movies to get started.

The Breakthrough Year for Streaming Video

In 2005, streaming video became a mass-audience phenomenon. Faster Internet speeds and new compression and streaming technologies helped a streaming video market to emerge. The Flash graphics and video streaming technology from Macromedia (later Adobe) was especially instrumental, since more computers had it installed globally in 2005 than the rival players from Microsoft, Apple, and RealNetworks. In January 2005, Google launched Google Video, a streaming service whereby users could upload their own digital videos to be streamed via the Internet. A month later, the Flash-based video site YouTube was founded with the same purpose (only to be acquired a year later by Google who merged the two services under the YouTube brand.) In March 2005, a similar site was launched in France, DailyMotion. A fourth video streaming service, Vimeo, beat all four of them by a few months, launching in November 2004. Flash has become obsolete and replaced by HTML5.

The explosive popularity of YouTube and other video sites in 2005 motivated the company to begin offering streamed feature films in early 2007. An international expansion followed, which presented an infrastructure challenge, as streaming video over such long distances can result in significant delays. This led Netflix to adopt what in 2020 is the most widely used principle for streaming media across the globe: placing the content closer to the consumer, geographically. The company lets Internet service providers host its servers, which are then filled up with new content during the less-busy nighttime in the specific region. The short distances between the local Internet service providers and the customers ensure minimal lag. In the same fashion, YouTube content, for example, is redundantly stored at multiple Google data centers around the globe, so that a user never has to receive the data stream from too far away.

The Arrival of Rivals

Several competitors emerged after Netflix's successful streaming launch, the first major one being the television content–focused Hulu, initially a collaboration of several Hollywood studios. Formerly download-based movie services such as Vudu, Amazon Prime Video, and Apple's iTunes Movie Store began offering movies for streaming rather than download, some with a similar subscription model as Netflix. Toward the end of the 2010s, such services became plentiful, especially as originally produced content became a competition parameter. Netflix launched its first, self-produced original series, *House of Cards*, which started a race among streaming services to create original, exclusive content that could attract new subscribers.

The large investments in television and movie productions across the streaming market boosted the entertainment industry, enabled the realization of otherwise less-commercially viable projects, and eventually led studios and television production companies to launch their own streaming services with original content, including CBS All Access, Disney+, NBC Universal's Peacock, and Warner Media's HBO Max. Companies that provided the technological platforms for streaming also launched services with original content, including Sony, Microsoft, Apple, Google, and Facebook, often with little success though. In the 2010s, Google/YouTube, along with Sony, Hulu, Sling TV, and a number of smaller vendors, began offering streaming of traditional flow-TV channels and on-demand content, in apps that resemble cable television packages, but were streamed via the Internet.

The Smartphone as Production and Broadcasting Tool

Toward the end of the 2010s, streaming video became even more ubiquitous. As smartphones became more powerful, and mobile data plans provided greater bandwidth and speed, they provided the ability to record, process, and upload videos to social media platforms where they could be seen by a wide audience. This led to a rise in apps and services that hosted user-generated videos, especially in short form. One example from the United States was the 2013 launch of Twitter-owned Vine, which became so popular with its emphasis on comedic content that the Facebook-owned photo-sharing app Instagram soon began offering a similar service. Since the latter had a larger user base, Vine quickly felt the competition and was eventually shut down, forcing many of the popular creators on the platform to migrate to YouTube. In 2018, the Chinese app and social media platform TikTok rose to prominence in the West, not only by presenting a similar concept as Vine but also by offering music bites that users could record themselves lip-syncing to. The latter came as a result of TikTok's acquisition of the social media platform Musical.ly.

The convergence of social media and streaming video was also spurred on by the introduction of livestreaming video to Facebook and Twitter, through Facebook Live and Periscope, respectively. Livestreaming technologies such as these enable smartphone users to stream video from their smartphone cameras to large audiences in real time through social media platforms. This has given rise to direct coverage of events otherwise inaccessible to news media. When Minnesota police officer Jeronimo Yanez fatally shot an African American man, Philando Castile, in 2016, the immediate aftermath was broadcast via Facebook Live by Castile's girlfriend, Diamond Reynolds. The same year, a sit-down strike by Democratic members of the U.S. House of Representatives was broadcast through Facebook Live and Twitter's Periscope as a means to circumvent an order from the then-ruling Republican majority to no longer deliver a camera feed from the changer to news organizations. These are two early examples of what has since become a common way to cover events, whether the broadcasters consider themselves citizen journalists or professional journalists.

Livestreaming and Streamed Games

Mobile livestreams are also integral to the livestreaming creators and producers who use platforms such as Twitch to reach an audience and earn an income through affiliate marketing and sponsorships. In a tradition that harkens back to Jennifer Ringley's JenniCam activities in the 1990s, livestreamers broadcast themselves doing any number of things live to both small and large audiences. While smartphones often provide the main production tool, a majority of livestreamers broadcast from home in more or less professional environments. Thus, Amazon-owned Twitch was originally named Justin.tv and was started as a platform for lifecasting, documenting the life of tech entrepreneur Justin Kan for eight months, beginning in 2007.

It evolved into a platform for self-broadcasting, organically switching its focus to gaming over the years. Gamers would stream their screens and webcams live, as they played popular games, watched by other gamers who might admire the skills on display, root for a particular player, or pick up some tips for their own engagements with the game. Twitch grew in popularity throughout the 2010s, bolstered by the increase in eSports viewership. It now hosts livestreamers who show their talents in disciplines other than gaming, particularly music, and has spawned a number of rivals.

In the early 2020s, actual computer games transitioned to streaming. As the delay between devices in the home and big cloud computing centers diminished due to improvements in Internet speeds, CPUs, and compression technologies, it became possible to play even advanced computer games via streaming. This was not possible previously, as a computer game must react within milliseconds when the player makes a move on the controller. By the early 2020s, the process of transmitting movement data to the server and observing a change in the streamed video on the screen could happen so quickly that the player would not know the difference between running the game on his local game console or on a remote server in the cloud.

Entering the third decade of the 2000s, most mainstream digital entertainment has become streaming-based.

Morten Bay

See also Internet: Impact on Media; Livestreaming; Social Media; YouTube

Further Readings

Alderman, J. (2008). *Sonic boom: Napster, MP3, and the new pioneers of music.* New York, NY: Basic Books.

Artwick, C. G. (2018). *Social media livestreaming: Design for disruption?* Milton Park: Taylor & Francis. https://books.google.com/books?id=g2N8DwAAQBAJ

Baxter, R. K. (2015). *The membership economy: Find your super users, master the forever transaction, and build recurring revenue.* New York, NY: McGraw-Hill Education.

Baym, N. K. (2018). *Playing to the crowd: Musicians, audiences, and the intimate work of connection* (vol. 14). New York, NY: NYU Press.

Burgess, J., & Green, J. (2018). *YouTube: Online video and participatory culture.* New York, NY: Wiley & Sons.

Craig, D., & Cunningham, S. (2019). *Social media entertainment: The new intersection of Hollywood and Silicon Valley.* New York, NY: NYU Press.

Dixon, W. W. (2013). *Streaming: Movies, media, and instant access.* Lexington: University Press of Kentucky. https://books.google.com/books?id=aY1q881PnNcC

Eriksson, M., Fleischer, R., Johansson, A., Snickars, P., & Vonderau, P. (2019). *Spotify teardown: Inside the black box of streaming music.* Cambridge, MA: MIT Press.

Holt, J., & Sanson, K. (2013). *Connected viewing: Selling, streaming, & sharing media in the digital age.* Oxfordshire: Routledge.

Randolph, M. (2019). *That will never work: The birth of Netflix and the amazing life of an idea.* Boston, MA: Little, Brown. https://books.google.com/books?id=m4aSDwAAQBAJ

Taylor, T. (2018). *Watch me play: Twitch and the rise of game live streaming.* Princeton, NJ: University Press.

STUDENT JOURNALISM

Student journalism has evolved with new platforms and technologies, much like its professional media counterparts. In the 21st century, student media organizations at many U.S. higher education institutions have faced similar challenges with reduced funding, loss of advertising, and declining audiences. High school newspapers report fewer editions or have moved exclusively to websites or news blogs. Likewise, some college newspapers are scaling back or entirely eliminating print editions in favor of digital-only publication, and some college radio stations' licenses have been sold. Nonetheless, student journalism is seen as providing a valuable forum for experiential learning, and in some cases reporting by student journalists at the high school or college level serves as a key news resource for the wider community. This entry first reviews structures of student media organizations and the platforms they utilize. It then looks at media law affecting student journalists in the United States, and how censorship or other attempts of oversight and control affect student journalists and the work they produce.

Student Journalism in High School and Higher Education

Student journalism, in the form of campus newspapers, existed well before formal journalism courses and programs. Today, at high schools and in higher education, student journalism occurs in both extracurricular and curricular classroom settings, across a wide variety of platforms. Student newspapers, radio stations, television outlets, podcasts, magazines, apps, and digital websites provide students experiential learning opportunities. Sometimes, the journalism performed is under faculty supervision and editing as part of a course or practicum. In other cases, it functions under the guidance of a faculty adviser to an extracurricular student media organization, with school or student government funding. At some colleges and universities, however, student media outlets are fiercely independent—both financially and editorially.

Student journalism organizations often strive to recreate professional-style newsrooms, reach audiences, cover their communities, break news, and master the tools, skills, and evolving platforms of the profession. These organizations have also had to confront the technical and financial challenges that have riven professional media. Increasingly, student newspapers have decreased or even eliminated costly print editions in favor of reaching audiences on digital platforms. For example, in 2019, American University's *The Eagle* transitioned to printing just once a semester, while continuing to regularly provide student journalism online. And in 2020, the 110-year-old University of Maryland student newspaper *The Diamondback*, transitioned to an online-only publication after dwindling advertising and expanding online readership. At the same time, student journalism organizations have embraced podcasts, social media channels, and other emerging platforms. For example, in 2015, the student newspaper at California's Mt. San Antonio College moved its print newspaper entirely to Twitter and the blogging platform Medium.

In radio and broadcast, colleges and universities have been increasingly selling off valuable Federal Communications Commission licenses to existing networks such as National Public Radio, or other media conglomerates, because of the value of the asset, the cost of running stations, and the burden of Federal Communications Commission compliance and possible fines. Since 2010, both large and small higher education institutions have sold licenses—sometimes for millions of dollars, for example: Brown University, the University of San Francisco, Vanderbilt University, Rice University, Georgia State, and Gadsden State Community College. As administrators have sold off broadcast licenses, increasingly college and university radio stations have turned to online streaming, whether they have an FM license or not, as younger audiences prefer these digital platforms.

The financial struggles of professional media, while mirrored in student-run journalism organizations, have also proved to be areas of opportunity. In some areas, as thousands of professional community newspapers have shuttered, student journalists have taken the lead in community coverage. For example, student-run *The Michigan Daily* has been the only daily newspaper in the city of Ann Arbor, Michigan, since 2009, covering both the city and the University of Michigan. In addition, student journalists are increasingly staffing statehouse bureaus and some institutions, including the University of Maryland, Arizona State University, and Northwestern University, operate student-staffed news bureaus in Washington, D.C., providing coverage of the U.S. Congress for local media outlets that no longer have Washington correspondents.

Censorship, Control, and Student Journalism

Student journalists in the United States, like their professional counterparts, rely on the protections of the First Amendment. Recent court rulings on student press freedom are inconsistent, however. The clearest direction from the U.S. Supreme Court is that any censorship of student journalism—at either the high school or college level—must be based on legitimate pedagogical concerns and may not exclusively be content-based and viewpoint-based.

A major ruling by the Supreme Court on student media, in 1988, limited the First Amendment protection for student journalists in K–12 schools. In *Hazelwood School District v. Kuhlmeier*, the court ruled that in the case of school-sponsored, curricular student publications at K–12 schools, administrators could regulate style and content "reasonably related to legitimate pedagogical concerns." Since *Hazelwood*, K–12 school administrators have used prior restraint or prior review to read high school student media publications before they are published, and censor student journalism prepublication.

Administrators' censorship has also extended to digital platforms and social media channels utilized by students. Since the *Hazelwood* ruling, some courts have applied this standard to college publications as well. In recent years, several states have passed "New Voices" legislation, explicitly protecting the First Amendment rights of student journalists and counteracting the impact of *Hazelwood*. Although it varies state by state, "New Voices" legislation generally seeks to protect high school journalists from the reach of *Hazelwood*, by reverting to a prior Supreme Court standard established in *Tinker v. Des Moines* (1969), which protects student speech unless it creates a clear and present danger or a substantial disruption to the school. "New Voices" legislation often also seeks to explicitly extend this protection to journalists at both public and private colleges and universities.

Aside from outright censorship or editorial influence, external control over student journalism is also exercised by cutting—or threatening to cut—student media funding, according to the Student Press Law Center. For example, in the wake of investigative reporting by Wichita State University's student newspaper, the Student Government Association approved dramatic reduction in *The Sunflower's* annual funding. Other schools have reported administration-approved funding cuts, as well as elimination of faculty adviser's pay or student journalists' salaries, according to the Student Press Law Center. However, research indicates that higher education journalism programs accredited by the Accrediting Council on Education in Journalism in Mass Communication at most public institutions had official rules governing student journalism freedoms and were not experiencing censorship issues.

Jacqueline Soteropoulos Incollingo

See also Censorship; Digital Distribution; Internships and Training Programs; Journalism Education; Supreme Court and Journalism

Further Readings

Carey, J. W. (2000). Some personal notes on US journalism education. *Journalism, 1*(1), 12–23.
Bickham, S. B., & Shin, J. H. (2013). Organizational influences on student newspapers. *Southwestern Mass*

Communication Journal, 28(1), 1–30. doi: 10.1177/146488490000100103

Harris, A. (2018, August 9). Student journalism in the age of media distrust. *The Atlantic*, https://www.theatlantic.com/education/archive/2018/08/student-journalism-in-the-age-of-media-distrust/567089/

Klein, A. (2018). Keeping high school journalism class on the cutting edge. *Education Week*. Retrieved from https://www.edweek.org/tm/articles/2018/10/03/keeping-high-school-journalism-class-on-the.html

Levin, D. (2019, Oct. 19). When the student newspaper is the only daily paper in town. *The New York Times*. Retrieved from https://www.nytimes.com/2019/10/19/us/news-desert-ann-arbor-michigan.html

Matsa, K. E., & Boyles, J. L. (2014). America's shifting statehouse press: Can new players compensate for lost legacy reporters? *Pew Research Center*. Retrieved from https://www.journalism.org/2014/07/10/americas-shifting-statehouse-press/

Policinski, G. (2019). Student journalism: More needed than ever. *Freedom Forum Institute*. Retrieved from https://www.freedomforuminstitute.org/2019/01/31/student-journalism-more-needed-than-ever/

Russo, C. J., & Hapney, T. L. (2013). Student newspapers at public colleges and universities: Lessons from the United States. *Education Law Journal, 14*(2), 114.

Spoont, J. (2014). Muting the airwaves: As colleges sell off their radio stations, student deejays grapple with their identities in the digital age. *Student Press Law Center*. Retrieved from https://splc.org/2014/11/muting-the-airwaves-as-colleges-sell-off-their-radio-stations-student-deejays-grapple-with-their-ide/

West, S. R. (2015). Student press exceptionalism. *Education Law & Policy Review, 2*, 131—151.

Stunt Journalism

Stunt journalism was a style of journalism common in the 19th century that involved the journalist's immersion in a story, sometimes under a false identity. Although often disparaged as little more than sensational storytelling, the history of stunt journalism is far more complicated as the way it is perceived is often a consequence of its results. As such, journalists who have engaged in it often found themselves either hailed as societal reformers or dismissed as little more than con artists or paparazzi who manipulated events to fit the narrative they wanted to tell in their stories. Even so,

the practice has informed the development of journalism and shades of it still exist today. This entry discusses some notable examples of stunt journalism and successor forms to this style of journalism.

What Is Stunt Journalism?

As a technique, stunt journalism is a practice that cuts across traditional journalistic beats, such as government, crime, or sports reporting, and is used to entice readers to follow a given story. Stunt journalism has more to do with the journalist's process of getting and writing a story than it does with the topic being covered. Problems can occur whenever journalists place themselves in a story and become part of the narrative they are covering, which is exactly what often happens with stunt journalism. The line between the journalist and the story become blurred, which can result in concern that truth is being manipulated.

The practice of using stunts in journalism was one of the reporting techniques used in what is often referred to as the *new journalism* of the late 19th century. The heyday for stunt reporting in the United States occurred in the decades following the Civil War, although it remained prevalent into the early 20th century. In general, the one attribute most early stunt journalism stories had in common was that they were found in what were often considered more sensational publications, such as the *New York Herald* and the *New York Journal*.

Prominent publishers such as James Gordon Bennett Jr., William Randolph Hearst, and Joseph Pulitzer used stunts as another way to grow their circulation and maintain their dominance in the post–Civil War newspaper realm. Journalism historian Frank Luther Mott and others considered stunt journalism to be exploitative and often referred to it as *surreptitious* or *undercover* reporting, as it most often required a reporter to don disguises or find other ways to misrepresent who they were and what they were doing. It was this deception that Mott and other journalism scholars have found distasteful and damaging to the craft of journalism.

Although stunt journalism is often framed as a style of journalism using various duplicitous reporting practices to gather information for a story, there were limits assigned to it. Stunt journalism was considered, especially by publishers who championed its use, far different from such made-up stories as the "Moon Hoax," a series of false articles published in Benjamin Day's *New York Sun* in 1835. Stories using stunts usually were not based on a completely false narrative founded on a lie for their premise. Instead, they focused on real-life stories that, for whatever reason, the publishers felt their readers would follow more closely if they had information not readily available to the public. Importantly, the publishers also believed interest in these stories had the potential to increase circulation and draw in greater numbers of subscribers. Despite questions over the methodology of gathering information, successful stunts often revolved around real societal ills that publishers and reporters thought needed to be brought to the public's attention.

Notable Examples of Stunt Journalism

One of the first acknowledged examples of stunt journalism was in the early 1870s when Bennett sent one of his young *New York Herald* reporters, Henry Morton Stanley, to go to Africa to search for a famously missing doctor, David Livingstone. The search took Stanley more than 2 years, but he eventually found Livingstone and included in his reports the famous greeting that is still part of popular culture today, "Dr. Livingstone, I presume?" Bennett's idea paid off handsomely and Stanley's stories about his pursuit of Livingstone garnered great excitement among newspaper readers of the day.

Nellie Bly

Not to be outdone, Joseph Pulitzer and his *New York World* also engaged in stunt journalism and were always looking for ways to best their competitors. Nellie Bly appeared at a most opportune moment when she managed to work her way into the offices of Colonel John Cockerill, the managing editor of the *World*. Bly offered her services and some story ideas, but when they met again the story they discussed was one based on complaints the paper had received about patient treatment at the Women's Lunatic Asylum on Blackwell's Island. Bly's task would be to gain access to the asylum to report on the rumors of bad treatment. Although there are conflicting narratives as to whether it was Cockerill, Bly, or Pulitzer who floated the story, there is no question that Bly agreed to go after it. To do so, she changed her name to Nellie Brown and pretended to be insane in order to have herself committed. She spent 10 days in the institution, gathering information and carefully concealing her notes, before Cockerill arranged for her release. In October 1887, her first articles on the conditions and mistreatment of the patients at the asylum ran under the headline "Behind Asylum Bars" and were an instant success. Readers clamored to know more, and the stories so shocked their sensitivities that reforms were instituted as a result.

Bly's next endeavor for Pulitzer's paper was lighter as she made her way around the world in 72 days, a race inspired by Jules Verne's book, *Around the World in Eighty Days*. It was a stunt that resulted in a copycat attempt by Elizabeth Bisland for *Cosmopolitan*, but Bly beat Bisland's time handily. By this time, Bly's stunts had made her a household name and she went on to use her fame to continue writing stories of social ills, especially those affecting conditions for working women and girls. These stories, especially her expose on Blackwell's Island, later earned her mention as one of the earliest muckrakers who broke new ground with their investigative reporting.

William Randolph Hearst

William Randolph Hearst, who was not about to be overshadowed by his nemesis, Pulitzer, also went about arranging stunts for his own papers, which he liked to refer to as *journalism of action*. One of the most famous instances involved a *New York Journal* correspondent, Karl Decker, who Hearst sent to Cuba to arrange for the escape of a 19-year-old political prisoner, Evangelina Cisneros, from a jail in Havana. It was a huge success, although there was some pointed criticism, especially from other newspapers, that Hearst had crossed the line and moved from journalism coverage to political activism.

Sob Sisters

As the 20th century came to a close, more women were finding their way onto newspaper pages, and stunt journalism was often a lucrative way to do it. Bly's work had proven that women were able to succeed in the newspaper world and that they often could get stories or provide different perspectives from those of their male counterparts. As their copy often presented stories in a highly emotional narrative, many of these women earned the moniker of *sob sisters*. For these women, their *stunts* often revolved around their ability to befriend criminals, victims, and their families to offer more personal coverage of crimes and tragedies with more intimate details. Even though they were becoming more accepted, such reporting still carried negative connotations for women, so many of them took on pen names to hide their identity. Two of the best-known female journalists to do so were Elizabeth Meriwether Gilmer, who used the pen name Dorothy Dix, and Winifred Sweet Black Bonfils, known as Annie Laurie.

Upton Sinclair

As the new century began, notable journalists such as Upton Sinclair, Lincoln Steffens, and Ida Tarbell advanced the investigative aspect of the journalism craft. They became known as *muckrakers* and were interested in promoting a progressive agenda in their works, which focused on societal concerns over poverty, class, and capitalism. For the reporting of his book *The Jungle*, Sinclair used a stunt similar to Nellie Bly's and took a job in a Chicago meatpacking plant so he could document the harsh working conditions of the workers there. His book changed the sanitary conditions of the plants but did not have as much of an impact on the workers' lives as he had hoped.

Successors to Stunt Journalism

In the mid-to-latter part of the 20th century, journalism styles emerged that clearly had their roots in stunt journalism. One, Gonzo journalism, gained popularity beginning in the 1970s with the work of Hunter S. Thompson. With the Gonzo style, the journalist becomes a part of the story and writes it in the first person. These types of stories make no journalistic claims of objectivity and are more aligned with commentary than straight reporting. Although this type of reporting often does highlight societal flaws and dilemmas, the journalist becoming a large part of the story separates it somewhat from stunt journalism. Thompson had a very edgy style, which gave rise to his popularity in a period of great upheaval, with Watergate and the Vietnam War playing a part in the backdrop.

The practice of journalists taking jobs under false pretenses, as Bly and Sinclair had done, became riskier after a 1999 court decision in *Food Lion, Inc. v. Capital Cities/ABC, Inc.* The case revolved around two reporters for the ABC show *Prime Time Live* who went undercover as Food Lion employees to investigate unsanitary food conditions. The two used hidden cameras to document their story for the couple of weeks they worked there. In the ensuing lawsuit, filed in 1995, Food Lion initially won damages, but most of those were overturned. Even so, in 1999, the U.S. Court of Appeals for the Fourth Circuit ruled that the reporters were guilty of trespass and that the First Amendment did not protect them from those charges. The ruling set a precedent that would make it difficult for a journalist to use a similar stunt for a story. This type of journalism, where a reporter assumes another identity, is not considered ethical in most cases and can often work to erode confidence in journalistic standards.

More recent tactics include reporters who are immersed in their story, but only in ways in which they identify themselves and their purpose. In 2003, journalist Adrian Nicole LeBlanc published her narrative nonfiction book, *Random Family: Love, Drugs, Trouble, and Coming of Age in the Bronx*. The book was the culmination of more than a decade of research where LeBlanc immersed herself in the lives of two teen girls and their extended family to document the struggles they faced growing up in a vicious cycle of drugs, poverty, and prison. LeBlanc's success in reporting and writing the book was due in large part to her ability to remain neutral in the telling of the story. At no point did LeBlanc misrepresent herself or her project to those on whom she was reporting. Everyone understood that she was chronicling their lives, and LeBlanc said that she became simply another part of the environment, unnoticed for the most part, but very much in the present.

Dianne M. Bragg

See also Bly, Nellie; Investigative Journalism; Muckrakers; Sensationalism

Further Readings

Bly, N. (n.d.). *Ten days in a mad-house* [Electronic resource]. Salt Lake City, UT: Project Gutenberg Literary Archive Foundation.

Hyde, J. (1991). The industrial press, 1865–1883: Professional journalism or pawn of urbanism? In W. D. Sloan (Ed.), *Perspectives on mass communication history*. Hillsdale, NJ: Erlbaum.

Kroeger, B. (1994). *Nellie Bly: Daredevil, reporter, feminist*. New York, NY: Crown.

Logan, D. A. (1998). Stunt journalism, professional norms, and public mistrust of the media. *University of Florida Journal of Law and Public Policy, 9*(2), 151–176.

Morris, J. M. (2010). *Pulitzer: A life in politics, print, and power*. New York, NY: Harper.

Peko, S., & Sweeney, M. (2017). Nell Nelson's undercover reporting. *American Journalism, 34*(4), 448–469. doi:10.1080/08821127.2017.1382297

Sachsman, D., & Bulla, D. (Eds.). (2013). *Sensationalism: Murder, mayhem, mudslinging, scandals, and disasters in 19th-century reporting*. New Brunswick, NJ: Transaction.

Sloan, W. D., Lucht, T., & Pribanic-Smith, E. (Eds.). (2020). *The media in America: A history* (11th ed.). Northport, AL: Vision Press.

Sumpter, R. (2013). Practical reporting: Late nineteenth-century journalistic standards and rule breaking. *American Journalism, 30*(1), 44–64. doi:10.1080/088 21127.2013.767686

Sumpter, R. (2015). "Girl reporter": Elizabeth L. Banks and the "stunt" genre. *American Journalism, 32*(1), 60–77. doi:10.1080/08821127.2015.999550

Swanberg, W. A. (1961). *Citizen hearst*. New York, NY: Scribner.

Whitt, J. (2015). Nellie Bly undercover: Reporting for the New York world (1887–1894). *American Journalism, 32*(3), 369–370. doi:10.1080/08821127 .2015.1064694

Sunshine Laws

In the United States, the term *sunshine law* is typically used to refer to state laws providing for public access to government meetings and public records as well as to the Government in the Sunshine Act (5 U.S.C. 552b), which governs access to business meetings of some 50 federal agencies, commissions, and boards. The Government in the Sunshine Act was signed into law on September 13, 1976, by President Gerald Ford. The legislation was sponsored by Senator Lawton Chiles (D-Florida) and Rep. Bella Abzug (D-NY) and was modeled on the earlier Florida Sunshine Act. This entry discusses the Government in the Sunshine Act, state sunshine laws, and new challenges to government transparency.

Government in the Sunshine Act

Passed partly in response to the Watergate scandal, the Government in the Sunshine Act and other anti-secrecy measures were enacted to make sure that government agencies deliberations were open to public scrutiny. The Government in the Sunshine Act works in concert with the Federal Advisory Committee Act of 1972, which required that meetings of federal advisory committees serving the executive branch be open to public observation.

The Government in the Sunshine Act calls for all agencies "headed by a collegial body composed of two or more individual members . . . and any subdivision thereof authorized" acting on behalf of a federal agency to open business meetings to public observation. While it does not stipulate that an agency must hold meetings, it does include procedural requirements that must be followed when the organization, board, or commission decides to meet, either in open or closed session. The law does not apply to Congress. While sessions for the House of Representatives are typically open, the Senate occasionally holds closed meetings to discuss treaties or personnel issues.

Generally, agencies must make a public announcement giving at least 1 week notice prior to each meeting. The notice must provide the time, place, and subject of the meeting. In addition, the agency must provide the name and phone number of a designated official or contact information regarding whether the meeting is to be open or closed. According to the law, meetings cannot be presumptively closed. To close a meeting, a board or commission covered by the law must vote in advance and make a written copy of the vote available to the public. A majority of the board or commission must vote in favor of closure and must also provide a full written explanation of its actions for closing part or all of a meeting.

The law provides for a limited number of exemptions under which meetings can be closed. The exemptions are similar to those included in the Freedom of Information Act; they can be summarized as:

1. Issues of national defense and foreign policy
2. Discussion of internal personnel rules and practices
3. Statutory exemptions provided under law
4. Proprietary information that would injure parties if made public
5. Accusation of crime or formal censure
6. Personal privacy
7. Investigatory records such as those collected by law enforcement
8. Financial institution reports
9a. Financial speculation and stability
9b. Frustration of proposed agency action
10. Issuance of subpoena, participation in civil action or proceeding, or formal agency adjudication

When an agency decides to close a meeting, the agency's general counsel must certify that the closure falls under one of the exemptions enumerated in the law. Some executive agencies, such as the Federal Trade Commission, hold many closed meetings because much of its work encompasses issues that fall under Exemption 10. Lastly, agencies must provide Congress with an annual report regarding their policies, an accounting of the number of meetings held, and whether exemptions applied to the meetings.

In addition to providing rules for conducting federal agency meetings, Section 4 of the legislation enacts a general prohibition on ex parte communication between government agency decision makers and other outside interested parties. This section of the law was included as a result of recommendations by the American Bar Association. The provisions of Section 4 apply to all executive agencies, regardless of whether they are headed by a board or an administrator.

The law requires that the agency keep a copy of the minutes of closed meetings for a minimum of 2 years. While the presumption of closure may be challenged by anyone through the federal district courts, the courts have generally interpreted the law strictly. In one example, the U.S. Circuit Court of Appeals for the District of Columbia ruled in 1985 that the law did not apply to the president's Council of Economic Advisors since the purpose of the council was strictly advisory. However, many examples illustrate the significance of the law. The law has opened the door for gavel-to-gavel coverage of important hearings and meetings on C-SPAN and has paved the way for creating electronic databases for services such as Congress.gov (formerly Thomas), a source for federal legislative information.

The law is not without detractors. Critics of the Sunshine Act assert that opening meetings has a tendency of subverting truly open debate at meetings since the participants may be concerned that their remarks will be transcribed or broadcast. Also, because meetings are open, many chairs of agencies and commissions are reluctant to bring an item to the floor unless they are sure of the outcome of a vote.

Journalists frequently complain that commission and agency meetings often seem scripted, with commissioners reading from prepared statements and voting in predetermined ways. Others have pointed to unintended consequences of the law. In 1995, Stephen Calkins, then general counsel to the Federal Trade Commission, noted that when two justices or judges are in discussions on how to reconcile divergent views, they could ask another judge sitting on a case to join the discussion. The Sunshine Act prevents commissioners at federal agencies from such informal discussions whenever the number of participants would constitute a quorum, such as at the Federal Communications Commission. As a result, critics point out that administrators can resort to using memos or deputizing aides to meet in a commissioner's place as examples of circumventing the Sunshine Act. Today, with growing concern over individual privacy, agencies need to balance public accountability without harming individual privacy rights.

State Sunshine Laws

Since the 1970s, most states have passed parallel legislation designed to open state and local government agencies to same level of scrutiny required in the federal law. All 50 states have enacted open meetings laws, but it is difficult to make generalizations about the success of these laws. In 2015, the Center for Public Integrity ranked each state's public records law and found that most states faired poorly because of many exemptions and loopholes. The Reporters Committee for Freedom of the Press concluded that the best laws are those that define a meeting by specifying the number of members of the board, agency, or commission who must be present to constitute a quorum.

Similar to the federal law, most state open meetings statutes provide for closed meetings or "executive sessions" in cases where personnel matters or invasion of privacy may be at issue. Other reasons for meeting in "executive session" may include issues of public safety and labor negotiations. Most states include a provision in their legislation that bars any final actions from being adopted in "executive session." Therefore, boards or commission must reconvene in public before adopting a final determination. Similar to the federal legislation, most open meetings statutes require a notification to the public as to when a meeting is to be held. The notification must be given far enough in advance so that interested parties can attend and most laws provide for actions to be taken if the law is violated.

Rapid advances in electronic communications have had a major impact on government transparency. For example, the Florida Sunshine Law mandates that cities keep a permanent record of all emails sent or received by public employees. The North Dakota law defines all email correspondence as a meeting and requires that emails to and from public officials must be made public upon request. Some states have enacted "sunshine laws" that require reporting of the amounts of money or emoluments that pharmaceutical companies pay physicians in connection with marketing activities related to new prescription drugs. One study in the *Journal of the American Medical Association*

found that reporting in some cases was spotty and that companies failed to provide specific information identifying the recipients of gifts.

Challenges to Transparency

As government administration evolves so do issues related to sunshine laws. New capabilities to engage the public through technology can provide more access for citizens; however, with the increasing use of private contractors for some traditional government functions, to whom open records laws apply becomes a legitimate question. There are also questions over the applicability of open meetings and open records laws to electronic data collection and the use of electronic memoranda.

Fritz Messere

See also Congress and Journalism; Freedom of Information Act (FOIA); Government, Federal, U.S., Coverage of; Government, State, U.S., Coverage of; Secrecy and Leaks

Further Readings

Brennan, T. A., & Mello, M. M., (2007). Sunshine laws and the pharmaceutical industry. *Journal of the American Medical Association, 297,* 1255–1257. doi:10.1001/jama.297.11.1255

Fleming, N. (2013). In digital age, sunshine laws turn hazy. *Education Week, 32*(28), 1–18.

Hirschhorn, E. L. (1977, January). Sunshine for federal agencies. *American Bar Association Journal, 63*(1), 55–59.

Pember, D. R., & Calvert, C. (2017). *Mass media law.* Boston, MA: McGraw-Hill.

Roberts, A. (2006). *Blacked out: Government secrecy in the information age.* Cambridge, UK: Cambridge University Press.

Roeder, C. B. (2014). Transparency trumps technology: Reconciling open meeting laws with modern technology. *William & Mary Law Review, 55*(6), 2287–2315.

U.S. House of Representatives & Committee on Government Reform. (2005). *On restoring open government: Secrecy in the Bush administration.* New York, NY: Cosimo Books.

Zubak-Skees, C., Qiu, Y., & Lincoln, E. (2015, November). *How does your state rank for integrity?*

The Center for Public Integrity. Retrieved from https://publicintegrity.org/politics/state-politics/state-integrity-investigation/how-does-your-state-rank-for-integrity/

SUPREME COURT AND JOURNALISM

The First Amendment to the U.S. Constitution reads in part, "Congress shall make no law . . . abridging the freedom of speech, or of the press." But what does this statement mean? Clearly "no law" does not really mean "no law" as there are a wide variety of laws in the United States that impact expression, including the expression of journalists.

While the words of the First Amendment appear to be simple, decisions by the U.S. Supreme Court have created a complex body of law and added meaning to the basic statement "Congress shall make no law." Adopted in 1791, the amendment now provides sometimes robust protection for journalists, although the U.S. Supreme Court has not always ruled the way journalists would like. It is also important to note that despite the wording of the "press clause," the Supreme Court has never granted journalists more First Amendment rights than other individuals. The First Amendment applies equally to journalists and nonjournalists alike. The amendment does not provide an institutional right to "the press."

Historically, the Court has attempted to balance the rights of journalists to gather and disseminate news with the rights of others. This includes the right to privacy and reputation, the right to a fair trial, the need for the government to keep some information classified, and the right of the government to maintain safety during protests.

Early Restrictions on the Press

In 1798, the United States passed its first law punishing journalists for their work. Intense rivalry between President John Adams's Federalist Party and Thomas Jefferson's Republican Party (sometimes called the *Jeffersonian Party*), together with a growing fear of a possible war with France, led

the Federalist-controlled Congress to pass the Alien and Sedition Acts of 1798. The sedition law prohibited and punished false, scandalous, and malicious publications about the U.S. government, Congress, and the president. Notice it did not apply to criticism of Vice President Thomas Jefferson. The law punished such expression with a $2,000 fine and a jail term of up to 2 years. The law was used to punish publishers of pro-Jefferson newspapers, many of which engaged in vicious attacks against President Adams. Of the 15 prosecutions under the law, eight were editors of Jeffersonian newspapers. Imagine today, Congress passing a law that said it was illegal to criticize Republicans but not Democrats and using it to jail the editors of *The New York Times* or *The Washington Post*. The law did not quiet criticism, however. In fact, the law provoked dissension among President Adams's supporters, and scholars have even argued it was a key factor in the election of 1800 when Adams lost to Jefferson.

Did the law violate the First Amendment? The Supreme Court never ruled on the law, but three members of the Court heard Sedition Act cases while riding circuit. All three justices held the Act was constitutional. The Act expired in 1801. Newly elected President Jefferson pardoned everyone convicted under the law and Congress eventually repaid all of the fines.

The First Amendment Takes Shape

Between the nation's founding and the early 1900s, the legal meaning of the First Amendment developed little and the guarantees of freedom of speech and the press were of limited value. There were few cases and almost no important First Amendment decisions by the Supreme Court before 1919 when the Court started hearing cases involving the Espionage Act of 1917 and the Sedition Act of 1918. The Espionage Act dealt with espionage problems, but some parts of the law were specifically designed to punish dissent and opposition to World War I. The Sedition Act, an amendment to the Espionage Act, made it a crime to attempt to obstruct military recruiting and to print, write, or publish disloyal or profane language that was intended to cause contempt of, or scorn for, the federal government, the Constitution, the flag, or the uniform of the Armed

Services. Cases involving these federal laws and other state laws designed to punish dissent, socialists, and communist sympathizers, such as *Schenck v. United States* (1919), *Abrams v. United States*(1919), and *Whitney v. California* (1927), would form the foundation of First Amendment law in the United States. It is important to note, however, that the Court was still years away from articulating a robust understanding of freedom of expression and the defendants in these cases did not win. Many went to jail for their beliefs and writings.

In 1925, the Court took an important step in advancing First Amendment rights in *Gitlow v. New York*. As noted earlier, the First Amendment reads "Congress" shall make no law. Read literally, this seems to suggest the amendment applies only to acts of U.S. Congress. This was the Court's approach to the entire Bill of Rights for years. In *Gitlow*, however, the Court ruled that the First Amendment also applied to actions of state governments. The case involved the prosecution of Benjamin Gitlow for printing *The Left-Wing Manifesto*, a document that reviewed the rise of Socialism, condemned "moderate Socialism," and advocated the necessity of accomplishing a "Communist Revolution." In this case, the Court linked the First Amendment to the 14th Amendment to the U.S. Constitution. The 14th Amendment guarantees that "no state" shall "deprive any person of life, liberty, or property, without due process of law." In *Gitlow* the Court ruled that the 14th Amendment's use of the term *liberty* incorporates (or includes) freedom of speech. Thus, the Court ruled that portions of the Bill of Rights place limits on the actions of state and local governments as well as the federal government. This doctrine is known as *incorporation*. Over the years, the Court has incorporated many of the provisions of the Bill of Rights, but the right to freedom of expression was the first.

Prior Restraints

Prior restraints—or prepublication reviews or censorship—have long been considered the most odious restriction on freedom of expression. Prior restraints can come in many forms. Most obvious are instances in which the government insists on giving prior approval before publication or broadcast or when the government simply bans the publication or broadcast of a specific kind of content or material. Prior restraint also occurs when courts ban the publication or broadcast of certain materials before a trial. They also occur if a court tries to preemptively block the publication of material that is considered defamatory or an invasion of privacy. Some laws provide for stopping the publication of material that violates another's copyright.

The Court has set barriers for the use of prior restraints in many of these situations. In 1931, in *Near v. Minnesota*, the U.S. Supreme Court declared that the primary purpose of the First Amendment was to stop the use of prior restraints. The case involved the publishers of a small Minnesota weekly newspaper called the *Saturday Press*. Jay M. Near and Howard Guilford were self-proclaimed reformers who repeatedly accused local officials of letting "Jewish gangsters" control gambling, bootlegging, and racketeering in Minneapolis. They also alleged that law enforcement agencies were not performing their duties. They made these charges using highly inflammatory language. They were ordered to stop publishing under a Minnesota state public nuisance statute that empowered a court to issue an injunction to stop the publication of any obscene, lewd, lascivious, malicious, scandalous, or defamatory publication. The only way Near or Guilford could publish another newspaper was to convince the government that their newspaper would be published in the public good and would contain no objectionable material. In 1928, the Minnesota Supreme Court upheld the constitutionality of the law, declaring that under the statute's broad powers, the state could regulate public nuisances including defamatory and scandalous newspapers.

On appeal, the U.S. Supreme Court reversed the ruling and declared the law unconstitutional. The statute, the Court wrote, was not designed to redress wrongs after the fact. Instead, the statute was designed to directly suppress the newspaper once and for all. The object of the law was not punishment. It was censorship. And the primary purpose of the First Amendment was to stop prior restraints, although the Court wrote that prior restraints might be permissible in some circumstances such as obscenity, incitement to violence, and information related to military operations during times of war.

Another momentous opinion about prior restraints came from the Court in 1971 in *New York Times v. United States*, a case now known as *the Pentagon Papers Case*. The case began when in the summer of 1971, *The New York Times*, followed by *The Washington Post* and a handful of other newspapers, started publishing a series of articles based on copies of a classified 47-volume government study of the United States' history in the Vietnam Conflict. Officially titled "History of the United States Decision-Making Process on Vietnam Policy," the top-secret document was leaked to the press in violation of national security law. When *The New York Times* refused to stop publishing the articles after being asked to by Attorney General John Mitchell, the government asked a court to issue an injunction to stop publication. A temporary restraining order was issued by the court against *The New York Times*. When *The Washington Post* started publishing similar articles, the government sought another injunction from a different court.

As the cases quickly made their way through the court system, the government made a number of arguments. First, it argued that publishing the material violated federal espionage statutes. When that didn't work, the government argued the president had the inherent power under the U.S. Constitution to conduct foreign affairs and protect national security, which included the right to stop the unauthorized publication of classified information. When this argument also failed to satisfy the courts, the government next argued the publication of classified information could irreparably harm the nation and the government's ability to conduct national affairs. The newspapers, on the other hand, argued that the government's classification system was flawed and that the government classified and declassified documents frequently, sometimes to sway public opinion or to influence a reporter's story. Second, the papers argued injunctions against publication violated the First Amendment. Finally, *The New York Times* lawyer, Alexander Bickel, argued that the government's action violated the separation of power under the U.S. Constitution. If Congress had never passed a law banning the publication of national security

information by a newspaper, that was not the job of the judiciary.

The Court ruled in favor of the newspapers. In a very short opinion, a majority of the Court wrote that prior restraints were presumed to be unconstitutional and that the government had not met the heavy burden to justify a prior restraint. The government had not established that the publication of the information would damage national security, only that it might. Bans on publication are presumed to be unconstitutional under the First Amendment. In this case, the government had failed to prove the ban was necessary to protect the nation. The Court did not say that prior restraints were always unconstitutional, however. It said the government had not shown why this injunction was needed. Thus, the decision fell short of the absolute declaration against prior restraints some hoped for.

The Court has also weighed in on judicial orders designed to prevent prejudicial information about trials from being published. Judges have long tried to compensate for prejudicial pretrial publicity using various remedies. As the mass media—especially cable TV channels and Internet blogs—have begun to cover sensational trials more and more, judges have continued to look for ways to stop information about trials from reaching the public. While some of these—voir dire (or jury selection), a change of venue, admonitions to the jury, sequestration of the jury—have no impact on the First Amendment rights of journalists, others do. When these other measures fail to prevent coverage of a trial some judges worry about the defendant's right to a fair trial and will use court orders, called *restrictive orders* or *gag orders*, on the press. These orders limit what journalists can say and can sometimes even be so sweeping that they prevent journalists from commenting on a case at all. Such orders raise serious First Amendment concerns.

In 1975, the U.S. Supreme Court heard a case involving a gag order on the press as part of a sensational murder trial and, eventually, set limits on when a gag order aimed at the press is constitutional. Erwin Simants was arrested and charged with the murder of all six members of the Kellie family in Sutherland, Nebraska, a town of 850 people. The search for and arrest of Simants drew attention from local and national news outlets. The media reported that Simants confessed and reported the grisly details of the crime, including speculation (later confirmed) that Simants had sexually assaulted some of the victims. Local judge Hugh Stuart responded to this unwanted attention by issuing a restrictive order that barred the press from publishing or broadcasting information about Simants's confession or any other statement made by Simants, contents of a note Simants wrote the night of the crimes, testimony from pretrial hearings, information related to the sexual assaults, or information about the gag order itself. The order as modified by the Nebraska Supreme Court prohibited reporting of only three matters: (1) the existence and nature of any confessions or admissions made by the defendant to law enforcement officers, (2) any confessions or admissions made to any third parties, except members of the press, and (3) other facts "strongly implicative" of Simants. The order was to be enforced until the jury was chosen. The press in the state appealed the decision to the U.S. Supreme Court.

In 1976, in *Nebraska Press Association v. Stuart*, a unanimous Supreme Court ruled Judge Stuart's order was an unconstitutional prior restraint of the press. Four justices—Potter Stewart, William Brennan, Thurgood Marshall, and John Paul Stevens—said this kind of restrictive order against the press could never be unconstitutional. Four other justices—Warren Burger, Harry Blackmun, William Rehnquist, and Lewis Powell—said that such orders were permissible in extraordinary circumstances. Justice Bryon White wrote there was really no reason why the Court should decide in this case whether other orders might be permissible. White, however, joined Chief Justice Burger's opinion establishing a test for when restrictive orders aimed at the press are constitutional. Under this test, called the *Nebraska Press Association* test, an order could be constitutional if a court shows there is (1) intense and pervasive publicity concerning the case, (2) there are no other alternatives that might mitigate the effects of the pretrial publicity, and (3) the restrictive order would in fact effectively prevent prejudicial material from reaching potential jurors. In Simants's case, the Court's majority opinion held there was no evidence that Judge Stuart's order would effectively prevent material from reaching potential jurors.

The small Nebraska community was already filled with rumors about Simants and what he had told police.

The traditional approach in U.S. law is that courts should not issue an injunction (court order) to stop the publication of an allegedly libelous statement before it occurs. The preferred approach in U.S. law, discussed in the next section, is to allow the allegedly libelous statement to be published and then to sue for monetary damages. Once a statement has been judicially determined to be libelous, however, some courts then allow an injunction prohibiting the defendant in the case from repeating the statement to be libelous. In addition, although prior restraints against Internet sites are generally ineffective because once information is posted on the web it can be copied and spread with ease, some research suggests courts are becoming more willing to issues injunctions against defendants who publish libelous material on the Internet.

Reporting on Public Officials, Public Figures, and Matters of Public Concern

Over the years, the Supreme Court has established strong protections for journalists when they report on government officials, public figures, or when they cover matters of public concern. These protections come from cases involving defamation, certain forms of invasion of privacy, and lawsuits involving intentional infliction of emotional distress. These protections can be extremely important when journalists are covering politicians, candidates for political office, famous individuals, individuals involved in public controversies, and matters that are important to the public, sometimes called *matters of public concern.*

Defamation is a tort or a civil wrong that attempts to redress damages to reputation. Defamation is a statement of fact that exposes the victim to hatred, ridicule, or contempt. Libelous statements are written and distributed. Historically, libel was most applicable to print media like newspapers, pamphlets, and books; however, in recent years, this is typically the standard for Internet communications as well. Slander is spoken defamation. The elements of a defamation lawsuit have different standards, depending on if the plaintiff is considered a private individual, a public official, or a public figure. For example, if a defamatory statement is made about a private individual by another private individual regarding a private matter, there is less constitutional protection for the statements. However, if a defamatory statement is made about a public figure regarding a matter of public interest, the statement will have heightened constitutional protections.

Throughout the mid-20th century, the Supreme Court worked to articulate these fundamentals of defamation law. The Court began the process of constitutionalizing the law of libel in 1964 in *New York Times v. Sullivan*. L. B. Sullivan claimed *The New York Times* had libeled him in a full-page advertisement that had been taken out by a group of Black clergymen from the state of Alabama. In its landmark decision, the Court held that the First Amendment requires a public official libel plaintiff to prove, with convincing clarity, that the defamatory statement was published with "actual malice." Actual malice means that a statement is published with knowledge of the statement's falsity or with reckless disregard for the truth. Later that year, the Court applied the actual malice fault requirement to criminal libel actions brought as the result of criticism of public officials.

In 1967, in the companion cases *Curtis Publishing Co. v. Butts* and *Associated Press v. Walker*, the Court held that "public figures" would also need to show actual malice to win libel actions. Neither plaintiff in *Butts* or *Walker* was a government official or employee. Both, however, were in the public eye, or what the Court called a *public figure*. In a concurring opinion, Chief Justice Earl Warren wrote that the actual malice fault standard—knowledge of falsity or reckless disregard for the truth—should apply to both public figures and public officials. The Chief Justice reasoned that both categories of individuals "often play an influential role in ordering society" *and*, importantly, have "ready access" to the media "both to influence policy and to counter criticism of their views and activities."

In *Gertz v. Robert Welch, Inc.* (1974), the Court broke down "public figures" into two primary categories. The first category, all-purpose public figures, included individuals who, based on their fame or notoriety, are public figures in every aspect of their life. The Court defined a second type of public figure as individuals who make the

conscious decision to enter the public sphere and engage in a topic the Court called a *public controversy*. These individuals, known as *limited-purpose public figures*, were defined by the Court as individuals who "have thrust themselves to the forefront of particular public controversies in order to influence the resolution of the issues involved." In either situation, public figures invite attention and comment.

In *Gertz*, the Court ruled that public officials and public figures must prove actual malice to prevail in libel suits while private individuals must prove at least negligence, with the states free to establish a higher standard of fault for private persons if they chose. The lower fault standard for private individuals, however, applied only to the awarding of compensatory damages. All plaintiffs, public and private, would have to prove actual malice to recover presumed or punitive damages, which are typically much larger than compensatory damages if the defamatory statements were about a matter of public concern.

The Court has also ruled that in defamation cases involving public figures or matters of public concern, the plaintiff has the burden of proving a statement was false. In *Philadelphia Newspapers, Inc. v. Hepps*, a 1986 case involving allegations, the plaintiff was involved in criminal activity, the Supreme Court ruled journalists do not have to prove their statements were true whenever they are covering public figures or when they are publishing information about private individuals so long as the subject matter of the allegedly defamatory statements involved a matter of public concern. Instead, the plaintiff would have to prove the statement was false. However, the Court has never defined "matters of public concern," although the phrase appears in a wide variety of cases involving speech by government employees, intentional infliction of emotional distress, invasion of privacy, and other areas of communication law.

In 1967, the Court applied similar protections to a false light invasion of privacy suits. False light invasion of privacy suits allows plaintiffs to sue when another publicizes material that places the plaintiff in a false light that would be highly offensive to a reasonable person and the publisher of the material was at fault when the publication was made. Unlike defamation, in a false light case, the plaintiff is not suing for damage to reputation.

Instead, they are suing for the damage caused to their right to be left alone. The plaintiff must prove the statements about them were false, caused them humiliation or embarrassment, and the defendant was at fault for publicizing the material. In *Time, Inc. v. Hill*, the Court ruled that plaintiffs must prove actual malice—knowledge of falsity or reckless disregard for the truth when suing for "false reports of matters of public interest." The Court did not say what standard was required when reporting on private matters and has yet to answer this question definitively.

Finally, in 1988, in *Hustler v. Falwell*, the Court applied a similar standard to suits for intentional infliction of emotional distress. The lawsuit started when *Hustler* magazine published a parody of a series of ads for Campari liqueur. In the real ads, celebrities would discuss the first time they tried Campari. The print ads, however, had very strong sexual overtones as the subject talked about their "first time" in the fake interviews. Although it was apparent by the end of the ads that the celebrity was talking about their first time drinking the liqueur, the ads played on the sexual double entendre of the general subject of "first times." In the *Hustler* parody, however, in a fictitious interview about his "first time," the Rev. Jerry Falwell, an evangelical preacher who in the 1980s led a group called the *Moral Majority*, described an incestuous encounter with his mother in an outhouse. He was also portrayed as a drunkard who often preached while intoxicated.

Falwell sued the magazine and was awarded $200,000 in damages by the jury for intentional infliction of emotional distress. On appeal, the U.S. Supreme Court reversed and ruled in favor of *Hustler* magazine and its publisher, Larry Flynt. The Court ruled that for a public figure or public official to win an emotional distress case, the plaintiff would have to prove the defendant made a false statement of fact that was published with knowledge of falsity or reckless disregard for the truth. In this case, because *Hustler* made no statements of fact about Falwell (the ad was a fictitious parody, after all), he could not collect damages. While many journalists may not approve of *Hustler* magazine or its depiction of Falwell, the decision adds an important layer of protection for media outlets that publish political satire, parody, or outrageous commentary. In 2017, for example,

John Oliver of HBO's *Last Week Tonight With John Oliver* won a lawsuit over Oliver's coverage of the coal industry because of the failure to prove actual malice.

Protections for Newsgathering

The Supreme Court has been less protective of the First Amendment right to gather information than it has been of the right to disseminate information. For example, the Court has been asked three times to give reporters a First Amendment right to gather news in a prison or jail. In *Pell v. Procunier*, decided in 1974, reporters in California asked to interview specific inmates in California's prison system. In a companion case, *Saxbe v. Washington Post*, reporters from a newspaper asked to interview specific inmates in federal prison in Lewisburg, Pennsylvania, and in Danbury, Connecticut. Journalists, along with the public, could tour and photograph prison facilities, conduct brief conversations with randomly encountered inmates, or correspond with inmates via mail. In the case of the federal prisons, journalists could also have a longer interview with randomly selected prisoners or a group of prisoners. In the cases, however, the media organizations argued that the press had a First Amendment right to interview specific inmates. The Court did not agree, writing in *Pell v. Procunier*, that the press "have no constitutional right of access to prisons or their inmates beyond that afforded the general public."

In 1978, the Court denied the press access to a county jail in *Houchins v. KQED, Inc*. An inmate at the jail committed suicide while held in facilities that were allegedly in poor condition. KQED television from San Francisco sought access to the facility to inspect and take pictures. The sheriff in charge of the jail said journalists could take one of the six yearly tours given to the public. The public tours, however, did not visit the area of the jail where the suicide had taken place. In addition, no cameras or tape recorders were allowed on the tours. As it had done in the previous cases, the Court ruled against the press. The Court noted nothing in the First Amendment "mandates a right of access to government information or sources within the government's control." Access to most governmental information and meetings, therefore, is governed by federal or state statutory law rather than constitutional law.

In addition, reporters may face civil liability or criminal prosecution when they trespass. The First Amendment will not protect a reporter who trespasses on private property or government-owned property in pursuit of a news story. This includes situations where a reporter accompanies law enforcement officials or firefighters onto private property. Finally, police and fire officials at the scene of disasters have the right to restrict access of the press and the public. Reporters must obey a lawful order from government officials or they may face criminal charges. The First Amendment, as noted, does not give journalists special access privileges.

The Court has upheld the right of the press— and the public—to attend trials. It has also said there is a First Amendment right of access to court documents. In 1980, in *Richmond Newspapers v. Virginia*, the Court ruled there was a common law and First Amendment right of access to criminal trials. In a series of cases over the next several years, the justices would extend this right of access to other judicial proceedings and records. The test for determining when a courtroom can be closed is complicated, however. In sum, the right of access to judicial proceedings and records is not absolute. Instead, it is a qualified or limited right of access. Once a judge determines that a proceeding or record is one that traditionally has been open or that there is some reason the proceeding or record should be open, the proceeding or record can still be closed (or sealed in the case of documents) after a judge follows five rigorous steps. In addition, there are some kinds of proceedings and records (like those involving juveniles) that are not considered open in the first place.

The Court has also ruled that the press has a right to use information that was unlawfully obtained by another. *Bartnicki v. Vopper* (2001) involved the radio broadcast of an audiotape recording of a cell phone conversation between two officials of a teacher's union. In the recording, the officials could be heard making threats against local school board members. The conversation was illegally recorded by an unknown party and then distributed to members of the press. After it was broadcast, the two union officials brought suit under federal wire taping statute. The Court ruled in favor of the journalist who broadcast the tape because the material was truthful, was about matters of public concern, and it had been obtained lawfully by the journalist even if the original source of the tape obtained it unlawfully.

Protection of News Sources

In 1972, the Court refused to provide protection to journalists and their sources when they are called to testify in criminal cases. In *Branzburg v. Hayes*, in a 5–4 decision, the Court ruled that there was no privilege for reporters to not reveal the names of confidential sources or other information when called to testify before a grand jury. The Court consolidated three separate cases. One case involved Paul Branzburg, a reporter who was called to testify about drug use in Kentucky after he wrote two stories about drugs and drug dealers. The second involved Paul Pappas, a television reporter called to testify before a grand jury about the time he spent at the Black Panthers headquarters. The final case involved *The New York Times* reporter Earl Caldwell who was also called to testify about the Black Panthers. In a highly fractured decision, the Court ruled the First Amendment did not provide a privilege from disclosing the identity of confidential sources to federal grand juries. While many lower federal courts have treated this decision as a very narrow ruling—applying it only to a reporter's responsibility to testify before a grand jury—journalists may want to be cautious when promising anonymity to sources. While some federal circuits recognize a qualified right to refuse to testify in other situations, other federal circuits do not.

Final Thoughts

Several major points can be taken away from the U.S. Supreme Court's rulings about journalists and the press. First, the Court has refused to read the press clause as giving journalists more rights or protection than others. The First Amendment applies equally to journalists and nonjournalists alike. The Court has also refused to rule that the First Amendment allows journalists to break generally applicable laws, like the trespass.

The Court, however, has provided broad protections for journalists when they report on public officials, public figures, and matters of public concern. In addition, although it stopped short in *New York Times v. United States* of saying a prior restraint of the press would always be unconstitutional, the Court placed a high burden on the government to demonstrate when such a restraint would be allowable.

Derigan A. Silver

See also Censorship; Espionage Act; First Amendment; Free Expression, History of; Free Press and Fair Trial; Freedom of Information Act (FOIA); Gag Orders; *New York Times*, The; Pentagon Papers; Press Freedom; Prior Restraint; Privacy; Zenger, John Peter

Further Readings

Amar, A. R. (2005). *America's constitution: A biography*. New York, NY: Random House.

Baker, C. E. (1978). The scope of the First Amendment freedom of speech. *UCLA Law Review, 25*, 964–1040.

BeVier, L. R. (1978). The First Amendment and political speech: An inquiry into the substance and limits of the principle. *Stanford Law Review, 30*, 299–358.

Bunker, M. D. (1997). *Justice the media: Reconciling fair trails and a free press*. Mahwah, NJ: Erlbaum.

Copeland, D. A. (2006). *The idea of a free press*. Evanston, IL. Northwestern University Press.

Davis, R. (2011). *Justices and journalists: The U.S. Supreme Court and the media*. New York, NY: Cambridge University Press.

Levine, L., & Wermiel, S. (2014). *The progeny: Justice William J. Brennan's fight to preserve the legacy of New York Times v. Sullivan*. Chicago, IL: American Bar Association.

Levy, L. W. (1985). *Emergence of a free press*. New York, NY: Oxford University Press.

TABLOID NEWSPAPERS

Tabloid newspapers, which began to flourish all over the world in the 1800s, notably in Britain and the United States, are defined by their size and content. Exact sizes of the publications may vary, but they are smaller than broadsheet newspapers and generally about 11 by 17 inches. More important than size, however, is the content of tabloids: large, arresting (often sans serif) headlines; splashy graphics, including woodcuts in earlier years and later photos; sensationalistic, terse, titillating writing; a focus on personalities, sports, entertainment, disasters, crimes (particularly crimes of passion); sexual and other scandals; and other provocative content. Many tabloids also carry a populist inclination, featuring crusades against corruption, incompetence, and elitist malfeasance. This entry discusses the origins of tabloid newspapers, concerns about their influence on other forms of media, and their ongoing popularity.

Origins

Bernarr Macfadden is probably best known for his founding of *True Story* magazine in 1919 and, in 1924, what would become *True Detective*. These magazines, true to the form of the "confessions" genre, featured lurid tales of illicit sexual misadventures, predatory relationships, and acts of passion or violence. Macfadden also founded the tabloid newspaper the *New York Evening Graphic*, usually just called the *Graphic*. The

Graphic arrived in September 1924 and quickly became one of the most reviled publications in the history of American journalism. It acquired the popular nickname "Porno-Graphic," but the *Graphic*'s raciness was only one of the attributes that earned it a place in the annals of sensationalism: It was to become well known for the use of what was called the *composograph*.

In 1936, the *Graphic* was covering a case involving a biracial woman who was being sued for divorce because her husband claimed he had been led to believe she was white. She argued that her racial background was apparent, and to support her case she partially disrobed in court. This story cried out for an illustration, especially in a newspaper called the *Graphic*. But the judge cleared the courtroom of photographers, so the *Graphic* hired a model to reenact the baring of her body in a setting resembling a courtroom, to make it appear as if the *Graphic* had a photo of the actual event. Only a tiny editor's note explained it was a reenactment. This caused a considerable increase in circulation, so the *Graphic* went on to repeatedly use composographs without much restraint.

Nothing is new in the practice of deception in the depiction of news. In ancient China, artists crafted elaborately detailed woodcuts for printed images; their use in newspaper journalism, with the more advanced form of woodblock engraving, became common practice in the 19th century in Europe, the United States, and elsewhere. These carefully detailed scenes could be based on eyewitness accounts or simply gossip, but the results were purported to be accurate illustrations. When combined with tall, arresting type and alarming verbiage as contrast, the illustrations and headlines became the foundations of tabloid journalism. If one looks closely at journalism history, one might say that "tabloidism" preceded tabloids.

The modern Latin term *oides* refers to "form," or "like," and is thus a convenient suffix for "tablet," a small slate or slab for an inscription or phrase. "Tablet" also refers to a pill in the more modern sense, and many popular sources trace the origin of the journalism term *tabloid* to a capsule developed by a London pharmaceutical company in the 1800s. A newspaper tabloid is both of these—a smaller form of a standard newspaper and also a readily digestible opioid for the masses.

One renowned use of tabloidism before tabloids—if one definition of the term includes sensationalism plus fancy—was by Benjamin Day in August 1835, when the Great Moon Hoax was concocted. In perhaps the most famous of journalism's early testing of the power of untruths, Day's New York *Sun* claimed that horned blue goats and man-bats lived on the moon and had been observed by a huge new telescope at the Cape of Good Hope. Further lending legitimacy to the stories was that articles about these beings were supposedly published in a Scottish science journal. After the publication of the Moon Hoax stories, the *Sun*, founded in 1833, saw its circulation leap by more than 20,000. The *Sun* was tabloid in size, measuring 7½ by 10 inches, but other than in its dimensions and whimsy, it resembled later descriptions and definitions of tabloids in no other way. Three columns of type were squeezed onto its pages, with barely an illustration or even what could be called a *headline* (some type was placed in all caps, with a slightly larger font or boldface to set off certain items).

Day's real contribution to tabloid journalism, perhaps, was the founding of the first successful penny paper in the United States, when most newspapers sold for 6 cents. This brought in the revolution of the penny papers (also tabloid in size), including James Gordon Bennett's *Herald* (1835) and Horace Greeley's *New York Tribune* (1841). The arrival of the Penny Press was important because the price was right for the working class, who became the key audience for later tabloids. This not only demonstrated that this market

existed, but that it had the potential for growth among working classes, of whom many were immigrants who were growing more literate, becoming more integrated into American life, and earning more leisure time and more pennies for entertainment.

The deception-as-entertainment marketing model is familiar to publishers, showmen, and hucksters of all types: Mythmaking, storytelling, gossip, and embellishment are part of the human condition. P. T. Barnum and others like him, including political leaders, made many fortunes off the idea that people want to hear the most compelling details about anything that strikes their fancy. Many have contended that readers probably knew that the claims in stories such as those found in the Moon Hoax were, in fact, hoaxes, or that exploits of all kinds of characters, whether they be sportsmen, heroes, or outlaws, were exaggerated. But that made them more attractive, not less—these readers were privy to a type of entertainment that was for *them,* not for the stuffy elite. The secret of the former printers and apprentices who founded or took over many newspapers was that they understood there was mass marketability in these tales. Much money was to be made, even a penny at a time.

The Penny Press helped revolutionize newspapers' look and feel, and it paved the way for the modern era of tabloids. But before the tabloid era exploded in the United States in the 1920s, it was preceded by broadsheet yellow fever that raged in the late 1800s and into the 20th century. The birth of "yellow journalism" was attributed to the New York competition in which William Randolph Hearst stole techniques (and personnel) from Joseph Pulitzer, and vice versa.

Hearst's and Pulitzer's newspapers lacked the tabloid size, and often therefore the impact, of tabloids' use of one or two photos and a headline plastered across an entire front page. But the competition was still that of modernized sensationalism that sold copies with the use of sometimes explosive reporting techniques and graphic exaggerations, along with simplicity in language, epitomized by Pulitzer's New York *World*. These newspapers sometimes went on populist crusades against the corruption of the clergy, failures of law enforcement, and excesses of robber barons. They exploited the human fascination with love, money, sin, violence, and death. They sponsored contests (Hearst brought to New York a lottery called *Lady Luck*) and stunts (the adventures of Nelly Bly, for Pulitzer's *World*, were among the most famous). Hearst, whose father had given him control of the San Francisco *Examiner* in 1887, bought the New York *Journal* in 1896 and hired, at significant raises, much of Pulitzer's prized editorial staff. From this era also came a comic-strip war that included the adventures of the popular character the Yellow Kid, whose name is thought to have given rise to the term *yellow journalism*.

Another precursor to tabloid newspapers could be called *tabloid magazines*, and among the most important of these was the *National Police Gazette*, especially after it was taken over in 1876 by Richard K. Fox, an ambitious Irish immigrant. Fox systematically built the *Gazette*'s readership dominion in barbershops and pool halls by featuring crime, particularly of a violent and sexually charged nature; sports, particularly boxing; and what were by that day's standards racy woodcuts of various classes of women with often deliberately disarrayed skirts and dresses, revealing their ankles and calves.

Often considered the first true tabloid in the United States was the New York *Daily Graphic*, which appeared in 1873, long before the *New York Evening Graphic* of the 20th century. The *Daily Graphic* was not to survive for long, and many trace the beginning of modern tabloids in America to the early 20th century. This history was colorfully described in the 1938 book *Jazz Journalism* by Simon Michael Bessie. For Bessie, the pre-tabloid beginnings on the North American side of the Atlantic gazed into the heart of a post–Civil War America. After the turn of the 20th century, they were part of an era that "included speakeasies, jazz, collegiate whoopee, bathing beauties, movie-star worship, big-time sports and many other gigantic exaggerations" (Bessie, p. 24), and the newspaper coverage of these excesses led Bessie to the coinage "jazz journalism." Bessie wrote in detail about the New York *Daily News* and some of its competitors. The book carries examples of headlines ("QUADRANGLE OF LOVE SHRINKS TO TRIANGLE"), photos, and tabulations of newspaper column inches devoted to categories such as "Crime," "Sex," "Sport," "Pictures," and "Features."

No history of tabloids can be complete without the inclusion of Alfred Harmsworth (later Lord Northcliffe), the British publisher who owed much of his success to the rise of compulsory education in England in the 1870s. This newly literate audience showed little interest in traditional English newspapering, with its endless columns of type and fusty styles. Harmsworth's approaches were more diverting and featured, as did Fox's and others', modern marketing techniques such as contests, awards, trivia, and other gimmicks to attract readers. In 1896, after experimental runs with other publications, Harmsworth launched the London *Daily Mail*. It was aimed at working men who had little time to peruse lengthier journals, much as later tabloids could be more readily scanned than bulky broadsheets on streetcars, buses, or subways. Harmsworth's success was so great that competitors quickly arrived, including the *Daily Sketch* and *Daily Graphic*, and in 1903 Harmsworth founded another famous title, said to be aimed at female readers, London's *Daily Mirror*.

A few years after the founding of the *Daily Mail*, Pulitzer, who often traveled abroad, was sailing from Liverpool back to New York, on December 19, 1900. As it happened, fellow travelers on the voyage included Alfred Harmsworth and his wife. On the ship, Pulitzer devised a way to involve Harmsworth in the celebration of the coming new year: He would issue a special edition of the *World* with the British innovator of the modern tabloid at the helm of Pulitzer's cherished *World*. So less than 2 weeks later, on the night of December 31, the *World* staff, uncharacteristically dressed in their finest, produced the January 1, 1901, edition under Harmsworth's direction. The first newspaper off the press on that morning, a second after midnight, was given to a messenger who rushed to catch a train to Washington, DC, to give the first 20th-century newspaper to President William McKinley. The *World* won that race, but perhaps more significant was that the newspaper's form was that of Harmsworth's English tabloids—9 by 19 inches. Thus, both Pulitzer and Harmsworth deserve credit for introducing the modern tabloid to the United States. The one-time edition sold more than 100,000 copies than usual, but Pulitzer regarded that as merely a stunt and returned the *World* to its broadsheet size the following day.

Harmsworth would not forget his adventure with Pulitzer, and he vowed to James Patterson of the *Chicago Tribune* that he would start a picture paper in New York if no one else did. Patterson took to heart the conversation and, together with Robert McCormick, began the New York *Daily News* in June 1919. At 11 by 15 inches, it was half the size of many newspapers of its day. An early issue covered a beauty pageant and an upcoming visit by the Prince of Wales. With large photos, glaring headlines, contests, beauties, sports, gossip, fiction, and advice, the *Daily News* roared through the 1920s, and by 1925, its circulation passed 800,000.

Tabloid fever eventually caught on all over the nation and indeed the world, and some international tabloids later escaped much of newspaper readership declines seen in the United States during the 21st century. There also developed a robust "clean" tabloid movement—serious newspapers that used the tabloid format without overt voyeuristic appeals. *Newsday,* founded in 1940, is one of the more well known of these.

Tabloids and Tabloidization

Tabloids have long played a role in the public imagination. The *Daily Mail* got a pop culture boost in the Beatles's 1966 song "Paperback Writer"; the New York *Post* won readers' admiration with classic headlines such as "Headless Body in Topless Bar"; media baron Rupert Murdoch used tabloids for sensational and political purposes after his News Corp. purchased London's *Sun* in 1969 and New York's *Post* in 1976; the *Chicago Sun-Times*, formed through the 1948 merger of the Chicago *Sun* and the Chicago *Daily Times* (which itself had a history dating back to 1844 when it was the Chicago *Evening Journal*), became renowned for its reporting and won multiple Pulitzer Prizes.

"Tabloidization" refers to tabloids' influence on other media—causing them to be more sensational in the pursuit of readers, viewers, or users—as well as on people's expectations of media and even their views of society. Such concerns have given rise to moral panics and crusades against sensationalism in media. Two of the best known crusaders against sensationalized, violent, and sexualized media images in U.S. history were U.S. postal inspector and anti-vice crusader Anthony Comstock and

German-American psychiatrist Fredric Wertham, who noticed that many of the juvenile delinquents he treated were fond of sensationalistic, often violent comic books. These men were born about 50 years apart, with Wertham's warnings coming in the mid-20th century and Comstock's in the last quarter of the 19th, but their alarms about the influence of violent and sexualized media content were similar. In more recent times, researchers have raised concern that tabloid coverage of crime and policing, particularly high-profile cases such as the murder trial of O. J. Simpson and the investigation into the death of child beauty pageant contestant JonBenet Ramsey, also can influence policies on criminal justice. Similarly, communications professor George Gerbner, who coined the term *mean world syndrome* in the 1970s, researched how audiences' exposure to sensationalized, violent media content can cause them to overestimate criminal dangers to society.

The merriment among tabloids' editorial excesses has also helped them solidify their position in journalistic lore. In the latter half of the 20th century, tabloid headline writers had a particularly jolly time of it, from "Ford to City: Drop Dead," to "Multiple Personality Man Charged Triple Room Rate!" to "Close but No Cigar," a description of the U.S. Senate's acquittal of President Bill Clinton in 1999 after his impeachment in the Monica Lewinsky affair. British tabloids, notorious for their own editorial leeway, produced some legendary headlines, not least of which was the "SUPER CALEY GO BALLISTIC, CELTIC ARE ATROCIOUS" in the *Sun*, regarding a 2000 football match.

The tabloid format is not confined to newspapers or magazines. Not long after the establishment of the Internet, news sites adopted large sans serif "clickbait" headlines, splashy graphics, photos, and videos that drew on tactics long used by tabloids. A news or gossip website displayed on a desktop or laptop screen, with large headlines and large graphics and photos, can be easily scanned at a glance, much in the same way that a newspaper tabloid can be. The Netflix documentary series *Trial by Media*, released in 2020, invoked newspaper tabloidism in its introductory credits to its episodes, which explored the media's use of sensationalism as a marketing strategy in crime coverage. Its opening included a typewriter clacking before the camera scanned upside-down newspaper columns as a large, all-caps headline with sans serif type was revealed: "NOTHING BUT THE TRUTH."

Bessie, who wrote about what he called *jazz journalism*, helped manage the literary careers of eight Nobel Prize winners, according to his obituary in the *Los Angeles Times*. He was probably best known for his work with Theodore H. White, who revolutionized American political coverage with *The Making of the President, 1960*, and three sequels, all of which Bessie helped guide. In his 1938 book *Jazz Journalism*, Bessie cited a headline in the *Daily News*, "FIREMAN STABBED TO DEATH," as an example of tabloidism's incitement of readers in 1920. Eighty-eight years later, in 2008, the year Bessie died at the age of 92, the *Daily News* carried the headline, "BERSERK! Crazed ex-cop gunned down in bizarre shootout in front of wife and three kids."

Guy Reel

See also Broadsheet Newspapers; Hard Versus Soft News; Hoaxes; Human Interest Journalism; News Values; Penny Press; Sensationalism; Tabloid Television; Yellow Journalism; Yellow Kid

Further Readings

Bessie, S. M. (1938; reissued 1969). *Jazz journalism: The story of the tabloid newspapers*. New York, NY: Russell & Russell.

Fox, R. L., Van Sickel, R. W., & Steiger, T. L. (Eds.) (2007). *Tabloid justice: Criminal justice in an age of media frenzy*. Boulder, CO: Lynne Rienner.

Mott, F. L. (1962). *American journalism: A history: 1690–1960*. New York, NY: Macmillan.

Reel, G. (2006). *The National Police Gazette and the making of the modern American man, 1879–1906*. New York, NY: Palgrave Macmillan.

Sparks, C., & Tulloch, J. (Eds.) (2000). *Tabloid tales: Global debates over media standards*. Lanham, MD: Rowman & Littlefield.

Swanberg, W. A. (1967). *Pulitzer*. New York, NY: Charles Scribner's Sons.

TABLOID TELEVISION

"Tabloid" originates in print journalism where it refers to a diminutive newspaper format. In keeping with their ease of handling, tabloid-sized newspapers are generally regarded as having little engagement with "serious" news, instead exhibiting a predominant concern with trivia and sensation. Just as tabloid newspapers are regarded as dealing with "less serious" news in an attempt to increase their market share, the pursuit of similar priorities in television has come to be referred to as *tabloidization*. Other related words include newszak, dumbing-down, infotainment, and, less disapprovingly, personalization and democratization. The variety of these terms attests to the different values that can be attached to this process: as detrimental to journalism or, more positively, as a key driver of the masses to news media. This entry discusses the development of tabloid television and its uses and effects.

Development

Across Western contexts, many believe there is an underlying obligation for media to foster citizenship and civic responsibility, as part of a public sphere. Since the 1980s, however, increasing competition from cable and satellite outlets, the information industries' growing internationalism, the dominance of online content, and a slackening of government and state regulation have combined to threaten this public service media model. This has resulted in a blurring of the boundaries between public and private and between information and entertainment.

Recent years have seen a conflation of news and talk programs as journalists shift to being journalist-hosts in studio-based shows that foreground audience participation. Indeed, even by 1992, there had been such a narrowing between news and entertainment that news/entertainment talk shows had become major forums for aspiring political leaders. One can trace this to Bill Clinton's 1992 saxophone-playing appearance on the *Arsenio Hall Show* during his campaign for U.S. president, while a more recent example is British Prime Minister Theresa May's shunning of conventional news interviews in favor of magazine program *The One Show* (BBC) during the runup to the 2017 United Kingdom general election.

In 1995, the national news event of the United States, extensively covered not only on talk shows but also on news programs, was the O. J. Simpson trial, during which television news programs routinely carried clips of reaction on the talk shows and talk shows carried clips of the footage gleaned from news programs. News thereby merged with and became dependent upon entertainment. Increasingly, it is the norm for "serious" broadcast news reporting to include stories about the personal lives of celebrities among the top stories, and for politicians to readily appear on news/talk shows such as *Fox & Friends*. This increased focus on personalities, one component of tabloidization, has become a feature of news and current affairs programming as broadcasters seek new audiences.

In addition to the choice of content, tabloidization indicates a series of journalistic practices that include a tendency toward more informality, characterized by the use of humor and colloquial speech. There has been an increase in the use of conversational styles in the media since the late 1970s, which has had the positive effect of allowing more people to better understand the complex social and political issues covered by the media. Linguistically, this informality can be as simple as the use of "Hi" rather than "Good evening" to greet an interlocutor, or exchange of unscripted, personal anecdotes among news anchors between stories (often dubbed "happy talk"). The viewer overhears personal comments about a journalist's life and thus may regard them as more familiar and trustworthy.

A well-known example of a journalist that built a sense of empathy with her audience is Katie Couric, who as a long-time NBC morning show host went through personal tragedies that served to emphasize her appeal and made her one of the most popular television figures of her generation. Yet her switch to become evening news anchor on Columbia Broadcasting System (CBS) didn't allow her the flexibility on the air she had long enjoyed, and her audiences dwindled. Drawing upon a similar focus on personality, when CBS correspondent Kimberley Dozier was badly injured while reporting from Baghdad in 2006, she returned to the network a year later to make a documentary about her experiences. This example of a correspondent becoming the story enabled her to produce personally informed reports that highlighted the experiences of Iraqi people as well as U.S. service personnel.

Similarly, within the course of an interview with a public figure such as a politician or company executive, questions might be asked about their private lives or personal opinions with the interviewer and interviewee exchanging anecdotes. Associated with this informality and bonhomie, the use of humor in tabloid broadcasting adds greatly to its entertainment value. Where this appears in programs traditionally devoted to serious news, it has given rise to the term *infotainment*.

Nowhere are the norms of infotainment more apparent than in parody, and programs such as *The Colbert Report* (Comedy Central, 2005–2014) satirize this entertainment approach to weighty content. Elsewhere, politicians regularly appear on talk shows where the associated informality and humor help them reveal a more personal, human side than would otherwise be visible in official appearances and, from another perspective, engaging audiences who might otherwise be unresponsive to more conventional media coverage of politics.

Developing this more positive view of the tabloidization of content, there are many advocates of personalization within the journalism business. Ian Hargreaves, former editor of a mainstream daily in the UK, favors a shift in focus toward the more personal components of a topic. Among the advantages of the personal in the news, he argues, is that journalists can direct resources toward neglected areas such as bioethics, birth technology, and the perceived breakdown in family life—all issues pertinent to the increasing public prominence of women. Journalism scholar Brian McNair also emphasizes the positive aspects of the rise in consumer and lifestyle content, arguing that this reflects recent advances of women in society which have feminized and humanized what had been a male-dominated news agenda, rendering it less pedagogic and more personal. Viewed this way, journalism has become more democratic, and its increased personalization enables more citizens to engage in issues.

Research into viewer responses to American news and current affairs programs suggests that human interest enables greater audience resonance. Viewers are able to relate personalized stories to their own experiences, producing a more vivid recollection of these news narratives and the associated issues. Conversely, it is more difficult for viewers to recall and discuss foreign news stories with the same confidence; where the items may not fit as readily with the demands of immediacy and personalization. Evidence of such a deficit of public attention to global matters is apparent in the American public's attitude to what is truly newsworthy. A 2018 report by the Pew Research Center shows that, in the middle of tumultuous global politics, most of those questioned were more interested in localized social issues such as health care, poverty, and education.

A growing focus on personalized, entertainment-oriented television news has been criticized by many academics. Hargreaves's support for the tabloidization of journalism is tempered by his condition that politics and foreign affairs should remain prominent topics. For some scholars, the concern is that traditional news values have been undermined by a new set of priorities, and infotainment has extended too far into the news media.

Scholars have also pointed to a link between tabloidization and commercial interests, with the prevailing motivation being profit and not journalistic standards. Craven financial imperatives can be seen as compromising the integrity of the journalist, particularly those involved in long-form investigative journalism and benchmark-standard news documentaries. Indeed, film scholar Bill Nichols suggests that documentary makers have been accused of compromising their agenda and abandoning the "discourses of sobriety" in order to meet the demands of program producers who require entertainment to fill their prime-time schedules.

Considering issues of "quality" in journalism requires drawing on value judgments that reflect long-held assumptions as to what are considered serious public matters and what is an appropriate mode of expression. Although scholar Martin Montgomery argues that there was not a noticeable tabloidization of British news broadcasting in the period 1985–2006 in terms of the news agenda, he also observed that there is an increasing tendency in broadcast news for correspondents to start their reports on even the most "serious" topics (such as reporting from war zones or disaster areas) with a comment about what it "feels like" rather than recounting events. This emphasis on emotion may well engage a wider range of viewers without necessarily making those viewers better informed about specific factual details.

It has been argued that the tabloidization of television and other media ignores the importance of engaging citizens who are, as a consequence, poorly informed and disenfranchised. The same features designed to make complex matters accessible are criticized for oversimplifying political issues or the nuanced dynamics of international affairs, reducing these to polarities of good and bad, winners and losers. Similarly, personalization of politics (on television and elsewhere) is criticized for shifting the emphasis away from polices to personalities.

Even the congenial forms of address and audience engagement are open to criticism, as the shift away from formality and associated personalization has led to accusations of a lack of decorum and deference toward those in authority, coupled with perceived declining standards of literacy in the wider society. However, this occasions a complex relationship with viewer expectation, and in Britain, attempts to introduce news presenters with marked regional accents and identities tend to excite as much controversy as praise, with accusations of "dumbing-down" prevailing.

Uses and Effects

The trend toward tabloid television has changed the way that many public figures engage with the medium. There appears to be an increasing willingness of politicians to appear on talk shows where they are subjected to questioning that veers away from tough issue-oriented questions or partisan debate, favoring instead questions that emphasize the personal and private in a nonconfrontational way. This does have its benefits. Research suggests that in this way, many Americans who might otherwise entirely ignore the presidential election campaigns are exposed to at least some information about the candidates. Potential voters who are otherwise unlikely to engage with "serious" news programs are more inclined to base voting decisions on the personal characteristics of the candidates than are their better informed and more policy-focused compatriots.

It is easy to sustain a set of links between forms of journalism and public engagement with the dominant news agenda. A December 2018 Pew Research Center report said that in a survey of people's sources of news and current affairs, those under 30 received their information from social media, with only 16% of them watching TV news, compared with 65% of the over-50s. A 2019 Pew Center report showed 52% of U.S. adults get news from Facebook. As this shift to online news continues, traditional broadcast news has sought to adapt. The dynamic, interactive elements of online news are now partially replicated in the visual appearance of broadcast news. There are multimedia elements, inviting viewers to "press the red button" to access additional material, while the screen itself is a dynamic mixture of scrolling headlines, talking heads, and subtitles and supertitles, simultaneously offering a variety of stories. In this way, broadcast media have come to resemble the visual appearance of a news website, with pop-up screens and hyperlinks, which in turn owes its origins to the design of tabloid newspaper front pages.

Elsewhere, political news is still to be found in the traditional format of programs such as *The Sean Hannity Show* and *Meet the Press*; broadcast television such as *PBS NewsHour*; and radio, such as NPR and Rush Limbaugh. However, a more nuanced account of the relationship between television, journalism, and public knowledge can be found in research by Jody Baumgartner, Robert Lichter, and Jonathan Morris (2014), which found that young Americans who watched *The Daily Show with Jon Stewart* reported increased confidence in their ability to understand complex contemporary political issues. That said, the researchers also concluded that the humor used to negatively portray politicians led to greater cynicism toward the political system and news media in general, resulting in less willingness to participate in politics among younger potential voters.

Much of the expressive power of the term *tabloid television* rests on its ability to cut across genres and media platforms and take on various meanings in different contexts. While some see it as being a positive development, for others it embodies declining standards in journalism. There is irony in the fact that tabloid television is able to present itself as being on the side of ordinary people, yet is itself driven by economic interests of media corporations. Yet if there is a need to engage a wide-ranging potential audience (which is, after all, the aim of commercial sponsors), it is argued that there must be a balance between informing and entertaining rather than seeing these as stark polarities.

Angela Smith

See also Hard Versus Soft News; Human Interest Journalism; Infotainment; Media Criticism; Media Literacy; News Values; Parody of News; Sensationalism; Tabloid Newspapers; Talk and News Radio

Further Readings

Baumgartner, J., Lichter, S. R., & Morris, J. S. (2014). *Politics is a joke! How TV comedians are remaking political life*. New York, NY: Routledge.

Franklin, B. (1997). *Newszak and news media*. London, UK: Arnold.

Macdonald, M. (2003). *Exploring media discourse*. London, UK: Arnold.

McNair, B. (2003). *News and journalism in the UK*. London, UK: Routledge.

Montgomery, M. (2007). The discourse of broadcast news: A linguistic approach. London, UK: Routledge.

Nichols, B. (1991). *Representing reality*. Bloomington: Indiana University Press.

Pew Research Center. (2007, April 15). Public knowledge of current affairs little changed by news and information revolutions: What Americans know: 1989–2007. Retrieved from http://www.people-press .org/2007/04/15/public-knowledge-of-current-affairs-little-changed-by-news-and-information-revolutions/

Postman, N. (1986). *Amusing ourselves to death: Public discourse in the age of show business*. London, UK: Methuen.

Shearer, E. (2018, December 10). *Social media outpaces print newspapers in the U.S. as a news source*. Pew Research Center. Retrieved from https://www.pew research.org/fact-tank/2018/12/10/social-media-outpaces-print-newspapers-in-the-u-s-as-a-news-source/

Shearer, E., & Grieco, E. (2019, October 2). *Americans are wary of the role social media sites play in delivering the news*. Pew Research Center. Retrieved from https://www.journalism.org/2019/10/02/americans-are-wary-of-the-role-social-media-sites-play-in-delivering-the-news/

Smith, A., & Higgins, M. (2020). *The language of journalism* (2nd ed.). London, UK: Bloomsbury.

Wike, R., & Castillo, A. (2018, October 17). Many around the world are disengaged from politics. *Pew Research Center*. Retrieved from https://www.pewresearch.org/global/2018/10/17/international-political-engagement/

TALK AND NEWS RADIO

Talk radio and news radio are the leading spoken-word formats in broadcast radio. The term *talk radio* tends to encompass all programming that involves one or more hosts discussing news stories or topics of interest to a community, often through interviews with leaders, experts, and other noteworthy people. The term *news radio* applies to programming that emphasizes coverage of breaking and ongoing news stories. This entry defines and compares talk radio and news radio, examines their history, the rise of the "shock jock" in the 1980s and beyond, and how both talk and news radio have continued to evolve in a digital era.

Talk Radio Versus News Radio

Audience interaction is an important part of the program; traditionally, this interaction has revolved around listeners calling the program and speaking with the hosts and/or interviewees. More recently, listeners have participated via text messages, e-mails, and social media posts directed to the host or program. The most popular subgenres of talk radio are political talk, sports talk, and business talk. *Political talk* typically involves a host giving opinions on current events; the host's viewpoints are well known to the audience and are expected to remain consistent over time. Hosts will often side with a particular political party about elections or legislative debates. Guests tend to be elected officials, authors, and other commentators. On a *sports talk* program, the hosts discuss topics relevant to local or national sports. Local hosts emphasize favorite professional and college teams from their broadcast area. Sports talk discussions revolve around recapping or previewing games, interviewing coaches and players, and debating associated topics like in-game strategy or

player transactions. *Business talk* usually centers on financial advice. The host and guests discuss issues that matter to investors, including market conditions, short- or long-term investment strategies, and the state of various companies or industries.

Hosts of talk radio programs are typically well-read and digest large amounts of news content to prepare their programs on a daily basis. They rely on producers to book guests, screen phone calls, and assist in preparing the topics and content to be featured during that day's program. Guests usually seek a talk radio audience to promote something, be it themselves, a book or some other creative work, or an upcoming event. Hosts seek guests whose promotional interests dovetail with the host's or the listeners' topical interests. Hosts are most successful when they can appear to be both realistic and relatable to their listening audience. Listeners engage in parasocial interaction with their favorite hosts; the host stands in for the listener in giving the opinions the listener would express to others and asking guests the questions the listener would want to be answered. Listener feedback, in turn, helps the host determine whether a given topic is connecting with the audience.

In contrast with talk radio, the term *news radio* is used to describe the coverage of breaking and ongoing news stories. Stations in major markets air news radio as a 24-hour-a-day format, while smaller-market stations air news blocks during morning or afternoon drive time, with briefer updates airing at the top of the hour during other dayparts. These stations often describe themselves as "news/talk." All-news stations are limited to larger markets because time spent listening (TSL) tends to be lower than other formats; news stations must make up for low TSL by having large cumulative audience numbers.

A news radio station or program features a format clock that ensures the repetition of important segments. Top news stories are repeated every hour or half-hour, weather and traffic updates are given concurrently (on 10-minute intervals such as the "10s" or the "8s"), and other topics like sports or business are also covered at a set time within the clock. News stations build their identity around the reliability of this repeated content. Perhaps the most famous news radio slogan in the

United States is that of New York's 1010 WINS: "Give us 22 minutes, and we'll give you the world."

News and talk radio stations regularly rank among the highest grossing commercial radio stations in the United States. The programming format allows plenty of commercial time each hour, and talk show hosts often provide a premium service to advertisers by endorsing products during program content, reading live commercials during ad breaks, and hosting sponsored segments or programs. Unlike with music radio, listeners are willing to sit through commercial breaks on talk or news radio because they await a specific (e.g., weather, traffic, sports) segment or they feel a greater sense of loyalty to a program host. As such, advertisers can rely on their spots to receive more attention. In addition, talk stations often feature paid programming on the weekends, in which sponsor companies promote themselves by supplying experts to answer listeners' questions about their chosen topic (e.g., health, garden, home/auto repair).

The Inventors and Early Years

All-news radio is believed to have originated with Gordon McLendon, a major-market station owner who played a large role in popularizing Top-40 music radio during the 1950s. In 1961, McLendon debuted a 24-hour news format at XTRA, licensed to Tijuana, Mexico, with a signal that blanketed most of Southern California. In 1965, Group W Broadcasting instituted their first all-news format at 1010 WINS in New York. The change was shocking at the time, given that WINS had been a popular Top-40 station and in heated competition with WABC for top ratings in the market. That same year, Group W also launched an all-news format at KYW in Philadelphia. In 1968, New York gained a second all-news station, as CBS flipped WCBS to the 24-hour format. All three stations have maintained the format for over half a century.

A key moment in the development of the news format was the formation of National Public Radio (NPR) in 1970. NPR's flagship news programs, "All Things Considered" and "Morning Edition," provided a national audience with high-quality radio news content that continues to the present day. These programs center on extended, long-form treatment of important news stories, emphasizing the creative use of live and ambient sound. This approach set NPR apart from commercial news stations' reliance on sound bites and brief summaries. Listeners increasingly found this approach to be a preferred alternative to mainstream broadcast news. NPR was able to build a network of over 1,000 member stations, many of which supplement national programming with their own local news segments and programs.

Talk radio evolved out of the "full-service" concept that dominated radio's early years. As radio formats became more standardized following the demise of network radio, many full-service stations scaled back music programming while supplementing their news operations with call-in or interview programs. In 1978, the Mutual Broadcasting System established the first true national talk radio star, picking up Larry King's overnight show. King's incisive interviews of authors and celebrities made for lively listening in the usually dead hours, making him a constant presence for third-shift workers and overnight truckers for the next 15 years. Meanwhile, NBC launched TalkNet, starring consumer information experts like Bruce Williams.

However, talk radio was a local phenomenon for the most part until the late 1980s. Within this framework, local hosts started to gain celebrity status with their commentaries and handling of local issues. Some, like Jean Shepherd at New York's WOR, found fame as master storytellers and conversationalists. Others did so by being harsh and confrontational in their style; examples include Joe Pyne, who earned top ratings in 1960s Los Angeles by urging unsympathetic callers to "gargle with razor blades," and Bob Grant, a New York radio staple for nearly 40 years.

Sports talk radio launched on July 1, 1987, when Emmis Broadcasting started WFAN-AM in New York, the first station dedicated to 24-hour sports. After a slow start, the station hit its stride when it moved from 1050 AM to a clear-channel signal on 660 AM, replacing WNBC, and adopted a lineup of Don Imus in morning drive and locally born-and-bred hosts throughout the day. WIP-AM in Philadelphia adopted sports talk shortly thereafter, and soon the format spread across the country.

In talk radio's early days, hosts were expected to keep their opinions to themselves; they could talk about politics, but only with political guests. This expectation was mostly due to the Federal Communications Commission's (FCC) Fairness Doctrine, which had been in effect since the 1940s, mandating that opposing viewpoints get equal air time when it came to controversial issues. If a show with one political slant aired for two hours, another show taking the opposite side would require two hours. The FCC stopped enforcing the Fairness Doctrine in 1987, and the removal of regulatory constraints on political opinions played a large role in the shift of talk radio toward a more politically minded format.

Talk Gets Political

The talk radio format received a boost in the 1980s, as AM stations that formerly played Top-40 and other music formats flipped to talk after losing most of their audience to better sounding FM. However, the moment when the format made its pivot toward national popularity took place on August 1, 1988, when Rush Limbaugh's national political talk show debuted in 56 markets. Limbaugh, a former Top-40 disc jockey, had reinvented himself as a conservative political commentator in the mid-1980s. Following a brief stint in Kansas City, Limbaugh's program took off at Sacramento's KFBK. In 1988, he moved his program to New York and went national when former ABC Radio executive Ed McLaughlin offered Limbaugh 2 hours of satellite time to syndicate his program.

Limbaugh's show grabbed attention and listeners immediately, both due to the host's irreverent personality and his penchant for courting controversy. His regular "update" segments featured collages of music and sound bites designed to upset liberal listeners. One example—the "Animal Rights Update"—featured singer Andy Williams's rendition of "Born Free" against a backdrop of animal noises and machine-gun fire. Limbaugh's invented language of catchphrases gave him linguistic solidarity with his growing audience, whom he termed *dittoheads* (the root "ditto" meaning "you're great, don't ever go away"). His most infamous turn of phrase labeled pro-abortion feminists as "Feminazis."

By 1992, Limbaugh's syndication audience had grown to an estimated 12 million listeners, heard over more than 500 affiliates. He debuted a nightly television show, which aired for 4 years, and wrote two best-selling books. Over the years, the satirical "updates" and parody songs dwindled in number as Limbaugh began to take on a more serious role as an opinion leader, someone whose listeners could make or break the legislation. He is credited with playing a major role in the Republican takeover of the House of Representatives in 1994, ending 40 years in the minority.

As Limbaugh's popularity grew, so did that of talk radio. By one measure, there were roughly 300 talk radio stations in the United States in 1989; by 1994, the number had tripled. The growing adoption of cellular phones during the 1990s also helped, as commuting listeners used the new technology to call in to their favorite shows. At first, leading talk stations featured lineups of mostly local hosts, representing a range of political viewpoints. However, when stations in San Francisco and Seattle took an all-conservative lineup to the top of the ratings, many stations elsewhere began to eschew opinion diversity for conservative sameness. Conservatives, feeling that they had few media outlets giving their political perspective, flocked to talk radio, entranced by the relatability of hosts who lived the same lives they did and empowered by the messages they received.

This trend was amplified by the passage of the Telecommunications Act of 1996, which removed limits on radio station ownership and led to many of the nation's top talk stations being acquired by a few major group owners. Using economies of scale, these companies found it much easier and cheaper to air a lineup of syndicated hosts delivered via satellite. Previously, talk radio had been an expensive format to produce because of the need to hire hosts and support personnel, which could be too expensive for cash-strapped small-market stations. Now, stations everywhere could switch to talk and import most or all of their programming; using the barter method, the station turned over some of its local advertising time to the syndicator as payment. Radio group owners rushed to adopt conservative talk formats, not to spread any kind of political message, but to cash in and maximize profits. Airing a lineup of like-minded hosts increased TSL and brought in more revenue.

This boom in talk radio syndication gave rise to a new wave of right-wing hosts who became prominent national radio stars. Some, like Glenn Beck, were former disc jockeys who adopted the same mix of comedy and commentary originally used by Limbaugh. Others, like Laura Ingraham and Mark Levin, came from a background in politics. Still others, like Sean Hannity and Michael Savage, found their way into talk radio with no prior broadcast training and became overnight sensations.

The Age of Shock Jocks

Concurrent with the rise of political talk in the early 1990s, many outspoken disc jockeys were taking talk radio in a different direction by evolving into "shock jocks." This term was mainly applied to on-air personalities who offered shocking opinions or catered to taboo-pushing topics, including sexual and other topics that often flouted the FCC's indecency rules. The roots of this form of radio date back to the 1970s, when midday and late-night talk shows engaged in what was known as *topless radio*, where young female listeners were invited to call in and discuss their sex lives at length with the hosts. This format gained popularity on many stations across the country but quickly subsided under threats of fines from the FCC. By the 1980s, radio therapists like Dr. Ruth Westheimer and Dr. Joy Browne had proven that relationship consultants could be popular without using graphic language.

Howard Stern receives most of the credit for popularizing shock-jock radio. He first gained infamy in the early 1980s at WWDC-FM in Washington, DC, where he displayed brutal honesty about his personal life and the contentious relationship with his superiors, along with irreverent and often controversial humor. In 1982, he moved to New York's WNBC-AM, where his afternoon show pushed boundaries and rankled NBC management. Despite high ratings, NBC fired Stern in 1985.

Stern soon landed at competing WXRK-FM, owned by Infinity Broadcasting. Infinity CEO Mel Karmazin became a champion for Stern and syndicated him to other markets. Within a few years, Stern's program held top ratings in New York, Philadelphia, Los Angeles, and other major markets. By the 1990s, the FCC had started to scrutinize Stern's program, fining Infinity repeatedly for indecency violations. Infinity appealed the fines on First Amendment grounds, but when the FCC threatened their broadcasting licenses, Infinity settled, paying $1.7 million in fines. Despite the staggering payout, Infinity considered the publicity Stern received to be far more valuable. Cementing his self-granted title as "The King of All Media," Stern published two best-selling autobiographies and made one of them into a movie, while a half-hour television version of his show aired nightly on cable's E! channel.

Based on Stern's success, Infinity's Westwood One network began to syndicate other controversial broadcasters, launching what came to be known as the *hot talk* format. Leading names in this trend included Don Imus, "Don & Mike" (Don Geronimo and Mike O'Meara), "Opie & Anthony" (Gregg "Opie" Hughes and Anthony Cumia), Tom Leykis, "Bob & Tom" (Bob Kevoian and Tom Griswold), and "Bubba the Love Sponge" (Todd Clem). This format proved very popular with mostly male audiences and helped to establish a beachhead for talk radio on the FM dial. After CBS acquired Infinity in 1997, shock jocks became the vanguard of a new CBS Radio.

As talk radio syndication of all kinds began to spread, several outspoken sports talk hosts began to gain national followings, including Jim Rome, "The Fabulous Sports Babe," and Scott Ferrall. ESPN launched ESPN Radio in 1997, quickly emerging as the gold standard of national sports talk. Most "hot talk" stations mixed in sports shows as part of their lineup to help appeal to the target male audience. Rock-music stations started adding syndicated shock jocks to their lineups, seeking the same result.

Listeners found these provocative hosts compelling because they enjoyed the biting pop-culture commentary and related to the personal stories. Listeners experienced parasocial interaction through the shared life experiences and a sort of voyeurism in the more risqué topics and segments. As with Rush Limbaugh and his fellow political commentators, part of the appeal came from not knowing what the hosts would say next. Would they be funny or offensive (or both)? Would they be poignant or absurd? As radio historian Susan Douglas explained, Stern and his ensemble cast employed a consciously mature brand of immaturity, appealing to white men who felt that their masculinity was endangered by the advance of social movements for women and people of color. Attracted to the mile-a-minute stream of sound bites and locker room humor, these listeners became extremely loyal. Similar to Limbaugh's dittoheads, many shock jocks named their audiences: Stern dubbed his the "Wack Pack," Opie & Anthony called their listeners "pests," and Rome labeled his audience as "clones."

The shock jock trend induced a backlash in the 2000s, following two very public controversies: an "Opie & Anthony" contest that resulted in the broadcast of a couple engaging in a sexual act at St. Patrick's Cathedral in New York, and the exposure of Janet Jackson's breast at the 2004 Super Bowl halftime show. Congressional hearings and increased minimum indecency fines followed, leading top radio companies to crack down on unruly behavior. Opie & Anthony and Bubba the Love Sponge were fired. In 2005, Stern left CBS for Sirius Satellite Radio (now SiriusXM), where he was free from content regulation. Two years later, CBS fired Imus after he made racially insensitive remarks about the Rutgers University women's basketball team.

News/Talk in the 21st Century

Beset by the technical limitations of the AM band, and audience perceptions that AM was "for old people," some news/talk programmers set their sights on a move to FM in the early decades of the century. Although many stations—mostly sports talk—succeeded, the decline of "hot talk" FM stations left most heritage stations apprehensive about moving to FM. Many industry-leading stations, such as New York's WABC and WOR, Cincinnati's WLW, and Los Angeles's KFI, still broadcast their primary signal on AM. The same is true of New York's all-news stations, WCBS and WINS, as well as Philadelphia's KYW and Boston's WBZ. A 2011 attempt at an FM all-news station in New York failed, lasting less than a year. However, NPR's mostly FM network continues to do well, staying competitive with or beating commercial news/talk stations in the ratings in many markets.

Current concerns surrounding broadcast talk radio mostly center on its audience and programming, which is perceived as older, white, and conservative. Few attempts have been made in recent years to format a station as something other than political, sports, or business talk; one prominent exception is the "lifestyle talk" approach at KMYI-FM (MyTalk 107.1) in Minneapolis. Although newer and younger political hosts, like Ben Shapiro and Dana Loesch, have attempted to bring in younger listeners, the programming still revolves around right-wing viewpoints. However, the power of conservative talk was still quite evident during the 2016 presidential election, when Republican nominee Donald Trump—whose penchant for shocking, controversial statements echoed many beloved talk radio hosts—rode a wave of talk radio support to the White House.

An attempt was made in the 2000s to counter all-conservative talk radio with an all-liberal network, Air America, led by former *Saturday Night Live* writer and future U.S. Senator Al Franken. Franken and fellow hosts such as Randi Rhodes, Lionel, and Thom Hartmann found it difficult to gain traction, as many radio companies put the format on their second- or third-tier AM station in a market, with far less signal strength and promotion than their primary, mainly conservative stations. The network also struggled with an ever-changing lineup and inconsistent management strategy, and it ultimately failed.

At the local level, the legacy of the Telecommunications Act of 1996 continues to affect talk radio in the United States. Since the turn of the 21st century, large radio owners have conducted several rounds of layoffs as a means of reducing corporate debt. In the talk radio format, these layoffs have largely resulted in local hosts being replaced by syndicated programming, especially at companies with their own syndication networks. Examples include iHeartRadio (owners of Premiere Radio Networks), Cumulus Media (current owners of Westwood One), and Salem Media Group. The lineups at sports talk stations are filled with syndicated hosts from ESPN Radio, Fox Sports Radio, and CBS Sports Radio. As a result, many medium- or small-sized markets lack a prominent space for discussing matters of local interest.

Many of the hosts who lost their jobs due to corporate restructuring or the decline of Air America and the shock-jock trend have resurfaced as successful podcasters. Examples include Marc Maron, Adam Carolla, Mike O'Meara, Steve Dahl, and Gregg "Opie" Hughes. In addition, NPR and its affiliated stations have seen a dramatic increase in the popularity of their programs since they began offering them as downloadable podcasts. In the world of podcasting, broadcast powers like ESPN and Fox Sports Radio battle for the most downloaded crown with digital entities like The Ringer and Barstool Sports. Podcasting has also greatly broadened the range of talk show topics; there is a show for every interest and pastime, from roller coasters ("Coaster Radio") to the 2000s TV series *Gilmore Girls* ("Gilmore Guys").

Satellite radio has created another home for talk radio hosts, as SiriusXM offers a range of different news, talk, and sports stations. There are talk stations for every political perspective—left, right, centrist, and more—and established sports talk networks like ESPN and Fox Sports stand alongside the insurgent Barstool and channels named for prominent hosts Dan Patrick and Chris "Mad Dog" Russo. SiriusXM's roster of talk hosts boasts former broadcast all-stars from Dr. Laura Schlessinger to Stephanie Miller to Michael Smerconish. Public radio news from around the globe is represented by NPR, the BBC World Service, and Canada's CBC. Meanwhile, Howard Stern continues to interview celebrities and occasionally stir up controversy on his "Howard 100" channel, where he has spent well over a decade.

Outside the United States, talk radio has become an avenue through which developing nations create their own political and cultural identities. The public forum that talk radio provides has enabled people to have a voice in debate and feel that they are becoming a part of an influential community. The aspect of geographically disparate listeners joining in an "imagined community" has been apparent in Western nations since the early days of radio, but in the current century, this phenomenon is growing throughout sub-Saharan Africa, as well as in ethnic and Indigenous communities from New Zealand to Canada to Spain. The regulatory apparatus controlling radio broadcasting in most of these countries has allowed more space for community radio to grow and flourish. This international aspect of talk radio—along with the versatility of the format across platforms—has fueled much of the recent scholarly literature on this art form, while also ensuring its viability for years to come.

David Crider

See also Broadcast, or Broadcasting; Newscasters, Radio; Sports Broadcasting

Further Readings

Crider, D. (2016). *Performing personality: On-air radio identities in a changing media landscape*. Lanham, MD: Lexington.

Douglas, S. J. (2004). *Listening in: Radio and the American imagination: From Amos 'n' Andy and Edward R. Murrow to Wolfman Jack and Howard Stern*. New York, NY: Times Books. doi: 10.1353/tech.2002.0056

Eastman, S. T., & Ferguson, D. A. (2013). *Media programming: Strategies and practices* (9th ed.). Boston, MA: Wadsworth.

Hilliard, R. L., & Keith, M. C. (2005). *The quieted voice: The rise and demise of localism in American radio*. Carbondale: Southern Illinois University Press. doi: 10.1080/08838150701457560

Hilliard, R. L., & Keith, M. C. (2007). *Dirty discourse: Sex and indecency in broadcasting*. Malden, MA: Blackwell.

McEwen, R. (2019). Iwi media in the era of media convergence: The opportunities and challenges of becoming "more than radio." *Pacific Journalism Review, 25*, 139–157. doi: 10.24135/pjr.v25i1.469

Moore, P. (2008). From the Bogside to Namibia: The place of community broadcasting in post-conflict cultural restoration. *The Radio Journal—International Studies in Broadcast and Audio Media, 6*, 45–58. doi: 10.1386/rajo.6.1.45_1

Rosenwald, B. (2019). *Talk radio's America: How an industry took over a political party that took over the United States*. Cambridge, MA: Harvard University Press. doi: 10.4159/9780674243224

TASS AND RUSSIAN NEWS AGENCIES

TASS, or Telegraphic Agency of the Soviet Union (translated from Telegrafnoye Agentstvo Sovyetskoyo Soyouza), is a Russian news agency that was prominent during the Soviet Union's Cold War with the United States and its allies. Its history goes back to the days of telegraphic news, but it has remained a propaganda distributor during its approximately century in existence. Lesser known is Rossiya Segodnya, created from two dissolved media operations that Russia President Vladimir Putin could use as a propaganda distributor. News agencies have a lot of influence because they distribute news to media outlets. They are especially useful to news outlets that cannot send correspondents to distant locations. For Russia, the news agencies are a way to get news to the media without having to cooperate with Western journalists working out of Moscow. This entry discusses the evolution of TASS and Russian News Agencies such as Rossiya Segodnya.

Brief History

As of 2021, Russia's modern news agencies evolved from previous ones with similar characteristics. In the early 1900s, there were two news agencies. The Russian Telegraph Agency was followed by the Trade Telegraph Agency. Tsar Nicholas II ordered a new agency be made from a merger, creating the St. Petersburg Telegraph Agency in 1904. It would be renamed the Petrograd News Agency. The Russian Revolution of 1917 resulted in the Bolsheviks taking power, and the new government established the Press Bureau of the All-Russian Central Executive Committee of the Councils of Workers, Peasants, and Soldiers Deputies to spread propaganda via the radio. The Petrograd and Press Bureau merged into the Russian Telegraphic Agency, commonly known as *ROSTA*. The propaganda role taken from the Press Bureau made some people distrust ROSTA, so propaganda activities were moved to the Agit-Collective. ROSTA evolved into the TASS and became one of the more respectable sources of Soviet information.

During World War II, the Soviet leadership wanted to improve TASS and its profile, so it acquired equipment from the United States and took what it could from the Germans. While the equipment, such as teleprinters, improved, reporting was not up to Western standards. The TASS employees had the opportunity to see the work of other news agencies, and they knew there were different expectations. Employees were afraid to offend the head of state, Josef Stalin, and were careful in what they reported for his daily reading.

As the Soviets expanded their control over European countries, they created a hierarchy of news agencies with TASS on the top. This helped raise TASS' power and authority over news agencies in invaded countries such as Estonia, Lithuania, and Ukraine. The Soviets tried to centralize many operations across countries, and this included TASS and the news agencies. TASS started training employees in other news agencies.

After World War II, TASS went from four divisions to two—INOTASS and RSI. INOTASS handled foreign news—both coming in and going out—and the RSI managed internal newsgathering and reporting. INOTASS' global operation required employees who were as fluent as natives in countries they covered, in addition to being well informed on the country or region. New employees started as translators and lower-level editors before becoming foreign correspondents. They would often return for a higher-level position after years away, or they would get a valued job in government.

TASS' budget came from fees paid by Soviet newspapers. It had a substantial budget because TASS had a near-monopoly on the news wire. But a monopoly in the Soviet Union did not equate to popularity. Where the oppositional press could exist in so-called satellite countries, Western news was valued more than TASS reports because of accuracy and objectivity. TASS' power also declined after the Korean War when China created its own news agency. It also lacked direct inroads to the American press until 1960, when TASS made a deal with the *New York Times*.

Russian Information Agency (RIA) Novosti's origins go back to 1941 during World War II, as the Soviet Information Bureau. Novosti focused more on feature stories, allowing TASS to spend more time on news and less on propaganda. Additionally, those feature stories could serve as propaganda.

Modern TASS

TASS became known as *ITAR-TASS* in 1992 after the Soviet Union fell and the Russian state became the Russia Federation. ITAR stood for the Information Telegraph Agency of Russia. But in 2014, the name changed back to TASS. The name has mattered less than the quality of reporting, or rather its role as a distributor of propaganda. Similar to TASS' obligation to represent the ideology of the Soviet Union's ruling party, as of 2021, TASS responds to the demands of the government under Putin.

Russian President Putin has attempted to reframe the Soviet past as part of his efforts to control the government, media, and elections. Part of this endeavor has been glorifying aspects of the Soviet Union that were reprehensible, such as Stalin, who was responsible for more than a million deaths—if not millions. Putin can frame much of the Russian news because of his control of state-owned media outlets and the pressure he can apply to owners of other media outlets. A recent example of how Putin has used TASS to share a fake narrative is the untrue accusation that Poland collaborated with Adolph Hitler on starting World War II.

In 2019, TASS agreed to a cooperation agreement with the North Korean news agency, Korean Central News Agency (KCNA), to share information, to help each other's journalists, and to fight what they called *fake news*. The KCNA is the means by which the North Korean government sends out official information. North Korea considers Russian media to be its ally in reporting on the country's relationship with the United States.

TASS has other agreements as well. One is with Getty Images to sell photographs produced by TASS. INFO-TASS is an electronic database service that serves as an archive of modern materials.

Rossiya Segodnya

Rossiya Segodnya is a news agency created by the Russian government from the RIA Novosti news agency and Voice of Russia radio, which the government dissolved in 2013. The redesigning of the previous entities into an effectively merged agency further strengthened Putin. RIA Novosti demonstrated the more objective style of journalism when covering anti-Putin protests connected to possible election fraud. Putin appears to have made the move against RIA Novosti and its management in order to reduce dissent against his rule. Even though RIA Novosti was owned by the state,

Putin was not able to control it. The new, Putin-controlled entity was initially called *International News Agency Russia Today*, or *Russia Today*, not to be confused with a television broadcaster by the same name. Rossiya Segodnya is part of the effort to centralize control of information and the large moneymakers, such as gas companies.

Rossiya Segodnya became controversial from the start. One reason is Putin's dissolution of RIA Novosti, which attempted objective journalism. Another reason is that Putin's government put a controversial figure in charge of Rossiya Segodnya, Dmitry Kiselyov, who made severe anti-gay remarks. Kiselyov was previously known as a proponent of journalism ethics and professionalism before becoming a propagandist for Putin, who also opposes democracy.

Rossiya Segodnya and Kiselyov's propaganda role went hand in hand with each other. Examples vary from the almost humorous to the serious. Sometimes the lies have sounded like those from the Soviet era, when propagandists would lie that the Soviet Union was responsible for many inventions. An old joke told by Russians was that the Soviet state created the elephant. The joke was told because of the outrageousness of Soviet lies. Kiselyov stated Russia created rap music, and he used a fake Nazi document for a report. He has also been a proponent of Russia's invasion of Ukraine. Because Kiselyov is the head of Rossiya Segodnya and reports on television, his statements are seen to represent the news agency.

Rossiya Segodnya is the official partner of the Russian Olympic Committee and the team, and has the responsibility of promoting them. It is a natural tie for Rossiya Segodnya because the agency has the assignment of projecting Russia's importance.

The agency has expanded its global operations. For example, it signed a deal in 2019 to open a bureau in Saudi Arabia. However, Rossiya Segodnya has not been welcomed everywhere. Latvia banned Rossiya Segodnya's Baltic news website for Russia's aggressions against Ukraine. Estonia froze Rossiya Segodnya's accounts in its country because Kiselyov is on the European Union's financial sanctions list. Wherever it has offices, Rossiya Segodnya and other state-owned media do not participate in objective journalism. They operate under the assumption that people need to be convinced as part of information warfare, not by appealing to reason and intellect.

Timothy Roy Gleason

See also Europe; Fake News; Press and Government Relations; Propaganda; RT and Sputnik; Russian Federation

Further Readings

Ennis, S. (2013, December 9). Putin's RIA Novosti ramp prompts propaganda fears. Retrieved from https://www.bbc.com/news/world-europe-25309139

Ennis, S. (2014, April 2). Dmitry Kiselyov: Russia's chief spin doctor. *BBC*. Retrieved from https://www.bbc.com/news/world-europe-26839216

Kruglak, T.E. (1962). *The two faces of TASS*. Westport, CT: Greenwood Press, Publishers.

Recknagel, C. (2014, September 2). ITAR-TASS looks ahead by traveling back to Soviet-era name. *Radio Free Europe/Radio Liberty*. Retrieved from https://www.rferl.org/a/itar-tass-rebranding-soviet-union/26563237.html

TELECOMMUNICATIONS ACT OF 1996

On February 8, 1996, U.S. President Bill Clinton signed the Telecommunications Act into law. The bill was designed to update, but not replace, major elements of the 1934 Communications Act. The 1934 act established the Federal Communications Commission (FCC; formerly the Federal Radio Commission), giving it the power to regulate telecommunications service and in some cases, content, in the name of the public's interest, convenience, and necessity.

To best understand the Telecommunications Act of 1996 and the subsequent challenges to it in the decades since its enactment, this entry begins with an overview of what, specifically, the Act did. How did it shape or change radio, television, cable, telephony, and Internet service? After reviewing each major element of the law, the entry examines the legal challenges brought against this legislation. The Communications Decency portion of the Act,

which tried to limit the transmission of sexually explicit content on the Internet in order to protect minors and was rescinded by the Supreme Court is examined. The entry discusses how the FCC has taken this mandate from Congress and used it to shape, although not always effectively, current limits on media ownership. Finally, the entry discusses the lasting impacts the Telecommunications Act has had on media consolidation, diversity of ownership, and Internet platform liability.

What the Act Did

In the late 1990s, developments in technology predicted the merger of television, radio, and telephone service, which prompted Congress to update existing legislation. As Thomas Krattenmaker noted in his 1996 article for the *Connecticut Law Review*, Congress believed that market forces and consumer choice should drive this transition. Congress was also concerned about the contradictory regulatory mandates that existed to govern telecommunications services, which are defined as the electronic transmission of information (in audio, video, or simple data form). The legislation sought to end what Congress saw as the monopolization of cable and wired telephone markets by breaking down barriers to entry.

The Act itself was far-reaching and extremely dense. It included 111 pages of mandates that sought to shape the ownership structure, service, commercial activity, and in some cases the content provided by the telecommunications industry.

The following discussion offers a breakdown, in broad brushstrokes, of what the Telecommunications Act sought to do.

Radio

The Act dropped all limits on the total number of AM/FM station licenses one company could own nationwide (more detail on this is provided in the section of this entry on "media ownership"). It also increased limits on the number of stations that a single company could own in a given market.

Television

As television technology shifted from VHF and UHF to HDTV and from analog to digital, broadcasters established rules for who would be eligible for additional spectrum space. The Act protected the deal that broadcasters had with the FCC that guaranteed existing broadcasters would be eligible for additional licenses.

Broadcasting

The Act made television and radio licenses long lasting and nearly impossible to lose. The Act increased the basic terms of the license to 8 years and mandated that the FCC grant renewal provided that the station had served the public interest and had no serious rule violations.

Cable

The Act repealed the ban on telephone companies offering cable service to their subscribers in their service area. It also repealed the "video dial tone" rules, which permitted phone companies to offer cable to customers if they operated as a common carrier and did not select the programming. The Act allowed telecom companies to offer cable and choose whether to be regulated as broadcasters, common carriers, or cable companies. The Act also removed rate regulations on existing cable companies.

Telephones

The Act allowed telephone companies to enter the cable market. It also moved all telephone companies to local exchange carriers (LECs), which is the system the Bell companies manipulated in order to become the monopoly that had to be broken up by the federal government in the early 1980s. The Act also said that any firm could acquire access to LEC facilities to offer competitive services. Finally, the Act allowed Bell companies back into LECs provided they were subject to regulatory constraints.

Universal Service

The Act codified the goal of universal service, which aims to provide everyone, everywhere access to telecom and information services at rates comparable to urban areas.

Media Ownership

Section 202(b)(1) of the 1996 Act set new ownership limitations. In a radio market with 45 or more commercial radio stations, a single party may own, operate, or control up to eight commercial radio stations, not more than five of which are in the same service (AM or FM); in a radio market with between 30 and 44 (inclusive) commercial radio stations, a party may own, operate, or control up to seven commercial radio stations, not more than four of which are in the same service (AM or FM); in a radio market with between 15 and 29 (inclusive) commercial radio stations, a party may own, operate, or control up to six commercial radio stations, not more than four of which are in the same service (AM or FM); and in a radio market with 14 or fewer commercial radio stations, a party may own, operate, or control up to five commercial radio stations, not more than three of which are in the same service (AM or FM), except that a party may not own, operate, or control more than 50% of the stations in such market. On the television side, the limits on station ownership were also increased to allow for additional consolidation. The new rules removed the caps on the total number of stations that a single company could own and operate, while extending the national cap on audience from 25% to 35% nationally.

When these rules were given to the FCC, the process of rulemaking for media ownership was also changed. To quickly comply with the dictates of the Act and implement the limits mandated by Congress, the FCC solicited no comments and collected no evidence on the state of the media industry. In the wake of this decision, a massive wave of station transfers and ownership consolidation followed, and between 1996 and 2010 the new ownership limits resulted in significant changes to the media landscape and rapid consolidation of ownership within the media industry.

Under the mandates of the Act, the FCC reviewed its ownership rules in 1998 and in 2000 without taking any notable actions. However, when concluding the 2002 biennial review, the FCC released a new set of ownership guidelines called the *Diversity Index*. Several legal challenges were filed to the decision, and those challenges were consolidated under the lead plaintiff Prometheus Radio Project in the Third Circuit, which released the first decision in 2004.

In 2007, the FCC released a new media ownership decision that was fairly narrow in scope, eliminating the ban on newspaper-broadcast cross ownership in the top 20 markets. The agency also released a new program designed to promote ownership by women and underrepresented groups. Both agency actions were part of a Third Circuit review in Prometheus II, which resulted in a harsh remand of the agency's action. In response, the FCC extended the then ongoing 2010 review into the review it was required to undertake in 2014.

Resolution seemed impossible, and the FCC's lack of efforts were noticeable. Then, in April 2016, the Third Circuit heard oral arguments again, and quickly issued an order requiring the FCC to resolve the impasse, and in August 2016 the agency released an order concluding the 2010 and 2014 reviews, as well as the associated proceeding dealing with minority ownership policy. The order maintained the status quo, offering no meaningful changes to the rules. Challenges followed, but before they could be resolved in court, a newly constituted FCC under the leadership of Trump appointee Ajit Pai issued an order on reconsideration in late 2017 as well as a new minority ownership proposal. The 2016, 2017, and minority decisions returned to the Third Circuit, and the panel again remanded the entire package of rules to the agency for a lack of evidence. Although both the National Association of Broadcasters and the FCC requested a full panel appeal, it was also quickly denied by the Third Circuit.

Media Content

In addition to regulating service and ownership of media, the Telecommunications Act of 1996 also put forth a handful of content-related rules. Unlike print content, broadcast content may be somewhat regulated without running afoul of the First Amendment to the U.S. Constitution because of the scarcity of spectrum space and the ubiquity of the medium itself. However, some of the content regulations included in the 1996 Act, particularly those that applied to Internet content, were

successfully challenged as violating First Amendment rights. The remaining pieces, such as Section 230, have gone on to shape the nature of content moderation on social media and other Internet platforms.

Cable

The Act included measures designed to reduce the amount of nudity on cable channels and to scramble channels with sexual content. It also allowed operators to refuse to transmit sexual content.

V-Chip

The Act attempted to facilitate parents' ability to limit children's exposure to programming with violent or sexual content by establishing a rating system for programs, which could be used with TVs that were built with embedded parental controls. The "V-chip" technology would allow parents to block shows not suitable for children over the age of 13 years, for example.

The Communications Decency Act

Section 502 of Title V of the Telecommunications Act of 1996 made it a crime to use

> an interactive computer service to send to a specific person or persons under 18 years of age, or [to use] any interactive computer service to display in a manner available to a person under 18 years of age, any comment, request, suggestion, proposal, image, or other communication that, in context, depicts or describes, in terms patently offensive as measured by contemporary community standards, sexual or excretory activities or organs, regardless of whether the user of such service placed the call or initiated the communication.

Concerns that the Communications Decency Act (CDA) would prohibit transmission of all kinds of material, including famous films, novels, and other content protected by the First Amendment, prompted the challenge to its constitutionality. In the landmark case *Reno v. American Civil*

Liberties Union (1997), the Supreme Court determined that this provision of the Telecommunications Act of 1996 was an unconstitutional content-based restriction because it restricted otherwise legal material from being made available online. The Supreme Court also held that the CDA's terminology was difficult to understand and thus unconstitutionally vague.

While the congressional restrictions on indecent or patently offensive material were overturned, the prohibitions against using the Internet to transmit obscene content remained intact because the First Amendment does not protect obscene speech. Subsequent efforts by Congress to regulate harmful content in the name of protecting children were dismantled by the courts (Child Online Protection Act of 1998).

The Supreme Court also left Section 230 of the CDA intact. This rule absolves computer service providers, including Internet service providers (ISPs) and social media organizations, of liability for what users communicate on their platforms. Specifically, Section 230 says,

> No provider or user of an interactive computer service shall be treated as the publisher or speaker of any information provided by another information content provider.

This statute was interpreted by the Supreme Court to mean that operators of Internet services were not to be construed as publishers and, therefore, were not legally liable for the words of third parties who use their services. The Court said that any law requiring ISPs to restrict or eliminate speech to avoid liability would create an "obvious chilling effect" on speech.

The impact of this portion of the Telecommunications Act of 1996 has been important as social media platforms came into existence. As private virtual spaces, social media companies are free to regulate expression as they see fit. Some activists have raised concerns that the lack of liability has allowed hateful and extreme speech to proliferate on these platforms.

Although the Reno Court said that any law requiring ISPs or social media platforms to restrict or eliminate speech to avoid liability would create an obvious chilling effect on speech, in 2018 Congress passed two pieces of legislation that run

directly counter to the Court's logic for protecting Section 230. The Allow States to Fight Online Sex Trafficking Act and the Stop Enabling Sex Traffickers Act, which are collectively known as *FOSTA-SESTA*, create an exception to Section 230 that increases civil and criminal liabilities for websites hosting ads for "prostitution." Activists and legal scholars have raised concerns about the chilling effect this creates. For example, the website Craigslist was forced to shut down some of its classified advertisements for fear of running afoul of this new law.

Lasting Impacts

Decades after the Telecommunication Act of 1996 was signed into law, its legacy is the deregulation of the industry, which has resulted in massive consolidation. Moreover, the FCC's quick adoption of the competition theory behind the Act fundamentally altered the structures of media and telecommunications in this country. An obvious impact is the regulatory lean toward larger media structures for purposes of economy of scale at the expense of both localism and diversity.

The FCC's inability to demonstrate the positive effects of these policies has created a regulatory paralysis that remains unresolved. Importantly, without a significant change in policy implantation, that paralysis continues to limit ownership of media outlets by women and people of color or to allow traditional media to adapt to changes in the marketplace.

The Telecommunications Act of 1996 is also responsible for what law scholar Jeff Kosseff refers to in the title of his 2019 book, the "26 words that created the Internet." When the CDA was rescinded by the Supreme Court in *Reno v. American Civil Liberties Union*, it sent a message to lawmakers that content-based restrictions on online speech would be viewed as a violation of the First Amendment and generally would not be tolerated.

In addition, by keeping Section 230 intact, the Supreme Court opened the door to nearly unrestricted expression on the Internet. By absolving computer services of liability for what third parties post on their sites, Section 230 helped establish the fairly hands-off approach many social media and other platforms take to regulating content. While extreme speech undoubtedly exists and calls to rework Section 230 to provide recourse for users facing harassment and threats seems warranted, the fact remains that Section 230 has enabled online free expression in a way that Congress could likely not have foreseen when they drafted the Telecommunications Act of 1996.

Caitlin Ring Carlson and Christopher R. Terry

See also Broadcast, or Broadcasting; Diversity in Journalism; Federal Communications Commission (FCC); Media Ownership; Section 230, Communications Decency Act

Further Readings

Kosseff, J. (2019). *26 words that created the internet.* Ithaca, NY: Cornell University Press.

Krattenmaker, T. G. (1996). The telecommunications act of 1996. *Connecticut Law Review, 29*(1), 123–174.

Nuechterlein, J. E., & Weiser, P. (2005). *Digital crossroads: American telecommunications policy in the internet age.* Cambridge, MA: MIT Press.

Reno v. American Civil Liberties Union, 521 U.S. 844 (1997).

Telecommunications Act of 1996, Pub. L No. 104-104, 110 Stat. 56 (to be codified at scattered sections of 47 U.S.C.).

Terry, C. (2019). Localism as a solution to market failure: Helping the FCC comply with the telecommunications act. *Federal Communications Law Journal, 71,* 327–352.

TELEGRAPH

The telegraph was an electrical network that enabled transmission and receiving of coded electrical signals across wires. The system, used first in Britain and then the United States, was largely developed by Samuel F. B. Morse and was first demonstrated publicly in 1844. Few new communication technologies have had the impact on society and culture that the telegraph did. It helped open the American West and maintain European colonial empires, revolutionized warfare and business, and changed the ways people thought about the world in which they lived. People could stay in touch with distant relatives, order products from distant stores, and remain connected to a broader culture. But perhaps its most profound effect was on the nature of news. Readers, through reports brought to their local paper by telegraph, came to understand events as connected, to think globally and to see similarities between themselves and those in faraway places. The public's perception of what was important was no longer limited to the local but evolved to encompass the national and international as well.

Origins

While a professor of design at New York University in 1835, Morse demonstrated that coded signals could be transmitted by wire. He had learned of the work of British inventors William Cooke and Charles Wheatstone, whose system of telegraphy began operating there in the 1830s. Morse used pulses of electrical current to deflect an electromagnet, which moved a marker to emboss a strip of paper with dots and dashes. Working with others, he developed what became the Morse code so that in different combinations, these dots and dashes represented individual letters of the alphabet. Morse transmitted his first telegraph message in January 1838 across two miles of wire near Morristown, New Jersey. Following that, he received a $30,000 grant from Congress to construct an experimental line from Washington to Baltimore, a distance of about 40 miles. Six years later, in May 1844, Morse sent the message "What hath God wrought" (quoting the Bible, Numbers 23:23) from the old Supreme Court chamber in the U.S. Capitol building to his assistant Alfred Vail at the Mount Claire railroad depot in Baltimore. The Post Office operated the line from 1844 to 1847, when they sold it to private interests.

Even before this first line had reached Baltimore, the telegraph had shown its worth in the rapid transmission of news. The previous month the Whig party had held its national convention in Baltimore and had nominated Henry Clay as its presidential candidate in the upcoming election. This information was carried by railroad to Annapolis Junction, which the telegraph wire had reached, from which Vail wired it to the Capitol. The news of Clay's nomination was published the next day in local newspapers. It was the first American news report dispatched by electric telegraph, an omen of the future of journalism. News could now be sent across great distances in a short amount of time, slowed only by the process of encoding and decoding the dots and dashes. For the first time, information could outpace land and sea transportation speeds.

These successes proved the reliability and utility of the telegraph, and Morse quickly obtained private funds to extend the line north to Philadelphia and New York. The New York to Boston line went into operation in 1846. By the end of that same year, state capitals in Albany and Harrisburg were connected to the main line. Small telegraph companies sprang up across the East and South, connecting cities and the towns by wire much as the railroads were doing—indeed the two services often used similar rights of way. Western Union, founded in 1851, opened its first transcontinental telegraph line in 1861, mainly along railroad routes. Spanning North America, the growing numbers of networks in the eastern states were connected to the small network in California by a line that ran from Omaha, Nebraska, to Carson City, Nevada, via Salt Lake City on October 24. (The famous Pony Express system for moving mail and messages ceased operations 2 days later.)

After three previous failures, the first successful transatlantic telegraph cable was completed in July 1866. With completion of the transatlantic cable, information and news could flow between European and North American cities in a matter of minutes. Further undersea telegraph lines expanded across the globe in coming decades.

Telegraphic News Agencies

The impact of the growing telegraph technology on journalism was soon obvious, for editors now could obtain information on events while it was still "new." Many newspapers hired reporters or established bureaus in other major cities to collect and send news back; however, this independent reporting was enormously expensive, not the least because each paper paid the full rate for transmission to the telegraph companies. It was common knowledge among newspaper editors that telegraph companies were selling news from their various offices to anyone, even though the staff of a specific newspaper gathered it. In 1848, David

Hale, publisher of the New York *Journal of Commerce*, learned that certain telegraph companies were even investigating the concept of setting up subsidiary organizations to gather and transmit news for sale. The dangers were obvious. With no government regulation or supervision, telegraph companies could make it impossible for any news but their own to move by wire. Newspapers would be forced to surrender the function of newsgathering, and those outside the journalism profession would reduce the news itself to a commercial and unreliable commodity. Hale approached James Gordon Bennett, publisher of the New York *Herald*, about the threat.

The two proposed resurrecting a previous scheme by newspapers to pool resources. In May 1846, Moses Yale Beach (1800–1868), publisher of the New York *Sun*, forged an agreement with four other New York papers to deliver news of the ongoing Mexican-American War. In the plan, dispatch riders from the front raced to Montgomery, Alabama, to place news reports on mail coaches, which carried them 700 miles to the nearest telegraph station. In offering an equal interest in the express venture to the other papers, Beach effectively created the first cooperative news service. In 1848, Beach formulated a similar venture to obtain and share European news from ships arriving at New York harbor, naming it the Harbor News Association. Hale and Bennett proposed to charter a new organization, forming the "General News Association of the City of New York" in 1851, including The New York Times and the New York Tribune with the earlier five. It was soon renamed the Associated Press (AP), America's first "wire service."

The AP, under the leadership of its first directors, Alexander Jones (1802–1865) and Daniel Craig (1811–1895), took on the task of joint telegraphic transmission of news stories to provide its members with a comprehensive summary of daily news. Spurred by the outbreak of the Civil War, the association expanded to include newspapers in other East Coast cities; this would be the first time that battles and developments of a war could be reported to the public within a day or so. Beginning in 1875, successive directors of the AP—over the objections and legal challenges of Western Union—secured leases on telegraph lines, allowing its messages to move untroubled by delays from other traffic. By 1892, the news agency was using nearly 23,000 miles of leased telegraph wires. The successes of the AP soon lead to the birth of other wire services including the Western Associated Press, Southern Associated Press, United Press, and International Press.

Use of the telegraph to transmit news stories also led, inevitably, to a more precise and concise journalistic style. Because early telegraph lines were unreliable and prone to failure, the opening paragraphs of a news story, which came to be known as the "lead," presented the most important facts. The rest of the story contained details and background. If telegraph service was interrupted during transmission, at least the most important part would reach the editor. AP correspondents during the Civil War were even ordered to put the most important news in the first sentence, with less crucial information following in the lead. The uncertainty and the expense of telegraph service contributed to reporters changing from a chronological style of reporting to a fact-based organization of information. Thus, the "inverted pyramid" style of writing was developed. Uncertainty also led to the practice of confirming both stories and sources, with editors often sending back messages asking for more details or ensuring that the original message was not a hoax (as might be transmitted by rivals).

Impact

Historians credit the technical shortcomings and expense of telegraph messages with a terse journalistic style and a shift away from the flowery 19th-century type of news writing. An experienced Morse operator could transmit or decode 40 to 50 words a minute. Lengthy stories took an inordinate amount of time to send and cost more. Hence, "telegraphese" evolved as an elliptical style of writing. Personal observations by reporters and other embellishments were eliminated as verbiage. The extensive use of abbreviations and code phrases to compress meaning into a small number of characters for ease of transmission over telegraph lines spread through journalism as well as business. Soon large commercial telegraph codebooks were

published, less for secrecy than for keeping costs down by letting a brief combination of letters or numbers stand for a complex transaction or idea. Getting the news reading public to accept the new form of news writing took some years, but that terse, impersonal, inverted pyramid style remains the norm for breaking news.

Despite its wonders, technical limitations led to the eventual demise of the telegraph. In 1913, Western Union developed multiplexing, making it possible to send up to eight messages simultaneously over a single wire (four in each direction). Shortly before, in 1906, the teleprinter, an electromechanical typewriter, allowed transmission of news stories directly to editorial offices, and in 1914, the AP adopted it for their wire service. By the 1930s, worldwide networks of 60-word-per-minute teletype machines were in use by major news agencies. And, at first within cities, and more slowly over distances, the telephone displaced the telegraph, doing away with the need for codes and letting reporters speak directly to editors. The telegraph remained an important mode of news communication through and even after World War II. Western Union announced the discontinuation of all telegram service in January 2006. Only 20,000 telegrams had been sent the year before, compared to 20 million in 1929.

The telegraph ushered in an era of rapid, regular, and reliable communications. As a result, the telegraph transformed the nature and style of journalism. Newspapers could deliver the latest information on events, and details could be quickly checked and confirmed. Readers came to expect newspapers to report national and global events in a timely manner.

Rex Martin

See also Associated Press; Cables, Undersea; Havas; Reuters; United Press International

Further Readings

Beauchamp, K. (2001). *History of telegraphy*. London, UK: Institution of Electrical Engineers.

Blondheim, M. (1994). *News over the wires: The telegraph and the flow of public information in America, 1844–1897*. Cambridge, MA: Harvard University Press.

Coe, L. (1993). *The telegraph: A history of Morse's invention and its predecessors in the United States.* Jefferson, NC: McFarland.

Schwarzlose, R. A. (1989–90). *The nation's newsbrokers,* vol. 2. Evanston, IL: Northwestern University Press.

Standage, T. (2018). *The Victorian internet: The remarkable story of the telegraph and the nineteenth century's on-line pioneers.* New York, NY: Bloomsbury.

Thompson, R. L. (1947). *Wiring a continent; the history of the telegraph industry in the United States, 1832–1866.* Princeton, NJ: Princeton University Press, (reprinted by Arno Press, 1972).

Winseck, D. R. (2007). *Communication and empire: Media, markets and globalization, 1860–1930.* Durham, NC: Duke University Press.

Winston, B. (1998). *Media technology and society, a history: From the telegraph to the internet.* New York, NY: Routledge.

TELEVISION COMMENTARY

"Television commentary" here refers to the added value journalists provide alongside the basic presentation of news that requires some degree of unpacking or analysis. Such added value is fundamental to debates about the wider quality of journalism and its contribution to democracy. In regions where television output is unregulated, any balanced, impartial journalistic analysis seems less frequent, given the entrenched editorial positions taken by the channels. Within regulated regions, theoretically at least, journalistic analysis would more likely adhere to the long-standing traditions of news reporting. In practice, though, the public's appetite for news might vary between a need for trenchant partisanship or scrupulous neutrality. This entry discusses the evolution of television commentary along with changes in broadcast regulation and technological advancements that have diminished the primacy of television news and, due to social media, complicated the efforts of some television networks to be seen as impartial.

Even within a media landscape where online engagement is the major area of growth in many developed countries, television has remained the primary source of news for adults. But broadcasting's dominance has been neither static nor emphatic; in the early part of the 21st century, research has consistently indicated that younger people consume their news online. Accordingly, television's grip might continue to decrease alongside the increase in the proportion of "digital natives"—those born into the Internet age and who have never known anything different. However, social media platforms such Facebook, Twitter, and Instagram frequently share clips from television news. Such viral content confirms television's continuing relevance and the establishment of a "hybrid" media where old and new modes of communicating the news live side by side.

As with other news, television news consists of beats including home affairs, crime, business, science, sport, and so on. For all such categories, there are general expectations that journalists should adhere to the noble ideals of professional reporting. These ideals include requirements that reporters should be truthful and factual, and that they should hold elected representatives and powerful corporate figures to account for the decisions they make. Accordingly, a "commentator" herewith refers to news anchors on broadcast networks who could reasonably be expected to provide analysis without necessarily giving their personal opinions.

For business reporters, for example, there are also expectations that they should explain and simplify complex stories. Similarly, it is reasonably anticipated that political reporters should not only report events but also explain the context and implications of policymaking and the details of the processes, parties, and individuals involved in legislation. Accordingly, political news is not confined to bulletins, but is carried within program formats embracing discussions, analysis, and live coverage of parliamentary debate.

Broadcast media are also used by political figures as a means of directly sharing their messages. In the United States, for example, President Franklin D. Roosevelt talked to the nation in his "fireside" radio chats during the 1930s and 1940s. In 2013, China's President Xi Jinping began to use the same Westernized approach to address his audience via their television screens. At election times in many countries, there will be campaign events, live debates involving party leaders, and perhaps live results programs lasting many hours.

Across all such programming, factual information and political messages may inevitably be accompanied by explanations, interpretation, and synthesis offered by specialist commentators. While such political commentary can be reasonably considered widespread within developed democracies, the regulatory conditions within which it operates might vary. In some countries, the principle of public service broadcasting exists as a defining structure for television and radio output, but even this is subject to variation.

Broadcast Deregulation in the United States

Often the United States is cited as exemplar of a deregulated broadcasting system, meaning that journalists have fewer rules to obey. After broadcaster deregulation gathered momentum under the presidency of Ronald Reagan in the late 1980s, the Federal Communications Commission (FCC) eliminated rules limiting media organizations that sought to build bigger portfolios of stations. In addition to a number of other concessions, commercials became limitless, and children's programming was no longer compulsory.

However, many felt that the most impactful move to deregulate the broadcast industry during this period was when the FCC stopped enforcing the fairness doctrine in 1987. The fairness doctrine had determined that TV and radio channels in the United States should ensure that important issues were adequately covered in a way that presented viewpoints representing a breadth of opinion. With the doctrine in place, many broadcast news professionals developed reputations for practicing objective, impartial journalism that made tangible contributions to public debate and citizens' knowledge of politics and current affairs.

Such trusted, personal reputations were typified by the esteem associated with news anchor Walter Cronkite. He had reported on World War II and the subsequent Nuremberg trials of top surviving German leaders, along with the Vietnam War, Watergate, and the assassinations of President John F. Kennedy, Senator Robert F. Kennedy, and Martin Luther King Jr. Accordingly, he was known as the "most trusted man in America." When he signed off each evening's newscast with his trademark "...and that's the way it is," the American public largely accepted that "it" was, indeed, the way that he had reported it. Many people felt that Cronkite and his generation of television commentators provided the gold standard of objective, impartial journalism.

After the fairness doctrine was lifted, new channels with more partisan television commentators began to thrive. Viewers keen to understand the parameters of public debate have no longer been able to use network or cable channels as a "one stop shop" featuring a full range of perspectives. Instead, many media organizations have positioned themselves at the extremes of political debate. Consequently, important matters are often discussed from entrenched and preset perspectives, with news narratives and those contributing to them either ignoring alternative views or delegitimizing them with ridicule.

The polarization of political debate in the United States in the early part of the 21st century is exemplified by Fox News and MSNBC. These two channels represent the extremes of political opinion, their editorial approaches amply demonstrated by the way that they each reported the first day of official proceedings in the attempted impeachment of President Donald Trump in 2019. On November 16, The *New York Times* reported that while MSNBC host Rachel Maddow asserted that the President was in considerable trouble as he had been "caught doing something illegal" at the "direct expense of the country's national interest," on Fox News Sean Hannity suggested that it has been "a great day for the United States, for the country, for the president" and "a lousy day for the corrupt, do-nothing-for-three-years, radical, extreme, socialist Democrats."

But even less obviously partisan U.S. news channels are not immune from imbalanced coverage and commentary that apparently offers more opportunities to one side than the another, although the tone of such coverage is usually rather more muted. Data generated by media monitor Andrew Tyndall noted that across the more moderate channels (ABC, NBC, and CBS) in the 2012 presidential election campaign, Republican candidate Mitt Romney enjoyed three times more airtime than his Democrat opponent (and incumbent President) Barack Obama. In 2016, Tyndall's data covering the same channels showed that Republican candidate Donald Trump enjoyed well over twice the airtime as Democratic candidate Hillary Clinton. It seems beyond doubt that 21st-century viewers in the United States wishing to find a range of ideologically driven punditry on the same TV platform will be disappointed. But, given the popularity of partisan channels, and the increasingly polarized political landscape within many nations, news audiences might also actually prefer their news content colored with emphatic opinions.

UK Broadcast Regulations

The prevailing broadcasting system in the UK is notably different, at least in theory. Ofcom—who regulate broadcast output—determine that TV channels must practice "due impartiality" in the way they present news and debate. This means that broadcasters should not show preference or favoritism or privilege one party, argument, or ideology over another. The principle, therefore, is to aid the democratic process by presenting the breadth of debate so that viewers might position themselves within that debate based on all options being given the same opportunities to persuade them. More specifically, this means that—unlike both Maddow and Hannity in the previous example—TV commentators should not reveal any preferences.

This has traditionally meant that audiences have recognized channels bound by impartiality as the most trustworthy. Indeed, principles such as fairness and lack of partisanship are often central in the ways that these channels promote their news provision. They are often claimed to be "enshrined" in the channel's ethos, and a founding principle for the way that they operate at every stage of news production.

However, the reality is more complex. The ways that impartiality can and has been breached have drawn considerable scholarly effort. Research claims to demonstrate, for example, that when editors and commentators omit some stories and not others, present only certain sides of a debate, and select some sources and contributors rather than others, impartiality can be subtly but tangibly compromised. Nonetheless, explicit tonal bias is unusual on regulated television programming in that rarely, if ever, will a broadcast journalist simply recommend one party over another.

However, this is not to say that broadcasters might not show preferences in other ways. Firstly, and while it could be more reasonably considered more about interviewing technique than "commentary," some might point to the different ways that some TV journalists interview different politicians. While many journalists would undoubtedly claim that they need to be appropriately combative and persistent in order to counter increasingly evasive politicians, critics would point to numerous examples of allegedly inequitable treatment. Political parties from all sides will often allege that they receive different treatment to their opponents and were asked harder questions, were probed more aggressively, and were interrupted more often, and that public perceptions might be influenced negatively as a consequence. During the 2019 UK general election, for example, the interview of Labour party leader Jeremy Corbyn by BBC political journalist Andrew Neil was described by Labour-party supporting website LabourList as "a brutal grilling," making for an "excruciating viewing experience" and "a grim day" for the party (Rodgers, 2019). When the BBC failed to secure a similar interview with Conservative Party leader and incumbent Prime Minister Boris Johnson, the corporation was widely condemned for a lack of balance.

But TV commentary has more contemporary challenges than just ensuring an equity of interrogative vigor. Technology presents a potentially problematic dimension to the media landscape in the United Kingdom and in other countries where broadcast output is regulated. The advent of the so-called "Smart TV," for example, means that on a split screen platform, unregulated Internet-based content sits alongside output that must meet regulatory demands. The conundrum for TV commentators was highlighted by Channel 4 presenter Jon Snow in July 2014.

Obliged to deliver the latest news about the bloody conflict in Gaza in a regulated bulletin, on July 26, Channel 4 also posted a video on its website—not subject to broadcast regulation—where Snow, speaking from the same studio from where he had read the news, gave a personal, moving, and at times visceral view of the conflict, and what should be done about it. While many were pleased to see such a notable journalist break away from the constraints of regulation, others claimed that his personal claims of impartiality were forever compromised.

Use of Social Media

The professional complexity of remaining impartial for those journalists obliged to it or preferring to practice it has also intensified in other ways. Social media has become a significant contributor to journalistic landscapes across the globe. It offers immediacy in terms of reporting news but can also be used to assist in establishing and maintaining news brands, directing more Internet traffic to its websites.

Much like Jon Snow's regulated and nonregulated journalistic activities existing side by side, social media presents another key challenge for contemporary journalists obliged to be nonpartisan. In essence, they are able to use a nonregulated medium to promote the content on a regulated medium. At particular times such as elections, for example, social media postings by BBC journalists, for example, are inevitably subject to particularly close scrutiny. In the 2019 general election, BBC journalists made the news themselves as a consequence of social media posts that many observers felt breached normal standards of impartiality, even if those standards did not actually apply to the medium the journalists were actually using. Shortly afterward, the corporation amended their own guidelines, advising that social media activity by journalists and commentators was subject to the same editorial standards as their broadcast output, and that their journalists and commentators should practice caution in their personal and private proclamations on platforms such as Twitter.

The response indicates that for the BBC at least, the quality and independence of their television commentary across a wide range of issues is a principle worth preserving. Indeed, considerable research suggests that audiences identify impartiality as a key requirement for a news provider that they could trust. The inference perhaps is that those who reject partisan news commentary on unregulated broadcast platforms should be rewarded with something demonstrably different in terms of editorial approach.

Redefining Impartiality

Even on regulated media where journalists are obliged to ensure that one side of a debate should not prevail over another, contemporary thinking suggests that for some issues, both sides of the story cannot reasonably be presented with equal treatment. By the second decade of the 21st century, for example, the climate emergency had been consistently shown to be scientific fact. In such a case, in order to prevent providing a "false balance," the growing consensus—reflected in the revised editorial policies of many media organizations—is that proper context should be provided if reports and broadcasts include contributors who are considered to be "deniers."

Richard Thomas

See also Bias; Election Coverage; Election Coverage, U.S.; Fairness Doctrine; Federal Communications Commission (FCC); Public Service Broadcasting

Further Readings

Alejandro, J. (2010). *Journalism in the age of social media*. Oxford, UK: Reuters Institute, University of Oxford.

BBC. (2019). *Guidance: Social media*. Retrieved from https://www.bbc.com/editorialguidelines/guidance/social-media

Cushion, S., & Lewis, J. (2009). Towards a 'Foxification' of 24-hour news channels in Britain?: An analysis of market-driven and publicly funded news coverage. *Journalism, 10*(2), 131–153. doi:10.1177/1464884908100598. Retrieved from https://www.ofcom.org.uk/__data/assets/pdf_file/0025/173734/bbc-news-review.pdf

Cushion, S., & Thomas, R. (2018). *Reporting elections: Rethinking the logic of campaign coverage*. Cambridge, MA: Polity Press.

Grynbaum, M. M. (2019, November 21). In prime time, two versions of impeachment for a divided nation. *The New York Times*. Retrieved from https://www.nytimes.com/2019/11/16/business/media/impeachment-media-fox-msnbc.html

Jackson, H. (2009). Obituary: Walter Cronkite: Legendary CBS news anchorman repeatedly voted the most trusted man in America. *The Guardian*, July 20, p. 31.

Kovach, B., & Rosenstiel, T. (2007). *The elements of journalism; what newspeople should know and their public should expect*. New York, NY: Three Rivers Press.

Newman, N., Fletcher, R., Kalogeropoulos, A., & Nielsen, R. (2019). *Reuters institute digital news report 2019*. Oxford, UK: Reuters Institute, University

of Oxford. Retrieved from https://reutersinstitute
.politics.ox.ac.uk/sites/default/files/inline-files/
DNR_2019_FINAL.pdf

Ofcom. (2019). *Review of BBC news and current
affairs*. Retrieved from https://www.ofcom.org.
uk/__data/assets/pdf_file/0025/173734/bbc-news-
review.pdf

Rodgers, S. (26 November, 2019). Labour's most grim
campaign day yet ends with Andrew Neil grilling.
LabourList. Retrieved from https://labourlist.org/
2019/11/labours-most-grim-campaign-day-yet-ends-
with-andrew-neil-grilling/

Simmons, S. (1978). *The fairness doctrine and the media.*
Berkeley, CA: University of California Press.

TELEVISION NEWSMAGAZINES

Television newsmagazines are programs longer than typical television newscasts, usually running an hour in length with some exceptions. Television newsmagazines often focus on one or only a few topics or stories. While many television newsmagazines present investigative reports, content often also contains interviews with celebrities, famous athletes, politicians, and human-interest or feature stories. Television newsmagazines continue to be a popular and important format in American broadcast journalism. Television programs in this genre are among the longest-running and highest-rated on American television. This entry examines the creation of a standard for television newsmagazines and the increase in popularity of the genre, as well as the evolution of some programs within the genre.

The first television newsmagazine, *60 Minutes,* has aired on the American CBS network since 1968 and has enjoyed high ratings from the beginning. It was created by Don Hewitt, one of the most successful television news producers of all time. Some, such as the Museum of Broadcast Communications, credit Edward R. Murrow along with producer Fred Friendly for inventing the television newsmagazine format with the program *See It Now.* That weekly program first aired in 1951 on CBS. Don Hewitt, the creator of *60 Minutes,* was a director on *See It Now.* Other popular and long-running programs in the genre include *20/20, Dateline,* and *48 Hours.*

Creating the Standard

In the United States in 1951, technology made it possible for television networks to broadcast programs on a regular basis. Before that, broadcast news programs aired over radio. Edward R. Murrow (1908–1965), American radio and television broadcaster, enjoyed success with his popular radio program, *Hear It Now.* But as television grew increasingly available and popular, Murrow and producer Fred Friendly (1915–1998) adapted the radio program *Hear It Now* into a television program called *See It Now,* which aired on the CBS television network. Murrow also hosted a show entitled *Person to Person* on which Murrow would interview celebrities in their homes.

See It Now aired from 1951 to 1958. Murrow hosted the program, which often covered controversial issues. One of the most historic of the controversial issues on *See It Now* was the episode that aired on March 9, 1954. The program explored the American Republican Senator Joseph McCarthy's anti-communist methods and the resulting so-called Red Scare. In this episode, Murrow gave the famous "Good night and good luck" speech, the title of the 2005 film about the conflict between Murrow and Senator McCarthy. Congress later condemned McCarthy's behavior.

Hewitt, creator of *60 Minutes,* also worked as a director on *See It Now.* Hewitt recalls in his memoir *Tell Me a Story* that his idea for the television newsmagazine format for *60 Minutes* came from his idea of combining Murrow's programs, *See It Now* and *Person to Person,* as well as the popular print magazine *Life.* Hewitt reasoned that combining hard news with soft news could be a successful formula for television. The formula would also be akin to *Life* magazine, which combined serious news with softer stories, without advertisements breaking up the individual stories.

The first broadcast of *60 Minutes* aired on September 24, 1968. During that broadcast, anchor Harry Reasoner (1923–1991) told the audience they were watching a new form for television. *60 Minutes* is one of the most successful programs in U.S. television history due to its ratings and longevity.

The format of *60 Minutes* is similar to that of a print magazine. The television program opens with an iconic video shot of a ticking stopwatch on the cover of a magazine. Hewitt recounts in his memoir

Tell Me a Story that he and others working on the program did not want to use music in the program, as they felt it would be a form of editorializing, but they did want some sound. He felt that devoid of any sound, the program may not get the attention of a potential viewer lingering in a room without a television but within ear shot. Hewitt writes that the program initially used a ticking stopwatch at the end of the broadcast. He had the idea of putting the stopwatch at the start of the program. The rest is broadcast history.

60 Minutes covers three stories including investigative reports, interviews, and feature segments on a variety of topics. Two of the three stories are often in-depth, hard news reports. The third story varies among feature and human-interest topics. Correspondents introduce their reports in front of a background resembling an open magazine with graphics and images relating to the story. As of 2021, *60 Minutes* is among the top 10 rated American television programs nearly every week. It airs on Sunday evenings and averages more than 10 million viewers.

Over the years, many famous news correspondents have worked on *60 Minutes*, including the first hosts Harry Reasoner and Mike Wallace (1918–2012). Wallace is known for his hard-hitting interview style. Other correspondents and contributors of *60 Minutes* include Morley Safer, Ed Bradley, Dan Rather, Leslie Stahl, Sharyn Alfonsi, Anderson Cooper, Charles Osgood, Meredith Vieira, Norah O'Donnell, Scott Pelley, Diane Sawyer, and Andy Rooney. Sawyer was the first female correspondent on *60 Minutes*. Rooney (1919–2011) is known for his humorous and curmudgeonly commentary at the end of most of the *60 Minutes* broadcasts from 1979 to 2011.

60 Minutes has won every major broadcast award and has won more Emmy Awards than any other prime-time program. It appears as number six in the 2011 *TV Guide 50 Greatest TV Shows of All Time*. Notable stories include compelling interviews with American politicians and world leaders, the crisis at the United States–Mexico border, and the coronavirus pandemic. In 1988, CBS debuted *48 Hours*, a television newsmagazine that investigates crime and justice cases. There is also an Australian version of *60 Minutes* that has aired since 1979.

Programs Increase in Popularity

Competing American television networks launched their own programs in the television newsmagazine genre. Television executive at ABC News and Sports Roone Arledge (1931–2002), who created *Monday Night Football*, also created the television newsmagazine *20/20* for ABC. The first episode of *20/20* aired June 6, 1978. The program's original anchors were magazine editor Harold Hayes and magazine art critic Robert Hughes. Following poor reviews, Hayes and Hughes were dropped less than a week after the premiere. The program was shifted to a more traditional television newsmagazine format. Television veteran Hugh Downs (1921–2020) was named anchor, a position he maintained for 21 years.

One of the most famous *20/20* anchors is American broadcasting icon Barbara Walters (1929–). Walters began as a contributor in 1979, made regular contributions starting in 1981, and became the program's cohost with Downs in 1984. Downs retired in 1999, while Walters remained a cohost until 2004. Walters is known for her unique interviewing style and the ability to get interviews with celebrities, politicians, and world leaders. She was also coexecutive producer and a former cohost of the television talk show *The View*. In 2020, the coanchors of the program were David Muir (1973–) and Amy Robach (1973–). Other contributors to *20/20* include John Stossel, Chris Cuomo, John Miller, Elizabeth Vargas, Diane Sawyer, Charles Gibson, Sam Donaldson, and Connie Chung.

NBC debuted its television newsmagazine *Dateline NBC* on March 31, 1992. It is the longest-running prime-time program on NBC. The original anchors of the program were Stone Phillips (1954–) and Jane Pauley (1950–). NBC has noted that *Dateline* is the network's signature newsmagazine. Lester Holt (1959–) became the main anchor of the program in 2011. Other anchors and correspondents associated with *Dateline* are Katie Couric, Tom Brokaw, Maria Shriver, Brian Williams, Elizabeth Vargas, Andrea Canning, Josh Mankiewicz, Keith Morrison, Dennis Murphy, Willie Geist, Natalie Morales, Meredith Vieira, Kate Snow, Ann Curry, and Craig Melvin.

The *Nightline* television newsmagazine on ABC was born out of the Iran Hostage crisis that began in 1979. Anchor Ted Koppel (1940–) hosted the then titled *America Held Hostage*. The hostage crisis lasted 444 days, ending in 1981, but Koppel and the renamed *Nightline* would last much longer. The program aired in a late-night time slot, after the late local news. Koppel was a calming presence who, at the same time, asked tough questions of his guests. He retired from the program in 2005, but *Nightline* continued in a somewhat different format. Following that format change at Koppel's departure, ABC announced in 2014 that the program would incorporate a digital component to appeal to younger audiences.

A Somewhat Different Angle

CBS News Sunday Morning is a 90-minute American television newsmagazine program that has aired on CBS since January 28, 1979. It was created by Robert Northshield and the program's first host Charles Kuralt (1934–1997). Kuralt is widely known for his segment, *On the Road,* that told the interesting stories of ordinary Americans. Charles Osgood (1933–) took over for Kuralt in 1994 and was the host for 22 years. Veteran news anchor Jane Pauley took over in 2016. *CBS News Sunday Morning* is a bit different than other television newsmagazines. While the program covers daily news and weather, it also spends time on politics, pop culture, and performing arts.

Another version of the television newsmagazine is *Inside Edition*, which has aired since 1995 as a syndicated program. Since the start of the *Inside Edition*, broadcast journalist Deborah Norville (1958–) has anchored the show. The program features a mix of hard news stories, entertainment news, and lifestyle features.

While news and sports often inhabit different spaces on television and the Internet, in the genre of television newsmagazines, they do intersect in some cases. *E:60* is a sports newsmagazine broadcast by ESPN. The series features investigative journalism and feature stories about sports. *Real Sports with Bryant Gumbel* is a monthly television sports newsmagazine on the subscription-based HBO channel that debuted on April 2, 1995. The program includes investigative stories and interviews with athletes.

Television newsmagazines are not confined to national network television. *Chronicle* is an American television newsmagazine produced by New England television stations WCVB-TV in Boston, Massachusetts, and WMUR-TV in Manchester, New Hampshire. *Chronicle* premiered on WCVB on January 25, 1982, and on WMUR in September 2001. *Chronicle* offers lifestyle, cultural, and news content.

American colleges and universities also produce television newsmagazines. The Broadcast Education Association (BEA) awards the best of those programs in an annual competition called the *Festival of Media Arts*. Criteria for submissions include any television newsmagazine including special themed episodes and allowing preproduced elements. In 2020, winners included television newsmagazines from Michigan State University, the University of Florida, California State Fullerton, San Jose State, and Syracuse University.

Television newsmagazines are also produced around the world. As noted, there is an Australian version of *60 Minutes*. *Sunday Night* was another Australian television newsmagazine show that featured a mix of feature stories and investigative reports. *Sunday Night* featured a live studio audience and a live call-in question and answer segment, which were eventually discontinued. *Sunday Night* as a whole was canceled in 2019.

In Canada, the television newsmagazine *16×9* debuted in 2008 and was canceled 8 years later in 2016. *The Fifth Estate* investigative journalism program is another Canadian television newsmagazine. It airs on the national CBC television network. The program has been on the air since September 15, 1975.

In Great Britain, *The One Show* is a television newsmagazine broadcast live on the BBC. BBC One promotes the program as a live magazine program that features topical stories and big-name studio guests. *The One Show* launched in 2006. Another British television newsmagazine *Nationwide* is a former BBC program that ran from 1969 until 1983. It was replaced by the British *Sixty Minutes*, which would eventually become *BBC News at Six*.

From the beginning, the television newsmagazine format has sought to combine hard news, investigative journalism, feature stories, celebrity news and gossip, and human-interest pieces into a program hosted by charismatic news anchors who can capture the attention of the audience. As *60 Minutes* creator Don Hewitt noted years ago, television news programs can both inform and entertain the audience.

Christine C. Eschenfelder

See also ABC News; Broadcast, or Broadcasting; CBS News; NBC News; Television News, History of

Further Readings

ABC News. (n.d.). 20/20. Retrieved from https://abcnews.go.com/2020

American Archive of Public Broadcasting. (n.d.). Structuring the news: The magazine format in public media. Retrieved from https://americanarchive.org/exhibits/newsmagazines

BEA Festival of Media Arts 2020 winners. Retrieved from http://beaweb.org/festival/2020-winners/

Biography.com (2019, July). Barbara Walters biography. Retrieved from https://www.biography.com/media-figure/barbara-walters

CBS News. (2020, September 1). About Us: 60 minutes. Retrieved from https://www.cbsnews.com/60-minutes/about-us/

de Moraes, L. (1999, May 6). Host Hugh Downs to leave 20/20. *The Washington Post.* Retrieved from https://www.washingtonpost.com/archive/lifestyle/1999/05/06/host-hugh-downs-to-leave-2020/ca432d48-d528-44fe-90e5-b13632e0081d/

ESPN. (2002, December 9). Arledge brought modern innovations to TV sports. Retrieved from http://www.espn.com/classic/obit/NEWarledgeobit.html

Hewitt, D. (2001). *Tell me a story: Fifty years and 60 minutes in television.* New York, NY: Public Affairs.

NBC. (n.d.). Dateline. Retrieved from https://www.nbc.com/dateline

Ranker TV. (2020, December 29). The best news magazine TV shows. Retrieved from https://www.ranker.com/list/best-news-magazine-tv-shows/reference

Shedden, D. (2015, March). Today in media history: Edward R. Murrow investigated Joe McCarthy on "see it now." Retrieved from https://www.poynter.org/newsletters/2015/today-in-media-history-edward-r-murrow-examined-joe-mccarthys-methods-on-see-it-now/

TELEVISION NEWS, HISTORY OF

Television news keyed the vision and imagination that accompanied the invention and development of television. Through most of the history of human communication, few dreamed that everyday people would see with their own eyes the same events later told in history books. Beginning with 15-minute news briefs at television's inception in the 1940s, television news grew into an endeavor available around the clock on multitudes of platforms to billions of people wherever they lived.

While diverse in journalistic, technological, and proprietary roots, television news grew from a single breakthrough. For the first time, people were able to not merely read about and listen to but see the unfolding of news. Television's capability for not merely showing events but for enabling people to participate in them explains its permanence as a fixture in mass communication. This entry examines the evolution of television news and discusses the transformation of television newscasting, as well as the development of CNN. The entry also offers an overview of challenges in the digital age.

Origins

Television news was shaped by three developments that accompanied TV's predecessor, radio. First and foremost, radio's introduction of commercial broadcasting influenced television news. Rather than using public tax money, founders opted to defray radio by having competing proprietors raise funds through the sale and broadcast of advertising. Vying for sponsors, proprietors' profits were determined by whose programs attracted the largest audiences. While a public service, television news did not transcend requirements it operate as a business.

Second, radio's introduction of national news shaped television news. While licensed to serve local communities, the first radio stations rose as affiliates of three networks—NBC, CBS, and latecomer ABC—which thrived by delivering programs to national audiences. From broadcasting's inception, the public identified broadcast news with national news. This was a significant departure in journalism, for centuries a function of locally published newspapers that carried from radio into television.

Finally, television news inherited from radio the form for news delivery. In radio, 15-minute broadcasts initially hosted by popular newspaper columnists evolved into a format known as the *newscast*. Scheduled between blocks of entertainment programs, the radio newscast was adopted by and became the defining structure of television news. Television further inherited the newscast's signature feature: the newscaster. On television, newscasters' personas were magnified. It was common for viewers to associate television news more with its newscast "anchors" than with the news itself.

Television news further drew from one more radio age experience. Radio dramatized the impact of on-the-scenes "live" news coverage. Orson Welles's 1938 "War of the Worlds," a fictitious broadcast of a Martian invasion that captivated the public, set a direction. The providers of television news were driven to overcome technological constraints, reconfigure journalism as a live eyewitness experience, and advance on Welles's effect.

The seeds of television news were sewn 2 years after the Welles broadcast when World War II began. It was during the war when radio news first excelled that experimental television commenced. In 1941, CBS conducted tests that led to the first newscasts broadcast on television. When TV was unleashed at the war's conclusion in 1945, provisions for network news already were under way. On both CBS and NBC, nightly newscasts were among the first programs televised when network broadcasting began in 1948.

The Rise of Network TV News

At first, television did not gleam as a news-and-information source. Limited to cumbersome cameras and equipment, early TV newsrooms rarely fulfilled expectations for picture coverage of news. Viewers saw few prominent broadcast journalists. Dubious of TV's picture component and fearing it would complicate reporting, lead news personnel stayed on radio. A result was the appearance of unlikely figures as the first network news anchors. CBS's Douglas Edwards had been a weekend radio announcer. NBC's John Cameron Swayze was a pitchperson for Camel cigarettes.

The first strides in television news were not accomplished on newscasts but in weekly documentaries. Teaming with producer Fred Friendly on the CBS series *See It Now*, Edward R. Murrow established stature as the "father of broadcast journalism." Observers acclaimed his 1954 documentary exposé on Senator Joseph McCarthy.

Yet television news barely had begun before its business requirements were evident. Profiting on hours of entertainment programs, the networks rigidly limited newscasts to 15 minutes. A stunning event in 1957 demonstrated that television news would cease as a public service unless it attracted large audiences. CBS canceled Murrow's *See It Now* series because of low ratings. CBS tripled its ratings when Murrow departed and the game show *The $64,000 Challenge* was televised instead. Murrow denounced CBS for reducing an instrument for enlightenment to "wires and lights in a box."

However, when in 1956 NBC ousted Swayze also because of low ratings, a pathway for growth opened. NBC paired Chet Huntley with David Brinkley on its nightly newscast named the "Huntley-Brinkley Report." Viewers flocked to the broadcast. Its popularity not only established the nightly newscast as the cornerstone of television news; it brought a turning point in U.S. journalism. A 1959 Roper Poll showed for the first time that television informed more Americans than newspapers. Television never relinquished its distinction as the public's main source of news.

The 1960s marked the most formative decade in network television news. Eclipsed by NBC as the decade began, CBS exerted momentum upon removing Edwards and reorganizing its nightly news in 1962. The network's new news anchor, Walter Cronkite, was destined to become the individual most synonymous with the development of television news. The two networks locked as rivals in 1963 when both expanded their newscasts from 15 minutes to a half hour. Viewers saw the first news shows comprised of polished filmed reports filed by the first domestic and foreign TV correspondents.

The expansions were propelled by—and helped propel—a decade iridescent in news. Night after night, the public witnessed the unfolding of history-making events including civil rights protests, the Vietnam War, riots, youth unrest, and missions into outer space.

The 1960s were most recalled for extraordinary moments when television news joined and gripped the U.S. population. Television's so-called "finest hour" followed the November 1963 assassination of President John F. Kennedy. The networks suspended entertainment programs with 4 days of continuous news coverage. Six years later in July 1969, 93% of Americans watched Neil Armstrong's first steps on the moon. The moon landing remained a promontory in television news for having drawn the largest audience (by percent) ever to view a television broadcast.

It was during the 1970s that CBS News ascended. Upon Chet Huntley's retirement in 1970, NBC ended the *Huntley-Brinkley Report*. The *CBS Evening News with Walter Cronkite* soared in popularity. A 1976 opinion poll ranked Cronkite as the most trusted man in America. A significant innovation was CBS's Sunday hour-long investigative series *60 Minutes*. Although a news broadcast, *60 Minutes* was the decade's most widely viewed attraction on American television.

Transformation of TV Newscasting

Yet throughout the 1970s, change had swept through television news. Although television had brightened from its conversion from black-and-white to color broadcasting and from entertainment programs increasingly venturesome and lively, CBS and NBC persisted with newscasts that were sober, dispassionate, and reflective of the tenor of the Cold War. While still the embodiment of television news, Cronkite personified its staid and serious image. Many observed that Cronkite and other network newscasters delivered news in the manner of gods speaking to the public from Mt. Olympus.

Insignificant in news since 1948, ABC achieved parity with CBS and NBC after introducing a new style of news in 1978. ABC had named sports producer Roone Arledge as head of ABC News. Arledge's 1978 *ABC World News Tonight* brought to television news sprite graphics, music, and personal story lines he had pioneered on ABC's *Wide World of Sports*. Under Arledge, ABC advanced on CBS and NBC by launching a second nightly

news broadcast called *Nightline* in 1979. A year later in 1980, CBS announced Cronkite's retirement.

Yet by this time, network news no longer was the endeavor's vanguard. Enduring innovation had risen not at the network but at television's local level. Long overlooked as a center of television news, the nation's local stations had two characteristics that foretold their capability to reconfigure the TV news process. Local stations controlled airtime. By the mid-1970s, stations in major cities broadcast 2 and 3 hours of news. Second, local newscast audiences in virtually every city had grown to exceed those of ABC, CBS, and NBC. Attentive to the public's restlessness with the network's traditional style of reporting, station owners and their news directors joined in pressing a new television news.

A transformation of television news commenced in the early 1970s when local stations introduced "electronic newsgathering." While network news persisted in filming news stories, local stations rushed the first miniature video cameras. The cameras provided viewers not only pristine images of news events; they enabled live reporting from wherever news occurred. Soon, television news was distinguished by newscasts in which almost all the content, either from a studio or from remote locations, originated live and at the same moment viewers saw it.

Yet more consequential were sweeping revisions in the concept of how television news was best communicated. In contrast to the networks' single male so-called Olympian newscasters, local stations introduced friendly and conversant anchor teams, content that stressed "news you can use," the personal involvement of reporters in news stories, and, notably, female and minority newscasters. Al Primo was a foremost innovator. At KYW in Philadelphia and WABC in New York, Primo perfected the newer elements in a local broadcast called *Eyewitness News*. Its techniques became standard in all forms of newscasting. Not only did the viewing of local news soar past network news in every major TV market, but also while network news lost money, local news became television journalism's first "profit center."

Amid the waves that stirred the 1970s were criticisms of television news. Many believed that reports by CBS News on the conservative Nixon administration hastened the Watergate scandal and Nixon's demise. The dispute flared into allegations that network news was slanted with a liberal bias. The allegations were never to disappear.

Nevertheless, the most vehement complaints about television news had come from inside the news profession. The most prominent figures in the national news media rose in attacking the innovations in local TV news. Cronkite, CBS News commentator Eric Sevareid, their colleagues, and numerous authors and writers scorned *Eyewitness News* for ushering what they called *show business news*.

Concerns escalated upon revelations that local stations in nearly every city had enlisted news consultants. The spread of the first news consultancies, McHugh & Hoffman and Frank N. Magid Associates, into local TV newsrooms changed journalism. For the first time, sophisticated market research was used widely in news decision-making. Initially an innovation in newsrooms' strategies for attracting No. 1 ratings, the consultants' research soon outmoded journalism's traditional "gatekeeping" function, in which journalists decided which news to report. With research, newsrooms could pinpoint news content that viewers most preferred. Although reviled for giving the public "not what it needs but what it wants," a research-consulting process soon was entrenched throughout television news.

CNN, News Proliferation, and Doubts

The upheaval of the 1970s culminated in a signal stride: the launch of the Cable News Network by local station owner Ted Turner in June 1980. CNN was the first 24-hour television news channel. Initially, ABC, CBS, and NBC ridiculed CNN as chicken noodle news. The debut of CNN was seen only by a small number of cable television subscribers. Yet as the first news source available around the clock, CNN rose to the forefront of television news.

Turner's venture was notable for an additional triumph. Pushing satellite technology, Turner delivered CNN not only to the United States but to every other country. World leaders appeared on CNN knowing they would reach a global audience. It played a key role in the fall of communism beginning in 1989. Televised across Europe, CNN's scenes of one country's democratic revolution promoted revolution in the next. The document that finalized the breakup of the Soviet Union in 1991 was signed with a pen that Soviet leader Mikhail Gorbachev gave to Turner.

Despite major newsgathering coups and credit for fulfilling Marshall McLuhan's vision of a TV "global village," television news never escaped the clutches of television's commercial system. By the mid-1990s, news providers reeled in a marketplace turned ravenous by competition. Audiences fragmented as television proliferated into a 500-channel environment. The public's shift to the Internet, and to infinite sources of news and information, had begun. For the first time, newsrooms downsized operations and laid off personnel.

The heyday of CNN ended. In 1997, no longer able to meet the enormous costs of 24-hour news, Turner sold CNN to Time Warner. The first competition in cable news further diminished CNN. In 1998, rival MSNBC premiered. More significant was the launch of the Fox News Channel by billionaire Rupert Murdoch the year before. Fox pursued a strategy not seen since the partisan press had ushered the advent of journalism 250 years before. It augmented news reporting with programs that showcased conservative commentators. Although accused of retreating on objective reporting, the Fox News Channel quickly tripled the audience of CNN. It would remain the leading provider of 24-hour news.

Another practice for winning viewers particularly jarred observers. Cable, broadcast, and local newsrooms seized on occasions in which they could concentrate on one high-profile news event. No longer did television news promise comprehensive summaries of the day's events.

While maligned for legitimizing "tabloid" news, a landmark was the arrest and trial of football star O. J. Simpson on murder charges in 1994 and 1995. Over 16 months when little else was reported, TV news massed viewers with each day's twist in the Simpson story. Spectacle treatment of lone events, in which a minor wrinkle could be headlined as "breaking news," became commonplace. Weeks of such coverage followed the death of Princess Diana in 1997, the Bill Clinton–Monica Lewinsky scandal in 1998, and the disputed presidential election recount in 2000.

Digital Age Challenges

At a needed moment, the September 11 terrorist attacks in 2001 revived the public's trust in the wherewithal and relevance of television news. The occasion resembled the Kennedy assassination. However, because audiences now had fragmented among hundreds of channels, most believed the JFK experience never would be repeated. Yet on the night of the attacks, almost every cable channel including MTV and shopping channels canceled regular programming. Together, diverse channels simulcast news coverage that CNN, Fox, and the broadcast networks provided. Again, television news unified the nation.

However, once transforming, television news soon was upstaged by a more sweeping revolution, that which marked the public's passage into the digital age. A fad at the time of 9/11, there were as many Internet users as television users 10 years later. At first, television newsrooms foresaw the Internet for its multitude of websites that promised more competition. Newsrooms added websites and Internet channels.

Yet it was apparent that the properties of television, a point-to-mass function, differed from and were lesser than those of digital communication. The newer technology was interactive. With the advent of social media, individuals for the first time communicated not only with one another but with news providers and even newsmakers. The public increasingly turned to digital colossus Google and the social media platforms Facebook and Twitter for all types of news. By 2020, television's ongoing role as the main source of news was unclear.

While few wagered to guess the newer direction of television news, its first achievement guaranteed an endeavor certain to carry far into the future. Since the 1940s, television had dramatized people's capability for seeing, visually experiencing, and sharing the world around them.

Craig Allen

See also ABC News; CBS News; CNN; Consultants, News; Fox News; NBC News; Television Commentary; Television Newsmagazines

Further Readings

Allen, C. (2001). *News is people: The rise of local TV news and the fall of news from New York*. Ames, IA: Iowa State University Press.

Barkin, S. M. (2002). *American television news: The media marketplace and the public interest*. New York, NY: Routledge.

Bliss, E. (1991). *Now the news: The story of broadcast journalism*. New York, NY: Columbia University Press.

Conway, M. (2009). *The origins of television news in America: The visualizers of CBS in the 1940s*. New York, NY: Peter Lang.

Cronkite, W. (1997). *A reporter's life*. New York, NY: Ballantine.

Friendly, F. (1967). *Due to circumstances beyond our control*. New York, NY: Random House.

Ponce de Leon, C. L. (2016). *That's the way it is: A history of television news in America*. Chicago, IL: University of Chicago Press.

Wolk, A. (2015). *Over the top: How the Internet is (slowly but surely) changing the television industry*. New York, NY: CreateSpace.

TERRORISM, COVERAGE OF

Terrorism generally refers to violence or threatened violence by nonstate actors against civilians to achieve a political or social objective. However, it is also a form of political communication—albeit a violent, public message—since publicity, transmitted by media outlets, is in fact part of its purpose, unlike most other crimes that attempt to avoid it.

The very nature of these events makes them irresistibly newsworthy. They are significant, exciting, dramatic, controversial, and emotional, all key ingredients for major news stories. Furthermore, the perpetrators of these acts recognize their attractiveness to the media. Media coverage helps create the "propaganda of the deed," as 19th-century Italian revolutionary Carlo Pisacane put it. A number of observers of the media scene believe terrorism has a symbiotic relationship with the media and journalism. Each benefits, at least to some degree, from the other. Terrorists need publicity to communicate their violent political message to target governments and publics, inspire and possibly build followers, gain support and prestige, and help achieve their policy goals in the process. The news media in turn are provided with a subject and story that appeals to audiences and journalistic values.

This entry discusses several key issues surrounding the journalistic practices regarding these events, including: how journalists go about covering them; evaluations of that coverage; the impact of terrorism journalism on the public, the government, and the perpetrators themselves; and policy responses to these perceived effects.

How Media and Journalists Cover Terrorism

Though every case of terrorism is arguably unique, journalists appear to approach major acts of political violence in similar ways. Journalists treat these events much like other major crises. Prominent, in-depth, and even saturation coverage generally follows, sometimes driving all other news off the front pages or lead broadcasts. The September 11, 2001, terrorist attacks dominated the news for weeks after, to the extent of almost eliminating other news. Similarly, the 1998 bombings of the U.S. embassies in Kenya and Tanzania remained the top story in newspapers in the two countries struck for almost 2 weeks, replacing other stories. Scholars such as Brigitte Nacos have argued that even relatively minor terror attacks—such as the World Trade Center bombing in 1993, or the burning of various new housing developments by "eco-terrorists" in the early years of the 21st century—merit substantial coverage, due to their newsworthiness.

Terrorism journalism borrows from other reporting genres, such as those for disasters, crime, and war. Like disasters, major terror attacks create a crisis atmosphere and lead to a focus on the rescues and emergency personnel, victims, and their loved ones left behind, the damage (physical or otherwise) caused, and the healing or repair of it in the aftermath. The search for those responsible; the investigation into the meaning, planning, and execution of the attacks; and later postmortem reports such as those by blue-ribbon panels parallel quite closely the motifs of crime journalism.

If a military or police-type response from the government is launched, such as is the case after major terrorist incidents, then a combat mode of reporting is utilized, as the retaliation is chronicled and evaluated for its degree of success. The degree of adherence to these elements depends upon the nature of the violence: a hostage crisis, for example, or a lone gunman will probably be portrayed only as a crime drama. Yet, in major terror attacks, a pattern does emerge: the initial shock, horror, and disaster response followed by the investigation, the pursuit of the culprits, and a judicial or military response.

On-the-spot, observational reporting may be limited by the context of these events, especially depending upon whether reporters are directly on the scene and what access they have. News organizations' competitive desire to be first can contribute to errors, such as when multiple people were misidentified as suspects in the Boston Marathon in 2013, though the initial coverage of a terrorist attack can also play an important public safety role in alerting the community.

On the other hand, the locus of the September 11, 2001, terror attacks in New York and the Washington, DC, area were easily accessible to journalists due to the concentration of national news outlets in those two cities. Indeed, this may have been one reason why buildings such as the World Trade Center were chosen as targets. Proximity also affects the type and amount of stories and subject matter. Comparative studies of media coverage of terrorism from North America, Europe, and Africa confirm that portrayal of these events is influenced by where they take place. Terror attacks that occur in the host nation or locality of a media outlet receive different treatment than those that occur on the other side of the globe. In particular, coverage is greater, and more likely to focus on the victims and impacts on the local level. Even coverage of attacks on foreign soil often contain a local component, such as listing victims from the outlet's own town or country, or official reaction from its own leaders in addition to the nation that was struck.

While globalization of media and international journalism may theoretically mean that cases of political violence in one locale will be covered by the media of another, it is nevertheless the case that local angles continue to influence the coverage of these events.

It is also clear that terror attacks promote a "journalism of unity" that celebrates or emphasizes community values in media portrayals. Indeed, media coverage of the aftermath, the victims, and mourning can help bring the community back together and help people see the ways they are connected. Such coverage may also help shape the collective memory of the event (or person) in the future, helping to construct powerful symbols that leaders, journalists, or others may subsequently draw upon. Examples include mediated memorial services for the victims at the Murrah Federal Building in Oklahoma City in 1995, the U.S. Embassy in Nairobi, Kenya, in 1998, and New York's World Trade Center in 2001, following the terrorist attacks there.

Other factors that influence the reporting of political news in general similarly impact coverage, such as competition between political actors for control of the news agenda and tone, and the nature and interests of the society within which journalists operate. Studies of coverage of the Palestinian *intifada* uprising and cross-national comparisons of terror attacks demonstrate that cultural or ethnocentric biases color the depiction and interpretation of acts of political violence. These differences may be related to audience tastes as well: Osama bin Laden may have been covered quite differently in Western as opposed to Arab media outlets after 9/11, for example, in part because of the differing political sympathies of their respective publics.

Use of Social Media and Impact on News Media

The rise of the Internet and social media outlets has transformed terrorism and journalism, as in other areas of life. Terrorist organizations favor them because they are open, international, interactive, and mostly unregulated and employ such outlets to gather information, coordinate activities, recruit followers, raise money, and of course advertise their actions and causes. Governments likewise use them to track, monitor, and prosecute terrorists. Media organizations use them as

sources, and even auxiliary outlets, for their reports.

These new communication devices also allow terrorists greater ease at setting the media agenda through dramatic and even orchestrated events that meet newsworthiness criteria. Anwar Al-Awlaki, an imam and leader of al Qaeda in the Arabian Peninsula, used YouTube, Facebook, and online magazines to promote jihad, recruit followers, and gain media attention before he was killed by a U.S. drone strike in 2011. Brenton Tarrant, the white nationalist shooter who killed 51 people in New Zealand mosques in 2019, posted a manifesto online and sent his list of grievances to government officials and media organizations via email just prior to livestreaming his attack on Facebook. Even before social media sites could remove the video of the attack, online followers had already posted it to YouTube, plus links and posts about it to discussion sites like Reddit and 4chan, overwhelming the attempts of social media companies to block it, and ensuring further coverage of the event through traditional media.

Indeed, some terrorists even employ sophisticated high-tech public relations experts. For example, the Islamic State of Iraq and Syria (ISIS) released slickly produced, edited, and choreographed videos of brutal executions, including people being beheaded or burned, to YouTube and Twitter in 2014 and 2015. While some news organizations refused to run the footage on television, nevertheless their references to them granted them a far wider audience.

Assessing the Nature and Content of Coverage

Several evaluations of how journalists and media perform in the coverage of terrorism can be found in the literature on this topic.

Biases and Stereotypes

Although one traditional journalistic norm is "objectivity," or the straightforward reporting of facts and events, actually doing so in practice is highly problematic if not impossible, leading to claims of bias or slants in coverage. While the meaning and identification of objectivity is almost as contentious as that of terrorism itself, and media portrayals are viewed to some extent through the eye of the beholder, not some neutral standard, nevertheless some scholars have identified particular patterns or features in coverage.

One criticism is that media coverage—due to space, time, and audience interest limitations—creates a simplification bias. Daya Thussu has written that a U.S. "global war on terror" frame has dominated coverage, and the message is that terrorism is caused by irrational extremists, especially Islamic radicals, who hate the West. This emphasis, also found by other scholars, omits important topics and keeps the audience from understanding the larger, more complex social, economic, and political roots of terrorism. How widespread globally this U.S.-driven image is, however, remains in dispute.

Similarly, Fouzi Slisli (2000) argues that sensationalism and a lack of in-depth reporting in Western media leads to vague labeling of whole groups into stereotypes like "fundamentalist Muslims" or "radical clerics." Indeed, Nacos, Yaeli Bloch-Elkon, and Robert Shapiro (2011) even argue that U.S. news coverage of global terror networks and military counterterror responses focuses too much attention on international, Islamic terror threats while at the same time there has been insufficient attention in the U.S. news media on domestic, home-grown threats such as those from neo-Nazis and white nationalists.

Nacos (2016) makes the further argument that gender stereotypes and notions of "traditional" roles have impacted the image of female terrorist participants. Although women have been members and even leaders of terrorist organizations throughout history, Western media depict them as outliers in a man's world. These biases frame women differently, as duped victims, often motivated by emotion, versus the political, religious, or ideological factors that drive men.

Excessive Coverage

One critique concerns the amount and intensity of coverage. Some observers argue that media "overplay" these events, giving them far more attention than they merit. As noted earlier, even relatively minor terror attacks and failed attempts result in heavy, and prominent, coverage by the news media. The botched first attack on New York's World Trade Center (1993), the failed missile attack on an Israeli jetliner in Kenya in 2002, or the 2013 Boston Marathon bombing (three dead, hundreds wounded) all received major coverage in their countries' news media, if not also overseas. One argument made by critics of terrorism coverage is that by making political violence so prominent, journalists aid the propaganda, prestige, and psychological impact of terrorists, providing them with the public attention they desire.

Overly Sensitive to Perpetrators

A related critique charges that media coverage is too sensitive to those who commit such acts. By treating them as major news figures, sometimes on par with government leaders, the media intentionally or unintentionally grant them and their political agenda a soapbox. For example, deadly Oklahoma City bomber Timothy McVeigh was able to express his views and perspectives in interviews with CBS News and two *Buffalo News* reporters; videotaped messages by leaders of the al Qaeda terror network can be instantly become big news in media outlets across the world upon release. Still, other studies have made the case that while indeed terrorists and the like do get coverage, the tone of that coverage is rarely favorable.

Overly Sensitive to, or Pro-, Government

Others argue instead that journalists may be too "pro-government" or cede too much control to officials and dominant elite perspectives following these incidents. While those who write from this perspective do not advocate that the press give "equal time" to terrorists, they argue that journalists go to the opposite extreme and grant the government too much unquestioned authority. By relying upon official sources and responses, becoming "cheerleaders for the system," and presenting "rally 'round the flag" depictions of national unity that follow, reporters give up their neutral observer status as well as fail to perform their critical, independent watchdog function. Instead, journalists can become openly biased toward the government in power, as when, in the weeks after September 11, American television reporters wore flag lapel pins, unabashedly cheered on the United States in the war against Afghanistan, or publicly proclaimed their support for the U.S. government. This approach in turn narrows the range of ideas presented by the press, thus stifling debate and depriving the public of information that might provide valuable reflection and democratic deliberation.

Sensationalism

Another perspective—not necessarily at odds with the others—criticizes journalists for sensationalism. Journalists hype the drama, focus on (some say exploit) the victims and the "human angle" of the tragedy, thus trivializing it. In this view, the journalistic focus on blood, gore, and chaos—or personalization and conflict—comes at the expense of discussions of the larger contexts that might help the public understand terrorism and political violence.

Fear-Mongering or Playing to Audience

A related critique attacks the media for playing on or creating public fears. The excessive amount and dramatic, sensationalistic coverage noted above has the effect of exaggerating the threat of terrorism and unnecessarily heightening public anxiety. Indeed, some studies have shown that attention to crime news promotes greater anxiety. While the evidence is less clear of a similar effect with coverage of terrorism, some evidence suggests a pattern in a similar direction where those who pay greater attention to news coverage of terrorism have greater fear and are more likely to support actions by their government in response to terrorism.

Who "benefits" from this supposed media fear-mongering isn't exactly clear. Critics who see journalism as aiding terrorists and the like believe that coverage of terrorism serves perpetrators' goals of terrorizing the population and undermines security efforts. Others, such as David Altheide in *Terrorism and the Politics of Fear* (2017), argue that journalists help create a climate of fear that helps governments justify increased security measures, reductions in civil liberties, and greater power and control over society in response, all in the name of fighting terrorism and political violence. Of course, both perspectives could be right.

Copycat or Contagion Effects

Perhaps the biggest issue concerning the journalism of political violence is what impact it has on future acts. Does media coverage of political violence beget more political violence?

Critics charge that by granting terrorists publicity and status, both for themselves and their causes, journalists encourage people to engage in violence for political ends. As former British Prime Minister Margaret Thatcher put it, the media provide the "oxygen of publicity" to the fire of terrorism. Just as media coverage of mass murderers may encourage copycats, so too does coverage of these actions. Proponents of this view believe that if the news media would not cover these events—or at least, would not cover them so extensively and/or favorably—much of the incentive to engage in political violence would cease to exist.

Such an argument would seem to have merit. Terrorists clearly know that media coverage and the publicity it generates is a key component of their actions. As September 11, 2001, showed, they clearly stage events to maximize their media impact. Some studies of this so-called contagion theory have found greater incidents of terrorism in an area following heavy media coverage of terrorism. Likewise, coverage of bomb threats against schools and nuclear power plants tend to increase future threats.

In addition, media attention to perpetrators grants them celebrity status that may help them achieve their own personal or political aims. Though most criminals shun public attention to their activities, many (but not all) who engage in political violence want it. The lavish media attention to McVeigh and bin Laden, as well as Olympic and abortion-clinic bomber Eric Rudolph and "Unabomber" Ted Kaczynski, who sent mail bombs to prominent scientists and business leaders in the 1990s, turned them into household names.

Yet others think the case for "contagion" is overstated and hard to prove. Furthermore, some believe that such claims may just be an excuse used by government officials to justify more control and censorship over the media. There exists a lack of long-term and concrete studies documenting subsequent linkages. The literature on the question remains inconclusive though anecdotally powerful.

Responses:
Censorship and Reporting Codes

Given the possible impact of coverage of these events on responding to and combating political violence in the future, policy responses have been proposed and implemented to mitigate its supposed negative effects. The two main types are censorship and journalistic codes of conduct.

Some analysts and policymakers believe that the stakes are so high that government secrecy toward and censorship of the media is required. They advocate governments withholding information or mandating blackouts of terrorist incidents. At the extreme, they believe governments should actively prevent media from disseminating certain information during or after such events, known as prior restraint.

Because of the core values of free speech and press underlying journalism, formal censorship is utilized much more often in authoritarian regimes like Pakistan and China than in Western democratic nations such as the United States. It is sometimes used even in those contexts, such as the United Kingdom's ban on media broadcasts or publications of statements by figures in the Irish Republican Army and its Sinn Fein organization during "the Troubles" in Northern Ireland in the 1970s and 1980s. The Russian legislature passed legislation in 2005 forcing all media organizations to clear stories beforehand with government counterterrorism agencies, in addition to other limits on the media.

Proponents of censorship argue that there are limits to free speech, and that the lives of actual or potential victims, and safety in general, outweigh unlimited freedom of the media to publish. Opponents retort that censorship rarely works, overstates the degree to which journalists cause or influence political violence, and destroys the very freedom that democratic governments are supposed to protect. In any event, the rise of "new media" outlets such as international cable and satellite television, the Internet, interactive wireless phones, and livestreaming on social media platforms have effectively decreased the ability of many governments to control coverage of political violence, much like other topics.

Less extreme is the argument that journalists and media organizations should practice informal self-censorship and not publicize information that might hurt law enforcement efforts or help terrorist aims. For example, the major American television networks delayed, heavily edited, or even refused to broadcast some videotaped messages from bin Laden and al Qaeda at the request of the administration of President George W. Bush so as to not help the terrorist organization pass on hidden messages to its followers or grant too much attention to it. This approach only works when the media organizations are sensitive to government calls or possible public backlash against the effects of their coverage.

Along these lines, media outlets, recognizing the ramifications of their actions, have developed formal reporting codes for use during terrorist attacks, hostage situations, and the like. A number of outlets such as CBS, the BBC, and some wire services and newspapers have formal reporting guidelines for covering terrorism. These policies vary by country and news organization.

Reporting codes give journalists ethical and practical guidelines to follow when dealing with terrorist attacks, including ways to avoid undermining legitimate government security efforts. David Paletz and Laura Tawney, in their study of such policies, concluded that in general, there was a strong sense that terrorism was a newsworthy topic, but also policy preferences toward avoiding sensationalism, coupled with "the desire not to legitimate terrorism or provide a platform for terrorists . . . and to avoid coverage which might endanger hostages" (Paletz & Tawney, 1992, p. 110). However, not all media outlets develop policies with such sensitivity. A cross-national study of newspaper editors found that while some editors were aware of the potential for their organizations to be used for terrorist ends, "the division of labor between the terrorist as fear generator and the unwitting editor as fear amplifier and transmitter has not been fully perceived by all those responsible for the media" (Schmid, 1992, p. 130).

No matter how formal the reporting codes may be, however, these voluntary restraints are just that—voluntary. Training of producers, editors, and reporters in these standards and codes of conduct may be varied or spotty. News organizations, in the heat of the moment, up against competition from rivals, facing time pressures, production constraints, and the like, especially given today's global "24/7" news environment, may throw such standards out the window in practice. The perceived lack of responsibility on the part of journalists is in fact one reason why governments and even publics in democracies often favor more heavy-handed controls on media coverage.

Conclusion

Finding the proper balance in tone or amount of coverage for these types of events is difficult. Journalists seem to be in a no-win situation in covering terrorism: They face criticism for giving too much coverage, or not enough; for being too easy on the perpetrators, or being too easy (or hard) on the government; for trivializing coverage by focusing on the human angle, or being insensitive to the needs of victims; and more.

On the one hand, news organizations are criticized by governments, law enforcement officials, and some "security-sensitive" scholars and related professionals for overblowing terrorism and assassination coverage and giving undue publicity to its perpetrators. On the other, they are criticized by other observers for passivity, following the government line, uncritically celebrating community values, feeding unreasonable fears, and/or exploiting they tragedy of the victims or allowing governments to do so for political ends. Yet it is hard to argue that major terror attacks should not be "news," or that the media should ignore the victims.

The question is how journalism can play its proper democratic function of independent and enlightening critic in the face of events that fundamentally strike the body and soul of the polity. There are no obvious answers. Still, there is no doubt that given the symbiotic relationship between journalism and terrorism, this genre of reporting will continue to be prominent, and contentious, just like its subject.

Todd Schaefer

See also Censorship; Criminal Justice and Journalism; Natural Disasters, Coverage of; News as Narrative; War and Military Journalism

Further Readings

Altheide, D. L. (2017). *Terrorism and the politics of fear* (Rev. ed.). Lanham, MD: Rowman and Littlefield.

Conway, M., & McInerney, L. (2012). What's love got to do with it? Framing 'JihadJane' in the US press. *Media, War & Conflict, 5*(1), 6–21. doi: 10.1177/1750635211434373

Conway, M., & McInerney, L. (2012). Terrorism in 'old' and 'new' media. *Media, War & Conflict, 5*(1), 3–5. doi: 10.1177/1750635211434349

Macklin, G. (2019). The Christchurch Attacks: Livestream terror in the viral video age. *CTC Sentinel, 12*(6), 12–29. West Point, NY: USMA Combatting Terrorism Center.

Nacos, B. L. (2016). *Mass-mediated terrorism: The central role of the media in terrorism and counterterrorism* (3rd ed.). Lanham, MD: Rowman & Littlefield.

Nacos, B. L., Bloch-Elkon, Y., & Shapiro, R. Y. (2011). *Selling fear: Counterterrorism, the media, and public opinion.* Chicago, IL: University of Chicago Press.

Paletz, D. L., & Tawney, L. L. (1992). Broadcasting organizations' perspectives. In D. L. Paletz & A. P. Schmid (Eds.), *Terrorism and the media.* Newbury Park, CA: Sage.

Schmid, A. P. (1992). Editors' perspectives. In D. L. Paletz & A. P. Schmid (Eds.), *Terrorism and the media.* Newbury Park, CA: Sage.

Seib, P., & Janbek, D. M. (2010). *Global terrorism and new media: The post-al Qaeda generation.* London, UK: Routledge.

Slisli, F. (2000). The western media and the Algerian crisis. *Race & Class, 41*(3), 43–57. doi: 10.1177/ 0306396800413004

Weimann, G., & Winn, C. (1994). *The theater of terror: The mass media and international terrorism.* New York, NY: Longman.

Wilkinson, P. (1997). The media and terrorism: A reassessment. *Terrorism and Political Violence, 9*(2), 51–64. doi: 10.1080/09546559708427402

THEORIES OF JOURNALISM

Theories of journalism define its nature and role within the context of different societies. These normative theories do not seek to predict or interpret news media phenomena, nor do they simply describe press systems. Instead, they reflect how news media ideally *should* be structured and operated under certain political conditions and social values. Press theories provide a framework to examine the relationship of journalism and society as well as what is expected of the media according to the social environment. A basic intent of the theories is to set out ideal standards against which the performance of each news media system can be evaluated. Another important goal is to compare key aspects of journalism in different societies and categorize news media systems around the world by the essential similarities and differences. Theories of journalism, therefore, serve as guides for journalists, media critics, and scholars in the field of mass communication.

Origins

Theories of journalism derive from multiple sources. The first attempt to study in a systematic fashion the role and function of mass media within a specific social setting was the work of the Hutchins Commission in the 1940s. In response to the increasing criticisms of the American press, which appeared to be moving toward sensationalism, commercialism, and monopoly—and away from objectivity—Henry Luce, cofounder of *Time* magazine, funded an independent commission of inquiry to deflect possible government intervention. Chaired by Robert Hutchins, chancellor of the University of Chicago, the commission was charged with investigating the state of journalism and the media more generally and making recommendations concerning their role. *A Free and Responsible Press*, the commission's 1947 report, provided a framework for assessing the social responsibilities of American journalism.

Subsequent studies by media scholars compared and contrasted news media systems in different social environments. Several theories of journalism have developed since the mid-1950s. Regardless of how many typologies may be suggested, there are only a few widely accepted approaches to society news media classification. They are known as *Four Theories*, *Five Concepts*, and *Three Movements*. Other perspectives are more or less variations of these three models.

Four Theories

No framework of theorizing the relation between journalism and society has been more influential than the University of Illinois Press's all-time nonfiction best-selling book, *Four Theories of the Press*. First published in 1956, it has been widely taught in journalism courses and translated into more languages than any other media textbook. The authors, Fred S. Siebert, Theodore Peterson, and Wilbur Schramm, proposed a typology of four theoretical categories for understanding news media systems: authoritarian, libertarian, social responsibility, and Soviet communist. The proposition underlying the *Four Theories* model was that news media always reflect a country's system of social control.

Authoritarian theory is the oldest concept of journalism, appearing in England in the 16th and 17th centuries. Johannes Gutenberg's innovation of printing with movable type in the 15th century led to a communication revolution that challenged both church and state monopolies on knowledge. In response, governments severely restricted the press to maintain absolute authority. The authoritarian concept evolved from the philosophy espoused by such thinkers as Plato, Niccolo Machiavelli, Thomas Hobbes, and Georg Hegel. They all consider the individual to be subordinate to society. Possession of knowledge is the province of authorities who justify their control as a means to protect social order. In an authoritarian system, the main purpose of journalism is to support and advance government policies. News media operate with government's permission, and they are subjected to government patents, guilds, licensing, and censorship. Although private ownership is provided, news media are obligated to endorse the version of the truth supplied by the national leadership. Journalism must function for "the good of the state" and cannot challenge, criticize, or in any way undermine government's authority. The authoritarian theory of journalism flourishes wherever a "strongman" type of government exists. The concept is widespread in several regions of the world, including parts of Asia, Africa, and Latin America.

Libertarian theory of journalism took root in England and the United States in the 17th century and arose in opposition to the authoritarian doctrine. Approval of the English Bill of Rights in 1689 laid the foundation for individual liberties. The concept of a libertarian press was drawn from the writings of John Stuart Mill, John Milton, John Locke, and philosophical principles of rationalism and natural rights. Libertarianism means that humans, as rational beings, are able to distinguish between truth and falsehood. The American Bills of Rights a century later expanded libertarian principles to include freedom of the press. In the libertarian view, news media must have an independent and autonomous role to help discover truth and to place a check on government. Libertarian journalism must be free to express ideas without fear of government interference. The separation of journalism and government ensures the right of all people with economic means to have access to news media. "The self-righting process of truth" in a "free marketplace of ideas" controls the media. In other words, individuals search for truth from competing claims. The libertarian news media, for the most part, are privately owned and free to inform, criticize, entertain, and sell. However, they are barred from defamation, obscenity, indecency, and wartime sedition. Libertarian journalism tends to exist in multiparty political economies featuring free market capitalism. The news media systems in countries like Germany, France, and Japan are typical examples.

Social responsibility theory is a modification of the libertarian notion. It was born in the United States in the 1940s, when increasing monopolistic conditions and questionable practices on the part of news media led to the advocacy of more moral restrictions on their freedom. The writings of the Commission on Freedom of the Press (the Hutchins Commission), the work of practitioners, as well as various news media codes of ethics formed the basis of the social responsibility concept. This theory differs from libertarianism in seeing the chief purpose of journalism as raising conflict to the plane of discussion rather than checking government. Under the social responsibility theory, everyone with something to say has the right to use news media. A socially responsible media are controlled by community opinion, consumer action, and professional ethics. Journalists must avoid serious invasion of privacy rights and vital social interests. Although the free news media are privately owned, government can take over to ensure public service. The social responsibility theory implies recognition by journalists that they must fulfill obligations to warrant their freedom. Those responsibilities include servicing the political system by providing information, discussion, and debate on public affairs; enlightening the

public so as to make it capable of self-government; safeguarding the rights of the individual by serving as a watchdog against government; servicing the economic system, primarily in bringing together the buyers and sellers of goods and services through the medium of advertising; providing entertainment; and maintaining its own financial self-sufficiency so as to be free from the pressures of special interests. Social responsibility theory guides most journalism operating in the United States.

Soviet communist theory of journalism stands at the other end of the spectrum. It flowed from the thoughts of Marx, Lenin, and Joseph Stalin with a mixture of Hegel and 19th-century Russian thinking. This theory is based on the premise that such ideas as rationalism and individual rights to know government business are unrealistic. Therefore, journalism in the Communist model functions to transmit governmental social policy rather than to search for truth. The press operates as a collective propagandist, agitator, and organizer to support the government and thus serve the people. Communist news media are considered integral parts of the state. The Communist party apparatus controls them. Within that system, self-criticism of failure to live up to Communist planning is encouraged, but journalists cannot criticize Party objectives. The Communist concept is an offshoot of authoritarianism but differs from its roots in several aspects. The Soviet news media model disapproves of private ownership, removes the profit motive, and emphasizes media as instruments of government. After the collapse of the Soviet Union in the early 1990s, news media in North Korea and Cuba became typical examples of communist journalism in its traditional form.

Revisiting Four Theories

Ralph Lowenstein, a media scholar, revised and expanded the four theories of journalism when he added a new category based on news media ownership. Slightly different titles were given to two of the four basic concepts proposed by Siebert, Peterson, and Schramm. Authoritarian and libertarian remained the same. Soviet communist was renamed as *social authoritarian theory* to remove the negative connotations of the original term and to broaden its application. Social responsibility became *social libertarian* to avoid the ambiguity in the original term and to reflect the roots of this theory in libertarianism. *Social centrist* was the new theory of journalism that institutes government or public ownership to assure the operational spirit of libertarianism.

In an attempt to broaden the social responsibility concept into a more active role, proponents of *civic* (or *public*) *journalism* suggested that news media should engage audience members in reporting important civic issues. Journalists are encouraged to reach out to the public, to give voice to the people's agenda, and to meet the needs of various social groups. Civic journalism moves beyond the role of a detached reporter in the marketplace of ideas to the role of a fair-minded participant in public life. Although the civic journalism concept has achieved only qualified success in the United States, it has been seen as a direct response to the call for socially responsible news media with a solid commitment to community service. The American civic journalism model has also been experimented with in other countries, including New Zealand.

Five Concepts

As the world's news media adapt to changing social needs, new theories of journalism have emerged to update the basic model proposed in 1956. The *Five Concepts* typology, first introduced by media scholar William Hachten in 1981, is a major deviation from the *Four Theories* approach. Significant changes have been made to sort global journalism into five distinct theories: Western, revolutionary, developmental, authoritarian, and communist. The basic tenet of this classification is that differing perceptions about the nature and role of journalism reflect the values of sociopolitical systems and historical and cultural traditions of the nations within which it operates.

The Western concept combines elements of both libertarianism and social responsibility. The theory holds that a government should not interfere in the process of collecting and disseminating news. News media are independent of authority and exist outside government. Under the Western concept, the press has the right to report and comment on as well as criticize government without restraints. To maintain its autonomy, news media must be financially strong and profitable. Meanwhile, the privately owned press system has obligations of public service that transcend moneymaking. The Western theory is practiced in democracies with market economies that have an established traditional of independent journalism. Examples of nations meeting these criteria include Britain, Canada, Japan, and the United States.

The revolutionary concept is concerned with illegal and subversive communication, using news media to overthrow a government or wrest control from alien or rejected rulers. Historically, effective use of communication has been a part of every revolution. In the United States, for example, Thomas Paine used pamphlets to help inspire the rebellion against Britain. In his writings, Jefferson advocated and justified the people's right to revolution. The theory of revolutionary journalism stemmed from Lenin's ideas of utilizing a newspaper as a cover for a revolutionary organization. By definition, revolutionary news media are those of people who believe that the ruling government does not serve their interests. Functions of revolutionary journalism include putting an end to government monopoly on information, organizing insurgents, destroying the legitimacy of the rulers, and bringing down the alien or rejected rulers. The words of the *Pravda* in the 1917 Russian Revolution and the underground press in Nazi-occupied France were classic examples of revolutionary journalism. A contemporary case was the use of audiocassettes and photocopiers by supporters of the Ayatollah Khomeini against the Shah's regime in Iran in 1979.

The developmental concept assumes that news media can function as multipliers of efforts to promote social change. This theory is a mixture of social responsibility ideals, communist ideas, as well as resentments against the West by impoverished and media-poor nations. In its basic form, the developmental concept posits that individual rights are necessarily subordinate to the larger goals of nation building. Therefore, the central government must control all instruments of mass communication to serve national goals in economic development, political education, and eradication of illiteracy. Development journalism should support authority rather than criticize or challenge it. News media freedom can be restricted according to the development needs of the society. Since information is a scarce national resource, news media are state property and are used to further national development. Along the same line, a nation can claim a sovereign right to control both foreign journalists and the flow of news back and forth across its borders. Although the concept of development journalism was seen as an emerging pattern associated with the noncommunist nations of the developing world, it appeared to be losing momentum by the mid-1990s. Good examples of developmental media can be found in Brazil, Ghana, Honduras, and Zimbabwe, among many others.

Authoritarian and communist concepts in Hachten's classification of news media systems are similar to those of Siebert, Peterson, and Schramm in *Four Theories of the Press*. In the *Five Concepts* model, the developmental and communist theories of journalism are variations of the traditional authoritarianism. Within authoritarian societies, diversity of views is wasteful and irresponsible, while consensus is a sensible goal for journalism. Therefore, journalists generally exercise self-censorship and maintain the status quo. Therein lies a major difference between authoritarian and communist concepts. The communist news media system is planned and built the process of change. Another distinction is related to media ownership. Communist news media are state property as opposed to the privately owned press in the authoritarian model.

Revising Five Concepts

Several modifications of the *Five Concepts* typology have been postulated since the mid-1980s. Within the Western concept, media scholar Robert Picard identified democratic socialism along with social responsibility and libertarianism as coequal subcategories. The *democratic socialist theory* was drawn from a mixture of modern Marxist thoughts and the writings of classic liberal philosophers. The roles of democratic socialist journalism are to provide an avenue for expression of diverse voices and to promote democratic governance. News media are operated for the citizen's use and for the protection of the citizen's social, political, and economic rights. In a democratic socialist system, the media are instruments of the people and

public utilities rather than tools of the state or privately owned institutions. To ensure the existence of news media plurality and the ability of citizens to access them, the state can intervene in media economics and ownership. Ultimately, this theory of journalism holds that ownership would be public and not-for-profit, through foundations, nonprofit corporations, journalist-oriented groups, and other collective organizations. Democratic socialist journalism lies somewhere between the social responsibility and developmental theories.

Along the same vein, *democratic participant theory* represents an effort to expand the boundary of the *Five Concepts* to include an alternative journalism approach. Media theorist Denis McQuail emphasized the role of news media in supporting cultural pluralism at a grassroots level. Public participation and empowerment of pluralistic groups are central to democratic participant journalism. The theory contends that individual citizens and minority groups have a right to be served by news media according to their determination of need. Therefore, group members rather than the powers of state or industry can directly control the organization and content of news media. Meanwhile, democratic participant journalism systems may receive government subsidies and training to provide their own audiences with nonmainstream, local, small-scale, interactive, and participative news media forms. The democratic participant and democratic socialist concepts represent a reaction against the abuses of private media ownership as well as state control of news media. These two evolving theories of journalism emerged in 20th-century Western Europe, and they are active in Scandinavian countries.

Two other concepts of alternative journalism reflect somewhat radical theoretical perspectives on the role of news media. One is emancipatory journalism, and the other is communitarian journalism. *Emancipatory media theory* calls for a reconceptualization of development journalism by charging news media with an activist role in social change. This theory requires bottom-up reporting in forms and formats that challenge and force oppressive structures to change. By disseminating the views and priorities for development of people at the grassroots level, emancipatory journalism empowers marginalized groups and mobilizes action against unequal power. Examples of emancipatory media can be found in, among other locations, rural areas of Bolivia, Uganda, and Zambia.

Meanwhile, the concept of *communitarian journalism* emphasizes the ethical imperative of news media to engage in dialog with the public it serves. This anti-libertarian theory urges journalists to abandon the role of neutral observer in order to help construct community identity. Under the communitarian view, news should be an agent of community formation, and the goal of reporting is not intelligence but a like-minded philosophy among the public. In some respects, the communitarian concept of journalism is reactionary to "mainstream" or "dominant" news media theory. This theory does not seem to have traveled far.

Three Movements

A new approach to theorizing the operation of the media in different social settings emerged in the 1980s when scholars challenged an ideological bias underlying the libertarian–authoritarian dichotomy. According to J. Herbert Altschull, all news media systems are agents of power, and beliefs about journalism in each system are held so passionately that they are not subject to rational or critical analysis. One system's faith may be another's folly. Therefore, the operation of a news media system can only be judged against the ideal values knowable for the specific society. In devising a value-free classification, Altschull conceptualized theories of journalism as three movements of a global symphony: market, Marxist, and advancing. The three movements differ in their journalistic purposes, articles of faith, and views on news media freedom.

Market journalism is assigned with the roles of (a) seeking truth, (b) being socially responsible, (c) informing the people in a nonpolitical way, (d) serving the people impartially, (e) supporting capitalism, and (f) being a watchdog of government. In the market movement, news media should be free of outside interference to serve the public's right to know. Journalists seek to learn and present the truth and must report fairly and objectively. In the market views on news media freedom, journalists are free of all outside controls and not servile or manipulated by power. No national media policy is needed to ensure free journalism. The market movement links to the First or Western World.

Marxist journalism also seeks truth and social responsibility as defined by its own standard. Marxist media educate the people in a political way and serve them by demanding support for socialism. News media, as collective organizers, are assigned the purpose of molding views and changing behavior. In the Marxist system, journalism helps transform false consciousness and educate workers into class consciousness. News media should provide for the masses and facilitate effective change. Journalists are believed to report objectively about the realities of experience. The Marxist theory of journalism views news media as part of the government. Consequently, a national media policy is required to guarantee that journalism takes a correct form. A free journalist should report the opinions of all people, not only those of the rich. Moreover, a journalist is required to counter oppression. The Marxist movement corresponds to practice in much of the former Soviet Bloc, China, North Korea, and Cuba.

Advancing journalism is the third model of the *Three Movements* classification. The roles assigned to the advancing media can be compared to those of the Marxist movement, but with some variations. In an advancing society, the first purposes of journalism remain serving truth, being socially responsible, and educating people in a political way. However, advancing journalists serve the people, by seeking, in partnership with government, beneficial social change. In addition, news media must be instruments of peace. The advancing movement believes that news media are unifying forces that serve the interests of the people by avoiding divisive reporting. The advancing journalist is meant to be a part of two-way exchanges, not merely one-way flow of information from journalists to the masses. Proper journalism is participatory. Under the advancing theory, news media freedom is less important than the viability of the nation. A national media policy is needed to safeguard journalistic freedom. Meanwhile, free media are not much concerned with freedom of mere information. It is more important that journalists be assured freedom of conscience than that they be flooded with information. The advancing movement applies to much of the developing or Southern World.

Closely connected to the *Three Movements* are the three world perspectives outlined by journalism researchers L. John Martin and Anju Grover Chaudhary. They chose the political designations of First, Second, and Third World as the basis for classifying press systems and theorized the three perspectives from six functions of journalism: the concept of news; the social, political, and economic role of the media; the educational, persuasive, and opinion-making function; the entertainment function; press freedom; and media economics.

Conclusion

Since the mid-1950s, increasingly complex theoretical ideas have expressed what news media should do under certain social norms. Normative theories of journalism, organized from various perspectives, have supplied different criteria for evaluating and comparing news media systems. By the turn of the 21st century, the *Four Theories* model continued to exert an immense influence. Despite its oversimplified and value-laden view, the work has been widely cited in journalism and mass communication.

Changing media, political, and economic landscapes across the world have outstripped the *Four Theories*, however, as well as two later typologies—*Five Concepts* and *Three Movements*. There have been criticisms that existing theories of journalism were constrained by the ideology and historical circumstances of their inception. The concepts of communist and Marxist media, for example, have been mostly voided with the demise of communism in the Soviet Union and Eastern Europe. In the post–cold war world, a more flexible version of media theory is needed to cope with the differences between orthodox communism (as in Cuba or North Korea) and the "pragmatic market socialism" of China, Laos, or Vietnam. Along the same line, changes in media technology have made it almost impossible to match a theory of journalism and a type of society. In the era of globalization, the World Wide Web has linked people across borders, enabling them to seek, receive, and disseminate information via transnational media that are beyond state control. On the other hand, the Internet has also provided an easy means for even the smallest groups to produce their own media, thereby creating a fragmented audience—an indicator of a Balkanization of the larger society. In settings where vastly diverse news media no longer operate as one system with shared ideals and values, traditional theories of journalism may become irrelevant.

Hai Tran

See also Alternative News Media; Civic Journalism; Comparative Models of Journalism; Development Journalism; Press and Government Relations

Further Readings

Altschull, J. H. (1984). *Agents of power: The role of the news media in human affairs.* New York, NY: Longman.

Baran, S. J., & Davis, D. K. (2006). *Mass communication theory: Foundations, ferment, and future* (4th ed.). Belmont, CA: Thomson Wadsworth.

Hachten, W. A., & Scotton, J. F. (2007). *The world news prism: Global information in a satellite age* (7th ed.). Malden, MA: Blackwell.

McQuail, D. (2005). *McQuail's mass communication theory* (5th ed.). Thousand Oaks, CA: Sage.

Merrill, J. C. (1991). *Global journalism: Survey of international communication* (2nd ed.). New York, NY: Longman.

Picard, R. G. (1985). *The press and the decline of democracy: The democratic socialist response in public policy.* Westport, CT: Greenwood.

Shah, H. (1996, May). Modernization, marginalization, and emancipation: Toward a normative model of journalism and national development. *Communication Theory, 6,* 143–166.

Siebert, F. S., Peterson, T., & Schramm, W. (1956). *Four theories of the press: The authoritarian, libertarian, social responsibility, and Soviet communist concepts of what the press should be and do.* Urbana, IL: University of Illinois Press.

Stevenson, R. L. (1994). *Global communication in the twenty-first century.* New York, NY: Longman.

THOMSON

The Thomson family of Canada controls a web of media businesses, which has grown and evolved from extremely modest origins in the 1930s to become one of the world's largest news and information empires. Now in a third generation of family ownership, their media holdings include the global Reuters news agency, *The Globe and Mail* national newspaper, many U.S. publishing companies, and several online databases. The corporate form of the family's holdings has also changed over the years from Thomson Newspapers and the Thomson Organization to the International Thomson Organization to the Thomson Corporation and now to Thomson Reuters. The family's privately held Woodbridge Company owns 62% of the shares of publicly traded Thomson Reuters, one third of the Canadian Press news agency, and 100% of *The Globe and Mail*. The hereditary peerage Baron Thomson of Fleet of Northbridge in the City of Edinburgh, which is often referred to as *Lord Thomson of Fleet*, was bestowed upon company founder Roy Thomson in 1964. It passed on his death in 1976 to his son Kenneth and in 2005 to his grandson David.

Company Origins

Roy Thomson was a serial entrepreneur who went broke selling auto parts in the 1920s but late in life founded an international media empire from the humblest of beginnings as a traveling radio salesman in the 1930s. His territory was in remote northern Ontario, far from his home in Toronto, but the business college graduate showed a knack for making money from media. To sell more radios, he founded North Bay station CFCH in 1931, which shared a building with the local newspaper. When Thomson learned how profitable newspapers were, even during the Great Depression, he decided to expand into that business. He bought the *Timmins Daily Press* in 1934 for $6,000, paying $200 down and the rest as installments of $200 a month. Thomson hired Jack Kent Cooke to sell advertising in 1936. The charismatic Cooke later took over management of Thomson's growing network of radio stations before branching out into professional sports, owning the NFL Washington Redskins, NBA Los Angeles Lakers, and NHL Los Angeles Kings. Thomson focused on newspaper acquisitions and eventually built one of the largest chains in Canada and the world.

Thomson Newspapers became notorious for penny pinching, paying low salaries, doling out pencils individually, and requiring reporters to use scrap paper instead of issuing them notebooks. Its titles as a result were not known for quality. Thomson once quipped that news was what separated the ads. He owned 19 newspapers in Canada by 1953, when he bought *The Scotsman* in Edinburgh. He moved to Edinburgh and bid successfully for a commercial television license there in 1957. He famously described Scottish Television on its opening as "like having a licence to print your own money" (Crisell, 2002, p. 108). He formed the Thomson Organization in 1959 to buy the Kemsley group, which was the largest newspaper chain in Britain. It included *The Sunday Times*, firmly establishing Thomson as a leading Fleet Street mogul at age 65. He bought *The Times* in 1966 from the Astor family and merged it with *The Sunday Times* as Times Newspapers.

Thomson was a new type of newspaper owner in Britain because he focused on profit, not on politics. He once famously said: "I buy newspapers to make money, to buy more newspapers to make more money. As for editorial content, that's the stuff you separate the ads with" (Anonymous, 1965). He branched out into the travel business in 1965, founding Thomson Travel and adding UK charter airline Britannia Airways in 1971. His most lucrative investment, however, was made in the early 1970s when he joined a consortium that struck oil in the North Sea. Those profits, which soon comprised most of the Thomson Organization's income, were mostly used to buy highly profitable small-town newspapers in the United States, where by the late 1970s Thomson had built one of the country's largest chains. The newspapers were inevitably squeezed for even more profits by cost controls, staff cuts, and steep advertising rate increases. Thomson Newspapers broke a long-standing taboo in American journalism by running front-page ads, perhaps as a result of its top executives being from Britain, where the practice was common. By the time Roy Thomson died of a stroke in 1976, the company he founded owned more than 200 newspapers in Canada, the United States, and the United Kingdom. The architecturally unique Roy Thomson Hall in Toronto, which opened in 1982, is named in his memory.

The Second Generation

Thomson's son Kenneth was Canada's first billionaire as a result of the fortune he inherited, but he was as private as his father was outspoken. He seemed to share only his father's frugality, reportedly waiting until a parking meter expired before feeding it, sorting through bargain bins for his socks, and even shopping for his own groceries to compare prices. He preferred to spend his riches on his extensive art collection. One of three children, he worked his way up in the family business, apprenticing as a reporter at the company's original *Timmins Daily Press* in 1947 and then selling ads for the *Galt Daily Reporter* before serving as its general manager from 1950 to 1953. He then took over as head of Thomson Newspapers when his father moved to the United Kingdom.

He reorganized the family's holdings soon after his dad died, and by the millennium had transformed the business from news and advertising to subscription information services. He sold Scottish Television in 1977 and the following year converted the Thomson Organization into the publicly traded International Thomson Organization Limited (ITOL) based in Toronto. He outbid George Weston Limited in 1979 for the Hudson's Bay Company, acquiring 75% of the historic Canadian department store chain for $400 million. A labor dispute at Times Newspapers prompted Thomson to lock out workers and cease publishing *The Times* and *The Sunday Times* for almost a year starting in late 1978, after which the newspapers were sold to Rupert Murdoch's News International in 1981.

Thomson Newspapers became Canada's second-largest chain in 1980 when it acquired FP Publications, which owned major dailies across the country, including *The Globe and Mail*, which it soon expanded into a national daily via satellite transmission. It prompted a Royal Commission on Newspapers later that year when it closed the *Ottawa Journal* and laid off 375 workers on the same day that rival chain Southam Inc. closed its *Winnipeg Tribune*. Thomson simultaneously sold the *Vancouver Sun* to Southam, which already owned the *Vancouver Province*, creating a third new local monopoly. The chains were charged with conspiracy to reduce competition but were acquitted in 1983 after a judge ruled the transactions were instead good business sense.

The 1981 Royal Commission on Newspapers report was harshly critical of Thomson's focus on the bottom line at the expense of journalism, noting that its spending on news and editorial content was 24% below the industry average. The report recommended that the chain be broken up by selling either *The Globe and Mail* or its other Canadian newspapers. Pointedly, it did not recommend breaking up the larger Southam, which it found published higher quality journalism. It recommended legislation to limit chain ownership, but none was enacted after the Liberal government of Prime Minister Pierre Trudeau fell. Perhaps as a result of the criticism Thomson received, the company never acquired another newspaper in Canada and instead bought U.S. titles and made non-newspaper acquisitions, increasingly adding specialized book, magazine, and business publishers.

ITOL bought textbook publisher Wadsworth in 1978 and renamed it Thomson Learning in 2000. The 1980s saw the company expand into a range of publishing areas. It acquired the publishing operations of U.S. defense contractor Litton Industries in 1981, and then bought a string of publishers including Warren, Gorham & Lamont (business); Delmar (educational); Callaghan & Company (legal); Clark Boardman (legal); Ward's (automotive); Gale (educational); Sweet & Maxwell (legal); Routledge (academic); Lawyers Cooperative Publishing; American Banker and Bond Buyer; MicroMedex Healthcare Series; Macmillan Professional and Business Reference; Medstat; the Institute for Scientific Information (Web of Science); Peterson's (educational); and Jane's. ITOL merged with Thomson Newspapers in 1989 to form the U.S.-based Thomson Corporation with headquarters in Stamford, Connecticut. It gradually divested its holdings in travel, oil, department stores, and even newspapers in favor of specialized online information services. It paid $3.4 billion in 1995 for Minnesota-based West Publishing, which owned 10,000 legal databases including the widely used Westlaw. By buying dozens more database companies, the Thomson Corporation expanded into one of the world's largest financial, taxation, scientific, and medical information providers. While other publishers posted their content on the open World Wide Web for all to access for free, it focused on buying specialized subscription databases, transforming itself into what its CEO described in 2005 as a Google for high-end professional users.

The corporate transformation may have been prompted less by foresight than by falling profits. From margins in excess of 30% in the 1980s, a recession in the early 1990s dropped the company's newspaper profits into the teens. They stayed there as a result of a drop in national advertising and structural changes in retailing, which moved from department stores to big-box stores such as Walmart that advertised less. By early in the millennium, the Thomson family had sold off its entire newspaper empire, which at its height included 233 titles in North America and 151 in the United Kingdom, except for their hometown *The Globe and Mail*. As a result, it avoided a financial catastrophe when the newspaper industry collapsed during the 2008–2009 recession as most classified advertising migrated to websites.

The Globe and Mail faced new competition in 1998 when Conrad Black founded the *National Post* after taking over the Southam chain, prompting a newspaper war between Toronto's four dailies. The Thomsons partnered *The Globe and Mail* with the CTV network in 2000 to form CTVglobemedia as part of the ill-fated "convergence" experiment in cross-media ownership. It lasted a decade, after which the Thomsons dissolved the joint venture as unworkable. By the time Kenneth Thomson died of a heart attack at his office in 2006, he was the world's ninth-richest person and had turned a family business worth $500 million into one worth an estimated $29.3 billion.

The Third Generation

The ever-growing Thomson family became increasingly secretive in its third generation. Its crowning media acquisition came in 2008, when it bought a controlling interest in the historic Reuters news agency, which was one of the world's oldest and largest with more than 200 bureaus in almost 100 countries. It had been founded in 1851 by Paul Julius Reuter, who got his start by sending stock quotes from Aachen, Germany, to Brussels by carrier pigeon. He soon moved his financial information business to London and expanded worldwide via undersea cable in the late 19th century. Reuter

built a reputation for scoops, including the first European report of U.S. President Abraham Lincoln's 1865 assassination. He thus soon added news to his subscriber services. His company Reuters was acquired in the 1920s by the domestic UK news agency Press Association but was restructured in 1941 as the private Reuters Trust to resist government pressure to transmit wartime propaganda. It later expanded into radio and television news, then in 1973 began to provide foreign-exchange rates to clients via computer. Reuters began facilitating electronic transactions in 1981 and later added electronic brokerage and trading services. It was floated as the public company Reuters Group plc in 1984 and its share price rose during the late-1990s dot-com boom but fell during recessions in 2001 and 2008.

The Thomsons acquired Reuters for $17 billion in 2008, merged it with the Thomson Corporation to form publicly traded Thomson Reuters, and moved its headquarters to Toronto. The new company had combined revenues estimated at more than $13 billion, making it one of the world's largest media conglomerates. The purchase was controversial because under the Reuters Principles, no entity was allowed to own more than 15% of its shares, but this was waived due to the news agency's precarious financial situation. According to the chairman of the Reuters Founders Share Company, he received assurances that the Thomsons would vote with the trustees on anything that might infringe on Reuters Trust principles. The exemption for majority ownership by Woodbridge would only be allowed, he added, as long as it was controlled by the Thomsons. Their takeover reportedly worried Reuters journalists, who feared they might be marginalized by the company's financial data business and that their reputation for unbiased journalism could be threatened by the influence of a majority shareholder. The purchase was reviewed by antitrust regulators in the United States and the European Union, which required the divestment of some competing divisions. Thomson Reuters, which sold a controlling interest in its Financial and Risk unit in 2018 for $17 billion, made $1.49 billion in profit in 2019 on $5.9 billion in revenues, for a 25.3% profit margin. In 2010, Woodbridge took over the faltering Canadian Press news agency in a joint venture with the Torstar Corporation, publisher of the *Toronto Star,* and Power Corporation, publisher of the Montreal newspaper *La Presse.* Established in 1917 as a co-operative owned by member newspapers across the country, the Canadian Press restructured as a for-profit company to focus less on news and more on subscription information services.

The private lives of the third-generation Thomsons are closely guarded by lawyers with nondisclosure agreements, lawsuits, and prenups. Their affairs sometimes leak out into the tabloid press but are rarely reported in Canada's mainstream media. David is the current Woodbridge chairman and 3rd Baron Thomson of Fleet. Like his father, David owns an extensive art collection and started as a reporter at the *Timmins Daily Press*, later managing a Bay department store. He was listed in 2019 as the wealthiest person in Canada with a net worth estimated at $37.8 billion. His sister Taylor (née Lynne) is a former actor and aspiring filmmaker. Peter, who is deputy hairman of Woodbridge, was a photographer for the *Brampton Times* and *The Globe and Mail* but made his name as a race car driver, winning the 2005 Canadian Rally Championship.

Articles about the third-generation Thomsons that are available in print are said to be missing from newspaper databases. *The Globe and Mail* reportedly refuses to sell photographs of the family, referring inquiries to Woodbridge. Otherwise the family is reported to have a hands-off approach to the media they own, allowing professional managers to run them.

Marc Edge

See also British Newspapers; Business Magazines; Convergence; Media Conglomerates; Media Ownership; Newspaper Chains, Ownership of; North America; Reuters

Further Readings

Anonymous. (1965, November 26). The collector. *Time, 86*(22), 53.

Braddon, R. (1968). *Roy Thomson of Fleet Street.* London, UK: Fontana.

Canada. (1981). *Royal commission on newspapers.* Ottawa: Minister of Supply and Services.

Crisell, A. (2002). *An introductory history of British broadcasting* (2nd ed.). London, UK: Routledge.

Goldenberg, S. (1984). *The Thomson Empire.* Toronto, Canada: Methuen.

Kingston, A., & Köhler, N. (2006, May 8). Canada's richest family, the Thomsons, are worth $23.8 billion . . . and they're just a little bit strange. *Maclean's, 119*(19), 22–32.

Kitty, A. (2000, June). Time for a change. *Quill, 88*(5), 14–17.

Krekhovetsky, L. (2003, December 7). Sentiment is for losers. *Canadian Business, 76*(23), 104–106.

Prochnau, W. (1998, October). In Lord Thomson's realm. *American Journalism Review, 20*(8), 44–61.

Thomson, R. (1975). *After I was sixty.* London, UK: Hamish Hamilton.

TIME IN JOURNALISM

The products of journalism are narratives, typically nonfictional and informative ones. Such narratives may refer to distant or recent past occurrences, report accounts regarding live incidents or ongoing trends, and reflect on future consequences and ramifications of current events. Thus, like other narratives, or even more so, time and temporality are constituting news narratives. From the production angle, time is an element that plays an essential part in newsmaking, as pressures such as deadlines or the desire to publish first exclusive items before colleagues are affecting journalistic practices in the accelerated news cycle. From the news technology and users' perspective, time is increasingly becoming a significant factor as the number of minutes spent in news sites is a measurable matrix. Hence, the "life cycle" of news stories depends on their consumption. That is, if the public does not click and spend time consuming them, then they vanish from the news sites' homepage and become less accessible and, by so becoming, they are, de facto, irrelevant.

The Past

The past is the focus of the narration within news stories that cover recent events of the same day or the immediate past in "breaking news" and real-time updates. Nonetheless, the past is an integral part of any news story, as previous knowledge assists media consumers in transforming the news into intelligible information (e.g., if they read an item on the president, they already know about that person's history in the public sphere). Thus, even when a connection between the past and the news is not directly manifested, all news items are, by default, related to a past that provides the background and context against which current affairs unfold.

Another meaningful connection between the past and the news is related to mediated collective memory. The most evident manifestation of mediated collective memory is "anniversary journalism," when news reporting marks the anniversary of culturally significant events, and the drive behind the coverage is to commemorate events and people. In such cases, journalism has a crucial role in shaping the collective memory by concretizing a narrative of the past into a functional sociopolitical construct.

Another use of the past in the news is when the past is utilized as a point of reference to the present, analogies that treat the past as a yardstick. This practice foregrounds the role of the past in the news to contextualize recent events. In the United States, from the 1950s to the 2000s the number of "contextual stories" increased in comparison to "conventional reporting" (Fink & Schudson, 2014).

Concluding this section, a distinction can be made between different journalistic uses and gratification of the past temporal orientation. In essence, the far past and collective memory are to be used as commemoration, the medium range past as deeper explanations to contextualize the news, and reports on recent occurrences from the immediate past as the news for itself.

The Present

News is usually associated with the present as the term itself suggests the connection to fresh information added to our previous knowledge. It also reflects the notion that the news should refer to and illuminate current affairs. From a wider narratological angle, the present is the anchor for all narratives and serves as the point of reference for both journalists and news audiences: the past is evaluated in the eyes of the current perceptions, and the future is assessed based on existing understandings. The newsmaking process can be interpreted as affording more than one deictic "present": the present of the reporter while producing the item, the present of the editorial staff while processing it, the present of the material production of the item, and the open present of its consumption. In the digital age, the gap between the production and consumption of news is very short.

In many cases, because of time pressures and the need to be relevant, there is a minimal lag between the occurrence of an event, its production, and its consumption. Moreover, different media exhibit varied relationships to this immediacy of news production and consumption. Within news narratives identify two primary forms of "present" can be identified. One is the "restricted present" which encompasses occurrences taking place during the report such as live events, both unexpected ("breaking news") for the journalists that the media covers as they unfold, or expected events, those that journalists are prepared to cover, such as media events. This form of the present has distinct temporal and spatial boundaries. The other kind of present is the "extended present," which refers to processes that started in the past, are currently evolving, and continue into the future (e.g., climate change). Research showed that event-centered reporting had declined in U.S. newspapers during the 20th century, as evidenced by an increasing number of references to the past and future in news stories.

The Future

A significant amount of news items assess the implications of ongoing trends and discuss the expectations of planned occurrences. Although newsmaking is not usually associated with covering the forthcomings, the discourse of the future has always been part of journalism. This phenomenon is mutual to all news platforms. Nevertheless, as digital media assumes the role of reporting immediately on breaking events and the recent past, the printed press becomes more inclined to an analysis of future implications. Thus, future temporal orientation is more evident in the printed media.

The discourse of the future is varied. On one extreme there are reports of the future at the most trivial and everyday level (e.g., weather forecasts) while on the other extreme, there are apocalyptical visions whose actualization would have the direst consequences (headlines such as "The epidemic is going to get out of control"). In between these extremes, there are varying levels of speculation (e.g., "the foreign minister will meet with the American ambassador today" or "budget cuts are expected after the election"). Those levels of speculation connote the degree of epistemic modality (i.e., the level of certainty or evidence the speakers have for the proposition expressed by the utterance). They are derived from the scope of time involved (short, medium, or long term, or an undetermined future) and the sources on which journalists base their stories: official announcements regarding scheduled events, the journalists' own assessments and interpretations based on similar past cases, and the sources themselves— parties of interest such as media advisors, politicians, and the military as quoted in the text. In response to the attacks of September 11, 2001, socially networked United States and global media worked to premediate collective effects of anticipation and connectivity, while also perpetuating low levels of apprehension or fear. Moreover, the news media may serve as agents of prospective memory insofar as they set the social "to-do list" by linking interpretations of the past to future-oriented tasks. Other studies of future-oriented news have pointed to its narratological qualities, including strategies of precontextualization, discursive manipulations of temporalities in reports of future events, and the creation of future-oriented suspense.

Journalism and Temporal Affordances

To evaluate the relationship between journalistic practices, temporal narratives, and news technologies, we can use the concept of "temporal affordances," which is defined as "the potential ways in which the time-related possibilities and constraints associated with the material conditions and technological aspects of news production are manifested in the temporal characteristics of news narratives" (Tenenboim-Weinblatt & Neiger, 2018, p. 39). Among such affordances are *immediacy* (to report on recent newsworthy events in close proximity to their occurrence; not prevalent in print stories), *liveness* (to report events simultaneously with their occurrence; more associated with TV news), *preparation time* (amount of time journalists can invest in developing a news story; shorter on digital outlets); *transience* (i.e., digital stories allows for incremental narratives and therefore gradual temporal layering) vs. *fixation in time* (the story as it is told in the print version of newspapers is thus a relatively fixed record); and *extended retrievability* (enables journalists to access, retrieve, and utilize previous item and big data in order to construct news narratives; e.g., hyperlinks within an item).

Thus, combining the different manifestations of time mentioned herein, from a temporal-functional perspective, news can be conceptualized as narratives "that provide: (a) accounts and updates regarding present states-of-affairs and/or unfolding events, (b) reports on recent occurrences, (c) deeper context and/or commemoration of a more distant past, (d) analysis of possible implications of current events and/or anticipation of upcoming events, and (e) projections that envision and address the far or conjectured future" (Neiger & Tenenboim-Weinblatt, 2016, pp. 155–156).

Motti Neiger

See also Liveblogging; Livestreaming; Longform Journalism; Simulcasting

Further Readings

Barnhurst. K. G. (2011). The problem of modern time in American journalism. *KronoScope, 11*(1-2), 98–123. doi:10.1163/156852411x595297

Barnhurst, K.G., & Mutz, D.C. (1997). American journalism and the decline in event-centered reporting. *Journal of Communication, 47*(4), 27–53. doi:10.1111/j.1460-2466.1997.tb02724.x

Bødker, H. (2016). The time(s) of news websites. In B. Franklin & S. Eldridge (Eds.), *The Routledge companion to digital journalism studies* (pp. 55–63). London, UK: Routledge. doi:10.4324/9781315713793-6

Fink, K., & Schudson, M. (2014). The rise of contextual journalism, 1950s–2000s. *Journalism, 15*(1), 3–20. doi:10.1177/1464884913479015

Marriott, S. (2007). *Live television: Time, space and the broadcast event.* London, UK: SAGE.

Neiger, M., (2007). Media oracles: The political import and cultural significance of news referring to the future. *Journalism: Theory, Practice & Criticism, 8*(3), 326–338. doi:10.1177/1464884907076464

Neiger, M., & Tenenboim-Weinblatt, K. (2016). Understanding journalism through a nuanced deconstruction of temporal layers in news narratives. *Journal of Communication, 66*(1), 139–160. doi:10.1111/jcom.12202

Reich, Z., & Godler, Y. (2014). A time of uncertainty: The effects of reporters' time schedule on their work. *Journalism Studies, 15*(5), 607–618. doi:10.1080/1461670x.2014.882484

Schudson, M. (1986). When: Deadlines, datelines, and history. In R. K. Manoff & M. Schudson (Eds.), *Reading the news* (pp. 79–108). New York, NY: Pantheon Books.

Tenenboim-Weinblatt, K., & Neiger, M. (2018). Temporal affordances in the news. *Journalism, 19*(1), 37–55. doi:10.1080/1461670x.2014.882484

Tenenboim-Weinblatt, K., & Neiger, M. (2015). Print is future, online is past: Cross-media analysis of temporal orientations in the news. *Communication Research, 42*(8), 1047–1067. doi:10.1177/0093650214558260

Zelizer, B, (2014). Memory as foreground, journalism as background. In B. Zelizer & K. Tenneboim-Weinblatt (Eds.), *Journalism and memory* (pp. 32–49). London, UK: Palgrave Macmillan. doi:10.1057/9781137263940_3

Trade Magazines

Trade publications have long offered specialized information to readers working in a specific trade, industry, or business sector. Their scope ranges from local and regional titles such as *Chicago Construction News* (though many of these are now zoned editions of larger operations) to international publications such as *Lloyd's List*, offering daily coverage of the global shipping trade. They are also sometimes referred to as *business-to-business* or *specialized business publications*. While originally issued in newspaper or magazine format, the trade press has expanded to include newsletters (now primarily digital), directories, industry surveys, and special reports. Publishers have built on their print brands to offer specialized industry-relevant information through a wide range of platforms including conferences, trade shows, webinars, awards programs, web portals, and e-newsletters.

Nearly every business field and profession is served by a trade publication, ranging from the *American Machinist* to *Hospitals & Health Networks* to *Wood Bioenergy*. These publications survive because they have made themselves indispensable to those working in the particular industry or profession they serve, providing targeted news and analysis of new products, business trends, government policy, and leaders in the industry. This entry discusses the purpose of trade publications, their historical evolution, changes to their distribution model, and recent trends in the sector.

Actionable Information

The number of trade publications is quite substantial, and despite not being available on newsstands many have circulations that rival specialized consumer magazines. Many publishers have developed strong presences in particular industries or sectors, offering a variety of publications serving different niches within them. Trade publications perform at least two major functions: delivering advertisements to decision makers in the targeted business sector, and providing specialized information those readers need to develop their businesses or further their careers. There is a fairly tight connection between the two, as nearly all of the advertising is business-to-business. In addition to advertising and other promotional services, trade publications earn revenue from selling marketing research and other industry-specific data, subscriptions and sales, and from conferences, seminars, and trade shows.

While their financial structure and delivery systems have shifted substantially over the years, trade publications continue to play a vital role in facilitating the flow of industry-specific information and perspectives both within those industries and to larger audiences including government regulators and through the business press. Yet there has been little scholarly analysis of the trade press, though it is sometimes considered as part of the study of magazines more generally. (Magazines dominated the field until recently—in large part because of their advantages as an advertising medium.)

The boundaries between trade and professional publications can be porous. There is also significant overlap with association publications in some fields. The American Booksellers Association's *American Bookseller* competed with commercially published trade magazines such as *Publishers Weekly* until 1998 (though the association's newsletter, *Bookselling this Week,* continued and is now distributed digitally). *Publishers Weekly* has gone full circle; launched in 1872 by a bibliographer, it was owned for several years by R.R. Bowker (publisher of Books in Print) until being sold to Xerox and then to Reed International (later merging with the Netherlands-based specialized publishing giant Elsevier, forming what became RELX), which sold it to former publisher George Slowik Jr. in 2010. (RELX publishes some 2,500 professional and scholarly periodicals, but sold its North American trade publications between 2009 and 2014. Reed maintained ownership of the annual American BookExpo trade show, which it bought from the Booksellers Association in 1995.) Since purchasing *Publishers Weekly,* Slowik has added email newsletters, podcasts, and an international book rights database to the weekly magazine.

Historical Evolution

Aside from a few studies finding that trade publications are an effective advertising medium, most scholarly research on the field has been historical in nature, often drawing upon trade publications as a vehicle for assessing the industry or market they cover. There has been much work on the agricultural press, relating the proliferation of titles to westward expansion (and hence new soil and weather conditions) and modernization, as individual holdings gave way to commercial agriculture. Early farm papers such as the *Agricultural Museum* offered an opportunity for farmers to share knowledge and first-hand experience, as well as develop a common

voice on issues such as railroad regulation. Later years saw the emergence of corporate publishers, increased specialization, and an emphasis on changing markets and economic conditions.

Professional journals serve the needs of their readers, but also document changing norms and practices in the industries they serve. *Nursing* magazine, for example, reflects the changing demographics of the profession, as well as the new challenges nurses face. (The magazine's ownership similarly reflects changes in the industry, from its 1971 launch by two medical editors to its current status as part of the Wolters Kluwer international stable of professional magazines and journals.)

While most trade magazines were issued on a weekly or monthly basis, there have been several daily trade newspapers as well, many of which continue as online publications. Like other major cities, Chicago hosted trade and professional dailies including the *National Hotel Reporter* (1872–1935, weekly in its last 3 years) and *Drovers Journal* (1873 to 1960, merging with the *Kansas City Drovers Telegram* in 1913 and continued as the monthly *Drovers* magazine by Farm Journal Media, which issues several online newsletters, the Agweb.com website, and print magazines serving different agricultural sectors).

Other daily trade newspapers included *Variety, Oil Daily,* and the venerable *Lloyd's List and Shipping Gazette,* founded in 1734. Lloyd's ceased printing its daily newspaper in December 2013, transitioning to all-digital publication, but launched a monthly print magazine in 2015 featuring longer-form analytical articles.

American Machinist exemplifies the evolution from occupational to trade magazine. Founded in 1877 as a weekly newspaper serving working machinists, it slowly evolved into a glossy monthly magazine aimed at engineers and managers employed in manufacturing and machine shops. Its editors were originally working machinists, as were most of its contributors, but they were gradually replaced by writers with a background in industrial engineering. In the 1960s, *American Machinist* moved from paid subscriptions and single copy newsstand sales to controlled circulation. In 2013, it shifted to online publication, offering a website, weekly email newsletters, webinars, and trade shows held in conjunction with other titles in Informa's manufacturing cluster.

Controlled Circulation

While trade publications originally circulated primarily through paid subscriptions, controlled circulation—providing the publication free of charge to individuals qualified by occupation or employer—is now the dominant distribution system for trade magazines and their Internet-based progeny. These publications are supported by advertising and sponsored content, and for fees for ancillary services including trade shows, webinars, and special reports.

However, many titles—particularly newsletters and dailies—continue to charge substantial subscription fees, even as they shift to digital platforms. *Beer Marketer's Insights,* for example, long known for the distinctive orange paper it was printed upon as well as its detailed coverage of the beer distribution industry, charges several hundred dollars to subscribe to its fortnightly newsletter, now distributed by email. As the beer business evolved and new technology facilitated the rapid dissemination of actionable news to subscribers, BMI launched several specialized titles: it also issues *Insights Express* 120 times a year, the semiweekly *Craft Beer News,* a newsletter on alcohol policy issues, and a newsletter on nonalcoholic beverages that might supplement beer distributors' lines—alongside an annual industry handbook, special reports, webinars, and conferences.

Many trade magazines have also resisted controlled circulation. Crain Communications's flagship *Ad Age* (the company also publishes city business newspapers and trade magazines for auto dealers and health care executives, among other titles) has been sold by subscription since it was founded in 1930, relying on solid news coverage, investigative reporting, and informative columns to persuade advertisers and media organizations alike that it is indispensable.

A Vibrant, Global Publishing Sector

While the circulation of most individual titles is relatively modest, collectively trade publications make up a large portion of the magazine industry, in the United States and around the world, and reach a highly desirable audience of influential industry executives and government policymakers. But given the proliferation of web-based publications, digital newsletters, and print titles it is difficult to reliably estimate either the number of trade publications or their combined circulation.

There has been a convergence of sorts in the trade press in recent years, exemplified by the recent convergence of three professional associations. Between 2012 and 2017, American Business Media (bringing together editors and publishers of trade newspapers and magazines), the Society of National Association Publications, and the Newsletter Publishers Association (which had renamed itself the Specialized Information Publishers Association a few years earlier) all joined the Software & Information Industry Association. Between them they include hundreds of companies and associations issuing thousands of print and online publications serving nearly every trade and industry.

Trade journalism is also an international phenomenon. While many titles are stand-alone publications or issued by small firms with a handful of titles, transnational media conglomerates have long held a dominant share of the trade press. These firms typically own several titles in related fields, closing or selling off titles that do not complement their portfolio. The resulting clusters facilitate the development of industry databases and other resources that can be shared across several titles. For example, Haymarket Media Group, the British publishing house that owns *PRWeek* (and conferences and digital newsletters serving United Kingdom, United States, Asian, and Middle Eastern markets), operates clusters of automotive, horticultural, marketing, and medical trade magazines, websites, and conferences.

Similarly, in 1998, Lloyds of London Press merged with International Business Communications Group, which issued financial publications and organized professional conferences, to form Informa. The company grew quickly, acquiring academic publisher Taylor & Francis, trade magazine conglomerate Penton, and other publishers of aviation, energy, finance, life sciences, and telecommunications newsletters and magazines. Today Informa has major holdings in Asia, Australia, Europe, and the United States, with some 1,500 print and online publications in media, transport, finance, commodities, law, and biomedical clusters. It also sponsors conferences and trade shows, and operates data and intelligence services drawing upon its global network of reporters and publications.

The trade press reflects trends in the broader economy. New business sectors give birth to new trade publications, even as legacy publications migrate to digital platforms and more interactive models. As industry becomes more complex and products more specialized, new publications emerge (often spun off from existing ones) to serve the new needs. Digital platforms have also facilitated the development of regional editions. Regardless of medium, trade publications provide essential information to their specialized readers and a highly efficient marketing mechanism for businesses. As a result, trade publications are well positioned to thrive in an otherwise challenging media environment.

Jon Bekken

See also Advertising; Business Journalism; Marketing; Media Conglomerates; New Media; Public Relations

Further Readings

Edwards, L., & Pieczka, M. (2013). Public relations and 'its' media: Exploring the role of trade media in the enactment of public relations' professional project. *Public Relations Inquiry, 2*(1), 5–25. doi:10.1177/2046147X12464204

Endres, K. (1995). Research review: The specialized business press. In D. Abrahamson (Ed.), *The American magazine: Research perspectives and prospects* (pp. 72–83). Ames, IA: The Iowa State University Press.

Endres, K. (Ed.). (1994). *Trade, industrial, and professional periodicals of the United States.* Westport, CT: Greenwood Press.

Hollifield, C. (1997). The specialized business press and industry-related political communication: A comparative study. *Journalism & Mass Communication Quarterly, 74*(4), 757–772. doi:10.1177/107769909707400407

Mott, F. (1938). *A history of American magazines* (3 volumes). Cambridge, MA: Harvard University Press.

TRANSPARENCY

Transparency in journalism implies that journalists make practices, processes, and sources open to public scrutiny. In journalism studies, it is considered an ethical principle and norm.

As a concept, transparency means a commitment to openness by individuals, institutions, and organizations. In public administration and governance, transparency is deployed as a counteracting measure against forms of institutional and organizational opacity and secrecy. However, as an organizational principle it can be understood as entailing *active disclosure,* meaning that beyond openness, the public is given the means and opportunity as well as the motivation to seek the truth. Scholars, such as Lars Thøger Christensen and George Cheney, consider that transparency practices signify the willingness of institutions to allow for public scrutiny and participation in oversight.

However, in journalism studies, the definition of transparency is fluid and proves challenging for journalists and news organizations. Some scholars have pointed to difficulties in putting transparency into practice. Oftentimes it is not clear what has to be made transparent—whether it is the motives of journalists or news processes—and how this should be done in order for journalism to fulfil its role in society.

Mark Deuze (2005) defines transparency as "increasing ways in which people both inside and external to journalism are given a chance to monitor, check, criticize and even intervene in the journalistic process" (p. 455). The definition implies that journalists and news media organizations undertake deliberate actions—such as declaring potential conflict of interests in news—to enable the public to inspect the news content and its production. Through transparency, journalists commit to be forthright about their intentions or interests to gain trust among audiences. While transparency does not necessarily promise change of journalistic behavior, it could serve as a bulwark against inaccuracies and false news. Scholars, however, doubt whether media organizations and journalists go to great enough lengths to make their practices, processes, and sources accessible, considering frequent criticisms over the faults and failures of journalism.

Transparency for Whom and About What?

Digital technologies have given more control to the public to scrutinize journalism, thus paving the way for a monitorial tradition of journalistic practices. Comments sections on digital news platforms, for example, provide audiences spaces to engage with journalists and interrogate the news. Many journalists of legacy news media organizations have responded through more accessibility to their audiences and the public. For example, on news pages online, some journalists have links to their social networks sites such as Facebook and Twitter, or their own blogs where they share contacts, details about their news context or programs, and their analysis and personal opinions, while inviting audiences to share sources, tips, or views about their content. On their part, citizen journalists through blogs, for example, have torn the curtain of traditional journalism by interpreting and sharing news or exposing biases and sources of legacy news media.

Emergence of the Norm of Transparency

Traditional journalism has tarnished its image in the eyes of the public through hidden practices and processes as well as anonymized sources. In the predigital age, one of the common practices that marked opaqueness of journalism was ghostwriting, whereby journalists wrote articles but celebrities or other popular individuals were credited as the writer. (Ghostwriting appears in forms such as speechwriting, opinion columns, or even through celebrity tweets.) Ghostwriters are used for a variety of reasons, including to make up for persons who may be inexperienced writers. In the 19th and 20th centuries, publishers and journalists accepted ghostwriting as a way to make publications popular through the use of names of celebrities in the bylines. In the American Jazz Age of the 1920s, these ghostwriting practices blurred the lines between public relations and journalism, according to John Carvalho and colleagues. Ghostwriting returned in the digital age in the form of journalists writing articles for blog posts of professional sports players. Critics consider ghostwriting as unethical, a form of deception and an impediment toward truth-telling, especially when it involves the news.

In the 20th century, news organizations provided audiences with platforms such as letters to the editors, correction boxes, and bylines to access and engage journalists. In the early 2000s, media

critics and scholars acknowledged that digital technologies had brought the "fortress" of journalism down by exposing newsroom and journalistic practices. During this period, transparency became such a buzzword that even scholars argued that as a norm it had become the "new objectivity." One sign that transparency had gained currency as a professional norm was when one of the largest professional bodies in the United States added the concept into its code of ethics. In 2014, the Society of Professional Journalists readjusted its fourth principle as follows: "Be accountable and transparent." Previously, it was simply, "Be accountable."

Social networks enhanced audiences' collaborative input to the production of news, for example, through the sharing of images, video, and text from scenes of accidents, disasters, or violent attacks, as it were for the 2005 London bombings. The integration of such user-generated content into news content and processes meant that newsrooms were openly inviting audiences to participate in journalistic production. Yet it also meant an increasing need for verification of audiences' content and a matching transparency in news processes and sourcing. News practices that became common included hyperlinking of news sources.

Initially, digital technologies opened up more possibilities for the practices of transparency through increasing platforms and actors engaged in public scrutiny. Tasks that used to be performed in hidden, such as sourcing, were brought to the public's attention through various digital technologies. For example, the use of hyperlinks meant the public could find out original sources used in news stories (e.g., government audit reports or further references to a scientific study). Sharing links meant audiences could verify for themselves the authenticity of the facts in the news. A commitment to transparency meant journalists deliberately provided access to the data they gathered for a story (e.g., full recordings of a news interview or transcripts). Today, many news organizations reinforce their commitment to transparency, especially in periods when the news they publish attracts public interest. In 2017, for example, *Frontline* (the investigative series of the American public broadcaster, PBS) published online its interviews with sources for a two-part documentary titled "The Putin Files." "The Putin Files" was an exposé into allegations that Russian President Vladimir Putin attempted to interfere with the U.S. elections in 2016.

Media critics and scholars consider transparency as weak when the news media fail to fully expose processes, editorial decisions, and practices in news production to the public. With digital technologies, an information overload to journalists and audiences hampers any processes toward complete scrutiny of journalism. At the same time, as a journalistic ideal, transparency fails when it does not transform the public's ability to interrogate journalism. There is a "double-sidedness" of transparency, according to Christensen and Cheney, when action toward openness generates light into institutional activities, but at the same time hides information necessary for the public to fully participate in the practice. Transparency's generation of darkness breeds the need for more information rather than insight into the actual faults and failures of journalism.

Transparency, Accountability, Credibility, and Trust

In their seminal practitioners' treatise, *The Elements of Journalism: What Newspeople Should Know and the Public Should*, Bill Kovach and Tom Rosenstiel (2001) consider transparency as a journalists' commitment, not only to truth-telling, but to being "truth presenters" (p. 289). The authors consider the "Rule of Transparency" as critical in reinforcing verification practices within the newsrooms by ensuring the audience is adequately informed about news processes. Audiences should therefore be empowered to interrogate the validity of the news as well as question journalists' biases and commitment to ethics and norms. However, scholars show that between journalists and audiences there is convergence of perspectives when it comes to truth-telling news practice, but not so in regard to the norm of transparency. Similarly, journalists do not rank transparency high in the scale of values, neither do audiences see it as central in news practice. Despite its low regard in journalism, transparency has become a value increasingly embraced because of the rise of digital technologies.

Journalists have instrumentalized transparency for the purpose of reducing delegitimizing discourses (public criticisms), which are detrimental to the authority of journalism as a profession. Legitimacy through transparency can be viewed in two ways: As a norm, transparency bequeaths the profession with authority; as through transparency, journalism earns approval or respect from its audience. According to Gaye Tuchman, transparency, as part of journalistic routines, brings order and predictability to the profession. Therefore, routines legitimize news practices and thus reinforce the authority of journalism.

In a democratic dispensation, scholars argue that individuals and institutions aspiring for good governance would consider transparency and accountability as inseparable. As such, there has been a contestation among media stakeholders whether accountability and transparency could replace each other. Accountability are practices through which the public keeps those in power in check. Scholars consider transparency practices to inadvertently promote accountability. The media is transparent when it embraces instruments meant to throw light onto its operations such as online profiles of journalists and active newsroom blogs, but at the same accountable because it makes journalistic actors accessible to answer to the public for their actions or inactions. When journalists engage with the public through digital platforms, they promote answerability—a form of media accountability that promotes deliberation between the public and the news media.

Transparency instruments are considered as important in journalism practice and a reinforcement to media accountability, especially in building credibility and trust of the news media, concepts that describes how well the public believe the news as a product of news organizations and journalistic practice. Transparency is about how to manage the way the public perceives journalism and thus the credibility and trust of the news media. There is a possibility that when the news media pays attention to their trust and credibility, they inadvertently make themselves open to public scrutiny and heed to the concerns of their audiences. The openness in which journalism is performed is critical among the public while essential in building and maintaining credibility and trust. Patrick Lee Plaisance noted that through transparent practices, news media and journalists also seek to reduce risks of trade (i.e., criticisms from the public and subsequently loss of credibility and trust by audiences).

However, more recent studies express doubts whether the presence or the absence of transparency instruments such as bylines and links to personal social media pages make journalists appear credible and trustworthy in the eyes of the audiences. Some transparency tools even go toward hurting the credibility of journalists, for example, when they express their political opinions via their personal Twitter accounts. In using a variety of digital platforms like Twitter, while offering themselves as transparent, journalists compromise on the journalistic norm of objectivity. While journalists need to connect with their audiences through self-representation and self-branding (thus subscribing to a form of transparency called *disclosure* as will be seen in the next section), they in the process compromise on journalistic objectivity.

Furthermore, research shows that even when the news media have made deliberate attempts to foster transparency—for example, through letters to the editors, correction boxes, or ombudsman's columns—there is little engagement between audiences and journalists. Some scholars have shown that more revealing transparency practices in digital news, such as footnotes in a story, attract more credibility among audiences.

As mentioned earlier, transparency ushers in practices to scrutinize journalistic processes. Thus, oftentimes trust and accountability are placed side by side with transparency through the argument that acts of openness in news practices can foster trust and improve the public outlook toward accountability of the media. With increasing disinformation in the digital spaces in the 2010s, scholars doubt that transparency can increase public trust in legacy news media. Onora O'Neill (2002) wrote that transparency "certainly destroys secrecy: but it may not limit the deception and deliberate misinformation that undermine relations of trust" (p. 70). O'Neill argued that instead of the focus on secrecy, the attention could be placed on "deception and lies" if the media are to regain trust. In curtailing unethical behaviors, transparency may fail as it is a preemptive practice (making journalists proactivily share information), but it could spur more secrecy.

Transparency in the Digital Age

Through the digitalization of journalism, there has been increased focus on the possibilities to provide a more transparent mode of journalism. A relevant enquiry in this context is to find out what journalists and news media actually *do* when they offer a transparent journalism and how this is evident for other journalists, legislators, and, not least, the general news-consuming public. What precisely are the everyday practices of journalists when they are being transparent? Because if transparency is supposed to achieve the functions discussed earlier, then it must

1. be performed at a regular basis,
2. be in a recognizable form, and
3. be open to evaluation.

Commonly used distinctions to separate different forms of transparency tools or techniques utilized by news media and journalists, as presented by Michael Karlsson, are disclosure transparency, participatory transparency, and ambient transparency.

Disclosure transparency refers to the way in which news producers explain and are open about how news stories are gathered, selected, and processed. This can be, for instance, the explanation of how and why a news story is published at all or framed in a particular way; forthrightness about errors being made, why they were being made, how they were adjusted and what measures that have been taken to prevent recurrence; or providing time stamps, make previous published versions of a news story, and in other ways highlight the draft character of online publishing. The distinctive features of disclosure transparency tools are that they are initiated by and in the hands of journalists and concerns the content of news stories.

Participatory transparency is openness whereby audiences are invited to and included in the various stages of news production. This can involve members of the audience sending in information (e.g., pictures, cell phone videos) that is incorporated in the news stories; commentary fields where the news story can be critiqued, thus shaping the framing and understanding of it, and revised; or instances where (portions of) a digital platform (e.g., website or channel) is open for citizens to provide their own reporting without necessarily being edited by professional journalists.

Finally, *ambient transparency* refers to techniques or tools that are used by news producers in the vicinity of news stories making it possible for news consumers to evaluate and form new meanings of news stories, through the association of content with the provided context. This, for example, can be hyperlinks that might be about an old news story or another topic but still shape the understanding of the original news story; the personal opinions and preferences of the journalists who put together the news story that does not change the content of the story itself but might influence the interpretation; or graphical markers indicating whether the story is an actual news story or a piece of advertising. Ambient transparency is distinct from the two other forms as it adds information around the edges of the news story (but does not explain or change the content directly) and disregards contributions from the public within the frame of the news story.

In general, the public are more positive toward disclosure transparency, thus indicating that this would be the most effective technique. However, although more research is needed, there are also studies that suggest that those with low trust in news media are generally negative toward journalistic transparency too, thus limiting its usefulness to restore lost credibility in the news.

Another issue that the later phase of digitalization has brought is the role of algorithms in journalism, again actualizing the concern of *what* it is that should be transparent to *whom*. Algorithms are essentially software that in various ways complement or replace journalists entirely in the gathering, selection, processing, distribution, and commenting of journalistic content and, thus, affecting it in the process. Research has, for example, shown that algorithms can be used to sort and analyze large amounts of data helping journalists find interesting patterns; identify trends on social media or search terms and make recommendations of what to publish; rank and curate user comments; pinpoint and target audiences based on geographical location, previous clicking patterns and predict what kind of news a specific target group (or even person) would prefer next;

and, perhaps the most prolific and debated function, write and publish news stories completely by themselves without human intervention.

The perhaps most startling consequence of journalism's algorithmization is that a potentially large part of news production becomes opaque even to journalists themselves. This is because algorithms are lines of codes in a computer program that are designed to produce a particular output and that code is most probably neither written nor understood by journalists or their managers. If transparency in journalism is about active disclosure, that the public, journalists, scholars, and other stakeholders have an opportunity to screen, criticize, and intervene in the journalistic process, then algorithms provide a real challenge. The persons, programmers, and designers best suited to explain how the algorithm works are most likely not journalists. They are probably not involved in the daily decisions that the algorithms make, or even employed by the news companies that use the algorithms. This means that there are several degrees of separation between the news output and the people as well as factors that are best positioned to explain the design, assumptions, rules, logics, bias, values, and ideologies behind that output. The issue becomes additionally complicated when machine-based learning is factored in. Machine-based learning is, for example, when an algorithm is making decisions or predictions without being supervised or explicitly programmed for them. It has some degree of independence, although it must be stressed that it is within a walled garden where human programing is foundational and the sample (*training data*) that the algorithm learns from is provided by humans.

Nevertheless, it still pushes editorial decision-making further away from the journalists. Consequently, as the decision-making processes become harder to localize, see, and understand, the journalistic accountability systems will face challenges too. Journalism risks getting black-boxed once again, this time with journalists also out of the loop.

Final Thoughts

As noted earlier, transparency implies journalists make practices, processes, and sources open to public scrutiny. In journalism studies, transparency is considered an ethical principle and norm. It is deployed through applications or tools that effect openness in journalistic practices, for example, hyperlinking of news sources. However, there is a discrepancy between the way transparency is conceptualized and its practice within the newsroom and its relative importance to the public. Furthermore, it is doubtful whether media organizations and journalists go to great lengths to make information accessible and complete considering frequent criticisms over the faults and failures of journalism. The additional layer of algorithms, their opaqueness, and their combination of a standalone role and intertwining with journalistic work and decision-making only enhances the complexity of the issues at hand. But the introduction of algorithms also increases the need for transparency in journalism for all involved parties, including journalists. However, to conclude, it is still uncertain whether the potential of transparency to transform journalism will be realized.

David Cheruiyot and Michael Karlsson

See also Credibility; Ethics; Media Criticism; Objectivity; Trust in Journalism

Further Readings

Carvalho, J., Chung, A., & Koliska, M. (2018). Defying transparency: Ghostwriting from the Jazz Age to social media. *Journalism.* doi:10.1177/1464884918804700

Christensen, L. T., & Cheney, G. (2014). Peering into transparency: Challenging ideals, proxies, and organizational practices. *Communication Theory, 25*(1), 70–90. doi:10.1111/comt.12052

Craft, S., & Heim, K. (2020). Transparency in journalism: Meanings, merits and risks. In L. Wilkins & C. G. Christians (Eds.), *The Routledge handbook of mass media ethics* (pp. 308–320). New York, NY: Routledge.

Deuze, M. (2005). What is journalism? Professional identity and ideology of journalists reconsidered. *Journalism, 6*(4), 442–464. doi:10.1177/1464884905056815

Karlsson, M. (2010). Rituals of transparency: Evaluating online news outlets' uses of transparency rituals in the United States, United Kingdom and Sweden. *Journalism Studies, 11*(4), 535–545. doi:10.1080/14616701003638400

Karlsson, M. (2020). Dispersing the opacity of transparency in journalism. On the appeal of different forms of transparency to the general public. *Journalism Studies, 21*(13), 1795–1814. doi:10.1080/1461670X.2020.1790028

Karlsson, M. (2022, Forthcoming). *Transparency and Journalism: A critical appraisal of a disruptive norm.* London, UK: Routledge.

Kovach, B., & Rosenstiel, T. (2001). *The elements of journalism: What newspeople should know and the public should expect.* New York, NY: Crown Publishers.

O'Neill, O. (2002). *A question of trust.* Cambridge, UK: Cambridge University Press.

Plaisance, P. L. (2007). Transparency: An assessment of the Kantian roots of a key element in media ethics practice. *Journal of Mass Media Ethics, 22*(2-3), 187–207. doi:10.1080/08900520701315855

Tuchman, G. (1972). Objectivity as strategic ritual: An examination of newsmen's notions of objectivity. *American Journal of Sociology, 77*(4), 660–679.

TRAUMA, COVERAGE OF

The lay definition of "trauma" can be quite broad (such Merriam-Webster's more general definition of "an emotional upset"). For the purposes of this entry, trauma is defined in accordance with the American Psychiatric Association's *Diagnostic and Statistical Manual of Mental Disorders, Fifth Edition* (*DSM-5*) involving close exposure to (or threat of) death or the experience of serious physical or sexual harm or violence. Importantly, exposure to a traumatic event does not necessarily trigger the psychiatric condition of posttraumatic stress disorder (PTSD), which the *DSM-5* states can result from directly experiencing the traumatic event, witnessing it in person, learning it has happened to a close family member or friend, or experiencing repeated or extreme vicarious exposure to details of an event through digital means if it is part of a person's job. Each possibility arises in relation to journalists, their sources, and their audiences. There is a dynamic interplay between journalism and trauma, and this entry covers four elements of that interaction: (1) traumatic events as news; (2) interviewing and photographing those who have been traumatized; (3) potential impacts on audiences; and (4) journalists and trauma.

Traumatic Events as News

Much news content involves topics or material that meet the lay definition of trauma as causing emotional upset. Conflict, consequence, and unusualness have been acknowledged as key news ingredients, and such events often involve content that has upset some people and whose content might evoke a strong emotional response in others. Within this broad category there is a considerable subset of news meeting the narrower medical definition of close exposure to (or threat of) death or the experience of serious physical or sexual harm or violence (*DSM-5*). At a global and national level, news of wars, terror attacks, mass shootings, natural disasters, air crashes, famines, and pandemics all involve death and serious injury which stand to traumatize the sources being interviewed, the audiences viewing them, and the journalists and photographers covering them. At a local level, the proximity of the event and the potential for audiences and journalists to know those affected can exacerbate trauma. Potentially traumatic local stories include serious car accidents, house fires, injuries to children, murders, criminal court reports, domestic violence, and sexual assaults. News not involving death or injury to humans might also trigger considerable shock and anxiety if not trauma, such as injuries to animals, environmental accidents such as oil spills, and financial and social crises such as stock market crashes and homelessness.

The modern history of the mass media has been punctuated by highly newsworthy events whose coverage has involved traumatized human subjects and sources, with the possibility to traumatize journalists and to enhance anxiety and emotional upset in audiences. Prominent examples from recent decades include the assassination of U.S. President John F. Kennedy, coverage of the Vietnam War (notably the images of the summary execution of a Vietcong fighter and the naked napalm-burned figure of the fleeing child Kim Phuc); the 9/11 terror attacks with the vision of the collapsing Twin Towers and victims in New York; the 2004 Asian tsunami; Hurricane Katrina in 2005; the 2020–2021 coronavirus pandemic; and public mass shootings such as those in Australia (1996), Norway (2011), New Zealand (2019), and the United States several times annually.

There are strong justifications for coverage of all traumatic events on numerous grounds including genuine public interest and concern; the Fourth Estate rationale of being a watchdog on the contributions of governments to the causes of the events and their actions in the aftermath; and the educative value of instructing audiences about the events that might assist them in the immediate aftermath and reduce the impact of like events in the future.

Nevertheless, there are different perspectives on the particularities of trauma coverage by the news media, with prominent debates centering on the ethics of photographing those who have died and those who have been injured or traumatized; interviewing vulnerable victims and relatives of the deceased; identification of the culprits in mass shootings and acts of terrorism; partisan or politicized assignation of blame or causes before formal inquiries; and of journalists putting themselves or others in danger or getting in the way of first responders during events.

A trauma-literate approach to newsgathering that includes an understanding of the individual, communal, and social impacts of trauma exposure has the capacity to not only enable journalists to apply appropriate self-care strategies in the face of trauma reporting but it also presents a knowledge base whereby reporters can make more informed and ethical news choices. Trauma literacy at an individual level includes understanding personal trauma reactions, some of which include nightmares, easy to startle response, fragmented thinking, and dissociation. Trauma literacy on a communal level includes understanding community survivor impact trajectories, some of which include a honeymoon period of communal euphoria which then descends into collective grief, frustration, anger, exhaustion, community fragmentation, and rebuilding. On a social level, it is not unusual for societies to be rendered silent regarding what has happened to them. Trauma has a disempowering impact. Many Holocaust and Khmer Rouge survivors never spoke of the atrocities they experienced. The trauma remains unspoken and integrates itself into the social fabric and ultimately can result in intergenerational and transgenerational trauma outcomes.

Interviewing and Photographing Those Who Have Been Traumatized

Interviews with, and vision of, the victims of traumatic events—and the witnesses to their death and destruction—have both ethical and legal dimensions. Most journalism ethical codes instruct against intruding upon the privacy of the grieving and vulnerable unless such intrusions are necessary because of an overriding public interest. For example, the Society of Professional Journalists' (SPJ) Code of Ethics counsels journalists to minimize harm by treating "sources, subjects and colleagues as human beings deserving of respect." To that end, it states "Journalists should:

- Show compassion for those who may be affected adversely by news coverage. Use special sensitivity when dealing with children and inexperienced sources or subjects.
- Be sensitive when seeking or using interviews or photographs of those affected by tragedy or grief" (SPJ, 2014).

The SPJ Code of Ethics continues: "Only an overriding public need can justify intrusion into anyone's privacy" (SPJ, 2014).

Restoring power to trauma-exposed interview subjects is important. Unlike interviews with business and political figures, informed consent is vital in trauma-focussed stories—more than in other stories, simply because of the amount of power and control that has been taken away from trauma-impacted persons. Simple strategies that can re-empower survivors such as asking where they would like to stand to do the interview; would they like someone with them; and the choice to stop the interview if they become distressed will help the interviewee feel in more control, often resulting in a better interview.

Despite such tips and guidelines, the controversial reporting phenomenon of the "death knock" has a long tradition, particularly in tabloid journalism, and survives into the 21st century. This is where reporters knock on the door of grieving family members after a tragedy (or telephone them) to seek out their tearful recollections of the deceased and the circumstances of the news event. The United Kingdom's Leveson Inquiry into the culture, practices, and ethics of the press in 2011 examined it closely. Journalists have typically justified death knocks on public interest grounds, arguing the human impact is an important part of the story and can inform public debate and policy. While journalists might argue a death knock interview can be cathartic for a witness, or close friend or relative, a trauma-literate approach suggests that people in grief or shock in the immediate aftermath of an event might not be of sound mind to offer informed consent to an interview and that in some cases the retelling of the circumstances may heighten the risk of negative post trauma impacts.

Another debate centers on news media access to victims' social media sites in the wake of a traumatic event, which can include appropriating photographs and publishing tributes and other quotes from comment streams. Many leading news organizations have editorial protocols regulating such practices.

The law of such intrusion varies markedly internationally, with privacy, confidentiality, trespass, nuisance, and surveillance device restrictions each active in different jurisdictions. In the United States, protections in the First Amendment to the U.S. Constitution apply to publication of material breaching privacy, but not to journalists committing unlawful intrusions in the course of their newsgathering. In the United Kingdom, the laws of confidentiality and privacy have been morphed to give legal recourse to celebrities and high-profile crime victims experiencing media intrusion into their grief or solitude. In Australia, the breach of surveillance devices laws underpinned regulatory action against a radio station who made a prank call to a London hospital impersonating the royal family and contributing to the suicide death of a nurse who had been duped in the lark.

With the advent of user-generated content, another legal issue includes the livestreaming of acts of terrorism, such as occurred during the Christchurch, New Zealand, mass shooting in 2019. Governments moved to pass laws—likely unenforceable—to require Internet platforms to take down such footage immediately.

Potential Impacts on Audiences

The phenomenon of "vicarious trauma" (or "secondary traumatic stress") emerged in the psychological literature in the 1970s and is defined as empathic exposure to the experiences of trauma in others. Yet communication researchers have long known the difficulty of demonstrating "media effects," and an assertion of vicarious trauma by definition is suggesting a particular effect of news media outputs upon those who watch them. Vision of the collapsing Twin Towers during the 9/11 attacks was played and replayed internationally in the aftermath, including footage of victims taking their own lives by leaping from the inferno. Psychological studies, such as the one conducted in 2007 by Michael W. Otto and colleagues, analysed the potential impact of such material, particularly on children. They found they had the potential to compound the trauma of those who had witnessed or survived the news event, and to contribute to the trauma of those who had not been involved but were essentially living the trauma via the media.

Those broadcasting or reporting using graphic imagery should take extra care during the editorial process and develop a series of questions for each situation that includes extreme graphic content including human beings and animals. The Radio, Television, Digital News Association (RTDNA) proposes points to help guide thinking around this. The organization does not distinguish between living or deceased human coverage and recommends approaches that ensure needless graphic content is not aired and avoiding repeated use of graphic content.

Journalists and Trauma

Studies have shown that 80% to 100% of news professionals experience at least one event during their careers that has the potential to cause significant psychological injury. While most media professionals are resilient and have no long-term effects, there are some who can experience impacts to their psychological functioning. The Dart Center for Journalism and Trauma was established in 1999 as a resource center and global network of journalists, journalism educators, and health professionals dedicated to improving media coverage of trauma, conflict, and tragedy. It is based at Columbia University Graduate School of Journalism in New York City, with international satellite offices in London and Melbourne, Australia. Since the 2000s, some news organizations have offered training and counseling to reporters and photographers to enhance their resilience in the face of such exposure, and more recently some have been training managers and editors in the duty of care responsibility to create policy and protocols around such reporting. This training is underpinned by the emergence of mental health and media research that has been examining the issue more closely in recent decades.

Signs of posttraumatic injury might include substance abuse, memory loss, and uncharacteristic or antisocial behaviors. Clearly war correspondents are prime candidates for mental health concerns, while other examples of impacts in journalists have arisen from coverage of disasters, famines, car crashes, and court trials of violent crimes such as sexual abuse and murder. In 2019, an Australian crime reporter was the first journalist in the world to successfully sue a news organization for lack of duty of care in regard to trauma exposure. The reporter, who had covered more than 30 murder trials, was awarded $180,000AUD in damages in a PTSD civil action where the court ruled her newspaper employer had failed to provide her with a safe workplace.

Traumatic responses can also stem from demeaning attacks and sexual harassment from the public during assignments, and can be exacerbated through ethical conflict, a sense of an unsupportive work environment, self-blame, and personal identification with the subjects of their stories. There is also the potential for compassion fatigue, particularly for reporters who have experienced other personal traumas in their lives. Some studies have examined vicarious trauma among journalists whose work has required them to view graphic and disturbing images and footage of traumatic news events. Editing and production roles across media involve the selection of such material—often user-generated content from witnesses or victims. Decisions have to be made about which images and footage are too confronting for audiences, but this involves the sourcing, viewing, and reviewing of much material that is so graphic that it might contribute to psychological trauma.

Mark Pearson and Cait McMahon

See also Criminal Justice and Journalism; Terrorism, Coverage of

Further Readings

American Psychiatric Association. (2013). *Diagnostic and statistical manual of mental disorders* (5th ed.). doi:10.1176/appi.books.9780890425596

Beam, R. A., & Spratt, M. (2009). Managing vulnerability: Job satisfaction, morale and journalists' reactions to violence and trauma. *Journalism Practice, 3*, 421–438.

Dart Center for Journalism and Trauma. (2020). Retrieved May 27, 2020, from https://dartcenter.org/

Dworznik, G. (2018). Personal and organizational predictors of compassion fatigue symptoms in local television journalists. *Journalism Practice, 12*(5), 640–656. doi:10.1080/17512786.2017.1338532

Houston, J. B. (2009). Media coverage of terrorism: A meta-analytic assessment of media use and posttraumatic Stress. *Journalism & Mass Communication Quarterly, 86*(4), 844–861. doi:10.1177/107769900908600408

Molnar, B., Sprang, G., Killian, K., Gottfried, R., Emery, V., & Bride, B. E. (2017). Advancing science and practice for vicarious traumatization/secondary traumatic stress: A research agenda. *Traumatology, 23*, 129–142.

Morales, R. F., Perez, V. R., & Martinez, L. (2014). The psychological impact of the war against drug-trafficking on Mexican journalists. *Revista Colombiana de Psicología, 23*, 177–193.

Novak, R. J., & Davidson, S. (2013). Journalists reporting on hazardous events: Constructing protective factors within the professional role. *Traumatology, 1*, 1–10.

Otto, M. W., Henin, A., Hirshfeld-Becker, D. R., Pollack, M. H., Biederman, J., & Rosenbaum, J. F. (2007). Posttraumatic stress disorder symptoms following media exposure to tragic events: Impact of 9/11 on children at risk for anxiety disorders. *Journal of Anxiety Disorders, 21*(7), 888–902. doi:10.1016/j.janxdis.2006.10.008.

Radio Television Digital News Association (RTDNA). (2020). *Guidelines for graphic content*. Retrieved May 27, 2020, from https://www.rtdna.org/content/graphic_content

Saylor, C. F., Cowart, B. L., Lipovsky, J. A., Jackson, C., & Finch, A. J. (2003). Media exposure to September 11: Elementary school students' experiences and posttraumatic symptoms. *American Behavioral Scientist, 46*(12), 1622–1642. doi:10.1177/0002764203254619

Society of Professional Journalists (SPJ). (2014). *Code of ethics*. Retrieved May 27, 2020, from https://www.spj.org/pdf/ethicscode.pdf

TRAVEL JOURNALISM

Travel journalism is broadly defined as any communication about a voyage outside one's immediate vicinity. An alternate, slightly more narrowed definition of travel journalism is any piece of consumable writing or media in which traveling plays a role in the story. By this definition, a story called "The Ten Best Coffee Shops to Visit on Your Portland Vacation" is travel journalism, whereas a story titled "The Business of Portland's Mail-Order Coffee Scene" would not be. The former aims to inform travelers about activities to engage in while traveling, whereas the latter is more focused on the business side of the coffee industry and not aimed at potential travelers. That said, whether a story is travel-related or not is often a matter of opinion, decided more by what publication or website the piece appears in rather than by a delineated set of parameters. Many magazines are devoted to the subject, myriad blogs and websites exist purely to help plan travel, and popular travel destinations readily provide their own online and print content about what to do in their towns and cities.

Travel writing can take the form of a guidebook on a vacation hotspot, an exposé on political unrest in a foreign country, a restaurant review from an out-of-town diner, or a feature story on a blog about what it's like to travel through an under- or overvisited location. Travel writing may appear glamorous to some people, so they may consider themselves amateur travel writers, imagining either an Indiana Jones–style of adventuring and raconteuring or that they can simply create a blog and start traveling the world for free. However, neither of these views are reflective of the current trends and challenges of the travel journalism landscape.

After briefly reviewing the history of travel journalism, this entry discusses several forms of travel journalism. The entry concludes with a discussion of current challenges and controversies related to travel journalism.

History of Travel Journalism

In the broadest sense, travel journalism has been around since the written word began. After surveying new land, explorers would come back with tales of new cultures and places. Marco Polo's *Il Milion* was widely popular among 13th-century Europeans, and publications from missionaries and explorers were published for those who remained at home (and who often financed the voyages). In later centuries, tales came back to the old country extolling the beauties and abundance of the new American continent. Early-19th-century writers became famous with tales of their voyages; notable authors like Herman Melville gained fame with his chronicles of voyages as a sailor (*A Narrative of Adventures on the South Seas*), as did Robert Louis Stevenson (*In the South Seas*).

As faraway destinations became less expensive and easier to reach due to the technological expansions of the 19th and 20th centuries, greater accessibility increased the demand and interest in travel writing. Early publications like *National Geographic* (first published in 1888) began as research journals but slowly changed to allow armchair travelers (those who read for entertainment value with no intention of traveling to the destinations covered) to go to remote, foreign locations via the page. Although the magazine was published irregularly for the first decade of its existence, it was a monthly magazine by the end of the 19th century. Initial readership was low but quickly escalated with the introduction of photography—most notably color photographs of the natural world—by 1910. Color photography, maps, and in-depth articles gave a boost to *National Geographic*, so much so that the magazine was lengthened in the 1950s, indicating the growing public demand for travel coverage. And many publications stepped into the growing market. *Travel and Leisure* (introduced in 1971) targets budget-minded travelers, while *Conde Nast Traveler* (introduced in 1987) caters to higher-end travelers, although both claim to appeal to both demographics.

By the 1990s, travel journalism was further aided by printing developments, including digital typesetting and inexpensive color printing, which enabled publications to easily and instantaneously publish at a minimal cost. Technological advances have led to developments ranging from travel blogs, which provide a venue for anyone to post photos and stories from vacations, to multimillion-dollar travel companies like the Travel Channel.

Forms of Travel Writing

This section discusses several kinds of travel journalism.

Destination and Experiential Coverage

A well-known style of travel journalism is the destination piece, which is usually a feature article in a magazine, website, or newspaper focusing on a specific journey or place. Such pieces aim to appeal to both armchair travelers and avid world explorers. Although *National Geographic* offers a mix of destination pieces and (more recently) exposés, these pieces are often in magazines that are mainly devoted to coverage of other topics like current events (*The Atlantic*), culture (*Vanity Fair*), or music (*Rolling Stone*).

Online travel sites like TripSavvy.com, LonelyPlanet.com, and OutTraveler.com are known for this style of writing, though travel guides and sponsored content (also called *advertorial*) have become popular in recent years. Although recently passed laws supported by the U.S. Free Trade Commission require all advertising and monetary or product transactions to be adequately disclosed to consumers, many consider this to be a grey area of travel journalism.

Exposés

A popular style of travel journalism related to destinations is exposés. These are usually investigative stories focused on a serious issue (e.g., illegal diamond smuggling, minority oppression) in a location foreign to the intended audience. These pieces are not intended to encourage travel, but rather to inform readers of what's happening somewhere else. They often have a political slant and may make judgments on the social, environmental, or humanitarian acceptability of the issue covered. Pieces falling into this category are usually aimed at consumers of hard news and are more likely to be found in news publications and websites like CNN or Time rather than niche or entertainment magazines and papers. Exposés are a popular type of story for television travel journalism as they tend to be informative, entertaining, and often have gripping visuals.

Travel Guides

One of the oldest types of travel journalism is the guidebook or travel guide. Created for travelers planning trips to specific destinations, they come in many varieties. Guidebooks are produced by both freelance and staff writers who work for such publishers as Fodor's and Lonely Planet and include reviews of hotels and restaurants, cultural advice, tips for pre-trip planning, maps and local information, and suggestions of what to do and see. They can cater to youth backpackers (Rough Guides) or older, more experienced travelers (AFAR.com). These publications, intended to guide day-to-day travel, include specific information rather than the anecdotal or emotional perspectives often found in shorter destination pieces.

Although guidebooks remain popular with travelers, their sales have been on the decline since the mid-2000s as online resources, often free, became more mainstream. Sites like Roadtrippers.com, TripAdvisor.com, WikiTravel.org, and ArrivalGuides.com offer hundreds of thousands of articles tailored explicitly to travelers' interests. The massive amount of online resources means that travelers can find guides that offer in-depth detail on their interests and leave out what they don't care about. Rather than buying a guidebook to everything Japan offers, a traveler can instead read 15 articles that go in-depth into topics they are most interested in; for example, "A complete guide to the best beignets in Kyoto," or "The Hello Kitty lovers guide to Tokyo's Harajuku district." To address this trend, many traditional guidebook companies have strong web presences that now have more readers than their print publications, such as Fodor's, Frommer's, and Lonely Planet. Many companies also offer their books in digital and phone-app editions.

Novels

Another mass-consumed style is the travel novel. These are intended for audiences reading at home, not for readers desiring a step-by-step guide. They are usually lengthy and often share more about the author and the author's life experience and takeaways than the location discussed. Famous examples of this genre of writing include John Steinbeck's 1961 novel about traveling with his French poodle, *Travels with Charlie*; and Ernest Hemingway's 1926 novel *The Sun Also Rises*, which follows a group of American and British expatriates living in France and traveling to Spain. Popular modern-day authors have achieved notoriety in this genre, such as Bill Bryson with his book *In a Sunburned Country*, which recalls his travels in Australia. Whether pensive, humorous, thought-provoking, or morose, travel-based novels are intended to contribute to the reader's literary repertoire, not necessary to encourage visitation.

Video

A more recent travel journalism format encompasses many of the aforementioned genres of writing but presents them via a different platform. Multimedia travel journalism combines television and online venues to present travel stories with video and sound. Viewers can find this type of journalism on television and streaming sources, such as the Discovery Channel and Netflix; in exposé form, as in programs like *60 Minutes* or *Anderson Cooper 360* that cover world issues; and in travel inspiration and guide form, such as *Andrew Zimmern's Bucket List* on the Travel Channel.

Blogging and Social Media

Since the mid-2000s, several new forms of travel-related content creation have entered the mainstream travel-planning process: social media, video sharing sites, podcasts, and blogs. Social media platforms (primarily Instagram) now allow travelers to produce and share travel-related video and photo content; indeed, some of the most popular Instagram accounts and "influencers" have several million followers. These content creators are often paid to visit destinations, create and post content, and, due to the ability to search networks by keywords or hashtags, reach thousands of people every day. As of 2020, it remains to be seen if this trend will continue or be replaced by a new medium entirely in a few years.

Video-sharing sites (e.g., YouTube) and blogs have also become accessible travel resources. To some readers, blogs like NomadicMatt.com and ThePointsGuy.com may be indistinguishable from corporate travel websites like TripSavvy.com. The blogging form of online journalism allows travelers to post photos and reviews of their travels for a personal audience of friends and family or a global audience of online readers. However, blogs can face conflict-of-interest and disclosure issues, especially if they are run by one person who receives free travel in exchange for coverage.

Video-sharing sites, such as YouTube.com, on which users can upload video content, are a mix of both professional video (e.g., compete travel programs uploaded and shared by the Animal Planet TV channel) and content made by bloggers and noncorporate travelers (e.g., travel blogger account Lost LeBlanc, whose YouTube channel has nearly 1.5 million subscribers as of 2020). Video content is increasingly available online, with many city, country, and travel-related organizations featuring video tours on video-sharing sites and/or their own websites.

Travel podcasts operate in a very similar vein to video-sharing sites, albeit audio only: Users can create and share a podcast. Many popular podcasts are created by corporate producer and smaller, independent podcasters alike.

Challenges

In this section, several current trends and challenges of travel journalism are discussed.

Economic Outlook

With the trend away from paid newspaper and magazine subscriptions and toward free (or very inexpensive) online travel content, many traditional forms of journalism have greatly reduced their staff and budgets. As a result, travel journalism (and journalism in general) in most forms is a low-paying field. It is not unusual for entry-level writers to be offered $10 for a 1,000-word article, or nothing other than "exposure." Many blogs do not pay contributing writers. Only the most senior and veteran writers are offered higher sums, such as $1 a word for a feature story in a major publication.

Objectivity

Objectivity arises in all facets of travel journalism, but especially with regard to guides and features on business or destinations. Because travel writers are usually paid little for a single piece, one of the ways they can afford to travel is on press trips (also called familiarization tours) paid for by destinations in the hopes that the writers will then publish stories about them upon the conclusion of the trip. However, this raises questions of objectivity, as some publications feel accepting free travel will cause the writer to want to please the destination and write only positive, biased stories. Those who contend stories from press travel should be accepted argue that editors ought not to work with writers who they don't trust to be unbiased, and that by only accepting stories from writers who can afford expensive travel, they're ensuring only wealthy, rather than diverse, voices get to tell stories. Occasionally, a publication will pay travel expenses for a writer. Still, given the reduced budgets across most publications, this is rare and usually reserved only for the few writers at the very top of their careers.

Parachute Journalism

Parachute journalism refers to the concept of an outsider quickly visiting a destination, seeing just a few sights, then leaving and writing articles that position themselves as an authority on the area or make sweeping statements about the destination. Given the desire for constant content and quick, poorly paid articles, parachute journalism is becoming more common. To address this issue, many publications aim to hire writers living in the areas they're writing about and/or may prioritize writers from specific groups or affiliations to tell stories from those groups.

Suzanne Dundas

See also Blogs and Bloggers; Environmental Journalism; Journalism and Globalization

Further Readings

Carlson, K. (2008, January 18). How to pitch: Travel & leisure. *Media Bistro*. Retrieved June 2008 from, http://www.mediabistro.com/articles/cache/a1114.asp

Conde Nast Traveler. (2006, March 12). *MagsDirect. com*. Retrieved June 2008 from, http://www.magsdirect.com/condenasttraveler-magazine.html

Eilperin, J. (2006). Despite efforts, some tours do leave footprints. *The Washington Post,* Retrieved April 2, 2006. https://www.washingtonpost.com/archive/lifestyle/travel/2006/04/02/despite-efforts-some-tours-do-leave-footprints/c179699a-53e4-46bc-bcbc-28282270880f/ retrieved December 20, 2021

Garrison, B. (2004). *Professional feature writing.* Mahwah, NJ: Lawrence Erlbaum Associates.

Hennessy, B. (2006). Subjects and treatments. In *Writing feature articles* (chap. 6). Boston, MA: Focal Press.

Il Milione (The Million or The Travels of Marco Polo). Publication information unknown, circa 1298.

National Geographic Press Room. (2008, June). National geographic fact sheet. Retrieved June 2008 from, http://press.national geographic.com/pressroom/index.jsp?pageID=factSheets_detail&siteID=1&cid=1047675381100

Pearson, P. (1990, June 5). Travels with Charley. *National Steinbeck Center.* (Revised June 1995). Retrieved June 2008 from, http://www.steinbeck.org/Travels.html

U.S. Department of Commerce, Bureau of Economic Analysis. (2008). U.S. economic accounts. Retrieved June 2008 from, http://www.bea.gov

TRIBUNE PUBLISHING COMPANY

The Tribune Publishing Company is a print and online media publishing corporation based in Chicago, Illinois, and incorporated in Delaware. Among the largest newspaper publishers in the United States, the company has 11 daily newspapers and commuter tabloids. Its portfolio includes the *Chicago Tribune*, the *New York Daily News*, *The Baltimore Sun*, the *Orlando Sentinel*, and the *Hartford Courant*, as well as other titles in Pennsylvania and Virginia. Syndication operations and websites also are part of Tribune Publishing's listings, plus several local newspapers in metropolitan regions of the United States.

Incorporated in 1847 with the founding of the *Chicago Tribune*, Tribune Publishing operated as a division of the Tribune Company until it spun off into a separate public company in August 2014. On June 20, 2016, Tribune Publishing adopted the name Tronc, short for "Tribune Online Content." In October 2018, the company reverted to its original name Tribune Publishing. In May 2021, the Tribune Publishing's shareholders approved a $633 million bid from Alden Global Capital, a New York–based hedge fund, to acquire the newspaper chain.

This entry traces the historical development of Tribune Publishing beginning in the mid-19th century under the leadership of Joseph Medill. The company, starting in the early 20th century, rose to become a national multimedia company through growth in acquisitions. Tribune's mergers and layoffs through the early 21st century, concluding with the company's acquisition by Alden, also are discussed in this entry.

The Early Beginnings

The history of Tribune Publishing is rooted with the publication of the *Chicago Tribune* newspaper, the leading newspaper in the Midwestern United States that launched on June 10, 1847, in a one-room plant at LaSalle and Lake streets in Chicago. Led by Canadian-born, later Ohio resident Joseph Medill as editor and part-owner after acquiring an interest in the bankrupt *Chicago Daily Tribune* in 1855, the *Chicago Tribune* was a strong pro-Union and antislavery paper during the American Civil War. Under Medill's tenure, the newspaper actively covered city news, generally avoided shaping news to conform to politics, and took editorial positions independent of their respective parties.

For four generations, the Medill family shaped the story of journalism in the United States. Joseph Medill influenced the political landscape that transformed the country during the mid-19th century by fostering the Republican Party, campaigning for the election of Abraham Lincoln, and serving as an engine for the outbreak of the Civil War. A 32-year-old lawyer at the time of his involvement with the *Chicago Tribune*, Medill opposed disunion and considered secessionists to be traitors.

After the Civil War, the Tribune Publishing Company built a four-story structure at Dearborn and Madison streets in 1869, known as the *original Tribune Tower*; however, the building was destroyed, along with most of the city, by the Great Chicago Fire in October 1871. Medill at this time was elected mayor and led the city's reconstruction. While Medill was mayor, Horace White—later editor of the *New York Evening Post*—gained editorial control of the *Chicago Tribune*. Post–Civil War, White shifted the paper's policies toward liberal positions. Subsequently, circulation declined among the vast Republican readership, although the paper continued to profit from advertising. However, when the paper lost money after the Panic of 1873, Medill gained full control of the newspaper's editorial decisions and operated it until his death in 1899. This 25-year span represented a monumental journalistic period of Medill's life in which he exercised increasing influence in municipal, state, and national affairs through the editorial columns of the *Tribune*. Throughout his time as editor, he promoted departmentalization of specialized news, including foreign, city, financial and commercial, books, religion, sports, and women. These changes were received well by readers.

Medill's two grandsons, cousins Robert R. McCormick and Joseph Medill Patterson, took over the company in 1911. That same year, the *Chicago Tribune*'s first newsprint mill opened in Thorold, Ontario, Canada. This led to the beginning of the Canadian newsprint producer later known as *QUNO*, in which Tribune held an investment interest until 1995. The Chicago Tribune-New York News Syndicate was formed in 1918, leading to Joseph Patterson's establishment of the company's second newspaper, the *New York Daily News*, on June 26, 1919. The Medill dynasty also included Joseph Patterson's sister, Cissy Patterson, who became the innovative editor of the *Washington Times-Herald*. In the fourth generation, Alicia Patterson founded Long Island's *Newsday*, an accomplished publication of post–World War II America.

In 1922, the *Chicago Tribune* organized an international design competition, an historic event in 20th-century architecture, for the new Tribune Tower to house the newspaper and its parent company. Under construction from 1923 to 1925, the new Tribune Tower was a 36-floor, neo-Gothic skyscraper, standing 470 feet tall on North Michigan Avenue in Chicago. It is listed on the City of Chicago's official website as a Chicago Landmark, a designation granted in February 1989.

Growth in Acquisitions

In the early 20th century, the Tribune Publishing Company gained its early start in print and broadcast acquisitions when McCormick guided the purchase of Chicago's WGN-AM radio in 1924 and WGN-TV in 1948. In 1963, the company acquired the Fort Lauderdale-based *SunSentinel* newspaper, and 2 years later, the *Orlando Sentinel*. A decade later, the company began sharing stories among 25 subscriber newspapers via the newly formed news service, the Knight News Wire. By 1990, this service was known as *Knight-Ridder/Tribune* and provided graphics, photo, and news content to its member newspapers. Knight-Ridder/Tribune became McClatchy-Tribune Information Services, when the McClatchy Company of Sacramento, California, purchased Knight-Ridder Inc. in 2006. Tribune later acquired the Newport News, Virginia-based *Daily Press* in 1986.

Since investing $5 million in America Online (AOL) in 1991, the Tribune Publishing Company moved toward becoming a national multimedia operation poised to distribute its news content via print, television, Internet, radio, cable, and broadband. By 1992, Tribune Publishing was running Chicago Online with AOL and working on creating an all-news cable TV station, Chicagoland TV. Five years later, the Tribune Company was committed to a future involving the Internet, as well as to the idea of having its newspapers work closely with broadcast and cable television in places where Tribune owned both. The company partnered with Time Warner Cable to launch a cable station in Orlando, leveraging the newsgathering operation of the Tribune-owned *Orlando Sentinel*.

In 1995, after setting the Tribune Company on the online path, Charles Brumbach retired as the company's chief. Jack Fuller became president of Tribune Publishing Company in 1997. As editor of the Tribune's editorial page, he won the Pulitzer Prize for Editorial Writing in 1986 and, in 1989, he became editor of the paper and later publisher and chief executive officer. Under Fuller's leadership, Tribune developed integrated multimedia approaches to newsgathering and distribution to create an interactive market.

The trend toward media mergers and corporate growth that started in the early 1990s grew ambitiously as the country started to enter a new century. In June 2000, Tribune created America's third largest newspaper corporation when it acquired the Los Angeles–based Times Mirror Company in a merger deal worth $6.5 billion, considered at the time to be the largest newspaper transaction in the history of the print industry. The merger added seven daily newspapers to Tribune's portfolio, including the *Los Angeles Times*, the Long Island–based *Newsday*, *The Baltimore Sun*, and the *Hartford Courant*. Along with its newspapers, the Tribune company owned 22 television stations. This meant that Tribune owned newspapers and TV stations in the nation's three top markets. Tribune Media Net, the national advertising sales organization of Tribune Publishing, was established in 2000 to take advantage of the company's expanded scale and scope.

Later in the first decade of the 21st century, Tribune launched daily newspapers targeting urban commuters, including the *Chicago Tribune's RedEye* edition in 2002. Scott C. Smith was promoted in early 2005 to president of Tribune Publishing. In 2006, Tribune acquired the minority equity interest in *AM New York*, giving it full ownership of the newspaper. However, in December 2007, Chicago-based investor Sam Zell bought the company, which fell into bankruptcy with $7.6 billion listed in assets against a debt of $13 billion—regarded at the time as the largest bankruptcy in the history of the media industry in the United States. More than 4,200 people lost jobs as a result of the purchase, and resources for the Tribune media outlets were reduced.

Tribune Deals, Rebranding, and Layoffs

On July 10, 2013, Tribune announced that it would split into two companies—its publishing division would become the Tribune Publishing Company, and its broadcasting, digital media, and other assets would remain with the Tribune Company. The spin-off was finalized on August 4, 2014.

After the split, in October 2014, Tribune Publishing purchased six daily and 32 weekly newspapers in the Chicago metropolitan area. On May 7, 2015, Tribune Publishing announced that it had reached a deal to acquire the *San Diego Union-Tribune* and its associated properties for $85 million, ending the paper's 146 years of private ownership. After the acquisition, the *Union-Tribune* and the *Los Angeles Times* became part of the new California News Group. Both papers maintained distinct operations, with content sharing between them.

In April 2016, Gannett Co., in a surprise move, sought to acquire Tribune Publishing, but Tribune's shareholders rejected the deal in May. Consequently, Gannett increased its offer from approximately $400 million to around $800 million. On May 17, 2016, Tribune announced it planned to make a bid to acquire Gannett instead. Then, in November 2016, Gannett announced that it would no longer pursue the acquisition.

In the middle of the sought-after acquisition by Gannett, the Tribune Company announced on June 2, 2016, plans to rebrand itself as Tronc. The rebranding was finalized on June 20, 2016, and Tronc began trading on NASDAQ under the symbol TRNC. In addition, that day, the company announced initiatives in content optimization, machine learning, artificial intelligence, and increasing the amount of video to 50% of all content by 2017—all were goals designed to increase reader engagement and ad revenue.

The newly branded company set to work on expanding its enterprise. On March 13, 2017, Tronc declared that it would license Arc, the content management system of *The Washington Post*. On September 4, 2017, the company announced that it had acquired the *New York Daily News*. Having been established in 1919 by the Chicago Tribune-New York News Syndicate, the *Daily News* had been owned by the Tribune Company before its sale to Robert Maxwell in 1991 and then to Mortimer Zuckerman in 1993. Tronc purchased the *New York Daily News* for $1 plus the assumption of its liabilities.

Despite its acquisitions, Tronc encountered financial challenges. On July 23, 2018, Tronc broke the news that massive layoffs were planned and ousted its editor in chief. Furthermore, the Tronc brand did not last. In mid-June 2018, it was reported that Tronc would return to its original name of Tribune Publishing.

After the company returned to its former identity of Tribune Publishing, in January 2019, newspaper industry veteran Timothy P. Knight became CEO, succeeding Justin Dearborn who had served in the role since 2016. The company's board of directors also elected former congressman and chairman of the House Rules Committee, David

Dreier, to succeed Dearborn as chairman. In February 2020, both Dreier and Knight stepped down as chairman and CEO, respectively. Knight was replaced by the chief financial officer, Terry Jimenez.

The New York–based hedge fund Alden Global Capital won shareholder approval in May 2021 for its $633 million bid to acquire the Tribune Publishing newspaper chain. Alden, which held a 32% ownership in Tribune, owns roughly 100 newspapers and 200 publications. Alden's founder, Randall Smith, is a member of Tribune's board. Heath Freeman is the fund's president who oversees Alden's newspaper holdings.

Alden is known in the newspaper industry for making recurring layoffs and buyouts to yield escalated profits. Prior to the shareholder approval for acquisition, union members in Tribune Publishing newsrooms had sought potential buyers in numerous Tribune markets who respected the public service role of journalism.

Melony Shemberger

See also Broadsheet Newspapers; Gannett; Media Conglomerates; Newspaper Chains, Ownership of; Publishers

Further Readings

McKinney, M. (2011). *The magnificent Medills: America's royal family of journalism during a century of turbulent splendor*. New York, NY: Harper Collins.

Rushton, W. (1916). *Joseph Medill and the Chicago tribune*. Madison, WI: Master's thesis, University of Wisconsin.

Shepard, A. C. (2000). Tribune's big deal. *American Journalism Review, 22*(4), 22.

TRUST IN JOURNALISM

Trust is considered an important concept for explaining why individuals are willing to consume and believe the news that media institutions distribute. A lack of trust in journalism has been linked to significant consequences for democracies, such as a less informed citizenry and a lower willingness of individuals to accept democratic decisions. Scholarly investigations of trust and related constructs have a long history, but they intensified with the advancement of the Internet and the global rise of populism, which also sparked fierce debates about so-called "fake news" and the "lying press."

This entry provides a definition of trust in journalism and outlines the state of trust in different countries. It illustrates ways of measuring trust, offers an assessment of causes and consequences of trust, and concludes with a brief discussion of future directions in research on trust.

Definitions

Trust is a key element of social interactions that aim at cooperation but involve a certain degree of uncertainty. The literature defines trust as a voluntary relationship between two actors, namely someone who trusts (i.e., a trustor) and someone who is trusted (i.e., a trustee). The trustee often possesses skills or resources that the trustor cannot acquire easily, thereby making the relationship asymmetrical. Trust reduces social complexity and substitutes the trustor's lack of knowledge about the future performance of the trustee; it is a hypothesis that the trustee will act in a way that is beneficial or at least not detrimental to the trustor. Consequently, trust is the willingness of a trustor to accept the risk of being vulnerable to the actions of a trustee. This willingness is usually based on some positive past experiences with the trustee.

Individuals are intrinsically motivated to monitor their social environment, yet they cannot acquire firsthand experiences regarding every possible event. The system of journalism selects and communicates information about the world outside people's immediate reach. From this perspective, trust in journalism is the willingness of people to take the risk of accepting journalism's depiction of social reality as accurate and appropriate. Defining journalism as the object of trust implies that people form trust-related judgments about the system of journalism as a whole rather than only evaluating the trustworthiness of single journalists or media outlets. Thus, trust in journalism is a form of generalized trust, largely independent from specific situations and trustees, which measures broad attitudes of the audience toward the system of journalism. As such, trust in journalism is related to concepts of institutional trust in the news media and other public institutions.

State of Trust

Globalization, digitization, and a changing political environment have intensified concerns about a decline of audience trust in journalism. Empirical evidence partly supports these concerns. Comparing findings from the World Value Survey and the European Value Survey in 45 countries between 1981 and 2014, Thomas Hanitzsch and colleagues reported declining levels of trust in the press in 24 countries. This decline was particularly severe in the Anglo-Saxon region, above all, in the United States. Countries in the Asian region, in contrast, have faced the opposite trend. In Europe, the average level of trust in the media and journalism is relatively stable over time. Still, a series of studies in Germany indicate an increasing polarization of trust perceptions: Over time, less and less people indicate that the media can be trusted sometimes, while the shares of people grow who either fully trust or distrust the media.

Various studies have reported associations between trust in journalism and trust in public institutions, such as the government or the federal congress. It has, therefore, been posited that developments regarding trust in journalism are often part of an overall societal shift toward a more critical assessment of institutions.

Measurement

As of today, there is no gold standard for measuring trust in journalism. Existing measures vary in terms of concept and objects, number of items and dimensionality, and scaling. Regarding concept and objects, studies that aim at measuring generalized trust have surveyed how much "trust," "confidence," or even "faith" people have in "the press," "the news media," "the news," or "journalism." The multitude of concepts and objects of trust studied likely impedes the comparability of findings. In terms of the number of items and dimensionality, large-scale and comparative studies often measure trust with a single item. An early example is the research conducted by the Roper

Center, which, starting in the 1950s, measured the credibility of television, radio, and newspapers over a longer period of time. This research was an important predecessor of various long-term studies that use single items to measure confidence in the press and other institutions. Such measures are highly efficient from practical considerations, yet their reliability and validity are disputable.

Other studies rely on multi-item scales that are more or less well established in credibility and news quality research. For example, researchers have asked respondents to indicate their agreement with statements such as "the news media are accurate" and "the news media are fair." Respondents' average agreement across these different items is then reported as a measure of trust. This research conceives of trust as a multidimensional construct, yet it seldom validates the dimensionality of the scales. Such validation is done by research that derives different dimensions of trust from theory and then uses confirmatory factor analyses across different samples. For example, the trust measure by Matthias Kohring and Jörg Matthes considers the tasks of journalists to select, communicate, and contextualize news. Using confirmatory factor analysis, the researchers suggest four dimensions of trust, namely, trust in selectivity of topics, facts, accuracy of depictions, and journalistic assessment. Subsequent research has adjusted this scale to measure generalized trust in the news media and compared it to established measures of credibility. While these scales are methodologically sound, an open theoretical question remains whether they actually reflect the concept of trust or rather different reasons why people trust or distrust journalism or the media.

Regarding scaling, measures differ in terms of numbers and value labels of response options. Choosing one scale over another can significantly affect the results. Although this is a general issue in survey research, it is particularly severe in non-correlational trust studies that primarily aim to report the share of people who trust or distrust journalism. For example, compared to five-point scales that allow respondents to choose that they trust the media "sometimes," four-point scales that do not include this response option seem to overestimate the share of distrusting people.

Causes and Consequences

Explaining differences in individuals' levels of trust in journalism is at the heart of trust research. One line of research suggests that varying levels of trust are a consequence of the (perceived) performance of journalism. If journalism performs well (or is perceived to perform well), people will be more likely to trust and vice versa. Low levels of trust in tabloid newspapers in many countries seem to support these assumptions. Research has also found that cynical and game-framed news reporting—as an example of low journalistic performance—can decrease peoples' trust in journalism. A seminal work by Kathleen Hall Jamieson and Joseph Cappella complemented this research by suggesting a reinforcing spiral between cynical political news coverage, trust in politics, and trust in journalism. Various studies also measure perceptions of news quality as an immediate indicator of trust, distrust, or skepticism. Critics of such approaches argue that news audiences have difficulties in judging news quality along normative criteria, such as balance and impartiality. Thus, performance-based approaches may not be able to comprehensively explain trust in journalism. This view is supported by comparative research that has found only limited associations between performance-based variables on the macro-level (e.g., freedom of press) and trust in the media.

Another line of research argues that the likelihood of individuals to trust journalism is rooted more deeply in their predispositions, values, and socialization. Findings are inconsistent regarding the associations between trust and various sociodemographics such as age, sex, and education. In contrast, research has reported stable correlations between the tendency of individuals to trust people in general and their levels of trust in journalism. This interpersonal trust is assumed to be rooted in childhood and further developed in early socialization experiences. On the macro-level, research has additionally found negative associations between people's embrace of postmaterialist values, such as freedom of speech or political participation, and trust in journalism. According to this research, postmaterialistic societies strive for more autonomy from public institutions and are, therefore, also less trustful of journalism and the media.

Political attitudes and ideologies constitute another area of research on the causes and consequences of trust in journalism. Research has consistently found that political cynicism, anti-elitism, ideological extremism, and endorsement of populist attitudes coincide with lower levels of trust in journalism. High levels of satisfaction with democracy, political trust, political interest, and political knowledge, in contrast, often go hand in hand with higher levels of trust. Different levels of trust, then, can have several political consequences: Distrust in the media and journalism increases the chance that individuals will avoid current information about politics, have biased perceptions of current social and political developments, and vote more in line with their party identification. Individuals with low levels of trust are also more likely to engage in violent forms of political participation, such as vehement protests against democratic decisions. Higher levels of trust, in contrast, are associated with an increased engagement of individuals in various forms of institutionalized and discursive participation.

Research has also investigated the associations between trust in journalism and media-related variables, such as media effects or the news consumption patterns of individuals. Regarding media effects, studies have found that distrustful individuals are less likely to share the news media's agenda of important topics in a society. At the same time, they are more resistant to news-induced persuasion than individuals with high levels of trust in journalism. Associations between news consumption patterns and trust are likely reciprocal: Since individuals build, to some extent, trust and distrust on past experiences, their experiences with journalistic products can affect their trust in journalism in the first place. This trust or distrust can then be used as a justification for consuming less or more news from legacy news media. In fact, empirical research has reported a relatively robust and positive influence of the exposure to various legacy media on peoples' levels of trust and vice versa. Typically, these relations are stronger the less abstract and less generalized the trust measure is.

Even individuals holding cynical attitudes toward journalism do not completely abstain from consuming its products. Explanations for this finding circle around peoples' need for cognition and their lack of functional alternatives for retrieving specific information. The Internet could provide such alternative information sources, which is why an increasing number of studies investigate relations between Internet use and trust in journalism. Findings are, however, inconsistent. Some studies report negative associations between the frequency of Internet use and media trust, which are explained against the background that Internet users could often be exposed to information that contradicts that from legacy news media. Other research, however, did not find significant correlations or called for a more nuanced view regarding which information users actually consume online. These studies report that the general frequency of news consumption on social media platforms is not associated with lower levels of trust in journalism. Yet, trust is particularly low among users who regularly consume alternative online media with an affinity to populism and among users who rely on social media platforms as their main news source.

Future Directions

While research has extensively investigated the factors associated with trust and distrust, it is still unclear how much trust people should have in journalism and the media. Researchers agree that too much distrust in journalism is dysfunctional to democracies, yet a certain degree of critical vigilance to question journalistic information is a vital component of enlightened societies as well. Therefore, research has begun to differentiate between a functional skepticism and a dysfunctional cynicism as two sources—or subdimensions—of trust and distrust in journalism. Disentangling the complex relationship between these factors and investigating ways to support skepticism and reduce cynicism appears as a fruitful avenue for future theoretical and empirical work.

Trust research could also benefit from conducting additional panel studies. Those could help to shed light on the role (i.e., cause or consequence) of the various political, social, and media-related factors associated with trust. Additionally, generalized forms of trust, such as trust in journalism, are often assumed to have a trait-like stability. Still, research suggests that the share of people trusting or distrusting journalism changes over time. Panel studies

could contribute to identifying when and why peoples' experiences with legacy news media matter for their development of trust in journalism.

From a methodological perspective, previous research has already proposed sophisticated scales for measuring trust in journalism and the media. Further methodological standards regarding the objects, dimensions, and scaling of trust measures would increase the comparability of different studies. Additionally, a short scale for measuring trust, one that combines the briefness of established credibility measurements with the specifics of the trust concept, would be highly valuable.

Finally, with journalists continuously worrying about a crisis of trust, interventions to rebuild trust should be developed and tested. Experimental research has already begun to test the efficacy of a more transparent news reporting and increased newsroom interactivity with the audience. Expanding such endeavors could provide newsrooms with knowledge regarding how they could build trust in their organizations and, potentially, also in the system of journalism as a whole.

Marc Ziegele

See also Audience Research; Credibility; Democracy and the Media; Fake News; Appendix: Journalism Organizations

Further Readings

Blöbaum, B. (Ed.). (2016). *Trust and communication in a digitized world: Models and concepts of trust research*. New York, NY: Springer.

Cappella, J. N., & Jamieson, K. H. (1997). *Spiral of cynicism: The press and the public good*. Oxford, UK: Oxford University Press.

van Dalen, A. (2019). Journalism, credibility and trust. In K. Wahl-Jorgensen & T. Hanitzsch (Eds.), *Handbook of journalism research* (2nd ed., pp. 356–371). London, UK: Routledge.

Hanitzsch, T., van Dalen, A., & Steindl, N. (2018). Caught in the nexus: A comparative and longitudinal analysis of public trust in the press. *International Journal of Press/Politics, 23*(1), 3–23. doi:10.1177/1940161217740695

Jackob, N. (2012). *Gesehen, gelesen, geglaubt? Warum die Medien nicht die Wirklichkeit abbilden und die Menschen ihnen dennoch vertrauen* [See, read, believe? Why the media do not reflect reality and why people still trust them]. Munich, GR: Olzog.

Kalogeropoulos, A., Suiter, J., Udris, L., & Eisenegger, M. (2019). News media trust and news consumption: Factors related to trust in news in 35 countries. *International Journal of Communication, 13,* 3672–3693.

Kohring, M., & Matthes, J. (2007). Trust in news media: Development and validation of a multidimensional scale. *Communication Research, 34*(2), 231–252. doi:10.1177/0093650206298071

Ladd, J. M. (2012). *Why Americans hate the media and how it matters.* Princeton, NJ: Princeton University Press.

Mayer, R. C., Davis, J. H., & Schoorman, F. D. (1995). An integrative model of organizational trust. *Academy of Management Review, 20*(3), 709–734.

Prochazka, F., & Schweiger, W. (2019). How to measure generalized trust in news media? An adaptation and test of scales. *Communication Methods and Measures, 13*(1), 26–42.

Tsfati, Y., & Ariely, G. (2014). Individual and contextual correlates of trust in media across 44 countries. *Communication Research, 41*(6), 760–782. doi:10.1177/0093650213485972

TWITTER

Twitter is a social media platform used for microblogging, the practice of expressing ideas and opinions through short messages. While communication is the primary function of Twitter, it is also utilized by a variety of users for purposes as varied as advertising, seeking employment, and gathering news. Twitter is unique among messaging applications in its open accessibility and public-facing user experience; unlike contemporaries such as Facebook or Instagram, Twitter does not require the permission of a user for others to be able to see their output except in rare instances when a user sets their account to private.

Increasingly, Twitter has become a platform used by journalists to break news and build their reputations in order to secure positions with larger institutions. Some news organizations look to Twitter as a proving ground for potential recruits based on their skills as well as the influence they've already established, although many news organizations also have struggled to draw clear lines about what they consider acceptable uses of the platform by employees. This entry further describes Twitter's users and some of its uses, before discussing its creation, functionality, and evolution. The entry then looks at some of the key events and figures in Twitter's history and concludes with a discussion of some concerns about Twitter as well as the implications of the platform for professional journalism.

The profile of the prominent Twitter user has evolved since the application's introduction in the mid-2000s. Celebrities have adopted the service as a way of growing their fan base through communication and notification, sharing updates on their creative endeavors as well as their opinions. Many news organizations were initially reluctant to use Twitter as a medium for sharing content but they have gradually adopted the platform. Twitter has also empowered a rise in so-called citizen journalists, or those other than professional journalists who break news on the platform. Politicians employ Twitter to garner support for initiatives, educate the public, and increase their own sphere of influence. Twitter has allowed like-minded individuals to connect with one another and making businesses, institutions, and political and organizational leaders more accessible to the average person.

In many senses, Twitter can be seen as the start of a large conversation. While it can be cumbersome to present an entire argument or article on the platform, a tweet or series of them can serve as the headline would in traditional news media to draw an audience in for the rest of the story. Content creators have found value in Twitter as a way to preview and entice consumption of blogs, websites, or even other social media services.

Creation

Jack Dorsey, a computer programmer, web designer, and entrepreneur, conceptualized what would become Twitter in early 2006 while working for the podcasting group Odeo. Dorsey refined existing short messaging system (SMS) technology that had been developed in the 1980s to serve as a communication method that would bridge the gap between different tools, allowing people to keep track of one another and to send a message via desktop computer that could be received by a cellphone or vice versa. Odeo cofounder Noah Glass coined the name "Twttr" for the prototype program and worked with Dorsey as well as cofounder Evan Williams and their colleague Biz Stone on its initial creation and launch. The basis of Twttr was creating short messages from a plug-in that would populate across multiple platforms.

The first iteration of Twttr launched on March 21, 2006, internally for Odeo employees with Dorsey sending out the first message—or tweet—that read "just setting up my twttr." In July 2006, the application, now called *Twitter*, went live to the public. Tweets constituted messages of up to 140 characters. Due to the instability of Odeo, which was unable to compete with Apple as a podcasting platform, Dorsey, Stone, and Williams purchased Twitter from the investors and broke away to form their own company.

Twitter made its first significant impact at 2007's South by Southwest Interactive Conference (SXSW) in Austin, Texas. Attendees adopted Twitter as their primary method of interacting and communicating with both others at the conference as well as the outside world. Over the course of the event, more than 60,000 tweets a day were sent. Twitter received the Best Blog award from SXSW and would continue to gain momentum at subsequent technology conferences throughout the remainder of 2007.

Functionality and Evolution

Initial versions of Twitter only allowed users to post to a mass audience without defining who they were directing comments at. It was customer feedback that led to the creation of the @ symbol as a method of specifying conversation targets. Users can place an @ sign before the name of their intended recipient and that person will be notified that they have been mentioned and given the opportunity to reply. It is common to employ the @ sign as a way to involve other parties in a conversation or to denote credit. Other social media platforms adopted variations on this function in the wake of Twitter innovating the method.

The concept of the hashtag also originated on Twitter before migrating across other avenues of social media. Using the # or hash symbol, a category, catchphrase, or other form of demarcation can be assigned to an individual tweet, grouping it with similar comments. Users can then access the search function to find all tweets that share a hashtag in common. The hashtag is used as much in casual conversation as it is in marketing as companies associate with larger trends in order to increase visibility of their message. Hashtags are also a convenient way for users to track events as they happen or develop.

Retweeting is one of the most popular and frequently used features of Twitter. The platform allows an option to duplicate another user's tweet on one's own feed, automatically providing the originator of the comment with credit while also sharing it with one's followers. Retweeting developed out of Twitter wanting to create a larger sense of community while also alleviating ill feelings over perceived plagiarism. While users initially retweeted "manually," Twitter would begin automating the operation in 2010 and later added the ability for additional comments along with the retweet as a quoted response.

As with most innovations associated to Twitter and its ongoing evolution as a digital media service, the @ sign, the hashtag, and the retweet all grew out of user exploration and were integrated into the application's functionality following development by Twitter participants. Robert S. Anderson, a digital creative director, is credited as the first Twitter user to employ an @ sign as a means of responding to a comment made by Buzz Andersen. The interaction occurred on November 2, 2006, early in Twitter's development; within the next year, the ability to reply to comments directly became a key part of the platform.

Another digital product designer, Chris Messina, suggested publicly the concept of using the # symbol to group content, what would become known as a *hashtag*, on August 23, 2007. Twitter proved initially resistant to the concept of hashtags, but the trend gained momentum among users until it was made an official feature by July of 2009.

On April 17, 2007, web designer Eric Rice used the phrase "ReTweet" to copy and paste an opinion social media expressed by Jesse Malthus. Up to this point, "ReTweet" had referred to restatements of your own tweet, but Rice continued using it—and the variation "Re-Tweet"—to reference others, a trend that caught on. In 2009, Twitter created a feature allowing users to retweet without creating a new thread, though even today some users prefer to perform the function manually.

Key Events

Twitter has been at the forefront of several social and political movements since its inception. Every major news outlet has adapted to the reality of digital media and its prominence in the 21st century. Because Twitter is the most open of the social platforms and provides real-time updates, it has been utilized in particular to break news and for journalists to corroborate stories. It has become a leading source for information sharing and dissemination.

In 2011, details about the May 1 assassination of terrorist Osama bin Laden surfaced on the platform more than an hour before President Barack Obama confirmed the event during a live address of the nation. Later in the same year, the Occupy Wall Street movement against economic inequality that began in New York City's financial district gained attention and spread to other cities in large part due to its organizers using Twitter to gather support. Around the same time, anti-government uprisings in Arab nations—collectively referred to as the *Arab Spring*—utilized Twitter and other social media platforms to organize. Initially, activists involved in calling for reform in countries such as Egypt, Tunisia, and Yemen, employed Twitter as a key method in sharing their sentiments and garnering support from around the world. Later, coordinators of rallies and other events would turn to the online service in order to plan their efforts across several regions.

Since the July 2013 acquittal of white police officer George Zimmerman in the shooting of Black teenager Trayvon Martin, "Black Lives Matter" has been used as a rallying cry for exposing racial inequality. While the first documented use of the phrase occurred on Facebook, the hashtag #BlackLivesMatter quickly became more commonly associated with Twitter. According to a 2016 study conducted by the Pew Research Center, over a 3-year period beginning in 2013, #BlackLivesMatter appeared on Twitter nearly 11.8 million times.

On October 15, 2017, actress Alyssa Milano repurposed the designation "Me too" from activist Tarana Burke as an identifier for women who had been victimized by sexual assault or harassment. This followed articles in *The New York Times* and *New Yorker* highlighting allegations brought forth by several women of sexual misconduct by film studio executive Harvey Weinstein. The Pew Research Center found a year later that the hashtag #MeToo had been used over 19 million times on Twitter, averaging out to roughly 55,000 tweets a day.

The 2012 and 2016 U.S. presidential elections unfolded in large part on social media, particularly Twitter, with both major political parties' nominees utilizing the channel to campaign and to gain support from a younger voting demographic. In some cases, campaign staffers "speak" for their candidates on social media, crafting messaging for their approval, but many politicians have begun to use Twitter directly. President Donald Trump in particular took to the platform as a substitute for traditional news releases or press briefings, placing increased onus of journalists to be vigilant in monitoring the channel.

Key Figures

After leaving the Missouri University of Science and Technology and subsequently dropping out of New York University prior to graduation, Jack Dorsey resettled in Oakland, California, during the late 1990s where he started a software provider in 2000. Dorsey pitched what would become Twitter to Odeo before breaking away to form a separate company of which he was CEO; he stepped down from that position in 2008 and remained as chairman. In 2010, Dorsey invested heavily in the social platform Foursquare and developed the Square mobile credit card payment application. As of 2020, Dorsey remained CEO of both Square and Twitter, a role he resumed with the former in 2015.

A software developer and cofounder of Odeo, Noah Glass headed up aspects of Twitter's early development—and coined the working title "twittr"—but did not make the jump to Dorsey and company's Obvious Corporation and later Twitter itself.

A Boston-born and educated designer, Biz Stone joined Odeo from Google along with Evan Williams in 2005. Stone accompanied Williams and Dorsey in the formation of Twitter and acted as the new group's creative director through 2011. After several outside endeavors on his own and with collaborators, Stone returned to Twitter in 2017.

A Google executive who founded Odeo in 2005, Evan Williams fostered Dorsey's initial ideas for a social messaging service and assigned Glass, Stone, and others to work on its development. Williams would cofound Twitter in 2006 and become its CEO following Dorsey stepping down in 2008. He ceded the CEO position back to Dorsey in 2015, but remained on Twitter's board until 2019.

Concerns and Implications for Journalism

Some critics of Twitter argue that it's too unregulated and fast-moving, with quality of content being sacrificed for immediacy and frequency. Many Twitter users will ignore the larger narrative and greater context that can be found beyond the platform and believe they have gleaned full stories from headlines, leading to misinformation as well as conflict and aggression. Yet Twitter has become an important tool for journalists both to collect news and report it. In awarding the Pulitzer Prize to The Denver Post for its coverage of a 2012 mass shooting at a movie theater in Aurora, Colo., the Pulitzer Committee noted the Post's use of Twitter and Facebook in capturing a breaking story with context. The newspaper noted that it was Twitter that alerted an overnight staff member to the shooting, which allowed staff to begin a series of late-night social media posts once the report was verified. A collection of tweets was part of the prize-winning package.

For better or worse, Twitter endures as a powerful social media tool that has impacted social and cultural events and landscapes and delivered a voice to millions of users. This can mean professional journalists are in some senses competing with amateurs who are breaking news but are not necessarily bound by the same ethics to do diligent reporting. Social media users may not always be able to distinguish between a thoroughly researched piece of journalism and a hastily assembled tweet. This adds a level of responsibility and challenge to the job of the journalist.

Benjamin Morse

See also Citizen Journalism; Facebook; Instagram; Social Media; Social Movements and Journalism

Further Readings

Anderson, M. & Hitlin, P. (2016, August 15). Social media conversations about race. Pew Research Center. Retrieved from https://www.pewresearch.org/internet/2016/08/15/social-media-conversations-about-race/

Bellis, M. (2019, July 3). Who invented Twitter. Thought Co. Retrieved from https://www.thoughtco.com/twitter-1992538

Brown, D. (2018, October 13). 19 million tweets later: A look at #MeToo a year after the hashtag went viral. *USA Today*. Retrieved from https://www.usatoday.com/story/news/2018/10/13/metoo-impact-hashtag-made-online/1633570002/

Bruns, A., & Highfield, T. (2012). Blogs, Twitter, and breaking news: The produsage of citizen journalism. In R. A. Lind (Ed.), *Produsing theory in a digital world: The intersection of audiences and production in contemporary theory* (pp. 15–32, Vol. 80: Digital Formations). Bern, Switzerland: Peter Lang Publishing.

Dominic, L. L., Seth, C. L. & Avery, E. H. (2012). Normalizing Twitter. *Journalism Studies*, 13(1), 19–36, doi:10.1080/1461670X.2011.571825

MacArthur, A. (2019, November 12). The real history of Twitter, in brief. *Lifewire*. Retrieved from https://www.lifewire.com/history-of-twitter-3288854

MacArthur, A. (2020, January 20). Twitter leadership: A Noah glass biography. *Lifewire*. Retrieved from https://www.lifewire.com/twitter-leadership-bio-noah-glass-3288878

The Pulitzer Prizes. (2013). The 2013 Pulitzer Prize winner in breaking news reporting: Staff of the Denver post. Retrieved from https://www.pulitzer.org/winners/staff-73

Seward, Z. M. (2013, October 15). The first-ever hashtag, @-reply and retweet, as Twitter users invented them. Quartz. Retrieved from https://qz.com/135149/the-first-ever-hashtag-reply-and-retweet-as-twitter-users-invented-them/

Swasy, A. (2017, March 22). I studied how journalists used Twitter for two years. Here's what I learned. Poynter Institute. Retrieved from https://www.poynter.org/tech-tools/2017/i-studied-how-journalists-used-twitter-for-two-years-heres-what-i-learned/

TYPE AND TYPOGRAPHY

Typography concerns the design, arrangement, placement, and usage of machine-printed type. Although the notion of mechanical printing predates Johann Gutenberg, the father of modern printing, by at least six centuries, essentially, the history of typography begins with the German goldsmith's invention of the letterpress around 1450. Gutenberg's invention was so well conceived that it remained the principal method of printing for more than 400 years. Gutenberg's process for printing from movable type brought together four skills: calligraphy, chemistry, metallurgy, and engraving. The key to the system was metal type.

Gutenberg used steel punches and brass molds to cast individual letters from an alloy of lead, tin, and antimony. Each character was cast hundreds of times as a separate block, and then the thousands of individual letters were assembled into pages. After printing, the pages could be disassembled and the type cleaned and reused. Type was stored in compartmentalized storage cases—capital letters in an uppercase and small letters in a lowercase (thus the terms we still use today)—and pulled out letter by letter to set the lines. The German inventor also had to develop a method of holding the type in place for printing, a slow-drying ink sticky enough to adhere evenly to the metal type, and a press capable of forcing the paper down onto the type for an even impression. Gutenberg modeled his printing press after the wine and cheese presses in use at the time and formulated a linseed oil–based ink, using lead and copper compounds for pigment.

The 42-Line Bible

Bringing all the elements together, Gutenberg began working on the first typographic book, a two-volume, folio-sized (11.75 × 15 inches) Latin Bible. The pages were printed in two columns; the first nine pages had 40 lines per column, the 10th page had 41, and the remaining 1,270-plus pages had 42 lines per column. He may have used this layout for the manuscript, or he may have started a 40-line Bible and increased the number of lines per column to save time and paper. Forty-eight copies of this landmark publication, out of an estimated press run of about 200, are known still to exist (one is always on display at the Library of Congress, for example). Gutenberg's 42-line Bible remains a magnificent example of the printer's art.

Development of the printing process and printing the 42-line Bible was expensive. Over a period of years, Gutenberg borrowed a considerable sum from wealthy Mainz merchant Johann Fust, putting his printing equipment up as collateral. In 1455, just as the Bible printing neared completion, Fust foreclosed on Gutenberg for nonpayment and seized possession of the equipment and all work in progress. Fust then hired Gutenberg's chief assistant, Peter Schoeffer, to finish production. It is unknown whether Gutenberg had any further hand in completing the project or reaped any financial benefits from his work. But his invention quickly spread throughout Europe. It is estimated that by 1500, there were already more than 1,000 printers operating out of some 200 locations in Europe. The basic printing process remained little changed for the next 400 years. Typography, on the other hand, began to change almost immediately. Gutenberg's heavy Textura typeface was quickly eclipsed by more graceful, easier-to-read letterforms.

Development of Typography

The 42-line Bible was designed and printed to look like a handwritten manuscript. According to early accounts, Fust tried to sell the Bibles as hand-copied originals before being found out in Paris. But during the first 50 years of printing, the so-called *incunabula* period (1450–1500), typographers such as Erhard Ratdolt and Claude Garamond started moving type design away from its dependence on calligraphic models to letterforms more in accordance with metal type and the technical possibilities of printing.

According to the best estimates, close to 10,000 different typefaces have been created since Gutenberg. Early on, printers began to experiment with the size, shape, weight, and spacing of the letters. In particular, they produced typefaces with the following variations.

- Letter strokes, the lines that are drawn to form the letters. These can vary from hairline to quite thick or can be monotonal, with little or no variation at all.
- Serifs, the finishing strokes at the end of a letter's main stroke. Serifs can be rounded or

flat, straight or cupped, bracketed or unbracketed—or missing entirely.

- Finials and terminals, the final or ending stroke forming a hook or a ball that is attached to some curved letterforms.
- Counters, the enclosed or partly enclosed white space within letters.
- Ascenders and descenders, the strokes which rise above or go below the main body of some lowercase letters such as b and h and p and y. No uppercase letters have ascenders and the Q is the only uppercase letter with a descender.
- X-height, the height of the body of lowercase letters in proportion to the ascenders and descenders. The measure is actually based on the letter *x*.

Letterforms also vary in posture—whether the letter sits straight or seems to lean; weight, which can range from light to extrabold; and width, which can expand or condense a standard shape. Over the centuries, typographers have tried in several ways to classify the multitudes of type designs. Perhaps the most common is to group typefaces according to common characteristics, into faces, subgroups, families, and fonts.

Faces of Type

Black Letter

Gutenberg modeled his first typeface after the calligraphy of the local German monks. The face of type that developed from Gutenberg's first font is known as *black letter* because of the heavy, compact strokes of the letters. This face is also known as *text* because of its early association with the text or body copy of printed books. Today it is sometimes referred to as *Old English*, although old English is actually a particular typeface of the black letter and not a face itself.

Black letter faces feature pointed letters that look as if they were drawn with a broad-nibbed pen. The vertical stems are tightly spaced with pronounced stroke contrast. The terminals often have diamond-shaped finishing strokes. Because of the centuries of tradition associated with this face, many newspapers still use black letter type for their nameplates.

Roman

Gutenberg purposely designed his type to look like the hand lettering it replaced. But within 20 years, printing had expanded south to Italy, and there a new face of type soon developed that has remained dominant through five centuries. In the spirit of the Renaissance, Italian printers moved away from handwriting as a model toward the simpler, more open letterforms chiseled on Roman buildings. Nicholas Jenson, a French-born Venetian publisher and printer, introduced the first truly successful roman typeface in 1470. Fellow Venetian publisher, Aldus Manutius, and his typographer Francesco Griffo refined Jenson's roman face. Griffo also produced the first italic typeface, although his design had only lowercase letters set with regular roman capitals. Another Viennese printer added matching italic capitals in 1524. The influence of Venetian printers soon made roman type dominant in all Europe outside the German-speaking areas. Development has continued through the generations, with the romans still the most numerous typefaces by far, and the most popular for text type. Most books, nearly all newspapers, and at least half of all magazines use roman typestyles for body copy. One of the most popular is Times New Roman, designed in 1931 under the direction of Stanley Morison. Times New Roman was designed for the exclusive use of *The Times of London* but was released for general sale a year later. It has become one of the most widely used typefaces in the English-speaking world, not just by newspapers but also by book and magazine publishers, advertisers, and printers.

Roman types are defined by contrasting thick and thin strokes and the presence of a finishing stroke or serif at the end of the major stem and hairline strokes. Because these faces are so profuse and so varied, they are usually divided into subgroups based on three characteristics: contrast in the thickness of letter strokes; stress—the angle or axis of the curves; and serif treatment. "Old face" or "old style" types feature strokes that make a gentle transition from thick to thin. Serifs are bracketed or molded into the terminals of the main strokes. The serifs of the ascenders in the lowercase slant and at the bottom of the uppercase E and top of the uppercase T extend outward.

The axis of the curves is inclined to the left. Giambattista Bodoni, the renowned Italian type designer and friend of Benjamin Franklin, popularized modern romans after French typographers introduced their prototypes in the late 1700s. In the moderns, the last vestiges of type's origin as handwritten letterforms disappeared. Rather, these faces have a distinct mechanical look reflecting strict emphasis on form and structure. These faces have a strong contrast between thick and thin strokes. Serifs are straight, thin, and unbracketed. The serifs on the lowercase ascenders are horizontal. Stress is vertical. Many designs fall somewhere between old style and modern with characteristics of both. Contrast between thick and thin strokes is not as pronounced as in modern, but more than in old style. Serifs are bracketed and those of the lowercase ascenders are oblique, but the slant is not as steep as old style. These faces are known as *transitional roman.*

Some typographers would classify italic typefaces as a separate face, but it is better to look at them as roman. Like the romans, their strokes vary in thicknesses with serifs (or curved finishing strokes) called *finials.* Their letter shapes correspond to their companion roman face. Their most striking difference is their slant to the right.

Romans come in every weight and size and are suitable for almost any application.

Sans Serif

Second only to romans in number and frequency of use are sans serif faces. Sans means "without" in French, and as the name implies, none of the members of this large face of type has serifs of any kind. Their variety comes from variations in stroke thickness and weight differences. Modeled after the flat, uniform strokes of ancient Greek letters, the first recorded sans serif typeface was introduced in 1816, but the designation sans serif was not applied until 1832. They had become very popular by the mid-1800s. Their stature was propelled further a century later by the German Bauhaus Institute, which emphasized functional design in furniture, architecture, product design, and typography. In the last half century, their popularity has increased to the point that today the use of sans serif faces rivals that of romans.

Sans serifs can be divided into two easily distinguishable categories: monolines and gothics. Monolines, sometimes called *true sans serifs,* have little or no variation in the thickness of strokes. They are geometric, precise, and elegant. Their letterforms are round and lightweight as compared to gothics. Gothics have some variation in the letter strokes, although the contrast is not as apparent as in romans. Thickness variations are often found where curved and stem strokes connect, causing them to look somewhat less graceful than their monotonal counterparts.

At one time, most newspapers set their headlines in a roman typeface, but now more than half use sans serif or a combination of serif and sans serif. The switch to sans serif for body type, however, has not been as pronounced. Roman typefaces are less monotonous, are considered easier to read than sans serif faces, and have been retained by most newspapers for text type. But sans serifs play an increasingly important role in advertising, magazines and newsletters, consumer product labeling, and web design.

Square Serifs or Egyptians

About the same time sans serif type was launched by William Caslon IV early in the 19th century, a fourth face of type was introduced by another English typefoundry, the Vincent Figgins Foundry in London. The first of the square serif faces was listed in the catalog as "Egyptian," and the name stuck. There was a great fascination at this time in both England and America with all things Egyptian, intensified by Napoleon's invasion and occupation of Egypt in 1798 and 1799, and the discovery of the Rosetta Stone in 1799. This tablet of black basalt had parallel inscriptions in Greek and Egyptian hieroglyphic characters that provided the key to deciphering the ancient Egyptian writing. Whether Figgins wanted the shape of his letters to call to mind Egyptian architecture or to suggest the visual qualities of popular Egyptian artifacts, the face became associated with the tremendous interest in Egyptian culture.

Egyptian faces are also called *square serifs, slab serifs,* and *antiques,* but the Egyptian designation is the most prevalent, leading to names such as Cairo, Karnak, and Memphis.

Pronounced square or rectangular serifs, uniform stroke formation, and short ascenders and descenders characterize Egyptian faces. Serifs vary from tall serifs thicker than the stem strokes of the letters, to monoline types with little or no contrast between the serif and letter thickness, to more moderate serifs, which contrast with stroke thickness.

The Egyptian faces were designed for advertising purposes rather than for book or newspaper printing. They are monotonous and tiring when used for body copy but work well for headings and headlines. In the mid-1800s, they were used extensively for large theatrical posters and often produced with wooden rather than metal type. Since then, they have gone through several periods of decline and revival. Today they are popular for newspaper and magazine ads, especially for reverses, white lettering on a dark background, and surprints, copy that is printed over photographic illustrations.

Hand-Formed

With scripts and cursives, typography comes full circle. These forms are designed, as was Gutenberg's first typeface, to resemble handwriting. They are meant to emulate letters written with hand-held instruments—first quill pens, then fountain pens, brushes, broad-nibbed lettering pens, or felt-tip markers. Together, scripts and cursives make up the hand-formed face, sometimes shortened to "hands."

Script letters generally slant to the right and the lowercase letters connect or appear to connect. The capitals are graceful and flowing and can stand alone without connecting to the lowercase letters. Cursives also slant like handwriting, but neither the upper or lowercase letters connect. Cursive faces often include flourished capitals and may include some alternate lowercase characters. Cursives are sometimes confused with roman italics, but italic typefaces have serifs that cursives do not. Some typographers refer to all hand-formed faces as "scripts"—those with connecting letters as "formal scripts," and those with letters that do not connect as "informal scripts."

Hand-formed faces, both scripts and cursives, have proliferated since the 1930s, but only a few examples produced before that time are still in use. These faces are much more difficult to read than serif or sans serif faces. Newspapers and magazines occasionally use them for titles, headings, and subheads. Their more common use is for announcements, invitations, letterheads, and in retail advertising.

Decorative

Gutenberg's 42-line Bible had blank spaces left for decorative initials to be drawn in later by a scribe. Soon afterward, printers were using two-part blocks to stamp in highly ornate capitals after the text was printed. From there it was but a short step for typographers to "embellish" existing, identifiable letterforms.

Actually, this sixth face is not a face at all. Rather, it is a catchall category for miscellaneous designs with indistinct characteristics. Also known as *novelty*, *specialty*, *ornamental*, or *mood*, this category includes standard forms that have been modified with outlines, inlines, shadows, and textures; typefaces that have been decorated with flowers or leaves or other designs; and specially created faces with letters fashioned from natural forms such as paper clips, wooden logs, or smoke.

These typefaces are very rarely used in news typography. In other uses, they are attention grabbers used almost exclusively for display type expressing ideas of a few words.

Families and Fonts

Within the faces and subgroups are the various individual typefaces. Most of these have a number of closely related faces, all very similar in design but varying in posture, weight, or style. The collection of related designs all bear the name of their parent typeface and are known as *families*. A font consists of the upper and lowercase alphabet, numbers, punctuation marks, and symbols in any one size of a particular typeface.

Before computerization, each font of a typeface had to be cast separately, and most type was available in fewer than a dozen standard sizes. Measurement was not standardized until the late 1800s, when the U.S. Type Founders Association adopted a point system. A point equals just under 1/72 of an inch. Another common measurement used by typographers is the pica. A pica equals 12 points. So there are approximately six picas or 72 points to the inch.

With the advent of photocomposition and digital composition, designers are no longer limited to a few faces in a limited number of sizes. The computer age has given every desktop publisher easy access to virtually every typeface that has ever existed.

But typography is more than just the development of typefaces. It is also their selection and arrangement to convey a message. In this respect, typography revolutionized human society. Printing—first books, then newspapers and magazines—became the basis for education and enlightenment that began the modern information age, to which the print news media are so indispensable.

Jim Martin

See also Editing, Print Media; Gutenberg Press; Printing

Further Readings

Baines, P., & Haslam, A. (2005). *Type and typography* (2nd ed.). New York, NY: Watson-Guptill Publications.

Craig, J., & Barton, B. (1987). *Thirty centuries of graphic design*. New York, NY: Watson-Guptill Publications.

Meggs, P. B. (1998). *A history of graphic design* (3rd ed.). New York, NY: Wiley.

Zapf, H. (1972). The expression of our time in typography. In C. B. Grannis (Ed.), *Heritage of the graphic arts*. New York, NY: R. R. Bowker.

U.S. International Communications

U.S. international communications encompass strategic efforts, funded or sponsored by the U.S. federal government, that seek to inform or engage foreign civil publics and actors regarding the interests, behavior, and image of the United States. It can also include U.S. communication intended for domestic audiences abroad, such as deployed servicemen and women, that also regularly reaches foreign nationals.

Facilitated in the 2020s by cutting edge fiber-optic and satellite communication infrastructure, the 21st century's speed and breadth of global information-sharing poses opportunities, challenges, and threats never before imagined. While the United States may not share the same unipolar dominance it once had in the immediate post-Cold War era, still, no country today has a stronger influence on global politics than the United States, making U.S. international communications a topic of paramount interest.

While a presidential State of the Union address or feature story in *The New York Times* or *The Wall Street Journal* carries substantial international reach, they do not constitute U.S. international communications as defined in this entry. Both examples lack a predominantly foreign target audience while the latter functions under private entities. This entry positions U.S. international communications as the outputs of the U.S. Department of State (DOS) and U.S. Agency for Global Media (USAGM) and, to a lesser degree, the U.S. Department of Defense (DOD). It first discusses the origins of U.S. international communications, then looks at the Voice of America (VOA), Radio Free Europe/Radio Liberty (RFE/RL), the more recent expansion of outlets under USAGM, and outlets for international communications run by the DOD.

Origins

The birth of U.S. international communications is embedded in the very founding of the country, with the adoption of the Declaration of Independence in 1776 serving as the Second Continental Congress' first formal communication with a foreign government. It was also the U.S. government's first attempt to manage its international image, framing itself in the international arena as a righteous, self-determined people seeking fundamental freedom from a tyrannical and oppressive government.

Systematic and sustained efforts at U.S. international communications, however, trace their roots to the early 20th century, when the Committee on Public Information (1917–1919) was founded during World War I. Similar efforts reemerged during World War II with the Office of War Information (1942–1945) and the U.S. Information Service (1953–1999), more commonly the U.S. Information Agency (USIA), during and following the Cold War.

In 1965, Ambassador Edmund Gullion coined the term *public diplomacy* as strategic communication with foreign publics carried out by the United States to advance its foreign policy interests. As of 2018, federal funding for public diplomacy initiatives was $2.19 billion. Responsibility for U.S. public diplomacy was initially spread across DOS and USIA. In 1999, USIA was dissolved, redistributing public diplomacy assets to DOS and the Broadcasting Board of Governors, which was renamed the USAGM in 2018.

The journalistic approach to U.S. international communications largely resides within distinct news networks operated formerly by USIA, and today, USAGM. The oldest, and most iconic, networks giving voice to U.S. international communications include the VOA and RFE/RL.

Voice of America

The VOA was established in 1942 to counter Nazi propaganda efforts in Latin America. Once the United States entered World War II, VOA was repurposed to broadcast to the United Kingdom, North Africa, and Italy. By the end of the war, VOA produced over 1,000 programs spanning 40 languages.

In 2020, VOA is the United States' largest governmental broadcast network, reaching 275 million people weekly in more than 100 countries on a budget of approximately $250 million. Surveys of VOA audiences between 2016 and 2020 show that, on average, 83% of audience members view the network as trustworthy. Broadcasting via television, radio, and the Internet, the network makes use of satellite, cable, FM, and medium-wave radio, and over 2,500 affiliate stations around the globe to report news and spread the democratic values of free press and free speech.

While VOA is directly funded by the U.S. federal government, it is an independent journalistic institution and member of the free press. A 1976 legislative mandate signed by President Gerald R. Ford established that final editorial decisions rest with VOA leadership, not members of the executive or legislative branches of government. This aims to protect the authenticity and credibility of VOA as a globally respectable and credible news outlet rather than a mouthpiece for U.S. propaganda.

Proof of such independence can be seen in recurring tense relationships between VOA, the White House, and Congress. In the 1950s, Senator Joseph McCarthy accused VOA broadcasts of being sympathetic to communism, leading to substantial staff, budget, programming reductions, and Congressional hearings. In the 1970s and 1990s, VOA journalists tirelessly reported on, respectively, the Watergate and Monica Lewinsky scandals, providing unfavorable coverage of the presidential administrations of Richard Nixon and Bill Clinton. Further, in 2020, President Donald Trump publicly criticized VOA coverage of the coronavirus pandemic, suggesting it overly favored China's lockdown approach in Wuhan; such criticism was the basis for the Centers for Disease Control and Prevention blacklisting VOA reporters and media requests.

VOA began strictly as a news information outlet, however, once President Dwight Eisenhower moved the network from DOS to USIA in 1953, programming was expanded to include entertainment and educational broadcasting. *Jazz Hour* with Willis Conover was an iconic way U.S. culture and values were spread behind the Iron Curtain. Beyond the creativity, freedom, and originality inherent in jazz improvisation, *Jazz Hour* regularly hosted artists such as Louis Armstrong, Ella Fitzgerald, and Irving Berlin who openly discussed their thoughts on societal issues of the time, including race and gender relations. While the 1950s and 1960s in the United States were plagued with social equality issues, giving voice to those who were critical of the government reinforced VOA's global credibility as an independent organization and the federal government's commitment to free speech and free press.

Radio Free Europe/Radio Liberty

Although a single network now, RFE/RL started as two separate entities with parallel missions. RFE launched in 1950, targeting audiences in Eastern Bloc countries including Poland, Czechoslovakia, Hungary, Romania, Bulgaria, and East Germany. RL launched in 1953, targeting audiences inside the Soviet Union itself. Where both organizations launched with substantial funding from the Central Intelligence Agency, ties were severed in 1971 when funding shifted solely to Congressional appropriations. The networks merged in 1976 to form RFE/RL.

Unlike VOA, which covers U.S. and global events, RFE/RL aims to provide region-specific coverage to each country in which it broadcasts. Headquarters were based in Munich until 1995 when they were moved to Prague. As of 2020, RFE/RL broadcast in 27 languages to 23 countries across Europe, the Middle East, and Central Asia, including Ukraine, Belarus, Russia, Iran, Afghanistan, Pakistan, and Kazakhstan. Funding for RFE/RL was $124 million as of 2018.

Much of RFE/RL's popularity came from rigorous investigative reporting and quality information sharing, starkly contrasting censorship by the Kremlin in both the Soviet Union and Eastern Bloc. RFE/RL openly reported on such events as the death of Joseph Stalin, the Berlin riots of 1953 and Poznań riots of 1956, and defections to the West, such as that of Polish public security minister Józef Światło. Following the Chernobyl nuclear accident, Soviet media did not cover the meltdown for up to 48 h and provided highly censored and often contradictory reports in the following months. Despite Kremlin efforts, audiences in Eastern Bloc countries were largely aware of the Chernobyl events thanks to continual coverage by RFE/RL.

Despite its popularity, the network was placed under intense scrutiny for the role it played in the failed 1956 Hungarian revolution. While a much contested and debated subject, RFE/RL broadcasts into Hungary supported the sentiment of the revolution and, whether intentional or not, suggested to Hungarian listeners that foreign assistance would be provided if the revolution achieved success early on. No such aid was ever provided, and the revolt was defeated by Red Army forces and Hungarian forces backed by the country's communist party. In all, some 16,000 Hungarians were killed or wounded in the failed uprising, with 200,000 displaced as refugees.

Following the collapse of the Soviet Union, the demand for broadcasting in Europe declined, and funding cuts in the early 1990s led to programming reductions across the network. In 1998, however, with growing tensions in the Middle East, RFE/RL launched an Arabic broadcast service called *Radio Free Iraq* that operated until 2015. Following a trend of growing U.S. interests in the region, in 2002, RFE/RL launched Radio Farda as a Persian language service

broadcast in Iran. With significant censorship by the Iranian government and IP address blocks on Facebook and YouTube, Radio Farda adopted an innovative approach stressing customized content for mobile audiences, such as an Instagram account with over 1.8 million followers as of March 2020. Given the rise of substantial populist sentiment in Europe over the 2010s, in 2019, Romanian and Bulgarian programming was reinstituted, with Hungarian services aimed for expansion by 2021.

RFE/RL's adoption of 21st century digital journalism has not been without issues. In 2018, RFE/RL used paid Facebook advertisements to push its content to audiences inside the United States. The Smith-Mundt Act of 1948 makes it illegal for USAGM networks to broadcast or provide their content inside the United States. Where 20th-century broadcasting was a function of physically pointing transmitters in certain directions, the boundaries of cyberspace are just now being tested both practically and legally in terms of international communications. The Smith-Mundt Modernization Act of 2012, signed into law by President Barack Obama, still restricts USAGM networks from broadcasting their content inside the United States, but it does allow them to distribute content to audiences inside the United States when directly requested by members of the public.

Post–Cold War Expansion

With the decline of the Soviet Union in the 1980s and eventual collapse in 1991, the United States began appropriating funding and assets more broadly. In 1985, Radio y Televisión Martí was launched as a Cuba-specific network. Based in Florida under the Office of Cuba Broadcasting (OCB), content aims to bring credible news in Spanish to Cuban citizens. Funding for the network reached $29 million in 2018. In 2019, USAGM reported that while the network's cultural and entertainment content was in good standing, its news content did not reflect quality journalism and, as such, was in need of substantial editorial reform.

The Middle East Broadcasting Networks, Inc. (MBN) oversees U.S. engagement with the Arab world, spanning the Middle East and North

Africa. Headquartered in Virginia, MBN has a budget of $110 million, broadcasting to 22 countries in various Arabic dialects. The organization operates two television networks, one radio network, five websites, and numerous social media accounts. Radio Sawa launched in 2002, seeking to engage with Arabic youth, and Alhurra in 2004 as a satellite TV channel. Alhurra reaches upward of 15 million viewers weekly, down from 26 million reported in 2011, and has consistently struggled to compete with regional competitors such as Al Jazeera, Al Arabiya, or Al Iraqiya. Given declining effectiveness, Alhurra underwent a substantial editorial transformation that launched in 2018, aiming to rebrand the service and provide a new look and feel that would resonate better with target audiences.

Radio Free Asia (RFA) is a private, nonprofit organization overseeing U.S. engagement in Eastern Asia. After a brief stint between 1951 and 1955, the 1989 Tiananmen Square protests renewed U.S. interests in a regional broadcaster, with President Clinton approving a relaunch of RFA in 1994. As a private entity whose mission is mandated by Congress, RFA operates on grant-based funding provided by USAGM, which makes us the network's board of directors. With an approximate budget of $44 million, RFA broadcasts in nine languages to six countries.

In June 2020, after substantial lobbying from the White House, the Senate confirmed conservative filmmaker Michael Pack as the new USAGM executive director. Pack's confirmation raised significant concerns among lawmakers and journalists about the safeguards ensuring the editorial independence of U.S. international broadcasters from the White House. In what was dubbed the "Wednesday Night Massacre," Pack fired the directors of RFE/RL, RFA, MBN, OCB, and USAGM's Open Technology Fund. The firings were followed by a handful of senior-level resignations in VOA. Pack also acted to weaken the regulatory firewall protecting USAGM's networks and their journalists' editorial autonomy and independence. Although the regulatory firewall is Congressionally mandated in the 1994 International Broadcasting Act, Pack claimed the rule is unconstitutional and undermined his own editorial oversight of the agency.

U.S. International Communications Through the DOD

Beyond DOS and USAGM, DOD also engages in international communications, primarily through the American Forces Network (AFN). Based in Maryland, AFN provides news and entertainment broadcasting in areas of U.S. military deployment. Despite U.S. target audiences, AFN has a history of functioning as an outlet for federal communication with foreign audiences. In the 1950s and 1960s, AFN was widely listened to across Western and Eastern Europe, particularly cultural programming like John Vrotsos' *Music in the Air*.

In the 1950s through 1970s, AFN radio and TV services in Tehran were widely popular among Iranian nationals, especially children. Following the nationalization of Iranian broadcast networks in 1969, AFN provided the only broadcast content not controlled by the Iranian government until its closure in 1976. Through the latter half of the 20th century, similar networks and affiliates were established in Vietnam, Thailand, Taiwan, the Caribbean, Panama, and Honduras. Armed Forces Radio Saigon's *Dawn Buster* with Air Force DJ Adrian Cronauer was the inspiration behind the 1987 hit *Good Morning, Vietnam*.

DOD also provides a newspaper service through the *Stars and Stripes*. With a Congressional mandate requiring editorial independence and providing an ombudsman to ensure quality journalism practices, *Stars and Stripes* is the only autonomous news outlet within the U.S. military. While the newspaper produces editions for Europe, Guam, South Korea, the Middle East, and Japan (with separate editions for mainland Japan and the island of Okinawa), all content is in English and available in print only at U.S. military installations. Target audiences include U.S. military servicemen and women, civil employees, veterans, contractors, and their families.

Stars and Stripes began publication in 1861 during the American Civil War and has offered daily newspaper coverage since World War II. The Pentagon's 2021 proposed budget stripped the newspaper of its federal subsidy, approximately $15.5 million. The remainder of the newspaper's annual revenue, approximately $15 million, is generated by sales, subscriptions, and advertising. Although the funding that went to *Stars and*

Stripes in previous Pentagon budgets was dwarfed by the overall size of the $705 billion budget proposal, then Defense Secretary Mark Esper argued the *Stars and Stripes*' funding needed to be redistributed to higher priority areas and proposed cutting its entire budget. In September 2020, following tweets by Trump in support of *Stars and Stripes*, the DOD reversed its position in a statement requesting Congress approve defense funding for the newspaper network through 2021.

DOD also engages foreign audiences through psychological operation efforts in support of stability operations. Where DOD wishes to provide foreign humanitarian and civic assistance, it does so through one of four routes: noncombatant evacuation operations, counterdrug operations, humanitarian mine action programs, and peace operations. If the U.S. Air Force plans to bomb a target in a densely populated urban area, for example, DOD can deploy personnel to inform civilians to evacuate for safety, making use of in-person, print, and broadcast communication. While psychological operations do not constitute journalism, they do constitute U.S. international communications.

U.S. International Communications in 2020 and Beyond

U.S. international communications have achieved global recognition over the latter half of the 20th century. While the 21st-century role and tactics of such U.S. efforts have been less clear, there is little question that programs across the DOS, USAGM, and DOD have paramount roles to play in the coming years and decades. While state-sponsored international journalism was largely limited in the 20th century, with a few networks such as VOA and RFE/RL, the BBC World News Service, and the Soviet Union's Radio Moscow, the 21st century has seen a growing number of countries launching their own international news services, including China's Global Television Network and Xinhua News Agency, Iran's Al-Alam News Network, Qatar's Al Jazeera, Saudi Arabia's Al Arabiya, Germany's Deutsche Welle, France's France 24, Japan's NHK World, Singapore's Channel News Asia, Turkey's TRT World, and Russia's RT (formerly Russia Today).

Along with global competition from other state-sponsored outlets, U.S. international communications outlets operate at a time when rising disinformation, fake news, and computational propaganda make the need for objective, transparent, and fact-based journalistic practices more critical the world over. For U.S. international communications to remain as relevant as they were in the 20th century, with a fast-growing list of competitors in an ever-growing segmented market, will require governmental support in the form of funding, commitment to editorial independence, new broadcasting models, and 21st-century strategies for effective journalistic storytelling. These strategies could include interactive multimedia presentation, data visualization, user-generated content, audience analytics research, and tailored content distribution.

Phillip C. Arceneaux

See also Agence France-Presse; Al Arabiya; Al Jazeera; Al-Manar; British Broadcasting Corporation (BBC); Deutsche Welle; Xinhua News Agency; Propaganda; RT and Sputnik; Stars and Stripes

Further Readings

Arceneaux, P., & Powers, S. (2020). International broadcasting: Public diplomacy as a game in a marketplace of loyalties. In N. Snow & N. Cull (Eds.), *The Routledge handbook of public diplomacy* (2nd ed., pp. 50–63). New York, NY: Routledge.

Comprehensive annual report on public diplomacy & international broadcasting: Focus of FY 2018 budget data. (2019). U.S. Advisory Commission on Public Diplomacy. Retrieved June 2, 2020, from https://www.state.gov/wp-content/uploads/2020/01/2019-ACPD-Annual-Report.pdf

Dillard, J. E. (2012). All that jazz: CIA, Voice of America, and Jazz Diplomacy in the early Cold War years, 1955–1965. *American Intelligence Journal, 30*(2), 39–50.

el-Nawawy, M. (2006). US public diplomacy in the Arab world: The news credibility of Radio Sawa and television Alhurra in five countries. *Global Media and Communication, 2*(2), 183–203. doi:10.1177/1742766506066228

Embarking on reform of the Office of Cuba Broadcasting. (2019, May 21). U.S. Agency for

Global Media. Retrieved June 2, 2020, from https://www.usagm.gov/wp-content/uploads/2019/05/Embarking-on-OCB-Reform-English.pdf

FY 2020 Congressional budget justification. (2019). U.S. Agency for Global Media. Retrieved May 31, 2020, from https://www.usagm.gov/wp-content/uploads/2019/03/USAGMBudget_FY20_CBJ_3-15-19.pdf

Hacker, K. L., & Mendez, V. R. (2016). Toward a model of strategic influence, international broadcasting, and global engagement. *Media and Communication, 4*(20). doi:10.17645/mac.v4i2.355

Petrinca, R. (2019). Radio waves, memories, and the politics of everyday life in socialist Romania: The case of Radio Free Europe. *Centaurus, 61*(3), 178–199. doi:10.1111/1600–0498.12232

Pospíšil, F. (2019). Inspiration, subversion, and appropriation: The effects of Radio Free Europe music broadcasting. *Journal of Cold War Studies, 21*(4), 124–149. doi:10.1162/jcws_a_00908

Roose, K. (2018, July 19). U.S.-funded broadcaster directed ads to Americans. *The New York Times.* Retrieved June 1, 2020, from https://www.nytimes.com/2018/07/19/technology/facebook-ads-propaganda.html

Stephens, M. (2017). *The Voice of America: Lowell Thomas and the invention of 20th-century journalism.* New York, NY: St. Martin's Press.

Workneh, T. W. (2020). Journalistic autonomy in Voice of America's amharic service: Actors, deterrents, and safeguards. *Journalism Studies, 21*(2), 217–235. doi:10.1080/1461670X.2019.1634484

Youmans, W. (2009). The War on ideas: Alhurra and US International broadcasting law in the 'war on terror.' *Westminster Papers in Communication and Culture, 6*(1), 45–68.

United Press International

United Press International (UPI), a 1958 amalgamation of the International News Service and United Press, was a major American news agency for more than seven decades. Owned in the early 21st century by News World Communications, UPI is now a remnant of its previous status as a major international news and information provider.

Origins

Though founded under its present name in 1958, UPI traces its roots to United Press Associations (UP). Publisher E. W. Scripps, in order to battle AP's then-restrictive membership policies, had formed three regional Scripps news services in the early 1900s and merged them to become the UP on June 21, 1907. He argued there should be no restrictions on which papers (369 of them at first) could buy his developing news service. He hired Roy Howard to lead the wire service and it is Howard who is largely credited for the spirit of innovativeness and doggedness at UP, pioneering the use of bylines on wire service reports and offering feature stories long before they appeared on the AP. In its early years, as the number of subscribers doubled, the UP scrounged and scraped to cover the Mexican revolution and the growing labor movement, and then it scored big with coverage of the tragic 1911 Triangle Shirtwaist Factory fire in New York City.

Among these stories of UP's early years was its handling of the Armistice ending World War I. Receiving word from a bogus informant, the U.S. Embassy in Paris passed word to UP that an armistice had been signed. On November 7, 1918, UP ran the bulletin pronouncing the war's end and tens of thousands of Americans poured into the streets to celebrate. For hours, the AP stubbornly held out for official word and was subjected to angry demonstrations and cries of being pro-German. When the AP was able to confirm that the Germans had not yet signed the agreement, UP was forced to issue a correction, and the AP was redeemed. Three days later, the war did officially end. The UP restored some of its reputation when roles were reversed in 1927 and the AP prematurely reported that Charles Lindbergh had landed safely after the first solo transatlantic flight from New York to Paris.

Competing after the war with "The Ring" news agency cartel operated by Reuters, Havas, Wolff, and the AP, UP became the first American news service to provide service to subscriber newspapers in Europe, South America, and the Far East. Indeed, its success was such that Reuters invited it to join the ring in 1912. UP turned down the offer and continued to expand. Direct service to Europe came in 1921, China a year later, and, through a subsidiary, colonies of the British Empire by 1922. By 1929, UP was serving nearly 1,200 newspapers in 45 countries. Despite the Depression, that number grew to 1,715 newspapers and radio stations

(UP was the first news agency to serve them, starting in 1935) by 1939.

UP staffers often toiled in less than optimum conditions and the agency was seriously under-staffed. But the circumstances became something of a badge of honor, and many who went on to television news fame with CBS, including Walter Cronkite, recalled their work for UP as demand-ing yet enjoyable. As a UP war correspondent, Cronkite covered D-Day, parachuted with the One Hundred and First Airborne, flew bombing missions over Germany, covered the Nuremburg trials, and opened the UP's first postwar Moscow bureau.

World War II helped boost the UP as newspa-pers sought the latest and most compelling accounts of the battles in Europe and in the Pacific. UP had the only news transmission system in Hawaii and helped break the news of the 1941 Pearl Harbor attack. Toward the end of the war, the UP scored major scoops with stories about the crossing of the Rhine River by Allied forces and the joining of American and Russian troops in Germany. The UP gave rise in this period to some of the biggest names in journalism. Besides Cronkite, UP claimed credit for the early careers of David Brinkley, Merriman Smith, Howard K. Smith, H. Allen Smith, Eric Sevareid, and Helen Thomas, among others.

Thomas (1920–2013), who joined UP in 1943, began as a radio news writer for the agency and was one of its longest-serving and best-known correspondents. Early on in her career, she cov-ered several capital beats including the Depart-ment of Justice, FBI, and Capitol Hill. In 1960, she began covering President-elect John F. Kennedy, and she reported on every White House adminis-tration since. She resigned from UPI in 2000, when News World Communications acquired the agency. She is known for her hard-hitting ques-tions and persistence during briefings and press conferences, and more recently stridently chal-lenged President George W. Bush on his reasons for going to war in Iraq.

When she first joined the UPI White House staff, Thomas worked for UPI's Merriman Smith—known to UP colleagues as "Smitty." Smith had covered the administrations of President Roos-evelt and President Truman, but he is most remembered for his coverage of the assassination

of President Kennedy. Riding several cars behind the President in the Dallas motorcade on Novem-ber 22, 1963, Smith was able to grab the car phone first, battling AP's Jack Bell, who pounded on Smith's back for the phone. Smith dictated to UPI that three shots had been fired at the motor-cade. Arriving at Parkland Hospital, he was able to confirm that the President had been hit and was first to report that the President had died, minutes ahead of AP. He flew back to Washington, DC, in Air Force One with new President Lyndon John-son and Mrs. Kennedy and witnessed Johnson's swearing in. For his coverage of the assassination, Smith received the Pulitzer Prize, one of 10 even-tually earned by the agency.

In the early 1950s, UP expanded its technology with the teletypesetter, which allowed news sto-ries to be set into type at subscribing newspapers. It began a newsfilm service for television stations as well as a facsimile service for news pictures in 1952. The news agency turned 50 in 1957. But all was not well behind the scenes.

Merger

The amalgamated UPI was formed in 1958 when UP merged with William Randolph Hearst's Inter-national News Service (INS) under Scripps's lead-ership. The merger was the ironic result of a 1945 federal antitrust action against the Associated Press, which, for many years, had refused mem-bership (and thus news service) to many of Scripps's and Hearst's newspapers. When the gov-ernment ruled that AP's actions constituted a vio-lation of antitrust law, the AP was forced to open up its membership to any paper or broadcast sta-tion willing to pay for its service. Many papers subsequently dropped the weaker agencies for the AP, leaving the UP and INS financially weak.

Discussions to merge the two wire services had taken place many times, some as early as the 1920s, but the changing competitive landscape created by the AP lawsuit made the situation one of some peril. On May 24, 1958, UP and INS became UPI serving roughly 5,600 print and broadcast clients. The AP at that point served more than 7,000 U.S. and international news organizations.

The coverage of Kennedy's assassination 5 years later was proof that despite the financial urgency of the merger, UPI could provide a lively news report of aggressive spot news and interpretation that often matched the AP's dependable and accurate, if more stodgy, news reporting. UPI began an audio service of news and actualities for radio stations the year of the merger. But UPI's doggedness would not be enough to sustain the agency as a long-term competitor.

UPI's Decline

During the 1960s, both UPI and AP were roughly comparable in terms of their financial security, technological innovation, and customer relations. UPI was at least marginally profitable. By 1970, however, UPI was beginning to suffer pressure from the costs associated with technology upgrades, aggressive news coverage by broadcast television, and the decline in number of local daily newspapers. The chief subscriber problem was that fewer papers could afford subscriptions to two at least partially overlapping news agencies—and given the choice, they nearly always chose the more robust AP. UPI was soon losing $3 million to $4 million a year.

The introduction of computers in the 1970s and satellites (where UPI was a pioneer) a decade later proved to be an enormous expense and led to major personnel shifts and some layoffs. On March 18, 1974, the reporters' Wire Service Guild struck UPI, the first strike ever in the agency's history. The financial stresses began to show. In the summer of 1974, UPI established a 15-member Newspaper Advisory Board to address common management concerns and policies for all UPI subscribers. By 1977, the board approved UPI rate hikes of 9.5% and ended its practice of price bargaining to gain subscribers. In 1978, during negotiations with the Wire Service Guild, UPI asked for a wage freeze for most of one year to help offset a $2.2 million annual jump in its costs of leased telecommunications circuits. The union agreed to the request. The situation grew dire enough by 1979 that UPI sought to entice more than 40 news organizations to become partners in UPI, but the request failed, and the Scripps Company put UPI up for sale in 1980, at which point UPI served more than 7,000 subscribers (including 2,250 in 92 countries), most of which were broadcasters. Indeed, UPI was the world's largest privately owned news service. But the inception of Cable News Network (CNN) that same year was another indicator of the changing news agency marketplace. UPI operated 177 bureaus around the world with some 1,200 staff in the United States and 580 abroad.

On June 2, 1982, Scripps sold the New York–based UPI for a nominal one dollar to Media News Corporation, a group specially formed to acquire the troubled agency. It was reported in the trade press that Scripps had given Media News $12 million in cash and forgiven debt to rid itself of the continued costs of operating UPI. The UPI Audio service became the UPI Radio Network in 1983. But the new owner could not stop the financial losses that continued to mount. In 1984, the guild at UPI accepted a 25% pay cut for 3 months and the firing of 100 staff. The atmosphere affected the leadership, and by 1985, just 3 years after the ownership change, UPI was forced to file for bankruptcy.

A year later Mario Vazquez Rana, a millionaire publisher of daily newspapers in Mexico, bought the agency and invested almost $7 million on new technology. But Rana's acquisition prompted cancellations by many subscribing newspapers and other clients and led to the resignations of several top managers. Industry leaders viewed the sale to Rana as further evidence of UPI's decline. Others viewed Rana's inability to speak English and his unfamiliarity with American journalism as significant hurdles to rescuing UPI. In 1988, Rana handed off control of UPI to Dr. Earl W. Brian and sold his World News Wire (WNW), part of the Financial News Network, an irrevocable proxy to operate UPI for at least 10 years. Under the agreement, Rana gave up all management and financial obligations, though he retained ownership. Dr. Brian was chairman of Infotechnology, Inc., an information technology company based in New York, and that company became a minority investor in WNW. But faced with rising costs and declining subscribers, WNW cut more jobs. In 1990, the Securities and Exchange Commission announced a formal investigation into the company, and WNW announced that it might be forced to sell due to UPI's increasing debt.

In 1991, UPI filed again for bankruptcy, listing total liabilities at $65 million owing to some

4,000 creditors. It was serving just 16% of American daily papers, down from more than half in 1966. It emerged from bankruptcy again in 1992, thanks to a group of Saudi investors. Middle East Broadcasting Center Ltd., a London-based television news and entertainment company, acquired UPI in bankruptcy court for nearly $4 million in cash. The court selected the Saudi investors over religious broadcaster Pat Robertson, who also sought control of the wire service. At the time, UPI had about 450 full-time staff members and 2,000 part-time employees. By 1997, however, those numbers were down to about 300 staff members and 800 part-timers, serving about 1,000 broadcast and 1,000 newspaper and Internet clients. The UPI Radio Network accounted for about half the new service's income but was closed down in August 1999. UPI adopted a new writing style for its main news feed, limiting its stories to no more than 350 words.

In May 2000, News World Communications, a conservative media group founded by the Rev. Sun Myung Moon that includes *The Washington Times* newspaper, purchased UPI for an undisclosed sum, pledging to retain its editorial independence. At the time of that sale, UPI had dwindled to 157 employees and the Washington, DC, headquarters building was soon put up for sale. The rest was a slow but continuing dwindling of people and capacity. By 2007, it appeared that UPI had only a handful of reporters, all based in Washington and no longer reporting breaking news.

Into the 21st century, UPI delivers an updated stream of breaking news from the United States, covering developments in science, health, technology, the economy, and in-depth coverage of space, as well as celebrity interviews, original photography, sports, and miscellaneous news to round out coverage.

Conclusion

UPI began in 1907 as United Press and became UPI in 1958 when UP merged with the INS. While UP and later UPI maintained an active competitive alternative to the Associated Press for much of the 20th century, it ultimately failed due to the costs of changes in information technology and within the newspaper business that began in

the 1970s. Surviving "Unipressers" left behind a record of which they could be proud.

Victoria Ekstrand and
Christopher H. Sterling

See also Associated Press; United Press International

Further Readings

Baillie, H. (1959). *High tension: The recollections of Hugh Baillie*. New York, NY: Harper.

Benet, S. V. (1933). United Press. *Fortune, 7*, 16–72, 97–104.

Gordon, G., & Cohen, R. E. (1990). *Down to the wire: UPI's fight for survival*. New York, NY: McGraw Hill.

Harnett, R. M., & Ferguson, B. G. (2003). *United Press International: Covering the 20th century*. Golden, CO: Fulcrum.

International Commission for the Study of Communication Problems. (1979). *Monograph 15 (on News Agencies)*. Paris, France: UNESCO.

Morris, J. A. (1957). *Deadline every minute: The story of the United Press*. Garden City, NY: Doubleday.

Peterson, I. (1997, March 31). In news business, U.P.I. plans to thrive in 350 words or less. *The New York Times*, p. D1.

Schwarzlose, R. A. (1990). *The Nation's Newsbrokers, Volume 2: The rush to institution from 1865 to 1920*. Evanston, IL: Northwestern University Press.

Stepp, C. S. (Fall 1984, Fall). Redefining the news service: An analysis of change at United Press International. *Newspaper Research Journal, 6*, 14–21.

UNESCO. (1953). *News agencies: Their structure and operation*. Paris, France: UNESCO (Reprinted by Greenwood Press, 1970).

USA TODAY

USA Today is a U.S.-based general-interest news product distributed digitally and with a printed edition published and distributed Mondays through Fridays from 37 sites across the United States. It is owned by Gannett Co. Inc. and is based in McLean, VA. *USA Today* is also part of a cooperative news operation, the USA Today Network, which utilizes newsgathering and production resources from more than 300 of Gannett's local news operations across the United States and in Guam. Since 1984, *USA Today* has also published an international edition tailored to American travelers, available in Asia, Europe, and Canada.

Launched in 1982 as a newspaper with a national audience, the circulation for *USA Today's* print product reached 2.28 million in 2000, making it the largest circulation newspaper in the United States at that time. However, the digital transformation of the newspaper business has caused a steady decline from that peak. By mid-2019, print circulation had fallen to 520,000, with nearly two thirds of those newspapers distributed to hotel guests. *USA Today* began digital distribution in 1995 with a website that did not employ a subscriber paywall. In 2019, the company reported a combined print and digital circulation for *USA Today* of 1.4 million.

USA Today was launched under the direction of Gannett's chairman, Allen H. Neuharth, who described the new venture as a paper with national distribution that would appeal to the television generation and would be "so different, so advanced in design and approach and content that it would pull the rest of the industry into the twenty-first century, albeit kicking and screaming" (Neuharth, 1989, p. 107). The antecedent to *USA Today* was *Today* (now *Florida Today*), which was launched by Neuharth in 1966 in Brevard County, FL, as "Florida's Space Age Newspaper" and featured many of the same design and features that would later be used in *USA Today*.

At the time *USA Today* was launched, the only American newspapers with limited national circulation were *The Wall Street Journal* and *The New York Times*, which were available in the largest cities. Prior to the launch, Gannett hired research firms to conduct thousands of personal interviews with prospective readers who responded positively to prototypes of the *USA Today* concept. Armed with that data, Neuharth was able to convince Gannett's board to approve the project, despite initial projected losses in the millions.

Gannett was uniquely suited to launch a newspaper with truly national circulation and distribution. Then the nation's largest newspaper chain, it already operated printing plants and production facilities across the country that could be used to put out a national paper. *USA Today* was produced at the company's headquarters in Arlington, VA, and distributed to production sites via satellite. With this system, *USA Today* managed to transcend geographic limitations on newspaper distribution that had been the dominant model in the United States to that time. Other Gannett papers also loaned staff to *USA Today* and contributed content to the national publication.

USA Today, which called itself *The Nation's Newspaper*, was divided into four sections (News, Money, Sports, and Life), each color coded (news, blue; money, green; sports, red; and life, purple). Major features were located in the same place in every issue for reader familiarity. Stories were shorter than in other major newspapers; only a small number of stories on the sections fronts jumped to inside pages. *USA Today* also made extensive use of spot color and graphics, including maps, charts, and informational graphics, which were then uncommon in U.S. newspapers. The front page was designed to attract readers buying the newspaper from blue-and-white vending machines that resembled a television set, which were installed on streets and airports around the country. In 1984, *USA Today* introduced full-color photographs, and in 1985, it launched a multi-million-dollar television marketing campaign, in which celebrities from the worlds of television, business, and politics sang, "I Read It Every Day."

Travelers were a key market for *USA Today*, which was distributed to hotel guests across the country and, eventually, internationally. Among the daily features was a national round-up with a single news story from all 50 states and a color national weather map and forecast, along with color comics.

News copy also used "USA" as an abbreviation for the United States, rather than "U.S.," as was dictated by the influential *The Associated Press Stylebook*. It also used personal pronouns "we" and "you" in an effort to be friendly and accessible, a style that was frequently lampooned by critics, particularly a 1983 headline which read, "MEN, WOMEN: We're still different."

With its graphics-heavy format and use of short, cohesive, tightly written stories, *USA Today* was roundly criticized as superficial and inconsequential by journalists at other publications and came to be dubbed as "McPaper," a reference to the fast-food franchise McDonald's. It would take 36 years for *USA Today* to win its first Pulitzer Prize. However, the newspaper proved enormously popular, breaking 1 million in circulation in just 7 months, and would have a substantial impact on the newspaper business, as other publications began imitating its use of color, graphics, maps, and charts.

On its editorial page, the newspaper uniquely took a centrist, nonpartisan approach; its editorials were often coupled with opinion pieces written from the contrary point of view for balance. *USA Today* had a long-standing policy of not endorsing political candidates until 2016, when it offered a "disendorsement" of Donald Trump that urged readers not to vote for him but stopped short of endorsing any of his opponents.

While circulation for *USA Today* was strong from the time of its launch, production and distribution costs outstripped circulation revenue and advertising, as national advertisers proved reluctant to take a chance on a new and unproven product. By 1984, losses for Gannett were totaling more than $10 million a month; during its first 5 years, *USA Today* lost more than $230 million. But in 1987, the newspaper finally became profitable, and circulation exceeded 2 million for the first time in 1988, when it published its largest edition ever with 78 pages, more than half carrying advertising.

However, mirroring a trend seen across the U.S. newspaper industry, *USA Today*'s print circulation began to decline starting in 2001, prompting Gannett to begin a slow shift to emphasizing the digital distribution space. USAToday.com was redesigned in 2001, broadening the navigation to include two new sections: Tech and Weather. That same year, *USA Today* moved its operations from Arlington to a more suburban site in McLean, VA.

In 2010, *USA Today* reorganized the structure of its staff around the content verticles on its website and mobile platforms, rather than the four-section paper. The digital focus accelerated in 2012 after Larry Kramer—the creative force behind the websites MarketWatch and CBS Digital Media—was named *USA Today*'s president and publisher.

USA Today launched a major redesign of the print product in September 2012 to allow better integration of content for digital and mobile platforms, which included new sections for travel and technology. It also replaced its iconic globe logo with a blue dot. Stock market tables were dropped; readers were referred to the website for that information.

Starting in 2013, *USA Today* also began distributing its content as an insert inside Gannett's largest local newspapers. Audit circulation rules allowed those copies to be counted as part of *USA Today*'s circulation, which allowed it to reclaim the title as the nation's largest circulation newspaper.

In 2014, Gannett split itself in two, spinning off its broadcasting properties into a separate company, Tegna, and leaving the newspaper properties as part of Gannett, with *USA Today* as the flagship. In 2015, Gannett launched the USA Today Network, a branded national digital newsgathering service that shared content between its national, digital, and local publications. Local subscription-based digital sites were branded with the network logo, and in 2017, local papers were rebranded to more closely resemble *USA Today*.

USA Today also built a national investigative team to focus on data-driven, collaborative projects between the national newspaper and other Gannett publications. In 2019, the network won its first-ever Pulitzer Prize for an investigation of President Donald Trump's proposed wall along the U.S.-Mexico border, a joint effort with the *Arizona Republic*.

In early 2019, Gannett began dropping cobranded *USA Today* content from its local newspapers, triggering speculation that it might be considering ending the print edition entirely, which company officials denied. In August 2019, Gannett announced that it would merge its operations with GateHouse Media Inc., combining the nation's two largest newspaper chains into an operation with more than 260 daily newspapers, along with nearly 270 weekly titles. The merged company, which kept the Gannett name, billed itself as a "digitally focused media and marketing solutions company," with *USA Today* again as the flagship property.

Rich Shumate

See also Broadsheet Newspapers; Circulation; Design and Layout, Newspaper; Digital Distribution; Distribution; Gannett

Further Readings

Neuharth, A. (1989). *Confessions of an S.O.B.* New York, NY: Doubleday.

Prichard, P. (1987). *The making of McPaper: The inside story of USA Today.* Kansas City, MO: Andrews, McPeel & Parker.

USER-CREATED CONTENT

User-created content, also called *user-generated content*, describes various kinds of content produced by Internet and social media users. Generally, user-created content is created by the user of a product or platform rather than the product or platform itself, represents a creative or original contribution, and is shared online and made accessible to other users. Content created by users has come to account for or shape much of the information, images, and videos that users encounter online, whether via social media or other sites. The relationship between user-created content and journalism is complicated, as user-created content can contribute to journalism, compete with it, or be used to promote and disseminate it. This entry describes the history of user contributions, defines various types of user-created content, explains the relevance to and influence of user-created content on journalism, and discusses criticism and concerns about it.

History and Types

The Internet, and social media in particular, was not the beginning of user contributions to public information. Newspapers had published letters to the editor and radio stations had allowed listeners to call in for years before the Internet was invented and widely adopted. Notably, the Oxford English Dictionary was written by public contributions in the 19th century. Amateurs had created their own newsletters, books, and radio broadcasts, particularly before the professionalization and regulation of those media. However, the Internet provided a platform that allowed users to contribute more easily and quickly than before, allowing more people to participate in information creation and leading to a massive increase in user-created content. Manuel Castells (2007) called this "mass self-communication" (p. 238) because every user was able to communicate to everyone else.

Cheap portable cameras, easy-to-use blogging platforms, and other technology made the work of capturing content and putting it online more accessible. From the late 1990s into the 2000s, a great deal of all kinds of content was being created by users. Blogging platforms allowed users to easily post personal reflections or comment on everything from the news to sports to their favorite shoes. Flickr, Snapfish, and other photo-sharing sites provided platforms for users to share hundreds of thousands of photos and even organize them with geotags and other tags that could make them useful to others. Many of these functions were later incorporated in tools such as Google's image search, which identifies the content in photos without user labor, and Twitter, which utilized hashtags to organize related information. YouTube provided the same possibilities for video sharing, creating a giant library of video content from amateurs, ranging from highly produced and edited amateur movies to recordings of users simply talking into the camera. Wikipedia, launched in 2001, provided a platform for users to collaborate in creating a massive online encyclopedia that was free to everyone and reflected the combined knowledge of users. Advocates promoted the value of mass participation, but most studies have found that less than 20% of users create content, and the vast majority only lurk and consume content.

Some sites allowed users to post links to news stories, creating curated news feeds reflecting the interests and opinions of users, rather than the editorial judgment of professional journalists. Reddit is perhaps the strongest example of a site that is built entirely by users posting stories. On curation sites, users generally do not report and write their own news stories or post their own photos or videos (although that also happens) but post stories or items from professional news organizations' websites and other online sources. These feeds are somewhat similar to the social media news feeds that users see, which are created by algorithms that select among the stories posted by a user's friends and other accounts they follow. Similarly, news aggregators, such as Google News, present users with lists of news stories generated by algorithms' interpretations of other users' behavior. In these cases, users are not directly—or even consciously—creating content but are nonetheless contributing to how content is filtered and selected.

User-created content also took the form of memes, mash-ups, fan fiction, and other activities in which Internet users took existing material, whether from professionals or other users, and remixed it to make something new, for comedic, critical, political, or creative purposes. In some cases, users simply organized information to provide context and perspective on reporting produced by professional journalists, but that kind of analysis or commentary can certainly constitute an original contribution. Axel Bruns called these users *produsers* and described the process of creating content in this way as produsage, in which users produce and use content.

By the end of the first decade of the 20th century, social media had grown significantly, becoming a central place for sharing content created by users. Several social movements, including protests against Iranian elections in 2009 and the Arab Spring in 2010–2011, made use of social media tools to organize and spread messages about their movements. While in some cases the significance of social media in aiding protests was later questioned, certainly the ability of the public to create original content that differed from the professional news media, particularly in countries where the news media was state-owned or state-controlled, gave an international platform to the movements.

In the United States, some movements effectively created awareness through the use of hashtags and user posts. The Black Lives Matter movement and #MeToo campaign spread through social media, in the latter case, as thousands of users sharing their personal experiences with sexual abuse and assault on social media. Some have questioned the effectiveness of users' online shows of support for social movements and the extent to which they translate into deeper engagement, however. The term *slacktivism* was coined to describe the desire to appear socially engaged

without contributing materially, whether through a physical presence at protests or donations to needy causes.

As new tools evolve, the definition of user-created content may evolve as well. Twitch is a livestreaming service primarily used by gamers to broadcast their game-play feeds. In 2019, Twitch claimed 3.7 million monthly broadcasters and 15 million daily active users. Although the majority of streamers play video games, there is an increasing number of channels dedicated to charity fundraising and education. While it is difficult to ascertain the income made by streamers, estimates claim that the top 10 streamers may be bringing in a combined $20 million annually. Streamers may have a variety of sources of income, including sponsorship, donations from followers, affiliate links, selling merchandise, and tournament winnings. Twitch partnerships are also available by invitation. This type of user-created content is different in that users stream live, rather than creating and sharing static content that can be viewed long after it is created.

User-Created Content and Professional Journalism

Not all content created by users is relevant to public information or journalism aside from competing for users' attention. Most individual social media posts might be considered to fall within the category of user-created content but are not relevant to a wide audience and would not be considered journalism by most widely accepted standards. In terms of information of public interest, user-created content can range from independent, random acts of citizen journalism, such as witnesses who record and share videos of police misconduct, to coordinated reporting efforts organized or overseen by journalists, as in the crowdsourced reporting done by *The Guardian* (UK), National Public Radio, and CNN's iReport.

One of the earliest examples of citizen journalism took place before the widespread use of the Internet. The video taken by George Holliday of Los Angeles police officers beating Rodney King was shown on local television news stations in Los Angeles in 1991. That video sparked an outcry against police brutality and riots when the officers were eventually exonerated. Videos of police abuse recorded by users remained a common theme on social media for decades.

Interest in and research about citizen journalism peaked in the first decade of the 2000s, when tools to capture and share news content first became widely available and adopted. Nonprofessionals are often the first and sometimes the only witnesses to major events, and when they are carrying phones with embedded high-quality cameras and Internet connections, they are uniquely positioned to document newsworthy events. In the first decade of the 21st century, citizens played key roles in reporting several major stories, such as the 2004 tsunami in Southeast Asia, the 2005 London Tube bombings, and shootings of unarmed citizens by police. Videos and images captured and shared immediately online by citizens provided firsthand documentation of significant events and gave a voice to many participants in news stories.

Citizen journalism was heralded as an opportunity for nonprofessionals to participate in the creation and selection of news content, upending journalists' roles as gatekeepers. Books such as Dan Gillmor's 2004 *We the Media* and Scott Gant's 2007 *We're All Journalists Now* reflected this enthusiasm. Proponents of citizen journalism saw the control exerted by a few professionals over the news agenda as problematic and hoped that bringing more contributors to the process would lead to news coverage that was more representative of the general public's issues and concerns. Critics of citizen journalism pointed out that nonprofessionals may lack training and awareness of ethics, while others noted that the term *citizen* was problematic, given the particular legal status it implies.

While many professional journalists were skeptical of, or even dismissive of, citizen journalism, there were some efforts to take advantage of public contributions. Participatory journalism, and especially crowd-sourcing, describes these more coordinated efforts, in which the collective efforts of a group of users are put toward completing a task or generating content. A notable crowd-sourcing effort organized by journalists was the work by *The Guardian* (UK) to acquire hundreds of thousands of pages of expense reports of members of Parliament and publish them to the web with a request for readers to help identify which

documents merited further examination. Within hours, the newspaper's readers had reviewed nearly half the documents. The site Talking Points Memo similarly posted on its site hundreds of Department of Justice documents it had received as part of a Freedom of Information Act request and sought reader participation in reading the documents to identify important information.

Professional journalists sought user contributions in other ways. One of the first steps in allowing users to contribute to news was the addition of comments sections to news stories that were posted online. Journalists are increasingly influenced by the audience, even if the audience is not directly involved in the creation of content. Many professional news sites feature most read or most shared stories, which are lists based on the behavior of other users in viewing, reading, and sharing stories. In this way, users are influencing the creation of news feeds by their behavior on the site.

It is important to distinguish between sites that are curated by a human who exercises news judgment and sites that are algorithmically aggregated based on user behavior online. The increasingly sophisticated audience metrics provided by online news can shape the behavior of journalists. New roles, such as engagement editor, social media editor, and audience editor, have been adopted in newsrooms to respond to audience data. While this might not strictly be considered user-created content, news produced by professional journalists may be increasingly user-shaped content. Some have argued that social media activity amounts to citizen journalism, but mostly citizen journalism appeared to have been displaced or subsumed by social media. In 2015, CNN dropped its iReport site, which had allowed citizens to upload original content and instead began sourcing stories directly from Instagram, Facebook, and Twitter, using the hashtag #CNNiReport.

User-created content has been viewed as a competitor to professional news media outlets or at least a threat to the authority journalists asserted over information and the financial viability of news organizations. User-created content is cheaper to produce and generally freely available, thus undercutting professional news media's control of the market. Many social media posts are links to professional news stories, which generate ad revenue for social media platforms when posted there, but not for the news outlets that reported the stories, unless users click through to the original source. As more advertising moved online and the news industry lost significant revenue, many daily newspapers closed or moved to online-only editions, while social media platforms often profited from the reporting newspapers had done.

Criticism

Although users may experience benefits from creating content, including potential emotional benefits from participating in crowdsourced projects and other similar efforts, much of the work done by users results in content that is served to other users by social media platforms and sites to generate revenue. The labor of users is uncompensated, and the content they create is used to sell ads and glean data from users, which can also be sold for marketing purposes. A political economic perspective might note the exploitative nature of this system. All social media users are somewhat exploited in this way; the value they receive is free access to the site, but in return their data and attention are sold, and the content they create, whether directly or through likes, comments, and shares, is shown to other users to attract their attention. Meanwhile, the apps and sites they use are designed to demand and keep their attention, and there is increasing evidence that heavy users of social media are more likely to be depressed.

Some content creators are compensated, and this also creates problematic incentives in the system. Influencers who receive benefits for promoting products are expected to disclose those relationships, but may not do so consistently. YouTube personalities who generate revenue from advertising depend on high numbers of views to make more money, so they are incentivized to create content that is more outrageous and likely to go viral. This often means appealing to the audience's biases and anger and trying to post videos immediately following a news story, rather than attempting to confirm facts and discuss them rationally.

User-created content also raises questions about ownership and intellectual property rights. It may be difficult for users in a digital environment to maintain control over the use of the content they

have created. Some efforts to address this include the creation of Creative Commons and public copyright licenses that allow a creator to give other users the right to share, use, and build upon content they have created.

On some platforms and social media sites, user-created content appears alongside and competes with content from professional news organizations, companies, and others. YouTube features channels from individual YouTube personalities but also major network shows and programs, such as HBO. The distinction between users and professionals is sometimes clear and other times not so obvious. In some cases, the presumed authenticity of a citizen report can be used to mislead audiences. For example, some prominent media personalities who have made a career of media agitation, brand themselves as "citizen journalists," when they are effectively media professionals with strong ideological positions, entirely dedicated to shaping media campaigns, who might be more properly considered entrepreneurial journalists.

Finally, the constant flow of information of all kinds places a strain on the capacities of users and especially voters to access, judge, and respond to information. The vast library of content online means that voters have more choice and information than ever before, but it also challenges their cognitive abilities, creating confusion, fatigue, and stronger emotions like anger or outrage.

Jessica Roberts

See also Audiences; Blogs and Bloggers; Citizen Journalism; News Aggregators; Participatory Journalism; Social Media

Further Readings

Allan, S. (2009). *Citizen journalism: Global perspectives.* New York, NY: Peter Lang.

Benkler, Y. (2016). Peer production and cooperation. In J. M. Bauer & M. Latzer (Eds.), *Handbook on the economics of the internet* (pp. 91–119). Cheltenham, UK: Edward Elgar Publishing.

Bruns, A. (2008). *Blogs, Wikipedia, second life and beyond: From production to produsage.* New York, NY: Peter Lang.

Castells, M. (2007). Communication, power and counter-power in the network society. *International Journal of*

Communication, 1(1), 29. Retrieved from https://ijoc .org/index.php/ijoc/article/view/46

Crowston, K., & Fagnot, I. (2018). Stages of motivation for contributing user-generated content: A theory and empirical test. *International Journal of Human-Computer Studies, 109,* 89–101. doi:10.1016/j .ijhcs.2017.08.005.

Gant, S. (2007). *We're all journalists now: The transformation of the press and reshaping of the law in the internet age.* New York, NY: Free Press.

Hermida, A. (2016). *Tell everyone: Why we share and why it matters.* Toronto, Canada: Anchor Canada.

Jenkins, H., Ito, M., & Boyd, D. (2015). *Participatory culture in a networked era: A conversation on youth, learning, commerce, and politics.* Cambridge, UK: Polity.

Khan, M. L. (2017). Social media engagement: What motivates user participation and consumption on YouTube? *Computers in Human Behavior, 66,* 236–247. doi:10.1016/ j.chb.2016.09.024.

Shirky, C. (2008). *Here comes everybody: The power of organizing without organizations.* New York, NY: Penguin.

Van Dijck, J. (2009). Users like you? Theorizing agency in user-generated content. *Media, Culture & Society, 31*(1), 41–58. doi:10.1177/0163443 708098245.

ViacomCBS

ViacomCBS was formed in 2019 after CBS Corporation and Viacom merged for the second time. It includes Viacom's three segments of TV channels: Music and Entertainment (MTV Networks, VH1, Comedy Central, the Paramount Channel, and others), Kids & Family (Nickelodeon channels), and Black Entertainment Television (BET) channels. It also includes Paramount Pictures, 30 television stations, 117 radio stations, various production companies, Showtime, the CBS Sports Network, and the Simon and Schuster book publishing company. The company is also the home of more than 140,000 premium TV episodes and 3,600 film titles. This entry opens with an overview of the origins of CBS and Viacom and then discusses the acquisitions and growth of Viacom, as well as the growth of CBS. The entry also examines the merger between Viacom and CBS Corporation, their subsequent split, and their eventual reuniting.

CBS Origin

The initial origin of CBS came from William Paley who managed to turn a handful of struggling radio stations in 1928, initially called *United Independent Broadcasters*, into what would later become known as the *Columbia Broadcasting System*. Within 10 years, CBS had 114 affiliates throughout the country.

Initial radio programming focused on dramas and entertainment, including shows featuring legendary entertainers Bing Crosby, George Burns, Gracie Allen, Jack Benny, Jack Haley, and Lucille Ball. Orson Welles broadcasted his famous Mercury Theater, presenting classic pieces of literature such as *A Christmas Carol* to the radio airwaves. Welles also famously produced *The War of the Worlds* in 1938, a fictional account of aliens landing on Earth that was so realistic that people panicked thinking it was actually happening.

CBS created its own news division in 1934. Edward R. Murrow was a key hire in 1935. CBS sent him to London in 1937 to develop a European bureau in London amid conflicts before and during World War II. During that time, his reporting gave CBS prominence by creating the European News Roundup, a series of reports from news correspondents from various European cities and anchored by Robert Trout. It gained immediate popularity and quickly became a daily show.

As CBS rose in stature in the 1940s, Paley led the charge in acquiring talent from rival NBC, including performers Freeman Gosden and Charles Correll (famous for their hit *Amos and Andy*), Charlie McCarthy, Red Skelton, and Jack Benny. By 1949, CBS overtook NBC in the ratings.

Television gained prominence in the 1950s. Popular hit shows such as *I Love Lucy* and *The $64,000 Question* boosted the network's television stature. In 1956, CBS announced that its radio operations lost money, while its television operations made money. The network dominated the television market in the late 1950s to mid-1960s with programs such as *Route 66*, *The Twilight Zone*, *The Andy Griffith Show*, and *The Beverly Hillbillies* among others.

Viacom Origin

In 1970, the Federal Communications Commission (FCC) forced CBS to split because of the ruling that television networks could not have financial stakes in cable television systems or syndication rights to the shows it aired. Viacom was officially developed in 1971 as a result and became one of the largest cable operators. The company also owned many popular previously run CBS programs for syndication, including *I Love Lucy*, which was a big source of their overall revenue early on.

Viacom created the premium network Showtime in 1976 to compete with Home Box Office (HBO). The move was significant because most of Viacom's revenue came from cable subscribers and sales of television series through syndication. Showtime's initial premise was to show recently run films that had just left movie theaters, similar to what HBO did. The following year, the network started transmitting to local cable stations. In 1978, Showtime signed a deal with Teleprompter Corporation, which was the largest cable provider in the United States at the time, to offer its customers Showtime instead of HBO.

By the 1980s, Viacom continued to invest in its cable infrastructure to expand its audience reach. However, the company also expanded its media portfolio. By 1981, it had added a number of radio stations in five markets including New York, Chicago, and Washington, DC. It had also acquired one television station in Albany, NY.

Viacom Acquisitions and Growth

Viacom merged with Warner-Amex in 1983 to create a joint ownership with Showtime and The Movie Channel. Warner-Amex sold its interest in 1985, giving Viacom sole ownership of both pay channels.

The company purchased the MTV Networks in 1984, which included MTV, VH1, and Nickelodeon. MTV was a channel devoted to showcasing music videos. VH1 had a similar model but focused on older video for an older audience.

Nickelodeon, originally developed in 1979, was a channel geared toward children. It did not have much success until it was acquired by Viacom, which ultimately gave it more of a flashy look to help distinguish it from other kids' channels.

That same year, Viacom merged its Cable Health Network with Hearst-ABC's Daytime cable television service. The new network was renamed Lifetime, which aimed itself toward women.

National Amusements, Inc. bought a controlling interest in Viacom in 1986 for approximately $3.4 billion. Sumner Redstone was the president of National Amusements, which was a large movie theater chain that had been in the Redstone family for 50 years. At the time, National Amusements had grown to 350 screens nationwide.

After Congress deregulated cable in 1987, Viacom sold some of their cable systems for large profits. The company started its own productions operations in 1989, developing feature films and producing network television series. The company made a series of acquisitions in the mid-1990s, purchasing Paramount Communications, Blockbuster Video, and Spelling Entertainment in 1994 and 1995.

Growth of CBS

The 1970s saw a time at CBS where they shifted their television programming away from rural America. Shows such as *Gunsmoke*, *The Beverly Hillbillies*, *Hee Haw*, and *Green Acres* were canceled to make way for *The Mary Tyler Moore Show*, *The Bob Newhart Show*, *All in the Family*, *M*A*S*H*, and others. The company's commitment to news programming paid off with *60 Minutes* and the *CBS Evening News*, which was anchored by Walter Cronkite.

On a corporate level, CBS battled to prevent an aggressive takeover attempt by Ted Turner, who owned Superstation WTBS and the Cable News Network (CNN), in 1985. The company spent approximately $1 billion to buy back some of its own stock in order to substantially drive up the cost of purchasing the company. Turner continued the challenge but eventually backed off to acquire Hollywood's MGM-UA Entertainment Co. CBS also sold off its book, magazine, and record business in the 1980s to focus solely on radio and television broadcasting.

By the mid-1990s, CBS had fallen to Number 3 in the national ratings, behind NBC and ABC. After decades of independence, CBS was sold to Westinghouse Electric Corporation in 1995 for $5.4 billion. The merger gave the new company operations of 15 television stations and 39 radio stations. Together, they reached approximately 35% of all households in the United States.

Two years later, Westinghouse Electric Corp. became CBS Corp. and also moved its headquarters from Pittsburgh to New York City. After the CBS acquisition in 1995, Westinghouse spent an additional $9 billion to acquire radio and television stations while selling off its industrial assets to focus solely on its media empire.

1999 Merger

In the 1990s, the FCC had a cap on television station ownership. Rules dictated that companies could not own stations that had a reach of more than 35% of the country's population. In 1999, Mel Karmazin, who was the president of CBS, engaged in talks with Viacom about purchasing some of their UPN network stations. However, the discussions became much bigger and led to a discussion of a complete merger between Viacom and CBS Corporation. The merger would give the new company a 41% reach to the country's population. The two companies announced an agreement on September 7, 1999, but still needed to gain approval from the FCC. The deal was completed in April 2000 after the FCC allowed the new company a 1-year window to shed some of its TV stations to comply with the previous rules. It became the largest media merger in the United States at $44 billion. The company kept the name Viacom, which became the second-largest media company behind Time Warner.

Redstone remained the chairman of the merged company, while Karmazin became president and the chief operating officer of Viacom. Karmazin had only been president at CBS Corp. for less than a year, but in that time, its stock had tripled and the network earned a Number 1 ranking in total viewers and households.

At the time, the merger gave Viacom an opportunity for the prestigious CBS network to reach out to the younger MTV generation and vice versa. It also allowed synergy between different networks from the two companies. Soon after the merger, the TV show *Survivor* premiered to huge ratings, which Redstone attributed to the power and reach of the newly formed union.

The merger produced other cross-platform opportunities as well. TV Land, a Viacom channel made up of syndicated programming, aired a weeklong marathon of *The Fugitive* in advance of CBS' revival of the franchise on their network. CBS created a Saturday morning Nick Jr. kids block of shows and also introduced an MTV-produced Super Bowl halftime show for Super Bowl XXXV and Super Bowl XXXVIII.

Unfortunately for Viacom, the halftime show during Super Bowl XXXVIII on CBS proved to be controversial. Justin Timberlake briefly exposed Janet Jackson's breast during the performance, resulting in a huge public uproar and numerous FCC complaints. As a result, the National Football League banned MTV from producing future halftime shows.

The relationship between Redstone and Karmazin quickly soured due to disagreements on how to manage the combined operations. Karmazin left in June 2004 due to his working relationship with Redstone. He split Karmazin's duties into two roles, naming Leslie Moonves and Tom Freston copresidents. Moonves was previously the chairman of CBS Inc., while Freston was the chief executive of MTV Networks.

2005 Split

Redstone announced a split of the company in June 2005, which became official in early 2006. He believed that each company would be more valuable as separate entities rather than together, claiming that the age of the diversified media conglomerate was over. The company was split into two: CBS Corporation and Viacom. Redstone remained chairman of Viacom and also the controlling shareholder for both Viacom and CBS Corp. Stockholders were offered shares of both companies with the split. Freston became CEO at Viacom, and Leslie Moonves became CEO at CBS Corp.

Viacom kept MTV Networks (which included MTV, VH1, Nickelodeon, Nick at Nite, Comedy

Central, CMT, Spike TV, and TV Land), BET, Paramount Pictures, Paramount Home Entertainment, and Famous Music. CBS Corp. combined the UPN and CBS networks, Viacom Television Stations Group, Infinity Broadcasting, Viacom Outdoor, Showtime, Simon & Schuster, and Paramount Parks. CBS Corp. also retained the CBS, Paramount, and King World television production operations.

Initially, industry experts, including Redstone, believed that Viacom would flourish with the split. However, CBS Corp. remained steady, while Viacom struggled to adapt to the digital age. CBS continued to find success with police programs, such as the CSI franchise (*CSI, CSI: Miami, CSI: NY*), *NCIS, Cold Case, Without a Trace, Criminal Minds*, and *NCIS*. Other programs such as *Two and a Half Men, Still Standing, How I Met Your Mother*, and the *Big Bang Theory* helped vault the network back to becoming the Number 1 most watched network in the United States in 2005–2006.

After Viacom shares stagnated, Freston resigned in 2006. He was replaced by Phillipe Dauman on September 5, 2006. Dauman had served in a number of senior executive positions at Viacom, including Deputy Chairman from 1996 to 2000, before leaving for a private equity firm between 2000 and 2006.

The Road to Reuniting

The year 2016 was a tumultuous year for Redstone and Viacom. Redstone stepped down as executive chairman of both companies at the age of 93 after reports of declining health and mental capacity. His daughter Shari Redstone was president of National Amusements, which was still the holding company for both Viacom and CBS Corp. Leslie Moonves, who had served as CEO of CBS Corp., was named CBS Chairman after Sumner Redstone stepped down. He was replaced as Viacom's executive chair by Dauman, who kept that role for only a few months until Shari Redstone ousted him as CEO and nonexecutive chairman later that year.

In Dauman's time as CEO, Viacom's stock increased approximately 130% during his tenure. Robert Bakish, who had worked at the company since 1997 in various roles, became the new CEO of Viacom in late 2016.

At the beginning of 2016, Shari Redstone sent a letter to Viacom and CBS urging the two companies to join together once again. However, she quickly withdrew the proposal after Bakish took over as CEO, citing his strategic plan to bring Viacom back to prominence. Moonves opposed the merger as well. Two years later, CBS rejected a second proposal by Shari Redstone.

Soon after merger talks were thwarted for the second time, Moonves was accused of numerous sexual misconduct allegations. In an interview, Moonves claimed that "there were times decades ago when I may have made some women uncomfortable by making advances." Moonves was stripped of his severance and CBS donated $20 million to organizations supporting the #MeToo movement and equality for women in the workplace. CBS Corp. COO Joseph Ianniello stepped in as president and acting CEO.

2019 Merger

After the departure of Moonves, merger talks quickly ensued and a deal was completed on December 4, 2019. The new company was named ViacomCBS, with Bakish becoming CEO of the newly formed company. Shari Redstone was named chairman of ViacomCBS. The merger was an all stock-swap transaction, with a total market capitalization of $26 billion. Ianniello shifted his role to chairman-CEO of CBS, a structure that was put in place as a part of the merger. He eventually left the company in March 2020 and was replaced by George Cheeks as CEO and president of CBS Entertainment Group.

Chris A. Bacon

See also CBS News

Further Readings

Berr, J. (2019, November 26). *Here is everything you need to know about the Viacom-CBS Merger.* Retrieved July 2, 2020, from https://www.forbes.com/sites/jonathanberr/2019/11/26/here-is-everything-you-need-to-know-about-the-viacom-cbs-merger/

CBS and Viacom Complete Merger. (2000, May 4). Retrieved July 2, 2020, from https://www.cbsnews.com/news/cbs-and-viacom-complete-merger/

Chmielewski, D. (2020, June 29). *Exclusive: For the first time Shari Redstone tells her side of the battle to merge Viacom and CBS*. Retrieved July 2, 2020, from https://www.forbes.com/sites/dawnchmielewski/2019/10/02/exclusive-for-the-first-time-shari-redstone-tells-her-side-of-the-battle-to-merge-viacom-and-cbs/

Fabrikant, G. (1985, July 4). *CBS, Trying to block Turner bid, to buy $1 billion of its own stock*. Retrieved July 2, 2020, from https://www.nytimes.com/1985/07/04/business/cbs-trying-to-block-turner-bid-to-buy-1-billion-of-its-own-stock.html

Forgey, Q. (2018, September 9). *Moonves ousted as CBS chief*. Retrieved July 2, 2020, from https://www.politico.com/story/2018/09/09/moonves-ousted-cbs-shief-813556

Goldman, M. C., & Johnson, T. (1999, September 7). *Viacom buys CBS for $35.6 billion*. Retrieved July 2, 2020, from https://money.cnn.com/1999/09/07/deals/cbs/

Hearst-ABC, Viacom in Pact. (1983, June 15). Retrieved July 2, 2020, from https://www.nytimes.com/1983/06/15/business/hearst-abc-viacom-in-pact.html

Schneider, M. (2019, August 13). *CBS-Viacom: 20 Years later, a look back at the high hopes and eventual collapse of that first merger*. Retrieved July 2, 2020, from https://variety.com/2019/tv/news/cbs-viacom-merger-20-years-later-moonves-redstone-karmazin-freston-1203265965/

Shari Redstone withdraws CBS-Viacom merger proposal. (2016, December 13). Retrieved July 2, 2020, from https://www.cnbc.com/amp/2016/12/12/shari-redstone-withdraws-cbs-viacom-merger-proposal.html

Viacom board opts to split company. (n.d.). Retrieved July 2, 2020, from https://www.cnn.com/2005/BUSINESS/06/14/viacom.split/index.html

Viacom completes split into 2 companies. (2006, January 2). Retrieved July 2, 2020, from https://www.nytimes.com/2006/01/02/business/media/viacom-completes-split-into-2-companies.html

Viacom names Philippe Dauman president and CEO, succeeding Tom Freston; Thomas Dooley named senior executive vice president and chief administrative officer. (2006, September 5). Retrieved July 2, 2020, from https://www.businesswire.com/news/home/20060905005560/en/Viacom-Names-Philippe-Dauman-President-CEO-Succeeding

VIDEO JOURNALISM

Video journalism is the practice of video news production whereby one person shoots, writes, and edits a news story, using digital technologies, for dissemination via broadcasting or broadband Internet. Video journalists (VJs) might also be called *backpack journalists* or *mobile journalists* or *multimedia journalists*. VJs might work for television stations, newspapers, websites, or citizen journalism organizations, or they might be independent freelancers. A VJ might shoot with a small video camera, a DSLR camera with interchangeable lenses, or increasingly, a smartphone.

Video journalism has taken hold in a variety of media institutions, changing journalistic narratives, practices, and identities. Shooting solo offers the possibility of a distinct style with filmic intimacy while at the same time it has led to concerns among many practitioners about quality, safety, and job security. The potential for narrative variability remains an inspiration for many VJs, and smartphone accessibility has put video's evidentiary power into the hands of human rights activists and marginalized groups. This entry discusses the history of video journalism, varying styles of VJs, controversies surrounding video journalism, and the use of video in citizen journalism.

History

While the term *video journalism* came into popular use relatively recently, its history goes back a century, and is rooted in both documentary filmmaking and photojournalism. Many of the earliest documentary filmmakers worked alone in spite of cumbersome, heavy equipment.

In the late 1980s, a former network television producer, Michael Rosenblum, saw potential in the new, highly portable Hi8 video cameras and titled a course he taught at Columbia University "video journalism." A few years later he established Video News International (VNI). VNI deployed VJs who, by working as solo international correspondents, constituted an operation that was cheaper to operate and more mobile than a conventional broadcast television network. VNI eventually became New York Times Television and years later was folded into the larger news-gathering operation of *The New York Times*.

So-called one-man-bands were the exception in television news and documentary film before media digitization. News production in the field began to change in the 1970s when ENG (electronic news gathering) video cameras started to replace film. While these units were not nearly as small and portable as today's technology, they made possible the earliest one-man bands in the 1970s and 1980s. During this era, single-person units were more often found in smaller markets, where young reporters would shoot, write, and edit as they worked their way into larger markets to work as part of a team with a photographer and occasionally a sound technician. This is no longer the case. As of 2018, the annual Radio-Television Digital News Association survey found that more than half of U.S. TV newsrooms in the United States "mostly" employed VJs, with the smallest markets relying most heavily on the one-man band model.

In Great Britain, the BBC has trained hundreds of VJs. In places such as Oxford, England, a nearly all-VJ staff produces a daily hyperlocal newscast for the area, something that was not financially possible prior to digitization.

Smartphones have accelerated the trend. Because smartphones are so small and easy to use, many more journalists might work as VJs full or part time, and a newsroom might easily double the number of staff who can shoot video. Amber Worthy, an anchor-reporter in Chattanooga, Tennessee, told documentary-researcher James P. Mahon "Our iPhone video—sometimes it's the only video we have" (Mahon, 2019). Indeed, as Mahon reported in his 2019 documentary *The MoJo Revolution*, some news organizations, such as Léman Bleu in Geneva and NDTV in New Delhi, rely entirely on mobile smartphone technology.

Many VJs now work for organizations once associated with print journalism. Often they are former staff photographers who were once assigned to shoot still photographs but now might shoot both formats for the same story.

VJ Narratives

The narrative style of video journalism varies, according to organizational needs. VJs who work for online organizations have had the freedom to experiment with formatting, but those VJs who work for TV news organizations tend to produce stories in conventional broadcast style, shooting their own standups and voicing scripts. A local television station in San Francisco, KRON, was among the first local television stations in the United States to convert to an all VJ staff; yet KRON's stories were almost indistinguishable from those produced by competing, non-VJ stations. In other cases, a TV VJ might adopt the more emotional and "experiential" style lauded by the pioneers of solo video journalism.

VJs who work for online organizations often adopt this more documentary style, using only natural sound and interviews to create a narrative. Dirck Halstead, one of the original members of VNI, was a leader in helping still photographers make this transition with what he called *Platypus* workshops where he encouraged students to avoid trying to copy TV news. The host of Australia's VJ-staffed *Dateline* program, Jana Wendt, noted that "One of the benefits and charms of this style is that you can get in where others cannot" (Fidgeon, 2004). On the mobile web, vertically oriented video, once a mark of amateurism, is now widely accepted and is even the official format of a show on NDTV in New Delhi.

Recognition of video journalism as a distinct form solidified after the turn of the new century. The flagship professional publication of the National Press Photographers Association, *News Photographer*, began using the term regularly in 2004, and 2 years later, the organization's annual Best of Photojournalism contest included an entry for solo VJs.

Controversies

Video journalism offers considerable advantages for newsrooms seeking to extend coverage and produce more digital content, but many VJs complain that they are being asked to do more work with less support. Photojournalists have trained themselves, and some have been compelled to learn video skills in order to keep their jobs.

Critics argue that in the rush to embrace video, journalists have lost jobs and quality has suffered. News organizations have cut back and in some cases eliminated their photography departments, expecting writers to learn how to shoot with their smartphones.

Researchers report that newspaper VJs enjoy their creative autonomy but worry about quality and often feel unsupported. Reporters complain that they've received video training but never use it because shooting and editing take time their organizations won't give them. Concerns about quality are valid, as research has found that users associate video quality with credibility.

TV journalists also harbor concerns about solo practice even though most of their newsrooms now employ VJs. Solo practitioners complain that it is hard to shoot and write well at the same time, particularly during breaking stories. There are gender discrepancies, too, as VJs in TV news might still be expected to wear business clothing, an added burden for women who might need to shoot in one outfit but carry a change of shoes, or more, for their on-camera appearances. Safety issues are also a concern, especially during live coverage.

Citizen Journalism

Video journalism's accessibility means nearly anyone can create online stories, blurring the distinction between journalists and the audience. In 1999, activists with lightweight video cameras produced a form of "counter coverage" of the protest against the World Trade Organization in Seattle. Since then, citizen video journalism has taken root with human rights groups such as Witness and other organizations devoted to giving voice to those underrepresented groups. Nongovernmental organizations use digital video to tell their own "news" about their efforts instead of relying on journalists. Police accountability activists, or cop-watchers, use video as part of their ongoing efforts to document and critique law enforcement.

Mary Angela Bock

See also Citizen Journalism; Convergence; Photojournalists

Further Readings

Assaf, C. T. (2019). Video convergence: Factors affecting photojournalists' satisfaction and adoption. *Annual Meeting*. Presented at the Association for Education in Journalism and Mass Communication, Toronto.

Associated Press. (2013, May 31). Chicago Sun-Times lays off all its full-time photographers. *The New York Times*. Retrieved from http://www.nytimes.com/2013/06/01/business/media/chicago-sun-times-lays-off-all-its-full-time-photographers.html?_r=0

Barnouw, E. (1993). *Documentary: A history of the non-fiction film*. Oxford, UK: Oxford University Press.

Bock, M. A. (2012). *Video journalism: Beyond the one-man band*. New York, NY: Peter Lang.

Canella, G. (2018). Video goes vertical: Local news videographers discuss the problems and potential of vertical video. *Electronic News*, 12(2), 75–93. doi:10.1177/1931243117705417.

Chen, G. M., Chen, P. S., Chang, C.-W., & Abedin, Z. (2017). News video quality affects online sites' credibility. *Newspaper Research Journal*, 38(1), 19–31. doi:10.1177/0739532917696087.

Fidgeon, R. (2004). The masters of DIY journalism. *The Herald Sun, Melbourne, Australia,* Retrieved from October 13, 2004, HO8.

Greenwood, K., & Reinardy, S. (2011). Self-trained and self-motivated: Newspaper photojournalists strive for quality during technological challenges. *Visual Communication Quarterly*, 18(3), 155–166. doi:10.1080/15551393.2011.599285.

Junnarker, S. (2006). Q&A with Travis Fox, video journalist for WashingtonPost.com. *Online Journalism Review*. Retrieved from September 16, 2006, http://www.ojr.org/qa-with-travis-fox-video-journalist-for-washingtonpost-com/

Madrigal, A. C., & Meyer, R. (2018, October 18). How Facebook's chaotic push into video cost hundreds of journalists their jobs. *The Atlantic*. Retrieved from https://www.theatlantic.com/technology/archive/2018/10/facebook-driven-video-push-may-have-cost-483-journalists-their-jobs/573403/

Mahon, J. (2019). *The MoJo Revolution: News from the palm of your hand*. East Tennessee PBS. Retrieved from https://www.pbs.org/video/the-mojo-revolution-news-from-the-palm-of-your-hand-5xxmps/

NPAA (n.d.). Training: News video workshop. Retrieved from https://nppa.org/training/news-video-workshop

Papper, R. (2018). MMJ growth is slowing down. Retrieved from December 30, 2019, http://bobpapper .com/wp-content/uploads/2019/07/2018-Release-3- MMJs-v5F.docx

Powers, M. (2014). The structural organization of NGO publicity work: Explaining divergent publicity strategies at humanitarian and human rights organizations. *International Journal of Communication, 8*(0), 18. Retrieved from https://ijoc .org/index.php/ijoc/article/view/2517

Websites

Rosenblum TV: www.RosenblumTV.com

VIDEO NEWS RELEASES

Video news releases (VNRs) are audio/video public relations and marketing tools generally designed to attract news outlets to cover the VNR-promoted product, service, or firm. The simple formula is that one makes favorable coverage of a client more likely if one makes that coverage easier by providing all the materials necessary for a newsroom to cobble together the story. Broadcast use of VNRs has U.S. federal regulators asking questions, and taking action in extreme cases, about whether VNRs violate sponsorship identification rules. This entry discusses the distribution of VNRs, how they are used, research on VNRs, and ethical concerns about their use.

VNRs started in the 1980s as three-quarter-inch videotapes mailed to local television newsrooms. Even these early versions had the basic elements of VNRs: suggested scripts, a complete television news package with reporter-style narration track, a "donut" (narration missing) version of the package so a broadcast news reporter or anchor could add his or her voice to the narration, extra footage fitting the topic or subject, extra expert or consumer sound bites, and still graphics of the product, company logo. These elements made it easy for any television news producer to craft the material into a story type such as voiceover (VO) or voiceover with sound bite (VO/SOT, originally standing for "voiceover/sound on tape"), and even have an over-the-shoulder graphic as the anchor speaks.

The distribution methods for VNRs have changed over time. For many years the primary source was satellite feeds. Broadcast newsrooms could record on videotape VNRs using the same satellite system they use to get shared news items gathered by affiliated news operations. Indeed, VNRs sometimes tag along on the actual network satellite feed. For example, an ABC affiliate in the 1990s in the United States may have had available to it the ABC NewsOne news satellite feed and may have even been an affiliate of CNN Newsource but also could record VNRs from a company then called MediaLink distributed on its own or sometimes mixed within network feeds.

Contemporary VNR distribution is more likely to occur via websites such as thenewsmarket.com or prnewswire.com. Though broadcast programming, notably television newscasts, remains a prime "target" of VNR distributors, one now can see VNRs being used as embedded clips on the websites of newspapers, magazines, specialty publications, and web-only news operations. VNRs also can become a component in an online corporate press kit made available not only to reporters but also to key audiences such as prospective investors and investment research analysts.

One day in early 2020, the following VNRs were available for download and use by television stations or any news entity with a website:

- Video and sound bites from International Monetary Fund spokesman Gerry Rice on the economic cost of the coronavirus outbreak.
- Still images, text, and video about Lamborghini introducing in Valencia, Spain, its "Surfaces" line of cars inspired by art and architecture.
- An array of promotional photos and stories from the Las Vegas Convention and Visitors Authority including video of a nighttime parade of very large trucks down one city street, the NASCAR Hauler Parade.

Documenting routine VNR use can be tricky. News directors in large newsrooms are news executives, not regularly involved in day-to-day coverage and story decisions. Producers are better sources but may underestimate daily VNR use or may not consider brief VNR shots in a larger package as a "use." The most reliable data come from SIGMA, an electronic verification service offered by Nielsen Media Research to advertising, public relations, and marketing firms. SIGMA tracks embedded codes and can be used to verify use of commercials, infomercials, VNRs, or public service announcements.

VNRs effectively exploit the current demands that television newsrooms produce more content, both online and on air, with fewer staffers. Within the realm of U.S. local television newscasts, VNRs tend to appear most frequently in health reporting segments or in VO format for light, amusing "kicker" stories toward the close of newscasts.

Scholars have approached VNRs from a variety of perspectives. Public relations practitioners have plumbed the usefulness of VNRs in an overall public relations strategy and the elements that make VNR content attractive to newscast producers. Journalism researchers, however, have explored the ethical dimensions of VNR use—namely whether the unlabeled use of VNR footage is deceptive. One relevant study appeared in the *International Journal of Advertising* in 2020. It involved native advertising on websites, in which material paid for by an advertiser was made to resemble the websites' editorial content. The study found that more detailed disclosure led audiences to see both the advertiser and the media in general as having more credibility. If true, then neither TV stations nor VNR producers should fear routine identification of the video source.

VNRs have been the subject of media criticism in recent years. In 2004, at least 40 stations aired at least part of a VNR made for the George W. Bush administration in support of a new Medicare prescription drug law that ended with a VO saying, "In Washington, I'm Karen Ryan reporting." After *The New York Times* reported on the use of the segments, other news articles highlighted government VNR distribution from agencies such as the Defense, Agriculture, and Census departments dating back for years, and getting extensive airplay. Journalists asked whether the airing of government-produced news reports that look like independent journalism betrayed the watchdog role of the press and deceived the public.

The Federal Communications Commission in 2011 entered the fray over VNRs when it fined two TV stations $4000 for airing VNRs without sponsorship identification. One was a Minneapolis station, which aired a piece on new General Motors convertibles, speaking only about that company and showing 12 different visuals of GM cars. The other was a New Jersey station, which reported on using zinc to shorten colds, but only specifically mentioned the Zicam product and showed images of it.

For all the introspection, however, government and corporate VNRs remain in use today. It takes a clever, informed viewer to spot their use across media platforms because notice of source or sponsor identification may be fleeting or even absent.

Mark D. Harmon

See also Credibility; Deception; Hard Versus Soft News; Newsroom Culture; Objectivity; Spin

Further Readings

Harmon, M. D., & White, C. (Summer 2001). How television news programs use video news releases. *Public Relations Review, 27*(2), 213–222. doi:10.1016/S0363-8111(01)00081-9.

Krouer, S., Poels, K. P., & Paulussen, S. (2020) Moving towards transparency for native advertisements on news websites: A test of more detailed disclosures. International Journal of Advertising, 39(1), 51–73. doi:10.1080/02650487.2019.1575107.

Nelson, M. R., Wood, M. L. M., & Paek, H. J. (2009). Increased persuasion knowledge of video news releases: Audience beliefs about news and support for source disclosure. *Journal of Mass Media Ethics, 24*(4), 220–237. doi:10.1080/0890052 0903332626.

Owen, A. R., & Karrh, J. A. (Winter 1996). Video news releases: Effects on viewer recall and attitudes. *Public Relations Review, 22*(4), 369–378. doi:10.1016/S0363-8111(96)90029-6.

Oxenford, D. (March 25, 2011). FCC fines two TV Stations $4000 for airing video news releases without sponsorship identification, even though the stations were not paid for the broadcast. *Broadcast Law Blog.* Retrieved from https://www.broadcastlawblog .com/2011/03/articles/fcc-fines-two-tv-stations-4000-for-airing-video-news-releases-without-sponsorship-identification-even-though-the-stations-were-not-paid-for-the-broadcast/

VIOLENCE AGAINST JOURNALISTS

Journalism has meant different things in different times and places, but however it has been defined, it has encountered some form of violence. In some cases, violence has been an unofficial form of media regulation. In other cases, violence has marked the continuation of political conflicts by other means. In yet other cases, violence has been primarily personal, growing out of a sense of outraged honor or acting as an assertion of sexual power. In every case, violence has had an expressive dimension; in some cases, it has been primarily symbolic. Although usually physical and material, violence in the 21st century has evolved to include "virtual" acts.

This entry is organized around patterns (rather than discrete acts) of violence. Violent acts are often chaotic and random, but recurring patterns of violence usually are generated by the structure of the media system and the prevailing definition and norms of journalism. Research has identified a number of patterns that are relatively common across space and time. The most prominent include conflict zone violence, majoritarian violence, personal violence, workplace-related violence, inclusionary violence, and virtual violence.

Conflict Zone Violence

The likelihood of violence has always been a feature of war reporting. War correspondents wear their nearness to physical danger as a badge of honor, and their memoirs always emphasize how deeply they shared the perils of combat with ordinary soldiers. The best-known example in the United States is columnist Ernie Pyle, killed by a sniper during World War II. By the late 20th century, violent conflicts had overrun the borders of conventional military action. In the 2010s, the most dangerous zones for journalists included Syria, where a complex civil war raged, and Mexico, where a quasi-military drug war targeted reporters.

Conflict zone violence has been a matter of concern for international journalism organizations for a long time and was a motivating factor behind the attempt to create an international credentialing body for journalists during the debate over the New World Information and Communication Order in UNESCO in the 1970s and 1980s. Organizations like Reporters Without Borders and the Committee to Protect Journalists monitor conflict zone violence, drawing attention to the extent of the problem as well as the fact that many victims are freelancers or local contract employees hired as translators or stringers by larger Western news organizations.

Conflict zone violence is unlike other patterns of violence in a number of ways. First, it exists in spaces where violence is expected. Second, it exists on the borders of social formations rather than within them. And third, it has a timelessness about it. One suspects that it will persist as long as journalism involves corporeal presence.

Majoritarian Violence

The most dramatic examples of violence against journalists typically come during riots and other crowd actions. In these cases, it is common for the crowd to present itself as the authentic voice of the people, emerging apparently spontaneously but as a stabilizing or recalibrating instrument rather than as a sign of disruption. The notion of the moral authority of the crowd was traditional in early modern Europe and became a common feature of democratic revolutions. During the American Revolution, both Patriots and Loyalists mobilized crowds to suppress opposition publications in areas under their control, asserting in effect that such voices were outside the legitimate political community. After the Revolution, crowd actions, like other techniques of mobilization, became a part of the repertoire of party politics. When reform movements, such as abolitionism, vexed majoritarian parties, their publications became targets of crowd actions.

Mass politics sometimes exacerbated violent intolerance, a dynamic that was particularly evident in the 19th-century United States. Antislavery activists provide the best example. Because the two major parties in the 1830s both required Southern support to win national power, neither could afford to be seen as "incorrect" on the slavery issue, and so both parties felt the need to make examples of abolitionists in their own territory. Democrat Martin Van Buren, while sitting vice president, took credit in private correspondence for an anti-abolitionist riot in his home turf of Utica, New York, while Usher Linder, Whig attorney general of Illinois, led the mob that attacked and killed abolitionist Elijah Lovejoy in Alton. In such cases, violent actions exemplify broader lines of force that curtail non-mainstream expression within the political system.

Partisan media systems in general seem to nurture more violence against journalists than professionalized or "objective" media systems. Journalists in partisan systems are seen as combatants in political conflict, and so are targeted whenever that conflict becomes heated. They are also more likely to be targets of personal violence.

Personal Violence

Violence against a journalist is always to some extent personal, but there are specific circumstances in which attackers claim to be motivated by a personal affront. Dueling is perhaps the most dramatic and certainly the most scripted form of personal violence. The typical case involved the subject of a published piece claiming that his (almost always) personal honor had been attacked and demanding satisfaction. Physical violence was thus seen as a proportional corrective to a rhetorical violation. Dueling was supposedly rule-governed and, although generally illegal, was understood by its practitioners to be orderly and gentlemanly—a way of restoring a damaged order.

In practice, personal violence, including dueling, was often a covert form of political warfare. A "gentleman," like anyone else, could find grounds for taking personal offense quite easily when engaged in political conflict. As late as 1882, Edward A. Burke, the treasurer of Louisiana, challenged C. Harrison Parker, editor of the New Orleans *Daily Picayune*, for remarks he considered personally offensive. Journalists could be attractive targets for several reasons: they were usually unskilled in combat, having chosen the pen over the sword; they could easily be characterized as ungentlemanly or cowardly for avoiding conflict; and by making the conflict personal and public, the would-be attacker stood a good chance of reputational gain. But the prevalence of personal violence in any given place or time cannot be shown to have succeeded in silencing journalists; in fact, they often took pride in having provoked a violent response, and personal attacks became a stock feature of occupational culture,

waning in the 20th century with the rise of professionalized news.

Rising levels of personal violence often correspond to periods of social change. The rise of dueling, for instance, followed the democratic revolutions in early modern Europe and North America and indicated fragility in the boundaries between elites and the larger public. In any situation, personal violence against journalists points to instability in the demarcation between public and private.

Workplace-Related Violence

Labor activism has occasioned violence in much of the industrializing world. Often that violence has visited reporters covering labor conflicts. But news organizations have themselves been part of the Industrial Revolution, and industrial news organizations have experienced labor violence in their own production systems. Sometimes striking workers have resorted to violence, including Luddite sabotage, to shut down production; more often, strikers and labor leaders have been targeted. Like majoritarian and personal violence, labor-related violence has been muted since the middle of the 20th century, a trend that can be attributed to the formalization of labor laws and policies as well as the fragmentation and diminution of news industry labor organizations. In any case, the workers at news organizations most likely to become entangled in violent conflict were more often press operators, typesetters, drivers, and even newsboys than reporters or editors, the occupations conventionally defined as journalists. Pressmen and drivers were the main combatants in the violent strikes involving Rupert Murdoch's Wapping printing plant in 1986 and at the *New York Daily News* in 1990.

As journalism has diversified, however, different forms of workplace-related violence have become familiar. In the 2010s, a series of spectacular reports of harassment of women journalists drew attention to the ways in which newsrooms had incorporated gendered definitions of key roles. It is fair to say that documented cases of sexual harassment point to a systemic disempowering of women in news workplaces; it is also likely that the sudden visibility of such cases indicates an emerging recalibration of the gendering of news.

Inclusionary Violence

As many sorts of violence diminished with the professionalization of journalism, other forms arose. Inclusionary violence refers to violent acts that are designed to force the inclusion of content that news organizations would otherwise ignore, as when James Hoskins occupied the newsroom of WCPO-TV in Cincinnati in an attempt to gain attention to inequality and injustice. The most dramatic examples of inclusionary violence are terrorist attacks: spectacular violent acts that are designed to force attention to non-mainstream ideas, groups, or movements. It is often asserted that terrorism would not exist without media. This is an overstatement, but especially since electronic media have become primary sources of news for most of the world, media coverage has become a fundamental element of terrorism. Even if terrorism has existed without media, there is no terrorist action today that does not aim at the media space.

Other forms of inclusionary violence are less disruptive. Activists print fake front pages of newspapers and insert them into newsboxes, for instance, in a relatively nonviolent form of inclusionary violence. In the 21st century, "hacktivists" attack news organizations' websites and upload content, and both news organizations and individual journalists have become anxious about digital security.

Inclusionary violence became important when news organizations became effective gatekeepers. This occurred when already industrialized news organizations acquired something like a monopoly position on a specific niche of the news ecosystem and adopted professional standards as a way of reassuring the public that they were exercising their vast power responsibly. That moment of modernist control has passed, and professionalized news no longer controls the media space. Instead, post-professional organizations in new media formats, particularly digital ones, provide avenues for public attention to non-mainstream groups and ideas.

Virtual Violence

In the age of digital media, new forms of violence have appeared, which can be provisionally grouped together as virtual violence. Some of these are native to social media, such as Twitter bots, which can be made to resemble the mobs of 19th-century majoritarian violence. Others are more palpably criminal, like ransomware attacks.

One can question whether virtual violence is violent at all. It is generally assumed that violence must be corporeal. Violence attacks the body, either immediately or, at one remove, by threatening bodily harm. No one would doubt that brandishing a gun is a violent act. Virtual violence sometimes can resemble brandishing a gun: "Doxxing" a journalist by publishing her home address or bank account numbers, for instance, is certainly understood as threatening violence and can have a powerful deterrent effect. Even seemingly whimsical acts, such as when a group of anonymous contributors to the website 4chan doxxed Anna Merlan, a reporter at the online news site Jezebel, by ordering pizzas delivered to what they seemed to think was her home, can seem to portend real danger.

Doxxing is characteristic of a social order that rigorously guards privacy in one sense while undermining it in others. Doxxing would seem mysterious to a 20th-century middle-class person in a Western country, for whom a listing in the phone book was an important sign of belonging to normal society. But the random personal material that appears on an ordinary Twitter feed or Facebook page would seem equally exotic. For journalists, as for others, a simple line between private and public has become a complex network of varyingly private/public spaces; as their boundaries multiply and blur, the opportunities for vandalizing them increase.

Conclusion

Journalists often think of their work as intellectual and therefore ideally remote from physical peril—except of course when braving conflict zones. But if journalism matters, it will likely be targeted by interests trying to influence it, peacefully if possible but forcibly if not. Journalists have been rudely reminded of this recently: by autocrats in the Philippines, by drug cartels in Mexico, and by police in the United States, where the Committee to Protect Journalists reported over a hundred acts of physical violence against journalists covering the Black Lives Matter protests erupting after the death of George Floyd. Violence against journalists in the United States in 2020 was reminiscent of earlier waves of civil unrest, such as when Chicago police targeted reporters covering protests of the Democratic National Convention in 1968.

Violence has always been a part of journalistic culture. But it is not a single thing. Rather, there have been and are many different forms of violence. They all are meaningful in understanding the structures of journalism as a practice, an industry, an institution, or a profession. For the most part, violent acts have been intended to silence voices, but a significant proportion have intended to force recognition of excluded voices. In some cases, violence has been a form of media regulation that has operated beyond the law while understanding itself as enforcing lawful behavior. In almost all cases, violence is strategic: Contrary to its image as a passionate outburst of spontaneous rage, violence has usually been calculated and goal-directed. If, on the surface, this fact makes violence against journalists seem more ordinary and manageable, on a deeper level it should raise concerns.

John Nerone

See also Freedom of Expression, History of; Labor Unions in Media; Partisan Press; Press Freedom; War Correspondents

Further Readings

Hughes, S., Mellado, C., Arroyave, J., Benitez, J. L., de Beer, A., Garcés, M., & Márquez-Ramírez, M. (2017). Expanding influences research to insecure democracies: How violence, public insecurity, economic inequality and uneven democratic performance shape journalists' perceived work environments. *Journalism Studies*, 18(5), 645–665. doi:10.1080/1461670X.2016.1266278.

Merlan, A. (2015, January 29). The cops don't care about violent online threats. What do we do now? *Jezebel*. Retrieved from https://jezebel.com/the-cops-dont-care-about-violent-online-threats-what-d-1682577343

Mindich, D. T. (2000). *Just the facts: How "objectivity" came to define American journalism*. New York, NY: NYU Press.

Nerone, J. (1994). *Violence against the press: Policing the public sphere in US history*. New York, NY: Oxford University Press.

Relly, J. E., & González de Bustamante, C. (2017). Global and domestic networks advancing prospects for institutional and social change: The collective action response to violence against journalists. *Journalism & Communication Monographs*, 19(2), 84–152. doi:10.1177/1522637917702618.

Richards, L. (1971). *Gentlemen of property and standing: Anti-abolition mobs in Jacksonian America*. New York, NY: Oxford University Press.

Sreberny, A. (2014). Violence against women journalists. In A. V. Montiel (Ed.), *Media and gender: A scholarly alliance for the global alliance on media and gender* (pp. 35–39). Paris: UNESCO.

Websites

Center for Media at Risk, Annenberg School for Communication, University of Pennsylvania: https://www.ascmediarisk.org/

Committee to Protect Journalists: https://cpj.org/

Reporters Without Borders: https://rsf.org/en

VIRTUAL REALITY

Journalism has changed due, in part, to the convergence of digital technologies, the Internet, and mobile media. Virtual reality (VR), sometimes referred to as artificial reality, is one of the formats journalism uses that integrates these phenomena. VR is defined as a computer-generated, three-dimensional environment that is interactive and immersive. For journalism, VR has three variants:

1. *Immersive journalism* is a first-person experience of a news event using a VR headset, or other VR technology. In the virtual environment, a user's body is represented digitally as an avatar, a 3D representation of themselves with a first-person view of the virtual environment. The avatar is situated in the scenario of the news story.

2. Another form of VR is called *augmented reality* (AR). For journalism, AR technology has two manifestations. The first is seen in virtual news

sets used for studio broadcasting. The second form AR can take is for journalistic storytelling in an AR-enabled media environment.

3. Third is a category of *virtual news writing* that has two subgenres: (a) news of, or about, VR technology and (b) journalism from virtual communities. The former is a type of science and technology journalism, and the latter is a journalistic form originating from virtual worlds that have their own newspapers, newscasts, and news organizations producing stories for and about virtual events, people, and communities.

VR lies on the far end of a continuum from reality to VR. Between the two ends of the continuum is mixed reality. Mixed reality refers to mixing the real with the virtual in varying degrees. AR is a form of mixed reality. In AR, the view of the real world is overlaid with computer-generated digital information or imagery (graphics, photographs, video, or animation). The yellow first-down line marker used for National Football League game broadcasts, Snapchat Lenses, and the Pokémon GO mobile game are popular examples of AR.

A Brief History

In 1935, science fiction writer Stanley Weinbaum wrote *Pygmalion's Spectacles*, in which a professor invents a pair of goggles that allows the main character to view a movie with sight, sound, taste, smell, and touch. The roots of VR, however, can be traced back to the 19th century in the form of panoramic paintings of battles and other scenes. Actual VR systems, as we know them today, have been around in experimental form since the 1950s. In 1957, filmmaker Morton Heilig invented the Sensorama, a large, booth-like contraption that was intended to give a user the illusion of being in a 3D immersive world complete with smell, stereo sound, and atmospheric effects like wind. Then, in the 1960s, head-mounted devices were being developed. Philco Corporation engineers created the first head-mounted system called *Headsight*, which had two video screens, one for each eye, along with a tracking system connected to a remote camera that allowed the user to look around an environment without physically being there. Computer graphics pioneer Ivan Sutherland

also developed a head-mounted system that displayed simple wireframe, computer-generated graphics in 1968. Around this time, the military was working on flight simulators for pilot training. In the late 1960s and into the mid-1970s, Myron Krueger worked on many interactive VR projects while earning his PhD at the University of Madison–Wisconsin. One of his later projects called *Videoplace* was an AR laboratory that combined projectors with video cameras that emitted onscreen images that surrounded users in an interactive environment. Through the 1980s, improvements in computer graphics and VR technologies made more advanced VR and AR possible. Stimulating wider interest in VR was the 1982 movie *Tron*, which depicted characters fully immersed in a computer-simulated videogame environment. Throughout the 1990s, VR continued to grow primarily in the console games and arcade sectors. In 1999, *The Matrix* came to theaters and enhanced the buzz about VR. In the 2000s, VR systems continued to improve, and although available to the consumer, the price tag for many VR systems was still too expensive for most people. One exception was Google Cardboard, a stereoscopic system that used a mobile phone inserted into the cardboard mounting device (more on Google Cardboard later in this entry). In 2010, 18-year-old inventor Palmer Luckey created the prototype for the Oculus Rift. The sale of his invention to Facebook for $2 billion in 2014 was both controversial and legitimizing for the technology. Currently, hundreds of companies are developing VR products.

The first phase in the use of VR for journalism was 360-degree video. Shot with specially designed cameras, or multi-camera rigs, everything is recorded along a panoramic plane. *The New York Times* was one of the early users of 360-degree video for news storytelling. The company published its first VR application (app) in November 2015 and distributed more than a million Google Cardboard headsets to home delivery subscribers. The first journalistic VR piece in *The New York Times* was an 11-min story about the global refugee crisis titled "The Displaced." It featured three children forced from their homes in Lebanon, South Sudan, and Ukraine. Since then, *The New York Times* has produced several VR news stories that have included topics such as the aftermath of the Paris terrorist attacks, the U.S. presidential elections, and stories about the planet Pluto. Other news outlets followed in the footsteps of *The New York Times*, including ABC, Vice, and The Verge.

Immersive Journalism

The idea of immersion is associated with a sense of presence (i.e., being in the virtual setting). For journalism, it refers to the production of news that induces a first-person experience of the place and events of a news story. Sometimes referred to as the "duality of presence," the person may feel they are there at the scene. A feeling of participating in the events of the news story creates a sense of being immersed in that event. The goal of the immersive journalistic experience is a greater sense of empathy for and, perhaps, a better understanding of the people and events that occurred.

There are various levels of immersion, from those in which a screen (computer, television, or mobile media) is used to view a virtual environment to higher level immersive systems with a wide field-of-view, high-resolution, stereo sound, head-tracked head-mounted display with real-time motion capture and auditory and haptic feedback. The latter is a "true" immersive experience. A "true" immersive experience is defined by the following:

1. 3D stereo vision via two screens—one in front of each eye;
2. surround vision—the real world is blocked from one's visual perception (i.e., as the user turns their head from side to side and up and down, they only see the virtual environment);
3. there is user dynamic control of viewpoint, which means that the user's head is tracked to update the display in real time according to where the user looks.

These immersive qualities allow the user to respond to the computer-generated situation as if it were real. Immersive journalism is a tool used to generate empathy and establish a connection with the story. Thus, VR journalism replaces journalism's core principles of objectivity with subjective involvement. With its purpose being to engage the audience emotionally, VR news calls ethical concerns to question.

Even with these immersive innovations that often have a wow factor, there are some restrictions to the VR experience. First, the image resolution is low compared to reality and to standard computer screens or high-definition television. Second, in spite of the immersive nature of VR, there is still the understanding that this is not real. There is, in other words, still a disconnect to reality due to the lack of full sensory involvement. VR CAVE experiences are a promising way to overcome some of these sensory issues (CAVE is a recursive acronym for Cave Automatic Virtual Environment). Invented at the University of Illinois's Chicago Electronic Visualization Laboratory in 1992, a VR CAVE typically has three or more projection walls where images display a surrounding environment. The user wears a pair of stereoscopic shutter glasses, which sync with the projector to generate 3D stereovision. The user can see through the glasses to view real objects in the environment (including their own body). The user can move through the CAVE environment and elements of touch, taste, smell, as well as simulated wind, and temperature changes are possible, all adding to the perceptual reality of the virtual situation.

In September 2014, the *Des Moines Register* was one of the first newspapers to use VR with one of their stories in a series titled *Harvest of Change*, which illustrated the life of today's American farmer using satellite map imagery, photographs of the farm, the Unity 3D gaming engine, 360-degree video, and coders and game designers. Reaction from the public was positive. However, making *Harvest of Change* cost $20,000, a price tag not many news organizations can afford.

Making VR Content

The production of journalistic VR content is different from traditional television news production and is divided into three stages. The first stage is capturing the content with cameras and microphones. The second stage is postproduction image processing with motion graphics and 3D modeling software. The third stage is distribution for headset, mobile media, or computer screen technologies.

Editing news stories for VR is changing the rules of journalistic work. For example, in making

VR content, the director has to work with non-fixed framing and edit content without using cuts, which is the traditional broadcast news editing method. In VR, there is a single piece of 360-degree video that creates the scene that users can explore as they want. The camera moves very little in most VR storytelling because camera movement can cause motion-related nausea for some users. This changes the narrative possibilities of news content. One solution has been to use video gaming techniques that allow users to explore scenes and discover characters and information at their own pace. Giving users this kind of freedom is a radical change to traditional journalism. Other considerations involve how much directed character action will take place in front of the 360-degree camera and how much computer-generated graphics or additional layers of video will be added to the news event in the postproduction phase. These concerns lead to issues about how much bias there may be with the production process and how much the virtual news story alters the facts of the actual event.

As with all media production, the audience should be considered. With the production of VR news content, however, audience considerations are different than for traditional news media. VR content producers have to decide which users they are trying to reach. A project with high-quality technology and interactive content requires a large budget and can include numerous VR specialists to create that content. This means that the end user will need to have high-end headset technology, thus reducing the audience size to those able to afford high-quality headsets. Lowering the quality is less costly but also means more limited technical and narrative possibilities. A larger number of users, however, can afford the less technically capable headsets needed to view the news story.

AR

AR technology was not initially designed as a media tool. Rather, in 1990, Preston Thomas Caudell developed the idea and coined the term "augmented reality" while working for Boeing where factory workers used AR to sort aircraft parts. AR technology then evolved into forms that could be used for other endeavors including journalism. Virtual news sets are one type of AR used for television broadcasting. In this form, AR combines people and other real objects with computer-generated environments and objects in a real-time, seamless way. Although still largely experimental, AR technology has also evolved into a wearable news storytelling technology.

Virtual News Sets

Virtual news set technology grew from traditional chromakey techniques. It debuted as a technology presentation by the American broadcasting technology company Ultimatte and German engineering firm IMP GmbH at the National Association for Broadcasters Convention in 1994. For routine broadcast applications, however, early virtual studio systems were challenging. They cost nearly $1 million, were very complex to use, were difficult for on-air performers to navigate, and, with jagged edges and other messy artifacts, they didn't look good.

To work flawlessly, a virtual set for broadcast has to allow the real-time combination of people or other real objects and computer-generated environments and objects in a seamless manner. A studio camera has to move in 3D space, while the image of the virtual camera is being rendered in real time from the same perspective. The virtual scene has to adapt at any time to camera movement (zoom, pan, tilt, dolly, track, or any other move).

There are many examples of the use of AR in news broadcasts. One example of its use came after the devastating fire that ravaged the historic Notre Dame cathedral in Paris in April 2019. France 2 used its main news studio to create a 3D AR model of the cathedral to showcase the damage and the planned repairs. The segment aired on the network's evening news, *Journal de 20h*. The model of Notre Dame was built using Avid's Maestro Virtual Set solution and Unreal Engine and provided viewers with sweeping views of the structure as well as detailed views at specific areas of concern. The AR model was positioned on the studio's floor and the news anchors could walk around the model as they spoke.

Wearable AR

In terms of journalistic use, AR can tell stories digitally. Using mobile, wearable computing systems that supplement the real world with virtual information, the goal is to engage people and provide contextual information about the news. Thus, AR devices can enrich a user's experience of the surrounding environment with computer-generated visual and auditory material. Early experimental work required the user to wear a bulky backpack and headset apparatus due to the need for the unit to provide both visual and sound information as well as GPS tracking technology.

Unlike the immersive forms of technology discussed earlier, this form of technology requires the user to be at the physical proximity where the news event took place. In other words, the AR experience allows the user to continue to see and hear the surrounding world but with additional computer-generated sights and sounds that are synchronized to the exact location of the user's geographic position (i.e., the actual location where the news event took place).

VR Journalism

VR journalism has two distinctive categories: news *from* VR and news *about* VR. The latter represents a host of publications about the technology and software used and being developed for VR systems, as well as the effects on users, including studies about the social, psychological, and behavioral aspects of VR technology use. This is a form of science and technology journalism found in consumer-oriented journals and magazines such as *Wired*, *AR/VR*, and *Popular Science*. Websites, blogs, and podcasts also disseminate a variety of social media information about VR products, technologies, and more to consumers. For professionals and academics, there are technical journals that publish original, multidisciplinary research such as *Virtual Reality*, the *International Journal of Virtual Reality*, the *Journal of Virtual Reality and Broadcasting*, and publications associated with the Institute of Electrical and Electronics Engineers, to name a few.

News *from* VR involves online games and virtual worlds where people, sometimes in very large numbers, interact socially. They have their own unique cultures, communities, geographies, currencies, commodities and markets, languages, holidays, events, sports, aesthetic look, and rules and regulations. The history of online games and virtual worlds parallels the development of the computer and computer networking. Online games have goals, or quests and puzzles to solve that help players progress, or level up. Virtual worlds usually have no goals or leveling and exist primarily as extensions of early textually based chatrooms, but with a visual component. Players exist in these virtual environments as avatars, or digital representations of themselves. Emerging out of these games and virtual worlds are a variety of journalistic forms that mirror reality, including newspapers, television-style newscasts, blogs, podcasts, and magazines. Most of these publications are available both within and external to the virtual world via the Internet.

Second Life is one of the more popular virtual worlds. Released to the public in 2003, Second Life saw rapid growth, and in 2013, it had approximately 1 million users. Numbers vary, but its use has diminished since then. From 2006 to 2007, Reuters inserted one of its technology reporters in Second Life. When the Reuters virtual reporter was called back from the virtual world, many believed the hype about Second Life was dead. News from Second Life and other virtual worlds, however, continues to this day. Content focuses on gossip, entertainment, fashion, well-known and notorious residents, and a variety of soft news. Shopping information about where the best deals can be found in the Second Life Marketplace is a popular form of information covered in various online publications. Occasionally, there are hard news stories about criminal activity in the virtual setting. For example, there are stories about nefarious individuals and organizations using virtual world economies for money laundering and fraud, as well as crimes involving underage sex and other aspects of pornography. On a more upbeat note, news about virtual world businesses and profit-making, educational opportunities, and celebrity and entertainment news can be found.

The transient, ever-changing nature of online communities, such as Second Life, means that news sources come and go (and sometimes come back again), changing names, editorial staffs, and writers with great frequency. *The Alphaville Herald*, *Second Life Enquirer*, and *Second Life Newser* are some of the current news publications. Others such as the *Metaverse Messenger* were short-lived enterprises, but old issues can still be found on the Internet.

The virtual environments of massively multiplayer online games such as *World of Warcraft*, *League of Legends*, and *Minecraft* have their own information outlets. Information about game strategies, new versions of the games, industry news, and more constitute a large amount of the flow of information about these virtual worlds.

Lawrence Mullen

See also Digital Journalism Ethics; Digital Journalism Tools; New Journalism; New Media; Objectivity; Science and Technology Journalism; Visual Journalism

Further Readings

Augmented reality, virtual reality and sets in broadcast. (n.d.). Retrieved from https://www.newscaststudio .com/category/augmented-reality-ar/

Brennen, B., & dela Cerna, E. (2010). Journalism in second life. *Journalism Studies, 11*(4), 546–554. doi:10.1080/14616701003638418.

Jones, S. (2017). Disrupting the narrative: Immersive journalism in virtual reality. *Journal of Media Practice, 18*(2–3), 1771–1185. doi:10.1080/14682753 .2017.1374677.

Owen, T. (2016). Can journalism be virtual? *Columbia Journalism Review.* Retrieved from https://www.cjr .org/the_feature/virtual_reality_facebook_second_life .php

Pavlik, J., & Bridges, F. (2013). The emergence of augmented reality (AR) as a storytelling medium in journalism. *Journalism & Communication Monographs, 15*(1), 4–59. doi:10.1177/ 1522637912470819.

Sirkkunen, E., Väätäjä, H., Uskali, T., et al. (2016). Journalism in virtual reality. In *Proceedings of the 20th International Academic Mindtrek Conference* (pp. 297–303). Tampere: ACM.

VISUAL JOURNALISM

Visual journalism includes all the ways in which the news is visualized and constructed for the human sense of vision. The visuality of journalism might also be called its form, visible structure, graphic design, or packaging. It is all the things that make a television production recognizable as a newscast. It includes the visual elements that make the *New York Times* look different from *USA Today* and the elements that make a newsmagazine distinct from an entertainment magazine. That a North Korean televised newscast looks so different from a newscast originating in the United States, or other western nations, shows how culture, politics, and tradition play significant roles in how news looks. News can take on different meanings depending on how it is visually constructed.

One can also think of such visual form as creating an environment that invites readers into a world molded to fit not only the habits of journalists and readers but also the current principles in political and economic life. The news provides a dynamic experience that appeals to the senses and is reassuring. The form seems natural to the audience—words, images, colors, patterns, shapes, and sizes, all reflecting and portraying events, some that are local or regional and others distant. The form of the news structures and expresses an environment, a space that represents something larger: the world-at-large, its economies, politics, sociality, and emotions.

Every visually oriented medium is designed with compositional choices for communicating ideas, moods, and identities. For example, newspaper layout is designed so the content speaks to a particular audience. And television news sets are designed so that the look of a newscast is appropriate for the brand of news programming and the attitude and mood it seeks to present to its viewers. Indeed, a lot of research goes into the way a newscast looks. The newscasters need to look good, the background should not be distracting, and the set should be properly lit. Research on television news and its look includes makeup, hairstyle, clothing, even whether the newscasters should wear eyeglasses. A whole research industry is built around television news, how it looks, and how the look of the newscast translates into audience ratings. This concern about the news and how it looks, especially in the area of television news, has led to controversial issues such as the firing of female newscasters when they get older, because they no longer have "the look" that gets a newscast good ratings. Although this form of age discrimination and sexism has largely been discontinued, instances of the practice may still occur.

These visual elements are part of the way news creates meaning, depicting social relations for the readers, users, and viewers. For example, should a newspaper have lots of white space on a page to suggest a sense of lightness, or fill as much of the page as possible with information to suggest a wealth of serious, valuable content? The latter treats the newspaper as a container for all the information needed by readers who wish to consider themselves well-informed. The condensed text and crowded pages signify this, even if it makes readability difficult and can, for others, signify pompousness, dullness, and conservativeness. Spreading text and other content out to include white space provides a new experience for a changing market, targeting a different kind of audience, perhaps younger, on-the-move, yet still with a desire to be informed. Such choices influence not only the meaning of the content but also the meaning of the medium itself—how it is perceived, and how the content is communicated—thus setting up a kind of social relationship between the medium and the reader.

Audience needs and technological limitations also dictate the look or design of a medium. There are economic, political, and other factors such as media convergence which play roles in the way our media look. Today's blogs and aggregator sites such as Google News and the Huffington Post have had a great economic influence on the whole field of journalism, including the way news is visualized. These sites compile news from other websites, and user preferences customize the news. The presentation of news stories on these sites makes a difference in what is seen and read. Readers generally will not scroll past the first page of a website, even if that is where the most significant information can be found. They tend to view the first available option presented to them by the aggregators. Aggregators use this idea to their advantage when laying out their sites and selecting their resources. This way of presenting the news attracts readers to a news site they might not have gone to before. For example, Google News has a powerful impact on the traffic that other news websites receive.

The accessibility of the Internet means that the public can more easily influence the look of the news. Internet access is possible anywhere, anytime, so we get news whenever we want on mobile devices. Amateur online journalists are putting this technology to use and creating weblogs ("blogs"), adding a grassroots dimension to the journalism landscape. Bloggers and other amateur journalists are also scooping mainstream news outlets as well as pointing out errors in mainstream articles, while people who have been made subjects of news articles are responding online, posting supplementary information to provide context and counterpoints. In all, the public is increasingly turning to online sources for news and having a greater influence on what is regarded as news and how news is visualized.

Regardless of platform (newspaper, television, or mobile device), visual journalism is what makes news recognizable as news. Every medium that relies on the visual sense has distinctive visual characteristics. Newspapers, magazines, television, news blogs, websites, and social media news feeds (e.g., Facebook) all have a unique look and that look is not stagnant. For example, the look of the front page of newspapers has changed significantly over the years. More pictures, more color, and more variation in font size and style are a few of the changes that can be noted.

Furthermore, the shift to online and multiplatform publishing has resulted in rapid changes to visual journalism. Newspapers and magazines now have websites and are accessible anytime, anywhere on mobile devices. Video content and interactivity are also possible in the digital sphere. In addition, the smaller frame sizes of mobile media have forced newspapers and other news media to adapt and format their news for smaller screens. Despite these technological changes, however, the core principles of visual journalism remain mostly unchanged. The communication of news, opinions, ideas, and information generally, as well as values and attitudes, requires the right kinds of visual materials, design, technology, production processes, and finances.

Readers, watchers, and users of news media often take the look, or form, for granted—not considering how the newspaper is laid out or why the lighting for a newscast is flat and without shadows. Only when an obvious mistake is made, or when a new form emerges, such as color photography in the newspaper in the late 1970s, does the audience take notice. Consideration of visual form is often left for academics to ponder. And although all media have visual qualities (arguably, even radio news broadcasts can have a visual aspect), the focus here is on explicitly visual media, and the discussion of visual journalism is organized around *text*, *images* (both still and motion imagery), and *presentation* (consisting of elements such as television set design, editing, screen or framing aspects including graphic layout, and acting). First, however, let us take a brief look at the relationship between human vision and the media used for journalistic purposes.

Human Vision and the Media

Understanding visual journalism begins with understanding the relationship between visual perception and mediated news imagery. The human eye and the brain's visual perception system are essential considerations for the way news, and indeed all media, are constructed. Indeed, as Marshall McLuhan pointed out, media are extensions of who we are at a biological level. Color, light, motion, patterns, contrast, facial recognition, and other variables are part and parcel of human visual perception, and our media reflect and utilize these qualities in ways particular to human vision.

As an extension of the human sense of sight, our media have particular characteristics. People have, for example, about 210 degrees of forward-facing horizontal field of view, or peripheral vision. The vertical range of the field of view is more restricted, around 150 degrees. This range of vision horizontally and vertically has implications for the media we have designed and their use for news dissemination. Media that are more horizontally than vertically oriented conform to the way the eyes see. Television screens are the best example of this. However, some media do not conform

precisely to the perceptual structures of the eyes. For instance, some media we use for news and information are more vertical than they are horizontal. Newspaper pages, magazines, smartphones, and iPods take on a more vertical dimension than horizontal. Our brain, however, is very good at adapting to a variety of visually constructed media environments, so no real problem is posed when media do not conform precisely to our visual perceptual construct. Additionally, many of these vertically oriented media can be folded (newspaper) or reoriented (mobile devices) to create the aspect ratio that conforms to the horizontal and vertical proportions indicative of television and human visual perception.

The positioning of our eyes on the front of our heads allows for binocular vision. Binocular vision, which is essential for depth perception, covers 114 degrees (horizontally) of the visual field in humans; the remaining peripheral 40 degrees on each side has no binocular vision (because only one eye can see those parts of the visual field). Our media, however, and the images seen within them, are two-dimensional (i.e., they lack any sort of "real" depth), so it is important to be able to create the illusion of depth perception with mediated images. In essence, our eyes are "tricked" into perceiving depth in a media image. The use of occlusion, size differences, linear perspective, spacing, light quality, light-and-dark color variation, and visual detail are some of the ways in which the illusion of depth is created for the two-dimensional frames of a photograph, television picture, or another image type.

Motion, as depicted in our media, is also an illusion. Because of the way our visual perceptual system works, we perceive motion in television and film images. Television is a series of 30 still images per second. In film, movement is depicted by showing 24 still images per second. The inability of our eyes and brain to process such a rapid succession of images allows us to perceive motion on television and in movie theaters and not a series of still images.

The perception of color is also important and has not always been a part of the news media landscape. Visual perception is concerned with the extraction of information from the external physical world, of which color is a dominant characteristic. Human color perception uses the part of the electromagnetic spectrum encompassing visible light (from roughly 400 to 700 nm, between ultraviolet and infrared light). The color we see is the effect of waves of photons that bounce off objects and stimulate cells on our retinas called *cones*. Most people are trichromatic, with cells in the retina that are sensitive to red, blue, and green light. Used in combination, these three colors allow most humans to distinguish between roughly a million different colors.

Color in the Media

Color has given journalists new ways to communicate. Colorization of the country's newspapers began as far back as 1891 when *The Milwaukee Journal* used a blue-and-red bar on its front page to commemorate the inauguration of a new governor. Today, 97% of North American newspapers print some of their news pages in color. There are still some traditionalists who say that color detracts from the news, but the debate about whether to use color is largely over. Newspapers in California and Florida led the way in the use of color decades ago, and the audaciously colorful *USA Today* accelerated the move to color when it started publishing in 1982.

In television, the transition from black-and-white to color was a slow process. Until the 1970s, television was, for the most part, a black-and-white medium. High-definition color imagery came to television in the 1990s and again changed how we see the news: in exquisite near-realistic detail. For humans, color vision is concentrated in the center of the visual field and is an important way in which we perceive news images. The realism color gives to mediated images, text, and other graphics is tied to objectivity and, along with motion, is a superb way to grab the attention of an audience. Thus, color, contrast, tone, shading, color combinations and color patterns, and lighting are important to the discussion of visual journalism.

Text

Text, or typography, includes font style, size, and other features such as italics, bold type, underlining, spacing, and use of white space. These variables influence the way news is perceived. Newspapers distinguish themselves by choosing and implementing typography to match their respective self-definitions. A serious newspaper of record might, for example, have headlines in several decks, stacked above a single column of text. Other newspapers might use banner headlines topping the pages with subordinate headlines moderately sized in contrasting typefaces.

Font styles come and go. In the late 1800s, fonts were bold, with thick and blocky serifs and a uniform stroke to make the newspaper printing process faster. This style is called *slab serif* and includes fonts such as Rockwell and Clarendon. In the digital age, thousands of font styles have become easily accessible, but only a relatively small number are currently used for newspapers. These include Times, Helvetica, Franklin Gothic, Century Old Style, Poynter, Utopia, Nimrod, Interstate, Bureau Grotesque, and Miller. There is also extensive use of custom typefaces or modifications made to existing fonts to make them fit the chosen look and feel of a newspaper. In all, the font chosen by a newspaper ought to be easy to read and become familiar, recognizable, and trustworthy to the reader.

Line spacing and text alignment are also important. They can influence the mood and attitude conveyed. Newer newspapers and webpage designs have used these qualities to create a sense of openness. Line spacing, or *leading* (a term going back to metal type and the use of strips of lead alloys to space out lines of type evenly), is the distance from the baseline of one line of type to the baseline of the next. When the spacing is small, there can be a sense of claustrophobia, crowding, or economy of space. Wider spacing suggests expansion, confidence, or even arrogance. There is a sense of modernism and openness when the line spacing is wide.

Alignment of typeface can be left, right, or justified, meaning that the left and right margins of each line are even. Justified lines give the appearance of being regimented. Some newspapers use justified lines to bring an attitude of efficiency, order, authority, and formality. But word spacing varies within a given line of justified type, especially when text is set in narrow columns. When the line lengths vary, there is a sense of informality, with a more organic look. The words are evenly spaced, and the mood induced has been described as more relaxed and natural.

Images

Images, especially photographic images, are what one typically thinks of when "visual journalism" is mentioned. But as discussed earlier in this entry, visual journalism is more than photography alone. Images come in two varieties: still images and motion picture images such as those of television and film. Still images can be photographs, cartoons, graphs and other data visualizations, drawings, and more. Motion images are any kind of image that depicts motion. They can depict photographic reality, computer-generated cartoons, animated characters and scenes, interactive data visualizations, or any combination of these.

The images we see in our newspapers and nightly newscasts are messages created by analog (not computerized) technology, or nowadays more likely by digital technology, and transmitted through a channel of communication to a point of reception, a viewing audience, or a reader. The image is the result of a process. A host of sociocultural factors and decisions come before the actual creation of the image that determined when the image is captured by a camera or made with computer software. Then a team or sequence of professionals, editors, and technicians choose, compose, crop (or edit in terms of motion images), and otherwise treat the image, give it a title, caption, or other textual treatment, and place it within the context of a news story. The point of reception is the audience that reads or sees it. The channel of transmission can be a newspaper, television, news blog, or other medium. The image is set within a complex of concurrent messages, various texts, graphic layout, frame size, and the ideology of the news source. Moreover, the dissemination and reception of the photographic image and the variety of messages and meanings it can have exist within a complex social milieu; the same image can take on wholly different meanings when seen in the context of different news sources.

Photographs are complex, because not only is there the literal reality they depict but also a symbolic meaning. There is, of course, a reduction in proportion, perspective, color, and other aspects of the reality depicted in a photograph. But the photographic image is an almost perfect analogy of the people, scene, and things within its frame. It is because of this convincingly accurate representation of visible reality that photographic images are tied to objectivity, truth, and factuality.

The claimed facticity of photography helped photojournalism to become an established practice in the 1920s. Before then, news events were often depicted through artists' illustrations. Before the 1930s, journalists commonly retouched, embellished, and manipulated photographs. In these early days of photojournalism, there was little in the way of an ethical code to govern what should or should not be done in terms of image manipulation. This situation did not change much in the years that followed. Decisions regarding the use of hidden cameras, posing and reenacting shots, using offensive imagery, invading the privacy of subjects, and other forms of image manipulation were ethical choices largely left up to the individual photographers or persons publishing the photograph.

In 1946, the National Press Photographers Association (NPPA) was founded (and then incorporated in 1947). Their Code of Ethics is, to this day, widely accepted as the standard for photojournalistic professionalism. Even so, the NPPA Code of Ethics is nonbinding, and although a breach in ethics might result in expulsion from the NPPA, membership is not required to work in the industry (though some employers may implement their own penalties). In the decades since NPPA's inception, ethical standards in photojournalism have been a process of trial and error and there have been several instances of photojournalistic image manipulation from the 1950s to the present day (see https://www.cc.gatech.edu/~beki/cs4001/history.pdf for examples).

The Digital Age brought about its own challenges with ethics involving news image manipulation. Indeed, the advent of digitization in the 1980s brought about historic changes in photojournalism. The acceptable things a photographer could do in the darkroom to enhance his or her photographs could now be done on a computer. Acceptable forms of photographic manipulation are those that make the photo more readable, such as dodging and burning, color, and contrast correction. These kinds of image changes are considered neither ethical nor unethical. Rather, they are the technical aspects of the grammar of photographic editing. However, the possibility of digitally enhancing a photograph beyond these technical aspects was now substantial and more difficult to detect.

But aspirations for objectivity in visual journalism continue to support the desire to be accurate, thus ensuring that photojournalistic imagery depicts people and events as truthfully and authentically as possible. Backing these claims of objectivity and authenticity are the aforementioned ethical guidelines for visual journalism that state that journalists should "not manipulate images or add or alter sound in any way that can mislead viewers or misrepresent subjects" (National Press Photographers Association, 2018, n.p.), and "never deliberately distort facts or context, including visual information. Clearly label illustrations and reenactments" (Society of Professional Journalists, 2014, n.p.). Visual journalists are also recommended to avoid staging and to "not intentionally contribute to, alter, or seek to alter or influence events" (National Press Photographers Association, 2018, n.p.).

Presentation

News is shaped by the visual constraints and liberties of the medium in which it is presented. Whether it's a newspaper, magazine, computer screen, movie theater, television screen, or mobile device, presentation encompasses the look of news within a frame, how people and objects are placed within the frame, and how they move and act within it. The combination of text and images communicates messages that journalists create, but the way they are presented using various visual tools adds another layer of meaning to their messages. Visual design is a fundamental part of the meaning of news content. To be successful, the design must speak the visual language of the audience. As the newspaper industry has changed, and as circulations have declined, especially for local news, much advertising has shifted to online formats. And, as readers themselves have changed their habits of information consumption, journalism has been called upon to create new identities for a struggling industry. Accordingly, design becomes instrumental in helping newspapers and other forms of news to portray ideas and attitudes

about the news that are shaping a new journalism landscape.

As noted above, font style and size, colors, borders, space, positioning, and images are among the many tools used for newspaper design. In the 1980s, computer technology enabled important changes to occur. Greater flexibility was one of the benefits. But change was slow. Much of the newspaper industry stuck with the traditional methods of production. The transition from older ways of laying out and printing the newspaper to new digital electronic forms was not without conflict. But since the 1980s, the creative processes of designing and editing a newspaper could be done at a computer screen. As a result, column widths, picture size, and line spacing became more flexible and could be edited with greater precision. Innovations in computer software brought new speed and versatility. Editing software has allowed cutout images, rapid collages, and other forms of graphics, charts, and compositional elements to be incorporated into designs much more creatively. This resulted in waves of redesigned newspapers through the 1990s and into the 21st century. Not all redesigns were successful, and some proved to alienate established readers. Merely redesigning a newspaper did not save those that failed to adapt to changing market and technological forces that were radically reshaping the industry.

As for television, the immediacy of the medium creates opportunities for live breaking news and the kinds of visuals associated with such broadcasts. No other medium provides the opportunities television does for live imagery, happening right now. The unrelenting flow of events, and the constraints of time and the need to limit what can be said and shown to an audience, the lack of indepth analysis, and reflection on the news of the day are some of the constraints of television news's look. At another level, there are the production components such as editing, live news, news packages, interviews, technologies to divide the frame into multiple images, lighting, background design, set furniture, and the physical appearance of newscasters that are among the multitude of visual components of television news.

In the early days of television news broadcasting in the 1940s and 1950s, film newsreels were the most readily available model for the visual presentation of the news. During World War II, they were filled with military stories that employed footage provided by the U.S. government. Besides that, newsreels specialized in events that were staged and of interest to the widest possible audience. These included celebrity weddings, movie premieres, beauty contests, and ship launchings. Newsreels showed only visual content recorded on film, with an unseen announcer providing commentary; the on-air newsreader sitting behind a news desk (also called a *news anchor*) would come later. In the mid-1940s, WCBW, CBS's wholly owned subsidiary in New York, developed several innovative techniques for visualizing stories for which they had no film and established the practice of sending a reporter to cover local stories. New, inexpensive video and microwave technology made newsgathering economically feasible in the 1960s; accordingly, many network affiliates expanded their news programming.

The advent of cable television, especially the founding of the Cable News Network in 1980, was a watershed moment in televised journalism that caused massive changes in the way we see the news today. Since then, the news that U.S. Americans watch on national cable channels and on their local news stations has continued to change significantly while network evening newscasts have remained largely unchanged. The parallel-like changes to the visual structure of the three cable news networks, Cable News Network, Fox, and MSNBC, has made them all look remarkably similar nowadays. Each contains a mix of interviews, packaged segments, and live coverage. Local newscasts have placed greater emphasis on traffic, weather, and sports and have reduced the number of edited packages and shortened the lengths of their news stories. These changes may reflect the economic strains affecting the industry. Many newscasts now include eye-catching graphics and updated sets. In addition, newscasters no longer just sit behind a news desk. Often they move around during the newscast to keep viewers interested. Many news sets also incorporate plasma television monitors, which provide flexibility by displaying pictures of different locations as backdrops for newscasters. Local broadcasters showcase their news anchors and rely on traditional visual elements such as skylines of their home cities.

Lawrence Mullen

See also Aerial Photography; CNN; Design and Layout, Magazine; Internet: Impact on the Media; Television News, History of

Further Readings

Barnhurst, K., & Nerone, J. (2001). *Forms of news: A history.* New York, NY: Guilford.

Barthes, R. (1977). *Image—music—text.* New York, NY: Hill and Wang.

Machin, D., & Polzer, L. (2015). *Visual journalism.* New York, NY: Macmillan International Higher Education.

McLuhan, M. (1964). *Understanding media: The extensions of man.* New York, NY: McGraw-Hill.

Mitchell, W. J. T. (2005). There are no visual media. *Journal of Visual Culture, 4*(2), 257–266. doi:10.1177%2F1470412905054673.

National Press Photographers Association. (2018). Code of ethics. Retrieved from https://nppa.org/code-ethics

Society of Professional Journalists. (2014). Code of ethics. Retrieved from https://spjdetroit.org/about-us/code-of-ethics/

Vox Pop

In the original Latin, "vox populi" means "voice of the people." Over time the phrase has become "vox pop." It is used to refer to both a type of interview and a structuring element in a story or a newscast. In a sense, what is now known as "vox pop" is what was once referred to as the "man (or woman) on the street." This entry examines vox pop style journalism and its utility for both story and newscast production. Specific attention is paid to the content, structure, setup, and editing of vox pop journalism and to its notable pros and cons.

Content Element

As an element of content, vox pops are generally used as a way to get short reactions from people "on the street," who might be asked about serious issues—a recent action by the government, for example. The opinions generated are then edited into a story, either a packaged piece or an anchor-read voice over B-roll around the constructed story. Most often, though, the vox pops are used to present more lighthearted stories since the sound bites are usually opinions. Using a vox pop in this manner is often referred to as "low-hanging fruit" because they are relatively easy to shoot and edit quickly.

Structuring Element

To producers of a newscast, vox pops can be used in a number of ways to help structure a story or a newscast. In either case, the format of a vox pop will be the same. Since this type of story normally runs short, the story can be placed within the local segment of the newscast to help give structure to that story block. Producers are often looking for stories that will change the pace within the newscast, and like readers, short vox pops can provide some variety to the story lengths that will help the producers give better flow to the newscast. If the piece is to be lighthearted, a good vox pop story can provide a nice finish to the segment or even the newscast.

A more serious story can also be helped by a vox pop element. To be sure, the structure of the bite itself remains the same; opinions would be sought and edited down to a solid sound bite that may include breaking stories since vox pops can be produced quickly and may help clarify the story for viewers.

Setup

In any case, shooting for a vox pop is relatively easy, with one camera recording all the sound bites. In an age of multimedia journalists, reporters are responsible for the entire production of their stories, from shooting and editing their stories to transcribing the story and, commonly, producing any graphics needed. The reporter sets up a camera on a tripod in a busy area where the prospect of getting enough material is assured. As people walk by, the reporter asks for opinions on whatever the story is about. The reporter asks for comments or opinions from passersby, making sure to get good, clean audio and framing each person in a slightly different pose. This is an important consideration, since the bites are "stacked" against each other to form one bite. If

each person faced the camera squarely, the edited cuts would look like jump cuts and would appear to be very two-dimensional.

Reporters need to visualize how the story will look on playback. This means the reporter should also record their own stand-ups. The stand-up may start the story off or the intro to the story could be read by an anchor in the studio. Reporters often will need to have a couple different versions of the story, so enough B-roll should be shot to allow for this eventuality. Stand-ups, bites, and B-roll are the three elements needed for a good story.

Editing

Standards of good editing need to be apparent in any story but are crucial in vox pop stories. In most cases, there will not be enough time in each of the clips for identifiers in the lower third of the screen. That means that imperfections in the editing process are more noticeable to the average viewer (things like jump cuts, flash frames, or bad audio). If enough B-roll was shot while in the field, the story could be compressed or expanded, depending on what the producer needs for that newscast. For example, a reporter may bring back five clips for editing into a vox pop, along with a stand-up. The reporter then edits each of the clips to about 5 seconds each and edits the opening stand-up, putting that clip into an editing sequence. All five of the edited clips are then put into the sequence, one after the other. The tag at the end of the story could be read by the anchor over B-roll. The total runtime for this type of story is generally no longer than 1 min. The reporter may also be asked to split the vox pop responses into slightly longer sound bites that can be used as voice-over or voice-over sound stories in a second newscast.

It is important to understand how each format of news story functions as journalists try to clarify the issues on the local, regional, and national scenes. Whether a reporter uses a voice-over, voice-over sound on tape, package, reader, or stories like vox pops, each has an important part to play in a good newscast. Producers often say that, even though there may be a dearth of producers, they don't want simple "stackers" but rather look for people who can make a newscast flow, who understand the relationship between story-type and viewer comprehension, and who can consider all these different story types as tools in their tool boxes.

Pro and Con

The great part about vox pop stories is their ability to be flexible in gathering local opinions about the issues of the day. Since they are easily constructed and quickly put into any show, vox pop stories are favorites of producers who seek a lighter story inside the newscast to relieve some of the downside that is seen in many shows.

The negative side of this type of story is its subjective nature. Since it is structured as an opinion piece, vox pop stories are sometimes criticized for being too one-sided, especially if the story concerns a local issue or notable person. Reporters and producers need to be careful with those issues since that "man on the street" will, undoubtedly, have an opinion to be shared. Often used as public opinion polls, vox pops become ubiquitous during election years and audiences can get tired of hearing the "results" since public opinion changes rapidly.

In the end, stories structured as the "voice of the people" can serve many uses in the production of a newscast, not the least of which is providing short stories with wide appeal among viewers. In particular, stories in reaction to unclean restaurants, faulty construction, and other targets of "activist journalism." In these cases, the stories are sometimes labeled a "franchise" that carries the signature of the reporter or anchor that does the work of the story and often leaves the follow-up

public responses to the end of the piece. This type of journalism is well-liked by the viewing public, many of whom believe that this addresses a needed solution to local problems. When people feel there is no one to help them, the "vox populi" stories in a newscast indeed give strength to the "voice of the people."

The use of vox pop stories as either content type or as structural elements within a newscast can be seen as having great utility. As audiences change over time, stories in this format can change with them. Most news consumers, like all persons on the street, want to give voice to the issues of the day, particularly if those issues have parts to play in the consumers' lived realities.

Gary W. Larson

See also Advanced Research Projects Agency Network (ARPANET); Digital Journalism Ethics; Interpretive Journalism; Sky News; Social Media

Further Readings

Beckers, K, Walgrave, S., &Van den Bulck, H. (2018). Opinion balance in vox pop television news. *Journalism Studies, 19*(2), 284–296. doi:10.1080/1461670X.2016.1187576.

Bergillos, I. (2019). Rethinking vox-pops in television news evolution of person-on-the-street interviews in Spanish news programs. *Journalism Practice, 13*(9), 1057–1074. doi:10.1080/17512786.2019.1635042.

Daschmann, G. (2000). Vox pop & polls: The impact of poll results and voter statements in the media on the perception of a climate of opinion. *International Journal of Public Opinion Research, 12*(2), 160–181. doi:10.1093/jpor/12.2.160.

WALL STREET JOURNAL, THE

The Wall Street Journal is an English-language, U.S.-based business and general interest news product with national and international distribution through digital and mobile channels and a print product that is published weekdays and Saturdays. The *Journal* is part of Dow Jones & Company, which is owned by News Corporation (News Corp.), with headquarters in New York City. Since 1996, the *Journal* has been distributed on WSJ .com, which was an early adopter of a paywall for digital content. In mid-2019, the newspaper reported a circulation of 1 million for its print product and 1.83 million paid digital subscribers. The number of digital subscribers surpassed 2 million in February 2020.

Through most of its history, the *Journal* focused on business and financial news, but it expanded its focus to political and general interest news coverage after being purchased by News Corp. in 2008. The *Journal*'s conservative editorial perspective is influential in U.S. conservative political circles, although it rarely endorses political candidates. The *Journal* has printed continuously since 1889, never missing an issue, not even after the September 11, 2001, terrorist attacks that damaged its newsroom in lower Manhattan. As of 2020, the *Journal* and its staff have won 37 Pulitzer Prizes.

Until a redesign in 2007, the newspaper had maintained the same six-column format, using small headlines and drawings instead of photographs. The newspaper's masthead, unusually, also contains a period at the end. An in-depth feature story—known as the "A-hed" because of the shape of its headline—was featured in the fourth column and influenced the structure of feature stories throughout the newspaper industry. A roundup of top news stories, called "What's News," has been a staple of the paper since 1941. The paper went to two sections in 1980, well after most other newspapers had adopted the format, and did not add color capacity until 2002. However, after the 2007 redesign, the newspaper began to look less distinct from its competitors, with increased use of color photography and graphic design elements.

The Wall Street Journal was launched in 1889 by Charles Dow, Edward Jones, and Charles Bergstresser, whose firm—Dow, Jones & Company Inc.—distributed information used by traders on Wall Street, New York City's financial center. The newspaper, originally published at the end of each trading day, was conceived as a way to make distribution of information more efficient than hand delivering it to individual subscribers. The object of the newspaper was "to give fully and fairly the daily news attending the fluctuations in prices of stocks, bonds and some classes of commodities" in order to present "a faithful picture of the rapidly shifting panorama of the Street" (Rosenberg, 1982, p. 10). In 1898, the paper began publishing both morning and evening editions; the evening edition was discontinued in 1934.

While *Journal* staff members were allowed to buy and sell stocks, the company required them to avoid conflicts of interest and not use inside information to manipulate stock prices or make trades, in order to bolster the newspaper's credibility. Among the most influential innovations of the *Journal* was the Dow Jones Industrial Average of leading industrial stocks, which was introduced in 1896 and remains among the most influential barometers of U.S. market health.

In 1897, the company launched the Dow Jones News Service, which operated alongside the newspaper to provide real-time market news that was distributed to subscribers on ticker machines. The newspaper prospered along with U.S. industrial development during the 1890s and began extending its coverage beyond Wall Street to any topic that impacted the nation's economy, including devoting two columns of coverage to Spanish-American War news in 1898. As described by one of the paper's early editors, William Peter Hamilton, the aim of the paper was "to make its news staff not second-rate specialists who might be able to explain a matter to someone already acquainted with the subject, but first-rate specialists who know the subject so well that they can make any portion of it clear to a school boy" (Rosenberg, 1982, p. 41).

In 1902, the original partners were bought out by Clarence Walker Barron, who owned similar financial publications in Boston and Philadelphia and had been the *Journal*'s Boston correspondent. Barron borrowed the money to buy the company from his wife, Jessie Waldron Barron, who held most of its stock and played a behind-the-scenes role in managing the company until her death in 1918. When Barron died in 1928, his stepdaughter and son-in-law, Jane and Hugh Bancroft, took over the paper, and their descendants controlled Dow Jones for the next 80 years before selling it to News Corp. in 2008.

Dow Jones and the *Journal* flourished in the 1920s, as the stock market boomed. In 1921, the company launched *Barron's*, a weekly financial newspaper with national distribution, and a Pacific Coast edition of the *Journal* in California, which made it the first daily publication available on both the East and West Coasts. As stocks began to gyrate in October 1929, the *Journal* tried to reassure its readers "conditions do not seem to foreshadow anything more formidable than an arrest of stock activity and business prosperity like that in 1923" (Rosenberg, 1982, p. 50). Three

days later, the markets crashed, ushering in a chain of events that led to the Great Depression and a market downturn that shrank the newspaper's advertising and circulation. The *Journal*'s editorial pages became a leading source of criticism of President Franklin Roosevelt's New Deal after he won the presidency in 1932.

In 1941, a new managing editor, Bernard Kilgore, sought to give the paper a wider reach and shift it from an emphasis on Wall Street to a national business newspaper. This effort gained traction on Monday, December 8, 1941, the day after Japan's attack on Pearl Harbor, when the newspaper published extensive coverage of the attack and its implications for the U.S. economy. Under Kilgore's leadership, the *Journal* launched a system of national distribution that would push circulation above 1 million by the 1960s.

The newspaper faced a crossroads in 1954, when General Motors—angered when a *Journal* reporter revealed details of designs for its new 1955 models—decided to pull its advertising from the *Journal* and block reporters' access to GM leadership. The newspaper went public with details of GM's actions and refused to back down to the pressure. Executive editor Bill Kerby would later say "this dramatic incident, and the spate of national publicity it engendered, firmly established in the public mind, including millions who never had read *The Wall Street Journal*, and presumably never would, that here was a newspaper of unshakable independence and integrity. GM had done us a priceless favor" (Rosenberg, 1982, p. 86).

In the 1965, the *Journal*'s Louis M. Kohlmeier won a Pulitzer Prize for an investigation into President Lyndon Johnson's finances, focusing on how the president had managed to amass a personal fortune despite spending years in public service. The public attention forced Johnson, infuriated by the coverage, to provide a detailed disclosure of his personal finances.

In 2007, News Corp., led by Australian-born media entrepreneur Rupert Murdoch, made an unsolicited offer to buy Dow Jones & Company and the *Journal* from the Bancroft family. Murdoch's history as an operator of tabloid newspapers and the politically conservative Fox News Channel engendered resistance to the offer from the newspaper's staff and some members of the

Bancroft family. After several months of negotiation, Murdoch bought the company for $5 billion, after agreeing to establish a committee to oversee the *Journal*'s editorial integrity. However, within a year of his purchase, both the newspaper's publisher and managing editor had departed, and the *Journal* began broadening its content to position itself as a competitor to *The New York Times*, which was a key motivation behind Murdoch's purchase, along with Dow Jones's financially lucrative news service.

Under News Corp., the number of lengthy stories in the *Journal* dropped sharply, with stories of more than 2,500 words virtually disappearing from its pages by 2011. While business coverage remained the largest topic addressed on the *Journal*'s front page, the amount of front-page business coverage had dropped by about one third by 2011, as coverage of government and foreign policy increased. In 2012, the company launched WorldStream, a streaming service featuring video shot by *Journal* journalists.

In 2013, the *Journal* and Dow Jones became a part of a new News Corp. when Murdoch splits his broadcasting and publishing properties into two companies. While the *Journal* is no longer part of the same company as the Fox News Channel, the Murdoch family still controls both entities.

In 2016, the print product underwent a major redesign, which reduced the number of sections, folding stories about sports, art, and culture into the first section and reducing coverage of metropolitan New York. Reporters were also instructed to reduce the length of stories and focus on the needs of digital and mobile distribution, as well as moving deadlines earlier in the day to boost readership.

The *Journal* also launched efforts to increase the number of digital visitors and their level of engagement, and the website and mobile app were redesigned in 2019.

Rich Shumate

See also Business Journalism; Murdoch, Rupert; News Corporation

Further Readings

Ellison, S. (2010). *War at the Wall Street Journal*. New York, NY: Houghton Mifflin Harcourt.

Rosenberg, J. M. (1982). *Inside the Wall Street Journal: The power and the history of Dow Jones & Company and America's most influential newspaper*. New York, NY: Macmillan.

Wendt, L. (1982). *The Wall Street Journal: The story of Dow Jones & the nation's business newspaper*. Chicago, IL: Rand McNally.

WALT DISNEY COMPANY, THE

The Walt Disney Company is an entertainment and media corporation with global holdings that span theme parks, merchandise, films, and broadcast and cable outlets. This entry includes a brief history of Disney, its key acquisitions in the media industry, and several connected journalistic issues, including conflict of interest, press control, and Disney's status as a media conglomeration.

A Very Brief History of the Disney Universe

The Disney universe traces its origins to 1923 in Los Angeles, California, with the production of short cartoons by brothers Walt and Roy Disney. The iconic Disney character Mickey Mouse made his debut in the animated film *Steamboat Willie* in 1928. The Walt Disney Studio started as a small, independent studio and eventually became an entertainment giant with full-length animated movies such as 1937's *Snow White and the Seven Dwarfs*, considered a "masterpiece" and after which the name Disney became synonymous with feature-length, animated films. *Pinocchio* and *Fantasia* followed in 1940. World War II saw the Disney studio producing military training films and propaganda starring the character of Donald Duck as a "loyal, dedicated American citizen," as described by Janet Wasko in *Understanding Disney: The Manufacture of Fantasy*. With the stalling of entertainment production, Disney experienced some financial troubles, but regained its place as the leader in animated film with *Cinderella* in 1950.

A television special on NBC in 1950 served basically as a promotional piece for the Disney film *Alice in Wonderland*, and Walt Disney saw TV as a medium through which to promote his idea for his Disneyland theme park. The production of an anthology show called *Disneyland* for ABC came with the network's $500,000 investment in the park. The children's daytime series *The Mickey Mouse Club* during the mid-1950s and *Walt Disney's Wonderful World of Color* in the early 1960s added to the company's presence on the airwaves. Disney continued to produce family-friendly entertainment in the form of live-action films throughout the 1960s and 1970s. Walt Disney died in 1966. The company continued to expand its theme park empire with the opening of Walt Disney World in Orlando, Florida, in October of 1971. Roy Disney, who had overseen the financing and construction of Disney World, died in December of 1971. Additional theme parks in Japan and France during the 1980s and 1990s accompanied the global reach of classic Disney characters, films, and merchandizing.

In terms of American culture, Disney in some form or another became a familiar part of everyday life. By the mid-1970s, the company relied more on its revenue from its theme parks and "was proving to be rather sluggish, both moving into newly developing distribution technologies (such as cable and home video) and in producing a wider range of media products" (Wasko, 2001, p. 26). In 1984, former television network executive Michael Eisner took over as the CEO, and annual revenues more than doubled. In 1986, the company known as Walt Disney Productions changed its name to The Walt Disney Company. Eisner would oversee changes in the Disney universe over the next two decades, which would establish Disney's reign as a corporate megapower—especially in the field of mass media entertainment.

Disney, the Mega-Media Company

Synergy—in terms of cross-promotion of all things Disney across all aspects of the Disney corporation—has made the company legendary in the business arena, as well documented in explanations of the Disney business model by scholars such as Wasko and Andi Stein. Media synergy within the Disney universe increased dramatically during the mid-1990s, as deregulation allowed for expansions in media companies' acquisition ability; the Federal Communications Commission had "unshackled" the three big television networks, ABC, CBS, and NBC, which let them make and distribute an unlimited amount of their own programming, as described by Geraldine Fabrikant.

It was under these circumstances that in 1995 Disney announced its $19 billion acquisition of Capital Cities/ABC, giving Disney control over not only the ABC network and its news and entertainment divisions but also several other media outlets, including the sports television and radio network ESPN, and cable channels Lifetime and Arts & Entertainment (A&E), as well as ABC-owned and affiliated television and radio stations. Prior to the merger, Disney had owned KCAL-TV, a television station in Los Angeles, and its cable outlet the Disney Channel. KCAL-TV was sold because of FCC regulations. The acquisition also gave Disney ownership over four newspapers, including the *Kansas City Star* and the *Fort Worth Star-Telegram*, which it soon sold to Knight-Ridder for $1.5 billion, as the newspaper holdings did not fit with Disney's synergistic agenda. Divestiture in its more than 20 radio stations in major markets followed during the 2010s, with an AM station in Los Angeles kept to be used as the originator for Radio Disney programming.

With its purchase of Capital Cities/ABC, "Disney firmly established its role as one of the dominant players in the U.S. media industry" (Wasko, 2001, p. 60). Synergy and cross-promotion between Disney and ABC soon appeared in network programming. Storylines of ABC sitcoms, such as *Roseanne*, featured visits to Walt Disney World. This practice continued in the 2010s, such as with the series *black-ish*, as well as ABC's *Good Morning America* weekday news programming. Through ABC and its affiliate stations, Disney reaches 99% of U.S. households, according to Sourcewatch, published by the nonprofit Center for Media and Democracy.

As Stein details in *Why We Love Disney: The Power of the Disney Brand* (2011), the expansion of the Disney media universe continued at a cosmic pace under Robert Iger, who took over as CEO in 2005, with the acquisition of Pixar Animation Studio in 2006 at a $7.4 billion price tag and the $4 billion purchase of Marvel

Entertainment—which included film, television, and digital properties, merchandising, and comic books—in 2009. As if to complete its universe metaphor, Disney bought Lucasfilm, with its franchise of *Star Wars* films and merchandise, in 2012 for $4.05 billion; by 2018 Disney already had recouped the purchase price.

In March of 2019, Disney acquired 21st Century Fox for $71.3 billion, which included the 20th Century Fox and Fox Searchlight film studios, the entire film library and every TV show made by 20th Century Fox, the FX and National Geographic cable channels, and a 30% stake in the streaming service Hulu, added to its already-held 30%. Excluded from the deal was the Fox broadcasting network, Fox News Channel, and Fox Sports Channel. The purchase created what Brooks Barnes, reporting in *The New York Times*, described as "an entertainment colossus the size of which the world has never seen" (p. B3).

Journalistic Issues and Implications of Media Conglomeration

Disney news topics over the decades since its founding include high-profile cases in which Disney either brought suit or threatened to do so against those whom the company accused of copyright violation. Garnering national attention were two stories in 1989 in particular: the televised 1989 Academy Awards which featured a stage number in which performers dressed as the Disney version of Snow White, and the case of a Florida day care center whose murals depicted Disney characters, as summarized by Wasko (2001). Neither case was prosecuted by Disney, but both illustrated the company's seriousness regarding what it saw as the unauthorized the use of its characters.

When ABC News became part of the Disney universe in the mid-1990s, the interconnectedness of the Walt Disney Company with a news organization that it owned brought to the fore issues of conflict of interest. In 1998, the quashing of a news story critical of Disney by the ABC news magazine program *20/20* received wide press coverage. The report was an investigation of lax hiring practices at Walt Disney World, which put into question the company's concern over security. While ABC executives cited editorial problems with the script, those problems were not made clear. Disney issued a statement saying that its own executives had nothing to do with the decision to pull the story. Questions surrounded the company's explanation, given that a second version of the script also did not pass approval. No written policy about Disney news coverage by ABC had been in place, although CEO Michael Eisner, in a 1998 NPR radio interview, had expressed his desire that ABC News not cover Disney. This, coupled with hazy rationales for canceling the story, and the inclusion of a story about dogs on Prozac in a subsequent edition of the show, made the case ideal for analysis as a conflict of interest. In their review of the incident in their 2001 chapter "Conflict of Interest in Journalism," Sandra Borden and Michael Pritchard considered the position of ABC and concluded that "a reasonable case can be made for the appearance of a conflict of interest, and this appearance cannot be resolved simply by an expression of confidence on the part of the decisionmaker" (p. 87). The *20/20* case thus presented the challenges that reporters have when investigating their own companies.

In 2017, Disney's treatment of a news organization became fodder for national news coverage as well as a short boycott of its films by other newspapers. In September 2017, the *Los Angeles Times* published a three-part investigative series of Disney's relationship with the city of Anaheim, California, home to Disneyland and other Disney resorts. In "Is Disney Paying Its Fair Share in Anaheim?," *L.A. Times* reporter Daniel Miller outlined the ways that Disney has benefited from various deals with city. "Over the last two decades or so," wrote Miller, "as Disney's annual profit has soared, the company has secured subsidies, incentives, rebates and protections from future taxes in Anaheim that, in aggregate, would be worth more than $1 billion, according to public policy experts who have reviewed deals between the company and the city" (p. A1). While Disney appeared to profit from those deals, "some of the city's working-class residents said they don't see enough of the upside," Miller further reported.

The *Los Angeles Times* story coincided with the impending release of a Disney-Marvel movie, *Thor: Ragnarok*. In November of 2017, it became public that Disney had imposed a ban on the newspaper's reporters from advance screenings of the film, citing the *Times*' "complete disregard for basic journalistic standards" in reporting the Anaheim story (Sims, 2017). In response to Disney's ban of the *L.A. Times*, film critics from other news outlets, such as *The Washington Post*, as well as four film critics' associations announced a counter-ban against Disney. Less than a day after the critics' associations issued a joint statement that it would not consider Disney-related films for its year-end awards unless Disney lifted its ban against the *Los Angeles Times*, Disney relinquished via a statement in *The New York Times*. The company said it had "productive" discussions with the *Los Angeles Times'* new leadership and would restore that newspaper's access to advance screenings of its films. The ban/counter-ban episode between Disney and the press lasted less than a week, but created negative publicity for Disney, belying the wholesome corporate image it has fostered for nearly a century. As David Sims, writing in *The Atlantic*, concluded, "Beyond the lesson learned about such bullying tactics, the message of the pushback should be clear—that even a behemoth like Disney can be vulnerable to bad press."

In her history of the Walt Disney Company, Wasko (2001) spoke to how not only has the name "Disney" become almost sacred regarding its stature and place within U.S. American culture, but how it has perfected the art of corporate synergy. As a, if not *the*, most successful purveyor of entertainment content on a global scale, Disney serves as a quintessential example of media conglomeration. The Disney universe appears to continue expanding, certainly beyond what scholars who have studied the implications of media conglomeration had previously considered. Henry Giroux and Grace Pollock, in 2010, noted how mergers like Disney's buyouts of ABC and Pixar Studios "consolidate corporate control of assets and markets, extending the influence of media conglomerates over public opinion" (p. 211). With its accumulative array of media outlets, Disney's influence continues to increase. In terms of how media conglomerations might affect democracy and the protection of a pluralistic media landscape, one must take into account the Walt Disney Company's political campaign contributions and lobbying efforts on issues such as copyright, advertising, and television broadcasting, as noted by Sourcewatch.

The complexities created when a media corporation owns a news organization include the scrutiny of coverage of the owner by the journalists in its employ, as well as questions regarding the integrity and ethical standards of those who supervise those journalists. How ABC news programs present stories about Disney leaves the news arm of the network open to inspection by others, including other news organizations. In the case of the *Los Angeles Times* in 2017, Disney's pushback to the newspaper's investigation of its business dealings with the city of Anaheim wherein one of its major attractions resides resulted in a pushback against Disney by the press itself.

Disney's recent acquisition of 21st Century Fox and its accompanying media properties has decreased the number of studios that produce cultural content. As media ownership looks to be held in fewer and fewer hands, Emily VanDerWerff (2019) observed that "while the most obvious concerns surrounding that possibility stems from how news might take on corporate interests, there are host of others than range from the political to the artistic." The decrease of voices and viewpoints, and layoffs that result in redundancies between media organizations that have real-life consequences for those who work in the industry are among the effects of almost endless media mergers. As VanDerWerff concluded, "The big fish are eating each other, and soon there may be only one left." That one last fish just might look more like a mouse.

Erika Engstrom

See also ABC News; Conflicts of Interest; Copyright; Ethics; Investigative Journalism; Media Conglomerates; Media Ownership; Television News Magazines

Further Readings

Barnes, B. (2019, March 20). As Disney gets gigantic, ripples may also be big. *The New York Times*, p. B3.

Borden, S., & Prichard, M. (2001). Conflict of interest in journalism. In M. Davis & A. Stark (Eds.), *Conflict of interest in the professions* (pp. 73–91). New York, NY: Oxford University Press.

Fabrikant, G. (1995, August 1). The media business: The merger, Walt Disney to acquire ABC in $19 billion deal to build a giant for entertainment. *The New York Times*, p. A1.

Giroux, H., & Pollock, G. (2010). *The mouse that roared: Disney and the end of innocence* (2nd ed.). Lanham, MD: Rowman & Littlefield.

Kurtz, H. (1998, October 14). ABC kills story critical of owner Disney. *The Washington Post*, pp. C1, C16.

Miller, D. (2017, September 24). Is Disney paying its share in Anaheim? *Los Angeles Times*, p. A1.

Sims, D. (2017, November 7). Disney's bullying tactics against the press failed. *The Atlantic*. Retrieved from https://www.theatlantic.com/entertainment/archive/2017/11/disneys-bullying-tactics-against-the-press-failed/545237/

Sourcewatch. (2017). Disney. Retrieved from www.sourcewatch.org/index.php/Disney

Stein, A. (2011). *Why we love Disney: The power of the Disney brand*. New York, NY: Peter Lang.

Treaster, P. (1997, April 15). Knight-Ridder to buy 4 newspapers from Disney for $1.65 billion. *The New York Times*, p. 35.

VanDer Werff, E. (2019, March 20). Here's what Disney owns after the massive Disney/Fox merger. *Vox*. doi:10.4135/9781529742176

Wasko, J. (2001). *Understanding Disney: The manufacture of fantasy*. Cambridge, UK: Polity.

Whitten, S. (2018, October 30). Disney bought lucasfilm six years ago and has already recouped its $4 billion investment. Retrieved from https://www.cnbc.com/2018/10/30/six-years-after-buying-lucasfilm-disney-has-recouped-its-investment.html

WAR AND MILITARY JOURNALISM

War and military journalism can be defined as journalism that covers war and armed conflict, internationally and intrastate. Literature in this field includes both perspectives about journalism practices in war and conflict zones such as pool systems and embedding with military forces, and analyses of disseminated content; military psychological operations (PSYOP); and spin and propaganda disseminated prior to, during, and after wars. Since journalism is both a professional practice and a "public good," the study of war and military journalism reveals a merge of scholarly traditions, where studies of professional practice and media content unite. Issues such as truth, bias, and objectivity—key issues in reporting from wars—cannot be discussed without reference to practice and individuality. Thus, studies of war

and military journalism tend to rely on various approaches and are found across disciplines. Research in this field may derive from both quantitative and qualitative traditions and use a wide scope of methods such as ethnographic studies, large-scale surveys, and content analyses of discourse, rhetoric, and narratives in the media.

War and military journalism scholarship is a well-established field within journalism and media studies largely related to other dimensions of the discipline. Affected by technological development, globalization, and market demands, this field of journalism relates to historical development, and aspects of technology, digitalization, and globalization are relevant to discuss within its scope. International relations and U.S. and allies' intervention abroad are also relevant for perspectives on censorship and media freedom. Another side to media freedom is legal issues, crime and impunity, and media ownership structures and economy.

This entry first sets the historical context of war and military journalism and defines some of the most prevailing and significant turns and developments in history of war and military reporting. It presents an overview of dominant discussions in the field, specifically the debate surrounding objectivity and truth, and divides in theoretical and practical approaches such as war and peace journalism. The local journalists and fixers in war and military conflict are discussed, prior to a section on the scholarly focus and development of research within the field. Contemporary approaches and subjects of study are outlined, including perspectives on information war and the subsequent violence against the press, which are closely related to issues of globalization and new media technology in contemporary war journalism. Views and discussions related to gender issues are presented where relevant throughout the entry.

The History of War Journalism

Attempts to control the media during war has taken various forms throughout history, and with somewhat different outcomes. The Vietnam War, also referred to as "the first television war" and "the living room war" for its role in narrowing down the distance between public and the media, demonstrated the important part media play to the outcome of war. While the U.S. public in the beginning showed support for the war, the loss of control over the news narrative both within and outside the United States brought about growing public dissent and ultimately defeat. The use of film was a new practice in journalism and turned out to have significant impact on a growing number of television viewers across the world. Despite attempts to control the media by embedding journalists with military units, circulation of uncensored news reports and critical perspectives from the approximately 600 accredited foreign journalists on the ground ensured that the world outside were exposed to eyewitness accounts of critical events. Some hold that stories that managed to escape U.S. censorship provided valuable information to North Vietnam, although very few security breaches by journalists were reported.

The lesson learned from the Vietnam War was to keep a closer tie to the media. The importance of maintaining public support in prolonged wars was manifest, and thus the U.S. administration imposed a pool system to control the narrative when invading Grenada in 1983 and Panama in 1989. By denying media staffs access to the frontlines and placing them in pools to receive military briefings and field visits only after battles had been fought, lesser uncensored information was disseminated. The denied access was justified with a concern for the safety of the reporters. However, the pool practice in Panama prompted harsh criticism of the system and resulted in public protests. While some 800 journalists would eventually arrive in Panama to cover the conflict after the invasion had begun, only 12 journalists were included in the pool that went with the U.S. forces. Their access was limited to staying at an air base and only entering the field accompanied by forces and never during battle.

The intentional exclusion of media during these wars represents a turn in the history of war and military journalism that would affect the position of reporters as neutral observers to conflict in wars to follow. And media safety has continued to increasingly become an argument to reduce freedom to report. Especially the confrontations of the Cold War exposed journalists to fragmented frontlines and information war. The war in former Yugoslavia was a turning point in which many journalists experienced for the first time that their status as neutral observers no longer applied.

Women in War Journalism

As war reporting has since the beginning been a strongly male-dominated job, some women journalists joined the line of work already during the European revolutions and the U.S. Civil War. Their numbers increased slightly in the First and Second World Wars and significantly during the Vietnam War. In more recent wars, women reporters have been regularly deployed to war zones while still facing restrictions both from military and editorial leaders. Their denied access is regularly explained by assumptions that women war reporters require extra facilitation and that the army units are unable to accommodate them, so-called pseudo-protectionism. Until today, war and military journalism remains male-dominated in participation and influence, although a rapidly increasing number of women are entering the field. The masculine traits of the military culture make women still vulnerable to assaults, sexist abuse, and discrimination. Attacks are not only perpetrated by sources and others in the field, but regularly occur in newsrooms by colleagues and supervisors. Physical and psychological attacks are particularly difficult to report for women war journalists because of the machoism and bravado in this field of work and the fact that their presupposed vulnerability has traditionally been the argument used by leaders to deny women staff access to wars.

Debating Objectivity: Peace and War Journalism

Manipulation of media content to promote either war or peace and reconciliation is a topic that has been problematized among practitioners and academics. The genocide in Rwanda in 1994 states an example of how media content can be skewed to sway public opinion, to play a critical role in inciting and prolonging violence. Strategically targeting and shaping public opinion, even inciting to act, radio, and other media platforms were utilized to plan and execute a genocide. Today, the case of Rwanda has, in contrast, become an example of how so-called constructive journalism can be used to reconsolidate a nation and build peace in postconflict situations.

While subject to academic criticism and dispute among scholars and practitioners of journalism, the theoretical discussion about the content of war and military journalism is to some extent divided in two: one that relies on the potential of the media to play a constructive role in war and conflict, and another that deals with criticism of their neglect. To some extent, the constructive approaches have responded to the criticism.

War Journalism and Mythmaking in the Gulf

The line of theory centering on the shortcomings of mainstream media is focused on their capacity to present objective news and stories from the battlefield, especially when embedded with military units. Departing from a focus on Western foreign correspondents covering international wars, this literature similarly to peace journalism directs a main concern toward the inquiry about journalistic ideas about truth and objectivity and how these are kept at the core of correspondents' work in the field. With main attention to the 2003 NATO led invasion of Iraq, the war correspondents' reflections about living dangerously and the impacts these dangers have on their work frequently surface throughout research on the foreign war correspondent.

This literature further focuses on dissemination of spin and constructed myths as part of military strategy to control the narrative and win public support. Examples of such myths are the narratives presented about Saddam Hussein in Western media in relation to the Iraqi annexation of Kuwait in 1990, resulting in international condemnation and a United Nations mandate for Western intervention. And so, the Persian Gulf War broke out with the massive U.S.-led air offensive Operation Desert Storm. In years to come, the stories about "weapons of mass destruction" (WMDs) circulated in the mass media leading up to the 2003 invasion of Iraq becoming a main argument for U.S. President George W. Bush and UK Prime Minister Tony Blair to go to war, along with ending Hussein's "support for terrorism" and to "free the Iraqi people." In 2003, Hussein was captured and sentenced to death in the United States.

Due to the lack of documentation of WMDs and the obviously skewed portrayal of enemy leaders, these arguments are being referred to as *myths* in the scholarship. A similar narrative of a "terrorist leader" was presented in Western media when NATO invaded Libya in 2011 and Muammar al-Gaddafi was overthrown and murdered. Although media mythmaking tends to frame leaders, the UN Security Council did not issue a mandate for regime-change in Libya. With mythmaking in war and foreign interventionism in the Gulf as starting point, a significant share of this literature pays attention to media strategies of the U.S. and NATO allies. Spin, PSYOP, and sentiment manipulation is a key topic in content of war and military journalism.

Peace Journalism

Peace journalism as a concept and method in journalism emerged first from the work of Johan Galtung and Mari Ruge's study about what makes foreign news newsworthy, in 1965. Suggesting that the media is inherently biased toward violence and conflict, they also noted that coverage from war and conflict presented news stories in which events were detached from the larger context in which they were situated, and by such did not contribute to foster understanding among its readership. Galtung then suggested peace journalism as an alternative to "war journalism," offering constructive guidelines for how to do "good" journalism. The peace journalism script encourages reporters to take active responsibility in explaining the context of news events. The approach also suggests that journalists may use certain skills and outlooks when reporting and that this can help avoid a natural bias otherwise tending to reinforce the conflicts and thus maintain a negative status quo.

The practice of *constructive journalism* is a newer concept within the media, which applies techniques from the field of positive psychology. Its fundamental idea is that audiences respond more positively and are more likely to engage in prosocial activities when exposed to stories about solutions or positive developments in society. *Solution journalism* is a similar kind of approach, aiming to present solutions to problems to the audience in order to avoid "compassion fatigue"— that is, apathy toward human suffering—but scholars who have tested solution-oriented content perception refrain from persisting it actually leads to (positive) action. It has similarities with peace journalism in the sense that both are prescriptive in their approach to how media can play a role in building peace and enhancing reconciliation or performing an otherwise responsible role in society for the better of the future. The social responsibility of journalism as an institution is the theoretical fundament for these perspectives.

The idea behind these approaches is constructivist in nature, assuming that complete objectivity is unachievable and that journalists should strategize and make well-considered choices in order to change a negative development, such as in war. It similarly assumes that if the journalists do not take that responsibility, other forces such as market or political demand will influence the coverage and uphold a potentially destructive bias. Its critics, on the other hand, understand this approach as a mere attempt to promote solutions for peace and to influence politicians, and that although unattainable, objectivity should still be a normative value to strive for. Criticism has concern for the so-called *journalism of attachment*, in which reporters in wars through history have taken sides with conflicting parties. It fears that objectivity and consequently truth will be compromised by the normative guidelines and tangible recommendations of peace journalism and that an approach that undermines the aim of objectivity (however unattainable) can be exploited by partisan press. That noted, the value of objectivity has a firm position in journalism across the world today, perhaps especially so in the international and mainstream media, and downplaying such a fundamental cornerstone in journalism is controversial at least. Despite this, peace journalism is listed on the curricula of journalism education programs across the world, and scholars still advocate for its potential and contribution to journalism education.

The Local Journalists and "Fixers" in War

War correspondents aside, local journalists covering intrastate wars is another side to war and military journalism. Local journalists, often working as "fixers" for national news staff travelling to the province or foreign correspondents coming from abroad, have a key position in making the news. Depending on the extent to which they are involved in their local environments, local journalists are easily accused of bias toward local conflicting parties. They are targets of illegal economic and political activity and their capacity to report on military operations in their area depends on how pronounced forces of crime, corruption, and impunity are in society. When it comes to covering intrastate military conflict, the local journalists often claim to be the ones who cover the war from the battleground while serving foreign correspondents or so-called "hotel-journalists" with footage from the field.

The extent to which local journalists have become targets of international war, which according to the United Nations Educational, Scientific and Cultural Organization (UNESCO) is significantly high, underpins a situation that is receiving growing attention from researchers globally. UNESCO estimate that more than 90% of journalist killed annually are local reporters.

While little research has yet investigated the role of the local journalists and fixers in war and conflict, they are argued to play a significant role in the newsgathering of foreign correspondents in war. This perspective on war journalism gained attention especially in relation to the 2003 to 2007 war in Iraq. Interviewing a number of "fixers" in Iraq during the war, Jerry Palmer and Victoria Fontan did a study of the practical details around choices and frames for the production of news stories in Iraq, finding that journalists who rejected embedding with forces relied instead heavily on the assistance of local fixers. The need for security was the main argument for them to rely upon help from locals, while language, network, and local knowledge were other important reasons. The extent of this reliance was illuminated by the fact that the fixers interviewed in the study stated that they even sometimes had to conduct full interviews on behalf of the correspondent and that the role of the correspondent was superfluous at times.

New Media and the Global Discursive Order

With increasing focus on security in what some scholars have called the "threat society," the mediated culture of fear is constructed in a dominant global discursive order disseminated by mass media. With reference to the narrative about the terrorist leader outlined earlier, the increasingly united media landscape constructed the global War on Terror. It is described as one of greater dimensions than wars before, representing a global divide between the rich dominating world powers and the poorer dominated peoples and cultures, and the media served as a conveyer of the discursive order that has constructed this divide. In the scholarship, this literature represents a merge between studies in war journalism and crisis communication, and centers on the idea that the hype of a crisis is used strategically to incite public concern for security and subsequent demand for knowledge and information. The strategy assumes that people will pay the price of civil liberty (such as right to information and expression of own opinion) at the cost of security and that they will settle with less accurate and documented information if they feel it is necessary and urgent.

Information War and New Threats to the Media

New literature suggests the postmillennium period brought deteriorated conditions for journalists in the shape of increasing economic pressure, new media platforms, and globalization. Centuries of military propaganda and information operations has contributed to directed attacks on journalists and media centers. The targeting of journalists in what scholars call the new world order includes the U.S. Air Force's bombing of Al Jazeera's headquarters in Kabul in 2001 and another 2 years later in Baghdad. A Serbian television station was targeted and bombed in 1999, and scholarly criticism points to Western media's inadequate coverage of the legal aspects of these wars. This context has also been brought to attention by academics in the United States addressing the lack of legal protection of foreign correspondents as a focal point to consider following criticism of U.S. foreign correspondents embedding with troops in Iraq. The censure of the academy is that the media are servants to control of the narrative, while placing emphasis on the role of its government as a threat and their consequent incapacity to protect their own journalists. While there is significant

focus on attacks by the U.S./NATO alliance, it is established that most killings of reporters in Iraq during the 2003 to 2007 war were perpetrated by Iraqi militants or insurgents.

The frontline to which the classic war correspondent was sent has been replaced by multiple fragmented frontlines while the use of drones, sent from bases and battleships far away, splits up the site of warfare. Reporters are increasingly on their own in differing locations. While the benefits of new media platforms such as WikiLeaks make it more difficult to keep information from journalists and the public, journalists continue to fight another battle to get access to the frontlines.

Journalist Safety and Restricted Media Freedom

Although journalists' possibility to operate in a conflict zone depends greatly on their options for security, this perspective was merely an underlying connotation in journalism research from war and military journalism until the latest decade. The threat and security perspective also concern scholars in the field of human rights and freedom of expression, and in 2015 UNESCO launched a research agenda on the topic that had significant impact on the growth of academic research in this field, including the issue of impunity for crimes against journalists. Although organizations working to promote the safety of journalists appear to be convinced of an increasing threat against the media, scholars are not united in this view. An increase may be logically explained as a direct consequence of a media out of state and military control, owing to new media technology and growing Internet access across the world. New communication systems and opportunities to participate, distribute, and obtain information are widespread and the traditional gatekeeper for editorial control weighs lesser on the output than it used to. New actors such as in the telecom industry are in position to gather information and surveil people, journalists among others. This has made it possible to trace and attack journalists in the field in recent wars such as was claimed with the killing of Marie Colvin and Rémi Ochlik in Homs, Syria, in 2012.

Recent wars in the Middle East have also contributed significantly to burgeoning media attention on the issue of journalists' safety. Media attention to the suffering and deaths of their own staff at work in the war zone has become an inescapable part of the narrative of war journalism since the turn of the 21st century. In competition for viewers and readership, the media displays themselves as an inevitably important and proximate witness to events in times where audiences could otherwise turn to a vast array of other sources for their information.

Concluding Thoughts

Media coverage of wars and armed conflicts has throughout the history of military warfare been an important asset to succeed in accomplishing their goal. Military forces depend on public support and trust to win the wars they are set to battle, and consequently how the media portrays that battle is essential to remain control over. Often, defeat is undermined, and success exaggerated. One's own loss is concealed to the possible extent, and victory over the enemy extensively displayed. Public support is a crucial element for winning a war. Recognizing that the media has since long been a significant player of war, it seems logical if they were increasingly targeted as a result of reduced opportunities for state censorship.

On the other hand, along with globalization and new media development, journalists are also more exposed than they used to be to surveillance and targeted reprisals. With global communication and social media, the journalist's work becomes more visible and they are more likely to be held personally accountable for what they publish. The traditional gatekeeper function in which responsibility rests on the editorial leadership is merged with new media systems where journalists are increasingly on their own. This puts them at extra risk for retaliations when publishing sensitive information or presenting critical political views. They increasingly pay the price for covering wars and armed conflict. The lack of security is reinforcing the need for protection in the field and thus journalists are still depending on travelling with military units to the war zone today. Another consequence of the attacks on journalists is that the increase in retaliation attacks may prompt higher levels of self-censorship among journalists, while a narrative of an unsafe profession may also keep them from wanting to enter the conflict hotspots and thus control of the press remains intact.

Marte H. Høiby

See also Military and the Media; War Correspondents; Objectivity; Self-Censorship; Violence against Journalists

Further Readings

Allan, S., & Zelizer, B. (Eds.) (2004). *Reporting war: Journalism in wartime*. Oxon, UK: Routledge.

Armoudian, M. (2016). *Reporting from the danger zone: Frontline journalists, their jobs, and an increasingly perilous future*. New York, Routledge. doi 10.4324/9781315733067

Carlsson, U. & Pöyhtäri, R. (Eds.). *The assault on journalism: Building knowledge to protect freedom of expression*. Gothenburg, Sweden: Nordicom.

Carlsson, U. (Ed.). *Freedom of expression and media in transition: Studies and reflections in the digital age*. Gothenburg, Sweden: Nordicom.

Carpenter, T. G. (1995). *The captive press: Foreign policy crises and the first amendment* (p. 315). Washington DC: Cato Institute.

Cottle, S., Sambrook, R., & Mosdell, N. (2016). *Reporting dangerously—journalist killings, intimidation and security*. London, UK: Palgrave. doi 10.1177/0267323117718318

Fisk, R. (2005, January 17). Hotel journalism gives American troops a free hand as the press shelters indoors. *The Independent*. Retrieved from https://www.independent.co.uk/voices/commentators/fisk/hotel-journalism-givesamerican-troops-a-free-hand-as-the-press-shelters-indoors-5344745.html

Galtung, J., & Ruge, M. H. (1965). The structure of foreign news: The presentation of the Congo, Cuba and Cyprus crises in four Norwegian newspapers. *Journal of Peace Research, 2*(1), 64–90. doi 10.1177/002234336500200104

Hanitzsch, T. (2007). Situating peace journalism in journalism studies: A critical appraisal. *Conflict & Communication Online, 6*(2). ISSN 1618-0747

Høiby, M. (2020). Covering Mindanao: The safety of local vs. non-local Journalists in the field. *Journalism Practice, 14*(1). 6--83. doi 10.1080/17512786.2019.1598884

Høiby, M., & Ottosen, R. (2018). Journalism under pressure in conflict zones: A study of journalists and editors in seven countries. *Media, War & Conflict, 12*(1), 69–86. doi 10.1177/1750635217728092

Kim, H. S. (2010). Forces of gatekeeping and journalists' perceptions of physical danger in post-Saddam Hussein's Iraq. *Journalism & Mass Communication Quarterly, 87*(3–4), 484–500. doi 10.1177/1077 69901008700303

Kim, H. S., & Hama-Saeed, M. (2008). Emerging media in peril. *Journalism Studies, 9*(4), 578–594. doi 10.1080/14616700802114365

Knightley, P. (1975). *The first casualty: From the Crimea to Vietnam: The war correspondent as hero, propagandist, and myth maker* (1st ed.). New York, NY: Harcourt Brace Jovanovich. doi 10.1086/ahr/81.5.1074

Knightley, P. (2004). *The first casualty: The war correspondent as hero and myth-maker from the Crimea to Iraq* (3rd ed.). Baltimore, Md: Johns Hopkins University Press. doi 10.2307/1852883

Lisosky, J. M. & Henrichsen, J. R. (2011). *War onwords: Who should protect journalists?* Santa Barbara, Ca: ABC-CLIO.

Loyn, D. (2007). Good journalism or peace journalism? *Conflict & Communication Online, 6*(2), ISSN 1618-0747

Lynch, J., & McGoldrick, A. (2005). *Peace journalism: Conflict & peacebuilding*. Stroud, UK: Hawthorn Press.

Lynch, J. (2008). *Debates in peace journalism*. Sydney, Australia: Sydney University Press.

McIntyre, K. (2015). *Constructive journalism: The effects of positive emotions and solution information in news stories*. Chapel Hill, NC: University of North Carolina at Chapel Hill Graduate School. doi/10.17615/g6sg-8p47

McIntyre, K., & Sobel, M. (2018). Reconstructing Rwanda. *Journalism Studies, 19*(14), 2126–2147. doi 10.1080/1461670X.2017.1326834

McIntyre, K. (2019). Solutions journalism. *Journalism Practice, 13*(1), 16–34. doi 10.1080/17512 786.2017.1409647

Mowlana, H., Gerbner, G., & Schiller, H. (Eds.) (1992). *Triumph of the image: The media's war in the Persian Gulf, a global perspective* (1st ed.). Boulder, CO: Westview Press. doi 10.4324/9780429503443

Murrell, C. (2010). Baghdad bureaux: An exploration of the interconnected world of fixers and correspondents at the BBC and CNN. *Media, War & Conflict, 3*(2), 125–137. doi 10.1177/1750635210363338

Nohrstedt, S. A., & Ottosen, R. (2014). *New wars, new media and new war journalism: Professional and legal challenges in conflict reporting*. Gothenburg, Sweden: Nordicog. doi 10.1177/1750481316659962b

Nohrstedt, S. (2016). The role of the media in the discursive construction of wars. In A. Schwarz, M. W. Seeger, & C. Auer (Eds.), *The handbook of international crisis communication research*. Hoboken, NJ: Wilec. doi 10.1002/9781118516812.ch13.

Ottosen, R. (2010). The war in Afghanistan and peace journalism in practice. *Media, War & Conflict, 3*(3), 261–278. doi 10.1177/1750635210378944

Palmer, J., & Fontan, V. (2007). 'Our ears and our eyes': Journalists and fixers in Iraq. *Journalism, 8*(1), 5–24. doi 10.1177/1464884907072419

Palmer, L. (2018). *Becoming the story: War correspondents since 9/11*. Urbana, IL: University of Illinois Press.

Peleg, S. (2007). In defence of peace journalism: A rejoinder. *Conflict & Communication Online, 6*(2). ISSN 1618-0747

Pendry, R. (2011). Sub-contracting news gathering in Iraq. *The International Journal of Communication Ethics, 8* (3/4).

Spector, R. H. (2016, April 27). The Vietnam war and the media. In *Encyclopædia Britannica*. Encyclopædia Britannica, Inc. doi 10.1108/err.1998.2.7.79.7

Steiner, L. (2017). Women war reporters' resistance and silence in the face of sexism and sexual violence. *Media & Jornalismo*. Versão impressa. doi 10.14195/2183-5462_30_1

Tumber, H. (2006). The fear of living dangerously: Journalists who report on conflict. *International Relations, 20*(4), 439–451. doi 10.1177/0047 117806069405

Tumber, H., & Palmer. (2004). *Media at war* (1st ed.). London, UK: Thousand Oaks, CA: Sage Publications, Inc

von der Lippe, B. & Ottosen, R. (Eds.) (2016). *Gendering war and peace reporting: some insight — some missing links*. Gothenburg, Sweden: Nordicom. doi 10.1177/0267323117739171b

Willis, J. (2010). *100 Media moments that changed America*. Santa Barbara, Ca: ABC-CLIO.

WAR CORRESPONDENTS

War correspondents provide accurate, reliable, and firsthand reports of armed conflicts, military operations and strategies, and the war's impact on civilian home fronts. These journalists are stationed in conflict zones or distant battlefields and perform a central role in helping the public follow, visualize, and understand past and present conflicts. War reporters access frontlines, cultivate sources, gather a wide range of perspectives (from authorities, noncombatants, and expert observers), and share their news with audiences all over the world. This type of reporting produces live footage, interviews, and close-up pictures of war that are usually outside of the reach of ordinary citizens. The work of war correspondents is both difficult and challenging.

War correspondents are impacted by the location and sociopolitical environments in which they operate, external and psychological pressures, and are expected to meet tight deadlines while engaging across multimedia platforms. Throughout the history of journalism, war correspondents have been jailed as spies or held back by military or police. Scholars of media and conflicts have documented governments' firm censorship efforts and goals to control information in the interest of security versus journalists' difficulties to provide comprehensive, let alone objective coverage of wars. The question of how journalists source information in times of national crisis has been subject of much debate. Over the past 200 years, the practice of war correspondence has evolved due to changes in technology, military-media relations, including self-censorship, and embedding practices. The job description is fluid but questions of access, balance, ethical responsibilities and the materiality of portraying human conflict, suffering, and death remain part of the job. In the digital age, changes and expansions in the use of technology, video livestreaming, multimedia platforms, and the rise of participant and citizen journalism have further impacted the work and demands of war correspondents.

This entry offers an introduction to the history and practice of war correspondence and reviews the biographies of noted American war correspondents from the mid-1900s up to the present.

History of Reporting
War and Early Pioneers

Historians have chronicled conflicts long before the concept of journalism was clearly defined. Athenian general Thucydides covered the Peloponnesian War (431–404 BCE) and was perhaps the first participant-observer and correspondent reporting on a long and divisive battle. In the modern era, correspondents were commissioned by British newspapers to cover the French Revolution and Napoleonic Wars (1789–1815). In the late 18th and early 19th centuries, journalists did not routinely cover battles as frontline correspondents. Instead, they gathered information from soldiers' letters, printed correspondence, other newspapers, and gossip. The practice of war reporting came of age during the Mexican-American War (1846–1848), when American newspapers—the primary vehicle of mass information—assigned full-time correspondents to cover military action. News from the battlefront was relayed via horseback, steamboat, and telegraph lines to American cities by reporters such as George Wilkins Kendall of the *New Orleans Picayune* or Jane McManus Storms Cazneau of the *New York Sun*. Scholars have noted that the rise of the commercial and penny press newspapers accelerated the need for war reporting in the mid- to late-1840s.

During the Crimean War (1853–1856), the British military practiced rigid censorship of all battlefield news and information was held back or not allowed to be published, which caused criticism among newspapers in London. In the United States, the American Civil War (1861–1865) was a turning point for military warfare, technology, the role of visual media, and war reporting. Black and white photographs became an important element of recording horrific battles as well as soldier's frontline experiences. In the 19th century, before the notion of journalistic objectivity or detachment was practiced, journalists engaged in advocacy and often shared partisan opinions and propaganda. By the 1890s, the "golden era" of wartime correspondence, professional reporters such as Richard Harding Davis (1864–1916) were widely known, and there was minimal pressure and military restriction on what to write and publish. The Russo-Japanese War (1904–1905) was a unique precursor to later 20th-century propaganda and information wars. In their goal to shape the news, Japanese censors delayed and regulated correspondents' access to news and used a pool system to share official information.

First World War and Second World War

By the start of World War I (1914–1918), the global public knew what a war correspondent was. At the onset of the conflict in August 1914, all British correspondents were banned from the fronts and the documentary of events was left to members of the military staff. In 1915, pressured by politicians and influential newspaper owners, the British government loosened its restrictions and allowed correspondents on the battlefields. American correspondents had covered the conflict from the start of the war. Some scholars have contended that American and British correspondents during the Great War served as an extension of the national propaganda efforts. Press historians have also chronicled the rise of women correspondents during the Great War, the unique challenges of female war correspondents, and their complex relationship to both authorities and audiences. In World War II (1939–1945) American radio journalists, who had covered the fighting during the Spanish Civil War (1936–1939), rose to new prominence but also faced stricter military censorship due to the medium's immediate and widespread distribution. Most famously, *CBS* radio journalist Edward R. Murrow was reporting from the rooftops during the London blitz raids. Murrow and his team of reporters, referred to as the *Murrow Boys,* followed in the footsteps of previous influential war journalists and correspondents and set a new standard for modern war journalists.

Wars in Korea and Vietnam

The Korean War (1950–1953) and Vietnam War (1959–1975) changed the relationship between military officials, government information officers, and war correspondents. Scholarship has found that journalists covering the Korean War continued to exercise self-censorship, which often meant leaving out the grim realities or photographs of combat. The Vietnam War influenced the professional ethos of journalists, as they became "participant-observers." News from correspondents in Vietnam hardened antigovernment attitudes and public criticism of then-president Lyndon Johnson. In the following years, military-press relations were at an all-time low and the military restricted journalists' reporting from invasions in Central America in the 1980s.

Gulf and Iraq Wars

The Gulf War (1990–1991) and Iraq War (2003–2011) marked the return of restricted access and the embedding of journalists with combat troops. In their effort to manage the perception of war and breaking news, military limited access to frontlines and journalists could no longer report with absolute autonomy. Military public affairs staff embraced publicity efforts to engage and embed journalists, and sustain a supportive media coverage. Independence, in turn, became a new hallmark for journalists who had to work with—but often around—official sources to verify information and provide a balanced picture. During the first Gulf War, CNN provided 24/7 live coverage of the war and became an immediate source for international viewers. People could watch the war unfold in almost real-time. Some journalists did not accept this restricted access policy. They wandered around and reported from enemy warzones without military protection. In the case of CBS News correspondent Bob Simon, he and his crew were jailed, which in turn created chilling effects for other journalists. During the beginning of the Iraq War, many journalists shared promilitary stances in favor of the U.S.-led invasion and commentators on cable news perpetuated the myth of widespread weapons of mass destruction, which did not exist, as U.N. inspectors concluded.

Elements and Demands of the Job

Together with foreign correspondence, some observers consider war correspondence to be the most difficult type of journalism. War correspondents have excelled at their job and received many Pulitzer Prizes and awards for their critical work. Reporting from war zones is dangerous and includes psychological, emotional, and physical costs that may impact correspondents for the rest of their lives.

War reporters perform a critical function through their eye-witnessing role that renders authority and proof during battles. From a cultural and theoretical perspective, historians of film, photography, and the press have also studied the significance of photography for memory and truth in war. James Carey (1987) argued that eyewitness accounts may be perceived as truth, but these perspectives are quick, subjective and incomplete (p. xxix). Scholars have suggested that the 9/11 terrorist attacks in 2001 were a turning for reporting on conflict and correspondents increasingly became part of the story.

Modern Forms of War Correspondence

In the digital age, freelance war correspondents have become an important source for news in addition to traditional reporters. These freelancers work across media platforms and mainstream news networks use their content, which raises questions of risk-transfer but also authenticity. Scholarship on conflict reporting and social media curation has found that people living amid armed conflicts increasingly act as microbloggers and contribute to warblogs. The widespread use of mobile phones and social media make it harder to restrict information from wars and conflict zones. In the 21st century, new types of warfare, global terrorism, and wars in Afghanistan and Syria have also added new risks and pressures to being an eyewitness of warfare. The Syrian civil war, which began in 2011—and has become too dangerous for many Western correspondents—has seen the rise of the collaborative news clip, in which legacy media use eyewitness content from citizen journalists in multimedia videos and live blogs.

Noted American War Correspondents

While most war correspondents—including journalists and photographers who perform the job of a war reporter, even if they do not bear that label—have to operate in dangerous battle zones, navigate relations with military officials, shift through official propagandas and viewpoints, interview observers, combatants, and civilians, and produce news

stories in a timely manner, throughout the history of journalism, some of these reporters stand out. This section provides nine profiles of important American war correspondents.

Christiane Amanpour

Christiane Amanpour (1958–) is one of the world's top war correspondents and has covered almost every conflict in the late 20th century up to the present. She was born in London to a British mother and Iranian father, grew up in Iran and escaped with the family after the Islamic Revolution in 1979. She graduated with a degree in journalism from the University of Rhode Island and worked as a reporter for WBRU, a local radio station in the early 1980s. In 1983, only 3 years after Ted Turner had created the 24-hour TV news network, she became an assistant at CNN's international desk. Amanpour quickly made a name for herself in 1985 with her report on the political situation in Iran, as well as her detailed reporting on the Bosnian crisis and Balkan conflicts in the late 1980s and early 1990s. She became well-known and respected for her coverage of the Persian Gulf War. Together with CNN reporter Peter Arnett, she provided live coverage of the war from a hotel in enemy capital Baghdad and helped establish the network as a serious source for international news. Amanpour has interviewed numerous heads of state, politicians, presidents, and leaders around the globe, including in the Middle East. She has won many Academy of Television Arts & Sciences Emmy awards and other accolades for her journalism. Throughout her career, Amanpour's reporting has emphasized the toll of war on civilian populations and the difficult ethical choices that journalists make in covering conflicts.

Peter Arnett

Pulitzer Prize-winning reporter and New Zealand-born Peter Arnett (1934–) is best known for his breaking news coverage from the Persian Gulf War in 1991, when he and a TV crew broadcast live news from a Baghdad hotel. He started his career as an Associated Press print reporter covering the Vietnam War and was an eyewitness on the ground for more than 13 years (1962–1975). In 1966, he won a Pulitzer Prize for his coverage, which exposed the confusion and chaos of the U.S. military's strategy. In 1981, Arnett started working for CNN and covered conflicts, war, and civil unrests in Latin America, the Middle East, Africa, and Central Asia. In 1991, Arnett and his TV crew provided live 24/7 coverage of the Persian Gulf War and the American-led invasion of the capital city from a Baghdad hotel room. Conservative leaders criticized the vivid pictures of nonmilitary casualties, including the bombing of civilian buildings, air raid shelters, and a baby milk factory. A majority of the American public, however, as a Gallup poll after the war showed, were in favor of Arnett's reports, which chronicled the brutality of U.S. warfare. In March 1997, he was the first Western journalist to interview the arch-terrorist Osama bin Laden in Afghanistan. Although Arnett ceased working for CNN in 1999, he continues to report and comment on wars for other networks.

Richard Harding Davis

Journalist and writer Richard Harding Davis (1864–1916) was the best-known American reporter at the turn of the 20th century. His view on war changed over the course of his career, and in later stories he often highlighted the human toll and bloodshed of modern warfare. At the beginning of his career in New York, Davis was the epitome of a masculine, handsome star reporter who had started out writing fiction and short story novels, including the bestseller *Soldiers of Fortune,* but he had longed to cover war. Newspaper magnate William Randolph Hearst (1863–1951) sent Davis to report on the Cuban rebellion against Spain in 1897, which led to the Spanish-American War (1898). During this conflict, Davis's colorful accounts and his narrative of the Rough Riders, an American volunteer unit in Cuba during the war, helped frame Theodore Roosevelt's reputation as a man of action. Scholars have argued that Davis also sensationalized his news, self-censored stories, and rarely reported on authorities' mismanagement or mistakes. Davis covered every major battle until his death in 1916, including the Greco-Turkish War

(1897), the Spanish-American War (1898), the Second Boer War (1899–1902), the Russo-Japanese War (1904–1905), and in 1914 the first weeks of World War I (1914–1918).

Martha Gellhorn

Maverick journalist, travel writer, and war correspondent Martha Gellhorn (1908–1998) started her career as a contributing writer for several publications, including the *New Republic* magazine. During the Great Depression, she traveled across the United States working for the Federal Emergency Relief Administration and in 1936 wrote the reportage *The Trouble I've Seen.* That next year, in 1937, Gellhorn left to report on the Spanish Civil War (1936–1939) for *Collier's Weekly.* During this time, she met American writer and correspondent Ernest Hemingway, and the two were married for a brief time (1940–1945). In the late 1930s, Gellhorn covered the rise of Adolf Hitler in Germany and during World War II, and was the only female journalist to land with Allied troops on the beaches of Normandy on D-Day in June 1944. Gellhorn was also one of the first reporters to witness the liberation of the Dachau concentration camp, and she described the horrific scenes she saw in vivid and illustrated pieces for *Collier's Weekly.* Her career spanned more than six decades, and she reported on pivotal events, including the Nuremberg trials, the Arab-Israeli wars (1967), parts of the Vietnam War, and the wars in Central America in the mid-1980s. In her 1988 antiwar autobiography, Gellhorn claimed to have followed the war wherever she could find it.

Marguerite Higgins

Trailblazing American journalist and war correspondent Marguerite Higgins (1920–1966) reported on World War II, the Korean War, and the Vietnam War. Her persistence, skills in frontline reporting, and the ability to get access and gather information demonstrated that war reporting was not exclusively a male career. In 1951, Higgins working for the *New York Herald Tribune* received a shared Pulitzer Prize for international reporting on her coverage of the Korean War. Previously she had covered World War II and rode with the Seventh Army, which liberated the Dachau concentration camp. She also covered the Nuremberg Trials after the war. In spring 1950, three weeks before the Korean War broke out, she became the *Herald Tribune*'s Tokyo correspondent. As one of the first journalists arriving in Korea, Higgins became an important eyewitness and reported on the clash between North Korean invaders and U.S.-and South Korean troops. She survived repeated gun shelling. Some U.S. Army officials tried to ban her and other female correspondents from the front (citing the lack of toilets as a reason) but General Douglas MacArthur rescinded this order and gave Higgins and other women equal access to news and army sources. Scholars have noted that Higgins's fearlessness and sense of competition increased when she and *Herald Tribune* veteran reporter Homer Bigart (1907–1991) became rivals. Higgins died at the age of 45 after having contracted the tropical disease leishmaniasis while on assignment in South Vietnam. She was buried in Arlington National Cemetery.

George Wilkins Kendall

In the mid-19th century, George Wilkins Kendall (1809–1867)—who trained as a printer and worked with Horace Greeley—cofounded the *New Orleans Times Picayune* in 1837 and was working as the first documented American war correspondent during the Mexican-American War (1846–1848). Kendall used the *Picayune* as a platform to advocate for westward expansion and he joined an expedition from Austin, Texas, to Santa Fe, New Mexico, that claimed to be searching for new trade routes in the west. His paper, which sold cheaply and reached a considerable audience, was strategically positioned as New Orleans was the closest American city to the Mexican interior and accessible via horse and steamship. When war between the United States and Mexico was declared in 1846, Kendall attached himself to the Texas Rangers under Ben McCullough and to Generals Zachary Taylor, William Jenkins Worth, and Winfield Scott, moving freely among the American lines and witnessing the battles first hand. The *Picayune* used a pony express service, nicknamed "Mr. Kendall's Express," as well as a system of steamboats to

deliver news, frontline reports, and relayed information to newspapers on the East Coast and in the North, often via railroads and telegraph lines. This pioneering communication system helped Kendall report news faster than military or political authorities. By the end of the war, Kendall had written more than 214 reports. His book *The War Between the United States and Mexico Illustrated* (1851) chronicled his experiences and became an authoritative account of the war.

Edward R. Murrow

American broadcast journalist Edward R. Murrow (1908–1965) was one of the 20th century's most influential journalists. His news reporting and war correspondence for CBS News–from Europe during World War II (1939–1945) and during the Korean War (1950–1953)–helped establish radio and television journalism alike as a pivotal and preeminent news media. Murrow graduated from Washington State College (now University) with a major in speech, learning how to "report for the ear." He served as president of the National Student Association (1929–1931) and joined CBS in 1935; in 1937 Murrow became CBS's European director in London. Murrow's reliable and dramatic eyewitness reporting from Europe in the late 1930s, including the German occupation of Austria and the Munich Conference in 1938, the Nazi's annexation of Czechoslovakia in 1939, and the German bombings raids of London during the Battle of Britain, known as *The Blitz* (1940–1941), brought him national fame and widespread recognition. In 1947, after the end of World War II, Murrow and journalist Fred Friendly (1915–1998) coproduced a weekly radio newsmagazine *Hear It Now*, which in 1951 turned into a television program, *See It Now*. The program aired information that exposed misinformation circulated by conservative Senator Joseph R. McCarthy who spearheaded the anticommunist hysteria of the postwar years. In 1954, Murrow broadcast the "Report on Senator Joseph R. McCarthy," which further criticized McCarthy's tactics and, in turn, shaped public opinion. In 1961, President John F. Kenney appointed Murrow as director of the U.S. Information Agency. During his career, Murrow won nine Emmy awards. Journalism scholars widely agree that Murrow's eyewitness reporting, his scrutiny of official information, and the creative use of modern media to tell his stories influenced later generations of war reporters, political journalists, and international correspondents.

Ernest Taylor "Ernie" Pyle

Pulitzer Prize–winning journalist Ernest Taylor "Ernie" Pyle (1900–1945) was one of the most influential war correspondents during World War II. He grew up on a farm near Dana, Indiana, and studied journalism at Indiana University but never graduated. After several smaller jobs, he became a reporter for the Scripps-Howard newspaper chain. In 1935, he became a roving reporter and traveled around the world, writing a successful column about the people he met. After the United States entered World War II, Pyle became a war correspondent and covered the military campaigns in North Africa, Sicily, Italy, and France in widely circulated stories. In 1944, he won a Pulitzer Prize for his reporting, which often emphasized the experiences and perspectives of the common soldier and average men. His direct and engaging style of writing resonated with readers and critics alike. Pyle called his observational skill *the worm's-eye view* of war. After his work in Europe, he also covered the U.S. military and Pacific Theater on Iwo Jima and Okinawa, and accompanied the 77th Infantry Division. Pyle was killed by Japanese machine-gun fire on Ie Shima, an island off Okinawa, in April 1945.

George Washburn Smalley

During the U.S. Civil War (1861–1865) George Washburn Smalley (1833–1916) was a correspondent for the *New York Tribune* and provided some of the war's greatest scoops. As a battlefield correspondent, Smalley made a name for himself, in particular reporting the Battle of Antietam, the bloodiest battle in American military history. His reporting style was marked by dense, accurate, and forceful prose. In September 1962, fewer than 36 hours after the fighting, the readers of the *Tribune* devoured Smalley's six-columns' long account of the Battle of Antietam. He moved with Union troops, running small errands for Union General Joseph Hooker, which allowed him unique observations and frontline experiences. After some of the most devastating battles in Maryland, Smalley took on numerous risks to get his stories to his paper in New York, having discovered that his first telegraphs were sent to the War Department and President Lincoln. In 1866, Smalley was sent to cover the war between Prussia and Austria. Having returned to New York for a few months, his editors sent him to London in May 1867 and tasked Smalley to set up a foreign bureau and organize a network of overseas reporters for the *Tribune*. He instituted a partnership with the *London Daily News* and later became the U.S. correspondent to *The Times* of London (1895–1906). Scholars have pointed out that Smalley had immense social capital; he had been educated at Yale University and Harvard Law School. He was a direct descendant of the Pilgrims, the son of a Congregational minister, and an antislavery advocate.

Outlook: Shaping News and Views on Conflicts

For almost 200 years, correspondents have covered battles, conflicts, and wars that have impacted societies and shaped geopolitical realities. War reporters remain important and critical eyewitnesses. Over time, their professional roles have evolved from being advocates who shared partisan perspectives during the mid- to late-19th century, to becoming more detached and independent observers in global wars in the mid-20th century, to embedded reporters in the late-20th century. The scope of their reports has continuously widened, from covering the on-the-ground warfare, military strategies, plans, and operations to providing more nuanced accounts that emphasize the civilian toll and social-political cost of armed conflicts.

Modern technologies, including the telegraph, radio, wireless, the television, and the Internet, have all revolutionized how stories, images, and information can be moved from distant frontlines to audiences at home or across the world. During the Vietnam War and the Gulf Wars, television provided live coverage of combat, in color, and journalists became correspondents-commentators. In an effort to build and expand viewership and trust, journalists and media pundits shared their opinions, which was often criticized. In today's digital world, war correspondents provide multimedia accounts of battles, terrorists attacks, and guerilla-style civilian wars. They share stories, blog, or tweet out their clips, images, and video reportage. In addition to broadcast and print news, correspondents everywhere use platforms such as YouTube, blogs, social media to television, podcasts, and online news. More fundamentally, the pressures of the job will remain extremely high, as correspondents seek balance between the notions of objectivity and advocacy, both of which inform their professional roles and personal conscience during wartime.

Elisabeth Fondren

See also Censorship; Embedded Reporters; International Journalism; Military and the Media

Further Readings

Allan, S., & Matheson, D. (2013). War reporting in a digital age. In *Digital sociology* (pp. 151–168). London, UK: Palgrave Macmillan. doi:10.1057/9781137297792_11

Allan, S., & Zelizer, B. (Eds.). (2004). *Reporting war: Journalism in wartime.* New York, NY: Routledge.

Alper, M. (2014). War on Instagram: Framing conflict photojournalism with mobile photography apps. *New Media & Society, 16*(8), 1233–1248. doi:10.1177/1461444813504265

Carey, J. (1997). *Eyewitness to history.* New York, NY: Harper Collins.

Cozma, R. (2015). Were the Murrow Boys warmongers? The relationship between sourcing, framing, and propaganda in war journalism. *Journalism Studies, 16*(3), 433–448. doi:10.1080/1461670x.2014.882098

Crozier, E. (1959). *American reporters on the Western Front, 1914–1918.* New York, NY: Oxford University Press.

Edy, C. M. (2016). *The woman war correspondent, the US military, and the press: 1846–1947.* Lanham, MD: Rowman & Littlefield.

Feinstein, A. (2006). *Journalists under fire: The psychological hazards of covering war.* Baltimore, MD: Johns Hopkins University Press.

Fondren, E. (2021). "The mirror with a memory": The great war through the lens of Percy Brown, British correspondent and photojournalist (1914–1920). *Journalism History, 47*(1), 1–26. doi:10.1080/00947679.2020.1837595

Frontani, M. R. (2004). Embedded: Weapons of mass deception-how the media failed to cover the war on Iraq. *Journalism History, 30*(2), 111.

Hallin Daniel, C. (1986). *The "uncensored war": The media and Vietnam.* New York, NY: Oxford University Press.

Kellner, D. (2008). War correspondents, the military, and propaganda: Some critical reflections. *International Journal of Communication, 2,* 34.

Knightley, P. (2004). *The first casualty: The war correspondent as hero and myth-maker from the Crimea to Iraq.* Baltimore, MD: Johns Hopkins University Press. doi:10.2307/1852883

Manning, M. J., & Wyatt, C. R. (2011). *Encyclopedia of media and propaganda in Wartime America (Vol. 1).* Santa Barbara, CA: ABC-CLIO.

Palmer, L. (2018). *Becoming the story: War correspondents since 9/11.* Champaign, IL: University of Illinois Press.

PBS, Reporting America at War. (2003). Retrieved May 20, 2020, from https://www.pbs.org/weta/reporting americaatwar/reporters/amanpour/poolsystem .html

Reilly, T. (2010). *War with Mexico!: America's reporters cover the battlefront.* Lawrence, KS: University Press of Kansas.

Sweeney, M. S. (2006). *The military and the press: An uneasy truce.* Evanston, IL: Northwestern University Press. doi:10.1080/08821127.2007.10678073

Sweeney, M. S., & Toft Roelsgaard, N. (2019). *Journalism and the Russo-Japanese war: The end of the golden age of combat correspondence.* Lanham, MD: Rowman and Littlefield.

Wall, M., & Zahed, S. E. (2015). Embedding content from Syrian citizen journalists: The rise of the collaborative news clip. *Journalism, 16*(2), 163–180. doi:10.1177/1464884914529213

Zelizer, B. (2007). On "having been there": "Eyewitnessing" as a journalistic key word. *Critical Studies in Media Communication, 24*(5), 408–428. doi:10.1080/07393180701694614

WarnerMedia

WarnerMedia is a United States–based mass media conglomerate and one of the world's leading news organizations. In 2020, WarnerMedia generated approximately $30.4 billion in revenues from its three operating divisions: Turner, Home Box Office

(HBO), and Warner Bros. While HBO develops and screens investigative and sports documentary specials and news-based comedy shows, WarnerMedia's News and Sports operations are principally based on the Turner's subsidiary Cable News Network (CNN), which, through its multiple digital distribution platforms, is central to the international production of television and online news.

In June 2018, WarnerMedia, then known as Time Warner, was acquired by AT&T Inc., the world's largest telecommunications company. Headquartered in Dallas, Texas, AT&T's 2020 revenues of $171 billion placed the company ninth on the Fortune 500 rankings of the largest U.S. corporations. The vast majority of these revenues ($139 billion, or 81%) came from its Communications division. AT&T is the largest wired and wireless telecommunication carrier in the United States and also the country's largest provider of direct broadcast satellite service. Through AT&T Mexico, the corporation is the third largest telecommunication services provider in Mexico. Although WarnerMedia produced just 17.7% of AT&T's revenues, WarnerMedia is the third largest media conglomerate behind the Walt Disney Company and Comcast: In 2020, Disney produced $65.4 billion in revenue, and Comcast's NBCUniversal and Sky operations produced combined revenues of $46.7 billion (or 45% of Comcast's total revenues).

After reviewing WarnerMedia's journalistic origins and operations, this entry focuses on cable news channel CNN, examining its editorial independence and political coverage.

WarnerMedia's Journalistic Origins

Although a comparatively small part of WarnerMedia's overall operations, news and journalism has been an integral part of the corporation's undertakings since its establishment in 1922. In that year, Henry Luce and Briton Hadden founded Time Inc. and a year later began publishing *Time* magazine. Although initially criticized as a "rewrite sheet" that was dependent on newspapers' journalism, the *Time* news magazine proved to be highly profitable and soon established its own professional standards and relative editorial autonomy with the formal separation of editorial and publisher functions. In the first half of the

20th century, Time Inc. published additional magazines such as *Fortune*, *Life*, and later *Sports Illustrated* and became a major force in U.S. journalism.

In the 1960s, Time Inc. sought to diversify away from its dominant magazine operations through investments in television production, book publishing (Time-Life books), and most consequentially the U.S. cable television industry (via Sterling Manhattan Cable). Time's corporate management had initially opposed involvement in television, viewing it as far removed from the practice of "quality journalism," but by 1958 Luce felt that TV offered an opportunity to provide a new "window on the world" for Time Inc.'s journalism. As Time Inc.'s editor in chief, Luce had sought to foster conservative, free market politics and an increasingly interventionist role for the United States through the notion of "the American century."

Faced with cable's heavy capital investment demands, in 1973 Time Inc. unsuccessfully attempted to sell its controlling share of Sterling Manhattan Cable to Warner Communications Inc. (WCI). When this failed, Sterling, and its newly launched pay TV cable program service, HBO, became wholly owned subsidiaries of Time Inc. In 1975, HBO became the first cable network to use satellites for regular transmission of television programming, and by the end of the decade, HBO and Time Inc.'s video group was the fastest growing and largest producer of profit for Time Inc.

In 1987, Time Inc.'s senior executives put forward a long-term strategy to produce "the new Time Inc." by combining Time Inc., WCI, and Turner Broadcasting System (TBS). Prior to its entry into cable television systems in 1973, WCI (formerly Kinney Services Corporation, a diversified conglomerate) had acquired Warner Bros. in 1969, giving it control not only of one of Hollywood's original film studios but also of Warner Bros.' substantial television program production and recorded music operations. Cable programmer TBS, based in Atlanta, Georgia, had pioneered the "superstation" concept in 1976 by transmitting its local channels via satellite to cable systems, a venture that signaled the further development of advertising-supported basic cable channels. In 1980, Turner Broadcasting had established CNN, the first 24-hour news cable channel, and by the late 1980s, TBS was the largest proprietor of successful cable networks, including TBS and CNN and the movie channel TNT.

In 1990, Time Inc. announced it would assume considerable debt to acquire Warner Communications Inc. and form Time Warner, the world's largest media corporation. In response to rapid consolidation in the cable and wider media industries, the deal united Time's cable systems and networks and Warner's cable systems, television, and motion pictures businesses. In 1996, Time Warner's preeminent position within the Hollywood-cable-TV complex was reinforced by its merger with TBS. Although Time Warner housed some of the world's largest operations in music, magazine, and book publishing, the corporation's overall strategy was driven by developments in the cable system and network industries and by a need to extract higher profits to manage debt.

In January 2001, as the so-called dot-com stock bubble was bursting, America Online (AOL), then the United States' largest Internet service provider, completed its purchase of Time Warner. Brought on principally by a write-down of its AOL unit's value, the renamed AOL-Time Warner announced a net loss of $98.7 billion in 2002, the largest in U.S. corporate history. The disastrous purchase served to highlight existing operational and financial problems that beset the corporation. This prompted a process of deconglomeration and a series of significant divestitures: in 2003 Time Warner dropped AOL from its name and sold its music group and then, in 2006, its book publishing operations. It spun off its AOL unit and cable division in 2009 and its magazine publishing company in 2014. This process left Time Warner with three principal, yet separate content-driven businesses: Turner, HBO, and Warner Bros.

Having rejected an $80 billion merger bid in 2014 from Rupert Murdoch's 21st Century Fox, in 2016 Time Warner accepted an $85.4 billion acquisition offer from AT&T, a deal which would give the telecommunications giant control of Time Warner's cable networks, filmed entertainment operations and sports rights. During 2017–2019, AT&T's acquisition survived a series of legal actions initiated by the U.S. Department of Justice. The Department of Justice's opposition to the potential market power associated with AT&T and Time Warner's vertical integration was echoed by the Republican presidential nominee Donald Trump, who stated that the deal represented "too much concentration of power in the hands of too few." As President, Trump derided CNN as "Fake News!" in response to the network's early reporting of the "Trump–Russia dossier" and for its strident criticism of the administration's treatment of the press. However, media and political speculation that AT&T would be forced to divest CNN, or the entire Turner division, to achieve the acquisition proved unfounded as the Department of Justice's legal action failed.

WarnerMedia's Operations

AT&T continues to report revenue and other financial information on three content-producing units of WarnerMedia (Warner Bros., HBO, Turner) as separate corporate divisions, as they were when acquired in 2018. However, between 2019 and 2020, AT&T introduced new management structures that sought to eliminate some of the operational partitions in the media conglomerate. WarnerMedia News and Sports combines Turner's CNN Worldwide, Turner Sports, and AT&T SportsNet regional networks. WarnerMedia Studios and Networks Group manages television series and motion picture development, production and programming across Warner Bros., HBO, and Turner's TNT, TBS, and TruTV networks. HBO Max, the subscription video-on-demand service launched in 2020, has been designated as a separately managed unit, reflecting the importance that WarnerMedia and AT&T place on it as a global competitor to services such as Netflix, Amazon Prime Video, and Disney Plus. AT&T has vowed to invest $4 billion in HBO Max between 2020 and 2023 to cover costs such as programming and the lost earnings from external buyers of WarnerMedia content.

In 2020, the HBO segment produced revenues of $6.8 billion, or 22.4% of WarnerMedia's total revenues, and operating income of $682 million. The Home Box Office segment operates premium cable and satellite television networks, HBO and Cinemax in the United States and in over 50 countries in Latin America, Asia, and Europe and reached over 35 million subscribers. AT&T's purchase of WarnerMedia has reinforced HBO's strategy of acquiring subscriber growth through an extended catalog of costly, high-quality original content such as *Westworld* and *Succession* and *His Dark Materials*. HBO content is also a mainstay of HBO Max and in 2020 HBO spent $1.8 billion on programming related to HBO Max. At the end of 2020, WarnerMedia had 41.5 million HBO Max and HBO subscribers in the United States and almost 61 million globally. In 2021, WarnerMedia plans to launch HBO Max in 60 markets outside the United States and a new ad-supported version of the streaming service. AT&T expects to reach between 120 million and 150 million HBO Max and HBO subscribers worldwide by the end of 2025.

HBO Max has also been used to distribute Warner Bros. films such as *Wonder Woman 1984* as the global COVID-19 pandemic shut down cinemas for an extended period in 2020. Despite a major reduction to its box office earnings in 2020, the Warner Bros. segment produced revenues of $12.2 billion, or 40% of WarnerMedia's total revenues, and an operating income of $2 billion. This segment of WarnerMedia principally produces and distributes motion pictures and television programming as well as videogames and live stage plays. It also distributes home video products and licenses rights to WarnerMedia's related intellectual property. These activities take place through three principal divisions: Motion Pictures (Warner Bros., New Line Cinema), Warner Bros. Television Group (WBTVG), and Home Entertainment. The segment also contains Global Brands and Franchises (home to DC Comics Superman, Batman, and Wonder Woman characters) and Kids, Young Adults and Classics (comprising former Turner operations Cartoon Network, Turner Classic Movies, Adult Swim, and Boomerang). WBTVG is the largest part of Warner Bros.' operations, producing $6.2 billion in revenue in 2020. As well as having production operations in 16 countries, WBTVG houses Warner's 50% stake in the CW television network, a joint venture with CBS Corporation, which owns and operates eight stations and is affiliated with some 200 stations in the United States. Based on total studio revenues, Warner Bros. was the second-largest television and film studio in the world in 2020, only overshadowed by Netflix.

The Turner segment primarily operates multi-channel basic television networks and digital properties from which it generates significant advertising and subscription revenues. Indeed, the largest proportion of WarnerMedia's 2020 revenue ($12.6 billion or 41.3%) was produced by Turner, which also produced the largest operating income ($5.3 billion). Turner earned $7.6 billion from subscription revenues and almost $3.9 billion from advertising. As noted earlier, the management of Turner operations has been subsumed under different areas of WarnerMedia. The leading entertainment cable networks (TBS, TNT, and truTV) are now managed together with HBO as part of the WarnerMedia Studios and Networks Group. For 2020, TBS and TNT ranked in the top five cable networks in terms of 25- to 54-year-old viewers in the United States. Turner International's distribution of entertainment and news brands in over 200 countries has now been assumed by WarnerMedia International.

WarnerMedia News and Sports brings together networks that can amass large, live audiences that are sought after by both advertisers and cable and satellite distributors. In 2020, CNN claimed to reach 96.2 million U.S. households and more than 402 million households and hotel rooms worldwide. It was coordinated from Atlanta and three regional headquarters in Abu Dhabi, Hong Kong, and London in a network of nine news bureaus and editorial operations in the United States 27 located outside of the United States.

CNN Worldwide is a portfolio of more than 20 news and information services in more than 200 countries and territories. These included CNN International, CNN Philippines, CNN Indonesia, CNN-News 18, CNN Turk, CNN en Espanol, HLN, CNN Chile, and CNN.com. The network claimed 900 affiliated local stations in North America, which received CNN content via the video newswire service CNN Newsource and which supplied news to the network in areas where CNN had no crews of its own. CNN has expanded its digital operations and as of 2020 ranks as the most trafficked news and information digital outlet for U.S. and global unique visitors, ahead of competitors such as the BBC and *The New York Times*.

CNN, Political Partisanship, and Editorial Independence

Having been appointed as president of CNN Worldwide in 2013, Jeff Zucker sought to improve

CNN's ratings, which at the time were hovering near 20-year lows. As well as significantly increasing investments in digital operations and reality-style documentary series, Zucker has focused the network's news coverage on two or three breaking news events and has sought a more aggressive, "crusading attitude" in its coverage, particularly of politics. Starting in 2015, CNN started concentrating on political coverage, often interrupting regularly scheduled programming for Trump's presidential nominee speeches. As well as relying heavily on a pundits-on-panels model of presentation and analysis influenced by sports channels, CNN recruited an additional 40 political reporting staff in the 2015 to 2016 period.

Along with the other main cable news networks in the United States, CNN has benefited from increased ratings during the 2016 election campaign and the subsequent Trump administration, as political partisanship in the country has grown. In 2020, according to Nielsen ratings, CNN finished third behind Fox News (average 3.6 million viewers) and MSNBC (average 2.2 million viewers) in news channels during primetime. CNN had an average of 1.8 million viewers, giving the channel its most watched year in its 40-year history. In the fourth quarter of 2020, CNN ranked first in all of cable viewership, not just news, in the United States.

While CNN was the third most watched cable news channel in the United States, its viewership was marked by the deep political divide in the country. Research conducted by the Pew Research Center suggested that political partisanship with regard to media usage and trust widened over the 2014–2019 period—none of the 30 news sources reviewed in the Pew survey were trusted by more than 50% of all U.S. adults. In 2019, CNN was the most distrusted source among conservative (67%) and moderate/liberal Republicans (43%), and this level of distrust has increased since 2014. Among Democrats and Democrat-leaning voters, CNN was the most trusted source, with 67% of such respondents trusting the network for political news; however, while this mirrors the level of trust that Republicans have for Fox News, Democrats trust and frequently use a wider range of news sources. Nonetheless, overall CNN's more assertive form of "journalistic objectivity" has been an effective response to the more partisan political coverage of Fox News and MSNBC.

Driven primarily by its U.S. news channel's improved ratings, in the period 2016–2019, CNN Worldwide has lifted its annual profits to more than $1 billion a year. On this basis, CNN's 2020 profits would represent at least 15% of WarnerMedia's annual profits. Cable news channels enjoy profit margins between 30% and 55% based on a robust dual-stream business model incorporating advertising and license fees, which they receive from cable companies and satellite operators (the latter can account for around 70% of total revenues). According to S&P Global Market Intelligence, during the period 2014 to 2018, the combined revenue of Fox News, MSNBC, and CNN increased from $3.6 billion to $5.3 billion, a 47% increase, and total profits for the three networks rose to $2.8 billion, almost a 70% increase.

When AT&T acquired WarnerMedia, its management sought to allay concerns it would interfere with the editorial independence of CNN. The profit upswing of CNN's operations has meant that, as compared to 2014 when it cut 300 jobs, the news organization has been relatively shielded from significant rounds of job losses at WarnerMedia. In 2020, WarnerMedia announced it would eliminate at least 1,800 jobs in the WarnerMedia Studios and Networks Group to reduce costs by at least 20%. As former CNN President Jon Klein noted, there is "nothing like profitability to shield a journalistic organization from pressure" (Flint, 2016). Nonetheless, CNN faces the uncertainty of the probable end of an electoral cycle rating bonanza as well as pressure from a corporate owner that has signaled that discretionary cash flow will go to paying down debt and developing WarnerMedia's streaming services. The issue of self-censorship over AT&T wider operations also looms large.

Scott W. Fitzgerald

See also Cable News; Media Ownership; Objectivity

Further Readings

Birkinbine, B. J. (2017). The AT&T-Time Warner Merger. *The Political Economy of Communication, 4,* 114–116.

Fitzgerald, S. (2016). Time Warner. In B. Birkinbine, R. Gomez, & J. Wasko (Eds.), *Global media giants* (pp. 51–71). London, UK: Routledge.

Fitzgerald, S. (2015). *Corporations and cultural industries: Time Warner, Bertelsmann, and News Corporation.* Lanham, MD: Rowman and Littlefield.

FitzGerald, D., Flint, J. & Mullin, B. (2020, October 8). WarnerMedia plans thousands of job cuts in restructuring. *The Wall Street Journal.*

Flint, J. (2016, October 24). In AT&T's Deal for Time Warner, CNN could be conundrum. *The Wall Street Journal.*

Mahler, J. (2017, April 4). CNN had a problem. Donald Trump solved it. *New York Times.* https://www.nytimes .com/2017/04/04/magazine/cnn-had-a-problem-donald-trump-solved-it.html and retrieved December 20, 2021.

McNair, B. (2017). After objectivity? *Journalism Studies, 18,* 1318–1333. doi:10.1080/1461670X.2017.1347893

Pew Research Center. (2020, January). U.S. media polarization and the 2020 election: A nation divided.

Vertically challenged: AT&T's merger with Time Warner goes on trial. (2018, March 17). *Economist.* https:// www.economist.com/business/2018/03/17/at-and-ts-merger-with-time-warner-goes-on-trial-retrieved December 20, 2021, [no author included]

WASHINGTON POST, THE

Founded in 1877, *The Washington Post* has been the leading newspaper in Washington, DC, since the 1950s. The quality, depth, and influence of its reporting on American politics and international affairs are unrivaled by any news outlet except *The New York Times.* It publishes a daily print edition and is one of the world's most popular online news destinations. Under the ownership of Amazon founder Jeff Bezos, who bought the paper in 2013, the *Post* has become one of the few major print newspapers to achieve economic success in the digital age. This entry traces the history of the *Post* from its founding through its purchase by Bezos. It discusses some of the *Post*'s journalistic innovations, its notable stories and approach to political coverage, and its financial ups and downs.

Founding and Early Years

Like many newspaper owners of the 19th century, *The Washington Post*'s founding publisher, Stilson Hutchins, was motivated by politics as well as profits. A staunch Democrat, Hutchins recognized that none of the five dailies being published in Washington during the 1870s represented his party (most newspapers in that era were openly partisan). He knew that if he put out a quality newspaper, Washingtonians who supported the Democrats would flock to it, and politicians of all stripes would read it. The first issue of Hutchins's *Washington Post* appeared on December 6, 1877, roughly a year after the disputed presidential election that put Republican Rutherford B. Hayes in the White House. Although the Democratic Party accepted the result (it was part of a compromise that allowed the Democrats to reestablish White supremacy and political dominance in the South), Hutchins did not. In news articles and editorials alike, the *Post* blasted Hayes for his alleged corruption and incompetence, referring to him as "the bogus President" and "his fraudulency."

Partisan vitriol aside, Hutchins built *The Washington Post* into a solid paper, with comprehensive coverage of politics and local news. Reliably profitable, its circulation hit a high of 54,000 the day after the presidential election of 1888. But Hutchins chose to sell it 2 months later to focus on promoting and selling Linotype machines—an invention that revolutionized newspaper production and would be a fixture in most newsrooms until the 1970s. The new owners of *The Washington Post* were a Republican (one-time Postmaster General Frank Hatton) and a Democrat (Congressman Beriah Wilkins). They toned down the *Post*'s partisanship and solidified its reputation as a good-but-not-great newspaper. After Hatton and Wilkins died, their heirs sold in 1905 to John R. McLean, a wealthy Democratic power broker and owner of the Cincinnati Enquirer. A friend of yellow journalism practitioner William Randolph Hearst, McLean jazzed up the *Post* with comics, reader contests, and large headlines about murders and love affairs, but he allowed the quality of its news coverage to deteriorate. It had never been the undisputed leader of Washington dailies before, but under McLean it sank to third place (out of four) in circulation.

The *Post* declined further when John McLean's son Ned took over after his father's death, in 1916. A volatile alcoholic and profligate spender (he lived in a 60-room mansion with a staff of 23 and purchased the Hope Diamond for his wife), Ned McLean alternately ignored and mismanaged the paper. When the Great Depression hit, the *Post* tanked. In 1933, the paper was $500,000 in debt and had to be sold at auction to avoid going out of business.

Purchase by Eugene Meyer

The man who snapped up *The Washington Post* in 1933 was Eugene Meyer, a brilliant financier who had made millions on Wall Street as a young man and had gone into public service, appointed to high-level positions by a series of U.S. presidents: Woodrow Wilson, Warren G. Harding, Calvin Coolidge, and Herbert Hoover. For several years, Meyer had toyed with the idea of buying a newspaper in Washington. He even offered Ned McLean $5 million to buy the *Post* in 1929, but McLean turned him down. Meyer got it in 1933 for $825,000. With his tremendous wealth, Meyer could afford to pump money into the paper to keep it afloat, and he had to do so for the first 22 years of his ownership. His main concern was the paper's editorial page, which would express the publisher's moderate Republican views: in favor of civil liberties, international cooperation, and free trade. Meyer had an eye for talent. He hired an unknown named Alan Barth to write editorials (in 1943) and an unknown named Herbert Block to draw political cartoons (in 1945), even though both held views to the left of Meyer's own. In short order, Barth established a reputation as the nation's best editorial writer and "Herblock" as its best cartoonist. During the Red Scare of the early 1950s, no major newspaper's editorial page opposed Senator Joe McCarthy more forcefully than *The Washington Post*'s.

Phil Graham as Publisher

Meyer wanted *The Washington Post* to stay in his family following his death. Passing over his daughter, Katharine Meyer Graham, he named her husband, Phil Graham, as publisher in 1946. Graham's greatest business triumph came in 1954 when the *Post* bought out its larger rival, the *Washington Times-Herald* (a deal that Graham and Meyer orchestrated with the *Times-Herald*'s aging owner Robert McCormick, the arch-conservative publisher of the *Chicago Tribune*). Although the *Times-Herald*'s isolationist, anti-elitist outlook was the polar opposite of the *Post*'s, roughly 75% of *Times-Herald* buyers converted to the *Post*—a remarkable achievement. It vaulted *The Washington Post* from a third-place position among Washington's dailies into a tie for first with the *Washington Star*, which published in the afternoon (the *Post* was a morning newspaper).

With *The Washington Post* profitable at last after acquiring the *Times-Herald*, Graham invested in it. From 1947 to 1962, the paper's news budget more than tripled (in inflation-adjusted terms), even as Graham expanded the company's media holdings by purchasing several TV and radio stations and, in 1961, *Newsweek* magazine. By the early 1960s, *The Washington Post* was the capital's dominant paper and Graham was one of the capital's most influential figures (he was a close friend and advisor to President John F. Kennedy). Privately, however, Graham had struggled for years with mental illness, and in 1963 he killed himself at his family's country home in Virginia.

The Katharine Graham–Ben Bradlee Years

When Katharine Graham took over the Washington Post Company following her husband's suicide, most people assumed she would be a hands-off publisher, serving briefly as a custodian then stepping down to make way for her oldest son, Donald, who was in college at Harvard. They were wrong. Graham soon realized that, apart from the editorial page, *The Washington Post* was a mediocre newspaper, and she set out to change that. Two years after taking over, she eased out the longtime managing editor in favor of Ben Bradlee, the brash, 42-year-old Washington bureau chief of *Newsweek*.

Bradlee and Graham forged a long, fruitful partnership. She increased his budget, and he hired a slew of ambitious young reporters to be based not only in Washington but also throughout the United States and overseas. Above all, Bradlee wanted to produce a lively, exciting newspaper. In 1969, he replaced the antiquated "For and About Women" pages with a new daily section called *Style*, which merged coverage of the arts and entertainment with lifestyle stories and cultural commentary. It succeeded both journalistically and financially, inspiring newspapers around the country to launch their own imitations.

The Washington Post would lead the press pack again 3 years later, on one of the biggest news stories in U.S. history. From June 1972, when five men were arrested for breaking into Democratic National Committee headquarters at the Watergate building, to August 1974, when President Richard Nixon announced his resignation, the *Post* owned coverage of the Watergate scandal. Because it was initially classified as a local crime story, the *Post* assigned it to two young reporters on the Metro desk: Bob Woodward and Carl Bernstein. As it became clear that the Nixon White House was involved, Bradlee and managing editor Howard Simons allowed Woodward and Bernstein to stay on the story, rather than handing it off to more experienced political reporters. This turned out to be a crucial decision. "Woodstein," as the pair became known, worked harder and more single-mindedly on Watergate than any other reporters. Rather than relying on longtime Washington insiders who might mislead them, they covered it as they would cover a police story—chasing down leads by knocking on doors and cold-calling sources on the phone, coaxing reluctant people to talk. Despite intense criticism from the Nixon administration, Graham and Bradlee steadfastly supported their reporters. (The duo had shown similar resolve in 1971 when they faced down tremendous legal and financial risks to publish revelations building on *The New York Times*'s Pentagon Papers exposé—an episode dramatized in the 2017 film *The Post*.) Woodward and Bernstein produced one scoop after another and won the Pulitzer Prize. Their 1974 book about the experience of reporting on Watergate, *All the President's Men*, became a bestseller and was adapted into an acclaimed Hollywood film, glamorizing and lionizing the two journalists, *The Washington Post*, and the enterprise of investigative reporting.

From the 1980s to the Digital Age

When Katharine Graham handed control of the Washington Post Company to her son Donald in 1979, it was thriving. The company's stock had risen steadily since its initial public offering in 1971, and the newspaper was still basking in the afterglow of its Watergate coverage. Its journalistic reputation took a serious hit 2 years later, when it published a story by reporter Janet Cooke called *Jimmy's World*, about an 8-year-old boy addicted to heroin. The article won the Pulitzer Prize, but shortly thereafter it emerged that no such child existed—Cooke had fabricated the story and none of the editors had detected it. Financially, the *Post* flourished throughout the 1980s, boosted by the closing of its longtime competitor the *Washington Star* in 1981. Another daily, the *Washington Times*, launched in 1982, targeting conservative readers put off by the *Post*'s alleged liberal slant, but it was a perennial money-loser and never dented the *Post*'s readership.

Signs of trouble appeared for *The Washington Post* in the mid-1990s, when its circulation began to decline after having increased steadily for decades. The decline accelerated in the 2000s, with many readers substituting free news on the web for the morning newspaper. As circulation dropped, so did advertising revenue, and the *Post* began shrinking its newsroom to cut costs. Four rounds of staff buyouts from 2003 to 2009 eliminated hundreds of jobs. The cuts likely would have been deeper if not for the Washington Post Company's fortuitous decision in 1984 to buy a small test preparation company called *Kaplan*, which had grown into a massively profitable giant by the 2000s. In 2008, Donald Graham announced that the Washington Post Company would become "an education and media company"—Kaplan was producing more than half of the company's revenue, while the newspaper was bleeding money.

Despite the *Post*'s financial struggles, it continued to produce outstanding journalism. Reporter Dana Priest, for example, earned two Pulitzer Prizes in 2 years; her investigations exposed the Central Intelligence Agency (CIA)'s use of "black site" prisons around the world to conduct extralegal interrogations of terror suspects (2006) and the horrific treatment of wounded veterans at the Walter Reed Army Medical Center (2008). Like most news outlets with well-known brands, the *Post* built a website (washingtonpost.com) that attracted millions of visitors each month, but the money it made from online ads was not nearly enough to offset the huge decline in revenue from print advertising. By 2013, the *Post* was losing over $50 million annually, and the Graham family, which had owned it for 80 years, was quietly exploring a sale.

Turnaround Under Jeff Bezos

The Grahams got the buyer they wanted in Jeff Bezos, Amazon's founder and one of the world's richest people. He purchased the *Washington Post* for $250 million in August 2013 and took it private, removing the stock market pressure to create quick profits (the newspaper is not affiliated with Amazon or Bezos's other holdings). Bezos and his leadership team engineered a remarkable turnaround. By 2017, the *Post* had doubled its web traffic, signed up over 1 million paying digital subscribers and created a lucrative sideline licensing its software to other online publishers. The paper was once again profitable even after going on a hiring spree—the newsroom employed more journalists than ever before.

The *Post* remains at the center of American politics. During the presidency of Donald Trump, it won Pulitzer Prizes for exposing the dubious nature of Trump's charitable giving, for showing the links between Trump's team and Russian interference in the 2016 election, and for revealing credible accusations that U.S. Senate candidate Roy Moore had engaged in sexual misconduct with underage girls. Trump labeled the paper "thoroughly disgusting," "crazed and dishonest," and "the enemy of the people." Marty Baron, then the paper's editor in chief, refused to respond in kind. "We're not at war, we're at work," he said of the *Post*'s approach to Trump. However, from the beginning of Trump's presidency, the *Post*'s opinion articles were almost uniformly anti-Trump, and its White House reporting often took an aggressive and critical approach (with good reason, its supporters say, given the Trump administration's misdeeds). Critics who accused the press of "normalizing" Trump and drawing false equivalencies between Democrats and Republicans in the Trump era focused their ire on *The New York Times* more frequently than on the *Post*.

Although the *Post*'s political coverage earns it the most attention, the newsroom also produces an array of niche online sections and reports enthusiastically on viral human interest stories. Some critics decry the viral content as "clickbait," but it has contributed to the *Post*'s digital success (washingtonpost.com often gets more than 90 million unique visitors per month). With a sustainable business model and a deep-pocketed owner, *The Washington Post* will likely continue to be an influential force in American journalism and politics for years to come.

Matthew Pressman

See also Graham, Katharine; *New York Times, The*; Pentagon Papers; Political Reporters; Pulitzer Prize; Watergate

Further Readings

Bray, H. (1980). *The pillars of the Post: The making of a news empire in Washington*. New York: W. W. Norton.

Halberstam, D. (1979). *The powers that be*. New York: Knopf.

Kennedy, D. (2016, June 8). The Bezos effect: How Amazon's founder is reinventing the Washington Post—and what lessons it might hold for the beleaguered newspaper business. Shorenstein Center on Media, Politics, and Public Policy, Discussion Paper Series #D-100. Retrieved from https://shorensteincenter.org/bezos-effect-washington-post/

Kindred, D. (2010). *Morning miracle: Inside the Washington Post; a great newspaper fights for its life*. New York: Doubleday.

Nolan, H. (2020, January 23). How the Washington Post pulled off the toughest trick in journalism. *Columbia Journalism Review*. Retrieved from https://www.cjr.org/public_editor/washington-post-fluff-news.php

Roberts, C. (1989). *In the shadow of power: The story of the Washington Post*. Cabin John, MD: Seven Locks Press.

Sherman, G. (2016, June 28). Good news at the Washington Post. *New York, 49*. Retrieved from https://nymag.com/intelligencer/2016/06/washington-post-jeff-bezos-donald-trump.html

WATERGATE

In June 1972, during President Richard Nixon's campaign for reelection, five men broke into the headquarters of the Democratic National Committee (DNC) at the Watergate complex in Washington, DC. The subsequent investigations by the media and Congress ended with Nixon's resignation 2 years later, in August 1974. "Watergate" refers to that break-in, Nixon's abuses of power, and the resulting congressional hearings. The press played a major, though somewhat mythologized, role in bringing to light those abuses. Watergate has been remembered as a watershed for political news coverage and became the namesake for future political scandals. Those scandals, which from the 1970s have had the suffix "-gate" appended, often also involved federal investigations into wrongdoing—for example, "Billygate" in 1980, when Jimmy Carter's brother was investigated for influence peddling; "Monicagate," the 1998 investigation into Bill Clinton's sexual misconduct; and "Bridgegate" in 2013, when New Jersey governor Chris Christie's staffers and appointees improperly closed lanes on the George Washington Bridge.

The Watergate Complex
Break-In and Early News Coverage

On the night of June 17, 1972, a security officer at one of the Watergate complex buildings, which then housed the headquarters for the DNC, found a piece of tape that had been placed over a door so that it could be reopened without a key. He called the police, who subsequently arrested five men, later found to have been there to repair listening devices planted 3 weeks earlier. Those men were Bernard Barker, Virgilio Gonzales, Eugenio R. Martinez, James W. McCord Jr., and Frank A. Sturgis. Carl Bernstein and Bob Woodward, two reporters on *The Washington Post*'s Metro desk—responsible for local news coverage rather than national politics—quickly linked McCord, a former Central Intelligence Agency (CIA) agent, to Nixon's reelection committee. Those two reporters would go on to write hundreds of articles about Watergate and its consequences.

The Washington Post continued reporting on the burglary and making connections between the break-in, the Committee to Re-Elect the President, and the White House, even as the White House denied any involvement. The *Post*'s 1972 coverage, which included Woodward and Bernstein's reportage, editorials, and the well-known cartoonist Herblock's editorial cartoons, would win them a Pulitzer Prize for public service journalism in 1973. The cartoons provide an especially vivid

record of how explicit the newspaper made Nixon's wrongdoing prior to his reelection. For instance, one September 1972 cartoon depicts Nixon and his top aides promising to investigate the break-in thoroughly, while in reality leading the American public in circles and carrying out criminal activities. In the cartoon, Nixon and his aides wear burglars' masks and carry sacks of money with labels that include "Secret Nixon Funds" and "Violations of Corrupt Practices Act" and have a tool bag labeled "Break-in and Political Espionage."

The press had made Nixon's complicity in the Watergate break-in as well as other crimes clear before Election Day. However, on November 7, 1972, Nixon won a landslide reelection victory: 520 votes in the Electoral College to Democratic presidential nominee George McGovern's 17 votes, and 60.7% of the popular vote compared to 37.5% for McGovern. Based on the outcome of the election, Nixon seemed to have been right when he privately told aides not to worry about the effects of Watergate.

Continuing Coverage
and a Special Prosecutor

In 1972, *The Washington Post* was, indeed, important to keep the Watergate story alive, as the Pulitzer Prize committee recognized. However, contrary to popular memory, *The Washington Post* was not the only media outlet pursuing stories related to Watergate, nor was the media the most decisive factor in the investigations. By early 1973, newspapers besides *The Washington Post* were covering the story intensively. *The New York Times*' Washington bureau knew it was at a disadvantage in reporting on Watergate because it did not have a good investigative or crime reporting team in its Washington office. In 1972, they had hired Seymour Hersh, who in 1969 had broken the story of the My Lai massacre, and they soon assigned him to the Watergate beat. On Sunday, January 14, 1973, Hersh broke the important story that the Watergate burglars were being paid hush money monthly out of a slush fund.

The New York Times was a leader in setting national news coverage, and their coverage of the Watergate story increased the coverage in other newspapers. Meanwhile, James McCord, one of the five burglars, wrote to the judge in his case, Judge John Sirica. He told Sirica that he and others had been pressured and paid off to plead guilty and remain silent and that there were others involved in the Watergate break-in. Sirica read that letter into the record, before handing down lengthy sentences for the burglars and ensuring the break-in would remain a news story. By early 1973, with Nixon beginning his second term as president, Watergate had risen to widespread public awareness and seemed to be a scandal with staying power.

Top White House staffers were soon implicated in the coverup of the Watergate break-in, and in April 1973, two of Nixon's closest aides—H. R. Haldeman and John Erlichman—were asked to resign. Nixon also fired the Attorney General, Richard Kleindienst, and White House counsel, John Dean. The new appointee for Attorney General, the Secretary of Defense Elliott Richardson, promised in his Senate confirmation hearings to appoint a special prosecutor to investigate Watergate independently. That special prosecutor, Archibald Cox Jr., a Harvard law professor, took on the independent investigation beginning in May 1973 and, along with the press and Judge Sirica, became an important factor in Nixon's downfall.

The Senate Investigation and the Saturday Night Massacre

Meanwhile, in February 1973, the Senate had voted to authorize its own investigation. The Senate Select Committee to Investigate Campaign Practices, also known as the *Ervin Committee* for its chair Sam Ervin, a Democrat from North Carolina, had broad powers of subpoena. As they subpoenaed records from the White House, they triggered a wave of defiance from the president. But after claiming for 2 months that executive privilege meant that his aides did not have to testify, Nixon relented on allowing the testimony. On May 17, 1973, the public hearings began, and Watergate for the first time was a national media spectacle.

The Senate hearings of the summer of 1973 were televised on the new public television network, which had only just been mandated 6 years earlier with the Public Broadcasting Act of 1967. The television played a central role in how ordinary Americans experienced the Watergate story—as entertainment. Indeed, many viewers tuned into the Watergate hearings every day, like they would a soap opera that had heroes, villains, confessions, and stories. The Watergate hearings were the first widely watched televised hearings since the Army–McCarthy hearings of 1954, and the Senate and its investigators, wary of being charged of being histrionic like McCarthy, were especially measured. The central question of the television hearings became one that most Americans could recite by heart: "What did the president know and when did he know it?" The hearings revealed a pattern of abuses of power. These abuses included instigating the so-called Plumbers' Unit, designed to plug and investigate leaks from the White House. The public also heard through these hearings about the White House using the Internal Revenue Service to harass political opponents. And, perhaps most significantly for the course of the investigations, the Senate and the American people found out that Nixon had secretly recorded all of his Oval Office conversations. The record of these conversations became known simply as *the tapes*. The Senate committee and the special prosecutor both subpoenaed the tapes, which the White House refused to hand over, claiming executive privilege. Judge Sirica ruled against the White House, which was determined not to release the tapes and appealed Sirica's decision.

On October 20, 1973, an evening that became known as the *Saturday Night Massacre*, and in an effort to prevent turning in the tapes, Nixon told Attorney General Richardson to fire the special prosecutor, Cox. Rather than reneging on his promise to the Senate that there would be an independent investigation, Richardson resigned. Nixon then told the Deputy Attorney General, William Ruckelshaus, to fire Cox, and when he also refused, Nixon fired him. The third in command at the Justice Department, Solicitor General Robert Bork, agreed to fire Cox, and the White House then sealed off the offices of the Watergate special prosecutor. They appointed a new prosecutor, Leon Jaworski, whom they thought would be more sympathetic to the White house. However, by now public opinion had turned against the president, whose behavior made it clear he had something to hide. As the decision on the release of the tapes continued making its way through the courts, it became clear that one tape was missing 18 and a half minutes, further implicating the president in criminal behavior in the public's mind.

Impeachment Hearings and Resignation

Just after the Saturday Night Massacre, on November 1973, Nixon gave his famous "I am not a crook" speech at a press conference. "People have got to know whether or not their president is a crook. Well, I'm not a crook," he said. Few people believed him by that point. Chief among those people who were suspicious of the president were members of Congress, who in November began steps to hold impeachment hearings in the House of Representatives.

In April 1974, as those hearings were organized and while still in a legal battle over the subpoenaed tapes, the Nixon White House released transcripts of some of the tapes to the House Judiciary Committee. People were horrified at the seemingly unpresidential language they heard Nixon using when the transcripts were released. At that point, even the conservative *Chicago Tribune* joined with other newspapers across the nation in calling for Nixon's resignation, hoping to save the country from the imminent impeachment hearings. They wrote that their opinion of Nixon had changed and that he was unfit for public office.

Nixon did not budge, and the House Judiciary Committee began televised impeachment hearings in July 1974. Again, public television carried gavel-to-gavel coverage, and again the country was gripped by the drama. Television had done more than print in conveying to the public the extent of Nixon's wrongdoing. On July 26, 1974, the House Judiciary Committee passed three articles of impeachment against Nixon: for obstruction of justice, misuse of power, and contempt of Congress. However, the full House of Representatives would never vote on those articles. At the same time as the impeachment, the Supreme Court was deciding *United States v. Nixon,* with the question of whether the president was immune from subpoena by executive privilege. The Court was split between liberals and conservatives, but in a unanimous decision on July 24, 1974, they decided that executive privilege applied only in certain cases, such as military and diplomatic affairs, but not others, including "the fundamental demands of due process of law in the fair administration of justice." The court ruled that the White House would have to hand over all subpoenaed material, including the tapes.

On August 5, 1974, the White House released what became called the *smoking gun* tape. That tape was a recorded conversation from June 1972, right after the break-in, when Nixon plotted to use the CIA in obstructing the FBI investigation into the break-in, a scheme that never materialized. Publicly, Nixon had been claiming to help the investigation, so the American public now had evidence of Nixon lying to them in addition to misusing the power of his office. On August 8, 1974, facing impeachment and without admitting any wrongdoing, Nixon announced he would resign the presidency. The following day he left the White House for California. He was never prosecuted for his crimes. Instead, a month later, in September 1974, his successor, President Gerald Ford, granted Nixon a full and unconditional pardon for any crimes he might have committed against the United States while president.

Memory and Legacy

Watergate has loomed so large in the public's imagination that political scandals for at least the next 50 years included the suffix "-*gate*." Depending on one's political perspective, Watergate could be interpreted in different ways, though—as the carrying out of justice, as a media conspiracy against Nixon, even, though more rarely, as a national security state conspiracy against the public. The most common, liberal view was that the system had worked but that it had only worked somewhat randomly. Watergate proved, they thought, that the Constitution needed to be reaffirmed and legislative reform was needed to prevent further abuses of executive power. The 1970s saw legislation that attempted to limit presidential power as well as acts like the Presidential Records Act of 1978, which decreed that all White House documents, tapes, and other material belonged to the American people and must be preserved.

The country also emerged from Watergate with myths about journalism. One of these was that journalistic initiative had led to a president's resignation, which was only partly true. In May 1974, Carl Bernstein and Bob Woodward, the reporters who pursued the Watergate story for *The Washington Post,* had published a book based on their experiences, *All the President's Men.* It was the fastest-selling nonfiction hardback in the history of American publishing, selling 300,000 copies. The paperback rights were sold for a record million-plus dollars. The famous actor Robert Redford meanwhile acquired the film rights and put together a team to make the movie, which came out in 1976 during the presidential primaries and assured that Woodward, Bernstein, and the *Post* had a secure place in the public memory of Watergate. The anonymity of their confidential source at the FBI, dubbed "Deep Throat" after the 1972 pornographic film, also made their reporting seem mysterious and glamorous. (White House tapes that were released in 1996 revealed that Deep Throat was an FBI agent, Mark Felt, and the tapes also made clear that the White House knew Felt was the leak as early as October 1972. In a 2006 *Vanity Fair* article, 2 years before his death, Felt confirmed he was Deep Throat, as many had long suspected.)

The popularity of the movie and the mystery surrounding Deep Throat made it seem in the popular imagination that Woodward and Bernstein singlehandedly solved the Watergate case and brought down a president. But the special prosecutor, the Senate committee, the House Judiciary Committee, and the judges overseeing the subpoenas had a much greater effect on the outcome. The myth that the media brought down Nixon remains a touchstone for Nixon supporters who believed in a media conspiracy to oust the president.

Another journalism myth holds that Watergate forever changed political reporting—making it more investigative and combative, creating a surge of interest in young people studying to be journalists, and increasing scandal reporting. None of these trends can be attributed solely, or even mostly, to Watergate. Journalism majors did increase, but the doubling of majors largely happened because of the student activism of the 1960s, prior to Watergate. There was also, indeed, more reporting on the private lives of public figures after Watergate. The American public had glimpsed the private and sordid life of a politician who never

expected his incriminating tapes would be heard, and that surely piqued public interest in salacious news. But there were other factors in scandal reporting, including the women's movement, which made the personal political, as well as events like Senator Edward Kennedy's apparent vehicular manslaughter at Chappaquiddick, and Ford's successor, Jimmy Carter, promoting his own character and morality, making that a requirement for the highest public office for decades to come.

Richard Nixon's legacy also remains contested, just as his reputation fluctuated during his lifetime. He almost immediately began to rehabilitate his image upon leaving office and styled himself a senior statesman until his death in 1994. Some historians have argued that his obstruction of justice and other crimes have overshadowed any legislative accomplishments, while others focus on his relatively liberal domestic agenda or internationalist foreign policy. Regardless of the impact of Watergate on journalism or on Nixon's reputation, it certainly had an effect on the public and public memory, cementing the idea of a "credibility gap"—the idea that politicians cannot be trusted to tell the truth. Journalists had coined the phrase in the 1960s and applied it to the Vietnam War, but polls after Watergate consistently showed that respondents trusted public figures, including the president, less than they had in the 1940s and 1950s when polling became popularized, and that Watergate played a considerable role in that deterioration of trust.

Kathryn J. McGarr

See also Investigative Journalism; Political Reporters; Presidential Scandals, Coverage of; Presidents, Coverage of; Press and Government Relations; *Washington Post, The*

Further Readings

Friedman, L., & Levanstrosser, W. F. (Eds.). (1992). *Watergate and afterward: The Legacy of Richard M. Nixon.* Westport, CT: Greenwood Press.

Greenberg, D. (2003). *Nixon's shadow: The history of an image.* New York, NY: W.W. Norton.

Kutler, S. I. (1990). *The Wars of Watergate: The last crisis of Richard Nixon.* Westport, CT: Greenwood Press.

Kutler, S.I. (Ed.). (2010). *Watergate: A brief history with documents* (2nd ed.). West Sussex, UK: Wiley-Blackwell.

Liebovich, L. W. (2003). *Richard Nixon, Watergate, and the press: A historical retrospective.* Westport, CT: Praeger.

Nixon, R. M. (1978). *The memoirs of Richard Nixon.* New York, NY: Grossett & Dunlap.

Olson, K. W. (2003). *Watergate: The presidential scandal that shook America.* Lawrence: University Press of Kansas.

Schudson, M. (1992). *Watergate in American memory: How we remember, forget, and reconstruct the past.* New York, NY: Basic Books.

Spear, J. C. (1984). *Presidents and the press: The Nixon legacy.* Cambridge, MA: MIT Press.

WEATHER JOURNALISM

The term *weather journalism* describes the publication and broadcast of information pertaining to climatic activity, precipitation, and atmospheric conditions. Often referred to as *meteorology*, the practice aims to study weather patterns and distribute predictions about future climate conditions. Weather journalism has historically been vital to predicting weather-related catastrophes where preventative measures can be taken to protect the lives of affected individuals in certain regions. Weather journalism allows modern methods of news spreading to compare current weather patterns with previously set records in categories such as temperature, rainfall, and air quality. Weather journalism is most prominently seen in forecasts on television, radio, online, and in-print. The significance of weather journalism is demonstrated through the broadcast of many notable instances of severe weather events, especially as climate change exacerbates the damage associated with these weather developments. Advancements in technology and distribution methods have greatly improved the ability to prepare for inclement weather and increased survival rates in severe weather instances. This entry examines the role of meteorologists, the presentation of weather-related information on television, in newspapers, and on the radio, as well as applications for weather journalism that encourage citizen participation. The entry also discusses improvements in weather forecasting technology, various types of weather warnings, and weather organizations.

Role of Meteorologists

Meteorologists are the face of weather journalism in most forms of media. Meteorologists use a combination of satellites, radars, and remote sensors to analyze and calculate how weather conditions will likely develop. Meteorologists present these predictions in the form of weather journalism to explain factors that are causing the weather conditions and give advice on how to best prepare for incoming conditions. Despite their frequent appearance on news media and prevalence in the broadcasting field, meteorologists typically obtain a bachelor of science degree in meteorology or atmospheric science. As of 2021, universities such as Texas A&M and the University of California–Los Angeles offer some of the top meteorology and atmospheric science programs for graduate students.

Meteorologists and weather broadcasters require an education balanced with journalist-style classes and atmospheric science–related courses. The American Meteorology Society (AMS) holds a Certified Broadcast Meteorology Program (CBM) which trains prospective meteorologists in the art of presenting weather forecasts and understanding a range of scientific and environmental topics. The program has ongoing professional development requirements that keep each CBM graduate informed of newly released scientific information and tools. Applicants to the program require at least a bachelor's degree in atmospheric science or meteorology from an accredited university or a designated list of coursework posted on their website. Subject areas that are covered in these education requirements include statistics, physics, remote sensing, and computer science. Meteorologists are expected to have strong analytical skills, interpersonal skills, critical thinking skills, and verbal communication skills.

Television, Newspaper, and Radio

Meteorologists in cities and towns are typically featured on TV news stations as hosts who present their findings on current and future weather patterns in their local region. The first TV meteorologist to present a weather forecast on a national network was Clint Youle in 1949. These TV personalities are a standard and customary part of most local news stations, especially during evening news hours. Among the information presented by these meteorologists are temperature, precipitation patterns, humidity levels, and incoming severe weather predictions. Daily newspapers also feature this information in print with predictions for the current day as well as up to a week's worth of weather predictions. In cases of inclement weather, local news stations are primarily responsible for keeping citizens informed on road, business, and school closures. News reporters film at remote locations to display real-time weather conditions in various locations that are of importance to news viewers. National news stations such as NBC and ABC offer broad United States weather updates to TV viewers. Morning talk shows on these stations feature the weather news segment within the period of the show.

The decline of paper newspapers has contributed to the rise of online platforms for weather forecasting. The circulation of daily U.S. newspapers reached a point of significant decline in the early 1990s. As of 2021, well-known newspapers such as *The New York Times* and *The Washington Post* are looking to expand the growth of their digital advertising. Weather reports on these online newspaper websites are presented in a variety of forms. *The New York Times* primarily features stories highlighting weather events that have already occurred in typical journalistic fashion. Other newspapers provide predictions for weather on upcoming days, mainly in 5-day or 7-day breakdowns.

The National Oceanic and Atmospheric Administration (NOAA) livestreams weather reports on the radio in cities across the United States. Listeners can tune in to the appropriate frequency by using a computer or mobile device. More than 750 transmitters are used across the United States, in Puerto Rico, and in the U.S. Virgin Islands. Radio reports include a daily summary as well as short-term forecast updates. The radio frequently performs test transmissions to ensure the reliability of their warning system. Weather radio devices can be purchased in-store and online. These devices scan through local weather radio stations to locate frequencies transmitted in the region that provide warnings and alerts.

Weather information is also available to listeners in the form of podcasts. Some podcasts share weather information in more localized regions of the country that is updated periodically throughout the day. Weather podcasts that do not provide updated forecasts draw on previous weather events to create a discussion. Podcasts such as WeatherBrains and Weather Geeks gather specialists who provide their own commentary on weather phenomena.

Modern Applications and the Rise of the Internet

Climate change and rising global temperatures have created further applications for weather journalism that encourage action by individuals. Journalists and citizens alike have taken to filming and detailing the devastation online to broad audiences in order to raise awareness of the catastrophes. These instances blend previous forms of weather journalism with more modernized methods of involving citizens in documenting weather events. Social media platforms such as Twitter and Facebook are frequently used to update individuals about weather events, especially with the decline of TV. Since its development in 2006, Twitter has become a popular social media for news updates. With more than 330 million monthly active Twitter users as of 2021, there is no denying the impact of the news media posted on the platform. Twitter features an option to search and view trending hashtags, with many tailored specifically to individuals in certain regions. Twitter released a restructured method of posting stories in October 2015 with a showcase called *Moments*. Weather journalism through Twitter Moments found new life as stories could be curated and collected in one central location accessible to Twitter users. Inclement weather events such as Hurricane Harvey in August 2017 were described and tweeted about in these Moments, and Twitter users across the world instantly received updates and posted their own related content.

Weather services have leveraged Facebook as a tool to share photographs and videos of weather events. Although launched as a primarily social application in 2004, Facebook has grown to become a popular news sharing platform. With around 50% of respondents in a survey by Wired claiming a preference for Facebook as a social media news source, Facebook remains a highly trafficked online site for live weather updates. The interactive nature of the platform increases engagement, which ensures that predictions and true weather events are accurate. Online users are encouraged to post weather conditions that are being experienced in order to provide warning to others who will soon be affected. Online profiles for national weather media outlets including The Weather Channel, AccuWeather, and the U.S. National Weather Service are frequently updated with weather news and related media content. Facebook users can then reshare, like, and comment on these posts.

The use of social media has changed the communication dynamic of weather journalism to be more two-way, rather than one-way. Social media users can post their own updates on weather they are observing to inform meteorologists and media outlets of the situation. Meteorologists can then improve existing weather predictions. Live updates from individuals experiencing weather events can lead to more accurate news reports. Hashtags on posts can aid in categorizing and localizing weather data to fit certain regions. Social media users can search for current weather events using these hashtags.

Another growing trend as of 2021 is the association of crowdfunding and fund-raising with disastrous weather events. The ease of publication and information transmission with modern technology has made it possible to raise money that helps victims of weather tragedies. Popular online sites such as GoFundMe and other specific organizations related to local weather catastrophes are often linked or promoted in news stories. Social media influencers, in particular, use their internet fame and power online to raise awareness of the events. Wildfires that began spreading across Australia in December 2019 were heavily documented and publicized on many media sites, and individuals across the world have raised unprecedented amounts of money in support of local firefighters using their influence online.

Online websites and platforms are popular sources of weather information. People often use these online weather centers in lieu of TV and print weather information as they can be updated in real time and provide the most accurate and reliable information on current weather conditions. Although the technology used to perform calculations and measurements is largely the same for all media sources, the speed of information delivery has allowed the internet to drastically change the way individuals are kept up to date. Media outlets reporting on the news frequently utilize designed social media pages and profiles to post weather updates or findings. Many local and national weather stations have created phone apps that give updated information on weather in various geographic regions. With certain location services preferences selected, app users can use radar and satellite features to see live precipitation or severe weather maps.

Text message and phone call updates have become popular forms of communication for weather alerts. The National Weather Service offers Wireless Emergency Alerts (WEA) to mobile devices across the United States. Governmental partners include organizations such as the Federal Emergency Management Agency (FEMA), the Federal Communications Commission (FCC), and the Department of Homeland Security. These updates speed the rate at which individuals can receive danger alerts without requiring the use of installed applications or subscriptions. Updates are provided as a free service through various phone carriers, but opt-out features can restrict the types of messages received.

Weather media outlets provide Doppler radar and satellite data to enable users to see and interact with weather projections. Doppler radars make forecasts by calculating the direction and velocity of atmospheric conditions, such as precipitation. Satellites monitor weather conditions from orbit and make observations using channels of the electromagnetic spectrum. Information collected from doppler radar and satellite data are condensed and made public to audiences using the Internet, especially through mobile apps. Opt-in mobile weather updates are available through some media outlets. Individuals sign up using a phone number or email to get alerts of incoming severe weather in their area. Once subscribed to receive these updates, individuals indicate their preference for event alert types ranging from typical timed weather updates to severe weather warnings.

Improving Technology

The importance of reliable weather updates cannot be overstated in cases of extreme weather. The speed with which these updates can take place relies entirely on improvements in technology and tools that can predict weather and transmit information. Weather forecasting equipment is evolving to utilize some of the technology industry's most innovative designs and systems.

Green screens were invented and put to use in the mid- to late 1900s, but they have continued to be heavily used for TV weather forecasting. The green screen, also called a *chroma key screen*, is a solid-colored wall behind a subject that can be altered to show another video projection in postproduction. On-screen meteorologists standing in front of these walls face a smaller screen to the side to see what is projected behind them. This helps give a reference for where to point and give hand motions toward weather patterns or predictions. The strategic use of green screens then allows for an interactive view of oncoming weather patterns.

Improvements in virtual and augmented reality technology are expanding the realm of possibilities for checking for weather updates in more lifelike settings. For example, 360-degree visual components in virtual reality (VR) and augmented reality (AR) goggles show upclose views of weather events. Animated weather scenes allow VR users to experience simulated weather events such as thunderstorms or tornadoes in a highly immersive setting. When goggles are paired with rooms that are altered to set the scene in the simulation, users can adjust temperatures and humidity levels to achieve the overall feel of a particular weather event. The use of this technology has practical applications in both the entertainment and educational sectors. Consumers can purchase headsets or sign up for VR experiences to view the technology. Trainings for future meteorologists can also be completed using the simulations. As technology continues to improve, these simulations are becoming more lifelike to give an authentic feel. As of 2021, an anticipated future recreational use for the technology displays idealized simulated weather conditions meant to provide a weather paradise away from the severe weather incidents occurring on Earth.

In May 2015, The Weather Channel's meteorologist Jim Cantore presented one of the first looks at virtual weather broadcasting. Simulations presented in this early stage demonstration featured a tornado seen from many viewpoints. Augmented reality from then on became a powerful medium to demonstrate the impact of various severe weather situations. Water surges displayed as a rising water wall next to on-screen meteorologists put into perspective the level of damage that could occur in severe floods. Since the introduction of these technological breakthroughs, The Weather Channel has produced augmented reality graphics for lightning strikes, hailstone formations, and precipitation formations in winter storms.

The Weather Channel won an Emmy for a weather segment from June 2018 featuring the use of immersive mixed reality. The technologically innovative media form presented information on how tornadoes form as well as details on safety tips and tricks. The segment was nominated for Outstanding Science, Medical, or Environmental Report. The Weather Channel was nominated again in the Outstanding Business, Consumer, or Economic Report category for its documentary entitled *Hidden Cost: Our Laws Have Not Kept Up With the Climate*, which won an Emmy award.

Types of Warnings

To appropriately inform the public of oncoming inclement weather events, a warning system with various degrees of severity is used. The National Weather Service divides weather alerts into three categories: watches, advisories, and warnings. Watches take place ahead of the severe weather event to indicate that risks for severe weather are heightened and that monitoring is still in process to determine when and where danger might strike. Common watches include Winter Storm Watches and Blizzard Watches. Advisories are issued when the likelihood of severe weather is fairly high, especially for instances of snow, sleet, and freezing rain. Winter Weather Advisories and Freezing Rain advisories address the nature of the weather events. Warnings are for the most severe weather events that pose a significant threat to life or property. Divisions such as Winter Storm Warnings, Ice Storm Warnings, and Blizzard Warnings are used in areas with incoming cold weather danger. Flash floods, tornadoes, and thunderstorms are severe weather events that are most frequently reported on news and radio stations.

Modern Weather Organizations

Prominent weather organizations of the 21st century include the National Oceanic and Atmospheric Administration (NOAA), the National Aeronautics and Space Administration (NASA), the National Center for Atmospheric Research funded by the U.S. National Science Foundation, the World Weather Watch under the World Meteorological Organization (WMO), and The Weather Channel.

The NOAA was founded in 1970 with a mission to track weather conditions and conduct research on the environment that ultimately improves the delivery of weather forecasts and warnings. The National Weather Service is a key component of the NOAA which offers continuous updates, including watches and warnings, over radio transmission and broadcast. In 2011, the National Weather Service launched an initiative to improve responses to severe weather warnings. Scientific and technological improvements combined with organizational and governmental pairings paved the way toward achieving this goal. Upgrades to the dual-doppler system improved rainfall, hail, and general precipitation predictions. Improvements to existing forecast models better account for space weather impacts on Earth. Also included within the NOAA are the National Ocean Service, the Office of Oceanic and Atmospheric Research, and the National Environmental Satellite, Data, and Information Service. The NOAA's Weather Radio (NWR) was founded in 1954 and features a network of radio stations that provide weather updates from regions across the United States.

NASA offers a complex weather tracking project called *SPoRT*, an acronym for the Short-Term Prediction Research and Transition Center. The online system associated with the project offers numerous highly specific and concentrated weather data. Originating in the Southeast region of the United States, the project has since expanded to include partners across the country. The program developed a plan in 2008 to highlight phases for expansion and strategic approaches to be taken over the next 5 years. NASA also hosts the World Weather Program which is an interactive, 3D simulation that is available online for users who can customize their weather information experience.

The National Center for Atmospheric Research was founded in 1960 by the National Science Foundation. The mission of the center focuses on expanding the use of state-of-the-art facilities across the world in universities and institutions. Included in the collection are extensive data sets, supercomputers, sophisticated computer modeling systems, and research aircraft.

The center also offers education and outreach opportunities with workshops and free public lectures. The World Meteorological Organization (WMO) is a United Agency given the task of observing the interaction between the Earth's atmosphere, land, ocean, climate, and weather. The organization was founded in 1950 and was officially designated as a specialized agency within the United Nations in 1951. The WMO promotes the unrestricted sharing of information pertaining to environmental issues to ensure environmental protection, as well as economic and social welfare. The WMO founded the World Weather Watch as a new initiative for the organization in 1963. The program aims to increase the exchange of meteorological information, especially through the dissemination of forecasts and weather warnings. To achieve this goal, the program's functions include coordinating the development of facilities, designing communication strategies, and improving the presentation of information for general audiences.

The Weather Channel was officially released in 1982 as a news broadcast channel. Cable satellite viewers have access to the channel, which can offer selected segments of national or localized forecasts. In an effort to expand to international audiences, the Weather Channel also hosts websites in regions including the United States, Latin America, the United Kingdom, France, and Germany. The Weather Channel websites are targeted to certain geographic regions when GPS and location preferences are activated. Map options include regional maps, classic weather maps, and radar maps. Videographic and photographic media for weather events are collected in galleries online. Previous series featured on The Weather Channel include *Atmospheres* in 2000, which featured three seasons, and *Storm Stories* in 2003, which featured nine seasons.

Georgia Shepard Barnes

See also Facebook; Twitter; Virtual Reality

Further Readings

Brooks, H., Witt, A., & Eilts, M. (1997). *Verification of public weather forecasts available via the media.* Norman, OK: National Severe Storms Laboratory.

Dwyer, E. (2014). *America's weather obsession.* Indianapolis, IN: Saturday Evening Post.

Hyvärinen, O., & Saltikoff, E. (2010). *Social media as a source of meteorological observations.* Boston, MA: American Meteorological Society.

Lachlan, K., Spence, P., Lin, X., Najarian, K., & Del Greco, M. (2014). Twitter use during a weather event: Comparing content associated with localized and nonlocalized hashtags, communication studies. Taylor & Francis Online.

Leon, D., & Talbert, M. (2002). *An intelligent user interface to support weather report generation.* Boston, MA: American Meteorological Society.

Silver, A., & Andrey, J. (2019). *Public attention to extreme weather as reflected by social media activity.* Hoboken, NJ: Wiley.

Sivle, A., & Aamodt, T. (2019). *A dialogue-based weather forecast: Adapting language to end-users to improve communication.* Hoboken, NJ: Wiley.

Waxberg, G. (2013). *Under the radar: National weather service aided by SKYWARN® Spotters.* Abingdon, UK: Weatherwise.

WEB ANALYTICS

This entry focuses on web analytics and how it is used in journalism. It begins with a discussion of what web analytics is. It then describes the extent to which newsrooms across the world are using web analytics and what they are using it for. It discusses factors that influence the use of web analytics as well as criticism of its use. The entry also provides insights into the implications using web analytics has on journalistic practices as well as traditional journalism norms.

Web analytics by definition work as the collection of measurements, analyses, and the reporting of data from the internet in order to understand and optimize web usage. Since the first web analytics companies were founded in the mid-1990s, web analytics have been widely used in marketing communications as part of strategies to boost sales through a stronger understanding of audience behaviors toward online advertising and marketing content.

As news began to move online in the latter half of the 1990s and in the context of dwindling resources, rising audience fragmentation as well as increasingly competitive markets, news organizations have gradually embraced web analytics, in an attempt to retain audience attention. Popular ways to track audience data to news sites include the use of free programs such as Google Analytics that are preferred by smaller news organizations with a limited budget. Larger news sites, despite some initial hesitance, have jumped on the bandwagon by turning to more sophisticated web analytics services such as Omniture, Chartbeat, and Stela, hoping to get the best insights about readers. Those insights to a news site can include numbers of hits, views, unique visitors, the geographical locations where users access the page from, what time they visit, how many comments there are on a story, how many times it is shared via email or social media, most used search terms, and amounts of time each user spends on a news item, among others.

Newsrooms' desire to learn about the audience is not new. In the traditional media environment, information on audience interests was pulled from several types of sources including market research, ratings, telephone calls, letters to editors, or simply from casual conversations with people at informal or formal gatherings. Even with these different ways of getting audience feedback, such information was provided sporadically, hence it did not help news producers and editors very much in adjusting their daily editorial decision making. In many cases, audience information only reached newsroom managers and not individual newsroom members. News, therefore, continued to be identified, produced, and published using a top-down, centralized approach, with stories being put together based on the assumption that whatever journalists find interesting will also be interesting to the audience. Research (e.g., Wendelin, Engelmann, & Neubarth, 2017) has demonstrated that journalists' news selection did not align well with audience interests and journalists were often accused of being aloof from their audiences. The Internet and digital technologies have offered news organizations unprecedented mechanisms to learn about the audience.

Nowadays, new digital tools can track every click and scroll and turn them into data to provide newsroom members in real time with myriad types of information on audience insights. At *The New York Times*, for example, the news analytics team has worked closely with the newsroom to use these insights in strategic content planning since 2013. The aim is for journalists at *The Times* to gain a better understanding of audiences in order to align their editorial decision making toward them. The team has helped newsroom members with tasks ranging from identifying potential readers and their interests and reading habits to planning for how a story should be covered in order to make it relevant to target groups.

Since its adoption of Stela, a digital tracking tool, *The New York Times* began to make audience insights open to its entire newsroom in September 2015. Stela displays all analytics about individual stories, from basic ones such as page views, referrals, and top comments to where readers of Nicholas Kristof's international column come from and whether they are subscribers or random visitors. Based on these data, newsroom members would make various types of editorial adjustments to their content ranging from tweaking headlines, promoting articles on social media, or reusing the language of the posts that perform well. On the morning of July 8, 2016, when five police officers in Dallas were shot, *The Times* changed the headline of its story more than a dozen times to add more information as its journalists monitored the changes in online traffic and audience response across platforms.

The recently adopted audience strategies at *The Times* reflect a change in the U.S. flagship newspaper, given the fact that not so long ago *The Times* was known for being "publicly dismissive, even scornful, of the idea of using web analytics to inform editorial processes" (Petre, 2015, p. 9). Such disdain subsided as *The Times* made changes in its leadership during the 2010s.

Like *The Times*, other newsrooms have developed initiatives to find out how to best use web analytics to support editorial strategies. At *The Dallas Morning News*, the audience and the breaking news and photo/video teams were the latest change to its editorial structure. The audience team, consisting of social media producers and data analysts, was responsible for pushing content to people and reaching audiences via social media. Mike Wilson, then editor of *The Morning News*, was quoted in an interview as saying that based on the data provided by the team, the organization began creating specific goals for every journalist to attract digital audience members. The *Morning News*'s editorial staff members were instructed not only to focus on getting clicks but also to develop a greater local, loyal audience and were provided support and strategies on how to do so.

Seeking to better understand the audience for editorial work is not happening only in the United States. In Europe, *The Financial Times* (FT) launched its own analytics tool, Lantern, in early 2016. The objective was to capture a more holistic picture of the readership and how audience members are interacting with FT's content beyond just page views and clicks. Lantern, which was part of the plan to increase FT's print and online subscriptions from 780,000 to one million, can provide FT's journalists with various types of web analytics such as time on page, retention rate, scroll rate, social performance, what type of devices readers are coming from, and whether they are subscribers or nonsubscribers. Another leading European publication, *The Guardian*, was among the earliest in the news industry to adopt metrics technologies. Since 2011, the organization began using Ophan, its own analytics tool, to make web analytics accessible to everybody in the newsroom in real time. *The Guardian*'s audience team has also been working toward the goal of integrating web analytics into newsroom routines by supporting subeditors in writing and tweaking headlines or involving journalists to consider audience data when producing content.

Other news organizations increasingly embracing web analytics include *The Wall Street Journal*, National Public Radio, HuffPost, and Quartz.

Several similar patterns across newsrooms about the use of web analytics can be observed. First, although page views and clicks remain important, audience monitoring has evolved into a more complex process of tracking and breaking down different types of web analytics data including how much time audience members spend reading, how they are interacting with content, what devices they use, whether they only stumble upon the page or are loyal subscribers, and which social media platforms take them to the page. Initially, web analytics was used to simply understand what stories or visuals draw in more traffic, which helped track how a story performs and also collected data for advertisement purposes. However, recent technological developments have fostered the use of web analytics to provide support for content planning both from short-term work such as writing and editing headlines and moving a story up or down to longer term strategies like tailoring content to specific audience groups and looking for ways to reach and appeal to those who have not visited or are not loyal readers of news sites.

Second, social media, among the different types of analytics, have become increasingly important to newsrooms as their user base has expanded and more readers are coming from such sites as Facebook and Twitter. With the influence of social media analytics on news production, scholars have suggested not binding news to being newsworthy but rather developing a new concept of shareworthiness in journalism.

Third, institutionalizing the use of web analytics to build it into the newsroom culture has been a priority for leading digital news organizations. Often, this initiative began with a structural change within the news organization through the addition of an analytics team, which works in tandem with the editorial body to collect and analyze web analytics to help the content team identify opportunities to reach audiences. Those with limited resources have made web analytics data available to journalists through other types of communications including erecting panels or screens with graphics in newsrooms or informing journalists about how stories have performed via emails or morning meetings. Results from a survey on the use of web analytics showed three quarter of newsroom managers in 25 countries indicated that the use of web analytics for audience insights is critically important to the future of news organizations.

Compared to marketing businesses, news organizations are laggards in adopting web analytics, mostly because of newsrooms' reluctance to using this type of audience data. The question then is: Why would such objective and benign information about audience interests cause concerns among journalists? While the new mechanisms allow for an improved understanding of what the audience wants, they have also challenged the journalistic authority. It invokes an important debate around the core value of journalism.

Traditional gatekeeping is based on the normative journalistic ideal that journalists have autonomy in deciding what the audience needs to know as the institutional role of journalism in the society is to inform the public of what is important. News, therefore, is a public good not a commercial product. Recipients of news are citizens not regular consumers. Allowing web analytics to drive news content may result in journalism heading down the market orientation road, which, according to some journalism scholars, will speed up tabloidization and lead to a dumbing-down of news.

Not all reactions to the use of web analytics in newsrooms are negative. In a 2016 report for the Reuters Institute for the Study of Journalism, Rasmus Kleis Nielsen and Federica Cherubini observed that journalists were curious in learning how to use web analytics, which was in contrast to previous findings about journalists' resistance to the introduction of various types of audience data in newsrooms.

This new shift in the newsroom culture toward incorporating web analytics into day-to-day and longer term editorial strategies does not necessarily mean that journalists' fear of losing their editorial autonomy over the gatekeeping process or declining news quality no longer exists. It means, however, that to some extent, the desire to stay connected with the audience as well as to salvage the industry from further shrinking has compelled journalists and news organizations to compromise. In addition, news, at the end of the day, is only relevant if it serves the purpose of informing and educating the public.

There remain grounds for concern, though. That is, whether the use of web metrics would shift journalism toward a direction that turned news into being data-driven instead of data-informed and sensationalized instead of educational and informational. The presence of technologists and audience development teams in the newsroom and how they work with journalists may easily be construed as paving the way to knock down the wall between the business and editorial sides in a news organization, a fear that many journalists have about losing their autonomy to web analytics for advertising purposes.

There is a growing body of scholarly literature on the use and impacts of web analytics on newsrooms, which has contributed to a better understanding of the transformation of news work in the digital media environment. However, extant research in this area has focused primarily on newsrooms in Western countries with democratic systems of governance. Perhaps, investigation into how newsrooms in countries in the global South where the news media are operating under different systems would provide a more complete picture of the use of web analytics.

Hong Tien Vu

See also Clickbait; Gatekeeping; Google; Search Engine Optimization (SEO)

Further Readings

Cherubini, F., & Neilsen, R. (2016). *Editorial analytics: How news media are developing and using audience data and metrics*. Oxford: Reuters Institute for the Study of Journalism. Retrieved from https://reutersinstitute.politics.ox.ac.uk/our-research/editorial-analytics-how-news-media-are-developing-and-using-audience-data-and-metrics

Nguyen, A. (2013). Online news audiences: The challenges of web metrics. In K. Fowler-Watt & A. Stuart (Eds.), *Journalism: New challenges* (pp. 46–61). Centre for Journalism & Communication Research, Bournemouth University.

Petre, C. (2015). The traffic factories: Metrics at Chartbeat, Gawker Media, and The New York Times. Retrieved from https://www.cjr.org/tow_center_reports/the_traffic_factories_metrics_at_chartbeat_gawker_media_and_the_new_york_times.php

Ross, A. A. (2016). "If nobody gives a shit, is it really news?" Changing standards of news production in a learning newsroom. *Digital Journalism, 5*, 1–18. doi:10.1080/21670811.2016.1155965

Tandoc, E. C., Jr. (2017). Follow the click? Journalistic autonomy and web analytics. In B. Franklin & S. Eldridge (Eds.), *The Routledge companion to digital journalism studies* (pp. 293–301). Milton Park: Taylor & Francis.

Trilling, D., Tolochko, P., & Burscher, B. (2017). From newsworthiness to shareworthiness: How to predict news sharing based on article characteristics. *Journalism & Mass Communication Quarterly, 94*, 38–60. doi:10.1177/1077699016654682

Wendelin, M., Engelmann, I., & Neubarth, J. (2017). User rankings and journalistic news selection: Comparing news values and topics. *Journalism Studies, 18*, 135–153. doi:10.1080/1461670X.2015.1040892

WECHAT

WeChat is the dominant smartphone-based messaging application in China developed by tech giant Tencent in 2011, which also owns the popular instant messaging software service QQ. To take advantage of its existing user base on QQ, when WeChat was first released, Tencent encouraged QQ users to move their QQ contacts and mobile contacts to new WeChat accounts. After its release in 2011, WeChat quickly reached 50 million users in 10 months. By 2018, WeChat had over 1 billion monthly active users. This entry discusses how WeChat works, the ways it is used, concerns about censorship and fake news on the platform, and security concerns raised by governments outside China.

Users can initiate text, voice, and video chat with friends on WeChat. Also, they can post and see friends' updates on the Moment page. Every user can have up to 5,000 friends on WeChat. Although WeChat also allows its users to form groups, it sets a limit of 500 members per group. Any one-sided following activity is not permitted on WeChat. In other words, users can only interact when both sides agree to be friends on WeChat. As a result, unlike many popular social media sites, WeChat focuses on limited person-to-small-group communication. It is not uncommon for celebrities who have millions of followers on Weibo, the Chinese Twitter-like microblogging site, to have far fewer friends, numbering in the hundreds, on WeChat because of this setting.

WeChat also has had a series of functions to help users find new friends on WeChat since its release. For instance, users can use the location-based "Look Around" feature to find people near them, the time-based "Shake" feature to find people who are using it at the same time, and message random strangers using the "Drift Bottle" feature.

The most popular function on WeChat is that users can leave a voice message instead of a text. It helped illiterate or semi-literate people to communicate with asynchronous messages. It is also easier for those who are literate but have trouble typing on small virtual keyboards on a phone screen to communicate on WeChat. WeChat can even convert most voice messages into text messages, so recipients can read when listening to voice messages is inconvenient.

WeChat also has some unique settings on its Moment page, where users check a newsfeed of updates from friends. Each time users post on the Moment page, they can decide among their friends who can and cannot see their posts. Only mutual friends can see each other's updates on the Moment page. In other words, WeChat users may be able to see a few recent posts when reviewing stranger's profiles based on their privacy settings, but strangers have to become mutual friends for further interactions. Also, likes and comments on the Moment page are only visible to mutual friends. In other words, people can only see likes and comments made by their own friends. For example, if Emily is not friends with April on WeChat, but they are both friends with Frank and commented on Frank's recent post on the Moment page, Emily cannot see April's comment or Frank's reply to April, and April cannot see Emily's either because they are not friends. Emily can still see all the likes and comments under Frank's post made by their common friends on WeChat. On social media like Facebook and Twitter, even on private pages, strangers may see each other's comments and reactions because of a mutual friend. This doesn't happen on WeChat because of its strict privacy settings. Scholars have argued WeChat's strong preference for interpersonal and small group communication limits the potential of online discourse and reduces its users' ability to create large online communities or spur social mobilization.

WeChat also has broad-based communication tools such as public or official account pages. Similar to personal blogs, an unlimited number of strangers can follow these public account pages to read, forward, and comment on their blog posts, as well as share them on their Moment page. Anyone who can provide a mobile phone number and government-issued identification document can apply to set up a public/official account page, and each page can post updates to its users once a day. Instead of the Moment page, those public account posts show up under the "subscriptions" tab on the WeChat home page called *Chats*.

Just as companies find it useful to advertise on social media platforms such as Facebook, Instagram, and Twitter, many businesses rely on WeChat to reach Chinese consumers. Research shows that users, especially young and well-educated ones, rely on WeChat for their entertainment, social, and information needs, as they enjoy sharing and communicating with others on WeChat about their personal lives, they also tend to recommend products and services they like to others. More importantly, many Chinese businesses also rely on WeChat to process payments. During the 2010s, Tencent, along with Chinese e-commerce giant Alibaba, played a role in shifting the Chinese economy to mobile payments from cash.

Every WeChat user has a WeChat Pay tab on their WeChat profile page, which is a digital wallet that can be connected to the user's bank account and allows users to transfer money to friends and send money gifts, also known as *virtual red envelopes*, on special occasions. WeChat Pay also gives each user a unique quick response (QR) code, which they can use to send and receive money immediately after scanning each other's code. In China, it's not unusual for WeChat Pay users to regularly pay for goods and services with their phones without any cash in hand. Small business owners, taxi drivers, and online merchants often ask customers to scan their WeChat Pay QR codes for payments without setting up a complicated system or expensive payment device. WeChat Pay not only has over 900 million monthly active users, but it is also considered one of the few potential competitors to Visa, Mastercard, and American Express. In recent years, the success of WeChat Pay has inspired Facebook to work on its own cryptocurrency, so that its messaging service users can send money to each other, although it is unclear whether Facebook can replicate the success of WeChat Pay in the West.

In 2020, to fight the spread of COVID-19, the Chinese government worked with Alibaba and Tencent to assign Chinese citizens a health QR code. To get a health QR code, WeChat users need to submit basic information, including any recent symptoms, travel history, the user's main residency, and government-issued identification documents. Once such information has been confirmed by authorities, a mini-program on WeChat assigned its user a personal health QR code that could indicate whether they need to be in quarantine or were allowed to enter public places with different color codes.

Censorship and Surveillance

Like many social media companies in China, Tencent is required by government rules to monitor users' conversations and mainly when specific political terms are used in those conversations. Although Tencent pays close attention to users who express anti-Communist Party opinions and even blocks users who repeatedly raise controversial political issues on WeChat, recent studies also show it seems to be unable to control the amount of fake news circulating on WeChat. For instance, right-wing anti–Hillary Clinton memes and conservative stories were viral on WeChat during the 2016 U.S. presidential election among first-generation Chinese immigrants in the United States. Most stories are not original news articles; rather, they are often repackaged news stories mixed with a biased reinterpretation of actual events in the United States. Because WeChat prioritizes person-to-small-group communication, the spread of rumor and fake news usually happen in private conversations or in small social groups. It is almost impossible for third parties such as journalists, researchers, or fact checkers to detect and trace the spread of fake news.

Moreover, censorship not only affects Chinese citizens' ability to engage in political discussion and organize political activities domestically, but recent research has also shown it affects how WeChat users who live overseas access information and express themselves. As the number of international WeChat users grows and a large percentage of Chinese who live overseas heavily rely on WeChat for personal communication and other information needs, foreign governments and the press have expressed concerns about privacy threats posed by the Chinese government's censorship on this platform. For instance, research shows that news published on WeChat accounts catering to Chinese immigrants living in Australia is very different from the news broadcast by the Mandarin service of the Australian government-funded Special Broadcasting Service. Specifically, political coverage on WeChat channels is similar to news published by Chinese news agencies, which reflects the position of the Chinese government. Many Australian government officials fear that the Chinese government still has control of the information that Chinese immigrants (who rely heavily on WeChat for news) receive through the censorship on WeChat. Foreign government officials also express concerns about the possibility that the Chinese government uses those popular Chinese apps, including WeChat, as powerful data collection tools as well as propaganda machines.

Security Concerns

In June 2020, the Indian government banned the use of WeChat, along with many other popular Chinese apps, because of reports on the misuse of users' data that could jeopardize the privacy of Indian people. Around the same time, the Australian government planned to investigate whether some popular Chinese apps including WeChat share users' data with the Chinese government. In the United States, the Trump administration also considered taking "strong action" against Chinese apps TikTok and WeChat for engaging in "information warfare" against the United States. As those attempts were blocked by courts, the new Biden administration appears to be distancing itself from such effort.

It is unclear how strict those actions taken by Western governments would be or how long those bans will last, many WeChat users, both individuals and businesses in mainland China and those locate overseas, are deeply concerned. Because most popular social networks and chat apps in the West, such as Facebook, WhatsApp, and Telegram, are banned in China, Chinese who live overseas heavily rely on WeChat to connect with family and friends in China and form local Chinese communities. Many businesses also rely on WeChat to reach their Chinese customers. It would not be easy for them to find a reliable alternative if WeChat is banned.

Meredith Wang

See also Asia, East and Southeast; Censorship; China; Facebook; WhatsApp

Further Readings

Gan, N., & Culver, D. (April 16, 2020). China is fighting the coronavirus with a digital QR code. Here's how it works. *CNN Business*. Retrieved from https://www.cnn.com/2020/04/15/asia/china-coronavirus-qr-code-intl-hnk/index.html

Harwit, E. (2017). WeChat: Social and political development of China's dominant messaging app. *Chinese Journal of Communication, 10*, 312–327.

Lien, C. H., & Cao, Y. (2014). Examining WeChat users' motivations, trust, attitudes, and positive word-of-mouth: Evidence from China. *Computers in Human Behavior, 41*, 104–111.

Munger, C. (2018, May). Berkshire Hathaway 2018 Annual shareholders meeting—11 May 2018 Afternoon session. Warren Buffett Archive. CNBC/Berkshire Hathway.

OGAP. (2019, September). *China: A Digital Payments Revolution*. Research & Analysis Publication. Retrieved from https://www.cgap.org/research/publication/china-digital-payments-revolution

Shen, X. (2020, July). WeChat users in the US say a potential ban of the app would cut them off from friends and family in China. *South China Morning Post*. Retrieved from https://www.scmp.com/abacus/tech/article/3093310/wechat-users-us-say-potential-ban-app-would-cut-them-friends-and-family

Yang, Y. (2020, July). Navarro says more U.S. action on TikTok, WeChat to be expected. *Bloomberg*. Retrieved from https://www.bloomberg.com/news/articles/2020–07–12/navarro-says-more-u-s-action-on-tiktok-wechat-to-be-expected

Yuan, L. (2019, March). Mark Zuckerberg wants Facebook to emulate WeChat. Can it? *The New York Times*. Retrieved from https://www.nytimes.com/2019/03/07/technology/facebook-zuckerberg-wechat.html

Wang, Y. (2019, February). How China's censorship machine crosses borders—and into Western politics. *The Washington Post*. Retrieved from https://www.washingtonpost.com/opinions/2019/02/20/how-chinas-censorship-machine-crosses-borders-into-western-politics

Weekly Newspapers

The term *weekly newspaper* (aka "weeklies") is a catchall for news media that publish less frequently than daily and usually serve distinct communities such as communities of place (rural communities, small towns, mid-sized cities, urban neighborhoods, or suburbs); communities of identity (based on, e.g., religion, race/ethnicity, avocations, sociopolitical ideologies); or combinations of both. In addition to more traditional community newspapers, the "weekly" sector of the newspaper industry includes alternative weeklies (aka "city papers"), regional farm newspapers, military-base newspapers, sports-centered newspapers, many scholastic and collegiate newspapers, and a variety of other niche newspapers. In some countries, small-circulation weekly newspapers outnumber larger daily newspapers—in the United States, for example, weeklies account for about 70% of all newspapers, and the vast majority have circulation below 10,000.

As the term indicates, most weekly newspapers publish one issue per week, but some publish more frequently (two or three issues per week) and some less often, such as biweekly or monthly. The term *weekly* has more to do with news cycle than publication frequency, however, with news and content compiled over multiple days rather than daily (or hourly), as is more common among daily newspapers. In the 2010s, some large-circulation daily newspapers shifted to weekly or twice-weekly print cycles, but those news operations maintained daily news cycles online. By contrast, weeklies that have shifted to publishing articles online first before print tend to maintain a weekly or twice-weekly news cycle even while publishing online. This entry first discusses the characteristics of weekly newspapers, including their news and opinion content, advertising and other forms of revenue, distribution, market penetration, and staffing. It then summarizes research on weekly newspapers.

Content

Content of weekly newspapers varies widely, but often includes articles falling into the traditional newspaper sections of local news, sports, business, and lifestyle. Regular content generally includes mostly local/communities news, especially coverage of local government and community institutions (or for communities of identity, news items about government actions, social trends, or organizational changes that resonate with those communities). Weeklies typically do not subscribe to news wires or syndication services, so the vast majority of content is produced by staff and community members. Weeklies are usually adept at "localizing" regional, national, and global news to provide community-specific information about larger news stories. The mix of weekly newspaper content also usually includes "micronews" about community members (e.g., births, graduations, marriages, promotions, anniversaries, obituaries), events calendars, and advertising from businesses within the community. Weeklies focused on proximate communities also include local sports coverage, often with an emphasis on subprofessional, amateur, or scholastic/collegiate sports.

Journalistically, weekly newspapers tend to focus on coverage of community routines and trends rather than emphasizing in-depth/investigative reporting or breaking news. Weekly newspapers often include reports of regular meetings by local governments and community agencies; summaries of police activities and fire calls, including the mundane (often including reports about minor disturbances and false alarms); previews of regular community events such as annual festivals and holiday activities; and news about the ongoing activities of youth and civic groups within the community. Much of the coverage is driven by announcements from governments or institutions, although some weeklies—especially alternative weeklies in major cities—are known for their aggressive investigations of government corruption and/or institutional malfeasance. By and large, though, the role of the weekly newspaper in the media landscape is to chronicle and facilitate community engagement.

Opinion sections are common in weekly newspapers, though unlike daily newspapers few weeklies publish syndicated columnists with national or global popularity. Rather, emphasis is on publishing unique opinions from the newspaper's community, often via letters to the editor and op-eds from community members. Because most weeklies have relatively small circulations, the volume of submissions to opinion sections tends to be manageable enough for the newspapers to publish all acceptable submissions and, in some cases, to encourage revisions of rejected submissions to meet the newspaper's publication guidelines. It is not unusual for weekly newspapers to devote several pages each week to local opinions and to publish additional commentary online.

Because of their relatively small staffs, most weekly newspapers rely heavily on submissions from the community, or so-called user-generated content (UGC), to fill pages. Beyond letters to the editor and community-sourced op-eds, such UGC can include wedding/anniversary announcements, press releases from local businesses and nonprofit organizations, obituaries, calendar items, news about military or professional promotions, scores from amateur and youth sporting events, and announcements of forthcoming public events. Many weeklies have regular "community columnists" who write summaries of news from their neighborhoods, often with little or no compensation—an extreme example of that is *The Budget* newspaper, which each week publishes dozens of pages of small updates from Amish and Mennonite communities around the world that are submitted by volunteer "scribes" in each community.

Revenue

Weekly newspapers often provide affordable channels for advertising by small and/or local businesses, local governments, and community institutions. In addition to affordability, weekly newspaper advertising delivers a default niche audience for community businesses. Many local businesses consider advertising in weekly newspapers as a form of sponsorship to support the local newspapers and its journalistic mission. Reciprocally, many weekly newspapers treat advertising as editorial content and will reject advertising requests that are inappropriate for their communities. Many weekly newspapers also have popular classified advertising sections featuring "help wanted" ads, personal announcements, public auction notices, and private sales of specific items. In many small towns and rural communities, weekly newspapers are considered "newspapers of record" and as such are suitable for public legal notices, which can constitute a significant portion of the weekly newspaper's advertising revenue.

Not all weekly newspapers charge for single-copy sales or subscriptions; many weeklies are free within their communities. As with daily newspapers, many "paid" weeklies offer a variety of purchasing options, with subscriptions costing much less per issue than single-copy prices and options for print only, online-only, or combined access.

Free newspapers may solicit "memberships" from audience members who wish to provide additional financial support. In some countries, government and industry-subsidized programs provide funding to weeklies with community service missions. Niche weeklies may also be underwritten by affiliated organizations such as religious organizations, regional consortiums, or nonprofit foundations.

Although many weekly newspapers had their own in-house presses through the mid-to-late 20th century, by the 21st century, most weeklies were printed externally. For independent weeklies, that usually involves production contracts with larger newspaper companies in the region; for chain-owned weeklies, printing is usually done at centralized hubs that service multiple newspapers owned by the same company. Independent weeklies with their own presses generally take on additional printing jobs to generate revenue, such as printing other newspapers in the region, scholastic and collegiate newspapers, advertising inserts, and commercial jobs such as catalogs, event programs, and specialty publications.

Distribution and Market Penetration

Distribution of weekly newspapers typically relies on box/newsstand delivery and, especially in rural communities, mail subscriptions. Home delivery of weeklies is more common in suburban areas where the major daily newspaper also publishes localized weekly editions for various neighborhoods and suburbs. In many large cities, alternative weeklies (aka "city papers") are usually free and available from street boxes and racks in supportive businesses. Niche weeklies may have more dispersed audiences and therefore rely entirely on mail and online-only delivery, such as regional farming newspapers and religious newspapers with regional or national circulations. Mailing costs for weeklies often exceed printing costs, even with postal discounts for news media and bulk mailing. Many weeklies offer limited mail subscriptions outside of their circulation areas to provide "news from home" to residents who are away for reasons such as military service, mission work, or higher education, or to seasonal residents who spend only part of the year in the community.

Market penetration varies widely among weeklies, often depending on the idiosyncrasies of the markets themselves. In urban and suburban markets, weeklies are typically considered a "second read" to provide granular local information to supplement the more regional news coverage of metro dailies and regional TV, radio, and online news sources. In such markets, weekly newspapers may only reach a small percentage of households and businesses in the community. In rural areas, however, weekly newspapers may be the only sources of local and regional news, and as such may reach most or all households and businesses in the coverage area. In some resort communities, market penetration of the local weekly may exceed 100% due to mail subscriptions by seasonal visitors who form emotional attachments to their vacation communities.

Weekly newspapers typically outnumber daily newspapers in their regions, and as such weekly newspapers often make up the bulk of the membership of regional, state, and provincial press associations. Those state/regional press organizations often provide training, limited legal advice, regional and national lobbying, and other support services tailored to the interests of weeklies and small-circulation dailies. Those organizations also often have annual or ongoing award programs that are focused specifically on recognizing high-quality work by weekly newspapers. Because of their emphasis on community news, weekly newspapers rarely receive national or international attention, although a small number of major awards have gone to weekly newspapers, mostly for commentary or criticism. In the United States, a handful of weeklies have won Pulitzer Prizes for public service or breaking news coverage.

Staffing

With the exception of large-circulation weeklies, most weekly newspapers are low-budget operations with relatively small staff. It is not uncommon for a weekly newspaper to be produced by only a handful of people—some are produced entirely by a single owner every week. Weekly newspaper journalists are usually generalists rather than specialists, being able to cover a broad range of issues and topics as well as the full gamut of newsroom skills: They not only report and write articles but also take photos, produce audio/video reports, copy edit, lay out pages, write opinion columns, update websites and social media accounts, manage submissions from the community, and handle all other "news side" operations. Many weeklies are produced by editor-publishers who manage both the "editorial side" and the "business side" of the newspaper, such as advertising sales and markup, circulation management, and accounting.

For professional journalists, weekly newspapers have long been considered essential entry-level publications for novices, whether interns, recent university graduates, or mid-career professionals entering the reporting field. Given the nature of the work, weekly newspapers give novices the opportunity to explore and develop a variety of skills in reporting, editing, and packaging for print and online media. Whereas larger news media may require new editors to have many years (even decades) of experience, many weekly newspapers offer subeditor positions to relatively new journalists with only a few years of experience, most of that gained while university students. However, a combination of factors—relatively low salaries, few benefits, and few opportunities for advancement—creates a "revolving door" culture at many weekly newspapers in which new journalists may only work there for a year or two before moving on to jobs at larger media. Top editors, publishers, and department heads tend to be the most stable positions at weekly newspapers, particularly "family newspapers" at which the editor/publisher is also the owner.

Research

Despite being the largest sector of the newspaper industry, both in terms of total newspapers and in terms of aggregate circulation, weekly newspapers tend to get little attention from media researchers and collegiate journalism educators. Few collegiate journalism programs offer coursework specifically focused on weekly newspapers (or, more broadly, community journalism across media platforms) or that provide students with significant exposure to high-quality weekly newspapers. Researchers who focus on the newspaper sector likewise often omit or ignore the weekly newspaper sector, even when making broad claims about the newspaper industry overall. Renewed interest in "community journalism" has reversed that trend somewhat in the early 21st century, particularly among professionals and scholars who believe society benefits from strong, consistent coverage of local and community news.

Bill Reader

See also Alternative News Media; Hyperlocal Journalism; Local Journalism

Further Readings

Brook, A. B. (2000). *The hard way: The odyssey of a weekly newspaper editor.* Bridgehampton, NY: Bridge Works Press.

Carey, M. C. (2016). Expression of culture in the Amish Press: Media and community maintenance in a religious diaspora. *Journalism & Communication Monographs, 18,* 3. doi:10.1177%2F1522637916656332

Lauterer, J. (2006). *Community journalism: Relentlessly local.* Chapel Hill: University of North Carolina Press.

Muller, J. (2012). *Emus loose in Egnar: Big stories from small towns.* Lincoln: University of Nebraska Press.

WELLS-BARNETT, IDA B.

Ida B. Wells-Barnett (1862–1931) was one of the most prominent African American political activists of the 19th and 20th centuries and a journalist known for her role as a daring anti-lynching crusader. While Wells-Barnett was well-known during her lifetime, her accomplishments were not fully recognized during her lifetime and were largely overlooked after her death until the 1970s. Wells-Barnett used all of the communication tools at her disposal—her voice, her pen, and her press—in advocating for human rights and social justice.

Wells-Barnett engaged in domestic and international lecture circuit tours and letter and editorial writing campaigns. She used investigative techniques to generate data-based reports designed to expose injustices, particularly the horrors of lynch law, and to prompt collective action that demanded equal rights for all U.S. citizens, regardless of color or sex. Though her work as an investigative journalist is often overlooked, she helped to pioneer a brand of data-based, investigative reporting that is still in practice today and her advocacy journalism remains a model for those who engage in the practice.

Wells-Barnett's tireless campaign to expose social injustices and her crusade for human rights contributed to the political enfranchisement and empowerment of women and people of color and the decline in lawless, barbarous acts of lynching. Moreover, her words continue to resonate with people of color who have long endured the carceral state and unjust police brutality. This entry discusses the development of Wells-Barnett as an investigative and advocacy journalist, public speaker, and nascent public relations innovator; her work to expose and end the injustice of lynching; her other efforts as an activist; and her ongoing relevance today.

Training Her Voice and Her Pen

Wells was born into slavery in Holly Springs, Mississippi, on July 16, 1862, 6 months prior to Abraham Lincoln's Emancipation Proclamation, the first of eight children born to Elizabeth "Lizzie" and James "Jim" Wells. Deeply involved in the Freedmen's Aid Society after the Civil War, Ida's father insisted that she attend classes at nearby Shaw University (now Rust College), the school he had helped to establish. In keeping with her father's passion, Wells became a teacher out of necessity after the death of her parents and youngest brother from a yellow fever outbreak in 1878. Over the next several years, Wells trained her voice and her pen in her diary, where she considered her future and critiqued racial inequities and emerging human rights violations. Wells moved to Tennessee in the early 1880s and taught in Shelby County, then in the Memphis public schools.

Amid emerging Jim Crow segregation practices, Wells tested her voice in mid-September 1883 when after boarding a train with a first-class ticket for the ladies' car, she refused to move to the smoker car. Moreover, after being forcibly removed by the train conductor, she sued the Chesapeake and Ohio Railway Company and won her case in the local court system. In doing so, she had taken a stand against the repeal of the 1875 Civil Rights Act, which the U.S. Supreme Court had overturned in 1883. But Wells's legal victory was short-lived as the local court ruling ultimately was overturned by the Tennessee Supreme Court in

1887. After the 1896 U.S. Supreme Court ruling in *Plessy v. Ferguson*, "separate but equal" became the law of the land.

Recognizing the failures of the legal system to protect civil rights, she turned to the pen and writing under the pseudonym "Iola," she critiqued the racial inequities she witnessed in the South, particularly the segregated Shelby County school system. Her journalistic exposes prompted the termination of her employment in the Shelby County school system in 1891, and shortly thereafter, she became part owner of the *Memphis Free Speech and Headlight*. From this vantage point, she would initiate her decades-long anti-lynching campaign.

Exposing that "Old Thread-Bare Lie": Transnational Anti-Lynching Crusade

On March 9, 1892, Thomas Moss, a dear friend of Ida B. Wells, and his two business partners were "murdered with no more consideration than if [they] had been a dog," the "barbaric retribution" for racial tensions and violence that ensued after they threatened the financial prosperity of a white grocer (Wells-Barnett, 1970, 52). In the days that followed, from her post as editor of the *Free Speech*, Wells critiqued the horrors of lynch law and encouraged the boycott of white businesses and migration from the city. After she penned a scathing editorial that exposed "the old threadbare lie that Negro men assault white women" on May 21, a white mob burned down her press and threatened her life. Nevertheless, she courageously persisted in unmasking criminal "lynch law in all its phases" and in revealing the injustices of Jim Crow laws that effectively nullified the Fourteenth and Fifteenth Amendments to the U.S. Constitution over the next four decades.

In the ensuing decade, her transnational anti-lynching campaign involved penning articles for Thomas Fortune's *New York Age*; publishing several influential pamphlets, including *Southern Horrors* (1892) and the *Red Record* (1895), and participating in domestic and international lecture tours from 1892 until 1894. To make her case against lynching, Wells turned to empirical evidence and investigative techniques that would come to define muckraking and data-based investigative journalism in the next century. Despite opposition of the vilest sort, Wells succeeded in changing public sentiment toward what had once been considered a type of vigilante justice frowned upon by polite society but otherwise tolerated.

Wells's efforts, which proved through empirical data that less than a quarter of those lynched from 1892 to 1894 were even accused of assaulting white women, prompted the proposal of anti-lynching legislation at state and federal levels and contributed to the slow decline of the practice. Despite the best efforts of Wells and her fellow activists and allies, the lynching of Black men continued and more than a century passed before the U.S. Senate passed anti-lynching legislation in 2019. The House followed with the Emmett Till Anti-Lynching Act in February 2020, but the two measures were slightly different and as of mid-2020 it was uncertain whether the Senate would pass a new bill that could be enacted into law.

As Wells exposed in the pamphlet *Mob Rule in New Orleans* (1900), based upon these conditions, the innocent who stood accused, men such as Robert Charles, "who in any law abiding community . . . would have been justified in delivering himself up immediately to the properly constituted authorities and asking for a trial by a jury of his peers," understood that "his arrest in New Orleans, even for defending his life, mean[t] nothing short of a long term in the penitentiary, and still more probable death by lynching at the hands of a cowardly mob" (as quoted in Roessner & Rightler McDaniels, 2018, p. 50).

The "Modern Joan of Arc": From National Activist to Local Reformer

When her image appeared alongside those of "race leaders" in a book published around 1900, Wells-Barnett was at the apex of her fame as a "lecturer [and] defender of the race," as the caption put it. However, some fellow human rights activists, including Susan B. Anthony, remained concerned that after marrying Chicago journalist, lawyer, and civil rights activist Ferdinand Barnett and starting a family, Wells might become less involved in the struggle for enfranchisement of women and people of color. Quite the opposite was true.

Over the next three decades, which marked Wells-Barnett's transition from national activist to local reformer, she remained committed to practicing the activism that she once orchestrated on the national stage on a local level. Counter to Anthony's presumption, the transformation in the trajectory of Wells-Barnett's advocacy campaign was not prompted by the "divided duty" of home and work, but instead, by her contemporaries. By privileging college-educated reformers and middle-class respectability, other activists elbowed Wells-Barnett to the margins of national movements and wrote her out of the historical narrative. Nevertheless, during this period, Wells-Barnett persisted in her activism, particularly in her primary advocacy efforts against lynching and for universal suffrage.

Wells-Barnett exposed the horrors of lynch law to shift public sentiment in favor of anti-lynching legislation through publicity pamphlets, such as *Lynch Law in Georgia* (1899) and *Mob Rule in New Orleans* (1900), and through advocacy journalism, such as "How Enfranchisement Stops Lynching," which appeared in former abolitionist Charles Metz's *Original Rights Magazine* in June 1910. She advocated for the enfranchisement and empowerment of women and people of color through local clubs and organizations, such as the Alpha Suffrage Club (1913) and the Women's Forum (1926); addressed poverty and injustices within her local community through her work as an advocacy journalist for the *Chicago Defender*, as the chair of the Negro Fellowship League (1908), and as a probation officer (1913–1916); and engaged in politics as a local organizer and candidate for an Illinois State Senate seat (1928–1930). In the aftermath of outbreaks of mob violence against African Americans in her new home state of Illinois (the 1908 Springfield race riot and the November 9, 1909, lynching of William "Froggie" James in Cairo), Wells-Barnett sought to stage a national intervention that demanded the voting rights of all Americans to ensure the halt of lawless, barbaric acts of "vigilante justice."

Despite her efforts to remain involved in leadership roles of national organizations, the militant social justice crusader often encountered the threat of marginalization by Black men and white women during this period. In 1909, for instance, though she later became a member of the organization's executive committee, W.E.B. Du Bois removed Wells-Barnett's name from the original list of 40 organizers of the National Association for the Advancement of Colored People. Likewise, 4 years later, in March 1913, National American Woman Suffrage Association leaders, based on threats of a boycott from Southern suffragists, attempted to relegate Wells-Barnett to the back of a parade with a procession of "colored women," but Wells-Barnett refused to be sidelined. When the Illinois delegation marched past, Wells-Barnett joined Alpha Suffrage club cofounder Belle Squire. Her defiant act prompted national media attention, prompting Robert Abbott's *Chicago Defender* to celebrate her as the "modern Joan of Arc" and the *Chicago Tribune* to recount her brave retort to Illinois suffragist leader Grace Wilbur Trout: "If the Illinois women do not take a stand now in this great democratic parade then the colored women are lost" (as quoted in Roessner & Rightler-McDaniels, 2018, p. 67).

Wells-Barnett was prompted to write her autobiography in 1928 after an exchange the year prior with a young woman who did not understand why she was once heralded as the "modern Joan of Arc." This work, alongside her budding experience as local political candidate, remained unfinished when she died of kidney disease at the age of 68 on March 25, 1931. Despite her national fame as a radical race leader three decades prior, Wells-Barnett's death went relatively unnoticed in newspapers across the nation, except for the *Chicago Defender*, one of the most prominent African American newspapers, which published several tributes to the local resident and national hero in the days following Wells-Barnett's untimely death. Even the nation's paper of record, *The New York Times*, failed to notice Wells-Barnett's passing in an obituary, a mistake only rectified in 2018 when it launched its "Overlooked" series on "remarkable people" who were not featured on its obituary page at the time of their deaths with an obituary of Wells-Barnett.

Wells-Barnett's Continued Relevance Today

Shortly after the death of Wells-Barnett, fellow *Chicago Defender* columnist and human rights activist Rebecca Stiles Taylor lamented the absence of a physical monument to Wells and encouraged those who were impacted by the social justice crusader to construct a spiritual monument to preserve her legacy. For more than a generation after her death, those closest to Ida, including her daughter Alfreda Duster, remained committed to preserving those spiritual monuments to her collective memory, but despite their best efforts to champion her legacy, Wells-Barnett remained relegated to the footnotes of American history until a new generation of historians, biographers, and documentarians reclaimed her story in the 1970s.

In the 2010s, based on the efforts of her descendants and those committed to preserving Wells-Barnett's legacy, including prominent journalist Nikole Hannah-Jones, the Ida B. Wells Monument Committee secured the necessary funding to commission sculptor Richard Hunt to carve a tribute to Wells-Barnett near her former home in Chicago's Bronzeville neighborhood. In 2020, the Pulitzer Prize board issued a special citation honoring Wells-Barnett for "her outstanding and courageous reporting" on lynching. The award came with a $50,000 bequest, with recipients to be announced at a later date.

Historians have suggested that the cultural surveillance of African Americans and incidents of police brutality toward Black men in the 21st century mark the continuation of the culture of lynch law that Wells-Barnett worked tirelessly to expose and eradicate. Through her advocacy campaign, which deployed empirical techniques later associated with data and investigative journalism, Wells-Barnett revealed the emerging carceral state at the turn of the 20th century and the coordinated surveillance efforts to police the behavior of Black men that often resulted in their unjust brutalization. Her anguished words of resolve upon losing her lawsuit in 1887 (as quoted in Wells-Barnett, 1970, xvii)—"Oh, God, is there no redress, no peace, no justice in this land for us"—remain particularly salient today for activists in the Black Lives Matter movement. Moreover, as some scholars have suggested, by returning to Wells-Barnett's advocacy campaign, particularly her use of data-based investigative journalism, social justice crusaders might raise awareness and address this emerging human rights crisis.

Lori Amber Roessner

See also Advocacy Journalism; African American News Media; Diversity in Journalism; Douglass, Frederick; Human Rights and Journalism; Investigative Journalism; Public Relations, History of

Further Readings

Bay, M. (2009). *To tell the truth freely: The life of Ida B. Wells*. New York, NY: Hill and Wang.

Broussard, J. C. (2003). *Giving a voice to the voiceless: Four pioneering Black women journalists*. Baton Rouge, LA: LSU Press.

DeCosta-Willis, M. (Ed.). (1995). *The Memphis diary of Ida B. Wells*. Boston, MA: Beacon Press.

DuRocher, K. (2016). *Ida B. Wells: Social reformer and activist*. New York, NY: Routledge Historical Americans.

Giddings, P. (2008). *Ida: A sword among lions: Ida B. Wells and the campaign against lynching*. New York: HarperCollins Publishers.

Lerner, G. (1992 [1972]). *Black women in white America: A documentary history*. New York, NY: Vintage Books.

McMurry, L. O. (1998). *To keep the waters troubled: The life of Ida B. Wells*. New York, NY: Oxford University Press.

Roessner, L. A., & Rightler-McDaniels, J. L. (Eds.). (2018). *Political pioneer of the press: Ida B. Wells-Barnett and her transnational crusade for social justice*. New York, NY: Rowman & Littlefield.

Schechter, Patricia A. (2001). *Ida B. Wells-Barnett and American Reform, 1880–1930*. Chapel Hill, NC: The University of North Carolina Press.

Wells-Barnett, I. B. (1970). *Crusade for justice: The autobiography of Ida B. Wells*. Chicago, IL: The University Press of Chicago.

WHATSAPP

Over the last decade, mobile instant messaging applications have radically transformed human communication. In addition to affordances offered by short message service (or text messaging), cross-platform mobile applications such as WhatsApp enable users to send and receive location information, record and distribute voice messages, and share video and images as well as documents and contacts in real time at no cost. Over time, WhatsApp has evolved into more than just a messaging system by adding features such as voice calls, video calls, and group calls to individuals and groups of friends.

When launched in May 2009, the application was intended only for interpersonal communication. The application was created by WhatsApp Inc. based in California, which was bought by Facebook in 2014. Since 2014, the app has used end-to-end encryption technology that allows for "data between communicating parties to be secure, free from eavesdropping, and hard to crack" (Endeley, 2018, p. 96). The ability to gather and share content for free has made WhatsApp a conducive tool for creating and distributing mass media content. Although it has a browser version for desktop computers, it is designed for use on mobile phones and is often used on smartphones. This entry discusses the global popularity of WhatsApp, its use in journalism, and the challenges presented by distributing news through WhatsApp.

The rapid proliferation of personal mobile phones combined with the low cost of mobile data prices has contributed to a sharp increase in WhatsApp's use worldwide. As of January 2020, the mobile application had over two billion users in 180 countries, which according to the company made it the most popular messaging app in the world. The application is ubiquitous in Asia, Africa, Europe, and Latin America. As of 2020, India is the biggest WhatsApp market globally, with over 400 million people using the application, followed by Brazil, where over 120 million people have adopted it for their day-to-day communication. The Netherlands had the highest market penetration, with over 85% of the mobile phone users using the application, followed by Spain (83.1%) and Italy (83%). The U.S. WhatsApp market was relatively small as of 2019, with only 68.1 million users embracing the mobile application. Unlimited data use offered by mobile networks in Asia and Latin America have also contributed to an exponential rise in the number of WhatsApp users in those countries.

WhatsApp and Journalistic Practices

The advantages of WhatsApp have turned the app into a useful tool in the production of news. For instance, its end-to-end encryption has made

WhatsApp an essential medium of communication for journalists and their sources, particularly in nondemocratic countries where state actors have often accessed off-the-record conversations to target and suppress reporters. For example, Marie-Soleil Frère reported in 2017 on how the application had become the main conveyor of information and the location for debate in Burundi, where journalists operate in a climate of constant fear and intimidation by the government. Likewise, researchers who investigated the use of WhatsApp in Malaysia during the country's 2018 general elections found that the application enabled journalists and citizens to engage in political chat and allowed them to circumvent government censorship and surveillance of more open social media platforms. WhatsApp also has seen exponential growth in countries such as Turkey, where citizens are wary about expressing antigovernment views on relatively open social media platforms such as Facebook and Twitter.

In addition, WhatsApp has had a significant impact on journalistic routines such as contacting sources, collecting information, communicating with collaborators, and transmitting audiovisual material from the field to the newsroom. COVID-19 related safety measures adopted in many parts of the world in 2020 put limits on the ability for journalists to report in the field and have only enhanced the usage of mobile phones and applications such as WhatsApp for journalistic newsgathering. Tomás Dodds (2019), who examined the use of WhatsApp in Chilean newsrooms, found that reporters, particularly from small journalistic projects, conduct interviews using the app, which drastically reduced their cost of news production.

The use of WhatsApp also diminishes the technological requirements that small newsrooms need to have for information gathering, including obtaining soundbites and quotes from sources. Besides, such news organizations, which made their way to a WhatsApp group of journalists, gained access to press releases, information about activities, pictures, and even the voice recordings of political candidates. In Dodds's study, journalists also reported that the informal communication style on WhatsApp helped them build a tacit level of intimacy and trust with their sources, which was "very different from the fatigued voices that picked up the phone . . . or the emails signed with perennial 'regards'" (2019: 732).

Similarly, Karen McIntyre and Meghan Sobel (2019), in their study on the use of WhatsApp by Rwandan journalists, found that reporters regularly used the app to generate story ideas, communicate with sources in remote areas, disseminate news, receive audience feedback, and invite the audience to submit tips. Journalists interviewed for their study claimed that official sources were more responsive to WhatsApp messages than phone or email requests. Research on WhatsApp as a communication tool for journalists also highlights the application's use to communicate with a network of reporters.

In addition to reaching sources and networking with fellow journalists, media personnel also use WhatsApp to engage with their audiences. According to research carried out in 34 countries by the Reuters Institute for the Study of Journalism, by 2018 WhatsApp use for news had almost tripled since 2014 and had surpassed Twitter in many countries. The increase in WhatsApp use coincided with a steady decline in Facebook use for news. With a growing user base, this mobile application has become an essential platform for news organizations to disseminate their stories, particularly among younger audiences who may have migrated from Facebook or Twitter to WhatsApp to discuss and share the news with their friends.

Since WhatsApp is a closed network, it does not provide a public platform for hate speech and trolling. This also makes the app appealing to an audience that may feel uncomfortable expressing their political ideas and opinions on more open platforms such as Facebook or Twitter. Although leading news organizations, including the BBC and *The New York Times*, have used the app in their coverage of the Ebola virus in Africa and Pope Francis's visit to Ecuador, Bolivia, and Paraguay, such efforts remained largely experimental.

However, more recently, news organizations have started paying more attention to WhatsApp by designing news content specifically for the users of the app. For example, *Oxford Mail* in the United Kingdom and inFranken.de in Germany deliver the most important news of the day to WhatsApp accounts of registered users. Unlike on other social media platforms, news organizations limit messages to two or five WhatsApp alerts a day. Similarly, several Spanish, Sudanese, and Chilean radio stations commonly ask listeners to send in short voice recordings via the service, and a large number of news portals have added share-to-WhatsApp buttons to their pages. Likewise, the WhatsApp channel, "Shotty," launched by Germany's Axel Springer Akadamie, has reported that the interactive and informal communication style on WhatsApp has enabled the creation of a strong bond to their community.

Ethical Questions and Concerns

The widespread use of WhatsApp for journalistic newsgathering has raised several questions related to its impact on journalists' well-being and the distinction between off-the-record and on-the-record communication between the sources and news reporters. The ubiquity of mobile phones and the ease of sending a WhatsApp message have allowed sources to contact journalists even at odd hours. Since the online rhythms of news production value immediacy, journalists are forced to respond to the sources immediately to ensure that the information is not shared with other news organizations. As a result, journalists are constantly on duty, creating a unique situation where they "find themselves hostage to the technology they celebrate" (Dodds, 2020, p. 731).

In addition, using emojis, gifs, and memes in the texts and informal tone of communication could blur the lines between what constitutes on the record and off the record. Technically, sources and news reporters understand that information exchanged is on the record unless the source clearly states otherwise. However, the informal nature of communication on WhatsApp requires journalists to make several subjective judgments each day and seek permission from their sources to publish information from their conversation on the messaging app. Also, in recent years, WhatsApp has been employed by several vested interests to spread misinformation and hoaxes, which have raised questions about the accuracy of the information obtained from the app. Many journalists have shared and published false information secured from WhatsApp forwards—forcing them to eventually issue a rejoinder and clarification.

Tool of Civic Engagement?

Studies have shown that the consumption of news on mobile phones is characterized by regular checks to receive news updates. A 2011 study by John Dimmick and colleagues also demonstrated that mobile users tend to consume news on their phones to fill the intervening spaces between things or small intervals of time in their day, which they referred to as "interstices." More recent research indicates that news sessions on mobile phones are much shorter than those on other devices. Scholars also contend that WhatsApp's affordances may lead the users to adopt a practice called "snacking," or "news grazing," which Meijer and Kormelink (2015, p. 670) describe as a habit of "grabbing bits and pieces of information in a relaxed, easy-going fashion to gain a sense of what is going on." Such short sessions of news consumption on mobile applications such as WhatsApp, coupled with exposure to low-quality news, do little to expand public knowledge on topics relevant for civic engagement. Further scholarly investigation is needed to gain insights into the relationship between the types of news content consumed by the audience and their ability to participate in public deliberation.

Challenges in News Distribution

Newsrooms using WhatsApp also face several challenges in distributing news content using the platform. For instance, since December 7, 2019, to crack down on "automated or bulk messaging or non-personal use" on the platform, WhatsApp blocked news publishers from sending out newsletters through the app (Owen, 2019). The app launched WhatsApp Business and WhatsApp Business API for large organizations, including media houses, to send bulk messages to the users.

In addition, with the proclaimed intent to prevent the spread of misinformation on its platform, WhatsApp has limited the number of participants in each group to 256 users. While some newsrooms have had to create several groups of 256 members in each, others have relied on unauthorized third-party software like WAppSenderPro and WhatsBroadcast to automate the process of communicating with their readers through the app. However, third-party software and chatbots don't support certain features, requiring news organizations to manage the distribution of content on various WhatsApp groups manually. The other disadvantage of sharing content via WhatsApp is that every image and video sent using the app takes up considerable space in the user's phone. Since many of these images seem like spam and intrude into the user's photo gallery, some mobile users may "unsubscribe" from a news channel. Besides, WhatsApp channels are an off-label use, that is, the audience must be persuaded to allow news organizations into their personal communicative space, and not many users might be accessible via WhatsApp channels.

Another challenge in using WhatsApp to distribute news content is its unwillingness to offer engagement metrics and analytics to the publishers. The limited analysis tools make it harder for newsrooms to assess click rates and link sharing data. Journalists and news organizations have asked WhatsApp to be more flexible to media houses and provide them with basic engagement analytics, create verified accounts for news organizations, and create a one-way publishing system through which publications can push content.

Prashanth Bhat

See also Facebook; Internet Impact on Media; Social Media; Twitter

Further Readings

Boczek, K., & Koppers, L. (2020). What's new about WhatsApp for news? A mixed-method study on news outlets' strategies for using WhatsApp. *Digital Journalism, 8*(1), 126–144. doi:10.1080/21670811.2019.1692685

Dimmick, J., Feaster, J. C., & Hoplamazian, G. J. (2011). News in the interstices: The niches of mobile media in space and time. *New Media & Society, 13*(1), 23–39. doi:10.1177/1461444810363452

Dodds, T. (2019). Reporting with WhatsApp: Mobile chat applications' impact on journalistic practices. *Digital Journalism, 7*(6), 725–745. doi:10.1080/21670811.2019.1592693

Endeley, R. E. (2018). End-to-end encryption in messaging services and national security—Case of WhatsApp messenger. *Journal of Information Security, 09*(01), 95. doi:10.4236/jis.2018.91008

Frère, M.-S. (2017). 'I wish I could be the journalist I was, but I currently cannot': Experiencing the impossibility of journalism in Burundi. *Media, War & Conflict, 10*(1), 3–24. doi:10.1177/1750635217698334

Iqbal, M. (2017, August 8). WhatsApp Revenue and Usage Statistics (2020). Business of Apps. Retrieved from https://www.businessofapps.com/data/whatsapp-statistics/

Jamshed, M. (2019). Encrypted exchanges: Whatsapp and the Malaysian General Election. Volume 37—*The New Malaysia* (2019).

Kelion, L. (2017, June 21). WhatsApp rises as a major force in news media. *BBC News*. Retrieved from https://www.bbc.com/news/technology-40340830

Kligler-Vilenchik, N., & Tenenboim, O. (2020). Sustained journalist–audience reciprocity in a meso news-space: The case of a journalistic WhatsApp group. *New Media & Society, 22*(2), 264–282.

McIntyre, K., & Sobel, M. (2019). How Rwandan journalists use WhatsApp to advance their profession and collaborate for the good of their country. *Digital Journalism, 7*(6), 705–724. doi:10.1080/21670811.2019.1612261

Meijer, I. C., & Kormelink, T. G. (2015). Checking, sharing, clicking and linking. *Digital Journalism, 3*(5), 664–679. doi:10.1080/21670811.2014.937149

Molyneux, L. (2018). Mobile news consumption. *Digital Journalism, 6*(5), 634–650. doi:10.1080/21670811.2017.1334567

Nahser, F. (2018, August 30). WhatsApp me the news. Medium. Retrieved from https://medium.com/global-editors-network/whatsapp-me-the-news-99651fbef0a5

Newman, N. (2018). Journalism, media and technology trends and predictions 2018. Reuters Institute for the Study of Journalism. Retrieved from https://reutersinstitute.politics.ox.ac.uk/our-research/journalism-media-and-technology-trends-and-predictions-2018

Owen, L. H. (2019, June 21). As of December, publishers will no longer be allowed to send out newsletters on WhatsApp. Nieman Lab. Retrieved May 26, 2020, from https://www.niemanlab.org/2019/06/as-of-december-publishers-will-no-longer-be-allowed-to-send-out-newsletters-on-whatsapp/

Schwär, H. (2017, July 10). 7 things I learned about WhatsApp journalism. Medium. Retrieved from https://medium.com/@hschwaer/7-things-i-learned-about-whatsapp-journalism-b66beb2cc017

WikiLeaks

Founded in 2006 by Australian publisher and activist Julian Assange, WikiLeaks analyzes and publishes censored and restricted materials. The United States government has increasingly used the Espionage Act, a law passed during World War I, to prosecute leakers of classified information, including those who have supplied information to WikiLeaks. The organization gained notoriety in 2010 when then-army intelligence analyst Chelsea Manning leaked hundreds of thousands of classified government documents to WikiLeaks, resulting in Manning being convicted under the Espionage Act and sentenced to 35 years in prison before President Barack Obama commuted her sentence in 2017. WikiLeaks has published material on its own, as well as shared materials with established news organizations so that they can independently analyze and report on the leaked records. Whether WikiLeaks's activities constitute journalism and founder Assange is a journalist have been the subject of debate. Such questions raise important ethical and normative implications for how "journalism" and "journalist" are defined, as well as important considerations in the United States for First Amendment jurisprudence governing the publication of national defense information and other materials that are lawfully obtained and truthful.

Background

In 2006, Assange launched WikiLeaks, an international nonprofit organization known for publishing leaked government documents and other classified materials. WikiLeaks has published more than 10 million restricted or censored documents and analyses, sometimes through its contractual relationships and secure communication channels with more than 100 news organizations around the world. Over time, WikiLeaks has shifted from releasing troves of documents on the Internet to working more closely with select news organizations to analyze, redact, and release information.

Espionage Act

Two months after the United States entered World War I, on June 15, 1917, Congress passed the Espionage Act, which prohibits the acquisition, recording, or copying of information that could injure the national defense or U.S. foreign relations. The Espionage Act was also passed to target individuals who authorities believed were disloyal to the United States or obstructed enlistment in the U.S. military.

In 1919, the U.S. Supreme Court upheld the convictions of three individuals who the government believed were dissidents and had threatened the war effort: Charles Schenck, the general secretary of the Philadelphia Socialist Party; Eugene V. Debs, the head of the American Socialist Party; and Jacob Abrams, an anti-war activist in *Schenck v. United States* (1919), *Debs v. United States* (1919), and *Abrams v. United States* (1919). However, in *Abrams*, Justice Oliver Wendell Holmes Jr. wrote a dissenting opinion in which he ruled in favor of Abrams, holding that the First Amendment to the U.S. Constitution protects the right to dissent and disagree with the government.

Chelsea Manning Leak

During President Obama's administration, the Espionage Act was increasingly used to target the sources of government leaks, including those who disclosed information to WikiLeaks. Perhaps most notably, in 2010, WikiLeaks published hundreds of thousands of classified military documents on its website. The documents, leaked by Manning, included incident logs from the Afghanistan and Iraq Wars, diplomatic cables from American embassies, and dossiers on Guantánamo Bay prison detainees held without trial. Among the classified military documents was also a video from a U.S. military helicopter as it shot and killed a Reuters photographer in Baghdad in July 2007, an incident referred to as *Collateral Murder* by WikiLeaks.

In July 2013, a military court found Manning guilty on six counts of violating the Espionage Act, as well as on 14 lesser charges. On August 21, 2013, Manning was sentenced to 35 years in prison, the longest sentence ever imposed for a conviction related to leaks of classified information. The day following her sentencing, Manning publicly announced that she was a transgender woman. In 2014, Manning and the American Civil Liberties Union sued the U.S. Department of Defense over their refusal to treat Manning's gender dysphoria, a condition requiring treatment through social transition therapy. On January 17, 2017, President Obama commuted Manning's sentence to seven years. Although Manning was jailed once more in 2019 for refusing to testify before a grand jury investigating WikiLeaks, she was later released.

"Vault 7" Leak

In ensuing years, WikiLeaks would obtain and publish emails, documents, and other materials, including U.S. State Department cables in 2010 and 2011, emails by Syrian political figures in 2012, Saudi Arabian government documents and cables in 2015, and details about many U.S. Immigration and Customs Enforcement officials and employees in 2018.

Another notable instance of WikiLeaks publishing a significant amount of classified government information occurred in March 2017 when the organization published over 8,000 documents exposing various types of software hacking programs, lines of computer code, viruses, and malware and other tools that the Central Intelligence Agency (CIA) may use to steal data from intelligence targets. The leak, known as the *Vault 7* leak, was regarded as the largest such acquisition of confidential information in the CIA's history.

Over 1 year later, in May 2018, the Federal Bureau of Investigation named Joshua A. Schulte, who formerly worked for the CIA and National Security Agency, as the prime suspect in the case. On June 18, 2018, prosecutors charged Schulte with 13 counts, including three under the Espionage Act, in addition to previous charges for possession of child pornography. The government contended that the leaked materials included national defense information, among other claims. In March 2020, the trial in the Southern District of New York against Schulte ended in a hung jury. However, Assistant U.S. Attorney David Denton said during court proceedings that the Department of Justice intended to retry Schulte on the Espionage Act charges. The retrial is expected to take place in late 2021.

WikiLeaks Versus Traditional Press Outlets

President Donald Trump's administration also targeted several leakers, including Assange himself. Although the Espionage Act has not been used to prosecute a traditional journalist who published leaked documents, the move marked perhaps the closest the federal government has come to prosecuting a news organization for its involvement in publishing leaked government documents.

In April 2019, U.S. prosecutors unsealed charges against Assange for conspiracy to "access a [government] computer without authorization" under the Computer Fraud and Abuse Act (CFAA), 18 U.S.C. § 1030. The indictment was originally filed on March 6, 2018, in the U.S. District Court for the Eastern District of Virginia but was kept secret until prosecutors mistakenly mentioned charges in an unrelated case's court filings. The charges were formally unsealed after British authorities, on April 11, 2019, arrested Assange at the Ecuadorian embassy in London, where he had been seeking refuge since 2012 after losing an appeal against extradition to Sweden, where he faced two sexual assault allegations. Although the sexual assault charges were later dropped, Assange was found guilty in Westminster Magistrates' Court of breaching his 2012 bail conditions. Ecuador's President Lenín Moreno had revoked political asylum and evicted Assange.

The count under the CFAA alleged that Assange attempted to assist Manning in cracking a password to log on to the U.S. Department of Defense computers under a username that did not belong to Manning. Assange also allegedly actively encouraged Manning to collect other classified documents. In addition, the indictment stated that Assange knew that Manning was providing WikiLeaks with classified records containing U.S. national defense information.

Following the indictment, some observers attempted to distinguish Assange from traditional journalists. For example, in an April 11, 2019, interview with *Vice News*, David A. Schulz, a First Amendment lawyer who advised *The Guardian* when it published documents leaked by Edward Snowden, said, "If you break into someone's home to get information, you don't have legal protection under the guise of sharing the news" (Uberti, 2019, April 11).

Other observers expressed concern that the CFAA charges were the next step in targeting journalists for reporting on leaked documents. Jane Kirtley, a professor at the University of Minnesota and director of the Silha Center for the Study Media Ethics and Law, told *Vice News* that the CFAA charges could be an "incremental step" toward charging traditional journalists under the Espionage Act (Uberti, 2019, May 24).

On May 23, 2019, the U.S. Department of Justice released an indictment alleging 17 counts under the Espionage Act against Assange. The indictment alleged that Assange and WikiLeaks had "repeatedly sought, obtained, and disseminated information that the United States classified due to the serious risk that unauthorized disclosure could harm the national security of the United States," among several other claims.

Once again, media law experts expressed deep concern with the charges. For example, Kirtley said in a May 24, 2019, interview with *HuffPost*, "This is serious . . . Everybody in the news business and frankly everybody who is a consumer of information needs to be paying attention to this . . . Whatever happens to Julian Assange could potentially happen to any journalist, anywhere—including someone who the government would acknowledge has a more traditional journalistic role" (Robins-Early, 2019).

Jameel Jaffer, director of the Knight First Amendment Institute at Columbia University, told *Vice News* on May 24, 2019, "I don't think there's any way to understand this indictment except as a frontal attack on press freedom." Jonathan Peters, a media law professor at the University of Georgia, agreed, calling the charges under the Espionage Act a "five-alarm fire for the First Amendment" (Uberti, 2019, May 24).

There are several implications of Assange being characterized as a journalist and WikiLeaks being classified as a traditional news organization. First, Assange's legal team would likely mount a First Amendment defense and emphasize that a traditional journalist had never been prosecuted under the Espionage Act. Second, the prosecution of Assange could raise the question of whether journalists soliciting information, such as tip lines or encrypted messaging systems, could be subject to criminal charges. Third, the debate around whether Assange is a traditional journalist further complicates determining who is a journalist and what constitutes journalism, which may have legal consequences, such as around the reporter's privilege. Finally, efforts by the federal government to criminalize the receipt and publication of classified information threatens journalists' ability to publish such information that would be in the public interest. It also establishes precedent for giving government greater control over what journalists can disseminate to the public.

On February 24, 2020, United Kingdom District Judge Vanessa Baraitser for the Woolwich Crown Court in London began hearing opening arguments for the United States' extradition request of Assange following the CFAA and Espionage Act charges. U.S. government attorney James Lewis reportedly contended during opening arguments that the case was not about First Amendment rights or journalistic practices, but instead about computer hacking and the publication of classified materials. Attorney Mark Summers, who represented Assange, countered that his client had not helped Manning crack a password or hack into a secure system, explaining that Manning already had access to the information. He added that WikiLeaks had partnered with news organizations around the world, including *The New York Times* and *The Guardian*, and that WikiLeaks had a procedure in place to identify and redact the names of individuals considered to be at risk.

On January 4, 2021, Baraitser refused to order the extradition of Assange to the United State to face the Espionage Act and CFAA charges. She reasoned that extraditing Assange would be "oppressive" to his mental health, citing the risk that he might commit suicide in an American prison.

Key Supreme Court Precedent

An important line of U.S. Supreme Court precedent implicating WikiLeaks and Assange is the First Amendment protection for lawfully obtained, truthful information. In *Cox Broadcasting Corporation v. Cohn* (1975) and *Florida Star v. B.J.F.* (1989), the Supreme Court held that the publication of a rape victim's name was protected by the First Amendment because the information was truthful and lawfully obtained. In *Landmark Communications, Inc. v. Virginia* (1978), the Court held that it was contrary to the First Amendment to convict a newspaper for publishing confidential complaints against a state judge. Finally, in *Smith v. Daily Mail Publishing Co.* (1979), the Court held that the First Amendment protected the publication of the name of a juvenile defendant obtained lawfully through routine newsgathering practices even though there was a state law against it. More recently, in *Bartnicki v. Vopper* (2001), the Court held that members of the press could not be held liable for publishing or broadcasting illegally obtained information if they were not involved in its acquisition.

Also relevant is *New York Times v. United States* (1971), also known as the *Pentagon Papers* case, in which the Supreme Court held that the federal government could not enjoin *The New York Times* and *The Washington Post* from publishing portions of a top-secret study about the Vietnam War, despite the government's purported national security interest. In a concurring opinion, Justice Hugo Black emphasized the importance of the press holding government accountable, writing, "In the First Amendment the Founding Fathers gave the free press the protection it must have to fulfill its essential role in our democracy. The press was to serve the governed, not the governors."

WikiLeaks Protected by First Amendment in Stolen Documents Case

In July 2019, Southern District of New York Judge John G. Koeltl dismissed a lawsuit filed by the Democratic National Committee (DNC) against WikiLeaks and Assange, among others, finding that WikiLeaks' publication of stolen DNC emails and documents was protected by the First Amendment. *Democratic National Committee v. Russian Federation* (2019) arose during the 2016 U.S. presidential election when WikiLeaks published thousands of emails and documents that Russian hackers had stolen from DNC servers. Because WikiLeaks published the materials one day prior to the Democratic National Convention, some observers argued that WikiLeaks was deliberately trying to influence the U.S. presidential election. Observers also cited several emails that contained information embarrassing to Democratic presidential candidate Hillary Clinton's campaign and the DNC.

In the ruling, Koeltl held that the First Amendment protected WikiLeaks and Assange "in the same way [the First Amendment] would preclude liability for press outlets that publish materials of public interest despite defects in the way the materials were obtained so long as the disseminator did not participate in any wrongdoing in obtaining the materials in the first place." Koeltl further held that WikiLeaks and Assange had not participated in the theft of the DNC's materials and instead had only requested the documents, meaning the First Amendment protected the publication of the stolen document, citing *Bartnicki*. Koeltl concluded that holding WikiLeaks and Assange liable "as an after-the-fact coconspirator . . . would eviscerate *Bartnicki*" because it would "render any journalist who publishes an article based on stolen information a coconspirator in the theft."

Criticism of WikiLeaks

WikiLeaks has been the subject of repeated criticism, accused of misleading or exaggerating descriptions of the materials it has obtained, violations of personal privacy, and lack of transparency. The organization also is alleged to have facilitated Russian influence in American affairs. For example, in 2016, the CIA concluded that Russian intelligence operatives disclosed materials to WikiLeaks in relation to Trump's election campaign. Other observers have cited a lack of whistleblowing or criticism of Russia.

Scott Memmel and Jonathan Anderson

See also Censorship; First Amendment; Freedom of Information Act (FOIA); Gag Orders; Investigative Journalism; Pentagon Papers; Prior Restraint; Secrecy and Leaks; Shield Law; Supreme Court and Journalism

Further Readings

Bauder, D. (2019, April 12). Journalism or not? WikiLeaks' status in media world complex. Associated Press. Retrieved from https://abcnews.go.com/Politics/wireStory/journalism-wikileaks-status-media-world-complex-62348606

Becker, J., Erlanger, S., & Schmitt, E. (2016, August 31). How Russia often benefits when Julian Assange reveals the West's secrets. *The New York Times*. Retrieved from https://www.nytimes.com/2016/09/01/world/europe/wikileaks-julian-assange-russia.html

Entous, A., Nakashima, E., & Miller, G. (2016, December 9). Secret CIA assessment says Russia was trying to help Trump win White House. *The Washington Post*. Retrieved from https://www.washingtonpost.com/world/national-security/

obama-orders-review-of-russian-hacking-during-presidential-campaign/2016/12/09/31d6b300-be2a-11e6-94ac-3d324840106c_story.html

Lawless, J. (2020, February 24). Hero or criminal? Court hears 2 views of WikiLeaks' Assange. Associated Press. Retrieved from https://apnews.com/article/90e6b341da5fd96fc6f3b1ddd6150d78

Memmel, S. (2018, Summer). Trump administration targets journalist, leaker of government information, and former government employees who took classified documents. *Silha Bulletin, 23*(3), 9–16.

Memmel, S. (2019, Summer). Federal prosecutors charge Julian Assange with seventeen counts under the espionage act, prompting renewed concern for journalists. *Silha Bulletin, 24*(3), 1–5.

Reporters Committee statement on latest Assange indictment. Retrieved December 31, 2020, from https://www.rcfp.org/may-2019-rcfp-assange-statement/

Robins-Early, N. (2019, May 24). Assange's Espionage act charge sets up a fight over the first amendment. HuffPost. Retrieved from https://www.huffpost.com/entry/assange-espionage-first-amendment_n_5ce8457ae4b00e03656dfc5e

Uberti, D. (2019, April 11). How Julian Assange's arrest could test the First Amendment. Vice. Retrieved from https://www.vice.com/en/article/wjvevy/how-julian-assanges-arrest-could-test-the-first-amendment

Ward, A. (2017, June 9). Chelsea Manning on why she leaked classified intel: "I have a responsibility to the public." Vox. Retrieved from https://www.vox.com/2017/6/9/15768216/chelsea-manning-interview-abc-news

Wiley, S. (2020, Winter/Spring). Julian Assange extradition hearing begins, delayed due to COVID-19 pandemic; Chelsea Manning released from prison. Silha *Bulletin, 25*(2), 45–46.

Zittrain, J., & Sauter, M. (2010, December 9). Everything you need to know about Wikileaks. *MIT Technology Review*. Retrieved from https://www.technologyreview.com/2010/12/09/120156/everything-you-need-to-know-about-wikileaks/

Websites

WikiLeaks: https://wikileaks.org/

Court Cases

Abrams v. United States, 250 U.S. 616 (1919)

Bartnicki v. Vopper, 532 U.S. 514, 522 (2001)

Cox Broadcasting Corp. v. Cohn, 420 U.S. 469 (1975)

Debs v. United States, 249 U.S. 211 (1919)

Democratic National Committee v. Russian Federation, 392 F. Supp.3d 410 (2019)

Florida Star v. B. J. F., 491 U.S. 524 (1989)

Landmark Communications, Inc. v. Virginia, 435 U.S. 829 (1978)

New York Times v. United States, 403 U.S. 713, 719 (1971)

Schenck v. United States, 249 U.S. 47 (1919)

Smith v. Daily Mail Publishing Co., 443 U.S. 97, 103 (1979)

United States of America v. Julian Paul Assange, 18-CR-111 (E.D. Va. Mar. 6, 2018).

WOMEN'S MAGAZINES

Women's magazines are publications aimed at female audiences that usually focus on entertainment, shopping, home improvement, and self-improvement. Early women's magazines were established as collections of reading materials presumed to address all of women's interests—unlike men's interests, which were represented across a variety of publications. Until the middle of the 20th century, the content of women's magazines encompassed traditionally feminine spheres, such as homemaking, cooking, child rearing, and romance—in other words, aspects of life representing women's presumably universal interest in finding a man and serving others. In the second half of the 20th century, however, more specialized women's magazines began to emerge, targeting women with spending power, while general-interest women's magazines began to incorporate additional topics of interest, such as career, health, fitness, politics, and personal fulfillment.

As a genre, women's magazines are entwined with consumerism and frequently feature content that encourages readers to assign oversized significance to conspicuous consumption and appearance. In promoting advertisers' economic interests, women's magazines have acted as cultural brokers between businesses and their female consumers. Often perceived as venues for soft journalism and focusing on trivial matters, women's magazines have nonetheless played a significant role as public spaces where gender and class are collectively constructed and continually renegotiated.

Furthermore, there are many exceptions to women's magazines' consumerism. In the past, many such periodicals have promoted art and literature, introducing new talent and encouraging aesthetic appreciation among their readers. For example, women's magazines were the first periodicals to start serializing novels in the United States, as early as the late 18th century. In times of war, women's magazines have sustained their readers' morale and favored patriotism and conservation over consumerism. Finally, activist women's magazines, such as *Ms.* (United States) and the now-defunct *Spare Rib* (United Kingdom), have eschewed the genre's obsession with conspicuous consumption by promoting meaningful political and social goals for women. This entry discusses the history and types of women's magazines, as well as their effects on their audience.

History

What is thought to be the first women's magazine was published in England in 1693 and called *The Ladies' Mercury*. It had branched out of a popular general-interest magazine at the time and lasted only a few months but was soon followed by a slew of other English women's publications. Their arrivals were linked to rising literacy rates and growing interest in reading among women. Some of the earliest women's magazines were annual almanacs containing calendars, recipes, and other useful bits of information, such as coachmen's rates. Others, like their contemporary counterparts, were published more frequently and offered content that was often salacious. They included articles, fiction, and numerous letters from readers, who often formed active epistolary communities around the periodicals. Until the second half of the 19th century, when advertising became an important revenue stream, most women's magazines in England had a high cover price (e.g., a shilling, or the equivalent of between $13 and $20 in today's buying power) and were almost exclusively intended for upper-class audiences.

In the United States, the first women's magazine was the *Ladies Magazine and Repository of Entertaining and Instructive Knowledge*, which appeared in 1792, almost a century after the emergence of the first women's magazine in England. This delay reflected lagging press culture and literacy rates in the early United States—for example, only half of the women living in New England in 1790 could sign their name. Nevertheless, more women's magazines began to emerge at the turn of the 19th century and in its first decades.

More than 100 women's magazines had been launched in the United States by the time *Godey's Lady's Book*—which would become famous for its record circulation—appeared in 1830. *Godey's* acquired the *Ladies' Magazine* and, after competing with Philadelphia's *Graham's Magazine* for over a decade, climbed to a peak circulation of 150,000 copies—a staggering audience reach for a magazine at the time. Although the most popular U.S. women's magazines of the day were published in New England, similar periodicals were emerging across the country. Most were intended for well-to-do housewives and carried no advertising. They also did not adhere to many contemporary standards. For example, many reprinted materials from magazines in England without credit or published articles that were unsigned or used generic bylines, such as "The Lady Editor." Magazines for factory girls as well as feminist and temperance magazines for a budding audience of women advocates also emerged before the Civil War.

The publishers and editors of most early women's magazines, both in the United Kingdom and the United States, were almost always men, but they frequently featured the work of female journalists and writers. Many of these women wrote anonymously or under male pseudonyms. Conversely, male writers sometimes attempted to adopt a woman's perspective. Regardless of the writers' gender, most of the magazines' content was intended to educate and, in a sense, empower the female readers but also to exert social control over them. A few British periodicals with upper-class audiences contended that their goal was to improve women's minds through enigmas, mathematical questions, and essays about current affairs. But the vast majority of women's magazines published before the 20th century were keen on instructing their readers how to be ladylike and abide by contemporary social norms—as evidenced by the use of the word *lady* in the titles of 27 such periodicals published from 1800 to 1850. These early periodicals advocated chastity for single women and obedience to husbands for married women. In polite society, unwieldy women's bodies were to be contained in tightly laced corsets, which began to be advertised in the 19th century.

Even when early women's magazines did not explicitly target "ladies," they acted as judges and enforcers of modesty and propriety. For example, the *Female Spectator*, published in the United Kingdom in the 18th century, defined what constituted immorality for women—the standards were different for men—by offering real-life examples, which readers were told to abhor. In the United States, the first popular magazine for African American women, the late 19th-century *Ringwood's Journal*, taught its readers to perform middle-class womanhood and be "respectable" (a strategy for attaining equality, not just a duplicate of white women's respectability) by wearing fashionable clothes. In England and France, women's periodicals featured affluent women writers who were also perfect mothers working from home to show their readers the proper way to "have it all."

In the late 19th and early 20th centuries, women's magazines on both sides of the Atlantic saw significant growth thanks to increased advertising. In the United Kingdom, magazines for middle- and lower-class women began to displace the society journals of previous decades. In the United States, advertisements—often disguised as editorial content—allowed women's periodicals to set low cover prices and reach a mass readership. For example, a quarter of the first issue of *The Ladies' Home Journal* in 1883 was filled with advertisements—a proportion that for most women's magazines in the 20th century would more than double. About the same time emerged *McCall's* (1870), *Woman's Home Companion* (1873), *Good Housekeeping* (1885), and catalog-like periodicals for sewing patterns, such as *The Delineator* (published first under the title *Metropolitan Monthly* in 1869) and *Pictorial Review* (1899), which would soon grow into full-fledged magazines. The audience reach of these so-called Big Six women's magazines soon skyrocketed; after the turn of the century *Ladies' Home Journal* became the first American magazine with more than one million subscribers. Though English women's magazines had modeled the genre for their late-to-the-game U.S. counterparts, in the early 20th century, the tables turned. American

titles such as *Vogue* and *Good Housekeeping* established highly successful British editions in 1916 and 1922, respectively, and they were joined by another game-changer—*Cosmopolitan*—in 1972. (Before launching its international editions, *Cosmopolitan* had already had a long history in the United States. It was established as family literary publication in 1886 and bought by William Randolph Hearst in 1905. It became a women's magazine only when Helen Gurley Brown, author of the 1962 bestseller *Sex and the Single Girl*, took over the editorial management in 1965.) World War II represented a watershed period that transformed the women's magazine industry yet again. Advertising became more plentiful after the war as the economy expanded and consumers' spending power increased. British women's magazines became increasingly profitable and gradually transformed into big business controlled by a small number of publishing companies, while American women's magazines entered a period of recession in the 1950s—only to recover to a roaring expansion in the 1960s. The second half of the 20th century was marked by women's magazines' contentious relationship with the women's liberation movement—especially in the United States, where the two leading voices of second-wave feminism, Betty Friedan and Gloria Steinem, drew many of their arguments about women's secondary role in society from their exposure to the genre and experiences as women's magazines' writers. In 1970, more than 100 women occupied the office of the now-defunct *Ladies' Home Journal*, demanding changes in the magazine's depictions of women.

Since the 1970s, women's magazines have more frequently covered issues that were central to the second wave of feminism, including equality in the workplace, freedom from sexual and domestic violence, and women's political representation. In part, these changes in editorial content have also been driven by the interests of advertisers seeking to reach women who make purchasing decisions not only for their homes and children but also for their own pleasure and personal fulfillment. But even as the genre recognizes and encourages women's economic and political power, much of the content continues to perpetuate heteronormativity and domesticity. Like the earliest women's periodicals, which acted to both empower and contain women, 21st-century women's magazines continue to send contradictory messages across the variety of publication platforms that are now available to them.

Production and Industry

The Association of Magazine Media divides women's magazines into three categories: lifestyle and service (e.g., *O, the Oprah Magazine*); fashion and beauty (e.g., *Vogue*); and home and garden (e.g., *Good Housekeeping*). It is important to note that, according to both contemporary data and historical research, men make up to a quarter of the audience of periodicals directly or obliquely aimed at women. In 2020, *Woman's Day*'s male audience was 5%, *Good Housekeeping*'s was 13%, *Cosmopolitan*'s was 14%, and *Southern Living*'s was 22%, as indicated by the magazines' media kits.

The business of women's magazines is shaped by various economic, cultural, legal, and technological forces. Some have influenced all printed media while others have been specific to women's magazines. For example, the introduction of the photogravure process in the 19th century and of color printing in the 20th century are examples of technological innovations that had positive effects on publishing across the board—but especially on the magazine industry, and especially on fashion magazines, which rely greatly on visual appeal. A change specific to women's magazines was the entry of large numbers of women into the workforce throughout the 20th century, due to both cultural changes and economic necessity.

Women's rising incomes and upward mobility led to increases in personal spending power, which in turn made female audiences more attractive to advertisers and created more business opportunities for publishers of women's magazines. These trends were especially evident in the late 20th century, when the growing numbers of upwardly mobile women in the United States and the United Kingdom led to the emergence of many new magazines, usually printed on light gloss paper, which became known as *glossies*.

Many women's magazines are still printed, distributed via subscription and sold in stores. However, with the advent of digital technology, many have also become branded content creation hubs, continuously producing text, video, and social media updates. But although the digital revolution has helped women's magazines reduce their printing costs, it has not necessarily been a positive development for the genre. Content has become more standardized, optimized for search engines, and shared between magazine brands owned by the same publisher. Women's magazine stories are often assigned and vetoed by digital specialists, who tend to be men, rather than by the female editors who have traditionally been central to the genre. Editors' duties have become more complex as they are asked to repackage content to meet the needs of different platforms as well as oversee user-generated content—in addition to the work of trained writers. Importantly, serving readers is no longer central to women's magazines, which increasingly earn revenues by retailing various products through their websites and offering services akin to those traditionally provided by advertising agencies.

The largest women's magazine publisher currently is the conglomerate Hearst Magazines, which owns *Cosmopolitan*; *Elle*; *Good Housekeeping*; *Harper's Bazaar*; *Marie Claire*; *O, the Oprah Magazine*; *The Pioneer Woman*; *Redbook*; *Woman's Day*; and *Women's Health* among others. The Hearst magazine empire represents the legacy of the publishing tycoon William Randolph Hearst, who in the early 20th century acquired many U.S. magazine titles as well as the National Magazine Company in the United Kingdom. Another large publisher of women's magazines is Conde Nast, which owns *Vogue, Glamour*, and *Allure,* along with digital-only titles such as *Self* and *Brides*. Several of the Hearst and Conde Nast titles have wide-spanning networks of international editions. For example, *Cosmopolitan* has 64 international editions, *Elle* has 45, *Vogue* has 26, and *Glamour* has 12. Last but not least, the Meredith Corporation publishes mostly home-oriented titles such as *Better Homes and Gardens, Real Simple, Southern Living*, and *Martha Stewart Living*.

In the digital era, women's magazines have faced increased competition from fashion, beauty, and food bloggers as well as social media influencers. Magazine-like online communities of women readers sometimes also emerge spontaneously on fan websites or around a Tumblr or Twitter hashtag. The diversity of such competition, combined with the pressures of catering to a variety of amorphous audiences across platforms, has led many women's magazines to cease publishing or to transition to digital-only presence.

The women's magazines that remain on the market, however, are among the top performers in the magazine industry. In 2019, according to the Association of Magazine Media, five of the top 10 magazines in the United States by total print and digital audience were titles that have traditionally been considered women's magazines: *Better Homes and Gardens, Good Housekeeping, Southern Living, Woman's Day,* and *Cosmopolitan.* The Association of Magazine Media reported that from 2014 to 2019 magazines in the category of women's fashion and beauty saw the largest across-platform audience growth—66%—among all magazine categories. During the same period, the total audiences of women's lifestyle and service magazines grew by 17%, and of home and garden magazines by 19%. Most of the audience growth for women's magazines since the mid-2010s has been driven by readers who access content via mobile devices or watch videos produced by magazine staff. This growth has offset the gradual decline of audiences who read women's magazines in print or on computer screens.

Women's Magazines' Functions and Effects on Audiences

Throughout their history, women's magazines have defined, whether explicitly or implicitly, what it means to be feminine and to be a woman—and how the reader can improve her mind, morals, skills, or body to fit the mold of a good woman. In that sense, women's magazines have always acted as teachers, but their curriculum has fluctuated over time. In the 1920s and 1930s, the audiences of U.S. women's magazines were encouraged to learn about politics and literature; by the 1950s, the readers could expect to learn only how to fix their marriage and how to prepare a dinner. Around that time, women's magazines increasingly began to rely on credentialed experts and scientific studies to establish their advice as credible. Audiences have continually recognized women's magazines as sources of guidance and fantasy as well as signifiers of the stages of womanhood—for example, as readers leave behind magazines for young women and replace them with periodicals that focus on parenting or cooking.

In the late 20th century, women's magazines began to face intense criticism for promoting visual stereotypes that set an impossible standard of beauty. At the center of such criticism typically have been the so-called cover girls—the women pictured on the magazines' covers with the intent to encourage audiences to see them as ideal or future selves. The covers of the early mass-circulated women's magazines were illustrations that represented prototypes of femininity, such as the housewife or the femme fatale. However, in recent decades, the covers have typically featured images, often digitally enhanced, of young models or show-business stars whose perfect appearance induces feelings of inadequacy among the readers. These feelings of insecurity are further reinforced by the magazines' editorial content, advertisements, and advertorials, all of which present the audiences with even more images of possible selves, potentially achievable if the reader buys a specific clothing item or makeup product.

Images in women's magazines often highlight body fragments—encouraging self-objectification—and depict models in situations that allude to stalking or abuse, as though experiencing violence is the ultimate proof of one's desirability. At the same time, editorial content promotes ideas that emphasize women's limited power in society. Because reading women's magazines is pleasurable, audiences may not always recognize that they are suspending critical thinking and allowing the magazines to serve as cultural authorities in their lives.

More recently, some women's magazines have made efforts to promote body positivity by sometimes featuring women who are not young or who are not thin. For example, the cover of the June 2020 issue of *British Vogue* portrayed then-85-year-old actor Judi Dench; the November 2020 issue of *Cosmopolitan* featured Barbie Ferreira, a plus-sized model and an actor, in a tightly fitting dress; and the October 2018 cover of *Cosmopolitan UK* showed American plus-sized model Tess Holliday in a swimsuit. However, the market forces that shape the survival of women's magazines, on any platform, continue to demand aspirational images that elicit clicks or purchases.

Such attempts at redefining beauty and femininity are therefore likely to remain isolated.

Miglena Sternadori

See also Feminist News Media; Hard Versus Soft News; Health and Medical Journalism; Human Interest Journalism; Lifestyle Journalism; Literary Journalism; Longform Journalism; Men's Magazines

Further Readings

Association of Magazine Media. 2020 magazine media factbook. Retrieved from https://www.magazine.org/mpa-factbook.

Adburgham, A. (2012). *Women in print: Writing women and women's magazines from the Restoration to the accession of Victoria.* London: Faber & Faber.

Aronson, A. (2002). *Taking liberties: Early American women's magazines and their readers.* Westport, CT: Greenwood Publishing Group.

Ballaster, R., Beetham, M., Frazer, E., & Hebron, S. (1991). *Women's worlds: Ideology, femininity, and the woman's magazine.* New York: NYU Press.

Barrell, J., & Braithwaite, B. (1988). *The business of women's magazines.* London: Kogan Page Ltd.

Beetham, M. (2003). *A magazine of her own? Domesticity and desire in the woman's magazine, 1800–1914.* Milton Park: Routledge.

Braithwaite, B. (1995). *Women's magazines: The first 300 years.* London: Peter Owen Publishers.

Damon-Moore, H. (1994). *Magazines for the millions: Gender and commerce in the* Ladies' Home Journal *and the* Saturday Evening Post, *1880–1910.* Albany: SUNY Press.

Dancyger, I. (1978). *A world of women: An illustrated history of women's magazines.* Dublin: Gill and Macmillan.

Duffy, B. E. (2013). *Remake, remodel: Women's magazines in the digital age.* Champaign, IL: University of Illinois Press.

Endres, K., & Lueck, T. (1995). *Women's periodicals in the United States: Consumer magazines.* Westport, CT: Greenwood Publishing Group.

Fraser, H., Johnston, J., & Green, S. (2003). *Gender and the Victorian periodical.* Cambridge: Cambridge University Press.

Gough-Yates, A. (2003). *Understanding women's magazines: Publishing, markets, and readerships in late-twentieth century Britain.* Milton Park: Routledge.

Kitch, C. L. (2001). *The girl on the magazine cover: The origins of visual stereotypes in American mass media.* Chapel Hill: University of North Carolina Press.

Landers, J. (2010). *The improbable first century of* Cosmopolitan *magazine.* Columbia: University of Missouri Press.

McCracken, E. (1992). *Decoding women's magazines: From* Mademoiselle *to* Ms. Berlin: Springer.

Mesch, R. (2013). *Having it all in the Belle Epoque: How French women's magazines invented the modern woman.* Palo Alto: Stanford University Press.

Rooks, N. M. (2004). *Ladies' pages: African American women's magazines and the culture that made them.* New Brunswick: Rutgers University Press.

Rooks, N., Pass, V., & Weekley, A. (eds.). (2016). *Women's magazines in print and new media.* Milton Park: Taylor & Francis.

Shevelow, K. (1989). *Women and print culture: The construction of femininity in the early periodical.* Milton Park: Routledge.

Walker, N. A. (2000). *Shaping our mothers' world: American women's magazines.* Jackson: University Press of Mississippi.

White, C. L. (1970). *Women's magazines, 1693–1968.* Michael Joseph.

Woodward, H. (1960). *The lady persuaders.* New York: Ivan Obolensky.

Zuckerman, M. E. (1998). *A history of popular women's magazines in the United States, 1792–1995.* Westport, CT: Greenwood Press.

XINHUA NEWS AGENCY

The Chinese national and international news agency, Xinhua, is one of the most influential news media organizations in the People's Republic of China (PRC)—and in the world. However, unlike its Western counterparts, Xinhua has rural and rather humble origins. Its state ownership remains controversial, though since the early 1980s (with some reversals in the early 2000s), it has decreased its dependence on state funding. This entry begins with an overview of the origins of Xinhua, then discusses its goal of financial independence, and finally examines the news agency's international expansion and addition of digital services.

Origins

Xinhua's predecessor, the Red China News Agency (Hongzhongshe), was established in rural Ruijin, Jiangxi province, in 1931, upon the foundation of the Chinese Soviet Republic under the rule of the Chinese Communist Party (CCP). Initially, Hongzhongshe shared staff, consisting of three to five full-time editors, with the CCP's central organ, the newspaper *Red China*, which was launched in the same year. Their news operations were suspended in 1934 when the CCP and its Red Army began the Long March, but revived a year later after the army reached Yan'an, Shaanxi province. As the situation in the Nationalist areas changed dramatically after the Japanese invasion, Chiang

Kai-shek, the head of the Nationalist Party, agreed to coordinate with the CCP to form a "National United Front" against Japan in 1936. As a response to these political changes, in 1937 the Red China News Agency and the newspaper *Red China* were renamed Xinhua (New China) News Agency and the *New China Newspaper*, respectively. They continued to share staff until 1939.

International news occupied only a small proportion of Xinhua's news output in the early 1930s. During World War II (1939–1945), the CCP's need for information about the war led to an increase in the proportion of international news in Xinhua's releases. In 1945, Xinhua established an international news desk consisting of four journalists. From 1947 to 1948, Xinhua launched its first overseas bureaus in Hong Kong, London, and Prague.

In early 1949, mere months before the foundation of the PRC, Xinhua's headquarters moved to Beiping (renamed Beijing in the same year). This was a turning point in Xinhua's history, marking the beginning of its transition from a rural-oriented Party organ into a city-based national news agency. In the early 1950s, Xinhua began to build a nationwide news collection network, covering the country's major cities and modelled on TASS, the former USSR's national agency.

In 1956, Xinhua signed its first news exchange contract with TASS. At about the same time, the Chinese agency reached agreements with the Agence France-Presse and Reuters (Thomson Reuters since 2008) in 1956 and 1957, respectively. By 1967, Xinhua had signed news exchange agreements with 22 foreign news agencies on the principle of free news exchange.

In late 1956, Xinhua set itself the goal of becoming a competitive international player within 10–12 years and planned its international expansion in the next 5–7 years. With support from then political leaders Liu Shaoqi, Hu Qiaomu, and Deng Xiaoping, Xinhua also began to modify its international news portfolio toward more balanced and accurate reporting in the middle of the "Great Leap Forward" in the late 1950s.

By 1956, the number of Xinhua's overseas bureaus reached 10, with 140 out of 2,416 Xinhua staff members working in these overseas offices. From 1956 to 1957, Xinhua sent almost 80 more journalists abroad. The agency also employed local residents for news collection in some developing countries. Many Xinhua journalists were sent to universities for foreign language training. In the late 1950s, the number of Xinhua's overseas bureaus tripled. Two thirds of the newly established overseas branches were located in Asia, Africa, and Latin America, including countries with no diplomatic relations with the PRC. During this period, Xinhua became the main news source for Chung Yang Tongshin, the North Korean news agency. Xinhua's influence also expanded to Southeast Asia, the Middle East, and North Africa where TASS had played a dominant role in the 1940s and the early 1950s.

Yet, the progress made by Xinhua in reporting international news was cancelled out by the events of the Cultural Revolution (1966–1976). Xinhua managers and Liu Shaoqi himself all became victims of the political struggles during the Cultural Revolution and lost their leadership positions. Many veteran journalists were sent to small villages for so-called reeducation. Some of them endured torture. All journalistic principles adopted earlier for reporting international news crumbled. Class struggles occurred in all divisions of Xinhua, including its overseas bureaus. However, under the direct leadership of Zhou Enlai, the first Premier of the PRC, Xinhua set up more overseas offices during this period, their number increasing from 51 in 1966 to more than 70 by 1976. From 1976 to 1980, Xinhua concentrated its efforts on recovering from the chaos caused by the Cultural Revolution.

Business Expansion in the Late 20th Century

Before 1980, Xinhua was fully funded by government subsidies. In the 1980s and 1990s, Xinhua endeavored to become a financially independent news institution, willingly receiving a reduced amount of state subsidies each year for nearly two decades. Throughout this period, striving for financial independence was part of Xinhua's ambition to become a "world-class news agency," on a par with the likes of Reuters and AP.

In January 1980, Xinhua began to charge domestic newspapers a subscription fee for using its news wires. In February 1980, Xinhua's *Reference News* daily sold the agency's first ever advertisement. In the early 1980s, Xinhua launched a series of new titles, including *Economic Information Daily* and the *Outlook Weekly* news magazine. In addition, Xinhua began marketing news services abroad. In September 1982, Xinhua launched a Spanish language news wire service aimed at Mexican media.

In March 1983, Xinhua started a 24-hour international news service operated by the headquarters and overseas bureaus. The number of its news wire subscribers reached nearly 5,300 in 1998, almost 9 times the number of subscribers in 1992. By the late 1990s, Xinhua had 30 domestic bureaus (at provincial levels) and 101 overseas bureaus in 92 foreign countries and regions around the world. Xinhua was able to provide news in seven languages, including English, French, Spanish, Arabic, Russian, and Portuguese. However, it was still reliant on leading western news agencies and the local media outlets of the host countries as sources for its international news stories.

Although Xinhua was able to cover more than 60% of its own operating costs by 1999, it had not achieved complete financial independence from state subsidies. After suffering a number of setbacks, including several corruption-related cases involving senior managers and journalists in the early 2000s, Xinhua turned back to the government, asking for more subsidies. In 2001, self-generated revenues and state subsidies contributed almost equally to Xinhua's overall income.

Since the early 2000s, Xinhua has adopted "news landing" as a branding strategy, as well as an indicator for evaluating journalists' performance.

"News landing" occurs when media outlets, including newspapers, TV and radio stations, news websites, and other news agencies, carry Xinhua's wire news or identify Xinhua as the news source. In the early 2000s, Xinhua surveyed about 470 domestic and 700 foreign news organizations in order to calculate its "landing rate." In order to make Xinhua's news wires more "attractive" to metropolitan dailies, the agency tried to speed up its responses to breaking news, as well as pursuing investigative journalism. In April 2000, Xinhua set up a new editorial desk—Xinhuashidian, which was responsible for investigative journalism. The agency also launched a new column available to all users of Xinhua's general news wires. Users could also access a bundle of selected reports on Xinhua's website.

In June 2000, Xinhua's domestic news became a 24-hour service. Technically, Xinhua has been able to break news around the clock since then. However, political constraints can still delay or prevent Xinhua from reporting breaking news. For instance, breaking news on politically sensitive topics such as strikes, demonstrations, religious conflicts, and natural disasters were, and to a large degree remain, subjects of censorship and self-censorship. After the SARS epidemic in 2003, Xinhua journalists were given more autonomy to break news about natural disasters for overseas audiences within a certain time frame. However, more restrictions were imposed in 2004, when "supervision by public opinion" (*yulunjiandu*) became a sensitive matter to Chinese officials.

Going Global and Digital in the 21st Century

In 2009, Xinhua began to accelerate its international expansion under the "Going abroad" project, partly in order to enhance China's soft power. In December 2009, Xinhua launched its TV news network, China Xinhua News Network Corporation, in order to reach out directly to foreign audiences. By the end of January 2017, Xinhua had established more than 180 overseas bureaus in major cities of the world.

Starting in 2015, Xinhua began to expand its online and digital services, aiming to transform itself into an online news agency. In 2016, more than 50% of Xinhua's annual income was generated by the agency itself, and the rest came from state subsidies. Since then, the share of self-generated income has been steadily increasing. It was expected to reach 75% by the end of 2019.

Xinhuanet Co. Ltd., the business entity which runs Xinhua's official news website, Xinhuanet.com, went public in October 2016 in Shanghai. Before this, Xinhuanet was the second most profitable enterprise owned by Xinhua. On March 6th, 2017, Xinhuanet's market capitalization reached RMB17.151bn (about US$2.49bn), nearly 3 times the value of Xinhua's total annual income in 2015. As of the end of May 2020, Xinhua still held nearly 60% of the shares in Xinhuanet.

In November 2018, Xinhua unveiled the world's first artificial intelligence (AI) news presenter, developed by the news agency in collaboration with a Chinese IT company. This is part of Xinhua's ambitious plan to integrate AI into its news production. In December 2018, Xinhua officially launched a novel news platform, called the "Media Brain," combining AI technology, cloud computing, Big Data, and the Internet of Things in news production.

Xin Xin

See also Agence France-Presse; Associated Press; Chinese Television; Comparative Models of Journalism; Reuters; TASS and Russian News Agencies

Further Readings

Xin, X. (2006). A developing market in news: Xinhua News Agency and Chinese Newspapers. *Media, Culture & Society, 28*(1), 45–66. doi:10.1177/0163443706059285

Xin, X. (2012). *How the market is changing China's news: The case of Xinhua News Agency*. Playmough, UK: Lexington Books.

Xin, X. (2018). Financialization of news in China in the age of the Internet: The case of Xinhuanet. *Media, Culture & Society, 40*(7), 1039–1054. doi:10.1177/0163443717745121

Websites

Xinhua English language website: http://www.xinhuanet.com/english

Yellow Journalism

No epithet in American journalism is quite as familiar, flexible, or widely invoked as "yellow journalism." The term was coined as a calculated sneer in the late the 19th century and lives on as shorthand for journalistic failings of all kinds. "Yellow journalism" is often equated to sensational treatment of the news, and to dressing up fakes and falsehoods as fact. It is an emphatic term of disparagement that slides easily off the tongue. It is an American idiom that resonates widely abroad, having found use in countries as diverse as Mexico, Thailand, Sierra Leone, Egypt, India, and France. Whether it's articulated overseas or in the United States, almost no one who invokes "yellow journalism" knows much about its origins or the practices it corresponded to when the term was coined.

The sneer emerged in early 1897 in New York City's highly competitive newspaper market, placed in the public domain by Ervin Wardman, an austere yet combative Harvard-educated editor. Wardman came up with "yellow journalism" while looking for a pithy putdown for the brash, lively, and self-promoting journalism of William Randolph Hearst. Wardman was a contemporary of Hearst and despised his rival's eagerness to flout norms of fin-de-siècle journalism by experimenting with vivid layouts, multicolumn headlines, and provocative illustrations in his *New York Journal*. Hearst, who was 32 years old when he burst onto the New York media scene in

1895, boasted that his techniques represented a "new journalism." And the *Journal* promoted that view in its columns and editorial cartoons. "New journalism" was a not-so-subtle rebuke to the practices of newspapers that were staid and conservative in appearance, including venerable titles such as Charles A. Dana's *New York Sun* and Edward L. Godkin's *New York Evening Post*.

Wardman, who enrolled at Harvard several months after Hearst had left the university without a degree, was a unambiguous, pro-tariff Republican. Hearst was a moderate Democrat. Partisan differences no doubt contributed to Wardman's enmity for Hearst and his journalism, and the editorial page of the *Press* reflected this antagonism. Wardman searched for an insult to apply to "new journalism" and landed on "nude journalism." It was a near-homophone for "new journalism" that appeared in a brief editorial comment in the *Press* on January 21, 1897. "Nude journalism" suggested newsgathering practices underpinned by few ethical sensibilities. At the end of January 1897, Wardman came up with an even more provocative pejorative: "yellow-kid journalism" which soon was abbreviated to "the yellow journalism." The sneer was born.

"Yellow journalism" owes its existence, indirectly, to a popular and innovative Sunday color comic that featured a bald, wise-cracking street urchin clad in a yellow nightshift. The character was known as the *yellow kid* and the comic first appeared in Joseph Pulitzer's New York *World*. The comic was immensely popular and Hearst lured the artist, Richard F. Outcault, to the *Journal* in October 1896. The *World* responded by commissioning another cartoonist to draw a rival yellow kid comic. So both newspapers were publishing and touting their yellow kids, much to Wardman's disgust. But not until 3 months later did the phrase "yellow-kid journalism" appear in the *Press*. Meantime, Wardman took to the newspaper's editorial columns to condemn the *Journal* and the *World* as "fake mongers, chambers of horrors, cesspools, sloughs, purveyors of mendacity."

Once he settled on "yellow journalism," Wardman invoked the phrase relentlessly to assail both the *Journal* and the *World* (which themselves were vigorous rivals). They also were the largest-circulating and most lively newspapers in New York, which surely grated on the ascetic Wardman. He mocked them in editorial page quips and one-liners that suggested Twitter-length comments of today. Few of the quips, though, were particularly inspired. Here's an example, from the *Press* of February 2, 1897: "The Yellow Journalism is now so overripe that the little insects which light upon it quickly turn yellow, too." A few days later, Wardman suggested that the yellow press publish this disclaimer in a prominent location of the front page: "YELLOW JOURNALISM IS A LIAR AND WE ARE IT."

After naming it, Wardman tried to destroy yellow journalism by cheerleading a boycott movement that took shape in the late winter and spring of 1897. It was a decency campaign that sought to banish the *Journal* and the *World* from libraries, reading rooms, social clubs, and other organizations across metropolitan New York. First to take the step was the Newark Free Public Library in New Jersey, the trustees of which declared the *Journal* and the *World* "chronicles of crime, of lust, and of general nastiness." The *Press* praised the ban, declaring in an editorial that the Newark library had "begun a reform which doubtless will be continued by similar bodies in other cities. In decent public esteem yellow journalism occupies the same place as brothels."

The *Sun* joined the cheerleading, saying it expected the boycott to "be pursued by decent institutions . . . generally. It is a movement whose natural impulse is in the disgust and indignation which have been increasing in all quarters against the licentiousness, the vulgarity, and the criminal spirit exhibited by those shameless papers with an effrontery almost without example in the history of journalism." The movement against the *Journal* and the *World* spread quickly. By May 1897, the *Press* figured that nearly 90 libraries, clubs, and reading rooms had banished the newspapers—among them the Century Club, the New York Yacht Club, and the Harlem branch of the YMCA. Other institutions, according to the *Sun*, kept the *Journal* and the *World* locked away, serving them only upon specific request by adult patrons. "The places where Yellow Journals are admitted," the *Press* declared, "are rapidly narrowing down to prisons, dives and brothels."

That was an exaggeration, of course, and after a few months the boycott movement faltered and quietly dissipated. It fell victim to its inherent self-limiting nature, in that institutions had no further way of censuring or punishing the newspapers after banning them. Besides, the grievances about the yellow journals were not very specific and tended to revolve around vague notions they were indecent and violated good taste. Even more fundamental to the boycott's collapse was that many New Yorkers *enjoyed* reading the *Journal* and the *World*. They were lively newspapers, not nearly as awful as Wardman and other critics asserted. There was more to "yellow journalism" than shrieking sensationalism or boorish excess. Close reading of the *Journal* and the *World* makes clear that in the late 19th century, "yellow journalism" embodied a distinct and robust genre of broadsheet newspapering that was defined by these features and characteristics:

- a variety of topics presented on the front page, including reports about politics, crime, war, international diplomacy, sports, and high society.
- a keen taste for self-promotion, for unabashedly calling attention to the newspaper's achievements. This tendency was especially pronounced in reporting about suspected corruption in public works contracts.
- the frequent use of multicolumn headlines, including those that stretched across the front page. Such headlines projected a typographic appearance decidedly more vivid than the cluttered, single-column look favored by most fin-de-siècle newspapers.
- the liberal use of illustrations including sketches and, as production techniques later allowed,

half-tone photographs. Locator maps and other graphic representations were commonplace.

- bold and sometimes experimental layouts, including those in which a single article and illustration dominated the front page. Such layouts, while not routine, anticipated the emergence of tabloid newspapers.
- a reliance on anonymous sources, especially in the dispatches of leading reporters, to whom bylines were often granted.
- a willingness to spend lavishly in gathering news. This was especially true for Hearst when he was establishing a high-profile presence in New York, where failed newspaper ventures were hardly unknown. In 1897, for example, Hearst hired Mark Twain, Stephen Crane, Richard Harding Davis, and other prominent writers for short-term assignments for the *Journal*.
- As those characteristics suggest, "yellow journalism" in its original, late 1890s incarnation was an complex genre, as inclined to experiment as it was eager to self-promote. As practiced at that time, "yellow journalism" was seldom dreary or predictable. Not surprisingly, the genre was popular in some cities beyond New York. By 1900 or so, newspapers in Boston, Chicago, Denver, St. Louis, and San Francisco—including but not restricted to titles owned by Hearst or Pulitzer—had adopted distinctive features of "yellow journalism." Among them were the old *Boston Post* and the *Denver Post*.

Hearst's *Journal* embraced the term "yellow journalism" in May 1898 and in doing so associated itself with heroic and risk-taking figures from the past. To be "yellow," the *Journal* reasoned, was to be audacious and even unconventional. "Caesar was yellow to the plutocrats of the Roman Senate," it declared in an editorial. "Napoleon was yellow to the traditional strategists whom he routed by scorning their rules. Washington was yellow to the Tories, and so were Jefferson and Franklin and Paine, and all the bold men who created this republic. The United States is doing an extremely yellow thing in waging this war [with Spain] to help another people instead of to fill its own pockets. And the sun in heaven is yellow—the sun which is to this earth what the *Journal* is

to American journalism" (Cited in Campbell, 2001, pp. 38–39).

While it didn't mind "yellow journalism," the *Journal* preferred to think of itself as a practitioner of the "journalism of action." This was self-actuating, participatory kind of newsgathering which, according to the *Journal*, obliged the press to inject itself conspicuously in public life and "fitly render any public service within its power." The newspaper "does not wait for things to turn up," the *Journal* said of its activist model. "It turns them up."

The "journalism of action" envisioned filling the voids left by government inaction or ineptitude and took expression in many ways. The *Journal* filed court injunctions to block or delay suspicious municipal contracts; it brought aid and charity to victims of blizzards and hurricanes; it unraveled the grim murder mystery of a headless torso that washed up in New York's East River. The *Journal* organized the successful jailbreak in Havana of 19-year-old Evangelina Cisneros, a political prisoner held without trial for months by Cuba's Spanish rulers.

The "journalism of action" is best understood as a subgenre of "yellow journalism," a Hearstian derivative that incorporated high-profile stunts with regular doses of self-promotion. It was energetic and attention-grabbing, but it did not win universal acclaim. The "journalism of action," as pursued by the *Journal*, often required the expenditure of substantial sums of money. Not all newspapers has access to such reserves.

The *Journal*, moreover, failed to distinguish itself during the crises and confusion of late winter and early spring 1898—a period bracketed by the mysterious destruction of the American battleship *Maine* in Havana harbor and the U.S. declaration of war against Spain. The *Journal* vigorously reported on the developments of those weeks, but not always accurately. It was notably mistaken, for example, in reporting that Spanish authorities were responsible for the explosion that sunk the *Maine*, a claim that a U.S. Naval Court of Inquiry did not corroborate. The court said it could not determine who blew up the battleship. But it concluded the *Maine*'s destruction was a deliberate act, that a mine likely had detonated beneath the battleship, igniting its ammunition magazines, and bringing death and injury to its crew.

The aftermath of the *Maine's* destruction was prime time for foes of yellow journalism to condemn the excesses of its reporting. It was during this time when the mythical claim took hold that Hearst and his were responsible for bringing on America's war with Spain. Foes of yellow journalism were keen to indict Hearst for warmongering and no critic was more eager to do so than Godkin, the Irish-born editor of the gray and sober *Evening Post.* Godkin assailed Hearst in print as "a blackguard boy with several millions of dollars at his disposal" and declared he had "more influence on the use a great nation may make of its credit, of its army and navy, of its name and traditions, than all the statesmen and philosophers and professors in the country."

Godkin's critiques rested more on assertion than evidence. But it was a convenient way to denounce Hearst and the reproach took hold—and was later reinforced by biographers of Hearst who didn't much like their subject. A more temperate and nuanced interpretation was offered by another Hearst biographer, Kenneth Whyte, who wrote: "Hearst's coverage [in the runup to the Spanish-American War] was part of an uproarious national dialogue. His voice sounds freakish when plucked out and examined in isolation, but in the context of the journalistic conversation that erupted as the *Maine* sank, it sounds quite different" (Whyte, 2009, p. 383).

The war with Spain was brief; hostilities lasted 114 days. The conflict was fought in the Caribbean and in the Pacific, which made it extraordinarily expensive for newspapers to cover. The two-front war also gave rise to embarrassments that hardly burnished the standing of yellow journalism. Hearst's *Journal* had no correspondent with the U.S. naval squadron that destroyed a decrepit Spanish fleet in Manila Bay in the first major engagement of the war. Instead, the *Journal* arranged to publish the dispatches sent by the *Chicago Record's* correspondent, a political cartoonist named John T. McCutcheon, with the understanding that the *Record* would print them first. The *Journal* broke that agreement and published under McCutcheon's byline an extravagant account about the U.S. naval victory—an account that only vaguely resembled what McCutcheon had written. It was an indefensible breach and signaled that the *Journal* would turn to fakery if competitive pressures were intense enough.

Other newspapers were guilty of fakery, too, as the *Journal's* evening counterpart demonstrated in laying a trap for Pulitzer's *World.* The *World* was suspected of lifting war-related news and presenting it as its own, without acknowledging the *Journal* as the original source. In June 1898, the *Evening Journal* printed a short, made-up item about the death in Cuba of an Austrian artillery expert whom the newspaper identified as "Colonel Refilpe W. Thenuz." Sure enough, in its editions the following day, the *World* reported the "death" of the Austrian colonel, saying he had "performed many acts of conspicuous gallantry." That afternoon, the *Evening Journal* revealed that "Refilpe W. Thenuz" was no military figure but an anagram for "We Pilfer the News." For days, the *Evening Journal* crowed about catching the *World* in a case of news piracy. The *World* suffered in silence until the controversy subsided. The episode was amusing and revealing. It demonstrated how plagiarism can be a temptation in newsgathering. It also illuminated the antics of the American press of the late 1890s and spoke to the intensity of newspaper rivalries of the time.

In November 1898, Pulitzer instructed his editors to tone down the *World,* to make it less flamboyant in appearance and in the treatment of news. The move was announced at a staff meeting and marked the beginning of a slow fading of yellow journalism. After the war, Hearst turned increasingly to national and New York politics while expanding his newspaper holdings by launching titles in Chicago, Boston, and Los Angeles. His attentions were divided, and he was unable to devote time to developing the "journalism of action" into a sophisticated model that could be widely adopted. "If I had stuck to one newspaper, I might by personal direction in detail have made a newspaper to suit me exactly," Hearst acknowledged in an interview in 1906. "But I went off starting other newspapers in widely separated places, and, of course, I can supervise all of them only in a general way. I can't give myself to any one" (Steffens, 1906, p. 12).

The aftermath of the Spanish-American War brought the rise of the antithesis of yellow journalism—the *New York Times* of Adolph Ochs. The *Times* of the late 1890s did not display multicolumn headlines. It eschewed dramatic layouts and seldom printed illustrations on its front page. It rarely awarded bylines. It lacked the resources for forays into activist journalism. Instead of exuberance, the *Times* offered a staid, serious-minded news report along with thoughtful coverage of the arts, sciences, and business. It sought to define itself as a moral counterweight to yellow journalism, an objective that took expression in its motto, "All the News That's Fit to Print."

The *Times* introduced the slogan in 1896, not long after Ochs acquired the newspaper, which had fallen into receivership. In February 1897, "All the News That's Fit to Print" was moved to the top left corner of the *Times*' front page—a place it has occupied ever since. The motto was an implied promise of restrained yet authoritative treatment of the news. It was intended as well as a rebuke to the extravagance of "yellow journalism."

Nonetheless, the *Times*' ascendancy seemed unlikely until Ochs abruptly lowered the newspaper's single-issue price to one cent from three cents in October 1898. The move came to seen as a historic turning point for the *Times*. It effectively made serious-minded journalism available at a yellow press price. And it prevented Hearst and Pulitzer from raising the price of their newspapers from a penny to two cents, as their representatives had privately discussed. A joint price hike would have helped the yellow press recover some of the expenses of their war coverage. But Hearst and Pulitzer shelved those plans to keep Ochs from cornering the one-cent market in New York. The decision locked the *Journal* and the *World* into a long-term revenue squeeze, further encouraging the decline of yellow journalism.

The genre faded for another reason, too: Its prominent features were gradually absorbed into the mainstream of American journalism. The use of bold headlines, multicolumn photographs, and dramatic page layouts all became commonplace in U.S. newspapers of the 20th century. So, too, did bylines for reporters. It's as if newspapers unintentionally became milder, tamer derivatives of yellow journalism as practiced more than a century ago in New York and beyond.

W. Joseph Campbell

See also Hearst, William Randolph; Publishers; Pulitzer, Joseph; Sensationalism; War and Military Journalism

Further Readings

Campbell, W. J. (2001). *Yellow Journalism: Puncturing the myths, defining the legacies*. Westport, CT: Praeger.

Craig, C. (2016). Breaking the news: Telegraphy and Yellow Journalism in the Spanish-American War. *American Periodicals, 26*, 2.

Shafer, J. (2009, March 30). Bring back Yellow Journalism. Slate.com. Retrieved from https://slate.com/news-and-politics/2009/03/bring-back-yellow-journalism.html

Steffens, L. (1906, November). Hearst, the man of mystery. *American Magazine*.

Stevens, J. (1991). *Sensationalism and the New York Press*. New York, NY: Columbia University Press.

Whyte, K. (2009). *The Uncrowned King: The sensational rise of William Randolph Hearst*. Berkeley, CA: Counterpoint.

YELLOW KID

The Yellow Kid was the popular narrator of the world's first comic strip, *Hogan's Alley*. The character's exploits were published in the *New York World* newspaper from 1895–1898 and the *New York Journal* from 1896–1898. Drawn first by Richard Felton Outcault (1863–1928) and later by George Luks (1867–1933), the Yellow Kid is remembered for his mass appeal and timely witticisms. Popular belief holds that yellow journalism is named for the Yellow Kid, as the reporting style and the cartoon hero were in vogue during the same period in late 1890s. This entry discusses the history of the Yellow Kid, the style and content of the comics where the character appeared, the character's popularity, and its effect on newspapers.

Publication History

The true date of the Yellow Kid's first appearance is contested by scholars. As the different aspects of his now iconic look were added on a little at a time, different historians point to different illustrations as the definitive start of the Yellow Kid. Outcault's first iteration of a dirty, jug-eared child dressed in an ill-fitting hand-me-down nightshirt was printed under the title, "Fourth Ward Brownies" in the magazine *Truth* on February 9, 1895. The black-and-white illustration was reprinted 8 days later in the *New York World* on February 17, 1895.

The "Brownie" child is similar in most respects to the Yellow Kid, but most scholars label this a prototype and not a true rendering of the character. Some point to April 1895 as the genesis of the Yellow Kid, when the character spoke for the first time through a message scrawled on his nightshirt, a tactic that would later become standard. Still others point to a quarter page *Hogan's Alley* comic titled "Circus in Hogan's Alley," published in the *New York World* on May 5, 1895, as the official start of the Yellow Kid.

The success of the character and his *Hogan's Alley* gang resulted in increased newspaper sales for *New York World* publisher, Joseph Pulitzer (1847–1911). Not to be outdone, rival newspaper publisher William Randolph Hearst (1863–1951) reached out to Outcault in later 1896 with a lucrative offer. Should Outcault leave Pulitzer and the *New York World* and work instead for Hearst's *New York Journal*, he would receive a hefty raise in wages. In October 1896, Outcault accepted the offer. The popularity of the Yellow Kid made the illustrator a lucrative asset, and his poaching by Hearst became a key part of a larger rivalry that ultimately resulted in a circulation war and spawned yellow journalism.

Unwilling to lose the Yellow Kid and the money the character brought in, Pulitzer hired Luks to continue drawing the comic. For more than a year between 1896 and 1897, Outcault and Luks created competing versions of the Yellow Kid for the *New York Journal* and the *New York World*. The *New York Journal* continued to use the title *Hogan's Alley* for the strip Luks created, while Hearst capitalized on the popularity of the comic's likeable main character by calling Outcault's panels *The Yellow Kid in The World*.

Publication of the Yellow Kid cartoons continued as a New York newspaper fixture through the end of 1897, but by early 1898 the character's popularity waned. The Yellow Kid continued on in the form of advertisements, humor periodicals, and curios for a little over a decade, but never again reached the same level of fame. By 1910, the Yellow Kid craze was over.

Style and Content

Hogan's Alley was the first weekly illustrated story told successively in five panels, making the Yellow Kid the hero of the first modern comic strip. The strip was printed weekly and often in color, an eye-catching feature in a time when most newspapers were primarily black and white. Early examples of the comic often place the Yellow Kid in the background in a subordinate role and without his signature yellow clothes. In these first comics, his nightshirt was printed in many different colors, including blue, orange, red, and green, and was sometimes published as a solid color or in a polka dotted or checkered pattern. It wasn't until September 22, 1895, that the Kid first appeared wearing his now iconic solid yellow nightshirt, which he wore consistently after January 1896. After this point, the Yellow Kid's look was fixed. He was thereafter always depicted as a barefooted, floppy-eared boy, and his nightshirt had a dirty hand-shaped smudge across the right hip.

Just how the Kid's look settled on this particular style is disputed, but Outcault stated in 1898 that the idea to color the Kid's nightshirt a bright sunshine yellow did not originate with him. Legend claims the Kid got his distinctive color after an engraving foreman for the *New York World* used the Kid's nightshirt as a handy place to test out a new process for printing yellow ink. There exists no verifiable evidence to lend credence to this story. The *New York World* had indeed struggled to perfect its yellow printing process but had resolved those issues months before the Kid's initial appearance.

Officially, the Kid was named Mickey Dugan, but the public dubbed the scamp the "Yellow Kid" in honor of his colorful nightshirt. Bald, filthy, and sporting a buck-toothed grin, the Yellow Kid found fame for his adventurous romps through New York and for the saucy banter written across his nightshirt spelled phonetically in street jargon. Each week, he tossed off pithy wisecracks and provided cultural commentary on everything from politics to conflict to the way children played in the streets. The dialogue often poked fun at authority and provided a joyful, if sarcastic, take on the day's news.

Outcault, who sympathized with the plight of poverty-stricken immigrants, drew *Hogan's Alley* in a chaotic, busy way that contrasted the innocent fun of the children with their squalid living conditions. Stray dogs, cats, and goats ran rampant in the *Hogan's Alley* comics, and the streets were crowded and dirty. The Yellow Kid's own look mirrored the circumstances of the immigrant children he was drawn to represent: his stained, ill-fitting clothes, lack of shoes, and head shaved bald to prevent the spread of lice all reflected the real-life living conditions of New York's poorest.

Popularity

The Yellow Kid was wildly popular, despite critics who claimed the comic was a cash grab that would ultimately destroy journalistic integrity and erode American values. His cheeky antics appealed to a wide range of audiences, including the growing number of semiliterate immigrants. By 1890, nearly half of New York's population was foreign-born, and the colorful pictures and limited text of *Hogan's Alley* became a major selling point for newspaper readers who hadn't yet mastered English. The Yellow Kid was also popular among the middle and upper classes, despite the poor reputation of the *New York World* and *New York Journal* among public libraries, schools, and the wealthiest inhabitants of the city. During the cartoon's heyday, tens of thousands of copies of the *New York World* were sold every Sunday to patrons eager for more colorful Yellow Kid capers.

The Yellow Kid's popularity peaked in 1896–1897, when the character's acclaim made him a star on and off the newspaper pages. During this period, the Yellow Kid became one of the first marketing icons in the United States. His image was featured on buttons, statuettes, puzzles, books, advertisements, billboards, matchbooks, blotters, cigars, postcards, cracker tins, soap wrappers, chewing gum cards, toys, and even whiskey bottles. In a nod to his upper-class fans, the Yellow Kid also inspired a Broadway play.

The Yellow Kid's popularity did not last. Both the *New York Journal* and the *New York World* quit running their respective Yellow Kid cartoons in spring 1898. The *World* published their last color panel featuring the Yellow Kid, "Casey Corner Kids' Dime Museum," on May 1, 1898. Four days later, the Yellow Kid appeared for the last time in the *Journal* printed as a single-column, untitled black and white box cut.

Legacy

Popular belief holds that the Yellow Kid inspired the term *yellow journalism*, a moniker used to describe the sensationalistic writing style that dominated the *New York Journal* and the *New York World* during the same period as the Yellow Kid's popularity, although some scholars have contested the point. Whether or not the one named the other, the two have become so intrinsically linked as to be nearly synonymous.

Perhaps the Yellow Kid's most lasting legacy can be found in the formatting of his cartoon world. The Kid was the first to incorporate and standardize the elements of the modern comic strip: color, minimal or absent text, recognizable characters, open-ended storylines told through sequential drawings, and balloon dialogue. In the full page, color panels of *Hogan's Alley* and the *Yellow Kid in The World*, the style of the modern comic strip was formed, tested, and proven a lucrative addition to newspapers.

Autumn Lorimer Linford

See also Comics; Hearst, William Randolph; Penny Press; Pulitzer, Joseph; Yellow Journalism

Further Readings

Blackbeard, B. (Ed.). (1995). *R.F. Outcault's the yellow kid: A centennial celebration of the kid who started the comics*. Northampton, MA: Kitchen Sink Press.

Horn, M. (1977). *Comics of the American west*. Winchester, ON: Winchester Press.

Horn, M. (Ed.). (1999). *The world encyclopedia of comics*. Philadelphia, PA: Chelsea House Publishers.

Silverman, F. (1994). Tracing the history of America's first modern comic character. *Editor & Publisher, 127*(48), 16.

Yaszek, L. (1994). 'Them damn pictures': Americanization and the comic strip in the progressive era. *Journal of American Studies, 28*(1), 23–38. doi: 10.1017/S0021875800026542

YOUTUBE

YouTube is at the top of the video-hosting industry, with hundreds of millions of visitors and billions of hours of videos played per month. At the start of 2020, YouTube had two billion logged-in monthly users. The platform has become a part of many people's daily routines and habits. YouTube is often considered to be part of Web 2.0—a shift most notably marked by the rise of digital platforms and applications that support and rely upon user-generated content. This entry examines the history and early use of YouTube, the birth of the YouTuber, and the platform's influence on news and journalism.

History of YouTube

YouTube was founded in February 2005 by Chad Hurley, Steve Chen, and Jawed Karim. All three were previously employees at PayPal. In April, the site's first video was uploaded. At that point, YouTube was one of many services that aimed to make it easier for people to share video online. Yet YouTube's platform has reached many milestones of success that weren't achieved by others. The first was in October of 2006 when Google acquired YouTube, purchasing it for $1.65 billion. But that was just the beginning.

In the early 2000s, YouTube offered a simple interface that allowed even the most novice users to share and view streaming videos. While there is some disagreement about why YouTube won the popularity contest among video sharing services, there are some key features that gave it an advantage over others. YouTube provided video recommendations, allowed easy video sharing, and made it possible for users to comment on content. The embedded video player made video content easily accessible. The platform's social networking capabilities also made the content easy to share.

Some of YouTube's success could have been in part due to increasing awareness of the platform. It was mentioned in a prominent tech blog in August 2005 which ultimately made many more people aware of the site, and thus lead to more content being uploaded to the site. Around the same time a viral *Saturday Night Live* skit "Lazy Sunday" became one of the initial YouTube hits.

The video was viewed 1.2 million times in 10 days before NBC demanded it be pulled off the site. This controversy brought more attention to YouTube. It was becoming clear that YouTube was a video sharing site first, and social networking site second.

A closer look at video sharing and what that can mean reveals a uniqueness of YouTube. The platform was a pioneer of the technology *to stream* video, not download video. This is an important differentiation because with streaming, viewers didn't "own" the content, they were given access to view it. That said, YouTube did offer the capability to upload content, so that viewers could become video creators. This user as creator focus was emphasized in the early days of YouTube. In 2005, their "About Us" page said the following:

> Show off your favorite videos to the world.
> Take videos of your dogs, cats, and other pets.
> Blog the videos you take with your digital camera or cell phone.
>
> Securely and privately show videos to your friends and family around the world . . . and much, much more.

This was very different than traditional broadcast of video content. Also in contrast to broadcast, YouTube didn't offer a constant flow of content to tune in to. Users could use filters or button searches for the "most popular" videos. Ranking and popularity guided content choices. The platform's search engines and ranking algorithms steered users' viewing. In 2020, 70% of what people watched was determined by a recommendation algorithm.

Original Creators and Audience

YouTube considers itself as a platform for video distribution and as an aggregator of content. This might seem to be obvious, but it is an important distinction. Because it is not a content producer, YouTube didn't consider itself to be a target for legal challenges that came its way. For example, companies like Disney battled YouTube to protect its intellectual property. They wanted the platform to enforce limitations on what users could use and/or share. But YouTube/Google's lawyers made the case that Disney can't hold a distributor responsible for copyright infringement. The platform told users to respect copyright laws. Their terms of service articulated warnings about the illegal copying of protected content. Still, many companies simply didn't want their content distributed on a platform they didn't control.

YouTube didn't make a profit in the first years, but once they realized how to tailor and distribute commercial messages to mass audiences, that changed. This shift was also due to collaborations with other online platforms, like Facebook and Twitter.

It wasn't long before the television industry bought into YouTube's approach, especially providing streaming on-demand content. After 2008, the platform had competitors like Netflix, Amazon, Apple iTunes, and Hulu. These companies were offering ad-supported subscription services, often for longer form content than YouTube provided. YouTube started to look more like television, and in 2011 changed its interface.

YouTube's evolution meant that instead of broadcast *being replaced* by social media content, broadcast *was becoming a part* of social media. An interdependence between television and video sharing platforms developed. Television was no longer just large screen in your living room, it was also that screen in your pocket. YouTube was not alone in thinking about television in this flexible way. Most, if not all, major American cable-television networks have their own online services and content portals that provide offer a wide variety of content.

Birth of the YouTuber

YouTube reorganized how users navigated content into channels or collections of videos. Thus, users were becoming more likely to be solely consumers and not content creators. The majority of those who viewed YouTube videos never uploaded a video themselves. Many didn't even make comments on videos. While YouTube started out telling users to "show off your favorite videos to the world," by 2011, 4% of YouTube users provided almost three fourths of the platform's content.

That 4% is important to know more about. These are the people who did videoblogging, or "vlogging." This is what most user-created content is called and it is a key part of the YouTube community. These are mostly videos where the subject talks directly to the camera, sometimes with clever editing. Vlogs tend to be easy to produce and don't require much more than a webcam and some simple editing skills. These videos tend to get responses, comments, and feedback from viewers.

Since 2006, there has been a growing number of guides proving details about how to make effective use of YouTube. The tutorials often teach readers how to create attention for their content so that it'll be widely circulated. The goal is for the video to go viral. This type of guidance is also provided to business who want to use the platform to market and advertise their products and services and get as many hits as possible. Sometimes it's difficult to figure out which vloggers are "real" and which are manufactured. The novice and professional uses of YouTube are clearly not separate, but they coexist and are evolving.

In 2019, 10% of the most popular YouTube videos draw 79% of views, according to a Pew Research study. The top content in late 2019 varied from compilations of trick shots and toy reviews to video game commentaries and conspiracy theories. Dude Perfect, Shane Dawson, and Mr. Beast are a few of the top YouTubers, all with over 23 million subscribers to their channels at the end of 2019. One of the creators at the very top of the list though is PewDiePie who was at over 100 million subscribers. He started his channel with videos of himself playing video games but has evolved into a personality who also gives commentary on internet memes and viral videos. As content creators become more attention, some of that attention ends up being negative. PewDiePie has been known to make anti-Semitic and other racist comments on his channel. In late 2019, he announced he was taking a break from the platform 3 days after YouTube posted new content moderation guidelines regarding hateful speech in videos.

In 2019, in an open letter to the YouTube community, YouTube CEO Susan Wojcicki addressed the challenge of balancing the creation of an open platform with these larger issues. While Wojcicki emphasized the need for the platform to remain committed to openness, she acknowledged that this sometimes means tolerating controversial and even offensive content.

While YouTube has taken some action, the company has been criticized for doing too little and not providing enough transparency. At one point, YouTube said in 3 months' time it had removed more than 100,000 videos and over 17,000 channels for violating its hate speech rules. They also said they took down over 500 million comments over hate speech. The company's updated policies included a ban on supremacist content and the removal of videos that deny well-documented points in history, such as the Holocaust, and the 2012 Sandy Hook elementary school shooting.

Videos can be removed from YouTube for a variety of reasons beyond hate speech, including copyright infringement, violence, and nudity. These last two get more at the concerns about children's use of the platform. A survey in 2019 by Common Sense found that 56% of 8–12-year-olds and 69% of 13–18-year-olds watch online videos every day. Younger generations are shifting from traditional television to streaming services, often viewed on smartphones, tablets, and laptops.

YouTube is supposed to be for users over the age of 13, because their parent company, Google, collects and markets user data. The U.S. federal Children's Online Privacy Protection Act exempts kids from data collection. But, it appears that plenty of kids have YouTube channels, such as Ryan Kaji of Ryan's World. His channel is family run, but the focus of the show is on Ryan who is under 13 years of age. The show is mostly based on his reviews of toys and has generated more than $22 million in revenue in one year. It's not illegal for kids under age 13 to create a YouTube account as long as a parent is aware of the account and knows user data is being collected.

Content for children can be marked "for kids" so that it doesn't go to the general YouTube viewers and comments are disabled on these videos. That said, parents still need to be aware of what their kids are watching. YouTube is trying to help by requiring content creators to designate any content as either made for kids or not made for kids. The change was part of a $170 million settlement with the U.S. Federal Trade Commission over alleged violations of Children's Online Privacy Protection Act. This meant targeted ads are restricted from running on kids' videos and certain features including being able to send push notifications are disabled. Also, anyone watching a video that's been designated as "made for children" will now be seen as a viewer under the age of 13 years old, regardless of how old the user actually is.

Redefining Journalism and News

In 2009, YouTube won a Peabody Award, a recognition that was usually given to more traditional journalistic outlets, such as cable television and radio. But that year the award committee said that YouTube is a Speakers' Corner, "where Internet users can upload, view and share clips, is an ever-expanding archive-cum-bulletin board that both embodies and promotes democracy."

Because YouTube is used by professional and amateur content producers to both entertain and inform, the public is increasingly faced with the challenge of figuring out what is and is not journalistic content. Journalistic publications and broadcast outlets will use YouTube to distribute their stories just like companies and community members who happen to capture a video. This means journalists need find a new place for themselves in the digital media landscape. The fact that most people can capture events and upload content just as easily as, and sometimes with more ease than, a journalist can means that citizens are often distributors of news. Still the platform was not intended for news, it was created to amuse.

In a 2006 *Washington Post* article, YouTube's marketing director explained that "we're really focused on democratizing the entertainment experience, so whether it's a user-generated content from aspiring filmmakers or from one of the networks, the reality is it's users who are in control. Our users decide what rises up" (Goo, 2006). That said, the site is not only a source of entertainment but provides many other services as well, both in the home and in the business world. YouTube is often idealized as a place where everyday content creators can reach mass audiences. Yet it is more than that, it is an interesting intersection of corporate and community participants, and the boundaries between and amongst these parties is not always clear. In the United States, YouTube's advertising revenue in 2020 exceeded $5 billion.

Kate Roberts Edenborg

See also Google; Instagram; Internet Impact on Media; Social Media; Video Journalism

Further Readings

Allocca, K. (2018). *Videocracy: How YouTube is changing the world…with double rainbows, singing foxes, and other trends we can't stop watching*. New York, NY: Bloomsbury Publishing.

Burgess, J., & Green, J. (2009). *YouTube: Digital media and society series*. Cambridge, MA: Polity Press.

Goo, S. K. (2006). Five months after its debut, YouTube is a star online video site could help create old-media celebs, too. *Washington Post*, Retrieved from May 1, 2006.

Lastufka, A., & Dean, M. W. (2008). *YouTube: An insider's guide to climbing the charts*. Cambridge, MA: O'Reilly Media.

Snickars, P. (2009). *The YouTube reader*. Stockholm: National Library of Sweden.

Z

ZENGER, JOHN PETER

John Peter Zenger was a printer in the American colonies in the 1730s who was involved in one of the most famous media trials in American history. Zenger's trial centered on whether newspapers could publish materials critical of the government without punishment. For Americans, this trial was one of the first events in the process of debating the issue of what constituted a free press, which would eventually lead to the adoption of the First Amendment. This entry discusses Zenger's background and the funding of his newspaper before looking at the trial and its impact.

Zenger's Background

Zenger had immigrated to the colonies from Europe at the age of 13 in 1710. His father had died on board the ship while crossing the Atlantic. At age 14, Zenger was apprenticed to William Bradford for 8 years. After completing his apprenticeship, Zenger settled in Kent County in Maryland as a printer. In 1720, he won a contract from the Maryland Assembly to print the laws passed by the colonial legislature. Zenger moved to New York in 1723 in the hopes of making more money. He went into a partnership with Bradford in 1725, but it did not last long. Zenger went into business for himself and printed primarily Dutch-language theological books and some political tracts, but he continued to seek other ways to make money by printing other materials.

Founding of *New York Weekly Journal*

In 1733, Zenger was recruited by the opponents of New York Governor William Cosby to publish a newspaper. The political faction that opposed Cosby was made up of wealthy New York merchants and landowners whose income and position were threatened by Cosby and his push for power. Cosby had been appointed as governor upon the death of the previous governor in 1731, but he did not arrive for 13 months. Rip Van Dam had served as acting governor during the interim. When Cosby arrived, he demanded that Van Dam give him half of the money he had earned as interim governor. Van Dam refused and Cosby took him to court to get the money. Chief Justice Lewis Morris sided with Van Dam and was fired by Cosby. This only led to more arguments and conflicts and the opponents of the governor sought the publication of a newspaper in order to share their views and opinions with the people.

With the financial support of Van Dam and Morris, Zenger began publishing the *New York Weekly Journal* on November 5, 1733. Zenger promised his readers "the freshest Advices, Foreign and Domestic." Lawyer James Alexander helped Zenger by writing many of the materials attacking Governor Cosby that were printed in the newspaper. Zenger also reprinted English essayists, including pieces by Joseph Addison, Richard Steele, and "Cato" by John Trenchard and Thomas Gordon. Advertisements in the paper also often included bogus materials that attacked Governor Cosby or his close advisors and hurt these men's reputations. In one advertisement,

Cosby was linked to a description of a monkey. Materials in the paper implied that Cosby was a crook and a French sympathizer, a damaging charge since England and France had been at war off and on for about 50 years.

Zenger's Arrest and Trial

After reading the paper for months, Governor Cosby was finally too mad to keep quiet. He sought a way to punish the printer. He ordered four issues of the *Weekly Journal* to be burned by the hangman in a public ceremony. He then leveled charges of seditious libel against Zenger. Seditious libel was a charge developed by the English monarchy in the early 1600s, and it could halt any publication that published criticisms or attacks on the government that could encourage people to resist or rebel against the government. Under this practice, printers could be imprisoned until they revealed the author of material considered seditious libel. To prove seditious libel, the government only had to demonstrate that the statements had been printed. Cosby sought an indictment, but the grand jury refused to indict Zenger. Cosby then asked the Assembly to indict him, but they also refused. Finally, a group of the governor's council agreed to start an action against Zenger, and he was arrested on November 17, 1734, on a charge of "raising sedition."

The *Weekly Journal* was not published the week following Zenger's arrest and his readers worried that the paper had ceased to exist. But it reappeared the following week, on November 25. Zenger explained that he had been arrested but promised his readers that he would continue to "entertain thro' the Hole of the Door of the Prison" with the aid of his wife and others who were ready to help keep the newspaper publishing. The paper continued to appear weekly while Zenger remained in jail for 9 months.

Zenger's trial finally took place in August 1735. Zenger's lead attorney was supposed to be James Alexander, the person who had written most of the newspaper copy that was being challenged, but Alexander and his partner were both disbarred shortly before the trial began. The court appointed a new lawyer for Zenger, but he was an ally of Governor Cosby so he would not have provided a good defense for his client. Alexander still developed a defense plan for Zenger's case and contacted Andrew Hamilton of Philadelphia, a friend of Benjamin Franklin and one of the best trial lawyers in the colonies. He agreed to take the case.

The trial opened on August 4, 1735. Attorney General Richard Bradley levied the charges of seditious libel against Zenger. The charges were based on several articles in the *Weekly Journal* that accused the government of jeopardizing the liberties and the property of the people. They also accused that the governor had tampered with numerous civil liberties including trial by jury and the right to vote. Bradley told the jury that their job was to determine if Zenger had published the articles in question. Hamilton's first move in court surprised many people. He admitted that Zenger had printed the newspaper issues in question which seemed to indicate that Zenger was guilty and should be punished according to the law. Bradley then called on the jury to immediately convict Zenger. But Hamilton declared that the case went beyond just the act of publication. He stated that the prosecution had to prove the materials printed in the articles were libelous, false, scandalous, or seditious before a guilty verdict was justified against Zenger. He argued that the jury must find Zenger not guilty if the printed materials did not meet that standard. Chief Justice James DeLancey stated that such an argument was not acceptable and told Hamilton to move on.

Hamilton did move on, but not in the way that everyone expected. Hamilton turned to speak directly to the jury. He asked the members of the jury to function as their own judges about the truth of the statements printed in the *Weekly Journal*. He stated that the charges that Zenger had printed were "notoriously known to be true" and that "therefore in your justice lies our safety" (Alexander, p. 75). Hamilton denounced unbridled power as exercised by Cosby and appealed to the individual juror's love of freedom and liberty as the only defense against tyrannical rulers:

[T]he question before the Court and you gentlemen of the jury is not of small or private concern, it is not the cause of a poor printer, nor of New York alone, which you are now trying. No! . . . . It is the cause of liberty; and I make no doubt but your upright conduct this day will not entitle you to the love and esteem of your fellow citizens; but every man who prefers freedom to a life of slavery will bless and honor you as men who have baffled the attempt of tyranny, and, by an impartial and uncorrupt verdict, have laid a noble foundation for securing to ourselves, our posterity, and our neighbors that to which nature and the laws of our country have given us as a right—the liberty both of exposing arbitrary power (in these parts of the world, at least) by speaking and writing truth. (Alexander, p. 99)

The basis of Hamilton's defense of Zenger thus became the idea that citizens had the right to criticize government officials and that citizens as jurors had the right to determine whether words were false. Hamilton argued that free speech was essential in the colonies to prevent governors from abusing their powers. When the trial ended, the jury found Zenger not guilty, which produced cheers from the audience in the courtroom. Technically, the not guilty verdict meant that Zenger had not printed the documents, although in fact he had. The verdict reflected that the jury members agreed with Hamilton's argument that the materials printed had to be false or seditious in order to constitute libel. So, Zenger was released from jail the next day. Following the trial, Zenger continued to be a successful printer. Two years later, he became the public printer for New York, and he continued to print the *Weekly Journal* until his death in 1746.

Impact of the Trial

The verdict in the Zenger trial did not set any legal precedents in America because truth and the right of juries to decide whether publications were libel or not were not established until the late 1700s. But the jury verdict did make it easier for publications to criticize government officials and would have a big impact over the years to come as Americans challenged the British government more and more. At the time of the trial, nothing was published about it outside of New York, but that changed in 1738. On May 11, 1738, Benjamin Franklin printed in the *Pennsylvania Gazette* that what happened in the Zenger case had not yet become law but that it really was "better than Law" and that it "Ought to be Law, and will always be law wherever Justice prevails." This statement reflects the slowly growing importance of the Zenger trial and the verdict which people increasingly saw as important to protect their liberty and freedom and the right to criticize the government and its actions.

Carol Sue Humphrey

See also Sedition Act of 1798; British Newspapers; Democracy and the Media; English Roots of the Free Press; First Amendment; Free Expression, History of; Free Press and Fair Trial

Further Readings

Alexander, J. (1736). *A brief narrative of the case and trial of John Peter Zenger.* Cambridge, MA: Reprinted by Harvard University Press in 1963, with an Introduction by Stanley Katz.

Cheslau, I. G. (1952). *John Peter Zenger and "The New-York Weekly Journal": A historical study.* New York, NY: Zenger Memorial Fund.

Kluger, R. (2017). *Indelible ink: The trial of John Peter Zenger and the birth of America's free press.* New York, NY: W. W. Norton.

Sloan, W. D., and Williams, J. H. (1994). *The early American Press, 1690–1783.* Westport, CT: Greenwood Press.

Smith, J. A. (1988). *Printers and press freedom: The ideology of early American journalism.* Oxford, UK: Oxford University Press.

Appendix
Journalism Organizations

The 50 organizations in the following list are of particular relevance to the field of journalism. While not exhaustive, this collection of names, websites, and annotations features a cross-section and representative sample of remarkable journalism and journalism-related groups with descriptions reflecting information gleaned from respective website content published in December 2020.

1. **Alliance of Area Business Publications (AABP):** https://bizpubs.org

    The Alliance of Area Business Publishers (AABP) represents 70 regional and local business publications in the United States, Canada, Australia, and Puerto Rico. AABP provides marketing and communications services, lobbying, educational programming, and new business development. AABP programs cover the sharing of information on electronic publishing, national polling of its members on business topics, providing sales and circulation targets, and conducting sales seminars. The organization was founded in 1979 as the Association of Area Business Publications.

2. **American Amateur Press Association (AAPA):** https://www.aapainfo.org

    The American Amateur Press Association (AAPA), a nationwide nonprofit organization of amateur journalists founded in 1936, promotes amateur journalism and the circulation of their work among members.

3. **American Journalism Historians Association (AJHA):** https://ajha.wildapricot.org

    The American Journalism Historians Association (AJHA), founded in 1981, advances education and research in mass communication history. Through regional conferences, committees, and publications, and an annual conference, members raise awareness of historical standards and ensure scholars and students recognize the importance of media history.

4. **American News Women's Club (ANWC):** http://www.anwc.org

    The American News Women's Club (ANWC) was founded in 1932 as the Newspaper Women's Club, with membership limited to women reporters and writers employed by newspapers. The ANWC includes a diverse group of journalists, independent authors, and professional communicators representing newspapers, radio and television stations, publishing companies, websites, public relations firms, corporations, academic institutions, and government.

5. **American Press Institute (API):** https://www.americanpressinstitute.org

    The American Press Institute (API) is among the oldest centers devoted solely to training and professional development for the news industry. API is an educational nonadvocacy nonprofit organization that in 2012 became affiliated with the News Media Alliance (formerly the Newspaper Association of America). It was initially located at Columbia University's Journalism School before moving in 1974 to Reston, Virginia.

6. **American Society of Media Photographers (ASMP):** https://www.asmp.org

    The American Society of Media Photographers ([ASMP], originally the Society of Magazine Photographers and later the American Society of Magazine

Photographers) is the leading trade association for photographers who photograph primarily for publication. ASMP promotes photographers' rights, educates photographers in better business practices, produces business publications for photographers, and helps buyers find professional photographers. Founded in 1944, ASMP has nearly 5,000 members and 38 chapters.

7. **Asian American Journalists Association (AAJA):** https://www.aaja.org

    The Asian American Journalists Association (AAJA) includes more than 1,500 members from the United States and Asia and promotes people of color for management positions in the industry. Reporters from the Los Angeles Times *helped create the organization in 1981. Membership includes broadcast anchors, print reporters, editors, producers, videographers, columnists, photojournalists, freelancers, academics, professors, students, as well as those who work in film and online media. The membership also consists of associates in business and public relations sectors. Close to one third of AAJA's members are students.*

8. **Association for Education in Journalism and Mass Communication (AEJMC):** https://www.aejmc.org

    The Association for Education in Journalism and Mass Communication (AEJMC) is a nonprofit organization of more than 3,700 educators, students, and practitioners from around the globe. It is the oldest and largest alliance of journalism and mass communication educators and administrators at the college level. It is a major international membership organization for academics in the field, offering regional and national conferences and refereed publications. It holds an annual conference each summer, featuring sessions on teaching, research, and public service in the various components of journalism and mass communication.

9. **Association for Women in Communications (AWC):** https://www.womcom.org

    The Association for Women in Communications (AWC) is a professional organization that champions the advancement of women across all communications disciplines by recognizing excellence, promoting leadership, and positioning its members at the forefront of the evolving communications era. With more than 1,100 members, AWC advocates on behalf of women in communications by providing opportunities for learning and by making connections across a nationwide network of women leaders.

10. **Association for Women in Sports Media (AWSM):** http://awsmonline.org

    Association for Women in Sports Media (AWSM) advocates for increased diversity in sports media. It is a volunteer-managed nonprofit organization founded in 1987 for women working in sports media. AWSM works to promote and increase diversity in sports media through career-enhancement networking and mentoring initiatives as well as the internship/scholarship program. It has placed more than 150 female college students in paid summer positions since 1990. It holds regional events and an annual convention.

11. **Association of American Editorial Cartoonists (AAEC):** https://www.editorialcartoonists.com

    The Association of American Editorial Cartoonists (AAEC) focuses on the promotion of the interests of editorial cartoonists and political cartoonists in the United States. It works closely with the Cartoonists Rights Network, an international organization looking to publicize oppression and attacks on political cartoonists by foreign governments, and stand with other international groups that support the human, civil, and artistic rights of cartoonists around the world. For over 60 years, the AAEC has been the professional association concerned with promoting the interests of staff, freelance, and student editorial cartoonists.

12. **Association of Healthcare Journalists (AHCJ):** https://healthjournalism.org

    The Association of Health Care Journalists (AHCJ) is an independent, nonprofit organization that aims to advance public understanding of health care issues. It seeks to improve the quality, accuracy, and visibility of health care reporting, writing, and editing. It does so through a number of training programs, online resources, and publications. There are more than 1,500 members of AHCJ.

13. **Committee to Protect Journalists (CPJ):** https://cpj.org

    The Committee to Protect Journalists (CPJ) is an independent, nonprofit organization that promotes

press freedom worldwide. Founded in 1981, CPJ has worked on behalf of scores of journalists who have been attacked or imprisoned each year. CPJ's networks are made up of journalists, researchers, and advocates, working together to support journalists and press freedom around the world.

14. **Corporation for Public Broadcasting (CPB): https://www.cpb.org**

The Corporation for Public Broadcasting (CPB) is a private, nonprofit corporation created by Congress in the Public Broadcasting Act of 1967. CPB seeks to ensure universal access to noncommercial, high-quality content and telecommunications services. It distributes more than 70% of its funding to more than 1,500 locally owned public radio and television stations. In 1969, the CPB started the Public Broadcasting System (PBS) and in 1970, the CPB formed National Public Radio (NPR), a network of public radio stations. On May 31, 2002, CPB, through a first round of funding from a special appropriation, helped public television stations make the transition to digital broadcasting, which was complete by 2009.

15. **Dow Jones News Fund (DJNF):** https://www.dowjonesnewsfund.org

The Dow Jones News Fund (DJNF) is a national foundation supported by Dow Jones & Company, Dow Jones Foundation, and others within the news industry. It emphasizes education for students and educators as part of our mission to promote careers in journalism, operating several high school and college-level grant programs. Editors of The Wall Street Journal *founded the Dow Jones Newspaper Fund in 1958, and it now provides internships and scholarships to college students, career literature, fellowships for high school journalism teachers and publications' advisers and training for college journalism instructors.*

16. **Editorial Freelancers Association (EFA):** https://www.the-efa.org

The Editorial Freelancers Association (EFA) is a national, nonprofit, professional organization of self-employed workers in the publishing and communications industries. Members are editors, writers, indexers, proofreaders, researchers, desktop publishers, translators, and others with a broad range of skills and specialties.

17. **European Journalism Centre (EJC):** https://ejc.net

Since 1992, the European Journalism Centre (EJC) has worked to produce sustainable, ethical, and innovative programs through grants, events, training, and media development. Headquartered in the Netherlands, EJC connects journalists as an independent, nonprofit institute for further training, a forum for journalists, media executives, and journalism educators. Its aim is to give further training to mid-career journalists and media professionals. The institute also acts a partner and organizer at the European level for media companies, professional organizations, journalism schools, and government bodies seeking to establish activities and projects.

18. **Fairness & Accuracy in Reporting (FAIR):** https://fair.org

Fairness & Accuracy in Reporting (FAIR) is a national media watch group that offers criticism of media bias and censorship. Founded in 1986, the group has worked to invigorate the First Amendment by advocating for greater diversity in the press. FAIR is opposed to corporate ownership of media entities and calls for the break-up of media conglomerates.

19. **Freedom Forum, The:** https://www.freedomforum.org

Established July 4, 1991, the Freedom Forum is a nonpartisan, international foundation dedicated to the protection of the free press and free speech. The organization works to raise awareness of First Amendment freedoms through education, advocacy, and action. It was founded when the Gannett Foundation, started by publisher Frank E. Gannett as a charitable foundation to aid communities where his company had newspapers, sold its name and assets back to Gannett Company for US$670 million. Retired Gannett chair and USA Today newspaper founder Al Neuharth formed the Freedom Forum.

20. **Fund for Investigative Journalism (FIJ):** http://fij.org

The Fund for Investigative Journalism (FIJ) provides grants to freelance reporters, authors, and small publications for investigative work involving corruption, malfeasance, incompetence, societal problems, or media criticism. FIJ provides grants and other support to independent journalists and news organizations to produce high-quality, unbiased, nonpartisan investigative stories that have an impact. It provides support to investigative journalists for news stories, books, documentaries, and podcasts that uncover wrongdoing by powerful people or institutions.

21. **International Center for Journalists, The (ICFJ):**
https://www.icfj.org

The International Center for Journalists (ICFJ) was established in 1984 to improve the quality of journalism worldwide. ICFJ works with journalists to promote news coverage of critical community and global issues and to build the storytelling skills of reporters. It is a nonprofit, professional organization located in Washington, DC, and it promotes journalism worldwide, working directly with more than 70,000 journalists from 180 countries.

22. **International Federation of Journalists (IFJ):**
https://www.ifj.org

The International Federation of Journalists (IFJ) is a global organization that was founded in 1926, and it is now the world's largest organization of journalists, representing 600,000 media professionals in 187 unions and associations in more than 140 countries. It is an associate member of UNESCO, and it has represented journalists at the United Nations since 1953. The IFJ supports journalists and their unions whenever they are fighting for their industrial and professional rights and has established an International Safety Fund to provide humanitarian aid for journalists in need.

23. **Journalism & Women Symposium (JAWS):**
https://jaws.org

The Journalism & Women Symposium (JAWS) brings together working journalists, journalism educators, and researchers for the sharing of resources, support, training, and information about issues that affect women in journalism. JAWS promotes the professional growth of women in journalism. The nonprofit grew out of discussions at a 1984 gathering at the Missouri School of Journalism about the representation of women in news media. It was incorporated as a nonprofit in 1995, and it has since grown into an organization of more than 900 journalists and educators.

24. **Journalism Education Association (JEA):**
http://jea.org/wp

The Journalism Education Association (JEA), founded in 1924, is among the largest scholastic journalism organizations for teachers and advisers. Among its 2,300 members are journalism teachers and publications advisers, media professionals, press associations, adviser organizations, libraries, yearbook companies, newspapers, radio stations, and departments of journalism. JEA is a volunteer organization. The headquarters office in Kansas State University in Manhattan, Kansas, is maintained as a clearinghouse for JEA members and programs, and provides essential office services.

25. **National Association of Black Journalists (NABJ):**
https://nabjonline.org

The National Association of Black Journalists (NABJ) is an organization of journalists, students, and media-related professionals that provides programs and services. Founded by 44 men and women in 1975 in Washington, DC, NABJ is the largest organization of journalists of color in the nation. Among its goals are strengthening ties among Black journalists, sensitizing all media to the importance of fairness in the workplace for Black journalists, expanding job opportunities and recruiting activities for veteran, young and aspiring Black journalists, while providing continued professional development and training, and increasing the number of Black journalists in management positions and encouraging Black journalists to become entrepreneurs.

26. **National Association of Broadcasters (NAB):** https://www.nab.org

The National Association of Broadcasters (NAB) is composed of members who represent the nation's radio and television broadcast industries. NAB works as an association and lobby group for broadcasters in commercial and noncommercial over-the-air radio and television. The NAB represents more than 8,300 terrestrial radio and television stations as well as broadcast networks.

27. **National Association of Hispanic Journalists (NAHJ):** https://nahj.org

The National Association of Hispanic Journalists (NAHJ) works toward the recognition and professional advancement of Hispanics in the news industry. Established in 1984, NAHJ consists of executive officers and regional directors who represent geographic areas of the United States and the Caribbean with approximately 3,100 members, including working journalists, journalism students, other media-related professionals, and journalism educators.

28. **National Association of Science Writers (NASW):** https://www.nasw.org

   The National Association of Science Writers (NASW), formally incorporated in 1955, is a community of journalists, authors, editors, producers, public information officers, students, and people who write and produce material intended to inform the public about science, health, engineering, and technology. NASW promotes the interests of science writers nationally and globally and advocates for copyright protections for writers. A dozen science journalists and reporters in New York City created the NASW in 1934 with the aim of improving the craft of science journalism.

29. **National Center on Disability and Journalism (NCDJ):** https://ncdj.org

   The National Center on Disability and Journalism (NCDJ) is an independent, impartial journalism education organization that works with journalists and educators, providing information about disability reporting issues in order to produce more accurate, fair, and diverse news reporting.

30. **National Federation of Press Women (NFPW):** https://www.nfpw.org

   The National Federation of Press Women (NFPW), a nationwide organization of professionals pursuing careers in communications, has promoted for more than 75 years ethical standards and offered professional development, networking, and protection of our First Amendment rights. NFPW offers community and connections to other professionals in 32 state affiliates and welcome at-large members from areas without affiliates.

31. **National Freedom of Information Coalition (NFOIC):** https://www.nfoic.org

   The National Freedom of Information Coalition (NFOIC) assists members through joint fundraising, project planning, and the interchange of ideas and information. It promotes press freedom, legislative and administrative reforms, dispute resolutions, and litigation to ensure open, transparent, and accessible state and local governments and public institutions. It was founded in 1989 in Dallas, Texas, as the

National Freedom of Information Assembly, and its first board was appointed in Washington at the organization's founding congress in January 1992.

32. **National Lesbian and Gay Journalists Association (NLGJA):** https://www.nlgja.org

   Founded in 1990, National Lesbian and Gay Journalists Association (NLGJA) is an organization of journalists, media professionals, educators, and students working from within the news industry to foster fair and accurate coverage of lesbian, gay, bisexual, and transgender issues. NLGJA works with the Centers for Disease Control as part of the Partnering and Communicating Together to Act Against AIDS (PACT) program.

33. **National Newspaper Association (NNA):** https://www.nna.org

   The mission of the National Newspaper Association is to protect, promote, and enhance America's community newspapers. NNA protects community newspapers through active and effective government relation programs that address the issues affecting community newspapers. Established in 1885, NNA's 2,200 current members make it among the largest national newspaper associations. The National Editorial Association changed its name to the National Newspaper Association in 1964.

34. **National Press Club (NPC):** https://www.press.org

   The National Press Club is a professional and social club for working journalists and communications professionals that has been a Washington institution for more than a century. Founded in 1908, the NPC has more than 3,500 members, and it offers over 2,000 events a year.

35. **National Press Photographers Association (NPPA):** https://nppa.org

   The National Press Photographers Association (NPPA) is an organization dedicated to the advancement of photographic journalism. The NPPA addresses issues connected to the First Amendment, including drone regulations, copyright, access, credentialing, cameras in court, unlawful assault on visual journalists, and cases that affect the ability to record events and issues of public interest. Founded in 1946, the organization is based in at the Grady College of Journalism and Mass Communication at the University of Georgia. Its members include still and television photographers, editors, students, and representatives of businesses that serve the photojournalism industry.

36. **National Scholastic Press Association (NSPA):** http://studentpress.org/nspa

    National Scholastic Press Association (NSPA) is a national community of student journalists and scholastic journalism advisers. NSPA advances journalism and media as a vital cultural force by connecting advisers, students, and professionals through national events. Formed in the 1920s, the organization has more than 1,500 member publications. The association is membership-based and annually hosts high school journalism conventions across the country.

37. **Native American Journalists Association (NAJA):** https://najanewsroom.com

    The Native American Journalists Association (NAJA) recognizes Native Americans as distinct peoples based on tradition and culture. The primary goal of the NAJA is to improve communications among Native people and between Native Americans and the public. The association was founded as the Native American Press Association in 1984 with initial funding provided by the Gannett Foundation. The organization was headquartered at the University of South Dakota in Vermillion, South Dakota, as of 2002. In 2003, it moved into the Al Neuharth Media Center, where it shared space with the Freedom Forum. In 2008, it moved to the Gaylord College of Journalism and Mass Communication at the University of Oklahoma in Norman, Oklahoma.

38. **NewsGuild, The:** https://newsguild.org

    Originally founded by print journalists in 1933, the Newspaper Guild, known today as The NewsGuild, is a union of 21st-century media. Its 25,000 members in the United States, Canada, and Puerto Rico are employed as reporters, photographers, editors, designers, advertising sales representatives, circulation workers, and business staff. In 2015, the union changed its name from Newspaper Guild to its current name, The NewsGuild, to reflect that newspapers are not the only publishers of news.

39. **News Media Alliance (NMA):** https://www.newsmediaalliance.org

    The News Media Alliance (known until 2016 as the Newspaper Association of America) is a trade

association founded in 1992 and headquartered in Washington, DC, representing approximately 2,000 newspapers in the United States and Canada. The organization has organized and hosted mediaXchange, the newspaper industry's annual conference.

40. **Online News Association (ONA):** https://journalists.org

    Members of the Online News Association (ONA) include journalists, technologists, executives, students, educators, and other digital media professionals. ONA creates programs focused on training and networking, leadership development, and diversity in newsrooms. ONA hosts the annual Online News Association conference and administers the Online Journalism Awards.

41. **Overseas Press Club (OPC):** https://opcofamerica.org

    The Overseas Press Club of America is the nation's oldest and largest association of journalists engaged in international news. It was founded in 1939 by nine foreign correspondents in New York City and has grown to nearly 500 members worldwide. The club advocates high standards in news reporting, the advancement of press freedom, and the promotion of fellowship among colleagues.

42. **Pew Research Center, The:** https://www.pewresearch.org

    The Pew Research Center is a nonpartisan organization that informs the public about the press, politics, and public policy issues, conducting public opinion polling, demographic research, content analysis, and other data-driven social science research. The Pew Research Center does not take policy positions and is a subsidiary of The Pew Charitable Trusts. It conducts public opinion polling, demographic research, media content analysis, and other empirical social science research.

43. **Poynter Institute, The:** https://www.poynter.org

    Founded in 1975, the Poynter Institute is a school for journalists, future journalists, and teachers of journalism. The school began when Nelson Poynter, the owner and chair of the St. Petersburg Times *(now the* Tampa Bay Times*) and Times Publishing Company, announced that he planned to start a small journalism school called the Modern Media Institute. Craig Newmark, a board member of the Poynter Foundation, donated $1 million to it in*

2015. In 2017, the Poynter Institute received $1.3 million from the Omidyar Network and the Open Society Foundations in order to support new projects in the areas of fact-checking technology, impact tracking, and financial awards through innovation grants and crowdfunding matches.

44. **Public Relations Society of America (PRSA):** https://www.prsa.org

The Public Relations Society of America (PRSA) consists of more than 30,000 professional and student members. PRSA is represented across the United States by chapters and professional interest sections. It was founded in 1947 by combining the American Council on Public Relations and the National Association of Public Relations Councils. In the 1950s and 1960s, the society created its code of conduct, accreditation program, and a student society called the Public Relations Student Society of America.

45. **Radio Television Digital News Association (RTDNA):** https://www.rtdna.org

The Radio Television Digital News Association (RTDNA) is a grassroots organization founded in 1946. Formerly the Radio Television News Directors Association (RTNDA), the organization consists of radio, television, and online news directors, producers, executives, reporters, students, and educators. Among its functions are the maintenance of journalistic ethics and the preservation of the free speech rights of broadcast journalists. The RTDNA is known for the Edward R. Murrow Award, given annually since 1971 for excellence in electronic journalism, and the Paul White Award, presented annually since 1956 as its highest award, for lifetime achievement.

46. **Reporters Without Borders (RSF):** https://rsf.org/en

Reporters Without Borders is an international nonprofit and nongovernmental organization with the stated aim of safeguarding the right to freedom of information. It describes its advocacy as founded on the belief that everyone requires access to the news and information, in line with Article 19 of the Universal Declaration of Human Rights, which recognizes the right to receive and share information regardless of frontiers. The organization provides information about the media freedom situation worldwide in French, English, Spanish, Arabic, Chinese, Russian, and other languages.

47. **Religion Newswriters Association (RNA):** https://www.rna.org

Religion Newswriters Association (RNA) was formed in 1949 to advance the professional standards of religion reporting in the secular press through education, contests, and mentoring. Since the 1970s, RNA has published an annual list of the top 10 religion-related news stories of the previous year.

48. **Scripps Howard Foundation:** https://scripps.com/foundation

The Scripps Howard Foundation supports philanthropic causes important to The E.W. Scripps Company and the communities it serves. Established in 1962, the foundation is the corporate philanthropy of The E.W. Scripps Company, a 134-year-old media company with newspapers and TV stations in more than 30 markets and an array of digital products and services, including social games. It is located in Cincinnati, Ohio, home to the Scripps Company. The Scripps Howard Foundation, along with Roy Howard's children, established the Roy W. Howard Archive at the Indiana University School of Journalism in 1983.

49. **Society of Environmental Journalists (SEJ):** http://www.sej.org

The Society of Environmental Journalists (SEJ) is the only North American membership association of professional journalists dedicated to more and better coverage of environment-related issues. SEJ was founded in 1990, and it now includes more than 1,500 journalists and academics working in news media in the United States, Canada, Mexico, and 43 other countries.

50. **Society of Professional Journalists (SPJ):** https://www.spj.org

The Society of Professional Journalists (SPJ), a broad-based organization that encourages the free practice of journalism, was founded in 1909 as Sigma Delta Chi. SPJ promotes the free flow of information vital to a well-informed citizenry. SPJ consists of more than 13,500 journalists dedicated to stimulating ethical behavior and perpetuating a free press.

Index